A COMPANION
TO
THE ROMAN ARMY

BLACKWELL COMPANIONS TO THE ANCIENT WORLD

This series provides sophisticated and authoritative overviews of periods of ancient history, genres of classical literature, and the most important themes in ancient culture. Each volume comprises between twenty-five and forty concise essays written by individual scholars within their area of specialization. The essays are written in a clear, provocative, and lively manner, designed for an international audience of scholars, students, and general readers.

ANCIENT HISTORY

Published

A Companion to the Roman Army
Edited by Paul Erdkamp

A Companion to the Roman Republic
Edited by Nathan Rosenstein and Robert Morstein-Marx

A Companion to the Roman Empire
Edited by David S. Potter

A Companion to the Classical Greek World
Edited by Konrad H. Kinzl

A Companion to the Ancient Near East
Edited by Daniel C. Snell

A Companion to the Hellenistic World
Edited by Andrew Erskine

A Companion to Late Antiquity
Edited by Philip Rousseau

A Companion to Archaic Greece
Edited by Kurt A. Raaflaub and Hans van Wees

A Companion to Julius Caesar
Edited by Miriam Griffin

A Companion to Ancient History
Edited by Andrew Erskine

A Companion to Byzantium
Edited by Liz James

A Companion to Ancient Egypt
Edited by Alan B. Lloyd

A Companion to Ancient Macedonia
Edited by Joseph Roisman and Ian Worthington

In preparation

A Companion to the Punic Wars
Edited by Dexter Hoyos

A Companion to Sparta
Edited by Anton Powell

LITERATURE AND CULTURE

Published

A Companion to Classical Receptions
Edited by Lorna Hardwick and Christopher Stray

A Companion to Greek and Roman Historiography
Edited by John Marincola

A Companion to Catullus
Edited by Marilyn B. Skinner

A Companion to Roman Religion
Edited by Jörg Rüpke

A Companion to Greek Religion
Edited by Daniel Ogden

A Companion to the Classical Tradition
Edited by Craig W. Kallendorf

A Companion to Roman Rhetoric
Edited by William Dominik and Jon Hall

A Companion to Greek Rhetoric
Edited by Ian Worthington

A Companion to Ancient Epic
Edited by John Miles Foley

A Companion to Greek Tragedy
Edited by Justina Gregory

A Companion to Latin Literature
Edited by Stephen Harrison

A Companion to Ovid
Edited by Peter E. Knox

A Companion to Greek and Roman Political Thought
Edited by Ryan K. Balot

A Companion to the Ancient Greek Language
Edited by Egbert Bakker

A Companion to Hellenistic Literature
Edited by Martine Cuypers and James J. Clauss

A Companion to Vergil's *Aeneid* and its Tradition
Edited by Joseph Farrell and Michael C. J. Putnam

A Companion to Horace
Edited by Gregson Davis

In preparation

A Companion to the Latin Language
Edited by James Clackson

A Companion to Greek Mythology
Edited by Ken Dowden and Niall Livingstone

A Companion to Sophocles
Edited by Kirk Ormand

A Companion to Aeschylus
Edited by Peter Burian

A Companion to Greek Art
Edited by Tyler Jo Smith and Dimitris Plantzos

A Companion to Families in the Greek and Roman World
Edited by Beryl Rawson

A Companion to Tacitus
Edited by Victoria Pagán

A Companion to the Archaeology of the Ancient Near East
Edited by Daniel Potts

A COMPANION TO THE ROMAN ARMY

Edited by

Paul Erdkamp

WILEY-BLACKWELL

A John Wiley & Sons, Ltd., Publication

This paperback edition first published 2011
© 2011 Blackwell Publishing Ltd

Edition history: Blackwell Publishing Ltd (hardback, 2007)

Blackwell Publishing was acquired by John Wiley & Sons in February 2007. Blackwell's
publishing program has been merged with Wiley's global Scientific, Technical, and
Medical business to form Wiley-Blackwell.

Registered Office
John Wiley & Sons Ltd, The Atrium, Southern Gate, Chichester, West Sussex, PO19 8SQ,
United Kingdom

Editorial Offices
350 Main Street, Malden, MA 02148-5020, USA
9600 Garsington Road, Oxford, OX4 2DQ, UK
The Atrium, Southern Gate, Chichester, West Sussex, PO19 8SQ, UK

For details of our global editorial offices, for customer services, and for information
about how to apply for permission to reuse the copyright material in this book please
see our website at www.wiley.com/wiley-blackwell.

The right of Paul Erdkamp to be identified as the author of the editorial material
in this work has been asserted in accordance with the UK Copyright, Designs
and Patents Act 1988.

Library of Congress Cataloging-in-Publication Data

A companion to the Roman army / edited by Paul Erdkamp.
   p. cm.
   Includes bibliographical references and index.
   ISBN: 978-1-4051-2153-8 (hardback : alk. paper)
   ISBN: 978-1-4443-3921-5 (paperback : alk. paper)   1. Military history, Ancient.
2. Rome—History, Military.   3. Rome—Army.   I. Erdkamp, Paul.

U35.C648 2007
355.00937—dc22

                                                                    2006009420

A catalogue record for this book is available from the British Library.

Set in 10/12pt Galliard by Graphicraft Limited, Hong Kong

1   2011

This book is dedicated with great respect and gratitude
to Lukas de Blois on the occasion of his retirement

Contents

Illustrations

Plates

Figure

Maps

Tables

Notes on Contributors

Clifford Ando is Professor of Classics and the College at the University of Chicago. He writes on the history of law, religion, and culture in the Roman world. He is author of *Imperial Ideology and Provincial Loyalty in the Roman Empire* (2000) and editor of *Roman Religion* (2003).

Anthony R. Birley was Professor of Ancient History at the universities of Manchester from 1974 to 1990 and Düsseldorf from 1990 to 2002. His publications include biographies of the emperors Hadrian, Marcus Aurelius, and Septimius Severus. He is Chair of the Trustees of the Vindolanda Trust.

Lukas de Blois is Professor of Ancient History at the University of Nijmegen. He has published on the history of the Roman Empire in the third century AD, the Late Roman Republic, historiography (Sallust, Tacitus, Cassius Dio), Plutarch's biographies, and Greek Sicily in the fourth century BC. He also published (with R. J. van der Spek) *Introduction to the Ancient World* (1997).

Will Broadhead is Assistant Professor of History at the Massachusetts Institute of Technology. His research is mainly on the history of Roman Italy, with a particular interest in geographical mobility and in the epigraphy of the Sabellic languages.

Pierre Cagniart has earned his doctorate in 1986 at the University of Texas. He is currently Associate Professor at the Department of History at Southwest Texas State University. He has published various articles on late republican warfare and his research interests also include Roman law and cultural history of the Roman principate.

Hugh Elton is currently associate professor in the Department of Ancient History and Classics at Trent University, Peterborough, Ontario. Previously he was Director of the British Institute at Ankara. He writes on Roman military history in the late empire, and on southern Anatolia (especially Cilicia). He is author of *Warfare in Roman Europe, AD 350–425* (1996) and *Frontiers of the Roman Empire* (1996).

Paul Erdkamp is Research Fellow in Ancient History at Leiden University. He is the author of *Hunger and the Sword. Warfare and Food Supply in Roman Republican Wars (264–30 BC)* (1998) and *The Grain Market in the Roman Empire* (2005). He is the editor of *The Roman Army and the Economy* (2002).

Gary Forsythe received his Ph.D. in ancient history at the University of Pennsylvania; and after teaching at the University of Pennsylvania, Swarthmore College, Bryn Mawr College, and the University of Chicago, he now is Professor in the Department of History at Texas Tech University (Lubbock, Texas). He is the author of four books, the most recent of which is *A Critical History of Early Rome: From Prehistory to the First Punic War* (2005).

Kate Gilliver is a lecturer in ancient history at Cardiff University and is a Roman military historian. She has particular interests in military reform in the republic and early empire, atrocities in ancient warfare, and in the relationship between ancient military theory and practice, on which she has published a book, *The Roman Art of War* (1999).

Norbert Hanel teaches archaeology of the Roman provinces at the universities of Cologne and Bochum (Ruhr-Universität) and has published *Vetera I* (1995). He has excavated in Germany and other European countries, particularly the Germanic and Hispanic provinces, and studied the naval base of the Classis Germanica Köln-Marienburg (Alteburg). His main research interests are the military and cultural history of the provinces especially of the western empire.

Olivier Hekster is Van der Leeuw Professor of Ancient History at the Radboud University Nijmegen. His research focuses on Roman ideology and ancient spectacle. He is author of *Commodus: An Emperor at the Crossroads* (2002), and co-editor of *Representation and Perception of Roman Imperial Power* (2003) and *Imaginary Kings: Royal Images in The Ancient Near East, Greece and Rome* (2005).

Peter Herz studied history, classics, and archaeology at the universities of Mainz and Oxford. He received both his D.Phil. and habilitation in ancient history at the University of Mainz. In 1994 he was appointed Professor of Ancient History at the University of Regensburg. His research interests include social and economic history, epigraphy, the ruler cult, and the history of the Roman provinces.

Dexter Hoyos was born and educated in Barbados. After taking a D.Phil. at Oxford in Roman history, he joined Sydney University where he is Associate Professor in Latin. His academic interests include Roman-Carthaginian relations, Roman expansionism and the problem of sources, the principate, and developing direct-reading and comprehension skills in Latin. His many publications include *Hannibal's Dynasty: Power and Politics in the Western Mediterranean, 247–183 BC* (2003).

Peter Kehne studied history, philosophy, classical philology, law of nations, and Roman law at the universities of Kiel, Hanover, and Göttingen. He received his D.Phil. in ancient history and is now Assistant Professor of Ancient History at the Leibniz University, Hanover. He has published on ancient history and historians, foreign policy, international relations, and "Völkerrecht" in antiquity, as well as on Greek and Roman military history, especially the Greek–Persian and Roman–German wars.

Wolf Liebeschuetz is Emeritus Professor of Ancient History at the University of Nottingham. He has published on various aspects of ancient history and late antiquity is a central interest of his. His most recent books are *The Decline and Fall of the Roman City* (2001) and *Ambrose of Milan: Political Letters and Speeches* (2005).

Luuk de Ligt is Professor of Ancient History at the University of Leiden. His research interests include the social and economic history, demography, legal history and epigraphy of the Roman Republic and Empire. His major publications include *Fairs and Markets in the Roman Empire* (1993) and numerous articles, most recently "Poverty and demography: The case of the Gracchan land reforms," *Mnemosyne* 57 (2004): 725–57.

Sara Elise Phang received a doctorate in Roman history from Columbia University in 2000. She has held a postdoctoral fellowship in Classics at the University of Southern California. She performs research at the Library of Congress and the Center for Hellenic Studies. Her first book, *The Marriage of Roman Soldiers, 13 BC–AD 235*, won the 2002 Gustave O. Arlt Award in the Humanities for Classical Studies. She is currently conducting research into Roman military discipline.

Louis Rawlings is a lecturer in ancient history at Cardiff University. His research interests include Italian, Greek, Punic, and Gallic warfare, especially the military interaction between states, such as Rome and Carthage, and tribal societies, and the roles warriors have in state-formation. He is the author of *The Ancient Greeks at War* (2006).

John Rich is Reader in Roman History at the University of Nottingham. He is the author of *Declaring War in the Roman Republic in the Period of Transmarine Expansion* (1976), *Cassius Dio: The Augustan Settlement (Roman History 53–55.9)* (1990), and articles on various aspects of Roman history, especially warfare and imperialism, historiography, and the reign of Augustus. He has also edited various collections of papers, including (with G. Shipley) *War and Society in the Roman World* (1993).

Nathan Rosenstein is Professor of History at The Ohio State University. He is the author of a number of works on the effects of war on Roman political culture and society, most recently *Rome at War, Farms, Families, and Death in the Middle Republic* (2004). He is also the editor, with Robert Morstein-Marx, of the *Blackwell Companion to the Roman Republic* (2006).

Denis Saddington studied English and classics at the University of the Witwatersrand, before being awarded a Rhodes Scholarship to Corpus Christi College, Oxford. He has taught in the universities of KwaZulu-Natal, South Africa, Witwatersrand, and Zimbabwe, and has written a book on *The Development of the Roman Auxiliary Forces* (1982). His main research interests are the early church, Josephus, Roman auxiliaries, and Roman provincial administration.

Walter Scheidel is Professor of Classics at Stanford University. His research focuses on ancient social and economic history, pre-modern historical demography, and comparative and interdisciplinary world history. His publications include *Measuring Sex, Age and Death in the Roman Empire* (1996) and *Death on the Nile: Disease and the Demography of Roman Egypt* (2001).

Timo Stickler is Akademischer Rat in Ancient History at the Heinrich-Heine-University, Düsseldorf. His research interests include the political and social history of late antiquity, especially in the western part of the Mediterranean. He is the author of *Aetius: Gestaltungsspielräume eines Heermeisters im ausgehenden Weströmischen Reich* (2002).

Oliver Stoll teaches ancient history at the University of Mainz and is research fellow at the Römisch-Germanisches Zentralmuseum, Mainz (RGZM). His research focuses on the Roman army, archaeology, and history of the Roman provinces. Various articles are included in his *Römisches Heer und Gesellschaft. Gesammelte Beiträge 1991–1999* (2001). He is the author of *Zwischen Integration und Abgrenzung: Die Religion des Römischen Heeres im Nahen Osten* (2001).

Karl Strobel is Professor of Ancient History and Archaeology at the University of Klagenfurt. His research is concentrated on the history of the Roman Empire, but also on the Hellenistic period, on the economic history of antiquity, and on the history and archaeology of ancient Anatolia. He has written numerous publications on the history of the Roman army, for example *Untersuchungen zu den Dakerkriegen Trajans* (1984) and *Die Donaukriege Domitians* (1989).

James Thorne studied archaeology at University College London before joining the British army in 1995, subsequently serving with the Royal Tank Regiment. His Ph.D. thesis (Manchester 2005) was entitled *Caesar and the Gauls: Imperialism and Regional Conflict*. His current teaching at the University of Manchester includes a course on "Roman Imperialism 264 BC–AD 69"; his other interests include warfare in classical Greece, on which he has published, ancient logistics, and a planned book on the transformation of empires into states.

Gabriele Wesch-Klein teaches ancient history at the University of Heidelberg, Germany. She is author of several articles concerning the Roman army during the principate. She has also published *Soziale Aspekte des römischen Heerwesens in der Kaiserzeit* (1998).

Everett L. Wheeler (Ph.D., Duke University) has taught history and classical studies at University of Missouri/Columbia, University of Louisville, Duke University, and North Carolina State University. Besides publishing numerous papers on ancient military history, the Hellenistic and Roman East, and the history of military theory, he translated (with Peter Krentz) Polyaenus' *Stratagems of War* (1994). His *Stratagem and the Vocabulary of Military Trickery* appeared in 1988. An edited volume, *The Armies of Classical Greece*, is forthcoming.

Michael Whitby is Professor of Classics and Ancient History at the University of Warwick. He is author of several articles on the late Roman army and has recently been responsible for editing the late Roman section of the *Cambridge History of Ancient Warfare* (2006). His many publications include *Warfare in the Late Roman World, 280–640* (1999).

Abbreviations of Reference Works and Journals

AE	*Année épigraphique*
AJAH	*American Journal of Ancient History*
AJP	*American Journal of Philology*
AncSoc	*Ancient Society*
ANRW	*Aufstieg und Niedergang der römischen Welt*
BASP	*Bulletin of the American Society of Papyrologists*
BGU	*Aegyptische Urkunden aus den staatlichen Museen zu Berlin; Griechische Urkunden*
BICS	*Bulletin of the Institute of Classical Studies of the University of London*
BJ	*Bonner Jahrbücher*
BMCRR	H. Mattingly and R. A. G. Carson, *Coins of the Roman Empire in the British Museum*, 1923–
CAH	*Cambridge Ancient History*
CBFIR	E. Schallmayer et al., *Corpus der griechischen und lateinischen Beneficiarier-Inschriften des römischen Reiches*, Stuttgart 1990
ChLA	A. Bruckner and R. Marichal (eds.), *Chartae Latinae antiquiores*, Basel 1954–
CIL	*Corpus Inscriptionum Latinarum*
CP	*Classical Philology*
CPL	R. Cavenaile, ed. *Corpus Papyrorum Latinarum*, Wiesbaden 1958
CQ	*Classical Quarterly*

CRAI	*Comptes rendus de l'académie des Inscriptions et Belles-Lettres*
Daris	S. Daris, *Documenti per la storia dell'esercito romano in Egitto*, Milan 1964
EA	*Epigraphica Anatolica*
FIRA	S. Riccobono et al., *Fontes iuris romani anteiustiniani*, 1940–3
FO	L. Vidman (ed.), *Fasti Ostienses*, Prague 1982
GRBS	*Greek, Roman, and Byzantine Studies*
IGBulg	G. Mikailov, *Inscriptiones Graecae in Bulgaria repertae*, Sofia 1956–1987
IGLSyr	*Inscriptions grecques et latines de la Syrie*
IGR (R)	R. Cagnat et al., *Inscriptiones Graecae ad res Romanas pertinentes*, Paris 1901–27
ILAlg	*Inscriptions latines de l'Algerie*, 3 vols., Paris 1922, 1957, 1976
ILS	H. Dessau (ed.), *Inscriptiones Latinae selectae*, Berlin 1954
InscrAq	J. B. Brusin (ed.), *Inscriptiones Aquileiae*, 3 vols., Udine 1991–3
JDAI	*Jahrbuch des Deutschen Archäologischen Instituts*
JHS	*Journal of Hellenic Studies*
JÖB	*Jahrbuch der österreichischen Byzantinistik*
JRA	*Journal of Roman Archaeology*
JRGZ	*Jahrbuch des Römisch-Germanischen Zentralmuseums Mainz*
JRMES	*Journal of Roman Military Equipment Studies*
JRS	*Journal of Roman Studies*
LA	*Liber Annuus* (Studium Biblicum Franciscanum Jerusalem)
LCL	Loeb Classical Library
Lib. Hist. Franc.	*Liber Historia Francorum*
LTUR	Eva Margareta Steinby (ed.), *Lexicon Topographicum Urbis Romae*, 6 vols., Rome 1993–2000.
MAAR	*Memoirs of the American Academy in Rome*
Mitteis, *Chr.*	L. Mitteis und U. Wilcken, *Grundzüge und Chrestomatie der Papyruskunde*, Leipzig 1912
MRR	T. R. S. Broughton, *The Magistrates of the Roman Republic*, 3 vols. (1951, 1952, 1986)

Not.Dig.Occ.	*Notitia Dignitatum Occidentis*
O. Amst.	R. S. Bagnall, P. J. Sijpesteijn, and K. A. Worp, *Ostraka in Amsterdam* Collections, Zutphen 1976
O. Bu Djem	R. Marichal (ed.), *Les Ostraca de Bu Djem*, Tripoli 1992
O. Claud.	J. Bingen et al., *Mons Claudianus. Ostraca Graeca et Latina*, Cairo 1992, 1997, 2000
O. Florida	R. S. Bagnall (ed.), *The Florida Ostraka. Documents from the Roman Army in Upper Egypt*, Durham, NC 1976
OJA	*Oxford Journal of Archaeology*
OLD	P. W. G. Glare (ed.), *Oxford Latin Dictionary*, Oxford 1968–82
P. Abinn.	H. I. Bell et al. (eds.), *The Abinnaeus Archive: Papers of a Roman Officer in the Reign of Constantius II*, Oxford 1962
P. Berol.	G. Ioannidou (ed.), *Catalogue of Greek and Latin Literary Papyri in Berlin (P.Berol.inv. 21101–21299, 21911)*, Mainz 1996
P. Brooklyn	J. C. Shelton (ed.), *Greek and Latin Papyri, Ostraca, and Wooden Tablets in the Collection of the Brooklyn Museum*, Florence 1992
P. Columb.	*Columbia Papyri*. Vol. I (1929)–XI (1998)
P. Dura	C. Bradford-Welles et al., *The Excavations at Dura-Europos. Final Report V 1. The Parchments and Papyri*, 1959
P. Fay.	*Fayum Towns and their Papyri*, B. P. Grenfell, A. S. Hunt, and D. G. Hogarth (eds.). London 1900
P. Fouad	A. Bataille et al. (eds.), *Les papyrus Fouad*, Cairo 1939
P. Grenf. 1	B. P. Grenfell, *An Alexandrian Erotic Fragment and Other Greek Papyri, Chiefly Ptolemaic*, Oxford 1896
P. Grenf. 2	B. P. Grenfell and A. S. Hunt, *New Classical Fragments and Other Greek and Latin Papyri*, Oxford 1897
P. Hamb.	P. M. Meyer (ed.), *Griechische Papyrusurkunden der hamburger Staats- und Universitätsbibliothek*, Leipzig/Berlin 1911–24
P. Mich.	*Michigan Papyri*. Vol. I (1931)–XIX (1999)
P. Osl.	*Papyri Osloenses*. Oslo. Vol. I, S. Eitrem (ed.), *Magical Papyri*, 1925. Vol. II, S. Eitrem and L. Amundsen (eds.), 1931. Vol. III, S. Eitrem and L. Amundsen (eds.) 1936
P. Oxy.	B. P. Grenfell and A. S. Hunt et al., *The Oxyrhynchus Papyri*, London 1898–
P. Panop.	T. C. Skeat, *Papyri from Panopolis in the Chester Beatty Library*,

Beatty   *Dublin*, Dublin 1964

P. Petaus   U. Hagedorn et al. (eds.), *Das Archiv des Petaus*, Cologne 1969

P. Strasb.   *Griechische Papyrus der kaiserlichen Universitäts- und Landesbibliothek zu Strassburg*

P. Yale   Yale Papyri in the Beinecke Rare Book and Manuscript Library

PBSR   *Papers of the British School at Rome*

PG   J.-P. Migne, *Patrologia Graeca*, Paris 1857–66

P.Gen.Lat.   J. Nicole and C. Morel (eds.), *Archives militaires du Ier siècle* (*Texte inédit du Papyrus Latin de Genève No. 1*). Geneva 1900

PIR   E. Klebs et al. (eds.), *Prosopographia Imperii Romani*, Berlin 1897–8

PIR^2   E. Groag et al., *Prosopographia Imperii Romani*, Berlin 1933–

PLRE   J. Morris et al. (ed.), *Prosopography of the Later Roman Empire*, Cambridge 1971–92

PSI   G. Vitelli et al. (eds.), *Papiri greci e latini*, Florence 1912–

RAC   *Reallexikon für Antike und Christentum*, Stuttgart 1950–

REB   *Revue des études byzantines*

REMA   *Revue des études militaires anciennes*

RIB   R. G. Collingwood and R. P. Wright, *The Roman Inscriptions of Britain*. Vol. 1. *Inscriptions on Stone*, Oxford 1965

RIC   *The Roman Imperial Coinage*. Vols. I–X, London 1923–94

RIU   *Die römischen Inschriften Ungarns*, Budapest, 5 vols., Amsterdam 1972–91

RMD   M. M. Roxan, *Roman Military Diplomas*, 1 (1954–77), 2 (1978–84), 3 (1985–93), London 1978, 1985, 1994

RMR   R. O. Fink, *Roman Military Documents on Papyrus*, Cleveland 1971

RPC   A. Burnett et al., *Roman Provincial Coinage*, London 1992–

RRC   M. H. Crawford, *Roman Republican Coinage*, Cambridge 1974

SB   F. Preisigke et al., *Sammelbuch griechischer Urkunden aus Ägypten*, Strassburg/Berlin/Leipzig 1913–

SEG   *Supplementum Epigraphicum Graecum*

Sel. Pap.   A. S. Hunt and C. C. Edgar (eds. and trans.), *Select Papyri* Vol. I: *Non-Literary Papyri Private Affairs*, Cambridge, MA: 1932, repr. 1988; and Vol. II: *Official Documents*, Cambridge, MA 1934, repr. 1995

Sylloge	W. Dittenberger, *Sylloge Inscriptionum Graecarum*
Tab. Vindol. 1	A. K. Bowman and J. D. Thomas, *Vindolanda. The Latin Writing Tablets*, Gloucester 1983
Tab. Vindol. 2	A. K. Bowman and J. D. Thomas, *The Vindolanda Writing Tablets*, London 1994
Tab. Vindol. 3	A. K. Bowman and J. D. Thomas, with contributions by John Pearce, *The Vindolanda Writing Tablets*, London 2003
TAPhS	*Transactions of the American Philosophical Society*
Waddington	W. H. Waddington, "Inscriptiones grecques et latines de la Syrie recueilles et expliquees," Paris 1870
W.Chr.	U. Wilcken, *Chrestomathie*, Leipzig 1912
YCS	*Yale Classical Studies*
ZPE	*Zeitschrift für Papyrologie und Epigraphik*
ZRG	*Zeitschrift der Savigny-Stiftung für Rechtsgeschichte (Romanistische Abteilung)*

Abbreviations of Works of Classical Literature

Aen. Tact.	Aeneas Tacticus
Appian, *B. Civ.*	*Bella civilia*
Appian, *Iber.*	*Iberike*
Appian, *Mithr.*	*Mithridateius*
Appian, *Pun.*	*Libyke*
Appian, *Syr.*	*Syriake*
Apuleius, *Met.*	Lucius Apuleius, *Metamorpheses* [= The golden ass]
Augustine, *Epist.*	Aurelius Augustinus (= St. Augustine), *Epistulae*
Aurelius Victor, *Caes.*	Sextus Aurelius Victor, *Caesares*
[Caesar], *B. Afr.*	[Trad. ascribed to C. Iulius Caesar], *De bello Africano*
[Caesar], *B. Alex.*	[Trad. ascribed to C. Iulius Caesar], *De bello Alexandrino*
Caesar, *B. Gal.*	C. Iulius Caesar, *De bello Gallico*
Caesar, *B. Civ.*	*De bello civili*
Calpurnius Piso, *Ann.*	L. Calpurnius Piso Frugi, *Annales*
Cic., *Brutus*	M. Tullius Cicero, *Brutus*
Cicero, *Agr.*	*De lege agraria*
Cicero, *Att.*	*Epistulae ad Atticum*
Cicero, *Fin.*	*De finibus bonum et malorum*
Cicero, *Flacc.*	*Pro Flacco*
Cicero, *Har.*	*De haruspicum responso*

Cicero, *Leg. Man.*	*Pro lege Manilia*
Cicero, *Nat. Deo.*	*De natura deorum*
Cicero, *Off.*	*De officiis*
Cicero, *pro Font.*	*Pro Fonteio*
Cicero, *Rep.*	*De republica*
Cicero, *Sen.*	*De senectute*
Cicero, *Sull.*	*Pro Sulla*
Cicero, *Tusc.*	*Tusculanae disputationes*
Claudianus, *B. Get.*	Claudius Claudianus, *Bellum Geticum*
Claudianus, *III Cons. Hon.*	*De tertio consulatu Honorii augusti*
Claudianus, *In Eutr.*	*In Eutropium*
Cod. Just.	*Codex Iustiniani*
Cod. Theod.	*Codex Theodosiani*
Corippus, *Laud. Iust.*	Flavius Cresconius Corippus, *In laudem Iustini*
De vir. ill.	*De viri illustribus*
Dig.	*Digesta*
Ennius, *Ann.*	Q. Ennius, *Annales*
Epictetus, *Disc.*	*Diatribae*
Epiphanius of Salamis,	
Adv. haeres.	*Adversus haereses*
Epit. de Caes.	*Epitome de Caesaribus*
Eugippius, *Vit. Sev.*	*Vita Sancti Severini*
Eusebius, *Vit. Const.*	*Vita Constantini*
Festus, *Brev*	*Breviarium*
Frontinus, *Strat.*	Sextus Iulius Frontinus, *Strategemata*
Fronto, *Ad M Caes,*	M. Cornelius Fronto
A. Gellius, *NA*	Aulus Gellius, *Noctes Atticae* [*Attic nights*]
Gregory of Tours, *HF*	Gregorius, Bishop of Tours, *Historiae Francorum*
HA, Ant. Pius	*Historia Augusta, Antoninus Pius*
HA, Aurel.	*Aurelianus*
HA, Avid.	*Avidius*

HA, Caracalla	*Caracalla*
HA, Comm.	*Commodus*
HA, Gall.	*Gallienus*
HA, Hadr.	*Hadrianus*
HA, Marc.	*Marcus Aurelius*
HA, Pert.	*Pertinax*
HA, Sev.	*Septimius Severus*
HA, Sev. Alex.	*Severus Alexander*
HA, Tyr. Trig.	*Tyranni Triginta*
Heliodoros, *Aith.*	Heliodoros, *Aethiopica*
Hieronymus, *Chron.*	*Chronica*
Hieronymus, *Epist.*	*Epistulae*
Hilarius, *Epist.*	*Epistula ad Eucherium*
Johannes Lydos, *Mens.*	*De mensibus*
Josephus, *Ant. Jud.*	Flavius Josephus, *Antiquitates Iudaicae*
Josephus, *B. Jud.*	*Bellum Judaicum*
Lactantius, *Mort. Pers.*	Lucius Caecilius Firmianus, *De mortibus persecutorum*
Libanius, *Orat.*	*Orationes*
Livy	T. Livius, *Ab urbe condita*
Livy, *Per.*	*Periochae*
Mauricius, *Strat.*	*Strategikon*
Mon. Anc.	*Monumentum Ancyranum = Res Gestae Divi Augusti*
ND	*Notitia Dignitatum*
Nov. Iust.	*Novellae Iustiniani*
Novellae Val.	*Novellae Valeriani*
Onasander	*Strategicus*
Pan. Lat.	*Panegyrici Latini*
Paulus, *Epit. Fest.*	Paulus Diaconus, *Epitoma Festi*
Petrus Patricius, *Exc. Vat.*	Petrus Patricius
Philo, *Flacc.*	*In Flaccum*
Philo, *Leg.*	*Legatio ad Gaium*

Philostratus, *VS*	*Vitae sophistarum*
Pliny, *Epist.*	C. Plinius Caecilius Secundus, *Epistulae*
Pliny, *NH*	C. Plinius Secundus, *Naturalis historiae*
Pliny, *Pan.*	[= C. Plinius Caecilius Secundus], *Panegyricus*
Plutarch, *Aem.*	Plutarchus, *Aemilius Paulus*
Plutarch, *Ant.*	*Antonius*
Plutarch, *C. Gracc.*	*C. Gracchus*
Plutarch, *Cam.*	*Camillus*
Plutarch, *Cato Mai.*	*Cato Maior*
Plutarch, *Crass.*	*Crassus*
Plutarch, *Def. Or.*	*de defectu oraculorum*
Plutarch, *Galba*	*Galba*
Plutarch, *Luc.*	*Lucullus*
Plutarch, *Marc.*	*Marcellus*
Plutarch, *Otho*	*Otho*
Plutarch, *Pomp.*	*Pompeius*
Plutarch, *Pyrrh.*	*Pyrrhus*
Plutarch, *T. Gracc.*	*T. Gracchus*
Plutarch, *Tim.*	*Timoleon*
Porphyr., *De Caer.*	Constantine Porphyrogenitus, *De Caeremoniis*
Procopius, *Aedificia*	*Aedificia*
Procopius, *Bella*	*Bella*
Ps.-Fredegar, *Chron.*	[ascribed to] Fredegar, *Chronica*
Ps.-Hyginus, *Mun. Castr.*	Ps.-Hyginus [ascribed to Hyginus], *De munitionibus castrorum*
Rutilius Namatianus, *Red.*	Rutilius Claudius Namatianus, *de reditu*
Sallust, *Cat.*	C. Sallustius Crispus, *Catilina*
Sallust, *Jug.*	*Iugurtha*
Seneca, *Nat.*	L. Annaeus Seneca, *Naturales quaestiones*
Socrates, *Hist. Eccl.*	*Historia Ecclesiastica*
Sozomen, *Hist. Eccl.*	Sozomenos, *Historia Ecclesiastica*

Stat. Silv.	Publius Papinius Statius, *Silvae*
Suetonius, *Aug.*	C. Suetonius Tranquillus, *Augustus*
Suetonius, *Cal.*	*Caligula*
Suetonius, *Claud.*	*Claudius*
Suetonius, *Dom.*	*Domitianus*
Suetonius, *Jul.*	*Iulius Caesar*
Suetonius, *Nero*	*Nero*
Suetonius, *Tib.*	*Tiberius*
Symmachus, *Epist.*	Quintus Aurelius Symmachus, *Epistulae*
Symmachus, *Relat.*	*Relationes*
Synesius, *Regn.*	*De Regno*
Tacitus, *Agric.*	Cornelius Tacitus, *Agricola*
Tacitus, *Ann.*	*Annales*
Tacitus, *Hist.*	*Historia*
Tertullianus, *Ad nat.*	Q. Septimius Florens Tertullianus, *Ad nationes*
Tertullianus, *Apol.*	*Apologeticum*
Tertullianus, *Cor.*	*De Corona*
Tertullianus, *Idol.*	*De idololatria*
Theophanes, *Chron.*	Theophanes Confessor, *Chronographia*
Ulpian, *Edict*	Domitius Ulpianus, *Ad edictum*
Varro, *L.L.*	M. Terentius Varro, *de lingua Latina*
Vegetius, *Epit.*	Flavius Renatus Vegetius, *Epitoma rei militaris*
Vell.	C. Velleius Paterculus
Vergilius, *Ecl.*	P. Vergilius Maro, *Eclogae*
Vergilius, *Georg.*	*Georgica*
Victor of Vita	Victor of Vita, *Historia persecutionis Africanae provinciae temporum Geiserici et Hunerici regis Vandalorum*
Xenophon, *Anab.*	*Anabasis*
Xenophon, *Cyr.*	*Cyropaideia*
Zacharias of Mytilene, *Hist. Eccl.*	*Historia Ecclesia*

Introduction

Paul Erdkamp

The guiding principle behind this companion to the Roman army is the belief that the Roman army cannot adequately be described only as an instrument of combat, but must be viewed also as an essential component of Roman society, economy, and politics. Of course, the prime purpose of the Roman army was to defeat the enemy in battle. Whether the army succeeded depended not only on its weapons and equipment, but also its training and discipline, and on the experience of its soldiers, all of which combined to allow the most effective deployment of its manpower. Moreover, every army is backed by a more or less developed organization that is needed to mobilize and sustain it. Changes in Roman society significantly affected the Roman army. However, the army was also itself an agent of change, determining in large part developments in politics and government, economy and society. Four themes recur throughout the volume: (1) the army as a fighting force; (2) the mobilization of human and material resources; (3) the relationship between army, politics, and empire; and (4) the relationship between the armies and the civilian population. Even in a sizeable volume such as this choices have had to be made regarding the topics to be discussed, but the focus in this volume on the army in politics, economy, and society reflects the direction of recent research.

Modern authors often claim that ancient Rome was a militaristic society, and that warfare dominated the lives of the Roman people. Interestingly, the first outsider in Rome to paint an extensive picture of Roman society and whose account has largely survived essentially says the same thing. Polybius was in a position to know, since he was brought to Rome as a hostage after the Third Macedonian War (171–168 BC) and was befriended by one of the leading families. The main task he set himself in his *Histories* was to explain Rome's incredible military success during the past decades. To Polybius, the stability of her constitution was one important element, but Rome's military success is explained by two other elements: manpower and ethos. At the eve of the Hannibalic War, Polybius informs us, Rome was able to mobilize 700,000 men in the infantry and 70,000 horsemen. To be sure, Rome never assembled an army of such size – even in imperial times her soldiers did not number as many as 700,000. But such a number of men was available to take up arms and fight Rome's opponents in Italy or overseas. In other words, almost all male, able-bodied citizens of Rome and her allies could be expected to serve in the army at one point or another. Military service was indeed the main duty of a Roman citizen, and military experience was widespread. The empires that Rome had defeated in the past decades – Carthage, Macedon, the Seleucid Empire – had lost the connection between citizenship and military service, instead relying largely on mercenaries. Polybius was also struck by the military ethos that Roman traditions instilled in the Roman elite and common people alike. Citizens and allies were awarded in front of the entire army for bravery in combat. Decorations were worn on public occasions during the rest of the soldiers' lives. Trophies were hung in the most conspicuous places in their homes.

> So when we consider this people's almost obsessive concern with military rewards and punishments, and the immense importance which they attach to both, it is not surprising that they emerge with brilliant success from every war in which they engage. (Polybius 6.39)

At the time that Polybius witnessed Roman society, the army and military ethos played important roles in the lives of almost all male Roman citizens. In that sense, Rome's was a militaristic society.

Although war and the army remained important aspects of the Roman Empire, it would be difficult to characterize Roman society at the time of Augustus (31 BC–14 AD) or Trajan (98–117 AD) as militaristic to the same degree. Just as the term "Roman" applied to ever widening circles, more and more recruits enlisting in the legions came from Spain, Gaul, and other provinces, while the people of the capital city did not serve in the armies anymore. Moreover, military service had become a lifetime profession for a minority of the empire's inhabitants. Recruits signed up to serve for up to 25 years. Many would die while serving in the army, though more of natural causes than due to military action. Many veterans from the legions became prominent members of local society, while those who had served in the auxiliary forces earned Roman citizenship at discharge. However, only a few percent of the empire's population served in the armies or fleets. Large sections of the empire hardly saw Roman armies at all during the next centuries, while many soldiers never saw combat. The army still held an important place in society, mostly so in the border regions where the majority of troops were concentrated, but this role had changed significantly.

Waging war remained the largest task undertaken by the state, and the army was the largest institution that the state created. It certainly was the most expensive, taking up about three quarters of the annual imperial budget. Mobilizing, equipping, and feeding the several hundred thousand men that were stationed between Brittannia's northern border and the Arabian desert was an undertaking that could not be sustained by the market alone, and required the direct intervention of the central and local authorities. On the other hand, the presence of Roman legions and auxiliary forces was the engine that drove crucial developments in the economy and society of the border regions. And it was through the army that many members of local aristocracies were integrated into the Roman Empire.

The army retained a central role in the power structures within the empire. Addressing the Roman Senate, Augustus used the phrase "I and the army are well," leaving no doubt about who ruled the empire and with what backing. Hence the close connection between emperor and armies was an important message to convey not only to the senators in Italy and peoples throughout the empire, but – most crucially – to the armies as well. While the Praetorian Guard, which was stationed near Rome, played an important role on the accession to the throne of Claudius in 41 AD, in the civil wars of 68–69 AD the armies of the Rhine, Danube, and the East decided who would be put on the throne. While the nature of the relationship between the emperors and the senatorial class (to which belonged many of the authors on whose historical narrative we nowadays rely) colors – and possibly distorts – our picture of individual emperors, the most important development in the position of the emperor during the next centuries may be said to have been the changing relationship between army and emperor. Whatever their qualities and intentions, emperors could not function without maintaining close relations with the troops. One of the problems was that many units were almost permanently stationed in the same region, and drew recruits from their locality. Troops developed regional ties that proved stronger in times of crisis than the ties with Rome or the emperor. In the mid-third century AD the position of emperor became the prize in a struggle between the various armies stationed in Britain, along the Rhine and Danube, and in the East. Diocletian (284–305) and Constantine (312–337) managed to restore control of the armies. In the meantime, however, Rome and Italy had lost their centrality, while internal threats played as much a role in the development of the army as did external wars.

The traditional view of the late Roman Empire held that, as the nature of the opponents along the borders changed and their strength became ever greater, the empire threatened to collapse under the stress, leading on the one hand to more state control of society in order to maintain military strength, on the other hand to a weakening army, consisting more and more of barbaric peoples or farmer-soldiers of dubious military value. This picture now seems largely untrue: the central authorities did not suffocate civil society in order to maintain the war effort, nor were the Roman armies of the fourth, fifth, and sixth centuries AD less capable of striking forceful blows at their opponents. In the fourth century, many Germanic peoples served in the Roman armies. The landowners paid money to hire men, and kept their own people on the land. The western half of the Roman Empire did indeed collapse, as after the battle of Adrianople large tracts of land came under the control of migrating Germanic peoples – in particular Vandals, Visigoths, and Ostrogoths – who were eventually allowed to settle under their own rule, but who increasingly made it impossible for the central Roman authorities to gather the resources necessary to sustain a sizeable army of their own. The armies of the emperor Justinian (527–565), which were backed by a populous eastern empire and reconquered Italy, northern Africa, and southern Spain from their Germanic kings, may be seen as the last Roman armies.

PART I

Early Rome

CHAPTER ONE

Warfare and the Army in Early Rome

John Rich

1 Introduction

By the mid-sixth century BC, Rome had become the largest city in western central Italy and one of its leading powers, but the reach of Roman power remained for a long time confined to the Tiber basin and its immediate environs. The Romans' penetration further afield began with their intervention in Campania in 343 BC and led in some seventy years to the conquest of all Italy south of the Po Valley. However, this advance and the ensuing expansion overseas cannot be understood without some examination of Roman warfare and military developments in the preceding centuries. This is the subject of the present chapter, and the following chapter considers some aspects in further detail.

The evidence for early Roman history is notoriously problematic. Roman historians developed extensive narratives, preserved most fully for us in two histories written in the late first century BC, by Livy and by Dionysius of Halicarnassus (the latter in Greek, and fully extant only for the period down to 443 BC). However, Roman historical writing only began in the late third century BC, and it is clear that the early accounts were greatly elaborated by later writers. For the period of the kings, most of what we are told is legend or imaginative reconstruction. From the foundation of the republic (traditionally dated to 509 BC), the historians give an annual record. This incorporated a good deal of authentic data, transmitted either orally or from documentary sources such as the record of events kept from quite early times by the Pontifex Maximus. However, this material underwent extensive distortion and elaboration in the hands of successive historians writing up their accounts for literary effect and expanding the narrative with what they regarded as plausible reconstructions. As a result the identification of the hard core of authentic data in the surviving historical accounts is very problematic and its extent remains disputed. There is general agreement that much of what we are told is literary confection, and this applies in particular to most of the accounts of early wars, which are full of stereotyped and often anachronistic invention.

Despite these difficulties, it is possible to establish a good deal about early Roman history and to make an assessment of the character of its warfare. We are helped in this by a range of further information, including data preserved by other ancient writers, for example antiquarian accounts of Roman institutions, a few inscriptions, and, particularly for the regal period, extensive archaeological evidence.[1]

2   Roman War and Expansion: The Regal Period

Rome's early success owed a good deal to its site: a group of defensible hills, at the Tiber crossing where the north–south route from Etruria to Campania intersected with the route from the interior to the sea and the saltbeds at the Tiber mouth. In origin Rome was just one of many communities of Latins, inhabiting the plain south of the Tiber and the immediately surrounding hillsides, and sharing the same Indo-European dialect and material culture and some common sanctuaries. North of the Tiber lived the Etruscans; these were non-Indo-European speakers, but in the early centuries the material culture of the southern Etruscan communities, and in particular Rome's neighbor Veii, had much in common with that of the Latins. East of Veii, and still north of the river, lived the Faliscans, linguistically close to the Latins. On the Roman side of the river, beyond the Latins lived other linguistically related peoples such as the Sabines. The wide range of peoples sharing and competing for these lands was to be an important factor in the Romans' early development.

Habitation began at Rome at least c. 1000 BC, and by the eighth century several hut-villages had formed, on the Palatine Hill and elsewhere. Grave furnishings in the region show increased social stratification and some spectacular wealth from the eighth century. In later seventh century Rome we can discern the creation of public buildings and spaces at Rome: by now it had evolved from a village community into a city-state.

Rome was now ruled by kings, perhaps more than the seven recorded by tradition. Modern writers have often supposed that under the last three kings (Tarquin I, Servius Tullius, Tarquin II) Rome was under Etruscan rule, but this doctrine has been refuted by Cornell. These reigns must have covered the mid- to late sixth century, and both the historical tradition and archaeological indications show that this was a period of enhanced prosperity, with Rome now established as the most flourishing city in Latium.[2]

The Roman historical tradition ascribed victorious wars and expansion against the Latins and other neighboring peoples to all but one of the kings, but very little of this detailed narrative can be historical. It is, nonetheless, likely that by the late sixth century Roman territory had reached roughly the extent which the tradition indicates for the regal period: there was a significant bridgehead on the right bank of the Tiber, and at least on the left bank Roman territory reached the sea, while to the southeast it extended up to the Alban Mount. Alföldi argued that much of this expansion did not take place till the later fifth century, but this must be wrong, since such substantial growth in that period would surely have been reflected in the tradition.[3]

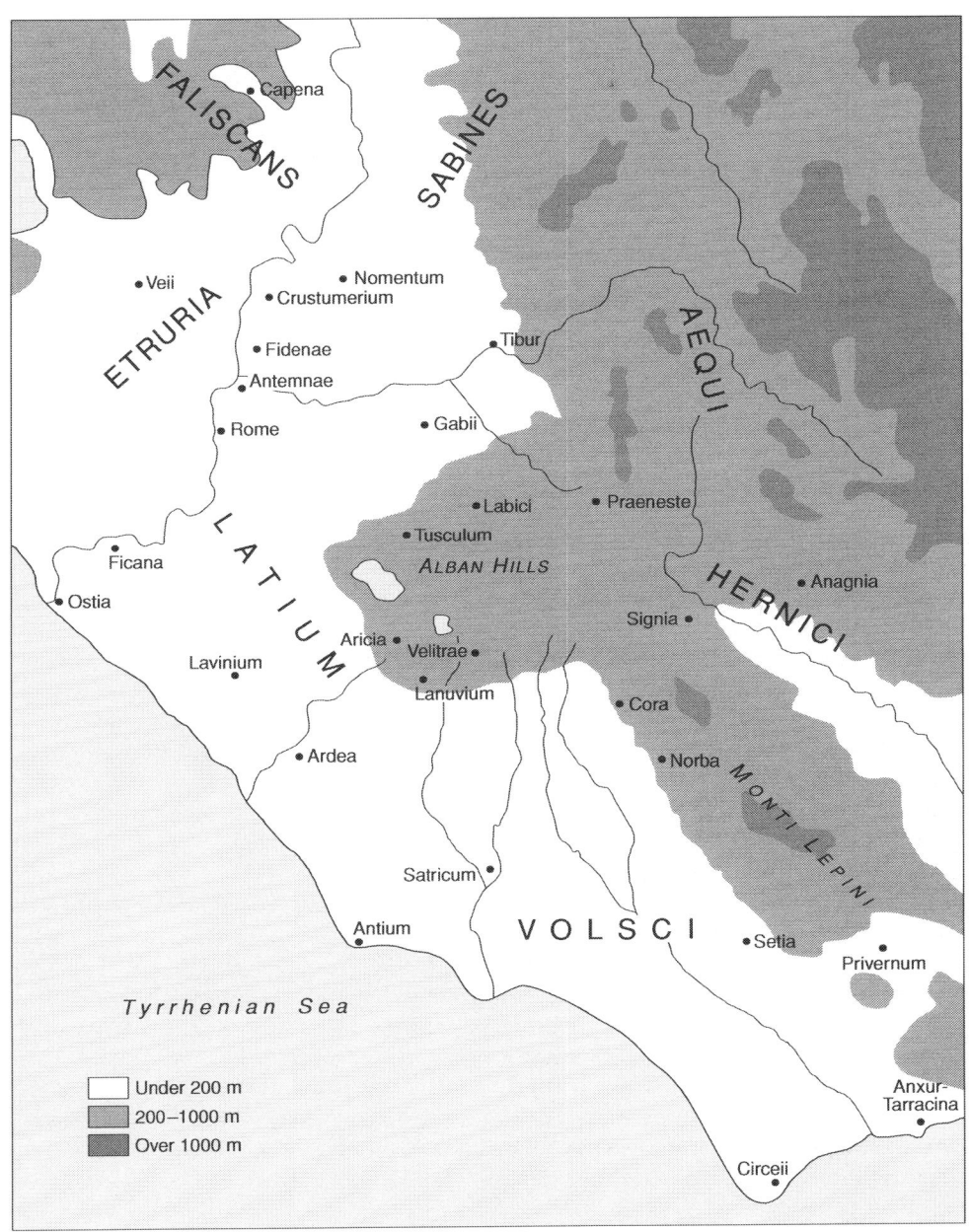

Map 1.1 Early Latium and its environs

Rome was not the only Latin community to expand in the archaic period, but its territory had become much larger than any other's. Beloch's estimates, though highly conjectural, are plausible approximations: he reckoned Roman territory at the end of the sixth century as 822 square kilometers, just over a third of all Latin territory (2,344 km²).[4]

The literary tradition represents Rome as seeking to assert supremacy over the other Latins from the reign of Tullus Hostilius on, with the Latins frequently mounting combined opposition. Little in this tradition is of any value, but, in view of the greater size of their city and territory, it is likely that the last kings were able to establish some form of hegemony over at least some of the Latins.

Remarkable evidence of the extent of Roman claims in the late sixth century may be afforded by their first treaty with Carthage, preserved by the second century BC Greek historian Polybius (3.22), in which the Carthaginians undertake not to injure "the people of Ardea, Antium, Lavinium, Circeii, Tarracina or any other of the Latins who are subjects." Although the alternative dating to 348 still has its supporters, most scholars now accept Polybius' dating of the treaty to the first year of the republic. Whichever dating is correct, the claim to rule over Antium, Circeii, and Tarracina probably represents an exaggeration of Roman power. These coastal towns, and the Pomptine Plain behind them, were occupied by the Volsci, and full Roman control was not established there until 338. It is commonly supposed that the Volsci were invaders who only arrived in the Pomptine region in the early fifth century. However, the tradition represents them as already present there in the time of the Roman kings, and we should accept its accuracy on the point. The supposed fifth-century Volscian invasion of the Pomptine region and ousting of the Latins would have been a momentous event, and it is most unlikely that no trace of it should have survived in Roman memory.[5]

Warfare was probably not the only means by which the Romans in the seventh and sixth centuries were able to extend their territory and their power. Nonetheless, despite its unreliability in detail, the historical tradition is probably right to portray them as often at war then with their Latin and other neighbors. The profits of such wars will have been one of the sources of the wealth of sixth-century Rome: the tradition that the great temple on the Capitol was built from the spoils from the last Tarquin's capture of Pometia may be well founded.[6]

The frequency of these wars can only be conjectured. Violent conflict between Romans and members of other communities may well have occurred most years. Ritual evidence has often been held to show that in early times, as later, war was a regular, annual occurrence for the Romans, with ancient rituals held in March and October being interpreted as opening and closing the campaigning season. However, the original significance of most of these rituals is disputed, and there is no ancient evidence that they constituted a seasonal war-cycle.[7]

One indication of the significance of warfare in archaic Latium is the spread of fortifications. Earth ramparts with ditches appear at some sites in the eighth century, and at numerous others over the seventh and sixth centuries. Some sites acquired complex defenses, like the three successive ramparts protecting the approach to Ardea. At least one town, Lavinium, seems to have acquired a stone circuit wall by the sixth century.

However, the large cities did not yet feel the need for such comprehensive defenses: the circuit walls at the southern Etruscan cities date to the later fifth and fourth centuries, and, although Rome acquired some partial fortifications in the archaic period, the first circuit wall, the so-called Servian Wall, in fact dates to the early fourth century.

3   Roman War and Expansion: The Early Republic

Little of historical value can be gleaned from the complex tales relating to the overthrow of Tarquin II, but there is no good reason to doubt the core fact, corroborated by the surviving magistrate list, that in the late sixth century BC (conventionally 509) the king was expelled and replaced by two annually elected chief magistrates, originally called praetors, but generally known from their later title, consul.[8] As already noted, the historians give an annual record from this point, in which wars bulk large, but any attempt to assess the warfare of the period must take full account of the record's deficiencies. The campaign details are generally obvious confections; there are some evident duplications, and at least some of the reported campaigns are probably the construction of historians, seeking to fill out the annual record with plausible invention.

It is often supposed that, as in later centuries, the Romans of the early republic were almost constantly at war, but that, whereas their later warfare was generally expansionist, in the fifth century they were mostly on the defensive against enemy attacks, and often fighting for their very survival.[9] This assessment requires modification.

The historical tradition itself indicates a striking fluctuation in the frequency of warfare: Roman forces are reported in combat in only fourteen of the years from 454 to 411, whereas before and after that period warfare is said to have occurred almost every year. Much of the recorded warfare may be invented, and much actual warfare may have left no trace in the record. Nonetheless, it is likely that this striking disparity has some correspondence to reality, and that the Romans were engaged in significantly less warfare in the later fifth century than before or after.

The expulsion of the kings appears to have ushered in a phase of widespread turbulence in the Tiber region. Rome may have been occupied for a time by the Etruscan adventurer Lars Porsenna, and, besides other conflicts, the Romans were confronted by a coalition of Latin states. However, they came out of these struggles well. Upstream on the Tiber left bank, they secured possession of Fidenae and Crustumerium.[10] The Latins were decisively defeated at Lake Regillus (probably located northwest of Tusculum; the battle is dated to 499 by Livy or 496 by Dionysius). A few years later, treaties of alliance were concluded first with the Latins and then with the Hernici, who lived in the upper valley of the Sacco, separated from the Tiber Valley by the watershed between the Alban Hills and Praeneste. According to tradition, both treaties were negotiated by Spurius Cassius, in respectively 493 and 486.

The treaties were probably formally equal, but it was a mark of the Romans' preeminence that the other Latin communities collectively made a bilateral agreement with the republic. Livy's and Dionysius' accounts of the subsequent warfare must exaggerate the subordination of the Latins and Hernici to the Romans, but it is doubt-ful whether the allied forces ever served under a non-Roman commander. Most import-antly, the alliances lasted. Livy (6.2.3) may exaggerate in claiming that there was no wavering in the loyalty of the Latins and Hernici until 389, but it is likely that there was little or no armed conflict between the Romans and their Latin neighbors in the intervening period, in marked contrast with the sixth century and earlier.[11]

Livy and Dionysius report very frequent conflict with the Sabines, Volsci, and Aequi, usually represented as starting with enemy raiding on the territory of the Romans or their allies. The Romans are portrayed as often suffering reverses, but generally gaining the upper hand, sometimes winning battles and capturing towns, but often contenting themselves with retaliatory plundering. Conflict with the Sabines is last reported in 449, but with the other two extends from the first notices, in 495, down to 388 for the Aequi and the later fourth century for the Volsci.

Modern writers commonly suppose that the historical reality behind these con-ventionalized reports is that, especially in the early fifth century, the Romans and their allies were under sustained and almost annual assault from mountain peoples pressing down on the plains. This interpretation depends heavily on the sources for the frequency of the conflicts and for the conception of the Romans' role as essen-tially defensive and reactive. However, the apparent frequency may partly result from the historians' invention of items to fill up the annual record, and their proclivity for presenting all Roman wars as justified responses to aggression is notorious. Moreover, the sources are much more upbeat about Roman successes than the bleak modern portrayals allow.

The Sabines of the Tiber Valley had had frequent contacts, both peaceful and viol-ent, with their Roman neighbors from early times. Intermittent conflict between Romans and Sabines probably continued in the early fifth century, but then tailed off, as the tradition suggests. The conflict with the Aequi and Volsci, however, arose from the early fifth-century regional turbulence and the ensuing alliances with the Latins and Hernici. The Romans themselves were separated from the Aequian and Volscian lands by the intervening territory of Latin communities, and the prospect of help against these enemies was probably one of the factors which attracted the Latins and Hernici to the Roman alliance.

The Volsci who came into conflict with the Romans and their allies dwelt in the coastal Pomptine plain from Antium to Anxur (their name for Tarracina) and the adjacent Monti Lepini. It is commonly supposed that they were invaders originat-ing from the central Italian mountains who had only recently arrived in this region, but, as we saw above, it is preferable to follow the ancient sources in holding that they had been present there from the sixth century or earlier. Whatever their origins, they were not now predominantly mountain dwellers: many dwelt in the plain or on the coast, and some of their settlements will have had an urban character.

The Aequi who clashed with the Roman alliance dwelt in the upper Aniene Valley and the surrounding mountains. From there they could cross easily into the upper Sacco valley, where some of them had evidently settled. The Aequi fit best with the model of mountaineers assaulting plainsmen, but it does not follow that their clashes with the Latins and Hernici always arose from Aequian marauding rather than the mutual disputes of neighbors. It is often supposed that in the early fifth century the Aequi occupied the Algidus, the main Alban Hills crater, and much adjacent territory, and that important Latin cities like Tibur and Praeneste either became subject to the Aequi or reached an understanding with them. If so, the Romans themselves would have been very vulnerable, but the sources give no warrant for postulating Aequian expansion on this scale. They are generally portrayed not as occupying the Algidus, but advancing into it to raid. It is most unlikely that the subjection of Tibur and Praeneste should have left no trace in the sources. Praeneste may often have clashed with the Aequi, but we hear little of this probably because this strong city was better able to defend itself than other Roman allies.[12]

The Romans on the whole probably did well out of the Aequian and Volscian wars. Only occasionally would these peoples' raids have reached Roman territory: such incursions are reported only in 488, 478, 470, 469, 465–463, and 446, all in narratives of doubtful historicity. The Romans' chief involvement was in dispatching armies in support of their Latin and Hernican allies, perhaps a good deal less often than the tradition implies. Such expeditions will have afforded much opportunity for booty. Moreover, the Roman alliance is reported as making significant territorial advances against the Volsci, notably in the late 490s, and in the late fifth and early fourth century, when they temporarily secured Anxur/Tarracina, and founded a colony at Circeii.

The early republic also saw three Roman wars with the city of Veii, their nearest Etruscan neighbor. The first war is reported as extending over the years 483–474 and the second (with intermissions) over 438–425. The issue in the second war was Fidenae: the war started with its revolt from Rome to Veii, and ended with the Roman capture of the town. These first two wars were typical conflicts between neighboring communities, but the third was a fight to the death. The Romans laid siege to Veii; resistance was allegedly protracted, but the city was eventually captured under the leadership of the celebrated Camillus (traditional date 396). Some of the inhabitants were made Roman citizens, and the rest sold into slavery. The land acquired from Veii all became public land (*ager publicus*), and much of it was soon afterwards distributed in small allotments to Roman citizens. This was a major expansion of Roman territory: Beloch (1926, 620) estimated the territory acquired from Veii as some 562 square kilometers and the total extent of Roman territory as now about 1,510 square kilometers.

There had been little or no Roman expansion in the period from the late 490s down to the late fifth century, but at the end of the century a new phase of expansion began, of which the capture of Veii was only the most notable instance. As we have seen, there were also advances at this time in the Pomptine region against the Volsci, and, following their success against Veii, the Romans went on in 395–394 to strengthen their hold north of the Tiber by exacting submission from the neighboring Faliscan communities, Capena and Falerii. However, the annexation of Veii and distribution of its land were actions on a different, and for the Romans, unprecedented scale, and have rightly been seen as the first step on Rome's advance to an imperial power. They also constitute a puzzle: the ancient tradition offers no adequate explanation for the Romans' decision to annihilate their neighbor.

The Roman advance received a sharp jolt in 387 (Polybius' date: the Roman tradition places the event in 390). A horde of invading Gauls defeated a Roman army at the River Allia, near Crustumerium, and the survivors were obliged to abandon the city except for the Capitoline Hill. The Gauls sacked the city and then departed. Further Gallic invasions ensued over the following century, but these passed off without Roman defeats. Although Gauls thereafter had a special menace for the Romans, the consequences of the Sack were neither grave nor long-lasting. The damage done to the city has left no archaeological trace and was probably less great than the tradition claims. To insure against a repetition, the circuit wall was constructed, enclosing an area of some 426 hectares, a huge undertaking which was itself striking testimony to Roman resilience.

The Romans were soon able to resume their expansion. The tradition is again unreliable in detail, but the main trend is clear enough. The Romans consolidated their position in southern Etruria with the foundation of the colonies of Sutrium and Nepet c. 383, and further warfare against Tarquinii and others in 358–351 ended in extended truces. In the south the Aequi were a spent force, attacking for the last time in 389–388, but frequent warfare is recorded with the Volsci. The gains made from them before the Sack were probably lost, but new gains were soon made, and Roman citizens received allotments of confiscated land in the Pomptine Plain. By the mid-fourth century Roman arms were approaching Campania.

Livy reports disaffection among the Latins and Hernici from immediately after the Sack. Its primary cause was probably increasing Roman dominance. In 381, at a hint of resistance, the strategically vital town of Tusculum was absorbed into the Roman citizen body, an unprecedented step for a community of this size. This peremptory act may have prompted the rebellion of Praeneste, defeated in 380. Further conflict followed in the mid-century: warfare is reported with the Hernici in 362–358 and with Tibur and Praeneste in 361–354. Widespread disaffection continued, and was to erupt in 340 in general revolt. When that rebellion was crushed in 338, most of the Latins, and many Campanians and Volsci, were incorporated into the Roman citizen body, a radical initiative which transformed the character of the Roman state and provided the springboard for the conquest of Italy.

Thus the period from the end of the fifth century saw a steady expansion of Roman power, only briefly interrupted by the Gallic Sack. This expansion and the resulting conflicts with Rome's allies probably led to an increase in the frequency of Roman warfare. However, even in the first half of the fourth century the Romans probably did not attain the level of more or less annual warfare which characterized most of the subsequent history of the republic. This was still more true of the preceding century. As we saw, the ancient historical tradition presents the later fifth century as, in Roman terms, an unusually peaceful period, and for most of the century there is in fact likely to have been significantly less warfare than the tradition claims. Moreover, such warfare as there was will have been mainly away from the Romans' own territory.

The first years of the republic were a turbulent time of shifting alliances and conflict with neighboring powers. However, the settlement with the Latins established in the 490s by the victory at Lake Regillus and the subsequent treaty of alliance inaugurated a comparatively peaceful period which lasted for the greater part of the fifth century. When warfare became more frequent again from the end of the century, the principal reason was the Romans' own expansionism in southern Etruria and against the Volsci and the tensions which this caused for their relations with the Latins.

4   Public and Private Warfare

Much of the conflict which occurred between Romans and their neighbors at least in the regal period was probably not at the communal level, but rather raiding and reprisals by individuals and groups. However, conflicts originating in this way will often have involved the community, and, more generally, the pressures of warfare and the need to mobilize armies are likely to have stimulated state formation and the development of communal institutions. The community in its turn may have sought to control private violence, and an instance of this may be afforded by the ritual of the fetial priests. Accounts of their procedure for declaring war often specify that the demand presented was for the surrender of "the plunder and the plunderers," and it seems likely that it originated as a communal response to private raiding, with the offenders' community being required either to make good the offense by handing them over or to accept the responsibility collectively.

Aristocratic warlords, accompanied by a retinue of armed followers and moving quite freely between communities, are widely held to have been an important feature of the society of west central Italy in archaic times, and a striking body of evidence supports this view. Such warrior bands may have been a survival from the pre-state world, and parallels may be drawn with other pre-state societies such as Homeric Greece.[13]

The best attested warlords are three figures from the Etruscan city of Vulci, the brothers Caeles and Aulus Vibenna and their associate Mastarna, known both from Etruscan art, especially the reliefs of the late fourth-century François tomb at Vulci, and from Roman tradition, according to which Caeles brought armed help to a Roman king and settled at Rome with his followers. The scholarly emperor Claudius reported an Etruscan claim that Mastarna had been king at Rome, and identified him with Servius Tullius. However that may be, the evidence does make it plausible to envisage the trio as Etruscan adventurers who intervened with an armed retinue in the affairs of Rome.

A band of comrades in allegiance to an elite leader also appears on a late sixth- or early fifth-century dedicatory inscription from Satricum (a site whose possession seems to have shifted between Latins and Volsci), usually translated as: ". . . the comrades (*sodales*) of Poplios Valesios set (this) up to Mamars." "Mamars" is an alternative name for Mars, and "Poplios Valesios" is an archaic form of the name Publius Valerius. If the dedicators were from Rome, this Valerius may be the famous Publius Valerius Publicola, whom tradition represented as playing a leading part in the foundation of the republic. However that may be, the inscription is vivid testimony to the importance of *sodalis*-groupings in the region in archaic times, and the temptation is strong to view them as a warrior band.[14]

Further warlords followed the example of Mastarna and the Vibennae in intervening at Rome after the expulsion of the kings: Porsenna's activity there is best interpreted in these terms, but the last reported attempt by a foreign adventurer to stage an armed coup at Rome, the Sabine Appius Herdonius' seizure of the Capitol in 460, was an abject failure.

The movement of such adventurers between communities is in fact part of the well-documented wider phenomenon of elite migration between the states of west-central Italy in the archaic period. At Rome the reception of non-citizens as kings is only one instance of this process. Another is the admission of the Claudian *gens*: according to the traditional story, the Sabine leader Attus Clausus (Appius Claudius) came over to the Romans in 504 with a large retinue. Such movement will have taken place from as well as to Rome, as the case of Gnaeus Marcius Coriolanus illustrates. According to the legend, this Roman war hero's opposition to the plebeians led to his exile from Rome; he joined the Volsci and led them on a campaign of conquest deep into Roman territory, ended only at the entreaty of his mother. This powerful tale was evidently developed in oral tradition before being embedded, with further accretions, in the historians' account of the years 493–488. The story must have a kernel of truth, and, as Cornell has recently argued, this must include a Roman renegade who took service with the Volscians.[15]

A related development to the activities of aristocratic warlords is often thought to have been private wars by individual clans (*gentes*), conducted by the clan-members and their dependents and focusing on the defense and expansion of their landholdings. However, this hypothesis, like the view that the Roman army was originally composed of clan leaders and their retinues, rests on highly problematic assumptions about the role and importance of the *gentes* in early times.

The only evidence for a *gens* engaging in warfare on its own is the story of the disaster suffered by the Fabii at the Cremera (the Tiber tributary on which Veii itself stood) during the republic's first war with Veii. According to most sources, in 479 some 306 Fabii manned a fort there accompanied (in some accounts) by 4,000 or 5,000 dependents, but in 477 they were ambushed, and only one Fabius survived. The episode has been much embellished, but must derive from an authentic memory of a Fabian disaster. It is often supposed that in reality the Fabii suffered their defeat while conducting a private war from their own landholdings, a late survival of independent gentilicial warfare. However, it is perhaps more likely that the disaster was, as the tradition claims, an episode in a public war. The Fabii, who were politically prominent at the time, could have undertaken the garrisoning of a raiding post which could not be maintained by the normal, short-term levy, perhaps an exceptional reversion to an older form of gentilicial levying. Alternatively, they may simply have suffered heavy losses in a regular battle, which is the version given by our earliest extant source, Diodorus (11.53.6).[16]

5   The Evolution of the Army

Weapons figure in grave-goods in west-central Italy from c. 1000 BC on, and from the eighth century graves of high-status warriors in Etruscan and Latin cemeteries are marked by combinations of iron weapons and bronze armor, much of it evidently intended for display rather than use. Grave-goods virtually disappear from Latin sites by the early sixth century. However, already by this time Greek hoplite equipment had begun to be adopted in the region, including the characteristic double-grip round shield and distinctive helmets and body armor. Hoplite equipment had appeared in the Greek world from the late eighth century, and its widespread use in Etruscan cities is attested from c. 650 on by grave finds and artistic representations. The evidence is thinner for Rome and the other Latin communities, but it seems likely that hoplite equipment came into use there about the same time or soon after its introduction in Etruria.

It has usually been thought that the introduction of hoplite equipment led rapidly to a new style of fighting, with the hoplites (heavy-armed troops) massed in close formation (the phalanx), using a thrusting spear as their main offensive weapon and also carrying a short sword. Greek city-states' defense, it is held, now depended on middle-class hoplites, serving alongside aristocrats in the phalanx line, and this had important social and political consequences. Difficulties have sometimes been found in applying this model to Etruria: it has been doubted whether an army of citizen hoplites is compatible with Etruscan social structure, commonly supposed to have been dominated in this period by aristocratic *gentes*, and it is notable that Greek equipment is often found in combination with Etruscan weaponry, as on the grave-stele of Aule Feluske of Vetulonia, shown armed with a hoplite shield and helmet but an Etruscan double-axe.[17]

Established views of hoplite warfare have, however, recently been subjected to radical critiques, notably by Van Wees.[18] He argues that close-formation fighting was not essential for the effectiveness of the new equipment, and that down to the early fifth century Greek hoplites continued to fight in a quite open formation, interspersed with light-armed troops. He also maintains that there was considerable disparity between working-class and leisured hoplites, with only the latter wearing much body armor. These conclusions fit well with the Etruscan indications, and, if they are correct, the difference between developments in Greece and Etruria may not be as great as supposed, and the adoption of Greek armor in Etruria may not have involved radical changes in fighting methods, let alone social structures. The same will also apply to Rome and Latium: here too fighting may have continued to be fluid and flexible, based on an open formation incorporating both light and more heavily armed troops, and especially at first, only the really well-to-do may have aspired to the new Greek-style shields and armor.

The Romans ascribed to King Servius Tullius the division of the citizen body into centuries based on wealth, and there is no good reason to doubt the attribution. The centuriate system in due course underwent radical modification and was to have enduring political importance as a basis for assembly voting, but, when introduced in the later sixth century, its purpose must have been primarily military. It is often supposed that in its original form the system divided the citizens simply into the "class" (*classis*), who served as hoplites, and the rest who served, if at all, as light-armed. However, although we know that in the second century BC the first of the (then five) classes could be referred to simply as "the class" and the rest as "below the class" (*infra classem*) (so Cato, cited by A. Gellius, *Noctes Atticae* 6.13), it does not follow that this was a relic of a much earlier one-class system. Although the details on equipment given by Livy (1.44) and Dionysius (4.16–21) are of questionable value, the tradition may be right that from its inception the centuriate system divided the infantry into multiple classes. King Servius will then have aimed to maximize the state's military resources by imposing an obligation of military service on all but the poorest citizens and regulating how they should arm themselves according to their means, with those who could afford it equipping themselves with some or all of the hoplite panoply, while the richest served as cavalry (perhaps true cavalry, rather than mounted infantry as in most archaic Greek states). The result will have been a heterogeneously equipped army with both hoplite and diverse other elements, which fits well with Van Wees' open-formation model of archaic warfare.

The Roman army must have changed greatly between the sixth and fourth centuries, but, although numerous attempts have been made to reconstruct its evolution, this can only be speculation. Even the best attested change remains problematic, namely the introduction of military pay. A well-established tradition (e.g. Livy 4.59–60) records its introduction, funded by direct taxation, in c. 406 at around the time of the start of the siege of Veii. It is not a difficulty that Roman coinage did not begin for another century: the payments could have been made in weighed bronze. But most warfare then still consisted of short, local campaigns, and the extended Samnite Wars of the later fourth century are a more likely context for the introduction of regular pay, although some payments may have been made to those manning the Veii siege.

By the end of the fourth century the Roman army must have reached much the form in which it was described for us by Polybius (6.19–26), a century and a half later. In this system the citizen troops were brigaded in legions of at least 4,500 men, of which the heavy infantry comprised at least 3,000. The equipment of these heavy infantry included an oval shield (*scutum*), heavy javelin (*pilum*), and short sword, and they fought in a flexible formation, deployed in three lines, each divided into ten maniples. The essential features of the system, the weaponry and the maniple as tactical unit, are often held to have been introduced only during the Samnite Wars, a doctrine supported by ancient claims that they were borrowings from the Samnites. However, this evidence is questionable and contradicted by other sources, and it seems unlikely that the Romans embarked on the struggle with the Samnites simply with a hoplite army. More probably, the manipular army was the product of a longer evolutionary process, in which a more diversely equipped force gradually became more standardized and tightly organized. Some features like the *scutum* may have been present much earlier, and Livy and Dionysius may perhaps be right in representing some elements in the Servian army as equipped with shields of this type. One important element of continuity from the Servian to the manipular system is likely to have been the maximizing of Roman military resources by imposing the obligation to serve on all but the poorest citizens.[19]

6   War and Society in the Early Republic

With the overthrow of the kings, political dominance at Rome passed to the patricians, a group of wealthy aristocratic families, who from the early years of the republic became a closed caste. The first two centuries of the republic saw repeated clashes between the patricians and the plebeians, the so-called Struggle of the Orders. In the fifth century the plebeians' gains were mainly defensive: in 494/3, the right to elect their own officers, the tribunes, and, in 451/0, a law code, the Twelve Tables. During the fourth century most of the patricians' political privileges were ended, giving wealthier plebeians access to office, while economic reforms, chiefly debt relief and the limitation of landholding, were enacted in the interests of poorer plebeians.[20]

Their military service was the plebeians' principal weapon. They are said to have carried out "secessions," withdrawing from the city in what was in effect a military strike, in 494, 449, and 287. We also hear frequently of tribunes obstructing levies in the hope of obliging the magistrates and Senate to accept their proposals. This tactic is not known to have been used in later times, and so, although the individual stories of obstruction are generally fictional, they probably draw on an authentic memory that this device had sometimes been employed in the early republic.

The original plebeians have sometimes been identified as the poorer citizens who served in the army, if at all, only as light-armed. However, in that case they would have had little political muscle, and there is no good reason to reject the sources' view that the *plebs* comprised all non-patricians. As we have seen, the make-up of the army was probably diverse, and all levels were probably represented both in the plebeian movement and among their opponents.

It is often supposed that in the fifth century incessant warfare and frequent enemy incursions had severe effects on the peasantry and produced a recession, and that all this fuelled the plebeians' discontents.[21] However, as we have seen, most of the fifth century was probably relatively peaceful. The supposed recession may be doubted: the decline in pottery imports (a regional phenomenon) and temple foundations are hardly certain indicators. Debt agitation is in fact attested in phases when we have identified comparatively high levels of warfare: in 494/3, and then not again until the fourth century (agitation from 385 and debt-relief measures in 367–342).

There was evidently much peasant land-hunger. The sources report frequent unsuccessful agitation for the distribution of public land in the fifth century, but the narratives are couched in terms which reflect the controversies of the late republic, and whether they have any authentic content is a matter of dispute. Settlements were, however, founded on land confiscated from defeated enemies. The foundation of a number of new communities (*coloniae*) is reported in both the fifth and early fourth centuries, of which at least some will be authentic; these ranked as new Latin states, and the settlers will have been drawn both from Roman citizens and their allies. In addition, numerous individual allotments of land were, as we have seen, made to Roman citizens in the early fourth century, in the former territory of Veii and on the Pomptine Plain. Land hunger may have been one of the factors which impelled the renewed expansion of the late fifth and early fourth century. By meeting it through substantial distribution of confiscated land, a precedent was set which was to be repeatedly followed, becoming one of the central themes in the history of Roman imperialism.

The pattern of almost constant warfare which was so central a feature of Roman life from the later fourth century on was not already established in the period before the great advance of c. 343 BC. Continuous war was the product, not the cause of Roman imperialism. Nonetheless, in much of this earlier period warfare was frequent, and many enduring features of the Romans' attitude to and conduct of war took shape then, for example military organization and fighting methods, the treatment of the defeated and ritual practices like the triumph.

Romans will have continued to be involved in piracy, but on land private wars will have died out from the fifth century. Warfare had become a civic activity, and fighting in the republic's armies was an obligation which fell on all but the poorest citizens. It helped to define what it meant to be a citizen, and gave ordinary citizens some leverage against the elite.

Warfare, then, was an activity in which both the elite and ordinary citizens took part. One illustration of this is afforded by the part played by individual combat in early Roman warfare. Fighting by individual champions may have played a leading part in the earliest warfare. Massed fighting later predominated, but individual acts of valor were still prized, both in and before the main engagements. The Roman practice of awarding decorations for outstanding feats must have gone back to the early republic, if not before. Individual combats between Romans and enemies were common before the main engagements, and some of these encounters became famous, like the duels fought against Gauls by Titus Manlius Torquatus (367 or 361) and Marcus Valerius Corvus (349). Sometimes, however, such combats were forbidden in the interests of discipline, and there were also exemplary tales of commanders enforcing discipline by executing their sons for contravening the ban.[22]

Individual acts of bravery were one of the ways by which aristocrats like Torquatus or Corvus could win personal distinction, but the rewards of valor were open to ordinary soldiers as well. The record for military decorations was said to have been held by Lucius Siccius Dentatus, tribune in 454, who "fought in 120 battles, won eight single combats after challenge, was distinguished by 45 scars on his front and none on his back" (Pliny, *Nat.* 7.101–2). The tally of Siccius' achievements is a later fiction, and he may be an altogether legendary figure. However, the tale remains an important exemplar of the possibilities which their military role opened to ordinary citizens. From the early republic on, aristocrats who sought to distinguish themselves for valor were striving to excel in activities in which ordinary citizens too were full participants.

NOTES

1   On the evidence for early Roman history see further Cornell 1995, 1–30; Forsythe 2005, 59–77. On the historical tradition see especially Oakley 1997–2005, 1.3–108. I shall explore the themes of this chapter in more depth in a forthcoming work on war, expansion and society in early Rome.
2   See further Cornell 1995, chapters 4–6 and 8.
3   Alföldi 1965, 101–75, 236–318. For refutation see e.g. Thomsen 1980, 130–8.

4 Beloch 1926, 169–79, followed e.g. by Cornell 1995, 208–9. See further Forsythe (in this volume).

5 For the Carthage treaty see e.g. Cornell 1995, 210–14; Oakley 1997–2005, 2.252–62. For the Volsci as already present in the Pomptine region from at least the sixth century see Musti 1992, 25–31; Gnade 2002, 138–56.

6 Cicero, *Rep.* 2.44; Livy 1.53.2–3, 55.7–9; Dionysius 4.50; Tacitus, *Hist.* 3.72. Pometia is perhaps to be identified with the town later known as Satricum.

7 The war-cycle interpretation is challenged by Rüpke 1990, 23–6.

8 See Cornell 1995, 215–41, refuting alternative views.

9 See, e.g. Oakley 1993, 14–16; Raaflaub 1996, 283ff. Cornell 1995, 293–326, gives the best available account of Roman warfare and external relations in the early republic. For the period after 390 see also Oakley 1997–2005, 1.344–65, 2.3–18.

10 The common view that Fidenae was held by Veii until the Second Veientine War rejects the ancient evidence for no good reason.

11 On the Cassian treaties see further Cornell 1995, 299–301; Oakley 1997–2005, 1.336–41. Dionysius 6.95 purports to cite the text of the treaty with the Latins. A fragment of the antiquarian Lucius Cincius (Festus 276–7 Lindsay) implies shared Roman and Latin decision-making and is most naturally taken to mean that commanders were sometimes supplied by communities other than Rome.

12 For the view criticized here see e.g. Cornell 1995, 306; Oakley 1997–2005, 1.338. It is true that Dionysius sometimes speaks of the Algidus as being in Aequian territory (10.21.1, 11.23.4, 28.1), but his topographical indications are confused: he envisages it as a city, and a full night's march from Tusculum. Ravaging of Praenestine land is reported for 462 (Livy 3.8.6).

13 See further Cornell 1995, 130–45, 157–8; Rawlings 1999. In general on private and public warfare in archaic Rome, see Cornell 1988; Timpe 1990.

14 See Stibbe et al. 1980; Versnel 1997 (interpreting the incomplete first word as "young men").

15 Cornell 2003, rightly observing that the common view that the historical Coriolanus was a Volscian or Latin enemy leader implausibly rejects an essential feature of the story. Cornell is less convincing when he argues that Coriolanus was already a warlord before he left Rome: the sources' references to him as accompanied at Rome by a retinue and leading a volunteer force against Antium (Dionysius 7.19, 21, 64; Plutarch, *Coriolanus* 13) are probably just literary elaborations.

16 Other main accounts: Livy 2.48–50; Dionysius 9.15–22; Ovid, *Fasti* 2.195–242. The private gentilicial war interpretation is advocated, e.g., by Richard 1988, and rejected, e.g., by Welwei 1993. The location of the tribe Fabia and Fabian landholdings on the border with Veii is merely a modern conjecture. On the role of *gentes* in early Roman society see now Smith 2006.

17 Snodgrass 1965; Spivey and Stoddart 1990, 127–39; D'Agostino 1990. For a comprehensive survey of military equipment in ninth- to seventh-century Italy see Stary 1981.

18 Van Wees 2004.

19 *Scuta* in the Servian army: so Saulnier 1980, 106–9; Connolly 1981, 95–6. In general on the evolution of the early Roman army see Rawson 1971; Kienast 1975; Thomsen 1980, 144–211; Cornell 1995, 173–97. On the themes of this section, and for a different view, see Forsythe (in this volume).

20 On these conflicts see especially Cornell 1995, 242–92, 327–43; Raaflaub 2005.

21 For example Cornell 1995, 265–6, 306–7; Raaflaub 1996, 286.

22 See Oakley 1985; Lendon 2005, chapter 8.

BIBLIOGRAPHY

Alföldi, A. 1965. *Early Rome and the Latins.* Ann Arbor.

Beloch, K. J. 1926. *Römische Geschichte bis zum Beginn der punischen Kriege.* Berlin.

Connolly, P. 1981. *Greece and Rome at War.* London.

Cornell, T. J. 1988. "La guerra e lo stato in Roma arcaica (VII–V sec.)," in E. Campanile (ed.), *Alle Origini di Roma.* Pisa, 89–100.

—— 1995. *The Beginnings of Rome. Italy and Rome from the Bronze Age to the Punic Wars (c. 1000–264 BC).* London.

—— 2003. "Coriolanus: Myth, history and performance," in D. Braund and C. Gill (eds.), *Myth, History and Culture: Studies in Honour of T. P. Wiseman.* Exeter, 73–97.

D'Agostino, B. 1990. "Military organization and social structure in archaic Etruria," in O. Murray and S. Price (eds.), *The Greek City. From Homer to Alexander.* Oxford, 59–82.

Eder, W. (ed.). 1990. *Staat und Staatlichkeit in der frühen römischen Republik.* Stuttgart.

Forsythe, G. 2005. *A Critical History of Early Rome.* Berkeley.

Gnade, M. 2002. *Satricum in the Post-Archaic Period.* Leuven.

Harris, W. V. 1990. "Roman warfare in the economic and social context of the 4th century BC," in Eder, 494–510.

Holloway, R. R. 1994. *The Archaeology of Early Rome and Latium.* London.

Kienast, D. 1975. "Die politische Emanzipation der Plebs und die Entwicklung des Heerwesens im frühen Rom," *BJ* 175: 83–112.

Lendon, J. E. 2005. *Soldiers and Ghosts. A History of Battle in Classical Antiquity.* New Haven.

Musti, D. 1992. "L'immagine dei Volsci nella storiografia antica," *Quaderni del Centro di Studi per l'Archeologia Etrusco-Italica* 20: 25–31.

Oakley, S. P. 1985. "Single combat in the Roman Republic," *CQ* 35: 392–410.

—— 1993. "The Roman conquest of Italy," in J. Rich and G. Shipley (eds.), *War and Society in the Roman World.* London, 9–37.

—— 1997–2005. *A Commentary on Livy Books VI–X.* Oxford.

Ogilvie, R. M. 1965. *A Commentary on Livy Books 1–5.* Oxford.

Raaflaub, K. A. 1996. "Born to be wolves? Origins of Roman imperialism," in R. W. Wallace and E. M. Harris (eds.), *Transitions to Empire: Essays in Greco-Roman History 360–146 BC, in honor of E. Badian.* Norman, 273–314.

—— (ed.). 2005². *Social Struggles in Archaic Rome.* Oxford.

Rawlings, L. 1999. "Condottieri and clansmen: Early Italian raiding, warfare and the state," in K. Hopwood (ed.), *Organised Crime in Antiquity.* London, 97–127.

Rawson, E. D. 1971. "The literary sources for the pre-Marian army," *PBSR* 39: 13–31 = *Roman Culture and Society.* Oxford 1991, 34–57.

Richard, J.-C. 1988. "Historiographie et histoire: l'expedition des Fabii à la Cremère," *Latomus* 47: 526–53.

Rüpke, J. 1990. *Domi Militiae: Die religiöse Konstruktion des Krieges in Rom.* Stuttgart.

Saulnier, C. 1980. *L'armée et la guerre dans le monde étrusco-romain (VIIIᵉ–IVᵉ s.).* Paris.

Sekunda, N., and S. Northwood. 1995. *Early Roman Armies.* Oxford.

Smith, C. J. 1996. *Early Rome and Latium.* Oxford.

Smith, C. J. 2006. *The Roman Clan.* Cambridge.

Snodgrass, A. M. 1965. "The hoplite reform and history," *JHS* 85: 110–22.

Spivey, N., and S. Stoddart. 1990. *Etruscan Italy.* London.

Stary, P. F. 1981. *Zur eisenzeitlichen Bewaffnung und Kampfesweise in Mittelitalien.* Mainz.

Stibbe, C. M., G. Colonna, C. de Simone, and H. S. Versnel. 1980. *Lapis Satricanus. Archaeological, Epigraphical, Linguistic and Historical Aspects of the New Inscription from Satricum.* The Hague.

Thomsen, R. 1980. *King Servius Tullius.* Copenhagen.

Timpe, D. 1990. "Das Kriegsmonopol des römischen Staates," in Eder, 368–87.

Versnel, H. S. 1997. "IUN]IEI. A new conjecture in the Satricum inscription," *Mededelingen van het Nederlands historish Institut te Rome* 56: 177–97.

Wees, H. van. 2004. *Greek Warfare. Myths and Realities.* London.

Welwei, K.-W. 1993. "Gefolgschaft oder Gentilaufgebot? Zum Problem eines frührömischen familiare bellum (Liv. II.48.9)," *Zeitschrift für Savigny-Stiftung, Röm. Abt.* 110: 60–76.

FURTHER READING

Cornell 1995 is a brilliant account of the period, though sometimes perhaps over-confident of the value of the ancient tradition. Forsythe 2005 is another fine account. There is much valuable information in the authoritative commentaries on the early books of Livy by Ogilvie 1965, and Oakley 1997–2005. The archaeological evidence is well presented by Holloway 1994.

The following are good essays on early Roman warfare and society: Harris 1990; Oakley 1993; Raaflaub 1996. Rawson 1971 is a classic study of the early Roman army. There are well-illustrated accounts for the general reader in Connolly 1981 and Sekunda and Northwood 1995.

CHAPTER TWO

The Army and Centuriate Organization in Early Rome[1]

Gary Forsythe

1 Introduction

This chapter examines the military and political organization of the Roman state during the period c. 550–250 as embodied in one of Rome's three voting assemblies,
the *comitia centuriata* or centuriate assembly. According to the later ancient Roman
tradition, during its earliest period of history, the regal period (traditionally dated
753–509), Rome was ruled by a series of seven kings, and the sixth king, Servius
Tullius (traditionally dated 578–534) created this institution. Hence, this military
and political system is often termed the Servian constitution. When the monarchy
was abolished and replaced by the consulship in 509, the period of the Roman Republic
commenced, and the *comitia centuriata* emerged as one of the most important political institutions in the Roman state. This body, which comprised all adult male Roman
citizens with the right to vote, remained in existence for over five centuries and finally
disappeared with the collapse of the republic and its replacement by a new sort of
monarchy, the principate established by Augustus.

The surviving ancient sources provide us with ample evidence concerning the nature
and functioning of the centuriate assembly for the periods of the middle republic
(264–133) and the late republic (133–31), but the origin and evolution of this institution during the early republic (509–264) is largely shrouded in mystery, because
the Romans did not begin to write historical accounts until the Hannibalic War
(218–201), by which time the *comitia centuriata* had completed its complex history
of development, and ancient Roman historians no longer possessed much reliable
information about how this institution had changed over time. Any attempt to explain
the origin and early development of the *comitia centuriata* must do so by placing
the institution in the context of the growth of the Roman state during the regal
period and early republic, including the military and political institutions that preceded it and shaped the environment in which it arose.

2 Rome's Earliest Political Institutions

Given what we know about other ancient city-states whose early political development is better documented, we may conjecture that by the end of the regal period the Roman state possessed a tripartite political organization: people, Senate, and king. The earliest organization of the Roman populace (ascribed by tradition to Rome's first king, Romulus) involved 30 units called *curiae*. These in turn were grouped into three sets of ten that were termed tribes: Ramnenses, Titienses, and Luceres. The exact nature, origin, and history of these divisions have been the subject of considerable modern discussion and speculation with little agreement having been reached, but what seems certain is that these tribal and curial units formed the basis of the earliest political and military structure of the Roman state. The earliest organized Roman infantry and cavalry must have been recruited from these divisions: for even in later times when the three archaic tribes and 30 *curiae* had long lost any meaningful significance, the cavalry units still retained a link to this structure by being organized into multiples of three: namely, the *sex suffragia* (six votes) and the other 12 centuries of *equites equo publico* (knights with a public horse) of the *comitia centuriata*. In fact, the *sex suffragia* were grouped into two sets of three and were named after the three archaic tribes. Similarly, the 60 centuries of the Roman legion might have originated as a doubling of the 30 *curiae*. According to the reconstruction of Roman antiquarians of the late republic, Rome's earliest army consisted of 3,000 infantry and 300 cavalry, recruited in groups of 100 and 10 respectively from each *curia*.

Besides providing a basis for military recruitment, the 30 *curiae* also served as voting units in Rome's oldest assembly: the *comitia curiata*. Thus, like the later *comitia centuriata*, the curiate organization possessed both military and political functions. In addition, it, like Rome's two later assemblies, was predicated upon the concept of the group vote. Citizens were organized into groups (*curiae*, *centuriae*, or tribes), and the majority vote within each unit or group became that unit's vote. A majority of such unit or group votes decided the issue.[2] Unfortunately, since the curiate assembly was almost entirely supplanted in later times by the tribal and centuriate assemblies, little is known about its original powers and functions. Even in republican times, however, it could be convoked in the Comitium (the place of assembly in the Roman Forum) to witness the making of wills and to give its assent to a special kind of adoption called *adrogatio* in which the adoptee was legally independent and not under paternal authority. Indeed, the term *adrogatio* indicates that this form of adoption was a legislative act in which a question (*rogatio*) was put to the curiate assembly, which then gave or denied its approval. The curiate assembly's military nature is also suggested by the fact that in later times the consuls needed to have their *imperium* affirmed by a *lex curiata* in order for them to have the right to conduct the auspices.[3]

The abolition of the monarchy and the establishment of the consulship presuppose that by the close of the sixth century there existed in the Roman state a well-established and powerful aristocracy. The rich graves discovered at sites in Latium dating to the seventh century (especially those containing chariots), as well as the traces of substantial town houses on the Palatine built during the late sixth century, corroborate and amplify this picture. Like other contemporary Greek city-states, the early Roman aristocracy was doubtless organized into an advisory or deliberative body used by the king. Under the republic it was called the Senate; and although it often met in temples, its own established meeting house was the Senate House, termed the Curia Hostilia, next to the Comitium. Its membership must have comprised the adult men of considerable wealth and social status.

According to tradition the Roman kings commanded the army in war, exercised judicial powers, and discharged religious duties; and when the monarchy was ended, these royal powers were neatly divided between the two consuls and the *rex sacrorum* (the king of sacrifices). This portrait has been widely accepted, but it must be stressed that even though the office of the *rex sacrorum* may render this view plausible, the later ancient tradition that paints the picture of complete and neat legal and constitutional continuity between the monarchy and the republic is not above suspicion. This major transition, especially in reference to the consulship, is unlikely to have been so tidy. Generally speaking, the historical process is a rather messy business and often works itself out in defiance of neat legal or logical schemes. On the other hand, legal and constitutional theory usually follows in the wake of major historical change and then constructs *post eventum* unhistorical, but logically coherent systems to justify the change and to demonstrate continuity. Given the unsatisfactory nature of the ancient evidence, we can say nothing certain about the kingship, but there might be some truth to the later ancient view that the kings were created through some process of nomination involving the Senate and ratification by the *comitia curiata*. It must also remain an open question whether, to what extent, and in what ways the king's authority was circumscribed by or exercised in conjunction with the will of the people and the approval of the Senate.

3   The Centuriate Organization and Hoplite Warfare

As already stated, the later ancient tradition maintained that Servius Tullius laid the foundations for the republic by his creation of the *comitia centuriata*, a popular assembly based upon the census and the military obligations of the citizens to the state. This assembly took its name from *centuria*, a military unit of the legion. In later historical times each legion was composed of 60 centuries, and in theory each century contained 100 men. The obvious military character of this assembly is indicated by its powers and place of meeting. Under the republic this body was responsible for electing all officials who exercised any form of *imperium*, which involved the raising and commanding of troops or the exercise of jurisdiction: consuls, praetors, censors, and curule aediles. These were the curule magistrates. Besides having the power to legislate by voting in favor of proposals placed before it by a curule magistrate, this assembly voted on declarations of war and ratified treaties and even acted as a high court in capital cases. Since it was considered to be an army sitting as an assembly, it was not permitted to convene within the sacred boundary (*pomerium*) of the city but always met in the Campus Martius, the Field of Mars, a large plain located on the northern fringe of the city and enveloped by the bend of the Tiber River.

The origin of the Servian organization does in fact seem to fit the historical context of Rome in the sixth century.[4] Our current state of knowledge, based upon rather limited archaeological evidence and a critical examination of Roman traditions, suggests that Rome began to emerge as a self-conscious embryonic state during the last quarter of the seventh century. At this time the level of the Roman Forum, which had hitherto been prone to flooding from the Tiber, was raised and paved over with gravel for the first time to serve as the political and religious center of the community. In this area, for example, were now erected the Senate House, the Temple of Vesta, and the Regia. Over the course of the sixth century more temples were built, testifying to organized public religion and a sizable economic surplus. It is also likely that the size of Rome's population and territory continued to expand, and the Roman community began to shape itself into a well organized city-state, so that by the beginning of the republic in 509 Rome was the largest of the Latin communities in Latium and probably rivaled the largest city-states north of the Tiber River in Etruria.

Part of this complex process of state formation during the sixth century is likely to have been the introduction of Greek hoplite warfare into Roman society.[5] The hoplite panoply consisted of a helmet, a corselet, greaves, shield, and thrusting spear. The first four items were worn to protect the warrior. The shield was circular, measured about three feet in diameter, and was held on the left forearm by an armband and handle. The spear was about six feet long, was grasped overhand with the right hand in the middle of the shaft, was held near shoulder height, and was used to stab at one's adversary. Hoplite warriors stood together in a tight formation, side by side and one behind the other in files usually eight to twelve men deep. They stood next to one another, so that their shields touched and presented a solid front to the enemy. Hoplite warfare originated in mainland Greece around 650, spread quickly throughout all Greek city-states (including the colonies in Sicily and southern Italy), and became the established method by which the Greeks fought their wars for the next three centuries until it succumbed to and was replaced by the Macedonian phalanx of pikemen.

The introduction of hoplite organization into Greek city-states during the seventh and sixth centuries is generally regarded as one of several important indications of state formation; and there is no reason why the same should not be assumed to have applied to the contemporary communities of central Tyrrhenian Italy, including Rome. The uniformity of the typical hoplite phalanx and the regularity with which it was imposed upon a state's adult male population clearly reflect the rise of the state with rational institutions and with the ability and need to organize its citizenry into a systematic scheme for warfare. Hoplite citizens had to provide themselves with their own armor and weapons. Thus, the existence of a hoplite class within a community was predicated upon relative economic prosperity and a society possessing a sizable number of independent peasant farmers and artisans. In addition, it was the general rule among these city-states that the obligation of arming oneself to fight on behalf of one's community entitled the hoplite warrior to the political right of belonging to and of voting in the citizen assembly.

Hoplite panoplies have been discovered in the so-called Tomb of the Warrior at Vulci on the Etruscan coast dating to c. 530, as well as in a tomb at Lanuvium in Latium dating to the early fifth century.[6] Thus, the later ancient tradition that ascribed a major military reform to Rome's sixth king in the middle of the sixth century can be associated with the introduction of the hoplite organization into the Roman state. The military system of the 30 *curiae* and three archaic tribes can probably be best dated to the period of Rome's early unification during the seventh century; whereas the centuriate organization that supplanted it came into being toward the close of the regal period. By that time the site of Rome had experienced considerable urban growth and development. Besides a rural countryside inhabited by an emerging landed elite and a peasant population, the city itself possessed a growing class of artisans and craftsmen of all sorts. Increased economic activity and opportunities must have attracted immigrants; and it is generally supposed that the centuriate organization was devised at this time to replace the now outmoded curiate system and to harness the military potential of Rome's growing population. The result was a hoplite phalanx recruited from new territorial districts called tribes.

4   Modern Estimates of Early Rome's Population and Manpower

Despite the unsatisfactory nature of the ancient evidence, some modern scholars have attempted to estimate Rome's size and military manpower at the end of the sixth century by making surmises based upon ancient religious and historical data suggestive of the size of Roman territory. Although the results are little more than educated guesses, the endeavor is at least instructive when the estimates are compared with estimates concerning other Latin, Etruscan, and Greek states.[7] For example, K. J. Beloch estimated that the Roman state c. 500 encompassed an area of 822 square kilometers = 317 square miles. This area would have constituted 35 percent of all Latium, and the next five largest states at this time according to Beloch's estimates were Tibur at 351 square kilometers, Praeneste at 262.5, Ardea at 198.5, Lavinium at 164, and Lanuvium at 84. The other nine towns of Latium (Ficulea, Crustumerium, Pedum, Aricia, Tusculum, Fidenae, Gabii, Nomentum, and Labici) had territories estimated as ranging between 37 and 72 square kilometers. Conversely, Alföldi argued that the Roman state at the end of the regal period was considerably smaller. Using his approximate boundaries, Ampolo calculates that according to Alföldi's reconstruction Roman territory would have measured only 435 square kilometers. On the other hand, there seems to be little doubt that Rome's urban area at the end of the sixth century was comparatively quite large.[8]

Rome's total population c. 500 has been variously estimated as having numbered in the low tens of thousands. Ampolo has demonstrated that Beloch's estimate of 50,000 is too high. Ampolo's own estimate of 20,000–30,000 can be taken as a reasonable guess, as well as his surmise that Rome could have put into the field 5,700–8,500 soldiers, corresponding roughly to a single legion of full strength (i.e., 6,000) or to two legions of three-quarters strength and each commanded by a consul. This would have been quite a substantial army with respect to neighboring states.

Ampolo's estimate for the size of Rome's population c. 500 compares well with Heurgon's estimate for the population of Etruscan Caere. Using demographic methods of analysis entirely different from those of Ampolo (i.e., the numbers of graves in Caere's famous ancient Banditaccia Cemetery), Heurgon concluded that from the seventh to the first century this state had a population of approximately 25,000. Finally, it should be observed that Ampolo's estimated size for Rome's entire military levy could have been convened in the Campus Martius to act as a citizen assembly. Thus, at the very beginning of the republic there is likely to have been an exact correspondence between Rome's hoplite army and the assembly that later evolved into the *comitia centuriata*.

5   The Later *Comitia Centuriata*

By the third century, when our ancient evidence becomes fairly reliable, the centuriate organization had gone through a very long and complicated process of evolution, which we cannot reconstruct in detail. We simply know of the final product of this evolutionary process. At that time the assembly consisted of 193 centuries or voting units that were organized into blocks according to property qualifications. Whenever the censors conducted a census, they assigned citizens to one of five economic classes based upon the assessed value of their property, and the members of each class were required to arm themselves for military service according to specified standards: the wealthier citizens being more heavily armed, and those of less means more lightly armed. In the centuriate assembly there were 80 units of the first class along with 18 additional units of knights (the *sex suffragia* and the 12 centuries of knights with a public horse) and two more of engineers for constructing siege machines. The second, third, and fourth classes were each allotted 20 units, and the fifth class was given 30 along with two additional ones for horn blowers used for issuing military signals. Those whose property fell below the minimum qualification of the fifth class were lumped together into a single century of the proletariate and were exempt from military service. The scheme can be outlined as follows:

Outline of the later centuriate organization[9]

Class	Qualification[10]	Centuries
Knights	100,000–>	12
First class	100,000–>	80
Sex suffragia	100,000–>	6
Engineers	100,000–>	2
Second class	75,000–100,000	20
Third class	50,000–75,000	20
Fourth class	25,000–50,000	20
Fifth class	12,500–25,000	30
Horn blowers	12,500–25,000	2
Proletarii	<–12,500	1

The voting in this assembly was sequential in the order of the classes and cen-turies as outlined above. Accordingly, since those citizens with a property qualification of the highest class were distributed among 80 units of the first class, 18 units of knights, and two units of engineers, this segment of the citizenry commanded a majority of the votes, although they numerically constituted a minority within the citizen body as a whole. Conversely, the single century assigned to those having a property qualification below the minimum of the fifth class must have been quite numerous. The Roman upper class of the republic was proud of this timocratic struc-ture that gave them control over the elections of the curule magistrates. They regarded it as superior to "the arithmetic equality" encountered in Greek democratic states like classical Athens, because the voting power of the centuriate assembly was dis-tributed according to one's wealth and military obligation to the state.

The centuriate assembly of the middle and late republic was intimately bound up with two other important Roman institutions: the census and the division of Roman territory into geographical districts called tribes. Although the latter had the same name as the three archaic tribes ascribed to Romulus, they formed an entirely new system of organizing the citizen body into units according to their residence within the confines of the Roman state. Before 387 when the territory of the recently conquered Veii was annexed and formed into four new tribes (Livy 6.5.8), Roman territory was divided into 21 tribes. The city itself formed four urban tribes, and the surrounding countryside was organized into 17 rustic tribes. The number of these districts was gradually increased during the period of Rome's conquest of Italy: pairs of tribes were created in the years 358, 332, 318, 299, and 241 until they reached a total of 35, which they never exceeded.[11] Moreover, the office of censor was created in 443, but if the later ancient evidence can be trusted, it was not until the late fourth century that the Romans began to elect censors regularly about every five years; whereas according to surviving sources, during the early history of the office (443–318) censors were elected on the average of about every nine years.[12] The censors were always two in number and held office for 18 months. Their primary duty was to conduct a census of the Roman people, which involved taking statements under oath from adult male heads of households as to the members of their family and their property holdings; and on the basis of these formal declarations every adult male was assigned to a tribe, to an economic class, and to a place within the *comitia centuriata*, and his taxes to the state were calculated according to the assessed value of his property. This entire nexus of the *comitia centuriata*, involving the census, economic classes, voting centuries, tribal districts, and state taxation, was attributed to King Servius Tullius by the later ancient tradition.

The historical accuracy of this claim is likely to resemble that of the so-called Servian Wall, the continuous stone wall built during the early fourth century that encircled the city of Rome and was designed to protect it from enemy attack. Although Servius Tullius was not responsible for the construction of this stone wall, the city in the sixth century might have been defended in places by earthen mounds and ditches; but later tradition ascribed the wall of the fourth century to a king of the sixth who might have been responsible for Rome's earliest defense works. Similarly, although

Servius Tullius was certainly not the creator of the fully developed centuriate system, archaeological data and comparative studies make it likely that hoplite warfare and organization were introduced into sixth-century Rome.

The centuriate structure itself and other ancient data offer clues as to some of the steps by which Rome's military organization evolved from an undifferentiated hoplite army of the sixth century into the highly differentiated centuriate system of the third century. The five classes of centuries were equally divided between those of military age (*iuniores* = 17–45 years old) and those over the age for military service (*seniores*): 40 units for the two groups in the first class, ten units for each in the second, third, and fourth classes, and 15 units each in the fifth class. Since the *comitia centuriata* had begun as an army acting as an assembly, it must have originally been composed solely of men of military age, but at some point when the body was viewed more as an assembly than an army, those over the age for military service must have been included and were given equal representation throughout the five classes. Unfortunately, there is no indication in the ancient sources that suggests when the distinction between *iuniores* and *seniores* became integral to the centuriate organization.

In a fundamental article on this subject Plinio Fraccaro interpreted the later structure of the centuriate assembly to mean that it had in fact originated during the late monarchy as an undifferentiated hoplite system, corresponding to a full military levy of 6,000 men (what the Romans later termed a legion), consisting of 60 centuries of 100 men each.[13] Fraccaro noticed that the armor and weapons required of the first three classes differ little and correspond to those of a hoplite infantryman: helmet, corselet, greaves, shield, spear, and sword for the first class, the same for the second class minus the corselet, and likewise for the third class minus the corselet and greaves. The members of the fourth and fifth classes, on the other hand, were light-armed skirmishers: those of the fourth class were equipped with only a thrusting spear and javelin, whereas the members of the fifth class were armed with nothing except slings and stones. Therefore, Fraccaro argued, it seems likely that the first three classes originally comprised Rome's undifferentiated hoplite army, in which all soldiers (except for the aristocratic cavalrymen) were equipped with a helmet, shield, and spear with the corselet and greaves possibly being optional. Moreover, these three classes of *iuniores* comprised 60 centuries (40 + 10 + 10), which is the number of centuries possessed by a Roman legion. According to Polybius (6.20–21), however, during the middle republic a Roman legion normally consisted of 3,000 heavily armed infantrymen (1,200 *hastati* of the first line, 1,200 *principes* of the second line, and 600 *triarii* of the third line) and 1,200 lightly armed men (*velites*). Thus two such legions would have comprised 6,000 infantrymen and 2,400 skirmishers, the latter apparently corresponding to the 25 centuries of *iuniores* of the fourth and fifth classes. Fraccaro therefore conjectured that the Servian reform doubled the earlier curiate system that had enrolled 3,000 soldiers from the 30 *curiae*; and when in 509 the king was replaced by two annually elected consuls, the Servian levy of 6,000 was divided equally between these two commanders, thus accounting for the fact that during later republican times the legionary *centuria* never numbered 100 men but about half that figure. Fraccaro's ingenious reconstruction receives support from

Ampolo's demographic estimate mentioned above that Rome c. 500 could have put 5,700–8,500 men into the field.

Information in A. Gellius (6.13, cf. 10.15.4) and Festus (Paulus ex Festo 100L s.v. *infra classem*) indicates that during the second century there existed a distinction between *classis* and *infra classem* = "the class" and "below the class," which referred to those of the first class versus those of the other four classes. But, as already described in the preceding paragraph, the armor and weaponry employed by the five different classes in later times suggest that originally the fundamental distinction would have pertained to those capable of equipping themselves to fight as hoplites and those who could not. This interpretation of the meaning of *classis* versus *infra classem* receives support from two other data. The Law of the Twelve Tables, Rome's earliest law code dating to the year 450, classified Roman citizens as being either *adsidui* or *proletarii*. The distinction was made in reference to who could serve as a legal stand-in for a litigant. According to A. Gellius (16.10.5) the law code specified that an *adsiduus* alone could be *vindex* for another *adsiduus*, whereas anyone could be *vindex* for a *proletarius*. The latter term derived from *proles*, meaning "offspring," and signified that the value of the person's property fell below the minimum census, and that the person's contribution to the state did not lie in paying taxes and performing military service but simply in producing offspring. Antiquarian information preserved by Cicero (*Rep.* 2.40) and Festus (Paulus ex Festo 8L s.v. *adsiduus*) suggests that these terms, *adsiduus* and *proletarius*, belonged to the Servian constitution and distinguished between those who qualified for military service at their own expense and those who did not.

The other relevant datum relating to the early distinction between *classis* and *infra classem* is an odd passage in Livy (4.34.6–7) concerning the year 426 that seems to preserve an archaic use of the term *classis*. After mentioning the dictator's celebration of a triumph for capturing Fidenae, Livy adds, as if by way of a final footnote on the Fidenate War, that according to some writers the Roman fleet (*classis*) had been deployed on the Tiber and had taken part in the battle. In criticizing this variant Livy first observes that the Tiber was too narrow for a naval action. He then conjectures that the use of a few ships in the river to block the escape of the enemy was later magnified into a naval engagement. Ogilvie correctly interprets *classis* as "army" and sees it as referring to the archaic Roman military levy of the *comitia centuriata* in contrast to those who were *infra classem*.[14] Interpreting *classis* as "fleet" seems to be a later annalistic misunderstanding of the term, which must have been found in some documentary source, such as a dedication in the Capitoline temple to commemorate the victory (see Livy 4.20.4). If so, as seems likely, we would have an important datum showing that in 426 the primary distinctions in the centuriate organization were among cavalrymen, *classis*, and *infra classem*. Although subdivisions could have already been made within the *classis* at this time, the dichotomy in terminology could have corresponded to a simple distinction between hoplite infantrymen and those below the hoplite census. Moreover, some provision is also likely to have already been made for a small number of light armed auxiliary forces.

In its initial stages hoplite organization does not need to have been very complicated, and two incidents from Thucydides' account of the Peloponnesian War clearly show how easy it was for a hoplite army to be the fundamental sovereign institution within a city-state. In the year 411 an oligarchy of 400 overthrew the democracy in Athens but was itself ousted and replaced by a simple hoplite constitution (Thuc. 8.97.1). After the Peloponnesian naval defeat of the Athenians off Euboea, the island revolted from Athens, which caused such a panic among the Athenians that they convened on the Pnyx and voted the 400 out of power. In their place they handed the government over to the 5,000, who were simply defined as "those who provided themselves with hoplite armor." In the spring of 418 the armies of the Argives and the Spartans and their allies confronted one another at Nemea, but instead of fighting a battle as the soldiers of both sides wished and expected, the young King Agis of Sparta conferred with two Argives, a general named Thrasylus and the Argive *proxenos* for Sparta. When these men agreed to a four-month truce and led the armies away, both armies were angry with the decision; and according to Thucydides (5.60.6) the Argives "on returning proceeded to stone Thrasylus in the Charadrus where they judge cases arising from a campaign before they enter the city. He took refuge at the altar and was spared, but they confiscated his property." This meting out of rough justice by an army outside the city reminds one of the *comitia centuriata* meeting in the Campus Martius outside the *pomerium* to elect its leaders, to decide on war and peace, and to try people on capital charges.

6   The Beginnings of Roman Expansion

The later annalistic tradition as preserved in Livy and Dionysius of Halicarnassus suggests that during the first half of the fifth century Rome and its Latin neighbors were hard pressed to defend the plain of Latium from the constant incursions made by Sabine, Aequian, and Volscian hill-folk; but after the middle of the fifth century Rome began to take its first steps toward territorial expansion with its capture and absorption in 426 of the small state of Fidenae, located upstream from Rome on the Tiber River. This success was followed a generation later in 396 by Rome's first really significant conquest, the capture of Etruscan Veii and the annexation of its territory. This acquisition has been estimated as having increased the size of the Roman state by about 60 percent. Moreover, the foundation of Latin colonies at Ardea in 442, Labici in 418, Velitrae in 401, Vitellia in 395, Circeii in 393, Satricum in 385, Sutrium and Nepet in 383, and Setia in 382 suggests that the threat posed by the encroachment of various hill-folk was on the wane, and Rome and the Latins were now instead expanding at their expense. Ancient historical evidence further indicates that the Roman state experienced considerable internal growth and development in its political and military institutions during the period c. 460–360. These major innovations are listed below in the form of a chronology of events. Although nothing is recorded concerning the centuriate organization, we may plausibly surmise that during this period this system must have likewise undergone various changes, as the Romans created new institutions and adjusted and adapted already existing ones to serve the expanding requirements of the state. Indeed, the creation of the offices of censor and quaestor indicates increased sophistication in Roman state finance and taxation, and this in turn might point to the creation or further elaboration of class divisions in the centuriate organization. Similarly, the institution of military pay for the first time in 406 and the expansion of the cavalry force in 403 testify to the growth of a more complex and sophisticated military system. We may further suppose that such changes resulted from or contributed to political tensions among different segments of Roman society; and that if any information concerning such alterations happened to survive into later historical times (but even this can be legitimately questioned), the ancient historical tradition, developed centuries later, misinterpreted the data and simplistically construed them in terms of the so-called struggle of the orders between patricians and plebeians.

Evolution of the Roman state c. 460–360

457   Increase in the number of plebeian tribunes from five to ten.[15]

451–450   Codification of the Law of the Twelve Tables.

446   Creation of the office of quaestor (two elected annually, perhaps to serve as state treasurers and/or quarter masters to the two consuls).

445   Creation of the office of military tribunes with consular power as a possible alternative to the annually elected consuls.[16]

443   Creation of the censorship.

426   Rome's capture and annexation of Fidenae.

421   Increase in the number of annually elected quaestors from two to four.

406   Supposed first instance of public pay for soldiers, possibly connected with Rome's war against Veii.

403   Recruitment of cavalrymen with their own horses to supplement the *equites equo publico*, possibly connected with Rome's war against Veii.

396   Rome's capture and annexation of Veii.

390   Gallic capture of Rome.

387   Creation of four new voting tribes out of the Veientine territory.

381   Rome extends citizenship to Tusculum.

380   Rome defeats Praeneste and its coalition of nine towns.

366   Reinstitution of the consulship along with one praetor for handling lawsuits and two curule aediles for managing various affairs in the city.

362   Henceforth the Romans elect every year six military tribunes who serve as subordinate officers under the two consuls.

Given the incomplete nature of our evidence for this early period of Roman history, it should come as no surprise that modern scholars have set forth different interpretations of how the military system of early Rome evolved. For example, G. V. Sumner has offered a reconstruction quite different from that of Fraccaro.[17] He argues that the original *classis* was not a military levy of 60 centuries, comprising what later evolved into the first three classes of the centuriate organization. Rather, he thinks that it did in fact correspond to the first class and thus made up an army of 4,000 hoplites, 40 centuries of *iuniores*; and that this was Rome's full military levy until 406/5 when Rome embarked upon its war against Veii. At this time, we are told, the number of military tribunes with consular power was increased for the first time from four to six, and the Romans also introduced military pay. Sumner conjectures that each of the consular tribunes was associated with 1,000 soldiers, so that their increase from four to six indicates that Rome in 405 increased its full military levy from 4,000 to 6,000. In order to do so, two new classes were created, the second and third classes of the centuriate organization, each consisting of ten centuries of 1,000 soldiers. Then when the consulship was reinstated in 366, the full levy of 6,000 was divided equally between the two consuls.

The principal difficulty with this alternative interpretation is the assumption that the phenomenon of military tribunes with consular power was entirely military in nature. The very facts of the reorganization of the Roman government in 367 strongly argue against this supposition: for six consular tribunes were then replaced by five curule officials, only two of whom (the consuls) were given specifically military duties, whereas the other three (the praetor and the two curule aediles) were attached to administrative matters in the city. It therefore appears likely that the preceding boards of six consular tribunes had been employed to satisfy both the external-military and internal-domestic needs of the Roman state.[18]

7 Divergence Between the Military Levy and the Centuriate Assembly

For the year 357 Livy (7.16.7–8) records the following curious incident:

> Nothing memorable was performed by the other consul except that through a novel precedent he passed a law with the tribes in the camp at Sutrium concerning a five percent tax on those who were manumitted. The senators gave their approval, because by this law no small amount of revenue accrued to a treasury in need of funds; but the tribunes of the plebs, prompted not so much by the law but by the precedent, sanctioned with death anyone who thereafter convoked the people far from the city; for if this were allowed, anything, no matter how harmful to the people, could be passed by soldiers sworn to obey the consul.

Despite Livy's mention of tribes, there can be no doubt that if this incident took place, the army ratified this proposal as a centuriate assembly convened while on campaign. Since this law was passed at Sutrium, the Latin colony on Rome's Etruscan frontier, it is likely that the army ratified this proposal either before or after a military campaign against non-Latin-speaking people, who were prime candidates for the Roman slave market. Nevertheless, this measure enacted by the army (presumably composed entirely of *iuniores*) did not sit well with civilian authorities back in Rome, and the latter ensured that such an incident would not be repeated. The episode therefore may represent the last occasion on which the army successfully asserted its archaic right to embody popular sovereignty. By this time, however, the idea had become outmoded, because the only military institution that exercised popular sovereignty was not soldiers on campaign but a centuriate organization that included *seniores* and perhaps other groups not fully represented in a field army.

8   The Growth in Roman Manpower

By the middle of the fourth century Rome had emerged as the single most powerful city-state in central Italy and was poised at the take-off stage for rapid expansion. The First Samnite War of 343–341 resulted in the merging of the Roman state and the league of northern Campanian communities headed by Capua through their sharing of citizenship. This augmentation in manpower was followed immediately by Rome's absorption of Latium into the Roman state. The Latin War of 340–338 ended in Roman victory and all the smaller communities of Latium being incorporated into Roman territory. Only the two larger states of Tibur and Praeneste retained their independence and were bound to Rome by bilateral treaties. During the Second Samnite War of 326–304 Rome continued to increase the size of its territory, as well as its manpower, both citizen and allied, available for military service; and the Romans' victory in this war placed them in the position of contemplating the conquest of peninsular Italy. Rome's rapid growth in territory, manpower, and other resources during the fourth century must have had major consequences for Rome's military organization. Under the year 311 Livy (9.30.3) records that the Romans began to elect 16 military tribunes to serve in four legions. The increase in the number of these annually elected officers from six in 362 (Livy 7.5.9) to 16 in 311 suggests a major change or restructuring of the Roman army. The six earlier military tribunes had probably been assigned three each to two legions, presumably reflecting a legionary organization that was still in part based upon the three archaic tribes of the Ramnenses, Titienses, and Luceres. The 16 military tribunes elected in 311, however, must have been assigned in groups of four to four legions, thus indicating a doubling in the size of the normal Roman military annual recruitment. Four legions still formed the usual yearly military levy of the Roman state 150 years later in Polybius' day (Polybius 6.19–20).

   With the first decades of the third century, i.e., the closing years of the early republic (300–264), our knowledge of the Roman state finally emerges from myth, legend, and murky twilight into the dawn of the historical period. The census figures recorded for these years are to be trusted. They represent the total number of adult male Roman citizens available for military service and show that Roman manpower at this time numbered more than a quarter of a million.[19] They are as follows.

Roman census figures for the early third century

Date	Census	Source
293/2	262,321	Livy 10.47.2
289/8	272,000	Livy, *Per.* 11
280/79	287,222	Livy, *Per.* 13
276/5	271,224	Livy, *Per.* 14
265/4	292,234	Eutropius 2.18

9 Epilogue

By 264 Rome had completed its conquest of Italy except for the Po Valley, and it was poised to embark upon its long succession of overseas wars of the middle and late republic. In large measure, however, Rome's political institutions (magistrates, Senate, and assemblies) were still those of a city-state. Rome never developed a system of political representation, but even throughout the middle and late republic all meetings of the assemblies were held in Rome; and given the extent of Roman territory and the difficult conditions of ancient travel, only a minuscule portion of the Roman citizens with the right to vote were able to come to Rome to exercise their suffrage.[20] Thus, over the course of three centuries the *comitia centuriata* had progressed from being an assembly of all of Rome's hoplites to a voting body that could accommodate only a very small percentage of Rome's enormous manpower. Nevertheless, whenever a census was administered, all adult male Romans were assigned to tribes, classes, and centuries within the centuriate organization.

By the close of the early republic Roman Italy consisted of three categories of people. Firstly, there were the Roman citizens. They occupied the territory of the Roman state, which now stretched across central Italy from the Tyrrhenian to the Adriatic, extended southward in a strip along the Volscian coast to the Bay of Naples, and included northern Campania. Secondly, there were the states allied to Rome. In terms of geography and population they formed the largest of the three categories. They were the various Etruscan, Umbrian, Picene, Sabellian, Messapic, and Greek communities of northern and southern Italy, who still exercised local autonomy over their own affairs but were bound to Rome by individual bilateral treaties. The third category of people were the Latin colonies scattered throughout the peninsula. Since their inhabitants enjoyed Latin status (a kind of half-Roman citizenship) and had Rome as their mother-city, they were closely bound to the Roman state by law, language, culture, and sentiment. Most important for Rome's future as an imperial power of the Mediterranean was the access which the treaties with the allied states gave Rome to the manpower resources of peninsular Italy. An overall picture of the impressive scale of the Roman military organization at this time can be obtained from Polybius 2.24, which lists the military manpower available to the Roman state in 225 at the time of the last major Gallic invasion across the

Apennines.[21] Besides cataloguing the various forces deployed against the Gauls, Polybius gives the total manpower for the different regions of Italy. Since Rome's earliest historian, Fabius Pictor, is known to have participated in this campaign (Orosius 4.13.5), Polybius must have taken these figures from his historical account, which in turn was based upon contemporary records. The numbers given below must correspond closely to what they were in 264. They add up to a total of 730,000 infantry and 72,700 cavalry.[22]

Infantry	Cavalry	Category
41,600	2,400	Romans in consular armies
60,000	4,000	Allies in consular armies
20,000	1,500	Romans guarding Rome
30,000	2,000	Allies guarding Rome
8,400	800	Forces in Sicily and Tarentum
50,000	4,000	Sabines and Etruscans
20,000		Umbrians and Sarsinates
80,000	5,000	Latin colonists
70,000	7,000	Samnites
50,000	16,000	Iapygians and Messapians
30,000	3,000	Lucanians
20,000	4,000	Marsi, Marrucini, Frentani, Vestini
250,000	23,000	Romans and Campanians

ACKNOWLEDGMENT

As I write these words on your birthday (July 29, 2004), I dedicate this chapter to you, my dearest wife Dorothy Alice (deceased March 8, 2003) in deepest gratitude for you having been the most perfect life-mate, love-mate, and help-mate whom anyone could ever hope to have.

NOTES

1   All dates are before the common era. The term "traditional," when used in reference to dates, means that these are the dates that became enshrined in the later ancient Roman historical tradition of the late republic. Their accuracy, especially with respect to the regal period, can be seriously questioned.

2   For Rome's assemblies see Botsford 1909, Staveley 1972, 119–216, and Nicolet 1980, 207–316.

3   For discussion of the significance of the *lex curiata de imperio* see Staveley 1954, 84–90.

4   For the Servian constitution in the context of Rome in the sixth century see Last 1945, 30–48. For the archaeological data from Rome and Latium during the regal period see Meyer 1983, Holloway 1994, and Smith 1996.

5   For Greek hoplite weaponry and warfare see Hanson 1991 and 2000.

6   For these finds see Torelli 1989, 35–6 and Drummond 1989, 170–1.

7   The modern works utilized in this and the following paragraphs are the following: Beloch 1926, 178 and 217; Alföldi 1965, 288–318; and Ampolo 1980, 15–30 and 168–75.

8   Rome's urban area at this time is estimated to have been 285 hectares, and the area enclosed within the so-called Servian Wall of the mid-fourth century measured 426 hectares. Ampolo (1980, 168) lists the urban areas of the following ancient cities. All figures are in hectares (1 hectare = 2.471 acres). Latin communities: Ardea and Satricum each c. 40; Etruscan communities: Volsinii-Orvieto 80, Caere 120, Tarquinii 150, Vulci 180, Veii 242; western Greek colonies: Selinus 29, Caulonia 47.5, Cumae 72.5, Velia 72.5, Massilia 75, Naples 80.5, Heraclea 110, Posidonia 127, Metapontum 141, Gela 200, Hipponium 225, Locri 232.5, Croton 281, Tarentum 510, Sybaris 515, Acragas 517; Greek mainland and Aegean communities: Megara 40, Thasos 52, Mytilene 155, Rhodes 200, Halicarnassus 250, Sparta 450, and Athens with Peiraeus 585.

9   The ancient sources that describe this organization are Livy 1.43, Dionysius 4.16–18, Polybius 6.22–23, and Cicero, *Rep.* 2.39–40.

10 These figures are in terms of *asses*, and the amounts reflect the census requirements of the late third and/or second centuries. Originally an *as* was one pound of bronze (one Roman pound = 324 grams), which was further subdivided into 12 *unciae* (whence the English word "ounce").

11 For the tribal system see Taylor 1960.

12 See Astin 1982, 174–87.

13 Fraccaro 1931, 91–7 = 1957, II. 287–92.

14 Ogilvie 1965, 583.

15 For the ancient sources that mention the events tabulated here consult Broughton 1951–2, vol. I. *sub annis.*

16 During the period 444–367 the Roman state was headed each year either by a pair of consuls or a board of military tribunes with consular power. At first the latter numbered three, but they were gradually increased to four and then to six. This change must have resulted from Rome's growing internal-administrative and external-military needs. For further discussion and modern bibliography on this question see Forsythe 2005, 234–9.

17 Sumner 1970, 67–78.

18 For the author's own argument that the increase in the number of consular tribunes was in part the result of these officials taking over the administration of justice from the pontiffs see Forsythe 2005, 211–13.

19 For what these figures represent see Brunt 1971, 15–25.

20 For modern attempts to estimate how many Romans could have possibly voted in the *comitia centuriata* during the late republic see Taylor 1966, 48–54, Staveley 1972, 186–90, Nicolet 1980, 290–7, and MacMullen 1980, 454–7.

21 For discussion of these figures see Brunt 1971, 44–60 and Baronowski 1993, 181–202; De Ligt (in this volume).

22 It is noteworthy that this total of slightly over 800,000 men capable of bearing arms during Fabius Pictor's lifetime is exactly ten times the figure which he attributed to the very first census conducted by King Servius Tullius (Livy 1.44.2). It therefore seems likely that Pictor estimated that from the first census down to his own day the manpower available to the Roman state had increased tenfold.

BIBLIOGRAPHY

Alföldi, A. 1965. *Early Rome and the Latins*. Ann Arbor.

Ampolo, C. 1980. "Le Condizioni materiali della Produzione: Agricoltura e Paesaggio agrario," *Dialoghi di Archeologia* 2.1.

Astin, A. E. 1982. "The censorship of the Roman republic: Frequency and regularity," *Historia* 31: 174–87.

Baronowski, D. W. 1993. "Roman military forces in 225 BC (Polybius 2.23–4)," *Historia* 42: 181–202.

Beloch, K. J. 1926. *Römische Geschichte bis zum Beginn der punischen Kriege*. Leipzig.

Botsford, G. W. 1909. *The Roman Assemblies from Their Origin to the End of the Republic*. New York.

Broughton, T. R. S. 1951–2. *The Magistrates of the Roman Republic*. Cleveland, OH.

Brunt, P. A. 1971. *Italian Manpower 225 BC to AD 14*. Oxford.

Cornell, T. J. 1995. *The Beginnings of Rome. Italy and Rome from the Bronze Age to the Punic Wars (c. 1000–264 BC)*. London.

Drummond, A. 1989. "Rome in the fifth century I: The social and economic framework," in *CAH* 7.2. Cambridge, 113–71.

Eder, W. (ed.). 1990. *Staat und Staatlichkeit in der frühen römischen Republik*. Stuttgart.

Forsythe, G. 1994. *The Historian L. Calpurnius Piso Frugi and the Roman Annalistic Tradition*. Lanham, MD.

—— 1999. *Livy and Early Rome. A Study in Historical Method and Judgment*. Stuttgart.

—— 2005. *A Critical History of Early Rome. From Prehistory to the First Punic War*. Berkeley.

Fraccaro, P. 1931. "La Storia dell'Antichissimo Esercito Romano e l'Età dell'Ordinamento Centuriato," *Atti II Congresso Nazionale di Studi Romani* 3: 91–7 = *Opuscula*. Pavia 1957, II, 287–92.

Hanson, V. D. (ed.). 1991. *Hoplites. The Classical Greek Battle Experience*. London.

—— 2000. *The Western Way of War. Infantry Battle in Classical Greece*, 2nd edn. Berkeley.

Heurgon, J. 1973. *The Rise of Rome to 264 BC*. Berkeley.

Holloway, R. Ross. 1994. *The Archaeology of Early Rome and Latium*. London.

Last, H. 1945. "The Servian reforms," *JRS* 35: 30–48.

MacMullen, R. 1980. "How many Romans voted?" *Athenaeum* 58: 454–7.

Meyer, J. C. 1983. *Pre-Republican Rome: An Analysis of the Cultural and Chronological Relations 1000–500 BC*. Odense.

Nicolet, C. 1980. *The World of the Citizen in Republican Rome*. Berkeley.

Oakley, S. P. 1997. *A Commentary on Livy Books VI–X, Volume I, Introduction and Book VI*. Oxford.

—— 1998. *A Commentary on Livy Books VI–X, Volume II, Books VII–VIII*. Oxford.

Ogilvie, R. M. 1965. *A Commentary on Livy Books 1–5*. Oxford.

Raaflaub, K. A. (ed.). 1986. *Social Struggles in Archaic Rome, New Perspectives on the Conflict of the Orders*. Berkeley (Updated edition 2005).

Smith, C. J. 1996. *Early Rome and Latium. Economy and Society c. 1000 to 500 BC*. Oxford.

Staveley, E. S. 1954. "The constitution of the Roman republic," *Historia* 5: 74–119.

—— 1972. *Greek and Roman Voting and Elections*. London and Ithaca, NY.

Sumner, G. V. 1970. "The legion and the centuriate organization," *JRS* 60: 67–78.

Taylor, L. R. 1960. *The Voting Districts of the Roman Republic*. Rome.

—— 1966. *Roman Voting Assemblies from the Hannibalic War to the Dictatorship of Caesar*. Ann Arbor.

Torelli, M. 1989. "Archaic Rome between Latium and Etruria," in *CAH* 7.2. Cambridge, 30–51.

Walbank, F. W., et al. (ed.). 1989. *CAH* 7.2: *The Rise of Rome to 220 BC*, 2nd edn. Cambridge.

FURTHER READING

Excellent modern treatments of the *comitia centuriata* as a political body of voting Roman citizens during the middle and late republic are to be found in Botsford 1909, Taylor 1966, Staveley 1972, 119–216, and Nicolet 1980, 207–316. But the student interested in how this institution fit into the larger military and political context of early Rome needs to become familiar with the complex history of that period. One should, of course, begin with the most important ancient sources, which happen to be the first ten books of Livy and *The Roman Antiquities* of Dionysius of Halicarnassus, both available in the Loeb Classical Library of Harvard University Press. These accounts, however, are highly problematic, because they were written long after the events that they purport to describe. They therefore must be read critically with the aid of modern scholarship. For Livy the commentaries of Ogilvie 1965 and of Oakley 1997 and 1998 are fundamental tools. Forsythe 1994 and 1999 offer further examination of the earlier annalistic tradition and of Livy's use and attitude toward his sources of information. The development of the centuriate organization is only one of many interrelated problems of early Roman history. Raaflaub 1986 (second edition released in 2005) and Eder 1990 are collections of essays by different scholars concerning numerous problems of early Roman history studied from various perspectives. The most recent attempts to narrate Rome's early history in English are Walbank 1989, Cornell 1995, and Forsythe 2005. Still useful are the older works of Alföldi 1965 and Heurgon 1973.[22]

PART II

Mid- and Late Republic

CHAPTER THREE

Army and Battle During the Conquest of Italy (350–264 BC)

Louis Rawlings

1   Introduction

Rome had developed into a significant power in central Italy by the middle of the fourth century BC. It had survived the threat posed by the tribes of the Aequi and Volsci in the fifth century, and had recovered from the sack of the city by Gauls in 390 BC. It was the dominant partner in its alliances with the Latin League and the Hernici. Diplomatic contacts and treaties further indicate its regional importance. In 354 it appears to have allied with the Samnites, a confederation of tribes that dominated the uplands of the central and southern Apennines (Livy 7.19.4). In 348 it also established or re-negotiated a treaty with the maritime empire of Carthage (Livy 7.27.1–2; Polybius 3.22), while in 343 BC it allied with the fertile and heavily populated region of Campania, famed for its cavalry (Livy 7.31).

Rome, however, was not the only power in Italy. North of the city, the 12 Etruscan city-states still remained prosperous and independent, and capable of fielding armies organized around phalanxes of heavy infantry spearmen (hoplites). Beyond them were tribes of Gauls, who dominated the Po Valley; one tribe, the Senones, controlled the Adriatic coast between Rimini and Ancona. Gallic armies possessed a strong warrior ethos and had a reputation for fearsome charges, but occasional brittleness in prolonged combat. The mountainous Apennine uplands that run like a spine down much of Italy were inhabited by various Oscan tribes. The Umbrians, Sabines, and Aequi, who were Rome's more or less immediate upland neighbors, possessed small and loosely organized tribal structures, but towards the southeast the Samnites, a numerous people with a warlike reputation, were formed into a powerful, albeit principally defensive, league. In the south of Italy were the Greek city-states of Magna Graecia, such as

Naples, Locris, Croton, and Tarentum, with their armies of hoplites and mercenaries, and the territories of Italic peoples, such as Lucanians, Apulians, and Bruttians.[1]

The 86-year period 350–264 BC was to see a radical expansion of Roman power in Italy and set the trajectory for future military and imperial development. Rome was to come into conflict with this diverse range of peoples, and, either by successfully overcoming them in warfare or by drawing them into its network of alliances, it would expand its power and influence to control the whole of Italy south of the river Rubicon.

2   The Roman Conquest of Italy

Historical overview

Rome's first challenge came from the Latins and Campanians, who waged a war to break free of Roman hegemony (340–338 BC). Its victory led to a significant enlargement of Roman territory and manpower. Rome also re-forged its system of alliances into a stronger and more dynamic tool for conquest (see below). It then waged a series of protracted wars against the Samnites in the central and southern Apennines. At times, the whole Samnite League appears to have been engaged, but, for the most part, cooperation between the constituent members of the confederation was not sustained and Rome seems to have been able to engage individual tribes and communities. Roman armies usually invaded Samnium, rather than the other way around, suggesting that Roman aggression was an underlying feature in the relationship between the two groups.[2] Despite a number of set-backs, notably at the Caudine Forks (321 BC) and at the battle of Lautulae (315 BC), by 304 the Romans had gained the upper hand against the Samnites. In fact, from 311, the Romans had also turned their attention to their other neighbors. The next 30 years (311–283) saw a dramatic enlargement of Roman territory and influence. In the last decade of the fourth century, the Romans returned to old allies, the Hernici (who were accused attempting to secede), and old enemies, the Aequi, and incorporated their lands into Roman territory. Sabinum suffered a similar fate after a campaign by M. Curius Dentatus (290 BC).

In the third century, the ravenous nature of Roman expansion provoked the formation of a multiple alliance of Samnites, Etruscans, Umbrians, and Gauls to oppose them, but Rome won major victories at Sentinum (295) and Aquilonia (293). These peoples struggled to maintain cohesion in the face of the Roman strategic advantages of territorial integrity, unified command and military organization. The Samnites and Umbrians were subdued by 290, and a few years later the Gallic Senones and their Etruscan allies were heavily defeated at Vadimon (283). Roman armies also increasingly intervened in the affairs of the Lucanians, the Apulians, and the cities of Magna Graecia. They met opposition from the principal Greek city of southern Italy, Tarentum, which was allied with the king and adventurer Pyrrhus of Epirus, trained in the arts of Hellenistic warfare, with his army of 25,000 men and 20 elephants. Despite winning victories over Roman armies at Heraclea (280 BC) and Ausculum (279 BC), and encouraging the renewal of Samnite, Lucanian, and possibly Etruscan and Umbrian hostilities against Rome, Pyrrhus was defeated by the Romans at

Beneventum (275 BC). He withdrew to Epirus, leaving the Romans free to complete the reduction of Tarentum (272 BC) and its allies, so that, by 264, the conquest of Italy had been achieved.

Patterns of warfare: predators and states

Understanding the developments of Roman warfare and military organization in this period presents some substantial problems. The paucity of material evidence for the Roman army in the middle republic has meant that most modern descriptions are dominated by the surviving accounts of Roman and Greek writers. However, there are considerable difficulties in using such sources. Our fullest narrative, written by Livy (59 BC–AD 17) some three centuries after this period, is only complete until 293 BC. The Greek historian, Polybius (c. 200–118 BC), gives some additional material, but his narrative interest really only begins in 264 BC. Other writers frequently offer only partial and fragmentary accounts. Furthermore, the sources tend to have their eyes fixed firmly on Roman history and we are told only rarely of conflicts in Italy that did not involve the Romans. It is clear, nevertheless, that warfare was a frequent feature of Italian life. Economic and demographic pressures encouraged many tribes in the upland regions of the Apennines to prey on their lowland rivals, or forced groups and individuals to leave their communities and enter mercenary service for overseas powers such as Carthage or the Sicilian tyrants. Much warfare in the Italian peninsula was undoubtedly relatively low-level, amounting to little more than raiding expeditions seeking plunder and glory, or asserting the prowess or dominance of one group over its neighbors. The people of Privernum, for example, are reported in 342 and 330 BC to have raided the territories of their neighbors, the Roman colonies of Setia and Norba (Livy 7.41.8–8.1; 8.19). The Romans too were not averse to plundering operations. In 310 BC, Q. Fabius Maximus Rullianus raided the lands at the foot of the Ciminian Mountain (Livy 9.36.11–14). His depredations escalated into full-scale confrontation when a large force of Etruscans and neighboring Umbrians engaged his forces near Sutrium (9.37). Although communities threatened by a Roman army might respond with such a large-scale muster, it appears often to have been a relatively short-lived reaction on a local scale. When offensive campaigns were mounted they usually targeted Roman allies that were closest. What appears striking about the Romans is how often they are presented as operating at a level and intensity that usually exceeded their rivals. Probably from 338, certainly from c. 312 BC, Rome frequently acted as a pan-Italian power capable of operating simultaneously in two or more theaters beyond the core of Roman territory. In the same year as Rullianus' operations at the Ciminian Mountain, another Roman army captured Allifae from the Samnites and "many other forts and villages were either taken intact or destroyed" (Livy 9.37). A Roman fleet was also sent to plunder the coast near Nuceria (9.38).[3]

The structures of Roman expansion

In the period 350–264 BC, there were only six years when Rome was not at war: 347, 344, 328, 288–7, and 285 BC.[4] Such bellicosity requires some understanding of the cultural, institutional, and economic pressures that drove Rome to war.

The Romans were clearly imbued with a war-like ethos. Success in war was a good way for some men to acquire prestige and influence. The martial achievements of aristocrats were remembered by future generations and sometimes took on a heroic status (Polybius 6.53–54). Valerius Corvus (348 BC, Livy 7.26) famously killed a Gaul in a duel and appears to have won his first consulship (of six) because of it. Roman generals sought glory and reputation in winning battles and, when successful, demanded recognition from peers and the wider community. Triumphs and ovations, military celebrations granted to victorious generals, feature increasingly in our records, particularly from c. 312. The desire to be remembered for one's military achievements is indicated by the surviving tomb of Lucius Cornelius Scipio Barbatus, (cos 298, *ILLRP* 309), whose epitaph claimed victories in Samnium and Lucania, and by the fragmentary fresco scenes found in a mid-third-century tomb on the Esquiline, which may represent the achievements of Fabius Rullianus during the Samnite wars.[5]

Triumphs recognized the elite's concerns with glory and prowess, but they were also opportunities for the community as a whole to celebrate the successes of the Roman army and to see the booty captured on campaigns being paraded through the city (e.g. Livy 10.46.5, 14). Later commentators recognized how Rome's gradually widening horizons increased the rewards of warfare; Florus' (*Epit.* 1.13.26–7) description of the triumph of Curius Dentatus over Pyrrhus at Beneventum imagined:

> Before then, the only booty you could have seen was the cattle of the Volscians, the flocks of the Sabines, the carts of the Gauls or the broken arms of the Samnites; but if you could have seen these captives, they were Molossians, Thessalians, Macedonians, Bruttians, Apulians and Lucanians; if you could have witnessed this procession you would have seen gold, purple statues, paintings and all the luxuries of Tarentum.

The economic benefits of warfare in this period should not be underestimated. As the fourth century progressed, notices about plunder recorded in our sources became more frequent. The imposition of indemnities on defeated enemies swelled the public treasury and plunder enriched the soldiers. Although the amounts of booty and tribute given by the sources must be treated with a good deal of caution, they are indicative of the fortunes of war flowing into Rome. Such profits had a considerable effect on the physical structure of the city, particularly during the upsurge in conquest from 312. Between 311 and 291, nine new temples were constructed. In 312/11 the first aqueduct into Rome, drawing water from as far as the Alban Hills near Gabii, was a major feat of construction (Livy 9.29.6). It indicates the resources available to the state and also suggests the degree of security and stability that the central core of Roman territory possessed. The laying of the Via Appia in 311 (Livy 9.29.6), along the coast into Campania, and the Via Valeria (307/6; Livy 9.43.25), inland to Alba Fucens, also indicates the resources of the city. As conduits for Roman armies to march out to campaign they demonstrate the state's widening foreign interests.

Essential to Roman success in the conquest of Italy was the effective exploitation of manpower, both from its own territory and that of its allies (*socii*). After the defeat of the Latins and Campanians (338 BC), Rome dissolved the Latin League and absorbed much of Campania into the *ager Romanus*, trebling its available manpower at a single stroke. A dynamic new alliance system was established that provided the resources to support expansion and was capable of integrating future allies and conquests. According to modern estimates, the amount of territory directly controlled by Rome, the *ager Romanus*, grew from 1,902 square kilometers in 340 BC to c. 5,525 square kilometers after victory over the Latins and Campanians in 338 BC. By 264 BC this had ballooned to 26,805 square kilometers; about a sixth of peninsular Italy (c. 125,000 km^2) and had been acquired primarily from defeated enemies. Some of this territory was parceled out in individual allotments (*viritane*) for citizens, but much of this massive area was controlled by colonies, usually of Latin status, that were expected to provide troops for Rome's armies when required. Cicero (*Agr.* 2.73) observed that they were situated like fortresses across the Italian landscape. Much of the territorial expansion, after the initial, but substantial, enlargement of *ager Romanus* in 338, appears to have occurred after 315 BC. While two Latin colonies were established in the quarter century before this date (340–315), eleven were set up in the following quarter (314–289), and a further six in the decade 273–263. In all, it has been estimated that the colonies established in this period required as many as 70,000 colonists and their dependants.[6]

3 Armies and Battle During the Conquest

Militiamen, mercenaries, and sworn bands

The Roman army was, in many respects, a militia whose recruits were expected to arm themselves at their own expense. Many of these would have been farmers who would have had little formal weapons-drill, but who would probably have been expected to pick up the necessary skills as they went along. Of course repeated, often annual, service would have increased familiarity with weapons, formations, and tactics, but armies were temporary and usually disbanded at the end of a campaign. By the end of the fifth century, the state appears to have provided some remuneration for the service in the army, the *stipendium* (military pay: Livy 4.59.11–60.8, 8.8.3; Diodorus 14.16.5). The award of pay theoretically enabled the Romans to keep their army in the field all year long if necessary, but the expectation was that most campaigns would only last for a few summer weeks. When the army of Publius Valerius Laevinus was ordered by the Senate to winter at Saepinum (280/279 BC), it was regarded as a punishment for military defeat at the hands of Pyrrhus (Frontinus, *Strat.* 4.1.24).[7]

Most states raised forces in response to threats or to prosecute their publicly approved wars. When Fabius Rullianus raided Etruria from his base on the Ciminian Mountain, Livy (9.36–7) described how he was first opposed by militias called up by local Etruscan aristocrats, and then by a larger assemblage of Etruscans and neighboring Umbrian allies. The armies of peoples such as Samnites, Lucanians, and Greek cities ought, for the most part, to be regarded as comprising men who regarded themselves as warriors (or possibly soldiers) only for the duration of the campaign. These forces were sometimes augmented by mercenaries, men who made their living primarily from their martial prowess. Campanians, Samnites, and Gauls are frequently named as mercenary material, but it is likely that any Italian with sufficient motivation might seek employment in this fashion. At least one Roman traveled to Egypt to take service with the Ptolemies (Griffith 1934, 243). Rome appears not to have employed mercenaries, mainly because it was able to draw upon large numbers of allies, but cities such as Tarentum employed mercenaries as a matter of course (Dionysius 20.1), and we also hear of the Samnites and Gauls (Livy 8.38; Polybius 2.19) using them in their local and regional conflicts.

Mercenary bands could be dangerous, particularly once they had been discharged. One group of ex-Syracusan mercenaries, Campanians who called themselves the Mamertines, took over the Sicilian city of Messana and proceeded to raid their neighbors (c. 289 BC: Diodorus 21.18; 22.7.4, 13; Polybius 1.7–8; cf. Plutarch, *Pyrrh.* 23–24). Another band of mercenary veterans discharged by Syracuse raided Bruttium, but they were intercepted by the local inhabitants, who raised a large force against them, stormed their stronghold and shot them all down with javelins (338 BC: Diodorus 16.82.1–2; cf. Plutarch, *Tim.* 30.1–2). Independently minded bands of predators, making a living from warfare and brigandage, seem to have been a frequent menace. One such group, operating out of caves in Umbria, appear to have been the target of Roman operations in 303 BC (Livy 10.1.4). Similarly, some stories about the Bruttii, a confederation that emerged in the fourth century, claimed that they had originally been mercenaries, brigands, outlaws, and ex-slaves. According to Diodorus (16.15.1–2), the Bruttii had survived by raiding their neighbors, but eventually grew in strength to besiege and capture Terina, Hipponium, Thurii, and other cities, and so to establish their own league. The activities of such bands of warriors indicate the ubiquitous and predatory features of violence in Italy in this period, but they also show how malleable the status of warriors might be. Men who at one time might have been considered brigands, at other times acted for pay, or for themselves when attempting to create new communities.

By calling themselves Mamertines (Sons of Mamers – the Oscan equivalent of Mars), the Campanian mercenaries who seized Messana were asserting their cultural and ethnic origins, and creating a strong sense of group identity. One story explained how these men had been dedicated in a *ver sacrum* ("sacred spring," Festus 150 L), a rite of expiation for a natural disaster, and had been expelled from their own community to make a new life for themselves through force of arms. Similar bands of warriors had long been a feature of Italian warfare, and the dedication of men in various rites that created bonds of military identity and aimed at enhancing commitment and obedience, continued into the third century BC. In 309 BC, men "who had dedicated themselves in the Samnite fashion," engaged the army of Papirius Cursor (Livy 9.40). According to Livy, they were only overwhelmed when a Roman commander offered them as a sacrifice to Orcus (the Oscan god of the underworld), a form of *evocatio* intended to draw away the magical power of their oath. The Etruscans, in 310 BC, applied a *lex sacrata* (sacred oath) to each man who was selected, which apparently led them to fight more bravely in battle (Livy 9.39). The Samnites of the so-called Linen Legion in 293 BC were "forced to swear a dreadful oath, a curse on himself, his family and household, if he did not follow where his generals led, or if he fled battle or did not kill anyone he saw in rout" (Livy 10.38). In Rome too, the soldiers swore an oath (the *sacramentum*) to obey the commands of their general. It reinforced the consul's power of coercion (*coercitio*), which allowed him to punish citizens summarily when on campaign (up to and including the death penalty). Personal and group discipline and subordination of the individual to the needs of the Roman state are regular motifs in our sources: "in war and peace bow to lawful authority," the dictator, Lucius Papirius Cursor, says in one of Livy's speeches (8.35). Exemplary stories of Papirius Cursor ordering the flogging of his subordinate officer, Fabius Rullianus, for engaging the enemy without permission, or of the execution by the consul Manlius Torquatus of his own son, were regarded as particularly severe and noteworthy.[8]

In addition to the *sacramentum*, Roman soldiers also appear to have sworn an oath (*coniuratio*) more informally among themselves, "not to flee the battlefield or to abandon their place in the battle-line" (Livy 22.38.2–5; Frontinus, *Strat.* 4.1.4). Such oaths undoubtedly fostered cohesion and identity in war, but, in this period, it was up to the soldiers themselves to exchange these undertakings. It was not until 216 BC that the state appropriated this latter oath and combined it with the *sacramentum* as an oath of loyalty to the commanders.

In the mid-fourth century, each consul usually commanded a legion of citizen soldiers, supplemented by allied contingents. By 311 BC, the number of legions that regularly took the field appears to have risen to four. In that year, the people were formally given the right to elect the military tribunes for each of the four legions, suggesting that popular prerogative was brought into line with a relatively recent military practice (Livy 9.30.3). From then on, each consular army usually consisted of two legions of citizens, perhaps numbering around 8,000–10,000 infantry and 600 cavalry and two *alae* of allies, probably amounting to at least as many infantry (but perhaps many more in some situations) and three times the amount of cavalry. Larger armies do appear to reflect the Romans' pan-Italian aspirations and coincide with the upsurge in bellicosity evident in the rising number of triumphs and colonies recorded from this point (see above). Such forces would undoubtedly have tested the resources of most of Rome's rivals and in the third century led to a number of anti-Roman pan-Italian alliances. In one of the largest battles fought by Italians in this period, at Sentinum (295 BC), it is possible that more than 40,000 combatants were involved on each side. The engagements fought between the Romans and Pyrrhus' forces were probably on a similar scale.[9]

Socii

As he rode onto the battlefield of Heraclea, Pyrrhus gained the distinct impression that he was being watched. It was not only that his cavalry bodyguard followed close upon his every move, nor that his polyglot army of Greeks and Italians drew inspiration from the sight of his purple cloak and glittering arms. One amongst the Roman forces appeared to be gazing at him. As the armies engaged, this enemy and his small body of companions cut their way through the ranks until the two men were face to face. In the shock of first contact, their horses were both killed. Pyrrhus was pulled to safety and re-horsed, leaving the dismounted enemy warrior to be overwhelmed in the cavalry melee. The single-minded man had not even been Roman. His name was Oblacus (or Oplax) Volsinius and he had been a leader of the Frentani, Roman allies from the Adriatic coast of Italy. It is possible that Pyrrhus recorded the encounter in his memoirs, which both Plutarch and Dionysius of Halicarnassus, our sources for the story, had read.[10] Even if he did not, and the story is little more than narrative color to enliven an otherwise dry battle account, nevertheless, it reveals a fundamental truth. Rome did draw upon allies such as the Frentani to fight its wars; in fact it relied very heavily on their bravery and commitment.

For the most part, the view of Roman military operations given by our sources hardly wanders from the actions of the citizen army, but it is clear that its success was based on organizing and integrating the *socii* (allies) to fight alongside the legions. It was fundamental that Rome was able to lead these allies effectively and was able to integrate ethnically and militarily diverse groups into its military system. It is highly probable that at least 50 percent of any army that Rome raised in this period would have comprised of allies, especially after the settlement of 338 BC. Not all allies were made to send contingents all of the time; the theater in which the army was campaigning probably determined which allies were called upon to assemble. The burden on individual communities of Roman recruitment would probably have been limited, and based upon a list kept in Rome known as the *formula togatorum*.[11] These troops were financed and supported by their own communities while on campaign (Polybius 6.21), which had the obvious effect of making warfare cheaper for the Romans to wage.

There are no surviving contemporary descriptions of how contingents of *socii* were armed or fought in this period. Our sources rarely notice their presence, let alone bother to describe them in action, but instead appear to have imagined them as Roman troops in almost every way. Livy claimed that when the Romans and Latins fought one another in 340 BC, their equipment and battlefield tactics were indistinguishable (8.8.15): "They knew that maniple would fight maniple, the whole line of *hastati* match *hastati*, *principes* against *principes*, while centurions must engage each other while the ranks remained unbroken." His description is probably anachronistic and reflects the homogeneity of the armies of the Social War, waged between Rome and its allies in the first century BC. Of course, in reality, this is unlikely to have been the case in our period. We know that individual contingents of allies were commanded by their own officers (Polybius 1.7; 6.21), such as Volsinius of the Frentani, and it is likely that the troops fought in equipment that reflected their own martial expectations and combat styles. As Rome absorbed the peoples of Italy, it is not clear how quickly they were influenced by Roman military methods, or indeed, how much the Romans themselves were influenced by their allies. The size of allied contingents and their internal organization would have probably varied considerably, due to the differences in the size of allied states and in the application of the *formula togatorum*; some units may have been assembled from the combination of several small communities. Our sources tend to call the infantry contingents "cohorts," (lit. the "corralled-together"), but at this time such units lacked the more formal structure that the legionary cohort was to acquire in the first century BC. In the third century, these cohorts of allies, it seems, were generally stationed on the wings (*alae*) of the army, and placed under the overall command of Roman officers, *praefecti sociorum* (Polybius 6.26.5), who helped to impose some order and centralized control on this multi-ethnic force. Allied horse, organized into *turmae* (troops of 30), played an important role on the wings, where they provided three-quarters of the cavalry strength of the army and covered the flanks during battle. It is probable that the Romans called on allies with suitable resources and expertise, such as the Campanians (e.g. Livy 10.29), or local elites, such as Volsinius and his followers, to provide the bulk of the cavalry. Some allied troops, perhaps the bravest or the best equipped, may have been selected to act as *extraordinarii* on campaign, who were stationed at the head of the advancing army, and may have fought separately in battle. Such contingents are first mentioned among the Hernici, who may have provided a model for Roman use (Livy 7.7).

The general reliability of the allies meant that, where necessary, they appear to have been entrusted with the duties of garrisoning towns and strongholds. On one occasion in 280, however, a contingent of Campanians, led by a certain Decius, appear to have mutinied and held the city of Rhegium for themselves for almost ten years. These Campanians were eventually captured and were scourged and beheaded in the Roman Forum. This exemplary punishment not only indicates the Roman concern for a reputation as protector of allies, but also chillingly reveals the potential consequences of disloyalty.[12]

Of course, Rome was not the only state to use alliances in war. When the Privernates and Fundani were allied in the 330s, overall command was held by Valerius Vaccus from Fundi (Livy 8.19). In the case of the Samnite League, when the four tribes resolved on a joint operation, they elected an overall commander, a *meddix touticus*, to conduct it (Livy 9.1.2; 10.12.2; 24.19.2). The League had a relatively formal existence and long-standing federal institutions, but other unions were not so closely integrated. Between allies who were relative strangers, such as members of the large pan-Italian alliances that were ranged against the Roman commonwealth in the early third century, command was held jointly and, in battle, allies were drawn up in separate contingents (e.g. Livy 10.27). Such division and lack of familiarity inevitably made cooperation and trust difficult, and allies might easily fall out amongst themselves (Livy 10.10; Polybius 2.18; 2.19).

The changing face of battle

> . . . the Etruscans, who fought in phalanxes with round shields of bronze, compelled them (the Romans) to adopt similar arms and, consequently, were defeated. Then, when other peoples were using shields such as the Romans now use, and were fighting in maniples, they imitated both and so overcame the originators of such fine models.
>
> (Diodorus 23.2.1)

Changes in military technology, when commented on by our ancient literary sources, are often seen in terms of the Roman assimilation of the enemies' equipment in order to defeat them. While this may reflect a genuine Roman openness to military innovation, in this period it also obscures a rather more complex process of cultural and military interaction and interchange throughout Italy and the Mediterranean. This process can be seen in the material record, and although archaeological evidence for military equipment from Rome and Latium is almost non-existent, there are representations of warriors in tomb paintings from Etruria, Campania, and Lucania and many examples on painted pottery from southern Italy. These can be supplemented by actual finds of weapons and armor across Italy.

The most common representations of equipment in fourth century art are of the fundamental elements of hoplite panoply: the large circular shield (*clipeus*), spear, and helmet. These basics are sometimes supplemented by greaves and body armor, usually linen or metal cuirasses. Although there is some regional variation in helmets and body armor, many designs were fairly widely dispersed, suggesting a climate of cultural and military exchange. Indeed, the majority of "Samnite" warriors depicted in Italian art are armed with, more or less, typical hoplite equipment. It appears that the hoplite panoply could be adapted to local conditions and preferences. For instance, although the basic weapon of many Italian infantrymen in this period was the spear, there was an enormous variety in the types used. Archaeological finds range from large blades, probably intended for thrusting and stabbing, to small light tips for javelins. In between, there are many types that might have been appropriate for throwing or thrusting. Representations of warriors in hoplite panoply, but armed with multiple spears, are not uncommon in Lucanian tomb paintings or southern Italian painted pottery. Clearly, some heavy infantrymen were not averse to engaging in missile combat. During the fourth and third centuries, there also appears to have been some rather unsystematic experimentation with what appear to have been proto-*pila*, spears with a narrow head and long iron shaft designed specifically to be thrown. The *pilum* was the primary weapon of Roman infantrymen in the second century, but the origins and date of its introduction are subject to some controversy. It is possible that some Romans were experimenting with the *pilum* in this period, but it may be the case that they converted to its use relatively late, after encountering Carthaginian mercenary Spanish and Celtiberian iron-necked spears in the mid-third century. Its introduction, however, might have been a more technological than tactical innovation; during the fourth century some Romans may already have been throwing spears in battle (see below).[13]

Diodorus suggested that the principal change in Roman equipment was the adoption of the oval shield, the *scutum*. In the fourth century BC this shield, with a central iron spine (*spina*), was popular among the Gauls of northern Italy and beyond. It occurs in a number of southern Italian vase and tomb paintings where it appears as a simple alternative to the circular shield in representations that might otherwise be regarded as typical hoplite scenes. In contrast to this visual evidence, some ancient commentators linked the *scutum* with tactical changes. According to Diodorus (23.2), just as the *scutum* replaced the circular shield, so the manipular formation replaced the phalanx. Our sources disagreed about when exactly the Romans made these changes, although most placed them in the fourth century. The changes appear to have been quite gradual; even in the second century BC one element of the Roman army (the *triarii*) appears to have acted in a manner that was similar to a hoplite phalanx. However, although the changes might have been slow and piecemeal, they reflect broader trends in warfare in this period. During the latter part of the fourth century, hoplites began to lose their primacy in warfare throughout the Mediterranean. At the same time, the oval shield (*thyreos*) began to appear in Greece, while Hellenistic armies increasingly included groups of specialized infantry performing different military roles. In third-century Boeotia, for example, groups of citizen infantry were called *thyreaphoroi* ("oval-shield-carriers"), *peltophoroi* (pelta-shield-carriers), *epilektoi* ("the chosen"), and *agema* ("the led"). The Roman move away from the hoplite phalanx was also accompanied by the emergence of different terms to describe the various elements of their infantry.[14]

Maniples and battle-lines

The Romans adopted a military organization that allowed a greater articulation of the citizen militia on the battlefield than had been possible earlier; in Delbrück's classic formulation, "the phalanx had been given joints." Fundamental to this organization was the creation of maniples ("handfuls"), which were small units numbering about 120 men and deployed, we are told, at intervals from one another (Livy 8.8.5). They were commanded by two officers (centurions) and two subordinates (*optiones*) (Polybius 6.24.1–2), indicating a concern with flexibility and with command and control that was paralleled in the Greek world, where there was an increasing emphasis on chains of command, with subordinate officers in charge of small units that were capable of combining or operating separately on the battlefield. Maniples appeared to have given the battle-line far greater resilience than larger and seemingly more solid formations. Plutarch (*Philop.* 9.1–2) claimed that the Achaeans in the third century, who used the *thyreos* and light spear, were effective when fighting at a distance. However, because they were deployed in a phalanx, rather than in maniples, they were easily forced back and scattered once melee was joined. Livy (9.32) reported that the Etruscans at Sutrium (311 BC), who were deployed in a single mass, became exhausted fighting the Roman front line and were defeated when the second line engaged. Resilience appears to have come from the fact that maniples facilitated the employment of reserves (e.g. Livy 8.8.9–14; 9.32; 10.14), although it is not well understood how the reinforcement or replacement of lines was achieved.[15]

The manipular legion is almost always described as operating in multiple lines (*acies*), but it is unclear when the subdivision of the early republican battle formation occurred, or how many lines there may have originally been. The sources appear to have known of at least two (possibly contradictory) formations. One was a two-fold (and therefore, perhaps, earlier) division between *pilani* ("columnists"), who were stationed behind the standards (*signa*) and *antepilani* (or *antesignani*), who were deployed in front of them. However, in Polybius' day, the *antesignani* themselves appear to have been divided into two lines. The first were called *hastati* ("*hasta*-users"), the second, *principes* ("the foremost," perhaps in the sense of being the best fighters), while the *pilani* had become more commonly known as the *triarii* ("third-liners": Varro *L.L.* 5.89; Ovid, *Fasti* 3.129). According to Polybius (14.8.5), the legion was deployed in a triple line (*triplex acies*) of 1,200 *hastati*, 1,200 *principes*, and 600 *triarii* (6.21.9); each line divided into 10 maniples (6.24.3). This has generally been preferred to Livy's statement (8.8.5, 7–8) that there were 30 maniples of *antepilani*, 15 each of *hastati* and *principes*, as well as 15 units (*ordines*) of *pilani* made up of *triarii*, *accensi*, and *rorarii* (on the latter, see below), not least because this would have produced a legion of over 8,000 men and contradicts Livy's own figure of 5,000 (8.8.14). In battle, the *hastati* engaged the enemy and were reinforced by the *principes*, while the *triarii* were allowed to sit or kneel (Livy 8.8) in reserve. They were usually only committed if the engagement was going very badly, thus spawning the phrase, "it has come to the *triarii*," for any serious situation (Livy 8.8), but they were rarely called upon otherwise, as is suggested in a comic jibe by Plautus: "Come now, everyone sit on the periphery, just like *triarii*" (*Frivolaria* frg. 5 Ritschl. = Varro *L.L.* 5.89).[16]

A substantial screen of skirmishers operated in front of these battle-lines, although they are often ignored in ancient battle accounts. In fact, in Polybius' description of the army, the light armed numbered over a quarter of each legion's strength (1,200 men out of 4,200). Polybius, writing in Greek, called them simply "javelin-fighters" (*grosphomachoi*), but Latin terminology seems to have been rather more fluid, leading to confusion among our sources. In his description of the army of 340 BC, Livy (8.8.5) used the term *leves* ("lights") for javelin and spear-armed contingents attached to the maniples of *hastati*. However, this may have led him into confusion about two other groups that he thought were present: the *accensi* and *rorarii* (8.8.8). Although he imagined them to be *triarii* of inferior quality, which is how he described them acting in his account of the battle of Veseris in 340 BC (8.9.14; 8.10.2–4), it is much more likely that Livy or his source misunderstood their role. Other evidence suggests that the *accensi* (lit. "attendants" – Cato in Varro, *L.L.* 7.58), were messengers and orderlies, although it is also possible that they had originally been attendants to the hoplites, analogous to the servants who carried the equipment of Greek infantrymen on campaign and who might have acted as light armed troops during combat. This practice may account for their mention in a battle that took place in 340 BC, if the Romans were still fighting with a hoplite formation. Livy's association of the *accensi* with the *rorarii*, however misguided he was in describing their battlefield roles, is also reflected in Plautus' early second-century comedy, *Frivolaria* (frg. 4 Ritschl. = Varro, *L.L.* 7.58), "Where are you, *rorarii*? They're here. Where the *accensi*? Look. . . ." They were elsewhere identified with *rorarii* and yet another term, *ferentarii*, as missile-throwing skirmishers (Paulus, *Epit. Fest.* 13). The *rorarii* were sometimes thought of as the men who opened battle, "like shower before the rain" (Varro, *L.L.* 7.58; cf. Paulus, *Epit. Fest.* 323), and *rorarii* was a term still in use in the second century, although by then it was giving way to a newer name for light infantry: *velites*. In social terms the light armed were generally those who were too poor to afford sufficient equipment to act as hoplites; this is implied in Livy's description of the Servian classes (1.43 cf. Dionysius 4.16–18). Even though the manipular army came to be structured primarily in terms of age, Polybius (6.21.7) observes that the poorest Romans remained as light armed. Unlike those who were better off, they appear never to have progressed into the *hastati*, *principes* and, finally, *triarii*.[17]

At the opposite end of the social scale Roman cavalrymen (*equites*) were drawn from the elite. They were men who had the leisure and resources to acquire the skills of riding and fighting from horseback. Judging by the disaster at the Caudine Forks (and indeed as late as 217 BC at Lake Trasimene), these aristocrats could not be relied upon to undertake any reconnaissance along the army's line of march. Three hundred citizen cavalry were raised for each legion, divided into ten *turmae*, but their role in battle is not easy to discern. Those depicted in a painting in the temple of Aesculapius were regarded as *ferentarii* (Varro, *L.L.* 7.57), a term principally applied to skirmishers. However, in Livy's account the *equites* sometimes attacked the enemy on the flanks or rear (8.39, 9.35, 9.40, 10.29), sometimes frontally (8.30, 10.14, 36), while at other times they dismounted to fight (9.22, 39). Usually their attacks appeared to have a disproportionately heroic and decisive effect (8.30, 39, 9.22, 27, 39, 10.28), which probably reflects an aristocratic bias in Livy's sources, although at Tifanum (297 BC) their frontal attack apparently failed and they withdrew from the battle entirely (Livy 10.14). Their true impact on Roman warfare and battle is difficult to assess, but according to the stock-theme of adaptation (see above), the Romans assimilated the cavalry tactics of the Samnites (perhaps Campanians), and the equipment of Greek horsemen (possibly Pyrrhic, or of Italiote Greek states).[18]

The Roman soldier's oath (*coniuratio*) "not to flee the battlefield or to abandon their place in the battle-line," had an interesting qualification: soldiers undertook to stay in the ranks "except to recover or fetch a weapon, save a friend or strike an enemy" (Livy 22.38.2–5). While the first part of the oath may have promoted group cohesion, the latter part suggests that there was considerable freedom of movement on the battlefield. As Livy reports it, the oath reveals an expectation that soldiers could leave the battle-line during combat to get new weapons (perhaps from an attendant), or that they might need to be recovered (probably after being thrown), and that they could move out in advance of the line to engage individual enemies, or indeed rescue friends in a similar situation. Such an oath might be inconsistent with the supposed orderliness (*ordinatio*) of a hoplite phalanx, but is rather more consistent with the kind of fighting undertaken by javelin armed soldiers organized into small groups such as maniples (particularly if the enemy fought in a similar style, as suggested in the depiction of combat in some Lucanian tombs in Posidonia). Indeed, during the battle of Sentinum, it is reported that the Romans spent time gathering up the javelins lying scattered on the ground between the two armies to reuse against their Gallic adversaries (Livy 10.29.6).

The move to maniples was a move towards missile combat. By the second century, the *hastati* and *principes* were armed with *pila*, while the *triarii* retained a spear (*hasta*) that could be used for thrusting, or could be stuck into the ground to present a bristling fence of spear-points. In the early second century Ennius could write "the *hastati* threw their *hastae*; an iron down-pour came." This is an image that resonates well with Varro's description of the *rorarii* as "shower before the rain."[19] The throwing of spears in battle, whether they were specialist *pila* or, initially, rather more multi-purpose *hastae*, would seem most plausibly linked to the period when the legion became organized into lines of maniples, since this appears to have allowed relatively small groups of men to run forward to throw missiles and retire, or to be replaced by a second line. As some sources suggest, the adoption of the *scutum*, which gave better protection, perhaps, than the circular shield in missile exchanges (Livy 9.19; Polybius 6.23) could be associated with this change in fighting.

4 Conclusion

The ancient literary evidence is often problematic, so any picture of Roman warfare in the fourth and early third centuries BC rests on a number of plausible, but by no means unchallengeable, inferences.

There appears to have been a gradual change towards multiple lines that allowed for fluid and independent movement of maniples (or even, possibly, individuals), with a tendency, in the early stages of battle, to rely on missiles. As these missiles ran out, or as men tired, maniples from the rear lines reinforced or replaced the front ranks, perhaps with an increasing commitment to hand-to-hand combat with thrust spears and swords. Changes in equipment may not have been sudden or universal, particularly in a militia army where men were expected to arm themselves from their own resources. For what it is worth, Livy's (1.43) description of the five Servian classes, which has sometimes been thought to reflect the period of the introduction of *stipendium* at the beginning of the fourth century BC, recognizes a variation in equipment throughout the army and the presence of both circular and oval shields among the soldiers.[20]

The bellicosity of the Romans and their willingness to undertake frequent wars on relatively large scales meant that despite the endemic nature of warfare across the peninsula, the citizen body as a whole was generally more battle-hardened and experienced than most of their enemies. On the other hand, Roman legionaries were far from professional soldiers, but rather militiamen who, at the end of a campaign, returned home to their farms or other occupations. Consequently, despite the almost annual experience of warfare, their weapons proficiency and tactical maneuverability was limited. The manipular formation somehow accommodated these militia features. The hoplites of the archaic and early republican army had been selected principally on wealth and property, but the manipular army, while still retaining a basic property qualification, came to be organized mainly by age. According to Livy (8.8.6–10) and Polybius (6.21.7–9), younger troops (*leves* and *hastati*) undertook the initial work in battle, but were stiffened by increasingly older and more experienced veterans (the *principes* in the prime of life and finally the "Old Guard" of *triarii*). Moreover, formal training and drill, although a feature of later Roman military service, was not essential in a system that fostered the natural fragmentation of battle-lines into small handfuls of men from the outset and made a military virtue of it. Polybius (18.32.10–12) observed that "every Roman soldier, once he is armed and ready, is able to meet an attack from any quarter, at any time or place. He is equally prepared and in condition to fight as part of the whole army, or a section of it, or in maniples, or singly." Resilience in relatively amorphous swarms of men raining missiles on their enemies was sustained through the use of the soldiers' oaths to one another and the fear of punishment that the consul might inflict after battle. Maniples were commanded by their own officers, centurions, which increased control, but also allowed for local battlefield initiative. It is not clear when standards became an integral feature of the legions, but they would have acted as invaluable rallying points on a fluid manipular battlefield, while the *pilani/triarii*, stationed in a dense mass behind the standards, ultimately gave the formation a veteran steadiness.

The legions were able to cooperate effectively in battle with the allied cohorts, perhaps suggesting that in a period when experimentation and cross-fertilization of fighting styles and weaponry was a widespread, if unsystematic, phenomenon, they too were comfortable with the sort of fighting that the Romans employed. Indeed it may have been the case that the success of Roman expansion contributed to a pan-Italianization of warfare that facilitated martial interchange. The Roman conquest of Italy did not happen in a vacuum and, despite the Romano-centric nature of the historical accounts, it is clear that other protagonists had roles to play. It is possible to understand some of the developments in Roman warfare in the context of wider processes that are apparent in Italian and Hellenistic warfare. In this, the ancient literary sources can be augmented by archaeological evidence from across Italy to create a clearer picture of the nature of Roman warfare.

Regardless of any shortfalls in the system, Roman and allied manpower increasingly gave the Romans the edge over their neighbors and enemies, so that their armies were, by Italian standards, large. Even when confronted with a well-drilled and organized army such as that of Pyrrhus, the Romans could recover from military defeats and replace their losses (Plutarch, *Pyrrh.* 19.5; Florus 1.13). Consequently, over the course of 85 years, their opponents, whether individual tribes or communities, or international and pan-Italian armies, found it difficult to compete with the flexibility and resilience of the Roman Republic and its armies.

NOTES

1   On Etruria see Saulnier 1980; D'Agostino 1990, 59–84. On Gallic warfare see Rawlings 1996, 86–9. Samnium, see Salmon 1967; Saulnier 1983; Cornell 1995, 346, 351.
2   Roman aggression in Samnium: Cornell 1995, 353–4; Harris 1979.
3   Material evidence: Bishop and Coulston 1993, 48. Literary sources: Rawson 1971, 13–31; Cornell 1995, 1–30. Italian mercenaries: Griffith 1934, 197–202, 208–211; Tagliamonte 1994. Predatory motives cf. Livy 7.28.3 (Auruncian raiding); Oakley 1993, 9–37, 14, n.1. Patterns of warfare: Rawlings 1999.
4   Harris 1979, 256–7; Oakley 1993, 15–16.
5   Warlike ethos: Harris 1979, 8–53. Single combat: Oakley 1985, 392–410. Triumphs: Cornell 1989, 363–4 table 7; Oakley 1993, 29; Rich 1993, 49–50. Epitaph of Barbatus: Cornell 1995, 359–60, 466 n.36. Esquiline tomb fresco: see Coarelli 1976, 3–11.
6   Manpower increase in 338 BC: Toynbee 1965, 141. Growth in *ager Romanus*: Afzelius 1942; Oakley 1993, 12; Cornell 1995, 380. Colonies: Cornell 1995, 381, table 9.
7   For Goldsworthy 2000, 44–5, 51–2, the introduction of pay began to turn the Roman hoplite militia into a "conscript army"; he rightly stresses the impermanence of Roman armies in the fourth and third centuries BC.

8   On early Italian war-bands see Rich, this volume. Papirius and Fabius: Frontinus, *Strat.*
    4.1.39; Valerius Max. 2.7.8; Livy 8.32. Manlian discipline: Livy 8.7, cf. Sallust, *Cat.* 52;
    Cicero, *Fin.* 1.7.23; *Off.* 3.31.112; Valerius Max. 2.7.6; Frontinus, *Strat.* 4.1.40–41.
9   On the election of military tribunes in 311: Salmon 1967, 232 n.2; Sumner 1970, 70–1.
    Pan-Italianization of warfare: Burns 2003, 60–85, esp. 62–3. Numbers at Sentinum: Cornell
    1989, 379; in Pyrrhic battles: Delbrück 1920, 298–300.
10 Dionysius 19.12, Plutarch, *Pyrrh.* 16.8–10.
11 *Formula togatorum*: Toynbee 1965, 424–7; Brunt 1971, 545–8.
12 Livy 28.28.3 and Livy, *Per.* 12, 15; Valerius Max. 2.7.15; Polybius 1.7.6–13; Orosius 4.3.3–5.
    Tagliamonte 1994. On the punishment of allies cf. the treatment of Frusino in 303,
    suspected of inciting the Hernici to revolt, Livy 10.1.3.
13 Minimum definitions of "hoplite" panoply, see Van Wees 2004. On helmets, metal cuirasses,
    and military exchange: Burns 2003, 68–73 and maps 1–5. Spears: Small 2000, 221–234.
    For tomb frescos in Posidonia/Paestum see Pontrandolfo and Rouveret 1992.
14 On the date of the *scutum*: Livy 8.8.3 (406 BC), cf. Livy 4.59.11, Diodorus 14.16.5;
    Plutarch, *Cam.* 40.4 (367 BC). Other sources ascribed the introduction of *scuta*, throwing
    spears and maniples, to the Samnite wars: *Ineditum Vaticanum* 3, Von Arnim p. 121;
    Sallust, *Cat.* 51.37–38; Athenaeus 6.273f, but note Diodorus 23.2.1 is vague. On round
    and oval shielded "hoplites" cf. Schneider-Hermann 1996, pl. 68 and 105. Oval shields
    in Italy: Stary 1979, 200–4.
15 Interchange of reserves: e.g. Delbrück 1920, 292–4; Sabin 2000, 1–17; Goldsworthy
    2000, 53–62.
16 *Pilani*: "columnists" is to be preferred to the more dubious etymology "*pila*-men,"
    Walbank 1957, 702 (against the definition offered by Varro 5.89). On the development
    of multiple lines, see, for example, Toynbee 1965, 514–18; Rawson 1971, 24; Oakley
    1998, 455–7.
17 Polybian numbers: Walbank 1957, 702–3. Livy's description (8.8.5–8) is too confused
    to calculate the size of contingents. Part of the problem surely comes from him imagin-
    ing *accensi* and *rorarii* to be different from *leves*. For textual problems see Oakley 1998,
    459–63. *Rorarii* in the second century BC: Lucilius 7.290, 10.393.
18 Roman cavalry: McCall 2002, esp. 13–25. Roman assimilation of cavalry tactics and equip-
    ment: *Ineditum Vaticanum* 3, Von Arnim p. 121; Polybius 6.25. Modern doubts, see
    Fredricksen 1968, 3–31, 14 ff.; McCall 2002, 27–33.
19 Macrobius 6.1.52 = Ennius, *Ann.* 8. frg. 281 Warmington = 287 Vahl. Varro, *L.L.* 7.58;
    Rawson 1971; Zhmodikov 2000, 67–78.
20 Late fifth-century date of the Servian classes: Cornell 1995, 186–8.

BIBLIOGRAPHY

Afzelius, A. 1942. *Die römische Eroberung Italiens (340–264 v. Chr.)*. Copenhagen.
D'Agostino, B. 1990. "Military organization and social structure in archaic Etruria," in
    O. Murray and S. Price (eds.), *The Greek City from Homer to Alexander*. Oxford, 59–84.
Bishop M. C., and J. C. Coulston. 1993. *Roman Military Equipment*. London.
Brunt, P. A. 1971. *Italian Manpower 225 BC to AD 14*. Oxford.

Burns, M. T. 2003. "The homogenisation of military equipment under the Roman Republic," *"Romanisation"? Digressus Supplement* 1: 60–85.

Coarelli, F. 1976. *Affreschi romani dalle raccolte dell'Antiquarium communale.* Rome.

Connolly, P. 1998. *Greece and Rome at War* (rev. edn.). London.

Cornell, T. J. 1989. "The conquest of Italy," in F. W. Walbank et al. (eds.), *CAH* 7.2 (2nd edn.). Cambridge 1989, 351–419.

—— 1995. *The Beginnings of Rome: Italy and Rome from the Bronze Age to the Punic Wars (c. 1000–264 BC).* London.

Delbrück, H. 1920 [1990]. *History of the Art of War, Volume 1: Warfare in Antiquity* (3rd edn.), trans. W. J. Renfroe. Lincoln, NB.

Fredricksen, M. W. 1968. "Campanian cavalry: A question of origins," *Dialoghi di Archeologia* 2: 3–31.

Goldsworthy, A. K. 2000. *The Punic Wars.* London.

Griffith, G. T. 1934. *The Mercenaries of the Hellenistic World.* Cambridge.

Harris, W. V. 1979. *War and Imperialism in Republican Rome, 327–70 BC.* Oxford.

McCall, J. B. 2002. *The Cavalry of the Roman Republic.* London.

Oakley, S. P. 1985. "Single combat in the Roman Republic," *CQ* 35: 392–410.

—— 1993. "The Roman conquest of Italy," in J. Rich and G. Shipley, *War and Society in the Roman World.* London, 9–37.

—— 1997. *A Commentary on Livy Books VI–X, Volume I, Introduction and Book VI.* Oxford.

—— 1998. *A Commentary on Livy Books VI–X, Volume II, Books VII–VIII.* Oxford.

Pontrandolfo, A., and A. Rouveret. 1992. *Le tombe dipinte di Paestum.* Modena.

Rawlings, L. P. 1996. "Celts, Spaniards and Samnites: Warriors in a soldiers' war," in T. J. Cornell, B. Rankov, and P. Sabin (eds.), *The Second Punic War: A Reappraisal.* London, 81–95.

—— 1999. "Condottieri and clansmen: Early Italian raiding, warfare and the state," in K. Hopwood (ed.), *Organised Crime in Antiquity.* London, 97–127.

Rawson, E. 1971. "The literary sources for the pre-Marian army," *PBSR* 39: 13–31.

Rich, J. 1993. "Fear, greed and glory: The causes of Roman war-making in the republic" in J. Rich and G. Shipley, *War and Society in the Roman World.* London, 38–68.

Sabin P. 2000. "The face of Roman battle," *JRS* 90: 1–17.

Salmon, E. T. 1967. *Samnium and the Samnites.* Cambridge.

Saulnier, C. 1980. *L'armée et la guerre dans le monde Etrusco-Romain (viiie–ive s.).* Paris.

—— 1983. *L'armée et la guerre chez les peuples Samnites (viie–ive s.).* Paris.

Schneider-Hermann, G. 1996. *The Samnites of the Fourth Century BC as Depicted on Campanian Vases and in Other Sources.* London.

Small, A. 2000. "The use of javelins in central and south Italy in the fourth century BC," in D. Ridgeway et al. (ed.), *Ancient Italy in its Mediterranean Setting: Studies in Honour of Ellen McNamara (Accordia Specialist Studies on the Ancient Mediterranean* 4). London, 221–34.

Stary, P. 1979. "Foreign elements in Etruscan arms and armour: 8th–3rd centuries BC," *Proceedings of the Prehistoric Society,* 45: 179–206.

Sumner, G. V. 1970. "The legion and the centuriate organization," *JRS* 60: 67–78.

Tagliamonte, G. 1994. *I figli di Marte: mobilità, mercenari e mercenariato italici in Magna Grecia e Sicilia.* Rome.

Toynbee, A. 1965. *Hannibal's Legacy: The Hannibalic War's Effects on Roman Life,* vol. 1. London.

Walbank, F. W. 1957. *A Historical Commentary on Polybius,* vol. 1. Oxford.

Wees, H. van. 2004. *Greek Warfare: Myths and Realities.* London.

Zhmodikov, A. 2000. "Roman republican heavy infantrymen in battle (IV–II) centuries BC," *Historia* 49: 67–78.

FURTHER READING

The best survey of the period is given in Cornell 1995, although Toynbee 1965 remains useful for detail. Roman expansion is analyzed by Harris 1979 and Oakley 1993. Rawson 1971 remains a fundamental discussion of the ancient sources. For archaeological evidence Burns 2003 is a useful starting point. Manipular battle is discussed by Sabin 2000 and Goldsworthy 2000 although most of their data comes from the Hannibalic War and later.

CHAPTER FOUR

The Age of Overseas Expansion (264–146 BC)

Dexter Hoyos

1 The Era of International Wars: Recruiting the Men

I became a soldier in the consulate of Publius Sulpicius and Gaius Aurelius [200 BC]. In the army which was shipped to Macedonia I was a private for two years against King Philip; in my third year, for my valour Titus Quinctius Flamininus appointed me centurion of the tenth maniple of *hastati*. After Philip's and the Macedonians' defeat, and after we returned to Italy and were discharged, I at once set out as a volunteer with the consul Marcus Porcius to Spain [195]. . . . This general considered me worthy to be appointed centurion of the leading *centuria* of *hastati*.

For the third time I once more became a volunteer, for the army which was sent against the Aetolians and King Antiochus [191]. By Manius Acilius I was appointed first centurion of the *principes*. . . . Twice thereafter I served in legions which campaigned yearly. Then twice I campaigned in Spain, once under the praetor Quintus Fulvius Flaccus, secondly under Tiberius Sempronius Gracchus [181–179]. By Flaccus I was brought home among those whom, for valour, he had brought home with him from his province; at Ti. Gracchus' request, I went back to the province.

Four times, within a few years, I have been chief centurion (*primus pilus*); thirty-four times, for my valour, I have been decorated by generals; I have received six *coronae civicae*. I have performed twenty-two years of service in the army and am more than fifty years old. . . . But please treat these remarks as simply about my situation. For myself, so long as anyone enrolling an army judges me a suitable soldier, I mean never to beg myself off.

(Livy 42.34, abbreviated)

So, according to Livy, spoke a veteran soldier-citizen in 171 BC, during the call-up of a new army to fight the Macedonians. The Senate and consuls were, as usual, anxious to enrol as many veterans as possible; Ligustinus and other former centurions demanded to be appointed to ranks matching their previous ones. But after his speech (we are told), they declared they would accept whatever positions the authorities thought fit. The speech is obviously a Livian elaboration, presenting the idealized figure of a solid, patriotically warlike farmer-soldier. Its itemized details, though, and the circumstances which Livy reports around it, suggest that it is based on a real episode and character.[1]

The details are vivid in any case. Blessed, if that is the right word, with only one inherited *iugerum* of land, Ligustinus found soldiering a more attractive métier. His many decorations in so many successful wars imply, too, a satisfying run of booty, so we may infer a bigger farm and better fortunes for the family by 171. Even so, 22 years of military service was a remarkably long run, and by 168, if Ligustinus returned safely, he will have completed a quarter-century's militia. His devotion to army service, though discontinuous, almost prefigures the professionals of later ages.

Idealized or not, Ligustinus' military life reveals much about the mid-republican citizen-soldier. The first two Punic Wars transformed the Romans' military system and had major effects on their society. To start with, campaigns outside Italy became the norm: fighting in Sicily, and at times other areas, went on for years in the First Punic War (264–241). Hannibal's war (218–201) added a further element – lengthy continuous service required of many troops in most theaters, best exemplified by the survivors of the battle of Cannae. Recruited between 218 and 216, these expiated their much-criticized survival by being kept under arms, first in Sicily and then in North Africa, until war's end. Ligustinus must have had plenty of predecessors – not all of them as fortunate in surviving to sturdy middle age.

Even though an era of shorter wars followed, his career shows how Roman citizen-soldiers might be discharged after one war only to be sought out for the next. Magistrates levying troops were keen to enrol experienced men, not a hard task if the war promised to be quick and profitable. The levy in 171 attracted many veterans who remembered the pickings from the previous Macedonian war (Livy 42.32.6). Indeed, Ligustinus and his comrades wanted to serve, but in their old posts as centurions. In 149 the consuls had no trouble calling up men for the Third Punic War because booty lured (Appian, *Pun.* 75.351) – a notable contrast with the resistance to levies for Spain just two years earlier (below).

But sometimes the authorities had to compel enrolment. Warfare that brought mere toil and risk, without counterbalancing rewards, rarely appealed. Compulsion was required, for instance, in 193 for a campaign against Ligurian mountaineers, and in 169 as Ligustinus' no-longer-enticing war dragged on (Livy 34.56.1–2, 43.14.6–7). In such wars, serving soldiers sometimes – rightly – felt exploited and they complained. It happened in Spain in 206, when a corps mutinied outright for a time (Polybius 11.25–30; Livy 28.24–29), and there again in 180 under one of Ligustinus' commanders, Fulvius Flaccus (Livy 40.35.5–7, 36.4, 36.10–11). Spain was an unpopular theater: the wars were hard, dangerous and, after the first three decades of Roman rule exhausted the readily available loot, mostly unprofitable. The outbreak of yet another Celtiberian war in 151 deterred even prospective young officers from volunteering, until Africanus' grandson Scipio Aemilianus set the example (Polybius 35.4.2–14; Livy, *Per.* 48).[2]

2 The Impact of Military Service

The economic and demographic impacts of these international wars are explored elsewhere. Here it is important to stress how constant a feature they were in Romans' and Italians' lives: a point well illustrated by Ligustinus' career. The regular demands for experienced recruits were one effect of another feature of Roman wars after 264: the unprecedented size of forces in service. Warfare had been a regular feature of Roman society from the outset, as Roman tradition itself recognized. The temple of Janus was closed, as a mark of total peace, supposedly only twice before Augustus' time – under King Numa (Livy 1.19.3) and in 235. But war-service from the third century on became more enduring and more large-scale.

Third-century legions consisted, in principle, of 4,200 Roman infantry and 300 cavalry (the latter recruited from well-to-do citizens), plus Latin and Italian allied troops up to twice these numbers. In the First Punic War two consular armies, each two legions strong, were levied yearly. From 261 until 249, and then again in 242–241, further recruits were needed for the Romans' ventures on the sea, mainly drawn not from Roman citizens but from their maritime Italian allies. On a conservative calculation, the fleet sent to invade Africa in 256 was manned by 69,000 crewmen; the one raiding Africa in 253 had nearly as many, and in 249, when two consular fleets suffered disasters thanks to the enemy and the elements, their combined crews may have exceeded 80,000 men.

The demands these efforts put on manpower were notable. When a big fleet and the legions both campaigned, as in 256 or 249, peninsular Italy had over a hundred thousand able-bodied men at war. On a rough estimate, in such years over 12 percent of available males were in arms. This was an unprecedented effort, although discontinuous and although its effects remain obscure.[3]

Even heavier demands ensued. There were some 155,000 men called up in 225 to face the Gallic invasion, and nearly as many (145,000 or so, for armies and fleets) at the start of Hannibal's war. At the height of this, in 212–211, with 25 legions in Italy, Cisalpine Gaul, Spain, and Sicily, and over 200 warships in commission, the total of Romans, Latins, and Italians under arms has been calculated at about 233,000. Even in the war's last year the republic's forces totaled around 110,000. These were extraordinary figures for a peninsula whose available manpower shortly before 218 totaled 770,000 according to Polybius (2.24); still extraordinary if, as has been argued, that figure should be corrected upwards to about 875,000 – very roughly, the military-age manpower of Iowa or East Anglia today.

After 200, with commitments across the Mediterranean from Spain to Asia Minor, numbers soon went up again: over 212,000 in 190; in the last year of the Third Macedonian War, still about 150,000; and in 146, when Carthage and Corinth were sacked, the fleet and 12 legions (each now 5,500 strong and with allied contingents to match) totaled roughly the same again. Every decade between 225 and 146 (it has been reckoned) had at least 8 percent, and during the Second Punic War up to 29 percent, of Romans aged 16 and over in arms. In turn, though citizen-to-allied

ratios varied during the same decades, the demands made on Latins and Italian *socii* will have been no lighter and often were heavier.

Society was thus war-permeated on virtually a permanent basis. Most Romans and Italians must, like Ligustinus, have seen military service themselves or had kinsmen who did so, or both.[4]

3 Risk Levels in the Great Wars

These great armaments had curiously contrasting fortunes in the third century and then the second. The first two Punic Wars were almost ruinously costly in lives. Fleets in the First Punic War were serious risks, thanks to nautical inexpertness and (occasionally) enemy skill. Polybius' naval figures, or some of them, have been suspected, but heavy ship- and crew-losses did occur, as mentioned above. Losses at sea hit the Italian *socii* especially hard, with the maritime allies providing most of the crews.

In the Second Punic War, it was Roman armies which suffered catastrophes, not only in Italy but also in Cisalpine Gaul and Spain. Even if Roman losses at Cannae, for instance, are estimated downwards (not entirely convincingly) to 30,000 killed besides the 10,000 captured – and likewise Appian's claim (*Pun.* 134.635) that Hannibal destroyed 400 Italian cities and slew 300,000 enemies – yet the Italian peninsula and especially its southern half suffered badly from 15 years of warfare. Roman territory itself, outside Campania, was not heavily harmed after 217: yet the census of 203, carried out with particular care (Livy 29.37.5–6), returned only 214,000 citizens (though it did omit several thousand now-disfranchised Capuans and other Campanians). The impact on the loyal Italian populations must have been proportionately harsher, while those who had defected not only had to provide forces for Hannibal's war-effort but later suffered for this at the Romans' hands.[5]

The wars following were a revolutionary contrast. None in the East lasted more than four years. Roman casualties were far fewer: 700 killed, as against 8,000 Macedonians, at Cynoscephalae in 197, in which Sp. Ligustinus no doubt fought (Polybius 18.27.6; Livy 33.10.7); allegedly 324 at Magnesia in 190, where Antiochus III was crushed (Livy 37.44.2); and, Livy affirms, 100 – mostly Italian *socii* – at Pydna in 168, where 20,000 Macedonians died (44.42.7–8). Defeats could occur – a notable setback at Callicinus in 171 against the Macedonians, for instance (42.57–60) – but none was shattering. There were few naval actions and no major disasters. Even allowing for deaths from wounds, skirmishes, and ailments, Roman forces in eastern wars must have come to feel almost damage-proof as well as invincible.

Although Spanish wars after 201 had fewer clear-cut endings – but instead much marching, many sieges, and opponents widely spread out and frustratingly resilient – Roman forces were smaller (usually a legion in either province), losses much lower, and a quarter-century, from 179 to 154, largely peaceful. Other second-century wars were small-scale, like the intermittent flare-ups in the Ligurian Mountains of northern Italy, in Sardinia and Corsica, and across the Adriatic in Illyria and Dalmatia; often enough, they were provoked by a general chasing booty, slaves, and *gloria*.

4 Why did Romans Fight?

Men were expected to serve Mediterranean-wide, as Ligustinus' 22 campaigns illustrate. This was a feature that Senate and magistrates took for granted. They took for granted, too, that able-bodied men would serve, whether as volunteers or as conscripts. This enduring war-willingness of the ordinary citizen was one of the many strands that gave the Roman and Italian communities their extraordinarily tough texture, as Hannibal discovered and Polybius praises.

Patriotic defense of a threatened *patria* gave Roman, and surely too Italian, soldiers a special esprit. Polybius stresses it in a contrast with the Carthaginians:

> [The Carthaginians] use foreign and mercenary forces, but the Romans native and citizen ones. . . . The Roman state rests its expectations on its own qualities and the support of its allies. Thus if ever they stumble at the start, the Romans fight back with all their strength, but the Carthaginians do the opposite. When struggling for their homeland and children they [the Romans] cannot relax at all from their fervour, but remain psychologically embattled until they master their foes. (6.52.4–7)

But, in the wars abroad, the vast armies and mighty fleets could not be effective merely through the fierce discipline and threats of punishment that Polybius elsewhere describes (6.36.6–38.4). Booty was a strong incentive, as we have seen; but not all wars yielded plentiful booty.

A centuries-old communal consensus and commitment was ingrained in the citizens of the *res publica*. Polybius brings out their cohesion and shared commitment: they all swore and kept the oath of obedience (6.21.1–3); every man mustered for service presented himself as and where ordered (6.26.1–4); the troops who formed the consul's bodyguard (*extraordinarii*) were selected from the allies' contingents (6.26.6–9), plainly a symbol of comradeship and trust; punishments and rewards motivated everyone equally – not only the soldiers, but their kinsfolk and neighbors at home (6.37.1–39.11). Roman armies' punctiliousness in gathering up and then distributing the plunder of a captured city, with allied troops too receiving their share, likewise impressed him (10.16.2–9).[6]

A prime example of Roman resolve in war, for Polybius, was their refusal to treat with Hannibal after Cannae, when practically the world judged all was lost; and a Roman prisoner-of-war who broke parole to stay on in Rome was summarily sent back to captivity (Polybius 6.58; Livy 22.58.9–10, 61.1–10). The long-suffering *legiones Cannenses*, despite some grumbles (Livy 22.5.10–7.4), gave solid service through the whole war: they captured Syracuse in 211 and destroyed Hannibal's last army at Zama in 202. On a smaller scale, Sp. Ligustinus and his fellow-centurions were both robust enough to protest at what they saw as unfair treatment, and then self-disciplined enough to accept what their commander decided – which (Livy surely implies) was in line with their request. At times, nevertheless, glimpses appeared of a more qualified attitude, noted above, to military service: not aversion to war, but skepticism about being called up for wars neither in defense of the *patria* nor with good prospects of profit.

Roman armies did not embody moral perfection, and their historians record many failings and atrocities. Booty, the prospect of riches, was a prime encouragement to enlist for wars abroad. Again, quite apart from the customary ruthlessness of battles and pursuits, city-captures and field-ravagings, troops could become demoralized, as in the melee at Trasimene (Polybius 3.84.2–14), or get out of hand as in the mutiny in Spain in 206 or the wild sack of Phocaea in 190 (Livy 37.32.10–13).

Leaders, too, could act badly. After Cannae, some young officers wanted to emigrate (Livy 22.53.4–13). Pleminius, Scipio Africanus' *legatus* at Italian Locri in 205, committed and allowed criminal outrages – even against his own protesting military tribunes (Livy 29.9, 29.16.4–19.2). The unscrupulous praetor Lucretius in 171 encouraged his troops to commit outrages in Greece, even against friendly cities (42.63.3–11; 43.6.1–3, 7.5–11). Spain in the 150s brought out the worst in some, like the violent governors Lucullus and Galba and the young officer-shirkers shamed by Scipio Aemilianus. But outrages did sometimes prompt a furore at Rome and sometimes earned redress; and at least some perpetrators were punished, like Pleminius who died in prison, and Lucretius who was fined 1,000,000 *asses* (29.19.3–21.3; 43.8).[7]

5   Military Structures in the Age of Expansion

Polybius, an experienced soldier himself, was impressed by almost everything about warfare at Rome. The Romans launched (he observes) the largest fleets in history in the first war with Carthage (1.63.4–9); the second war was the greatest ever known, save for its predecessor (5.33.4). He gives us an invaluable survey of the Romans' military system during the great wars; later on he explains why Roman camp-palisades were superior to Greek ones, and discusses how the legion's formation out-matched the phalanx's (6.19–42; 18.18; 18.28–32). He shows that the Romans had available manpower, citizen and allied, huge by Greek and even Seleucid standards, and his history illustrates repeatedly their resourcefulness in using it. "Naturally then," as he remarks, "the results of their enterprises in war prove successful and splendid" (6.39.11).

The army had originally been the Roman citizenry in arms, with the Campus Martius their traditional mustering-ground. Annually the consuls, and other qualified magistrates as necessary, recruited the forces they needed from able-bodied citizens aged between 17 and 46 (Polybius 6.19.5–21.10). Organizing the levies into the appropriate legionary ranks took place at Rome (though Africanus in 205 organized his in Sicily: Livy 29.1.1); probably so did the bulk of the preliminary mustering. Latin and allied Italian communities meanwhile levied their own contingents, as specified by the terms of their alliances with the Romans, and sent them to join the Roman forces. The process could take time, but if enough eligible men came to Rome ahead of the levy, as in 169 (Livy 43.14.2–15.1) and perhaps also in 264, it could be completed in as few as 15 days.

From the second century on, an army sometimes included small bodies of specialist support troops too, like Balearic slingers whose accurate hurling of stones and lead bullets was legendary, or Gallic and Iberian cavalry – more maneuverable (and expendable) than citizen or Italian horse. Polybius (6.19–42) vividly depicts how the early to mid-second-century army functioned: the procedures for recruitment, the armament, the efficiently laid-out and maintained marching camp, the fearsome discipline. Much of his account is illustrated by further evidence, including arch-aeological: second-century Roman siege-camps near Numantia in Spain, like the famous site at Renieblas, obey Polybian principles so far as the terrain permits. Finds there and elsewhere support his description, too (6.23–24), of the legionary *pila*, heavy oblong shield (*scutum*), *gladius*, and armor (breastplate or, for wealthier soldiers, chain-mail coat).[8]

Before 300 BC, the legion had moved from its older phalanx formation to a more flexible array, based on small companies or *manipuli* deployed normally in three lines (the *triplex acies*, "three-fold line") – *hastati* (younger men) in front, *principes* (men in their prime) in the middle, *triarii* (the oldest and most experienced) in the rear. Each line had ten maniples, with a maniple of *hastati* and *principes* numbering in theory 120 soldiers, the *triarii* 60 apiece. The maniple in turn was made up of two platoons, *centuriae*, each led by a centurion. For battle the centuries deployed one behind the other – so the two centurions in a maniple were termed *prior* and *posterior* respectively, as in Ligustinus' speech – while across the *triplex acies* the maniples were deployed in alternating sequence like black or white chessboard squares. An army had numerous light-armed soldiers, too, by 211 termed *velites*: most likely citizens, of all fighting ages, who could not afford expensive armor or weaponry. In a legion of some 4,200 men, some 1,200 – nearly one in three – were *velites*, with the job of harassing and, if possible, softening up the enemy before battle, then after victory helping in the pursuit (and the plundering).

Livy (8.8.9–13) describes the manipular formation as existing by 338, although not all his details match Polybius' second-century legion: for instance, he ascribes 15 maniples to each line, and gives spears (*hastae*) only to the *triarii*. Implicitly then the other two lines now used the javelin (*pilum*) and *gladius*, although Polybius is the first to attest these. Two *pila* for hurling, one heavier than the other, replaced the phalangite spear or pike; eventually the *triarii* too would give up their *hastae*.

All legionaries also had a short, two-edged sword for thrusting and slashing, which Polybius and others term "Spanish" (6.23.6; cf. 2.30.8, 33.5–6; Livy 31.34.4, etc.). Trade or other contacts may indeed have brought it from Spain, for very similar swords have been found at Spanish archaeological sites of earlier date. With it, the Romans wrought massive slaughter against their foes. Livy graphically, if rather complacently, records the horror the Macedonians felt after a skirmish with Roman cavalry in 200:

> those who had seen wounds done by spears, arrows and occasionally lances, in their regular fighting with Greeks and Illyrians, saw bodies beheaded by the Spanish sword, arms and shoulders hacked off or necks entirely cut through to separate heads from bodies, entrails gaping, and hideous other wounds; in a panic they realised what weapons and what men they must fight against. (31.34.4)[9]

How accurate Livy is on the mid-fourth-century legion is debated, for his contem-porary Dionysius of Halicarnassus writes in an excerpt on Pyrrhus' war – using the present tense – that "those who fight in serried ranks with cavalry spears gripped in the middle by both hands, and [who] often decide things in battle, the Romans call *principes*" (20.11.2). As this was not the case in his and Livy's day, Dionysius may be copying a Pyrrhic-era source which saw the *principes* armed in the old way. But Plutarch, drawing on another source from that same era, Hieronymus of Cardia (who in turn had utilized Pyrrhus' *Commentaries*), contrastingly describes the Romans in their second battle with the king as resisting his phalanx with their swords, but unable to maneuver in their usual flexible style (Plutarch, *Pyrrh.* 21) – the new way. Conceivably, old and new types of legion were both still serving in 279, but a simpler possibility is that Dionysius or his Greek source mistakenly wrote "*principes*" when he should have written *triarii*. The description fits Livy's account of the *triarii* – and it was they who proverbially gave the decisive push in a desperate battle.[10]

If so, Livy's mid-fourth-century legion need not be anachronistic. It would hardly be surprising if some features changed over the next century and a half (like the number of maniples per line, and the disappearance of rear-line fighters called *rorarii*). By the 220s the *pilum, gladius,* and manipular array were standard, as Polybius' accounts of battles against the Gauls in 225 and 223 show. Here we find javelins hurled to break up enemy ranks, the maniples attacking with cut-and-thrust swords and, in 223, the *triarii* lending their *hastae* to the front maniples to blunt Gallic swords – after which the front lines drew their own swords and cut the enemy to pieces (Polybius 2.30.8, 33.4–6).

At some date, maniples began to be associated – one each of *hastati, principes,* and *triarii* – in units called *cohortes.* Polybius, recording Scipio's victory at Ilipa in 206, mentions a body of three maniples that "is called a cohort by the Romans" (11.23.1, *coortis;* cf. 11.33.1). This grouping may have been borrowed from allied formations, for the first cohorts that are mentioned, in 294, 217, and 212, were Latin or Italian (Livy 10.33.1, 23.17.11, 25.14.4; cf. 28.45.2). Livy mentions a *cohors Romana* in Spain in 211 (25.39.1, unfortunately in a battle-narrative exaggerated at best) and one in 207 at the Metaurus (27.49.4). The cohort would in time become the main unit of the legion.[11]

6 The Armies' Other Half: *Nomen Latinum* and *Socii*

Latin cities (the **nomen Latinum**) and the rest of the Italian allies (*socii*) were obligated to furnish specified contingents under the terms of their agreements with the Roman Republic. Their register of military obligations is conventionally termed the *formula togatorum.* Various seafaring allies, notably the Greek cities of the coastal south like Naples, Rhegium, Locri, and Tarentum, supplied warships, transport ships, and crews, while Roman and allied infantry served aboard the warships as marines (Polybius 1.20.13–14; Livy 26.39.5, 36.42.1–2). The great fleets of the First and Second Punic Wars, though, were not reproduced in second-century wars.

Latin and allied army units were equipped and disciplined like their Roman counterparts, with variable numbers of infantry and cavalry assigned to each army. For instance, the six legions levied in 218 totaled 24,000 Roman foot and 1,800 horse, plus 40,000 allied foot and 4,400 horse (Livy 21.17.1–2, 17.5). But at Cannae, allied infantry numbers equaled Roman (Polybius 3.107.12), as they did in Polybius' time (6.26.7). Second-century near-equality was perhaps due to a realization that the Hannibalic war's ravages, and continuing Roman recruitment demands, were damaging allied military resources. Some recovery in allied resources perhaps developed later in the century, or at least the Romans thought so, for the ratio seems once more to have climbed to about 2:1 by 90 BC.[12]

7   The Romans in Battle

A Roman army's objectives were conceptually straightforward: to seek out the enemy's army and shatter it, to take his strong-points (and of course loot them), or both. Supplies, like reinforcements, were supposed to come from home but, in practice, an army often had to live off the land. It moved carefully; once the opposing army came into view, battle did not automatically follow, save when it was an ambush like Trasimene or an accidental blundering together as at Cynoscephalae. A good deal of watchful maneuvering commonly occurred, each general looking for a site favorable to his own force and avoiding any that might favor his foes. This went on, for instance, in Apulia over months in 217–216; though Hannibal did once catch part of the Roman army off-guard, it was rescued by Fabius Cunctator with the other half. In Spain decisive battles were rare, with combat often occurring as light or heavy skirmishes and with attacks on the country's many fortified centers.[13]

A major battle between advanced armies, when it came, could determine the outcome of the war. The only exceptions were when the Roman army lost. Then the war ground on.

What a classical Roman battle was like is now a much-discussed subject. It could be long – three hours at Trasimene and supposedly a longer one against the Ligurians in 172 (Livy 22.6.1, 42.7.5) – or short, like the 40 to 50 minutes in the afternoon for victory at Pydna (Plutarch, *Aem.* 22; cf. Livy 44.40.7). After skirmishing by the light-armed of both sides, a battle usually began with the *hastati* hurling their two *pila* from close quarters at the enemy to disorganize them. Surprisingly perhaps, these rarely had a similar gambit in reply. Against unprotected foes, like the inadvisedly nude Gaesatae at Telamon (Polybius 2.30.1–5), *pila* could wreak havoc, but they seem to have caused much less consternation to Punic, Macedonian, and other sophisticated forces.

Next, the main bodies of infantry advanced on each other, and now, if not earlier, the cavalry on the wings were likewise launched against the enemy horse.

Face-to-face infantry combat was not normally a grindingly unrelieved melee with hours of thrusting and hacking. Soldiers bearing armor, heavy shields, and iron-bladed weapons could not physically sustain this. Instead, a complex pattern prevailed, the hostile lines clashing physically for some minutes, then pulling back to draw breath and redress formation, and after that surging forward anew. At Zama Scipio was able, in mid-battle, to pull back and re-align his entire army for the final attack, using trumpet-signals and much helped by the quiescence of Hannibal's powerful third line, looking on immobile at the annihilation of the rest of its army (Polybius 15.13–14; Livy 30.34).

Appian, writing of a civil-war battle between veteran legions in 43 BC and drawing on a good source, depicts face-to-face combat vividly:

> . . . they raised no battle-cry . . . nor did any of them utter a sound as they fought, whether they were winning or losing. [Hemmed in by marshes and ditches], unable to push each other back, they were locked together with their swords as if in a wrestling contest. . . . If a man fell, he was immediately carried away and another took his place. . . . When they were tired, they separated for a few moments to recover . . . and then grappled with each other again. When the new recruits came up they were amazed to see this going on with such discipline and silence. (*B. Civ.* 3.68.279–81; cf. 4.128.533–537, Philippi)

This could be Cannae before the trap closed, or Zama in its decisive third phase.

Against enemies in phalanx array or in less-disciplined formations, like Gallic hordes or Spanish tribal units, these methods had to be modified. The phalanx could be irresistible – so long as it advanced steadily across level ground. So the thing to do was wait until it became disordered on the rough, as at Pydna, or charge into its unprotected rear or flank as at Cynoscephalae and Magnesia. Cavalry often decided a pitched battle's outcome, as Hannibal's famously did at Cannae; likewise the praetor Varus against Mago in Liguria in 203 (Livy 30.18.1–13) and Masinissa and Laelius at Zama, as well as King Eumenes of Pergamum at Magnesia.

Gauls and Spaniards seem to have fought in closely-ordered ranks (cf. Polybius 2.28.6–11, on Telamon). But Gauls, while full of élan which might carry the day, were less disciplined, and most had little armament save their shields and slashing swords. Spaniards were by contrast well equipped, though (it seems) properly drilled only when enlisted in Carthaginian service. Gallic or Spanish forces could put heavy pressure even on a firm legionary array; but at some stage in the battle this array – again often aided by a timely onslaught of cavalry or the light-armed – would normally overcome them (e.g. Polybius 2.28.9–30.8; Livy 29.2.4–18, on a difficult victory over northern Spaniards in 205).[14]

One area in which Roman military prowess in these centuries was serviceable, but did not greatly shine, was sieges. The destructive inventiveness of Hellenistic engineers had created attack-towers, battering-rams, and varieties of catapult, famously used by Alexander and his successors. Roman armies sometimes tried these, as in the protracted sieges of Lilybaeum and Drepana during the First Punic War, but success was far from guaranteed: these towns were still untaken when the war ended. If a place could not be taken at first assault – like New Carthage one day after Scipio swooped on it in 209 – circumvallation and rams were standard (and, occasionally, underground tunneling). For two years (212–211) two consular armies simply surrounded Capua with ditches and ramparts until the starving city capitulated. Besieging Oreus in Greece in 200, the Romans did use mantlets and rams, but left the technical military sophistication (stone-hurling catapults "and every type of artillery") to their Pergamene allies (Livy 31.46.10). The siege of Ambracia in 189 involved rams and tunneling, but still dragged on for months until the Aetolians sought terms (Polybius 21.27.1–6, 21.28.1–18; Livy 38.5–7). And Marcellus' assaults on Syracuse, from 213 to 211, were frustrated memorably by the ingenious engines of Archimedes, to the effectiveness of which the general could reply only with a quip (Polybius 8.6.6). In the end, as so often, Syracuse fell through treachery. It was Carthage, in 146, that had to be captured street by street and house by house.[15]

8   Enemies on Three Continents

Until 264 the Romans had fought only in Italy. In that year, they abruptly undertook a major international war against both the Syracusans (whom they quickly forced into peace) and the Carthaginians (who took much longer). Hannibal's war was then the first of four further extraordinary conflicts which, by 167, made the republic the arbiter of the Mediterranean world. In 149–146 a couple of short sharp wars ended the effective independence of all Greek states, including Macedon, while a much more painful one physically extinguished Hannibal's city. All these conflicts were accompanied by intermittent, often serious fighting against less-organized but combative peoples, notably the north-Italian Gauls, the Ligurian mountaineers, and Spanish communities and confederacies – none convinced of their theoretical annexation by the republic.

It was the momentous period from 219 to 167 that prompted Polybius' famous question, "who is so petty or inert as not to wish to know how, and through what political system, practically the entire inhabited world in not quite fifty-three years fell under the Romans' mastery?" (1.1.5, cf. 3.1.4–3.3.9). The anciently ingrained Roman habit of regular, almost yearly warfare thus endured, but enemies of the imperial republic were now to be found on all three continents – in Hannibal's war on all three at once.

The Romans' good fortune, and another major factor in their success, was never to face all-out war with more than one first-class enemy at a time. The nearest they came to this was in 215–211, when Philip V of Macedon made his ultimately ruinous decision to ally with the seemingly all-conquering Carthaginians, and Syracuse with still worse judgment followed suit: yet both proved feeble allies. Again, during the earlier wars with Pyrrhus and Carthage, the formidable north-Italian Gauls gave no trouble, while in the Second Punic their threat was sporadic. Later, the allies of Macedon and the Great King (Aetolia and Epirus, for example) were secondary dangers at worst, while Hannibal's vision of an anti-Roman coalition between Antiochus and Carthage remained a dream.

Individually, the other side sometimes tested the Romans severely and even won victories. An all-out alliance between two or three could, conceivably, have brought the republic to disaster: for Carthage, Macedon, and the Seleucid Empire could field armies comparable to the Romans' in size and training. At Agrigentum in 261, for instance, the Punic general Hasdrubal reportedly had 56,000 horse and foot (Diodorus 23.8.1, citing the Agrigentine historian Philinus). Polybius, perhaps optimistically, reports 74,000 Punic troops at Ilipa in 206 (11.20.2; cf. Appian, *Iber.* 25.100), Livy a more economical but still impressive 54,500 (28.12.13–14). Antiochus the Great supposedly fielded 72,000 variegated troops at Magnesia – though Livy's detailed figures, whether from Polybius or not, add up only to about 57,000 (37.40; Appian, *Syr.* 32.161). Philip V's army numbered 25,500 at Cynoscephalae (Livy 33.4.4), while the assembled military might of Macedon in 171 is reported as 43,000, the largest since Alexander the Great's (42.51.11). On the other hand, such armies were hard to replace if destroyed, a complete contrast to Roman capabilities.[16]

In these eastern states, a regular army consisted of a closely massed infantry phalanx, wielding formidably long pikes (*sarissae*), and of cavalry units and light-armed foot of various types, as Livy's detailed breakdowns of Antiochus' and Perseus' forces illustrate. A phalanx was subdivided into large brigades, but normally fought as one powerful mass charging with the leading ranks' *sarissae* leveled. The great eastern powers had found no good reason to change military methods which had worked for them ever since Philip II and Alexander, despite external intruders like the horse-riding Parthians of central Asia and the light-armed Thracian foot and horse of the lower Danube lands (who were often hired as mercenaries).

Some variations were tried. Pyrrhus faced the legions at Asculum with Italian allied maniples between his phalanx brigades (Polybius 18.28.10–11); he was able to drive the enemy off the field again, but with dispiriting attrition to his own side. At Cynoscephalae – a battle that developed unexpectedly – Philip V had a right and a left phalanx, which got themselves separated (this proved disastrous). At Magnesia the Great King's 16,000-strong phalanx was deployed in ten columns, each 32 ranks deep, with a pair of elephants in each intervening lane (Livy 37.40.1–3) – perhaps an experimental variant of Pyrrhus' method, but it did not avert defeat.

Manipular array need not have taken the eastern powers by surprise, for Pyrrhus had had to cope with it 70 years earlier. More probably, military traditions and organizational inertias prevented more innovative adaptations. Besides, Cynoscephalae might – optimistically – be regarded as a fluke, and Magnesia as a standard-model cavalry victory after all, for the Romans' energetic ally Eumenes precipitated the rout of Antiochus' infantry with a flank charge quite in the Alexandrian style. One or two later attempts at imitating Roman methods, like Antiochus IV's mail-coated 5,000-strong "Roman" legion (Polybius 30.25.3; I *Maccabees* 6.35), never proved very lasting.[17]

Roman armies, as the impressed Polybius saw, were organizationally, technically, and tactically superior to any others in the third and second centuries except Hannibal's. Hannibal's armies were a different challenge. Like earlier Punic armies, they began as a Hellenistic combination of African phalanx-troops, more lightly armed Spanish and other units, and cavalry. Regrettably, Polybius' only comparison of Punic with Roman war-making is stereotyped and generalized (6.52.3–7, quoted earlier). But Hannibal thought highly enough of Roman equipment to re-equip his own African infantry with captured weapons and armor (3.87.3) and in doing so may have also imposed a more flexible infantry array, though not a manipular one. His tactics especially at Cannae, and even at Zama (Polybius 15.12–15), suggest this, for in fighting the sword-wielding legionaries his heavy infantry, too, wielded swords. This contributed to the gigantic killing-machine of Cannae, for, as described above, the *gladius* was a frightening weapon in experienced hands (cf. Livy 22.51.6–9).

Ambushes, swift marches like the one to Rome in 211, followed by a thrust south to threaten Rhegium, and the fact that, as time passed, his army consisted more and more of Italians, point again to a modified and more versatile formation.

Ironically, the military arm imagined as quintessentially Hannibalic – elephants – played little useful part in his battles. Of the ones he brought to Italy, all but one died during winter 218–217, while his biggest-ever contingent, 80 at Zama, were easily disposed of by the Romans (Polybius 15.12.1–4).

Hannibal did make the mistake of arriving in Italy with fewer than half the men he had led across the Pyrenees. But during his stay (218–203) he not only built up a field army able to defeat the Romans, but for some years kept another operating independently in the south, while also sustaining garrisons in friendly cities across central and southern Italy – a total military roll hardly short of 90,000. In 208–207, with armies in Spain and his brother Hasdrubal leading some 30,000 fresh troops to Italy, the Carthaginians must still have had something like 150,000 soldiers all told between Spain and Italy (and not counting any home-based troops). Of course, few of these were citizens, for the Punic Republic relied largely on African and Spanish conscripts and foreign mercenaries, and in Italy, as mentioned, increasingly on local recruits. But it remains striking how, a decade after the war began, the Carthaginians' military effort still matched that of the Romans.[18]

9   Leadership

Of course the legions were not guaranteed instant or constant success. Skilful phalanx-tactics like Pyrrhus' could overcome them, if at a cost. Gallic élan almost did so at Telamon in 225, and a Gallic forest ambush in northern Italy in 216 nullified Roman technical superiority, destroying a consul-elect and his two legions in a disaster almost as great as at Trasimene (Livy 23.24.6–13). Leadership could not get much more abysmal than in 137, when the consul Mancinus in Spain let himself be trapped and forced to capitulate to the indomitable Numantines. Generals' unimaginative tactics, too, could throw away the legions' advantages, like their virtual reversion to phalanx formation at Tunes in 255 and at Cannae. Similarly with overconfident strategy, most strikingly the Scipio brothers' in southern Spain in 211, which led them piecemeal to destruction.[19]

Necessary along with high-quality arms, organization, and commitment, then, were adroitness in leadership and – it should also be stressed – a degree of initiative at all levels (preferably against an enemy lacking both). After the disaster to the brothers Scipio, it was a military tribune, L. Marcius, who rallied the surviving forces and led them north back to the Ebro, with (at best) half-hearted harassments from the victorious Carthaginians. It was similarly an unnamed tribune's stroke of inspiration at Cynoscephalae to lead 20 maniples from Flamininus' victorious right wing – the legion's *principes* and *triarii*? – into the unsuspecting rear of Philip V's still intact other phalanx. At Pydna, despite the phalanx's successful early charge, uneven terrain then opened gaps in its fearsome *sarissa*-array to allow the flexible Roman maniples to seize the initiative and break it up into ruin.

Nor did enemy leaders shine often. Energy without brilliance characterized, for instance, Philip V and his son Perseus, likewise Antiochus III and the Achaean leaders of 147–146, Critolaus and Diaeus. Among the Carthaginians, few indeed were the generals – perhaps only Xanthippus in 255, Adherbal in 249 (both soon lost to view), Hamilcar and Hannibal – who rose above indistinction when warring with the Romans; Carthage paid for this limitation in one war after another.

The Roman military genius of the era was Scipio Africanus, whose strategic and tactical breadth of thinking was perhaps not matched until Caesar. He trained his armies, in Spain and then in Africa, to a remarkable level of sophistication, winning each of five successive victories from 208 to 202 with different – and often complex – maneuvers to which not even Hannibal had an answer. At Ilipa in particular, he put his divisions through a series of moves of nearly baffling intricacy (to judge from Polybius' effort at describing them: 11.22–23) to achieve the enemy's total overthrow. His armies' skills were a counter, and a tribute, to the professionalism of Carthage's land forces in the Barcid era.

Yet this was a sophistication difficult for other Roman generals, however capable, to match – not to mention their armies. Leaders and armies of the first half of the following century did remain skilful and successful, partly because they had to confront sophisticated opposing military systems. Even so they did not need to reproduce Scipio's tactical finesses, and once the Hellenistic kingdoms were toppled and Carthage left smouldering, the quality of Roman armies and commanders fluctuated between average and poor. Ligurian mountaineers, the hardy highlanders of Corsica and Sardinia, Illyrians and Dalmatians, Gallic peoples from time to time in or beyond the Alps, and slave rebels in Sicily were tough to fight, but hard or impossible to crush by Scipionic, or even Flamininian, methods. In the harsh and dispiriting Spanish wars after 154, the troops performed indifferently when not badly, although Scipio Aemilianus did restore some old-fashioned discipline to his in 134–133. It would take a fresh round of major wars after 112 to bring the Romans' military system back to first class.

NOTES

1 All translations, save of Appian (n.14), are the author's. On Ligustinus: Cadiou 2002, 76–90.
2 *Legiones Cannenses*: Brunt 1971, 419–20, 648, 652, 654–6. Conscription and its discontents: Feig Vishnia 1996, 147–52.
3 Janus closed in 235: *MRR* 1.223. Origin of crews and fleet totals: Thiel 1954, esp. 73–96; Lazenby 1996, esp. 61–141. 12 percent of adult males: in 265, 292,000 citizens were censused (Eutropius 2.18); in 225 the ratio of Romans to all Italians, on Polybius' figures (n.4), was about 1:2.8, so for 265 this would mean about 817,000 Italians in all.
4 Brunt 1971, 417–28, 432–3, 669–70, and 671–86 (estimating about 300 sailors and 40 marines per ship). Polybius' figures for 225 are extensively debated: see Walbank 1957, 196–203; Brunt 1971, 44–60. "Corrected" estimate: Brunt, 54. Men in service between 200 and 146: Brunt, 422–8, 669–70; Hopkins, 33–5; Erdkamp 1998, 263–8.

5   Naval and other losses 264–241: Lazenby 1996, 161–4. Cannae's losses: Brunt 1971, 419, 694–5; Lazenby 1978, 84–5; Goldsworthy 2001, 191–5. Rebel allies punished: David 1996, 62–9.
6   Roman plundering (not always as tidy as in Polybius): Ziolkowski 1993, 69–91. Booty only one factor: cf. Erdkamp 1998, 265.
7   Lucullus and Galba: *MRR* 1.455–7. Cowardice and other vices in Polybius' Romans: Eckstein 1997, 179–81.
8   Keppie 1984, 44–51. Levy in 264: Hoyos 1998, 64–5. Camps: Schulten 1933, 41–8, 93–129. Equipment: Walbank 1967, 703–6; Connolly 1981, 130–3.
9   Manipular army: Rawson 1971, 19–20, 24–31; Keppie 1984, 21–3, 63–6. *Velites:* Walbank 1957, 703; Sekunda et al. 1996, 21–3. Macedonians' horror: cf. Zhmodikov 2000, 75.
10 A different interpretation in Rawson 1971, 24–6; Potter 2004, 70–2. Livy on 338 is criticized by Sekunda and Northwood 1995, 40–1.
11 Allied cohorts: Lazenby 1978, 12–13, 22; cf. Walbank 1967, 302. Roman cohorts: Kromayer and Veith 1928, 299–300 (Ilipa "die erste Belegstelle"), 427–34; Keppie 1984, 63–6 (dating them to Marius' time).
12 Fleets from 264 on: the standard works are still Thiel 1946 and 1954. After 200: cf. Brunt 1971, 669–70. Strengths of allied contingents: Toynbee 1965, 2.128–35; Brunt 1971, 677–86.
13 Supply and logistics: above all, Erdkamp 1998, 46–155, 297–301.
14 See Sabin 1996, 59–79, and 2000, 1–17; Goldsworthy, 2001, 118–43. Zhmodikov 2000, 67–78, holds that javelins and spears were in use throughout a battle, but leaves unclear how the supply could be kept up. Gauls and Spaniards at war: Connolly 1981, 113–26, 150–2.
15 Siege-warfare: Kromayer and Veith 1928, 244–5, 373–6; Kern 1999, 251–98.
16 Ilipa armies: Walbank 1967, 296–7 (preferring Livy); Lazenby 1978, 145 (plausibly preferring Polybius). Antiochus' at Magnesia: Bar Kochva 1976, 8–9, 167–9; Grainger 2002, 314–23, estimates only 50,000. Macedonian numbers: Hammond and Walbank 1988, 436–7, 540–2.
17 Hellenistic armies: also Garlan 1984, 353–62. Antiochus' "legion": Bar-Kochva 1976, 41, 55–6, 60, 180–3.
18 Hannibal's forces: Hoyos 2003, 108–19, 127–9, 227–8. Punic armies: Ameling 1993, 155–94, 210–24.
19 Mancinus: *MRR* 1.484–5. Battle of Tunes: Lazenby 1996, 103–6. Cannae: Goldsworthy 2001, esp. 95–156. Scipio brothers: Hoyos 2001, esp. 83–9.

BIBLIOGRAPHY

Ameling, W. 1993. *Karthago: Studien zur Militär, Staat und Gesellschaft.* Munich.
Bar Kochva, B. 1976. *The Seleucid Army. Organization and Tactics in the Great Campaigns.* Cambridge.
Brunt, P. A. 1971. *Italian Manpower, 225 BC–AD 14.* Oxford.
Cadiou, F. 2002. "À propos du service militaire dans l'armée romaine au IIe siècle avant J.-C.: le cas de Spurius Ligustinus (Tite-Live 42, 34)," in P. Defosse (ed.), *Hommages à Carl Deroux*, vol. 2. Brussels, 76–90.
Connolly, P. 1981. *Greece and Rome at War.* London.

Cornell, T., B. Rankov, and P. Sabin (eds.) 1996. *The Second Punic War. A Reappraisal.* London.

David, J.-M. 1996. *The Roman Conquest of Italy.* London.

Eckstein, A. M. 1997. "*Physis* and *Nomos*: Polybius, the Romans, and Cato the Elder," in P. Cartledge et al., *Hellenistic Constructs: Essays in Culture, History and Historiography.* Berkeley, 175–98.

Erdkamp, P. 1998. *Hunger and the Sword. Warfare and Food Supply in Roman Republican Wars (264–30 BC).* Amsterdam.

Feig Vishnia, R. 1996. *State, Society and Popular Leaders in Mid-Republican Rome 241–167 BC.* London.

Garlan, Y. 1984. "War and siegecraft," *CAH* 7.1. Cambridge, 553–62.

Goldsworthy, A. 2000. *The Punic Wars.* London (reissued as *The Fall of Carthage. The Punic Wars,* 2003).

—— 2001. *Cannae.* London.

Grainger, J. D. 2002. *The Roman War of Antiochus the Great.* Leiden.

Hammond, N. G. L., and F. W. Walbank. 1988. *A History of Macedonia,* vol. 3. Oxford.

Hopkins, K. 1978. *Conquerors and Slaves,* Cambridge.

Hoyos, B. D. 1998. *Unplanned Wars: The Origins of the First and Second Punic Wars.* Berlin.

—— 2001. "Generals and annalists: Geographic and chronological obscurities in the Scipios' campaigns in Spain, 218–211 BC," *Klio* 83: 68–92.

—— 2003. *Hannibal's Dynasty. Power and Politics in the Western Mediterranean, 247–183 BC.* London.

Keppie, L. 1984. *The Making of the Roman Army. From Republic to Empire.* London.

Kern, P. B. 1999. *Ancient Siege Warfare.* Bloomington, IN.

Kromayer, J., and G. Veith. 1928. *Heerwesen und Kriegführung der Griechen und Römer.* Berlin.

Lazenby, J. F. 1978. *Hannibal's War. A Military History of the Second Punic War.* Warminster.

—— 1996. *The First Punic War. A Military History.* London.

Potter, D. 2004. "The Roman army and navy," in H. I. Flower (ed.), *The Cambridge Companion to the Roman Republic.* Cambridge, 66–88.

Rawson, E. 1971. "The literary sources for the pre-Marian army," *PBSR* 39: 13–31.

Sabin, P. 1996. "The mechanics of battle in the Second Punic War," in Cornell et al., 59–79.

—— 2000. "The face of Roman battle," *JRS* 90: 1–17.

Schulten, A. 1933. *Geschichte von Numantia.* Munich (repr. New York, 1975).

Sekunda, N., and A. McBride. 1996. *Republican Roman Army 200–104 BC.* London.

Sekunda, N., S. Northwood, and R. Hook. 1995. *Early Roman Armies.* London.

Thiel, J. H. 1946. *Studies of the History of Roman Sea-Power in Republican Times.* Amsterdam.

—— 1954. *A History of Roman Sea-Power before the Second Punic War.* Amsterdam.

Toynbee, A. J. 1965. *Hannibal's Legacy. The Hannibalic War's Effects on Roman Life,* 2 vols. Oxford.

Walbank, F. W. 1957, 1967, 1979. *A Historical Commentary on Polybius,* 3 vols. Oxford.

Ziolkowski, A. 1993. "*Urbs direpta,* or how the Romans sacked cities," in J. Rich and G. Shipley, *War and Society in the Roman World.* London, 69–91.

Zhmodikov, A. 2000. "Roman republican heavy infantrymen in battle (IV–II centuries BC)," *Historia* 49: 67–78.

FURTHER READING

Society, economy, and demography have been studied by Toynbee 1965 and Brunt 1971. Feig Vishnia 1996, is a major contribution on society and politics. The Romans' relations with their Italian allies is treated by David 1996. On technical military matters, the classic treatment is Kromayer and Veith 1928; on naval warfare, Thiel 1946. More recent works include the excellent (if unfootnoted) Connolly 1981, which devotes special attention to Hannibal's war, Sekunda, Northwood, and Hook 1995, and Sekunda and McBride 1996. The important, often neglected questions of supply and munitions are studied by Erdkamp 1998. Hellenistic warfare is described succinctly by Garlan 1984. Notable modern works on the Punic Wars, in turn, include Lazenby 1978 and 1996, and Goldsworthy 2000. Military, political, and social aspects are stimulatingly canvassed in Cornell, Rankov, and Sabin 1996. Hoyos 2003 may also be consulted.

CHAPTER FIVE

The Late Republican Army (146–30 BC)

Pierre Cagniart

"It should be remembered that throughout the Roman Republic the soldiers fighting for Rome were their own citizens for whom the defense of the state was a duty, a responsibility and a privilege." Such a noble picture, quoted from Lawrence Keppie's *The Making of the Roman Army*, may have been appropriate for most of the republican era but, for the period we are studying (from 146 to 30 BC), it no longer conforms to reality. After the middle of the second century and, definitively in the first, Roman soldiers did not join the army "as a duty, a responsibility and a privilege." In the first century, a legionary fits Tacitus' definition: a man who had failed in all other walks of life and who had joined the military as the last resort (Tacitus, *Ann.* 4.4) and, we may add, a man who had found a new identity in a non-civilian life, in the society of the legions.

In this chapter, we will discuss the transformation of the Roman army from a militia-citizen to a professional army (section 1), the change in its tactical organization, from the manipular to the cohortal system (section 2), the equipment used by the Roman soldiers (section 3), and conclude with a discussion of how these soldiers used their weapons and combat formations on the battlefield (section 4). The period under study, 146–30 BC, is one of the most fascinating and the most dramatic periods in the evolution of the Roman military, from the army that subjugated the Mediterranean world to the army that presided over the centuries of peace and security of the empire.

1 The Roman Army: From a Militia to a Professional Army

Republican Rome was a timocratic society: the duties and privileges of the citizens depended on their wealth. Every five years, the heads of Roman families had to declare the value of their properties to the censors who, accordingly, distributed the families among classes and centuries. To be eligible for the draft a citizen must have registered as an *assiduus*, that was as a citizen with a minimum property qualification. At the beginning of our period (146 BC) this minimum amount was 4,000 *asses* (Polybius 6.19.2). Below this amount, a citizen was classified in the category of the *proletarii*, who were, except in case of emergency, exempted from service in the legions. An *assiduus* was not necessarily a rich citizen: a farm between two and seven *iugera* would be enough to qualify him for service in the legions. It was in 212/11 BC, after the catastrophic defeats suffered at the beginning of the Hannibalic War, that the minimum of property qualification was reduced from 11,000 to 4,000 *asses*.[1]

Although current scholarship is divided on this issue, this minimum property qualification was probably further reduced to 1,500 *asses* (Cicero, *Rep.* 2.40), either in 140 BC or between 133 and 125 BC.[2] Finally, in 107 BC, Gaius Marius, in levying an army for the war against Jugurtha, the king of Numidia, accepted volunteers without asking for any property qualification (Sallust, *Jug.* 86.2; Plutarch, *Marius* 9.1). The progressive lowering and, with Marius, abandonment of property qualification for recruits used to be explained by a growing shortage of Roman manpower in the second century.[3]

In 1983, J. Rich convincingly demonstrated the fallaciousness of "The supposed Roman manpower shortage of the later second century BC." In 2004, N. Rosenstein offered a new interpretation that revolutionized our understanding of the social, economic, and military history of the last centuries of the Roman Republic.[4] According to Rosenstein, the Senate believed that the population of Italy was in decline when, in reality, it was increasing regularly. He explained the decrease in the census reports by the fact that many citizens did not register with the censors for fear of being drafted for the war in Spain.[5]

The war in Spain, from 218 to 133 BC, is essential for understanding many aspects of the transformation of the Roman military at the end of the republic. Rome had acquired Spain from Carthage at the end of the Second Punic War, but it took nearly a century to pacify the Iberian Peninsula. Spain was the nightmare and the cancer of Roman foreign involvements. It drained the resources and the morale of the army. Fighting against a fierce enemy who used guerrilla tactics perfectly suited to the terrain, the Romans were unable to reach any decisive conclusions despite repeated campaigns. To be drafted for the war in Spain was financially unattractive, not to say disastrous. The *stipendium* the soldiers received was pitiful and, after the deduction of the cost of their equipment, clothing, and food, there was nothing left to bring back home. The poverty of the country where they were fighting made looting a dismal prospect and neither their commanders nor the Senate would provide any financial reward at discharge. In such conditions, the morale, discipline, and fighting motivations were, not surprisingly, very low. It is telling that, when P. Cornelius Scipio Aemilianus, consul in 134, was given Spain as his province, he did not draft a new army but brought with him 4,000 volunteers (Appian, *Iber.* 84.365).

The citizens who volunteered for Marius' army were these landless citizens and, if we accept Rosenstein's conclusions, they had become landless not as the result of long overseas military service or of competition from large estates worked by slaves, but because there was no land available for them. Even Tiberius Gracchus discovered this fact when the commission in charge of implementing his *lex agraria* found out that there was, in reality, very little land available for redistribution. Marius' recruits were motivated by the hope that they would be rewarded, at the time of their discharge, with land and thus would become independent farmers. They were not disappointed: Marius' veterans, both from the Numidian War (107–105 BC) and the war against the Germans (105–101 BC), received land (most of them in Africa and North Italy). Consequently, from 107 onward, soldiers joined the army expecting their generals to provide financial rewards at the end of the campaign. In addition to the booty soldiers could gain from a war, the anticipation of tangible benefits at the time of discharge became the motivation to serve, and this transformed the Roman soldier into a mercenary. Soon, another logical consequence was to follow: soldiers understood that their future depended on their commander, the only one able to provide for them. This is at the root of professional and private armies.[7]

A new stage in the transformation of the Roman army occurred in 88, with L. Cornelius Sulla. Sulla, who was consul that year, received the command of the war against Mithridates, king of Pontus. He was with his legions at Nola ready to lead his army to Greece, when he was told that his command had been transferred to Marius. For Sulla, the command of an eastern war held the promise of glory, fame, and wealth. As for his soldiers, a war in the East was less important for military glory than for the financial rewards to be expected. Greed was the main motivation for his legionaries, and Sulla was clever enough to ensure they understood that his loss of command also meant that they would lose out on benefiting from a lucrative campaign. So both the consul and his legions marched on Rome to reverse the law that had deprived Sulla of his command, an unprecedented move made possible by the nature of the new army, an army of mercenaries. It was the logical consequence of the reforms of the draft Marius himself had made. Sulla set an example that would be followed during the last 50 years of the Roman Republic when the loyalty of the Roman soldiers was no longer with the state but with the man who could bring them fortune.

We do not know the composition of the army under the command of Sulla in 88, and it would be futile to speculate on the percentage of recently enfranchised Italians. However, we may consider here the consequences of the Social War for the composition of the Roman army. After 88, all Italians were Roman citizens and, as such, could join the legions. Italy offered an unlimited number of potential soldiers, especially poor rural Italians who had, for the same reasons as the Roman citizens before them, lost hope of inheriting a sustainable piece of land. We have seen how the Roman army, before the Social War, had become proletarized. After the Social War, it was possible for well-off citizens to avoid being drafted. Most of the men who joined the legions were volunteers. The large Italian component in the Roman army after the Social War would be an important factor in its political uses by their generals. Many poor Italians had never been to Rome and had limited loyalty for the republican oligarchic institutions (some of them had fought Roman legions during the Social War). After 88 BC, Roman armies were mostly made up of rural Italians.[8]

Sulla was a great general and a good judge of the new soldiers he was commanding. He knew why they had enlisted. So, as long as they fulfilled their military duties and fought with the discipline and bravery he expected of them, he accommodated their lust for riches. Indeed, after the long and difficult siege of Athens (87/6), he let his soldiers vent their frustrations by opening the city to slaughter and looting (Plutarch, *Sulla* 14.4–10). Similarly, after the two brilliant and hard fought battles of Chaeronea and Orchomenos (86), he allowed them to freely sack and loot Boeotia from end to end (Plutarch, *Sulla* 26.7; Appian, *Mithr.* 51; 54). When Sulla concluded the peace settlement at Dardanus with King Mithridates (summer of 85), his soldiers complained bitterly. The peace deprived them of the opportunity to loot the riches of the East. Sulla understood their frustrations perfectly but had no intention in getting involved in an eastern war when he had his mind turned toward Rome. So, the province of Asia Minor served as a good substitute for the greed of his soldiers. He billeted his troops in various cities, ordering the inhabitants to provide not only for food and clothing, but money (Plutarch, *Sulla* 25.3–4; Appian, *Mithr.* 61.63). He also closed his eyes to the exactions of the soldiers in charge of collecting tributes, unpaid taxes, and penalties for the past treason of the province. Obviously, they found a way to enrich themselves without having to fight for it. In the spring of 83, when Sulla was to lead them to Italy, his soldiers had accumulated enough booty to offer to lend him money for the coming civil war against his enemies in Italy (Plutarch, *Sulla*. 17.3; 27.1–5; Appian, *B. Civ.* 1.79).

In Italy, Sulla was faced with leading his army against Roman legions. Would his soldiers fight for him in the coming civil war? The key moment came when, near Capua, Sulla's legions were to face the legions of the consul Norbanus. A detail is telling: Sulla did not put his army into regular battle order but let his veterans rush without pause against Norbanus' raw recruits. Sulla did not want both armies to stand against each other for any length of time because they would have to face the reality that they were fighting against fellow citizens (Plutarch, *Sulla* 27.10–16). Sulla's victory at Capua sealed his legions' commitment to him. Although the years 83 and 82 saw hard fighting, they stayed loyal to him until the very end; defections came from the opposite armies, not his own.

Sulla's proscriptions and the confiscations of land from the various Italian communities that had sided with his enemies gave him enough land for the veterans of the 23 legions. With the money they had looted from Asia Minor and Greece, Sulla's veterans also acquired lands in Italy (particularly in Campania, Etruria, and Umbria) (Appian, *B. Civ.* 1.104).

However, the veterans of Sulla were quite different from those of Marius, some 20 years earlier. For many of Sulla's veterans, the return to, or the discovery of, the hard and unexciting life on a farm was an unpleasant outcome. So, through disillusion or inexperience, many lost or sold their farms, not to mention those who cashed in their land before settling on it. This left a large number of veterans with no alternative but to re-enlist and to become professional soldiers.[9]

We now turn our attention to the next great Roman general, L. Licinius Lucullus. Lucullus' reputation – that of a hard disciplinarian, an aristocrat from the old school of commanding soldiers, not buying them, a general who denied his soldiers the opportunity of looting, and who was to pay the price by facing mutinies and, ultimately, the desertion of his army – is too simplistic an interpretation. Lucullus' ultimate failure in keeping his army under control was not caused by his supposedly old-fashioned character. His objection to letting his men loot is totally unfounded. So much so, that it was precisely because his soldiers had amassed so much loot that they objected to more campaigning and deserted him.

Indeed, in 68, when preparing a campaign against Parthia, his legions mutinied. According to Plutarch, "full of gold and used to luxury," they had been on enough campaigns and thought they deserved a rest from hard fighting (Plutarch, *Luc.* 31.9–32.4). As for their desertion in 67, the testimony of Appian needs no comment: "When Lucullus was already encamped near Mithridates, the proconsul of Asia sent heralds to proclaim that Rome had accused Lucullus of unnecessarily prolonging the war, and had ordered that the soldiers under him be dismissed, and that the property of those who did not obey this order should be confiscated. When this information was received, the army disbanded at once . . ." (*Mithr.* 90). It would be difficult to find a better illustration of the nature of the Roman army in the sixties, an army of mercenaries willing to follow their general until they amassed enough loot, and who were totally indifferent to the goals and significance of the war they were fighting.

The next general to discuss in connection to our subject is Pompey the Great. In 83 BC, at 23 years of age, having not held any public offices, Pompey recruited three legions from the clients and veterans of his father in Picenum, a private army that he provided with food, transport animals, and all the necessary equipment (Livy, *Per.* 85; Appian, *B. Civ.* 1.80.366; Plutarch, *Pomp.* 6.5). From then on, Pompey's military career was a series of brilliant wars, including his startling campaign in 67 BC, when, in three months, he cleared the Mediterranean of endemic piracy, and culminating with his brilliant eastern campaign from 66 to 62 BC when he subdued and completely reorganized the Roman Empire in the East.

Like Sulla, Pompey had no illusions about the motivations of his soldiers. In his triumph (September 28–9, 61), he distributed the fantastic amount of 384 million sesterces to them, each soldier receiving a minimum of 6,000 sesterces, with higher amounts for his centurions and officers (Plutarch, *Pomp.* 45.4; Appian, *Mithr.* 116). This was in addition to the looting and lavish distributions they gained during their campaigns. Even with such lavish financial benefits, Pompey's veterans, like all veterans since Marius, were given land.

The true professional army was Caesar's making, the last stage of the transformation of the Roman Republican army. Since 58 BC, most of his legionaries had spent years together without returning home, finding in the life of the camp, in the numerous marches in enemy territory, in countless raiding and counter-raiding operations, and on the battlefield, a feeling of belonging to a distinct society with its own rules and codes. Caesar himself let them know, on many occasions, how different, not to say superior, they were. They came to look at their commander as the supreme authority, the only authority. Caesar's leadership, courage, military expertise, personal flair, and individual charisma made him a hero for his troops. The men who fought for Caesar had become dissociated from civil society. They found in their comrades in the *contubernium*, the century, the cohort, and the legion, a new world, a new way of life, the life of professional soldiers.[10]

2 Formations and Units

The legions

In the first century, the structure of the Roman military was fundamentally transformed, from manipular to cohortal formation. At the beginning of our period, the legion was still organized into 30 units, the maniples, ten for each of the three lines that constituted the battle formation. The Greek historian Polybius describes the manipular system of his time as follows: the first two lines, the *hastati* and the *principes*, were made of ten maniples, each maniple consisted of two centuries. The third line, the *triarii*, was composed of ten maniples with only one century each. A century was, on paper, 60 infantrymen strong. The legion included 1,200 light skirmishers, the *velites*, who were the first to engage the enemies. In all, a legion was 4,200 men strong (1,200 *hastati*, 1,200 *principes*, 600 *triarii*, and 1,200 *velites*). The legion was also supported by 300 cavalry (Polybius 6.19–26).

In the manipular legion, the distribution among the three lines was based on age and wealth. Each soldier being responsible for his equipment, the *velites* were the poorest recruits and, since their task was based on speed and mobility, they were also young soldiers. The rest of the formation was distributed strictly according to age. The soldiers of the first line, the *hastati*, were the youngest, the third, the *triarii*, the most experienced soldiers. The manipular legion was suited to one style of fighting, at which it excelled: this was the straightforward, large-scale battle, involving little or no prior tactical maneuvers that characterized most of what the Romans and their enemies were used to in the third and second centuries.[11]

However, the manipular system came to be superseded by a new formation: the cohortal system. The cohort, as a fighting unit, was first used by P. Cornelius Scipio in Spain, during the Hannibalic War (Polybius 11.23.1 and 11.33.1) and, after the war, by his successors. All earlier references to cohorts as fighting units were connected with the war in Spain (there are 17 references to the use of cohorts in Spain from 210 to 195 in Livy). The manipular legion was not well suited for fighting in Spain. The Spaniards were using hit-and-run tactics and Spain, a country of hills, mountains, and deep valleys, was ideal for such type of warfare. Furthermore, the country was poor which made it difficult to feed a large army. On many occasions, Scipio needed to use speed – a difficult task with a legion of more than 4,000 men – but also concentration – a nearly impossible task with maniples of only 120 men. In combining three maniples together he was able to solve both problems since the new unit, the cohort, could respond more efficiently to the tactics used by the enemy. According to requirements, he could create offensive units made up of varying numbers of cohorts. The Spaniards, in addition to guerilla warfare, were also using massive frontal assaults that could not be easily absorbed by maniples but could be dealt with more appropriately by larger cohorts.[12]

The war in Numidia, as recorded by Sallust, gives an interesting picture of the transitional period during which the Roman army was still organized in manipular formation, but when both Metellus and, after 107 BC, Marius made occasional uses of cohorts of ethnic allied troops (Ligures: Sallust, *Jug.* 77.4, 88.6, 93.2, 100.2; and Pelignians: Sallust, *Jug.* 105.2), as well as legionary cohorts (Sallust, *Jug.* 51.3 [Metellus], 56.3–4, 94.3, 99.1 and 100.4 [Marius]). Furthermore, it is during the war against Jugurtha that we have the last reference to the use of the *velites*, the light skirmishers who disappeared with the definitive adoption of the cohortal system (Sallust, *Jug.* 46.7). It is also worth noting that it was during the battle of the Muthul that we have the last mention of a manipular formation (Sallust, *Jug.* 49.6, with Metellus).

Cohorts, as combat formations, remained the exception in the second century with the manipular system being the rule. And yet, in this century, the Romans faced more enemies using either guerilla warfare (e.g. Scordisci and Ligurians) or massive frontal assaults (e.g. Gauls or Germans), for which cohorts were better suited. Finally, to face the Cimbri and Teutones, Marius chose to organize his legions on the cohortal model and, with his other reforms, made the cohortal system the new standard formation of the Roman military. After Marius, all Roman legions were made up of cohorts.

So, in the last decade of the second century, the legion of 30 maniples was replaced by the legion of ten cohorts. Each cohort consisted of three maniples with two centuries each; a century was made up of 80 men and was commanded by a centurion. Although our sources do not specify the officer in command of a cohort, it certainly had one; otherwise, it could easily become a mass of unorganized men. Very likely, it was the senior centurion (the *pilus prior*) who was in command, having authority over the remaining five centuries. A cohort was between 480 and 600 men strong.

On the battlefield, the cohorts could be distributed, according to the topography of the battlefield or the size and combat formation of the enemy, on a single line (Caesar in Africa: *B. Afr.* 13.2) or on two lines (Crassus in Aquitania: Caesar, *B. Gal.* 3.24.1); however, the three-line formation (the *triplex acies*) was the most common (4–3–3 system).

In the cohorts, the distinction between age, wealth, and equipment disappeared. This new order did not include units of light skirmishers, which were now integrated in the cohorts. Cohesion and uniformity were the landmarks of the cohortal system. In addition of being part of a legion, a cohort, and a century, a legionary was member of a *contubernium*, a group of eight soldiers who shared their meals and their tent. Living together, sharing the burdens, anxieties, and exaltations of years of campaigning, these men were likely to develop strong friendship and solidarity ties. In combat, these men would be eager not to disappoint their comrades and to support and protect them.

If Marius could not be credited with the creation of the cohort, his organization of the army in the years 104–103, while waiting for the German tribes in southern France, perfected the system. Marius improved the legion's mobility and independence of movement by getting rid of the mass of non-combatants who had traditionally followed the Roman armies: slaves who carried the equipment of soldiers, slave traders and other merchants looking for opportunities to enrich themselves, even prostitutes. Marius, who was disdainful of this mass of civilian parasites, although he may not have gotten rid of all of them, threw out of the army those who carried military equipment, and transferred to the soldiers the care of their weapons and what was needed for campaigning, and reorganized the baggage train – pack animals or wagons if the terrain allowed them – as part of the legion and under supervision of slaves (*calones*). Otherwise, each soldier was to carry his weapons, food, cooking utensils, and the various tools necessary to build the camps. All these items were in a sack attached to a forked pole which was carried on their shoulders. They looked like beasts of burden and soon gained the popular nickname of "Marius' mules." With Marius, the legion gained the mobility, independence, and readiness that had been lacking or seriously compromised before his reform (Frontinus, *Strat.* 4.1.7).

In addition, Marius was very much concerned with the proper training of his soldiers. To the daily marches with full equipment and the building (and dismantling) of camps, Marius added training and mock fighting with weapons, on the model used in gladiatorial school, a method of training introduced in the army by P. Rutilius Rufus, the consul of 105 (Val. Max. 2.3.2). Finally, by making the eagle (*aquila*) the standard for all the legions, Marius improved the unity of the armies and gave the soldiers a symbol that expressed their attachment to an all-encompassing body, an institution to which the soldiers' loyalty could be directed (Pliny, *Nat.* 10.16).

The military reforms made by Marius drastically improved the fighting ability of the Roman military. The crushing defeat of the Ambrones and Teutones at Aquae Sextiae (102 BC) and the Cimbri at Vercellae (101 BC) tested Marius' army. Later in the first century, generals like Sulla, Lucullus, Pompey, and Caesar would confirm the fighting excellence and superiority of the cohortal system, the formation that would be maintained during the entire imperial period.[13]

Cavalry

In the last two centuries of the republic, the Roman cavalry, like the infantry, went through dramatic changes: by the first century, Roman and Italian cavalry attached to the legions were replaced by foreign units, mostly composed of Numidians, Spaniards, Gauls and, from Caesar onwards, Germans with, on occasion, auxiliary foreign units.[14]

Cavalry, by combining speed, mobility, and independence, played an important role in Roman military strategy and tactics. During a campaign, the cavalry was used for reconnaissance, for gathering information on the enemy's forces and movements, for protecting foraging troops, and for securing the army on the march. Conversely, the Roman cavalry was used to harass the enemy on the march and to disrupt its supplies and foraging. On the battlefield, the cavalry was used to protect the flanks and rear of the infantry's lines and, if successful in defeating or forcing the enemy's cavalry off the field, to disrupt the cohesion and morale of the enemy's battle formation by attacking its flanks and rear. Its most effective contribution was the pursuit and massacre of a routed enemy.

On paper, the role of the cavalry looks impressive but, in reality, the ancient cavalry had inherent shortcomings that limited its role on the battlefield. Without stirrups, high-backed saddles, and horseshoes, a cavalryman was always at the risk of

losing his balance. Before the Hannibalic War Roman cavalrymen, fighting without
defensive protection, could maintain better stability but were vulnerable to infantrymen who could oppose them efficiently with their spears, javelins, and swords. They
were also easily routed by better equipped enemy troopers. By adopting cuirass and
greaves, heavier shields and sturdier spears, they became more competitive but, at
the same time, they lost mobility and stability. The added weight increased the risk
of losing balance. Furthermore, horses do not charge and penetrate obstacles they
cannot see through or jump over. So, a line of infantrymen having the nerve to keep
its formation would not be vulnerable to a direct assault.

    Roman soldiers knew these limitations; with discipline and courage, they learned
how to fight effectively against cavalry. They knew that horses would not collide
with them. They knew that a horseman closing in on them was more vulnerable
than themselves: an infantryman could wound or kill the horse, he could move to
the left side, forcing the cavalryman to fight in an awkward position, because he would
have to twist his body to the left to use his spear or his sword. The best illustration
of the cavalry's vulnerability was seen during the battle of Pharsalus (June 29, 48 BC)
when Pompey's cavalry, 7,000 strong, attacking Caesar's right flank, was restrained
and finally routed by six cohorts that Caesar, anticipating his adversary's battle plan,
had moved to face the assault (Plutarch, *Pomp.* 69–71; Caesar, *B. Civ.* 3.86–93).

Auxiliary units

In addition to highly specialized units like the Balearic slingers and the Cretan archers,
the Roman army used foreign troops as auxiliaries. Unfortunately, we have little information about the details of the organization of these foreign contingents fighting
alongside Roman soldiers. They are merely listed in our sources, in the composition
of armies, especially during the civil wars, but little is known of their military organization and importance as fighting units. Most of them were provided by client kings
and one may remain skeptical about their will to sacrifice their lives for a foreign
cause they had been forced to join. We have many allusions to their unreliability and
the distrust of Roman generals for their contribution on the battlefield. The organization of permanent and reliable auxiliary forces in the Roman army is a legacy of
the imperial period.[15]

3   Equipment and Weapons

The legions

With one exception, the offensive and defensive weapons used by the legionaries
between 146 and 30 BC did not change.[16]

    We may begin with the exception, the abandonment of the heavy spear (*hasta*)
that had equipped the *triarii*, the third line of the manipular formation (Polybius
6.23.16). The spear was a weapon intended for thrusting. The heavy spear was made
of three parts: an iron head of various shapes, a thick heavy wooden shaft, and an

iron butt. The iron or bronze butt was, primarily, for the protection of the wooden shaft against moisture when the spear was stuck into the ground. It would also, in case the lance was broken, be used as a weapon. A row of spears was very effective against charging enemies. The Romans abandoned the spear because it was a weapon unfit in a cohort formation, not because it was inefficient.

In the cohortal system, the offensive weapons of the legionaries were standardized: the javelin (*pilum*), the short sword (*gladius hispaniensis*) and, of much lesser importance, the dagger (*pugio*). The *pilum* was a throwing javelin of great penetrative power. It was a close-range javelin of 2.1 meters long (7 feet) with a maximum range of 30 meters (100 feet) and an effective range of 15 meters. A *pilum*, according to some modern experiments, could pierce 30 millimeters of pinewood or 20 millimeters of plywood and, possibly, the man behind the shield if thrown at a distance of 5 meters. It was designed to penetrate deep into the shield so as to make it difficult or impossible to take it off and, most importantly, either to break or to bend upon impact thus giving the enemy no opportunity to throw it back.

At close quarters, the legionary used his Spanish sword. This was a thrusting and slashing sword, extremely well adapted to close-order fighting. It was 75 centimeters (30 inches) long and 47 millimeters (2 inches) wide; its weight was perfectly concentrated one-third from the tip. It was a lethal weapon, possibly the best in the ancient world. Although Polybius does not mention it, the legionary was also equipped with the *pugio*, a sidearm held either on his left side or across his belt (the sword was held on the right side). Obviously, one may question the use of a dagger on the battlefield; it was certainly no challenge to an enemy and it could not substitute for the *gladius*. This has led some modern scholars to see the *pugio* more likely used for the daily routine of the soldier than for combat.[17]

For defensive weapons, the Roman legionary wore a helmet, a shield, a cuirass, and greaves. The most common form of helmet was in the shape of a bowl with cheek pieces and neck protection (the Montefortino type). Helmets were made of iron or bronze. The helmet offered the best protection while leaving the soldier with unobstructed vision and hearing, this lack of obstruction being vital since the manipular or cohortal formation depended upon orders that had to be seen (*signa* of the units) or to be heard (*cornu* or trumpet). On the top of the helmet was a device intended to hold horsehair or a hole intended to hold feathers. This caused the soldier to look taller and thus more impressive.

Legionaries were protected from the neck to knee by the *scutum*, a heavy shield (10 kg; 22 lbs), oval and curved, made of two or three layers of plywood (the boards were laid at right angles to each other and glued) and covered with calfskin. It was some 1.2 meters (4 feet) in length and 76 centimeters (2 feet 6 inches) in width. Its rim was protected at the top and bottom by bronze or iron binding, a protection against sword slashing and against the elements when resting on the ground. A spine and a boss of iron riveted to it added protection from missiles (arrows and javelins) but also made it a powerful weapon with which the bearer, by applying all his weight when clashing with an enemy, could easily unbalance and even throw him to the ground. The Roman soldier held his shield with his left arm, grasping an attachment located just behind the boss.

Legionaries wore cuirass, the most common and effective being the coat of mail armor (the *lorica hamata*). It was made of linked iron rings and offered excellent protection without hampering movement. It was generally reinforced on the shoulders by another layer of mail. The mail shirt offered the best protection but was heavy (10 kg or more). To better distribute the weight, soldiers wore a belt that transferred some of the weight into the hips, relieving them of some of the burden; the belt also had the advantage of stabilizing the mail cuirass, keeping it tight.

The cost of a mail armor was prohibitive to many recruits when each soldier was responsible for its equipment. Polybius tells us that soldiers who were too poor to use it protected themselves with a pectoral plaques, a plate of iron or bronze, either square, rectangular, or round, kept in place by leather tongues. Another full body protection could be obtained with scale armor (*lorica squamata*), made of small bronze plates. It was much less expansive than the mail cuirass, easier to manufacture, and easier to repair. When polished, it also gave the bearer a splendid and frightening appearance. But it was heavier than the mail cuirass and offered less freedom of movement.

The last type of cuirass was the so-called muscle cuirass. It certainly looked impressive and offered great protection, but it had too many shortcomings: it was expensive, heavy, and very uncomfortable on the battlefield. For these reasons, it remained of limited use, mostly for the parade field and for rich aristocrats. It was better suited for cavalrymen, its weight and lack of flexibility being less important than for the infantryman.

In his description of the equipment of the legionary, Polybius mentions the greave (in the singular; Polybius 6.23.8). Greaves were uncomfortable, especially when on the march. So it was very likely that, when using it, the legionary protected only his left leg, the one always vulnerable. Indeed, when fighting, a soldier, holding his shield on his left arm, when throwing his *pilum*, or when using his sword for a thrusting attempt, would put his left leg forward in order to put all his weight behind the blow he intended to deliver. The greave was either bent to fit the leg or attached with leather thongs.

For centuries, all drafted citizens armed themselves at their own expense, the consequence of the nature of a citizen militia in a timocratic society. But, even during the first centuries of Roman history, in case of military emergency (when the *tumultus* was declared), when *proletarii* (citizens below the property qualification necessary to serve) were called to defend the commonwealth, the state armed them at public expense.

At the time when Polybius wrote his *History* (the last books of which were written after 133 BC), the state was sometimes compelled to provide the military equipment for a growing number of *assidui* who did not have the means to buy their equipment or part of it. The lowering of the property qualification from 11,000 *asses* to 4,000 *asses* forced the state to equip many *assidui* at public expense. And yet, there were financial consequences for those who benefited from state funds since the principle of a citizen militia was maintained and the soldiers, in addition to the cost of food and clothing, would reimburse the cost of their equipment through installments, by deduction from their *stipendia* (the money received by soldiers during campaigns) (Polybius 6.39.15).

The situation became critical when the minimum property qualification was again lowered and went down from 4,000 to 1,500 *asses*. A very large number of citizens who could be drafted could not afford the cost of their equipment and the deductions from the *stipendium* became so large that they deprived the drafted citizens of any of its benefit. So, in 123 BC, the tribune of the Plebs, Gaius Gracchus, sponsored a law that declared it illegal for the state to make any kind of deductions (food, clothing, or military equipment) from the soldiers' pay (Plutarch, *C. Gracchus* 5.1 following Gabba's interpretation [1976] 10). And yet, the conservative nature of Roman society kept the principle of deduction alive, even if it was done in a purely symbolic way. Indeed, even when the citizen militia ceased to exist and was replaced by a professional army, equipped entirely at public expense, such symbolic deductions were still in effect; such was the situation in AD 14, according to Tacitus (*Ann.* I.17.6). Originally, the state bought military equipment from private manufacturers (Liv. XXII.57.11). It is not until around 100 BC that we have reference to state-owned armories and arsenals (Cicero, *Rab. Perd.* 20).

Cavalry

Polybius describes the reform of the cavalry's equipment without precision about the period this reform was implemented (Polybius, 6.25.3–11). Modern scholars date the change to the Second Punic War, the years following the series of disasters of the years 218–216.[18] The troopers' earlier equipment was, according to the Greek historian, limited and defective: they had no body protection, riding "nearly naked," and their lances were so slender and pliant that "the shaking due to the mere motion of the horse caused most of them to break"; furthermore, as Polybius notes, their lances had no butt-ends, so that a horseman "could only deliver the first stroke with the point and after this if they broke they were of no further service." As for the shield, it was made of ox-hide, too light to be of any use for attacking and rendered unserviceable when the rain and moisture peeled off and rotted the wood. Such deficient equipment was totally inadequate when the heavier equipped troopers serving in Hannibal's army challenged the Roman cavalry. The Romans had to adapt themselves to the situation and adopted a new steady and strong lance with a heavier head and spike at the butt end (that could be used in case the lance was broken by a stroke). They were also equipped with a heavier shield made of a solid and firm texture that offered good service for both protection and assault. Although Polybius does not mention helmets, mail cuirasses, and protection for the legs, other sources, as well as depiction of cavalrymen on monuments (e.g. the monument of Aemilius Paullus at Delphi celebrating Roman victory at Pydna in 168 BC), confirm that cavalrymen were equipped with such protective gear.

We have no information concerning the equipment of the foreign cavalry that replaced the citizen cavalry in the first century BC or of the auxiliary troopers that, occasionally, reinforced them. They equipped themselves according to the customs and traditions of the countries they came from, so one can expect variations in the protective gear and weapons they were using.[19]

4 The Order of Battle

We need to begin with the obvious: pitched battles are exceptional occurrences in war. Soldiers spent most of their time on the march, in their camps, on garrison duties, and in training. Soldiers, in presence of the enemy, were not, in general, fighting pitched battles, but engaged in skirmishes, fighting unexpected raiding incursions, or involved in counter-raiding expeditions; they engaged in tactical maneuvers that often did not end with direct confrontations, either because they failed to achieve their tactical intentions or because the enemy succeeded and avoided entrapment, or because the success of the maneuver forced the enemy to surrender without fighting. Roman soldiers were spending much more time in siege warfare than in facing the enemy on a battlefield. It is a common saying that the Romans won their wars with spades rather than swords. Any person reading Caesar's war commentaries knows the fundamental importance of siege warfare during the Gallic and the Civil War: Caesar's legionaries spent most of their campaigns besieging cities and camps, or trying to immobilize enemies by entrenching them.

As for the actual battles, it is an illusion to believe in a single model, in the existence of sets of rules that could be applied uniformly to a so-called "Roman art of war." How could it be otherwise? Topographic and climatic factors are never predictable, the respective sizes of the armies on the field, the fighting skills of the soldiers on both sides, and the different tactics used by the adversaries, all these factors, and the list is far from being exhaustive, render illusory the belief in a "model" systematically followed by Roman generals. In the period under consideration, the Roman army fought guerilla wars, slave insurrections, pirates, and, of course, civil wars. Wars against foreign enemies were never comparable and forced the Romans to face challenges, to respond to different enemy fighting skills. The strategies and tactics used by Rome's enemies were always different: Jugurtha in Numidia, Mithridates or Tigranes in the East, the Parthians across the Euphrates, the Celtic tribes in Gaul, the Germans both in Germany and during their migration across the Rhine, the Britons, the Spaniards, to name but few, were different peoples, different societies, using different ways of fighting.

This is not to say that Roman generals and Roman soldiers were not fighting according to general principles of engagement. We have discussed their combat formations (the cohortal system), their weapons, and their training. In ideal conditions, they expected to fight as follows: the legionaries would face the enemy by standing in three lines (although, as we have seen, two lines or even a single line may be used depending on numerical and topographical considerations), their flanks protected either by cavalry, natural obstacles, or man-made fortifications. The general would address the soldiers before the signal was given for the assault. Then the legionaries would start marching slowly and silently toward the enemy's lines until reaching a distance from which they could effectively throw their javelins. It was only at that point that they would run, discharge a volley of *pila*, and shout the war cry. If the enemy had not disbanded, they would draw their swords for hand-to-hand combat. In most cases, such disciplined and determined charges would break the enemy's will and both cavalry and infantry would slaughter the routed enemy. But if the enemy had not been defeated and firmly stood their ground, the battle would be decided by the fighting skill and the courage of the legionaries, the leadership of the centurions, and the general's skill in shifting cohorts where needed or in using reserves at the appropriate moment.

This is generally how modern Roman historians describe a battle and this scenario can be found in some ancient accounts. The main problem came when a battle was not decided speedily, namely in those few minutes when an infantryman could physically fight. This was the key question addressed by P. Sabin[20] and explained by his concept of "sporadic close combat," describing Roman infantry clashes "as a natural stand-off punctuated by periodic and localized charges into contact." Sabin's interpretation is probably the best explanation of what happened on the battlefield when battles were fought for hours. And yet, Sabin's "model" applies only to prolonged infantry battles and, ultimately, remains a "model." It is logical and it may have worked, but it is still an explanation founded on the need for historians to impose, in the words of A. K. Goldsworthy, "a neat order on chaos," the chaos of the battlefield.

In conclusion, I would like to insist on the fact that there were no "models" in battles fought by the Romans. In the first six books of Caesar's *De Bello Gallico* (from 58 to 52 BC), we find the descriptions of seven pitched battles: (1) against the Helvetii in 58 BC (1.24–26); (2) against Ariovistus in 58 BC (1.51–52); (3) against the Belgae in 57 BC (2.8–11); (4) against the Nervii and their allies in 57 BC (2.19–28); (5) against the German tribes of the Tencteri and Usipetes in 56 BC (4.7–15); (6) two battles under the command of Labienus against the Treveri in 53 (6.7–8); and (7) against the Parisii in 52 BC (7.57–62). None of these battles followed a common pattern, but all depended upon circumstances and these circumstances were always specific. Circumstances could also be created by the generals themselves who wanted to avoid an enemy able to predict their strategy and tactics: as Appian quotes Caesar: "the most potent thing in war is unexpectedness" (*B. Civ.* 2.53). This conclusion is valid for all the wars fought by the Romans and, we may add, for all wars in world history.

It is with Julius Caesar that this chapter concludes. The army recruited, organized, and trained by Julius Caesar in Gaul marks a turning point in Roman military history – the birth of a highly efficient professional army and the model of the imperial army. And yet, Caesar did not create a new army and did nothing new in terms of tactics and strategy. In its structure, the Roman army that Caesar commanded was not much different from those under the commands of Marius, Sulla, Lucullus, or Pompey. What was different was Caesar's soldiers' image of themselves, as soldiers. The concept of the Roman soldier fighting for Rome "as a duty, a responsibility and a privilege" was dead. Soldiers were now highly trained and highly efficient professionals. They fought because they lived for fighting. There was no "revolution" in the nature of the Roman army in the middle of the second century BC, only a progressive evolution of what soldiers came to be. We may say of Caesar what we said of Marius: he did not change the army, but made the best possible use of the armed forces as they existed, and he had the genius of making his soldiers "realize" who they "really" were – potentially the best soldiers in Western history. And, on this model, the Roman army made it possible for the Roman Empire to achieve peace and security for more than two centuries.

NOTES

1 Gabba 1976, 5–6. Rosenstein 2004, 57–8.
2 Discussion in Rosenstein 2004, 276–7 n.76. Gabba 1976, 6–8; De Ligt (in this volume).
3 References and modern interpretations are perfectly summarized in Brunt 1962, 69–86. Tiberius Gracchus' land law: Shochat 1980.
4 Rich 1983, 287–331.
5 Rosenstein 2004, 12–17, 53–7, 156–7. Evans 1988, 121–40.
6 Rosenstein 2004, 57. Rathbone 1993, 144–5.
7 Gabba 1976, 1–19 and nn.171–81; Rosenstein 2004, 167–9.
8 Gabba 1976, 24–6.
9 Gabba 1976, 46–9. For the growing importance of volunteers and mercenaries in the Roman army of the late republic: Harmand 1967, 245–62, 272–99; Watson 1958, 113–20; Messer 1920, 158–75; Brunt 1962, 69–86.
10 For a detailed argumentation: Harmand 1967, 409–82.
11 Keppie 1984, 19–36.
12 Bell 1965, 404–22.
13 For a discussion of the changing military quality and performance of the Roman army after Marius' reforms (by contrast to the progressive decline in the second century): Harmand 1967, 8–20. Goldsworthy 1996, 12–38. Warry 1980, 130–87. Keppie 1984, 57–79.
14 McCall 2002. Dixon and Southern 1992, 20–5. Harmand 1967, 46–51.
15 Recruitment and poor military aptitude of auxiliary troops: Harmand 1967, 41–5; Yoshimura 1961, 473–95.
16 Bishop and Coulston 1993, 48–63; Harmand 1967, 55–98.
17 Goldsworthy 2003, 30.
18 Rawson 1971, 45. McCall 2002, 33–45.
19 Harmand 1967, 81–8.
20 Sabin 2000, 1–17.

BIBLIOGRAPHY

Bell, M. J. V. 1965. "Tactical reform in the Roman Republican army," *Historia* 14: 404–22.
Bishop, M. C., and J. C. N. Coulston. 1993. *Roman Military Equipment from the Punic Wars to the Fall of Rome*. London.
Brunt, P. A. 1962. "The army and the land in the Roman revolution," *JRS* 52: 69–86.
Connolly P. 1989. "The Roman army in the age of Polybius," in J. Hackett (ed.), *Warfare in the Ancient World*. London, 149–68.
Dixon, K. R., and P. Southern. 1992. *The Roman Cavalry*. London.
Evans, J. K. 1988. "Resistance at home: The evasion of military service in Italy during the second century BC," in Yoru Yuge and Masaoki Doi (eds.), *Forms of Control and Subordination in Antiquity*. Leiden, 121–40.

Feugere M. 1993. *Les armes des romains de la République à l'antiquité tardive*. Paris.

Fuller, J. F. C. 1965. *Julius Caesar. Man, Soldier, and Tyrant*. New Brunswick.

Gabba, E. 1976. *Republican Rome. The Army and Allies*. Oxford.

Goldsworthy, A. K. 1996. *The Roman Army at War, 100 BC–AD 200*. Oxford.

—— 2003. *The Complete Roman Army*. London.

Harmand, J. 1967. *L'armée et le soldat à Rome de 107 à 50 avant notre ère*. Paris.

Keppie, L. 1984. *The Making of the Roman Army. From Republic to Empire*. New York.

McCall, J. B. 2002. *The Cavalry of the Roman Republic. Cavalry Combat and Elite Reputations in the Middle and Late Republic*. London.

Messer, W. S. 1920. "Mutiny in the Roman army. The republic," *CP* 15: 158–75.

Rathbone, D. H. 1993. "The census qualifications of the *Assidui* and the *Prima Classis*," in H. Sancisi-Weerdenburgh et al. (eds.), *De Agricultura: In Memoriam Pieter Willem de Neeve (1945–1990)*. Amsterdam, 121–52.

Rawson, E. 1971. "Literary sources for the pre-Marian army," *PBSR* 39: 13–31.

Rich, J. 1983. "The supposed Roman manpower shortage in the later second century BC," *Historia* 32: 287–331.

Rosenstein, N. 2004. *Rome at War. Farms, Families, and Death in the Middle Republic*. Chapel Hill.

Sabin, P. 2000. "The face of Roman battle," *JRS* 90: 1–17.

Shochat, Y. 1980. *Recruitment and the Programme of Tiberius Gracchus*. Brussels.

Warry, J. 1980. *Warfare in the Classical World*. New York.

Watson, G. R. 1958. "The pay of the Roman army. The republic," *Historia* 7: 113–20.

Yoshimura, T. 1961. "Die Auxiliartruppen und die Provinzialklientel in der römischen republik," *Historia* 10: 473–95.

FURTHER READING

Keppie 1984 and Goldsworthy 2003 offer a modern and complete survey. Goldsworthy 1996 is possibly the best on the subject. For a more specific and very complete survey, Harmand 1967 is excellent.

For the evolution of the recruitment and the professionalization of Roman soldiers, E. Gabba's studies remain essential: "Le origini dell'esercito professionale in Roma: i proletari e la riforma di Mario," *Athenaeum* XXVII, 1949, 173–209; "Ricerche sull'esercito professionale romano da Mario ad Augusto," *Athenaeum* XXIX, 1951, 171–272. Both studies are published in English translation (by P. J. Cuff) in Gabba 1976. Rosenstein 2004 offers a new interpretation that challenged many of Gabba's conclusions. It is essential reading for this question.

Tactical issues are discussed by Connolly 1989; Bell 1965. Military equipment: very complete guides in Bishop and Coulston 1993 and Feugere 1993. On the Roman cavalry in the republican period, the most comprehensive study is to be found in McCall 2002. Sabin 2000 is an original and thought-provoking discussion on tactics and human behavior on the battlefield. Fuller 1965 remains a classic military biography of Caesar.

CHAPTER SIX

War and State Formation in the Roman Republic

Paul Erdkamp[1]

1   Introduction

At the start of his Iberian campaign in 195 BC, Cato the Elder sent the army suppliers back to Italy, remarking that the war would sustain itself. The Roman soldiers subsequently plundered the land far and wide (Livy 34.9.12–13). The older literature on the Roman army used to hold that it was a principle of Roman warfare that the legions sustained themselves by living off the land. We now realize that that was usually not the case. The Roman armies needed money, food, fodder, horses, pack-animals, weapons, clothing, building material, ships, and wagons. The institutions and mechanisms that were created to fulfil these needs were not brought into existence at once – they emerged as Roman wars expanded in terms of the number of men involved and in geographical scale. At the end of the republic, during the civil wars, Rome was able to mobilize and sustain armies that numbered hundreds of thousands of men. The civil wars demonstrate the organizational ability of the Roman state at this time, although they exhausted Italy and the provinces. Military historians of the early modern period often compare the Roman logistical feats to those of later wars. One scholar, describing the problems that the British government at the time of the American Revolution had in sustaining its armies of up to 65,000 men across the Atlantic (and which it failed to solve), observed that "no European government had faced such a task since Roman times."[2]

2   State and State Formation

Modern historians emphasize the organization of war as the driving force behind the emergence and growth of the state in Europe. They argue that the "state" as a form in which the political community was organized in Europe emerged in the fifteenth to seventeenth century. Those states that had the strongest armies were the most successful, which was not only a strong impetus for other rulers to improve their instruments of war, but also caused the disappearance of many entities whose rulers failed to do so. This development applies as much to internal strife as to external conflicts. Strengthening the armies meant the creation and continuous improvement of means to control human and material resources. Traditionally, the development of the state was perceived in terms of "force" and "coercion": the armies and bureaucracies provided the rulers with the instruments with which to impose yet more obligations on their subjects. Recently, more emphasis has been put on the element of bargaining, as rulers and subjects agreed on measures that were to their mutual benefit. Rulers who could show (or successfully claim) that strong armies meant peace and prosperity could persuade their subjects to offer more resources for the purpose of war.[3]

There are many similarities between the problems that faced ancient Rome and the early modern states. For one, the process of state formation in early-modern Europe had a domino effect, as one state was forced by the growing power of its neighbors either to take the same path or to disappear. Rome too had been forced to improve the performance of its military organization by the strength of the opponents it faced, many of which were highly developed states when Rome met them on the battlefield. Nevertheless, many differences mean that the comparison between the process of state formation of the Roman Republic and the European states is not straightforward. The rulers of late-medieval Europe shaped their states in a feudal society and had to deal with an urban bourgeoisie that was no integral part of feudal power structures. In Rome, control within the state was and remained in the hands of an urban-based elite of landowners. Rulers in early-modern Europe created and were faced with a military revolution, as the use of gunpowder led to an arms race in which an increasingly powerful and expensive artillery was developed, which in turn required much larger and more costly fortifications than the medieval castles had been. The development of weaponry from archaic to imperial Rome is of no comparable degree.

One important issue is whether one is allowed to talk about the ancient world in terms of "state" and "state formation," since many modern historians claim that the state originated in post-medieval Europe. Although there is one crucial difference between the Roman Republic and early-modern states like France, Spain, or the Dutch Republic (on which more below), there are sufficient similarities to allow the term "state," and to make war and state formation a useful concept for the ancient world. The government of the Roman Republic, embodied in assemblies, the Senate, and magistrates and expressed as *senatus populusque romanus* (SPQR), claimed sovereignty over all members of the body politic. As part of this, the legitimate use of force was confined to representatives of the state. Their power to act as representatives of the state, symbolized by the *fasces*, was called *imperium*. Hence, it was not their noble birth that legitimized them to wage war or engage otherwise on behalf of the state, but the *imperium* that was given to them by the Senate and popular assemblies. The existence of private wars in early Rome may be assumed, but warfare had very soon become the prerogative of the state.[4] The community created magistracies as its executive and provided them with an apparatus in the form of institutions and a body of law that was neeeded to perform their tasks. As in early-modern Europe, the army was by far the largest and most expensive of these institutions, which is not surprising, since the waging of war was the largest task that ancient states faced.

The term "state formation" refers to a dual process. On the one hand, it is concerned with the growth of central authority, of the organizations and institutions used by the authorities, and of the resources needed by the authorities to perform their tasks. On the other hand, state formation reflects the widening scope of tasks that are perceived by the authorities as the responsibility of the state, which means that the state is getting involved in terrain that originally had been in the private sphere.

This chapter will deal with four aspects of state formation in the Roman Republic. First, the control of human resources for war is related to the geographical expansion of the Roman state. Second, the role of material resources that allowed Roman armies to function. Third, the mobilization of material resources, which went hand in hand with the growth of various institutions, including magistracies and law. Fourth, the means that were created to improve the workings of the army which could be turned to other uses, thus leading to a larger spectrum of state functions.

3   Human Resources: Citizens, Allies, and Provincials

In one respect, the Roman Republic differed significantly from the early-modern states, since the latter were sovereign in a well-defined and clearly delimited territory. Roman authorities claimed sovereignty not only within their own political community, but also outside the Roman territory (*ager Romanus*). In other words, the *ager Romanus* was not identical with the Roman state. In at least one important respect, the state comprised also the communities of the Latins and other allies. Moreover, modern states are perceived as territories, while ancient states were predominantly communities of citizens.

Rome claimed sovereignty over other states in the sense that, from the late fourth century BC onwards, citizens of various communities served in her army. Half of them were the citizens (*cives*) of Rome itself. These citizens either lived in the city of Rome or in towns of Roman citizen-status within the *ager Romanus*. The other soldiers either were citizens of communities that shared a common Latin status (*nomen Latinum*) or of communities that each had made a unilateral treaty with Rome (*socii*). In the third century BC, consular armies consisted normally of two legions of Roman citizens and two units of similar size that were manned by Latins and other allies (Polybius 6.26.7; 6.30.2). Italy was perceived as a perpetual military alliance under Roman hegemony. The Italic allies were therefore clearly distinguished from the non-Italic troops, such as Cretan archers or Numidian horsemen. Rome was clearly sovereign, since the Latin and allied communities only contributed troops to the Roman army and never fielded armies independently. In other words, the Latin and allied states had lost sovereignty over their troops. In all other respects, though, the Latin and allied communities functioned as independent communities, but that largely holds true for the towns of Roman citizens as well. Two things are noteworthy. First, since sovereignty in the Roman Republic was a multi-layered affair, the Roman state of the republic had no clearly defined territory. Second, this complex structure had its origins in war.

Citizens

When the republic was created, war was the most important function of the state. Status and political division of the citizenry was indissolubly connected to their role in the army. At the start of the republic (traditionally 509 BC), two magistrates (later called consuls) were annually appointed to command the armies. The authority of the consuls was sometimes suspended and for a period of up to six months (the duration of a campaigning season) was taken over by one dictator. From 443 BC onwards, censors were regularly appointed whose main task was to register the citizens' age and property class, which was the basis both for military service and for voting in the assembly that decided on war/peace and elected the consuls. This so-called *comitia centuriata* probably had its origin in the assembly of the army, consisting of all the able-bodied citizens. In the early republic, one's role in the army and one's weight in the assembly depended on one's property class. The wealthiest citizens served in the cavalry, the land-owning farmers in the heavy infantry. Poorer citizens either served as light-armed troops or contributed to the Roman war-effort as non-combatants. The wealthiest classes serving in the cavalry counted most in the voting process in the assembly, although the cavalry was less crucial than the heavy infantry on the battlefield. Despite their numbers, the people in the lowest property class had practically no vote in the *comitia centuriata*. As a result of internal strife other magistracies and other forms of assembly emerged in the fifth and fourth century BC, in which the poor citizens had an equal vote to the rich, but neither the people's tribunes nor the *comitia tributa/concilium plebis* had a role in war.[5]

In comparison to the times when aristocratic warriors fought each other in highly individual actions, the deployment of propertied citizens fighting in more or less heavily armed infantry forces had increased the number of men that were effectively fielded against neighboring peoples. One can imagine that such a development in one community quickly forced other communities to follow. The increased importance of wider sections of society also caused a shift in political power and social status. Henceforth, the army consisted of men who performed their duty as citizens by fighting their community's enemies.

Allies

Annexation of defeated neighbors obviously led to an increase in Roman military manpower, but a characteristic feature of the republic was that Rome did not depend on direct incorporation to achieve this result. Rome conquered Italy by creating a complex system of unilateral alliances with other states that allowed the exploitation of their manpower.

This system was not created from nothing, but it adapted instruments that had been developed for the alliance with the Latins in 493 BC, which the Hernici joined in 486 BC. From the start of the fifth century, the sources mention continuous wars against the Aequi and Volsci, peoples that had recently appeared to the south and east of Latium. Hence, the alliance was based on common interests and common enemies, which did not preclude, however, the regular outbreak of internal hostilities.

Authors writing centuries later depict Rome as the leading power of this alliance, but it is possible that Rome was just one of its members, albeit a powerful one. The sources tell us that command was shared between Rome and the Latins. Most importantly, Rome and the Latins joined in the establishment of common colonies on conquered territory. It was not so much Rome as their more direct Latin neighbors that the Aequi and Volsci threatened most. Rome's main enemy was the Etruscan city of Veii on the northern side of the Tiber. When this city was destroyed in 396 BC, Rome annexed its territory and settled its own citizens on the land. After Rome's rise in power and the successes against the Volsci and Aequi, which diminished the need for cooperation, increased tension led to a large-scale war (340–338 BC), during which Rome finally subjected the Latins.

The settlement of 338 BC put control of the military resources of the former alliance firmly in Roman hands. Part of the Latin communities, such as Lanuvium and Aricia, was incorporated in the Roman citizen body. The citizens of these Latin communities became Roman citizens, and in that sense Lanuvium or Aricia ceased to exist as states. However, these citizen-communities continued to function as self-governing towns. The character of independent communities was even more clearly retained in the case of those communities that were given a restricted Roman citizenship. This was, for instance, the case with Capua (340 BC) and the Volscian towns of Fundi, Formiae, and Arpinum (338 BC). The so-called *cives sine suffragio* were not given the vote in citizen assemblies (although they voted in their own assemblies). Rome's leading families probably did not want to give voting power to the inhabitants of such a populous city as Capua, or to peoples who, in contrast to the Latins, lacked a common cultural background with Rome.[6] The rulers of Rome, however, secured what they wanted most: direct control of the military manpower of these communities. According to a fragment from a much later writer, the *cives sine suffragio* served in legions of their own. When Polybius (following the senator and historian Fabius Pictor) says that in 225 BC the Romans and Campanians (i.e. Capua) could muster 250,000 soldiers, this only makes sense when they were perceived as all serving together.

Finally, Rome made unilateral treaties with allied communities that kept their own citizenship. Even these allies lost part of their sovereignty, however, because their troops could only fight under Roman command and their authorities could no longer engage in diplomatic relations with other states. Between 338 and 270 BC, Rome expanded this system throughout the Italian peninsula, mostly in the form of unilateral alliances.[7]

Rome continued to establish Latin colonies on land taken from its opponents. The Latin colonies established by Rome in this period had the same status as the Latin states that continued to exist in 338 BC. Remarkably, the settlers of these colonies were mostly Roman citizens, who exchanged Roman for Latin citizenship when enrolling in the colony. Men with Latin citizenship served in the allied units that fought alongside the legions. In other words, Rome created strongholds far from Rome to increase her control in these regions, but rather paradoxically did so by creating formally independent towns, and by taking away citizenship from the Roman citizens who settled in the colony.[8] Hence, colonies increased the manpower pool of the allied units at the cost of that of the legions. This is a clear illustration of the multi-layered nature of sovereignty in the republic.

Coercion and cooperation

Rome gained control of Italy on the basis of coercion, and as long as wars continued to be fought in Italy, Roman allies defected to the other side, as for instance during the war against Pyrrhus (280–275 BC). From then on, the local rulers seem to have concluded that more was to be gained by loyalty than by opposition. As long as they provided Rome with troops and ensured local stability, Rome offered internal backing. Besides, Rome presented itself as protector against external threats. Polybius (2.23) writes that, when Gauls threatened to invade Italy (225 BC), the allies rallied around their hegemon, since Rome offered protection against this common enemy. Much of this is Roman propaganda. Nevertheless, when Hannibal invaded Italy a few years later, only some of the allies defected to his side, and this only after a series of Roman defeats had shattered Rome's image. More than a century later, the Social War (91–89 BC) forced Rome to grant Roman citizenship to its allies. The preceding analysis has shown that this did not imply a sudden increase of the Roman "state." From the start, Rome had taken over sovereignty in the field of war, and the allies and Latins gradually lost more and more of their independence. Although many administrative changes followed the grant of citizenship, it was not as great a step as might appear.

Rome did not look for manpower in its provinces. Some communities in the provinces were given Latin status, but this was exceptional and had little to do with exploiting manpower. However, from the time of the Second Punic War onwards, Rome increasingly began to employ units of non-Italic peoples, such as Numidian and Iberian horsemen, or Ligurian and Thracian light-armed troops, among its infantry. At no time did Rome include units of, for instance, Macedonian pikemen, since these, just like Roman legionaries and their allied counterparts, were heavy infantry fighting in close formation. Rome used foreign troops to supplement its infantry. Increased use of non-Italic auxiliary forces allowed Rome to disregard the Italic cavalry and light-armed units. The *velites* and legionary cavalry disappear from the sources at the end of the second century BC.[9] From now on, Rome used its own manpower and that of the Latin communities and its Italian allies, covered by the *formula togatorum*, exclusively to man a uniform heavy infantry. Property was no precondition any more. Because not all of these men were able to finance their own weapons and equipment, recruits were equipped at the cost of the state from the late second century BC. This development is indissolubly connected to the exploitation of the human and material resources of the regions outside Italy.

4 Material Resources: The Needs of War

To bring a massive army into the field was one thing, to equip and sustain it quite another. Rome needed to supply its armies with weapons and armor, uniforms, blankets, and tents, horses, pack animals, and wagons. The real logistical challenge, however, was to provide the armies with sufficient amounts of food and fodder. Not only were the volumes involved much larger, the consequences of supply failure were disastrous.[10]

Food and fodder

The staple food of the soldiers was wheat. Polybius (6.39) informs us: "The infantry receive a ration of wheat equal to about two-thirds of an Attic *medimnus* a month, and the cavalry seven *medimni* of barley and two of wheat. Among the allies the infantry receive the same and the cavalry only one and one-third *medimni* of wheat and five of barley." Two-thirds of a *medimnus* (a Greek measure) equals four Roman *modii* or approximately 26.5 kilograms. There is no reason to assume that the rations were changed in subsequent years. Rations of approximately 830 grams of wheat per day provided nearly the entire daily energy requirement of the soldiers. The rations of wheat, which were supplemented with meat, olive oil, wine, and vinegar, could not be guaranteed at all times, and the availability of the other items depended even more on regional and military circumstances. Wheat would sustain less loss than other foodstuffs when stored for long periods or transported over long distances. It had furthermore a good ratio between volume and nutritious value. Since flour was more vulnerable, the rations were usually issued as unmilled corn and had to be milled by the soldiers themselves using handmills. Logistical restraints determined this cereal-dominated diet and prohibited any significant change of the diet while on campaign.

The Roman horsemen received a ration of wheat that was three times that of an infantry soldier, while allied horsemen received a double ration. The extra rations were meant for the servants who accompanied these upper-class combatants, which indicates that all members of the army received equal rations, although officers and horsemen had more money to spend on additional items of food. In the second century BC, generals are often said to have restored discipline by turning away sutlers selling food. Polybius also stated that the horsemen received monthly seven *medimni* of barley in the case of the Roman cavalry and five *medimni* in the case of the allied cavalry. This equals about 7 and 5 kilograms of barley a day. Again, we may assume that the difference implies that the rations were meant for more than one horse. It is likely that the Roman horsemen had recourse to a mule that was fed by the commissariat, while Roman and allied horses received the same amount of barley, which was supplemented by grazing and dry fodder.

The servants and pack animals added to the food and fodder requirements of the Roman armies. The above figures imply a number of 1,000 servants accompanying 800 horsemen. In addition, there were many muleteers and servants in the various unit and army trains. Exact numbers cannot be given, because these depended very much on the conditions and nature of each campaign, but we should think of some 20 percent on top of the number of combatants. The mules consisted mostly of pack animals needed in the army train. Taking as an example an army of some 40,000 men (including non-combatants), we should reckon with 4,000 horses and 3,500 pack animals. The daily consumption of such an army would be approximately 60 tonnes of corn and 240 amphorae of wine and olive oil. On top of this was the food and fodder needed for the men and mules bringing the provisions from the supply base to the army.

Logistical restraints

The logistical requirements constituted a severe hindrance of the strategical functioning of the army, since it limited the size of armies, the range of their maneuvers, and the duration of campaigns. Hence, it is often supposed that generals preferred their armies to "live off the land," seemingly being able to go wherever they wanted, not being restrained by supply lines and bases. In one sense, all armies lived off the land, since the horses and pack animals required such large amounts of feeding that no army could do without grazing or the occasional plundering of stores of dry fodder. This almost daily chore, which is called the *pabulatio* by Latin authors, is not to be confused with the *frumentatio*, which is the gathering of food either by harvesting standing crops or by gathering civilian stores. The *frumentatio* was a well-organized maneuver, using part of the infantry to collect the food, while the cavalry, light-armed troops and the rest of the units were engaged in defending the area. Living off the land could indeed be successfully done by small, but tactically strong, armies operating in hostile territory for a limited time at the right time of year. In other words, "living off the land" created its own set of restraints, limiting the location and duration of campaigns.

The opposite solution was to ensure adequate provisioning from overseas or nearby supply bases. Each option posed its own limitations on strategy. The choice a general had may be summarized as one between logistical security and operational flexibility, the latter meaning the opportunity to operate where and when one wanted. The aims of security and flexibility were often contradictory. Caesar opted for flexibility and surprise during the civil wars of 49–45 BC, but this also often meant near disaster, such as at Dyrrhachium, from where his army was forced to withdraw because starvation threatened his troops. In contrast, the Roman armies fighting Macedon (200–197, 171–168 BC) and the Seleucid Empire (191–188 BC) in the first half of the second century BC could count on huge amounts of wheat and barley from the provinces of Sicily and Sardinia and from the newly won allies Numidia and Carthage. During the wars in the East, an elaborate supply system, relying on an existing infrastructure, allowed the Romans to continue their operations in wintertime, to lay siege to cities until they fell and to concentrate large forces in hostile territory until the enemy was defeated on the battlefield. Geography played a role too, however. The fighting that broke out in inland Iberia in 154 BC demonstrates some of the problems that armies were facing in regions that could not be reached from the Mediterranean Sea. In 153 BC, the town of Ocilis, in which the Romans had collected all their provisions, defected to the enemy, forcing the Roman commander Q. Fulvius Nobilior to abort the siege of nearby Numantia. When, in 136 BC, Aemilius Lepidus Porcina besieged the town of Pallantia, he relied on foraging parties collecting supplies from the surrounding countryside. As the land became exhausted and the food supply failed, the army had to withdraw.[11] In short, food supply determined whether the Romans could employ the full potential of their manpower. Relying on the regular shipment of external resources had clear strategic advantages.

The low capability of ancient transport meant that armies could take along food for only a limited number of days. For example, an army of 40,000 men would need an equal number of mules to haul all the food and fodder it consumed in 30 days, which would not only mean an unwieldy train of at least 50 kilometers in length, but also multiply the army's food requirements. The Romans used mules in their army trains because these offered access to all kinds of terrain. Wagons were more efficient when traveling along roads, and they were also needed to transport larger items, such as parts of siege engines, since pack animals could only carry packs of maximally 50 kilograms on each side.

We can distinguish three phases in the transportation of supplies. First, provisions were brought to supply bases, which tended to be located near rivers or on the coast, because large volumes of supplies could only be transported over long distances by ship or boat. Second, a shuttle system regularly transported the supplies to the army, or the army would replenish its stocks at the supply base. For instance, during the Second Macedonian War, Flamininus would regularly send cohorts from the army laying siege to Thessalian towns to the supply base at Ambrakia, which is a return trip of some six days (Livy 32.1.7). If the supply lines became too long, the number of mules involved would rise steeply, thus adding significantly to the amounts of fodder needed. The colonies established by Rome throughout Italy may have served as supply bases in the conquest of Italy. The third element in the supply system was the army train itself, which carried supplies for at most 15 days.

It may be obvious to say that armies could not function without adequate provisioning, but two important points follow from this. First, the ecological, economic, and technical limitations of the supply system shaped to a large degree the ways that Roman wars were fought. Second, those states that managed to supply their armies in a way that offered most security and operational flexibility had a crucial advantage on the battlefield. Hence, the increase in scale of Roman wars had to be matched by the exploitation of the material resources of the empire. In other words, the Romans did not win an empire for its resources, but winning an empire forced them to exploit its resources.

5　The Mobilization of Resources

The requirements of food and fodder – and the additional provisions necessary for an army that campaigned in overseas territory for years on end – compelled the government to find or create means of acquiring the necessary foodstuffs, goods, money, and services. In some conquered areas, Rome took over existing systems of taxation; in others the continuous though fluctuating need for corn and other supplies by the armies present in that area turned ad hoc solutions into permanent levies in money and kind. War thus provided the impetus to increase the state apparatus consisting of magistrates (and their staff), laws, and institutions.

Money and monetization

The introduction of army pay may be related to the intensification of warfare and to the widening of the groups serving in the army to include men who welcomed additional income. Traditionally this is dated to the year 406 BC, at the start of the decisive campaign against Veii (trad. 406–396 BC). According to Livy (4.9.11), the Senate introduced army pay (*stipendium*) to compensate the men serving in this struggle for the labor they lost on their family farms. It is possible that later Roman historians wrongly dated the introduction of pay to this period in order to emphasize the intensity of the war against Veii. Some scholars believe that prolonged campaigns that kept the soldiers away from their farms only occurred from the later fourth century onwards, during the wars against the Samnites, Etruscans, and Gauls; others argue that army pay was indeed introduced at the time of the war against Veii.[12]

The increasing intensity of warfare required the introduction of more permanent and efficient means to bear the cost of the army. The main argument in favor of the late fifth-century introduction of army pay is the connection consistently made in the sources between the *stipendium* and the introduction of the *tributum*, the tax that was imposed on citizens in order to finance army pay. Not only is the *tributum* mentioned regularly from roughly 400 BC onwards, we also hear of the payment of indemnities, which were imposed for the first time in 394 BC on Falerii. Livy informs us that, when the Senate introduced army pay, the tribunes of the *plebs* warned the people that they would have to pay for their wages themselves, since the Senate would be obliged to introduce a tax to finance it all. However, the *tributum* seems to have shifted most of the burden to the highest property classes. Its height was determined by the military requirements. Livy sometimes mentions the imposition of a double or triple tax. The money was repaid after the war, but only if the treasuries held sufficient reserves. After the end of the Third Macedonian War (171–168 BC), the financial state of the republic was such that no *tributum* was levied between 167 and 43 BC.[13]

Livy also explains that, because there was no silver coinage yet, the senators, who were eager to show their willingness to bear their part of the burden, literally carted their payments of heavy bronze money (*aes grave*) to the state treasury. Whatever the truth of this, if army pay was introduced at the end of the fifth century, it pre-dated the introduction of Roman coinage. There is little evidence, moreover, that the coinage of other states was much used at Rome before the third century BC. Michael Crawford observed that the late appearance of coinage at Rome is "to be related to the fact that she did not demand tribute from her Italian allies, but men."[14] The earliest issue of a Roman silver coinage dates to the last years of the fourth century, in other words, during the wars against the Samnites. However, this issue of silver coins was an isolated event, which has led to the suggestion that the coinage was not so much related directly to the wars, but more to the building of the Via Appia from Rome to Capua (which was also not unrelated to the wars of that time). The war against Pyrrhus (280–275 BC) and the First Punic War (264–241 BC) were crucial for the monetization of large parts of Italy. Rome began to issue coinages regularly from the war against Pyrrhus onwards, while many other states struck coins in huge numbers in these years. Those allied communities who previously hardly had used coins began to do so in this period, probably due in part to the fact that the Latins and allies had to pay their own troops for serving. Most coins were issued in bronze, moreover, because the troops were paid in such coinage. After the Second Punic War (218–201 BC), Italy was not only monetized, but also used Roman coinages.[15]

In summary, the introduction of taxation, the monetization of Rome and Italy, and the nature of the coinage up to the late republic were solely determined by military needs.

Taxes in kind

Despite the use of coinage and the monetization of society, Rome relied on taxes in kind to fulfil the army's food requirements. The strategic advantages and security offered by organized provisioning encouraged the Romans to gain access to food as directly and forcefully as possible. Due to the paucity of sources, we remain in the dark about the food supply of the armies before the First Punic War. However, the measures introduced in the first provinces – Sicily, Sardinia, and Hispaniae – illustrate the development of ad hoc to structural solutions.

The Second Punic War, in which for many years food supply was a pressing concern for the authorities, was crucial in the development of taxes on Sicily and Sardinia. According to Livy (23.48.7), both islands paid some kind of tax (*vectigal*) after the First Punic War, this being a levy of grain and possibly other crops. It is likely that the *vectigal* was mainly meant for the sustenance of the troops stationed on both islands, which was disrupted, Livy says, when hostilities broke out during the Second Punic War.[16] When Sicily was pacified, a tithe system was introduced that was governed by the *lex Hieronica*, named after the former king of Syracuse. The tithe consisted of one tenth of the harvest of grain and other food crops. The Romans intended to make full use of the productivity of the islands at a time when a huge number of men had been brought under arms to fight in different war zones. In the final phase of the war, both Sardinia and Sicily played an important role in feeding the overseas armies. This role was continued during the wars in the East. The tax on Sardinia and Sicily ensured a steady flow of grain that was undoubtedly used to provision the armies that had now become a permanent feature of the Mediterranean. In times of increased requirements, such as the wars in the East, a double tithe was levied and other sources of grain were utilized.

Rome could not take over an existing tax system in Hispaniae. The taxes gathered there during the Second Punic War and afterwards consisted of ad hoc levies demanded by the Roman commanders from the Iberian peoples to pay and feed the Roman army. Tribute was demanded from defeated peoples, as when in 205 BC the Ilergetes were ordered to supply six months' worth of corn to the Roman troops (Livy 29.3.5; cf. 21.61.7ff.). Such tributes were supplemented with ad hoc contributions from Rome's allies in Iberia and overseas shipments. At first, the yield of the tribute was still very much dependent on Rome's position in the peninsula and on the Roman military demand. In 181 BC the Senate was informed that in that year the usual supplies of corn and money were not necessary, since the successes in Iberia ensured sufficient supply from local resources (Livy 40.35.4). With the expansion of Roman rule, the situation improved. In 171 BC, the Roman Senate regularized the various exactions and enforced purchases (paid at a rate fixed by the Roman governors) imposed on Hispaniae (Livy 32.2.12). Despite much which is unclear, the lack of Roman or Iberian coins in wide circulation before 150 BC seems to point to the predominance of taxes in kind in this period.[17]

Allied rulers who had their own system of subtracting resources from their subjects, such as Carthage and Numidia, provided assistance on a grand scale. When these areas became provinces, existing systems were turned into provincial taxes. Allied contributions still played a role in the first century BC. Caesar's army in Gaul received grain from allied tribes and the province of Gallia Narbonensis. The Senate allocated the provisions and troops for each provincial governor annually. This is implied, for instance, by Cicero (*Att.* 6.3.2) regarding his own governorship of Cilicia in the late 50s BC, when he notes that the provisions for his province had been allocated before the threat of a Parthian invasion had emerged. During the civil wars, the sustenance and financing of the Roman armies caused widespread impoverishment in the provinces. Caesar, Pompeius, and the other adversaries ordered troops, money, and food supplies from provinces and individual communities according to their need, and on their own accord sent them to other provinces.

In short, Rome created a system consisting of fixed taxes-in-kind in the provinces, offering a steady flow of food stuffs to feed the armies, which was supplemented by ad hoc contributions from allies and subjected peoples as the need arose.

Administrative structures

The apparatus created from the third century BC onwards could obviously not be managed by the few magistrates who commanded the armies and supervised civilian affairs in Rome. It has often been remarked that at the end of the republic the empire was governed with the administrative tools of a city-state. Although this is somewhat of a simplification, it is clear that the Roman state could not function without reliance on local elites.

The executive apparatus of Rome was limited to the magistrates and their staff. When commanding an army, consuls were assisted by quaestors, possibly from the fifth century onwards, who had a direct role in ensuring the supply of corn to the armies. The responsibilities of the quaestors, who are later seen as the treasurers of the armies and provinces, may have originated in the management of supplies. In 267 BC, the number of quaestors seems to have been increased to eight. In the second century BC, the quaestors posted in the provinces were involved in taxation and the management of public corn. An official staff assisted consuls, praetors, and quaestors. These so-called *apparitores*, who included scribes, heralds, messengers, and lictors, were appointed by the state. In the first century BC, when the system was fully established, their importance should not be underestimated: the highest-ranking scribes could be of equestrian status. Moreover, they formed a permanent part of the Roman executive apparatus, while most magistrates remained in office for only one or two years. Apart from the *apparitores*, all officials used their own private staff for their public functions.[18]

Most of the tasks involved in the mobilization of resources were executed by the local elites. Rome's retention of local administrative structures ensured that the available executive instruments were sufficient to fulfil the tasks that Rome needed. As we have seen, Rome usually left local taxes in place when turning regions into provinces. In the operation of the tithe system in Sicily, for instance, the towns still played a crucial role. The Roman governor made contracts for the acquisition of taxes in each particular area. Most of these contractors were local rich Sicilians and sometimes the towns themselves. To provide the state and potential tax farmers with the necessary information, city officials had to draw up a detailed annual report of the agricultural resources in their community. Rome clearly relied on the cooperation and knowledge of local elites. The situation was no different during the civil wars, when we often see commanders ordering local councils to contribute money or provisions to the war effort. As long as local rulers provided Rome with money, troops, and supplies, there was no reason to alter local power structures, let alone replace them with Roman administrators.

Polybius (6.17) provides clear evidence for the large role played in the second century BC by state contractors (*publicani*). An immense number of contracts, he says, were rewarded for the construction and repair of public buildings, and for the collection of revenues from navigable rivers, harbors, mines, and lands. "In a word, every transaction which comes under the control of the Roman government is farmed out to contractors." The reason that the supply of food or other provisions to the army is not included in Polybius' text is obvious: the Roman state did not resort to contracts to provision its armies with essential goods.[19] *Publicani* were only involved in the provisioning of armies as transport contractors, but if Rome needed many ships, requisitioning offered a more direct course to fulfil this need. This is not to say that armies did not attract numerous traders, who were eager to sell food, horses, wagons, and so forth. Caesar tells us for instance that during the Gallic War, outsiders had gathered in the cities of Noviodunum and Cenabum, in which the army's winter stores were being collected, for the sake of trade (Caesar, *B. Gal.* 7.3.1).

The expansion of its power gave Rome the opportunity to use the resources from beyond its own hinterland, but the impulse to do so did not arise automatically. Rome did not expand in order to use its subjects' wealth and resources. The impetus to create taxes in money and kind and to build up the required apparatus in the form of magistrates, staff, and law was provided by war.

6   The Spin-Offs of War

The growth of the state in republican Rome went beyond expansion of its territory or institutions. Instruments that were created on behalf of war were used for new functions, increasing the scope of the involvement of the state in society. In that sense, many state functions – in antiquity as well as later times – can be seen as the spin-offs of war. Three examples of this will be discussed: (1) the food supply of the capital, (2) the creation of "provinces," and (3) intervention in local affairs.

Feeding Rome

In 123 BC, C. Gracchus introduced the grain dole in Rome, which meant that cheap grain was distributed to part of the capital's populace. Some scholars assume that the food supply of the city of Rome had always been regarded as a responsibility of the state. Hence, it is thought that Rome took control of the provinces' food surpluses in order to feed the capital. However, feeding the capital was only a secondary use of provincial grain.

The first instances of the distribution of grain occurred at the end of the Second Punic War. In the years 203–200 and again in 196 BC, grain was shipped from Sicily, Sardinia, Hispaniae, and Africa to Rome and sold there at low prices. All these shipments can be related to the end of large-scale operations (in Iberia in 204 BC, in Africa in 202 BC, and in Greece in 197 BC), which led to military reserves becoming available, army demands diminishing, and levies taken from vanquished peoples increasing. In other words, these shipments were not the result of a structural policy to supply Rome.

During the decades preceding Gracchus' measure, two developments occurred. First, due to its expansion, Rome's income in money and kind increased, while at the same time the number of troops did not significantly grow. The annexation of Africa in 146 BC in particular turned one of the major corn-producing regions of the Mediterranean into a tax-paying province. Undoubtedly this increase of Rome's annual tribute opened up the opportunity in peaceful years to divert some tax-corn to the ever-growing multitudes in Rome. Second, the involvement of the Senate and magistrates in the provisioning of the capital city gained its own momentum, as it showed Roman politicians a way to popularity and raised expectations in the Roman populace. In 129 BC, an aedile purchased supplies in Thessaly. A governor of Hispaniae gathered grain in his province in 124 or 123 BC and sent it to Rome (Plutarch, *C. Gracc.* 6.2). In short, Gracchus' law was not as revolutionary as it might seem. It was meant to regularize the ad hoc actions that individual magistrates had taken and which were unintended side-effects of the state's control of grain.[20]

Provinces

At the end of the first century BC, the Romans had turned most of the lands bordering on the Mediterranean into provinces. Egypt, which was put under direct Roman control after Actium and the death of Cleopatra (32 BC), was the last acquisition of the republic. However, when the first provinces were created in the aftermath of the First Punic War, "province" had been a totally different concept.

Originally, the term "provincia" referred to the task of a magistrate. The *provincia* of the *praetor peregrinus*, for instance, was the jurisdiction between Romans and foreigners (*peregrini*). At first, *provincia* did not have a territorial meaning. The first provinces were little more than campaigns assigned to army commanders. Due to the stressed situation after the First Punic War, Rome stationed troops under the command of a Roman magistrate on Sardinia and in the western part of Sicily. In this way, the first "provinces" were created.

The case of Iberia, which became a war zone at the start of the Second Punic War, was no different. The troops remained there after Carthage had been defeated, because the internal division between many hostile tribes in Iberia made it impossible to impose a final solution on the entire region that would allow withdrawal of all Roman troops. In contrast, the armies operating in Africa and Greece were withdrawn after the Carthaginian Senate and Philip of Macedon surrendered. Even after Macedon had been defeated for the second time, ending the Third Macedonian War, no direct control was imposed, even though the kingdom was broken up into four separate states. In short, Rome had no desire to retain troops or magistrates in every war zone.

In the mid-second century BC, the attitude of the Roman rulers changed. The continuous presence in Sicily, Sardinia, and Iberia resulted in the emergence of fixed solutions and the regularization of relations between the army commanders and the "provincials." Army commanders had become governors and provinces had become subjected territories. Experience had shown that provinces offered material resources that could be utilized in war and politics. Hence, wars were deliberately sought in Africa and Greece in mid-century, and provinces were established in both regions in 146 BC. Further provinces were created in Asia Minor (129 BC) and southern Gaul (125 BC). In short, when provinces, which had originally been no more than war zones, were turned into institutionalized instruments of control, the creation of such provinces gained its own momentum.[21]

Local intervention

The sovereignty that the Roman state claimed for its provincial governors was at first limited to strictly military affairs and was only gradually widened in scope. A similar development occurred in Italy, which in theory remained a military alliance of self-governing states. The matter of sovereignty, which was unclear to begin with, was made even less clear in the second century BC by the growing presence of Roman citizens throughout Italy as a result of commerce, migration, and the founding of Roman colonies. Under these conditions, it was inevitable that Roman influence in local affairs increased, even if Roman rulers did not seek it. There is little evidence that the Roman government deliberately encroached upon local sovereignty, but the authority of Roman representatives naturally superseded that of the local magistrates. Allied states could not settle land disputes between themselves on the battlefield anymore, and turned to Rome.[22] The same applies to the provinces, where communities involved in local disputes would approach the highest Roman official. Maintaining local peace meant solving local conflicts. In one of his letters, Cicero is proud to have solved a local food shortage during his governorship of Cilicia (51 BC):

> Wherever I went, without force, without legal process, without hard words, by my personal influence and exhortations, I induced Greeks and Roman citizens, who had stored corn, to promise a large quantity to the people. (Cicero, *Att.* 5.21.8)

Even if idealized and one-sided, this passage shows that the governor was not merely an army commander anymore. The relationship between rulers and the ruled changed, which is best reflected in the measures taken by the Senate to curb the governors' abuse of power in the provinces. Already in 171 BC, embassies from Hispaniae objected in Rome to the greed and behavior of some of their governors. As part of the institutionalization of provinces, the way Rome dealt with such complaints was regularized in 149 BC, when a permanent court was established to hear cases against magistrates and promagistrates. Many laws on such cases followed, whose importance is not diminished by the fact that the courts did not function well in practice. These courts show that, as Roman sovereignty *de facto* increased, Roman rulers became more and more involved in local affairs. New institutions were created to deal with the provinces.[23]

7 Conclusion

As a state, Rome changed significantly in the period of the republic, not only in the sense of geographical expansion, but also in terms of of sovereignty and institutions. The state became more complex, comprising Roman citizens, allies, and provincials, in whose lives the state became more and more involved, broadening the spectrum of state functions. Public functions in the earliest states may be reduced to three fields: religion, justice, and war. Much of the process of state formation originated in war. The creation of an empire went hand in hand with bureaucratization, institutionalization, and regularization. In particular the wars against Pyrrhus and Carthage boosted the development of various institutions, including magistracies, taxation, and coinage.

Rome expanded geographically, but it took over only part of the sovereignty of the states it subjected. The provinces did not differ significantly from the alliance in Italy, as both consisted of largely self-governing communities. Sovereignty in war was monopolized by Rome, but involvement was limited in other fields. Rome's military power grew by the exploitation of the manpower of the Italian states and material resources of the provinces. Coercion on the basis of military stength was part of the power structure of the republic, and would remain so under the empire. However, the functioning of the empire was also based on the cooperation of the allied and provincial elites with Rome.

The end result may be seen in the period of the civil wars. Having taken control of the instruments of the state, a handful of generals mobilized armies of hundreds of thousands of troops. It reflects the leveling within the empire that Italy was hit just as hard as the provinces by the costs of war on such a scale. Augustus, having emerged from this struggle as sole ruler, fully understood that maintaining power was based not only on coercion, but also on bargaining with the people who mattered.

NOTES

1 I am very grateful to Toni Ñaco des Hoyo and Luuk de Ligt for their helpful comments.
2 Bowler 1975, 40.
3 Among the vast literature, Tilly 1990; Porter 1994; Glete 2002.
4 Timpe 1990.
5 See Galsterer 1976, 21ff.; Forsythe and Rich (in this volume).
6 Hantos 1983, 109ff.
7 Galsterer 1976, 65ff.; Hantos 1983, 150ff.; Harris 1984.
8 Hantos 1983, 122ff.

 9   Keppie 1984, 63–77. On the cavalry: McCall 2002, 100–13.
10   On the food supply of republican armies, see Erdkamp 1995, 1998; Roth 1999.
11   On these campaigns, Richardson 1986, 126ff.
12   Late fifth century: Cornell 1995, 187, 313. Late fourth century: Raaflaub 1996, 290.
13   Schwahn 1939, 7–8; Nicolet 1978.
14   Crawford 1985, 17.
15   Crawford 1985, 29–51; Harl 1996, 21–37. Challenging old assumptions is Wolters
     2000/2001.
16   On the *vectigal*, Ñaco des Hoyo 2003.
17   Howgego 1994, 17f.; Ñaco del Hoyo 2003, 165. Cf. Richardson 1976; 1986, 112ff.
18   Lintott 1993, 50ff.; Richardson 1994, 580ff. On the *apparitores*, Purcell 1983.
19   Livy (23.48.4–49.4; 25.3.8–5.1) does contain a story about fraudulent *publicani* ship-
     ping grain to Spain during the Second Punic War, but – in my opinion – the story has
     to be rejected as complete fiction. However, the older literature assumes that large-scale
     contractors took care of all aspects of the military food supply. See in particular, Badian
     1972. Although accepting that this was not normally the case, some might want to argue
     that the story in Livy reflects the unusual situation of those years.
20   Erdkamp 2000. Cf. Garnsey 1988, 182ff.
21   Richardson 1994, 564ff. On the *lex provinciae*, Lintott 1993, 28ff.
22   Harris 1972; Galsterer 1976, 149ff. See Campbell 2000, 454ff. for a list of such disputes
     in Italy and the provinces.
23   Lintott 1993, 55ff.; Richardson 1994, 577ff., 594ff.

BIBLIOGRAPHY

Badian, E. 1972. *Publicans and Sinners. Private Enterprise in the Service of the Roman
    Republic.* Oxford.
Bowler, R. A. 1975. *Logistics and the Failure of the British Army in America, 1775–1783.*
    Princeton.
Campbell, B. 2000. *The Writings of the Roman Land Surveyors.* London.
Cornell, T. J. 1995. *The Beginnings of Rome. Italy and Rome from the Bronze Age to the Punic
    Wars (c. 1000–264 BC).* London.
Crawford, M. H. 1985. *Coinage and Money under the Roman Republic. Italy and the
    Mediterranean Economy.* London.
Erdkamp, P. 1995. "The corn supply of the Roman armies during the third and second
    centuries BC," *Historia* 44: 168–91.
—— 1998. *Warfare and Food Supply in Roman Republican Wars (264–30 BC).* Amsterdam.
—— 2000. "Feeding Rome or feeding Mars? A long-term approach to C. Gracchus' *lex
    frumentaria*," *AncSoc* 30: 53–70.
Galsterer, H. 1976. *Herrschaft und Verwaltung im republikanischen Italien.* Munich.
Garnsey, P. 1988. *Famine and Food Supply in the Graeco-Roman World.* Cambridge.
Glete, J. 2002. *War and the State in Early Modern Europe.* London.
Hantos, T. 1983. *Das römische Bundesgenossensystem in Italien.* Munich.
Harl, K. W. 1996. *Coinage in the Roman Economy, 300 BC–AD 700.* Baltimore.
Harris, W. V. 1972. "Was Roman law imposed on the Italian allies?" *Historia* 21: 638–48.
—— 1984. "The Italians and the empire," in W. V. Harris (ed.), *The Imperialism of Mid-Republican
    Rome.* Rome, 89–109.

Howgego, C. 1994. "Coin circulation and the integration of the Roman economy," *JRA* 7: 5–21.

Keppie, L. 1984. *The Making of the Roman Army. From Republic to Empire*. London.

Lintott, A. 1993. *Imperium Romanum. Politics and Administration*. London.

McCall, J. B. 2002. *The Cavalry of the Roman Republic. Cavalry Combat and Elite Reputations in the Middle and Late Republic*. London.

Ñaco del Hoyo, T. 2003. *Vectigal Incertum. Economía de guerra y fiscalidad republicana en el occidente romano. Su impacto histórico en el territorio (218–133 aC)*. Oxford.

Nicolet, C. 1978. "Le stipendium des allies Italiens avant la guerre sociale," *PBSR* 46: 1–11.

Porter, B. D. 1994. *War and the Rise of the State*. Toronto.

Purcell, N. 1983. "The apparitores. A study in social mobility," *PBSR* 51: 125–73.

Raaflaub, K. A. 1996. "Born to be wolves? Origins of Roman imperialism," in R. W. Wallace and E. M. Harris (eds.), *Transitions to Empire. Essays in Roman History, 360–146. In Honor of E. Badian*. Norman, 273–314.

Richardson, J. S. 1976. "The Spanish mines and the development of provincial taxation in the second century BC," *JRS* 66: 139–52.

—— 1986. *Hispaniae. Spain and the Development of Roman Imperialism, 218–82 BC*. Cambridge.

—— 1994. "The administration of the empire," *CAH* 9. Cambridge, 564–98.

Roth, J. 1999. *The Logistics of the Roman Army at War (264 BC–AD 235)*. Leiden.

Schwahn, W. 1939. "Tributum und tributus," *RE* 7a, 1–78.

Tilly, C. 1990. *Coercion, Capital and European States, AD 990–1990*. Oxford.

Timpe, D. 1990. "Das Kriegsmonopol des römischen Staates," in W. Eder (ed.), *Staat und Staatlichkeit in der frühen römischen Republik*. Stuttgart, 368–87.

Wolters, Z. 2000/2001. "Bronze, silver or gold? Coin finds and the pay of the Roman army," *Zephyrus* 53/54: 579–88.

CHAPTER SEVEN

Roman Manpower and Recruitment During the Middle Republic

Luuk de Ligt

1 Introduction

During the third and second centuries BC, the armies of the Roman Republic lost many battles but not a single war. Part of the reason why Rome was able to recover from even the most disastrous defeats lies in the vast manpower resources upon which she could draw. One of the aims of this chapter is to outline the methods of recruitment that enabled the Romans to deploy between 150,000 and 200,000 fighting men (including marines) during the most critical phase of the Hannibalic War, and a roughly equal number of troops in the Second Macedonian War.[1]

A closely related theme is the development of Roman manpower resources during the second century BC. Basing their opinions on Appian's description of the background to the Gracchan land reforms and on a particular interpretation of the census figures for the second century BC, many ancient historians have argued that constant warfare and the expansion of rural slavery caused the citizen population – and indeed the free population of Italy as a whole – to decline. Against this, I shall argue that the citizen body continued to grow throughout the second century BC. It will also be suggested that this steady demographic expansion had the seemingly paradoxical effect of reducing the number of citizens eligible for legionary service. My reconstruction of demographic developments implies that lowering the property requirement for military service could easily enlarge the number of potential legionaries. In the final section of this chapter, it will be argued that this is precisely what happened. This finding lends support to the views of those ancient historians who have argued that the Roman army became increasingly "proletarianized" during the final decades of the second century BC.

2   Methods of Recruitment

In his account of the Roman constitution Polybius describes the methods by which Roman citizens were recruited into the legions during the mid-second century BC. When the consuls were about to enroll soldiers, they announced at a meeting of the popular assembly the day on which all Roman citizens of military age had to present themselves. On the appointed day the popular assembly or the consuls divided the 24 military tribunes into four groups, corresponding to the four legions that were going to be created. The distribution of the foot soldiers then took place on the Capitol on a tribe-by-tribe basis, with the recruits being led forward in groups of four and the officers of the four legions being given the right of first choice in turn. According to Polybius this procedure continued until each of the legions comprised 4,200 foot soldiers or as many as 5,000 "in times of exceptional danger." Finally, each of the legions received a complement of 300 cavalry. Polybius also describes the method used for recruiting and mobilizing allied units: "The consuls send their orders to the allied cities in Italy which they wish to contribute troops, stating the numbers required and the day and place at which the men selected must present themselves. The magistrates, choosing the men and administering the oath . . . send them off, appointing a commander and a paymaster" (6.19.1–21.5).

In view of the fact that Polybius was a well-informed contemporary observer, one would expect his account to be reliable. Yet there are some difficulties. One of these is that Polybius' figure for the size of a normal legion, 4,200 + 300 men, is out of line with the figures provided by Livy for the early decades of the second century BC. If we are to believe Livy, the size of a standard legion was 5,200 men from at least 184 BC onwards.[2] In principle, Livy's higher figure could be a retrojection of a later reality, for which one of his annalistic predecessors might be held responsible. A strong argument against this theory is that Livy's statements concerning the number and disposition of legions in the early second century BC are generally reliable. Moreover, since Marius is reported to have increased the standard size of a legion to c. 6,000, the figure of 5,200 does not reflect the size of the Roman legion in the time of the late-republican annalists. These considerations make it difficult to question the validity of Livy's statements concerning the size of legions in the early second century BC. It would seem to follow that Polybius' description of the levy contains some anachronistic elements, which can be explained by assuming that he adapted an earlier account. It has plausibly been surmised that this source was a kind of handbook for military tribunes that was written during the first or second quarter of the second century BC.[3]

A more serious problem has to do with Polybius' statement that "all Roman citizens of military age" were to present themselves at the levy. To begin with, even according to the most pessimistic estimates, at least 75,000 adult male citizens aged between 17 and 46 were liable for military service during the first half of the second century BC.[4] It would surely have been extremely inconvenient to convene all these men at Rome in order to select the c. 20,000 men that made up four legions. A closely related difficulty is that the *dilectus* is said to have taken place not on the Campus Martius (as in the first century BC) but on the Capitol. Even if the levy was spread over several days, this seems an unlikely point of assembly for a very large number of potential recruits.[5]

In the case of the allied communities we happen to know that their magistrates and representatives were summoned to Rome, where the military quotas demanded from them were fixed in discussions that took place on the Capitol (Livy 34.56.5–7). We must surely suppose that the same procedure was followed in the case of self-governing *municipia* and that the requirement of universal attendance applied only to citizens resident in or near the city of Rome. This means that the levy involved two stages: a first stage in which recruits were enlisted by the local authorities and a second one in which the men thus selected were distributed among the legions. Polybius' description refers solely to the second stage.

Another point that needs to be made concerns the number of legions that were created using the method described by Polybius. Although his account reflects the well-known practice (which can be traced to the Second Samnite War[6]) of entrusting an army of two legions to each of the consuls, the number of legions in the field was generally much larger than four, especially from the Second Punic War onwards. In fact, there are good grounds for believing that in 212 BC, when the Roman war effort reached an all-time high, as many as 25 legions were fielded in the struggle against Hannibal. It has been calculated that this huge force represented c. 30 percent of the adult male citizen population.[7] Not long after the conclusion of the Second Punic War another peak was reached during the war against the Seleucid king Antiochus III, in which 12 or 13 legions were put into the field.[8] In the decades that followed the number of legionaries on active service gradually fell, with some 15 percent of all adult male citizens serving in 173 BC, and between 8 and 11 percent during the mid-second century BC. By comparative standards even the low percentages of this last period are very high. In fact, in Europe a comparable rate of mobilization would not be reached until the rise of Prussia in the seventeenth and eighteenth centuries.[9]

Following his account of the *dilectus* Polybius describes the consuls as instructing the allies to furnish contingents of a certain size; they then specify the place and time at which these units were to muster. Elsewhere, in his description of the Roman war preparations on the eve of the Gallic invasion of 225 BC, he tells his readers that the allied communities were ordered to compile lists (*katagraphai*) of all men of military age (Polybius 2.23–24). More than a century later, the epigraphic *lex agraria* of 111 BC refers to "the allies or members of the Latin name [i.e. the Latin allies], from whom the Romans are accustomed to demand soldiers in the land of Italy *ex formula togatorum*."[10] This phrase seems to hint at the existence of a document that was used to distribute the burden of military service equitably among the allies. It has been conjectured that this schedule was constructed using the *katagraphai* referred to by Polybius, and that the year 225 BC marked the birth of the *formula togatorum*.[11]

Unfortunately, the exact nature of the *formula togatorum* is obscure. Some 40 years ago Toynbee argued that it was a list specifying the maximum number of troops that Rome could demand from each city.[12] At first sight, this interpretation would seem to be supported by an incident that took place in 177 BC. In that year the Samnites and Paeligni complained that their military obligations had remained the same as before, despite the fact that 4,000 of their families had migrated to the Latin

colony of Fregellae. They asked the Senate to remedy this injustice by compelling
the emigrants to return (Livy 41.8). This episode does not, however, show that the
number of troops demanded from the Samnites and Paeligni had been fixed once and
for all: what they complained about was simply that the formula used to distribute
the military burden did not reflect recent demographic developments. According to
Dionysius of Halicarnassus (6.95.2), the *foedus Cassianum* of 493 BC had required the
Romans and Latins to assist each other in war "with all their forces." Some passages
in Livy seem to point in the same direction. Thus we are told that the consuls of
219 BC were empowered to levy "as many" allied troops "as they thought fit" (Livy
21.17.2: *quantum ipsis videretur*). Similarly, a decision taken by the Senate in 217 BC
empowered Quintus Fabius Maximus "to enroll from the citizens and the allies as
many horsemen and foot-soldiers as seemed good to him" (Livy 22.11.2: *quantum
videretur*). Most probably then the bilateral treaties that regulated the relationships
between Rome and its allies in later centuries put the latter under the obligation to put
every able-bodied man into the field at Rome's request.[13] On this view, the *formula
togatorum* did not limit the requirements that Rome could make: it was no more than
a schedule used by Rome to apportion the annual military quota among its allies.

An impression of Rome's aggregate military potential can be gained from Polybius'
enumeration of Roman and allied manpower resources in 225 BC (2.24). From his
survey it appears that a theoretical total of c. 750,000 men could be mustered from
south and central Italy (including Cispadana and the Veneto). Even if many ancient
historians have found fault with Polybius' estimates and calculations,[14] there can be
no doubt that Rome could draw upon an enormous reservoir of soldiers, and that
this goes a long way to explaining its swift rise to superpower status in the second
century BC. It also appears that even if we ignore the c. 20,000 soldiers supplied
by the two Cisalpine tribes, allied forces accounted for some 60 percent of the
manpower resources available to Rome. Commenting on the origin of the Social
War of 91–88 BC, the early-imperial writer Velleius Paterculus (2.15.2) claimed that
the allies furnished twice as many soldiers as did the citizens. This is almost certainly
an exaggeration. It is true that the proportion of allied troops went up to c. two-
thirds between 200 and 190 BC, but this was a temporary increase that reflected the
high demands made on allies who had been disloyal during the Hannibalic War. In
the 170s BC the ratio of allied to Roman troops appears to have been close to
parity, and even in the late second century BC, when the burden on the allies is thought
to have been increased, their contribution was never higher than 60 percent.[15] Despite
this there can be no doubt that Velleius was right when he said that the allies had
made a crucial contribution to the wars that had won Rome a Mediterranean empire
in the second century BC.

3   The Demography of a Warrior State

It is commonly thought that the annual recruitment of tens of thousands of soldiers
had a detrimental effect on peasant smallholders in Italy and eventually undermined
Roman manpower resources. Another widely held assumption is that the Gracchan

land reforms of 133 BC were an attempt to deal with this demographic and military problem. On the face of it, Appian's account of the background to these reforms would seem to support this theory. In one passage, for instance, he describes Tiberius Gracchus as making a powerful speech in which the people of Italy (*Italiotai*) were characterized as excellent fighters but also as declining into poverty and depopulation (Appian, *B. Civ.* 1.9). Similarly, Tiberius Gracchus is said to have defended his proposal by rhetorically asking whether a citizen was not always a better man than a slave, and a soldier more useful than a non-soldier (Appian, *B. Civ.* 1.11). The same demographic and military theme is found also in Appian's description of the undoing of the Gracchan reform program, as a result of which "the numbers of both citizens and soldiers diminished still more" (*B. Civ.* 1.27).

At first sight, the census figures for the period 160–130 BC seem to tell a similar story: whereas the censors of 164/3 BC had been able to register some 337,000 adult male citizens, the census figure for 130 BC is only 319,000. Although a decrease of less than 20,000 in more than three decades may not seem huge, the general

Table 7.1 Census figures for the period 265 BC–AD 14

Year	Census figure	Source
265/4 BC	292,234	Eutropius 2.18
252/1 BC	297,797	*Per.* Livy 18
247/6 BC	241,712	*Per.* Livy 19
241/0 BC	260,000	Hieronymus, Ol. 134.1
234/3 BC	270,713	*Per.* Livy 20
209/8 BC	137,108	Livy 27.36
204/3 BC	214,000	Livy 29.37
194/3 BC	143,704	Livy 35.9
189/8 BC	258,318	Livy 38.36
179/8 BC	258,794	*Per.* Livy 41
174/3 BC	269,015	Livy 42.10
169/8 BC	312,805	*Per.* Livy 45
164/3 BC	337,022	*Per.* Livy 46
159/8 BC	328,316	*Per.* Livy 47
154/3 BC	324,000	*Per.* Livy 48
147/6 BC	322,000	Eusebius, Arm. Ol. 158.3
142/1 BC	327,442	*Per.* Livy 54
136/5 BC	317,933	*Per.* Livy 56
131/0 BC	318,823	*Per.* Livy 59
125/4 BC	394,736	*Per.* Livy 60
115/4 BC	394,336	*Per.* Livy 63
86/5 BC	463,000	Hieronymus, Ol. 173.4
70/69 BC	910,000	Phlegon fr. 12.6
28 BC	4,063,000	*Res Gestae* 8.2
8 BC	4,233,000	*Res Gestae* 8.3
AD 14	4,937,000	*Res Gestae* 8.4

trend for these years is in sharp contrast to the steep increase indicated by the census figures for the first 35 years of the second century BC. Unfortunately, there are no comparable figures for the allies.

Given the existence of this seemingly converging data, it comes as no surprise that many ancient historians have subscribed to Appian's view that Tiberius Gracchus' aim was to resolve a manpower shortage, although no agreement has been reached as to the severity of this demographic and military crisis.[16] For a long time the main challenge to this theory came from a group of specialists in the field of Italian survey archaeology, who claimed to have discovered traces of numerous small farms dating to the second century BC. Unfortunately, the realization that many of these farms may have to be dated to the period before the Second Punic War has done much to question the credibility of this attempt to undermine the prevailing orthodoxy.[17] For the rest, one of the few to dispute the notion of a pre-Gracchan manpower crisis has been John Rich, who pointed out that the slight demographic decline of the mid-second century BC must be set against the much faster decline in the average number of legions in the field that can be observed after the conclusion of the Third Macedonian War.[18] According to Rich, we must conclude that the Gracchan land reforms were not meant to deal with an acute recruitment problem. More probably the Gracchi were guided by a much vaguer concern over a slow contraction of the free Italian population, whose quantitative fate was in marked contrast to that of the proliferating foreign slaves employed on the estates of the elite.

In my view, this challenge to the traditional interpretation is convincing to the extent that it has become difficult to explain the Gracchan land reforms as an attempt to alleviate an immediate shortage of recruitable citizens. On the other hand, even if Rich's re-interpretation of the background to the *leges Semproniae agrariae* does not require us to subscribe to the traditional theory of population decline, it is at least compatible with such a theory. In short, although the idea that the Gracchi tried to solve an acute manpower crisis has lost much of its original appeal, the basic assumption that the free citizen population was in decline remains very much on the table. Yet if we want to achieve a better understanding of Roman manpower resources and of the causal connections between recruitment practices and social and economic developments, we must surely try to establish whether the Roman citizen body (and the free population of Italy as a whole) declined, stabilized, or increased during the second century BC.

One of the theories developed to account for the alleged population decline of the second century BC centers on the contrast between warfare in the third and second centuries BC. The basic idea is that, as long as Roman wars were fought in or near Italy, they were compatible with the requirements of subsistence-oriented agriculture. During much of the third century BC campaigns are thought to have been short and to have taken place mainly during the summer season, when the labor requirements of traditional agriculture were minimal. Since the legionaries returned home in autumn, they had enough time to plant and cultivate the next year's crops. This essentially harmonious relationship between war and agriculture is supposed to have been disrupted during the late third and second centuries BC. When Roman wars began to be fought in distant parts of the Mediterranean world, the old

practice of allowing citizen-soldiers to return to their farms at the end of the campaigning season was given up. Their families, unable to cultivate their plots, faced starvation
or financial ruin. As a direct result of this, many families sold or abandoned their
lands, causing the free country-dwelling population to decline.[19]

   In a recent book the American ancient historian Nathan Rosenstein has highlighted
the weaknesses of this theory.[20] For one thing, there are clear indications that as early
as the second half of the fourth century BC many Roman armies campaigned well beyond
the end of the summer season, with some armies carrying on their operations until
December or early January. Part of the explanation for this is that by the end of the
fourth century BC the Romans had introduced a system of military pay (*stipendium*) and
devised a sophisticated logistical system that freed their armies from the constraints
imposed by the harvest dates of the enemy's crops. These two developments greatly
increased the length of the Roman campaigning season, making it possible for them
to do far more damage to the enemy's economic infrastructure and to conduct lengthy
sieges. At the same time, as campaigns began to be fought in distant parts of Italy
and on Sicily, it became more usual for Roman armies to be kept in barracks during
the winter months, for the obvious reason that this dispensed with the need to start
from scratch at the beginning of the next campaigning season. In short, from the
late fourth century BC onwards there is no evidence to support the traditional notion
that furloughs in the fall and winter allowed Roman legionaries to return to their
farms in order to see to the autumn planting. In this respect the wars of the late
third and second centuries BC were not qualitatively different from those of the period
343–218 BC. The only important difference was that from 218 BC onwards *more*
Roman citizens came to take part in this system of quasi-year-round warfare.

   It could, of course, be argued that the dramatic increase in the number of citizens
in the legions that undoubtedly took place after 218 BC must have reduced the overall fertility rate by diminishing the pool of male candidates available for marriage. In
the long term this could have undermined Roman manpower resources. There are,
however, some serious problems with this theory. To begin with, the notion that
heavy recruitment led many men to postpone marriage does not take into account
that a Roman legion was structured by age groups in such a way as to reduce the
burden placed on older men.[21] As Polybius explains, a Roman legion of the third
century BC consisted of 1,200 *velites*, 1,200 *hastati*, 1,200 *principes*, and 600 *triarii*
(6.21–24).[22] Some 2,400 of these legionaries appear to have been younger than 25,
and a further 1,200 younger than 30. This means that men in their late twenties
and early thirties made up less than 15 percent of the legions. If this finding is combined with the well-known fact that it was customary for Roman men to marry in
their late twenties,[23] it follows that the wars of the late third and second centuries
BC are unlikely to have depressed the fertility rate by removing large numbers of
men from the marriage market. In any case, from the perspective of demography
the age at which men marry is less important than that of women.[24]

   If Roman warfare is unlikely to have depressed the overall fertility rate, it remains
plausible that the large-scale wars of the years 264–168 BC pushed up the number
of Roman war casualties. Did this perhaps undermine Roman manpower resources
in the long term? One of the few scholars to have explored this line of inquiry is
Dominic Rathbone, whose analysis centers on the coastal town of Cosa, founded as

a Latin colony in 273 BC.[25] From a handful of literary data it would appear that Cosa originally had between 3,500 and 5,000 colonists, living there with their families. Livy (33.24.8–9) reports that the colony was permitted to take on a further 1,000 families in 197 BC, which suggests that by then its original population had declined by about 20 to 30 percent. According to Rathbone, a decline of this order can be accounted for by assuming that on average around 700 adult men from Cosa were doing military service at any one time, that the annual casualty rate was just over 7 percent, and that when a smallholder was killed on campaign his family would then abandon his allotment in one out of four cases. Against this theory it has been pointed out that the annual call-up rate assumed by Rathbone is excessive, and that he takes insufficient account of the Roman census figures.[26] There are also some grounds for thinking that many rural households were perfectly capable of dealing with the negative consequences of heavy recruitment and high casualty rates. It has been pointed out, for instance, that much of the productive work normally carried out by men could equally well have been done by women, many of whom are likely to have become the *de facto* heads of their households during the absence of their husbands or sons.[27] Moreover, many rural households are likely to have contained an extended multi-generational family or two co-resident nuclear families. Such households would have been in a good position to adjust to temporary or permanent changes in their man-power. We cannot, in fact, rule out the possibility that in strictly economic terms the effects of conscription may have been largely positive, since many rural house-holds suffered from a structural labor overcapacity.[28] Finally, Sallares has recently argued that the free population of Cosa's rural territory in particular may well have declined not because of military death rates, but because of malaria.[29]

More recently, Rosenstein has tried to arrive at a grand estimate of Roman war losses during the years 200–133 BC. Based on an analysis of the Roman casualty figures reported by Livy he concludes that the annual rate of mortality among all recruits must have been in the order of 4.75 to 5.45 percent. Even if we assume that some 1.5 percent of all conscripts would have died of other causes if they had remained civilians, the excess mortality rate may still have been as high as 3.95 per-cent. If we apply this estimate to the total number of men conscripted between 200 and 133 BC, it appears that the wars of this period resulted in an excess mortality of approximately 200,000 among the Romans and their Italian allies.[30] Interestingly, however, there are strong indications that the early decades of the second century BC, when Roman casualties were higher than in the period 167–133 BC, witnessed a rapid expansion of the Roman citizen body (cf. below).

If these observations are combined, it would seem to follow that the demographic system of post-Hannibalic Rome was characterized not only by a high mortality rate but also by a very high fertility rate that allowed the citizen body to expand despite the excess mortality caused by large-scale warfare.

4 More Slaves, Fewer Soldiers?

As is well-known, the decline of military manpower that allegedly lay behind the Gracchan land reforms has been attributed not only to the deleterious effects of military service abroad but also to the fast expansion of rural slavery that is thought to have taken place after the Second Punic War. One prominent proponent of this view was Keith Hopkins, who emphasized the causal connection between Roman imperialism and the growth of a "slave society." As Hopkins observed, the wars of the early second century BC, especially those in the Hellenistic East, generated an enormous flow of wealth in the shape of booty and war indemnities. Most of this income flowed into the purses of the Roman elite, and a significant part of it was used to buy Italian land, partly because there were few alternative opportunities for investment and partly because landowning conferred social status. Since much of the most desirable land in central and southern Italy had previously been cultivated by free peasants, the inevitable outcome of this development was a drastic decline in their numbers. Their places were taken by foreign slaves, of whom an abundant supply was available in the form of the captives taken by Roman armies.[31]

One weakness of this reconstruction has to do with the quantitative importance of rural slavery. Although Hopkins offers no estimate for the second century BC, he thinks that urban and rural slaves made up about one-third of the Italian population in the time of Augustus. There can be little doubt that this estimate was inspired by the fact that slaves accounted for roughly 33 percent of the population of the southern part of the United States before the outbreak of the American Civil War. But why should the percentage of slaves in republican Italy have been of the same order of magnitude? In fact, some simple calculations are enough to show that even during the early empire, when Italy was far more heavily urbanized than in the second century BC, no more than about 250,000 slaves were needed to produce all the wine and all the olive oil consumed annually by the joint population of all Italian cities, including Rome. Even if during the second century BC a large proportion of the rural slave population was used to grow grain, it would seem to follow that the quantitative importance of rural slavery in pre-Gracchan Italy has been exaggerated.[32]

In the absence of hard data on the number of slaves, the theory that a fast increase in the number of slave-run *villae* caused the free population to decline has relied heavily on the census figures for the second century BC. Unfortunately, the interpretation of this vitally important data is not without its difficulties. From the late nineteenth century onwards some distinguished scholars have argued that the census figures should be interpreted as referring to those Roman citizens eligible for military service (the so-called *assidui*). This would mean that the censors were not expected to register *proletarii*. This theory is now generally believed to be incorrect.[33] More recently, Lo Cascio has suggested that the censors registered only a small proportion of the adult male citizen population because Rome was the only place where Roman citizens could register.[34] In his view, up to 70 percent of the adult male citizen population may have remained unregistered.[35] Perhaps not surprisingly, this theory has failed to convince many specialists. Overall, the most plausible reading remains that of Brunt, according to whom all census figures relating to the middle and late republic are to be interpreted as comprising all male citizens aged 17 years and over, including those aged over 45.

What then do the census figures tell us about the development of Roman manpower resources during the second century BC? As has already been noted, the figures for the period 200–168 BC suggest that the citizen body recovered quickly from the blows of the Second Punic War. For our purposes, however, the most interesting period is that between 168 and 114 BC. If we restrict ourselves to the first seven census figures that have been preserved for this period, we are left with the impression that the late 160s BC marked the beginning of a long period of slow but steady decline in the number of adult male citizens. It is, of course, tempting to follow Brunt and many others in interpreting this downward trend as the demographic background to the Gracchan land reforms of 133 BC.

There are, however, some serious problems with this superficially attractive theory. To begin with, there is the basic fact that the relatively low census figure for 130 BC is followed by much higher figures for the years 124 and 114 BC. If we are to believe these figures, the censors of 124 BC were able to register some 395,000 adult male citizens, around 75,000 more than had been registered six years earlier. This data is clearly incompatible with the theory that the Roman citizen body was in continual decline from the late 160s BC onwards. This explains why Beloch and Toynbee took the drastic and methodologically dubious step of lowering the census figures for these years by eliminating one of the initial Cs.[36] In other words, the theory of a gradual contraction of the citizen body can only be maintained by manipulating the surviving evidence.

How then do we account for the fact that the census figures for the 130s BC are lower than those for 168 and 163 BC? In my view the most plausible answer to this question remains that the relatively low census figures for the period 160–130 BC reflect the growing reluctance of many Roman citizens to serve in the army. This does not, of course, mean that every Roman citizen who lived in the country had started trying to avoid taking part in any military campaign whatsoever. Increasingly, ancient historians are becoming aware that attitudes to military service were affected by many variables, such as the amount of land held in private ownership, access to additional resources (including leaseholds), and the varying size of peasant households. Sources also indicate that the willingness of Roman citizens in general to go on campaign varied according to the cause in question, the expedition against Carthage in 149 BC proving particularly popular.[37] These important qualifications notwithstanding, the traditional view that an increasing number of citizens became less willing to serve in the army during the second century BC retains much of its original plausibility. As early as 169 BC we hear of consuls trying to avoid unpopularity by not enlisting citizens who were reluctant to serve (Livy 43.14.2–6 and 15.1). No reading of the evidence, moreover, can leave us in any doubt that the protracted and unrewarding wars fought in Spain from 154 to 133 BC resulted in considerable discontent. Sallust's description of the background to the levy of 107 BC points in the same direction: according to him the optimates reckoned that the recruitment of even a few thousand legionaries would make Marius unpopular, since the Roman *plebs* were so reluctant to serve as legionaries (*Jug*. 84.3). Put together, these snippets of information make it difficult to deny that there was considerable antipathy to military service amongst Roman citizens, especially at the time of the Spanish wars.

At this point, a few words must be said about the recent theory that many impoverished citizens were keen to serve in the army because this would provide them with supplementary income. It is true that there are good grounds for thinking that the daily *stipendium* received by Roman legionaries of the second century BC was three *asses* and that this sum equaled the value of approximately two kilograms of Sicilian grain in the time of Cicero.[38] This may seem generous. However, it should not be forgotten that deductions were made for food and clothing. Moreover, a passage from Polybius suggests that as early as the mid-second century BC many, if not all, legionaries received their weapons from the state and that the cost of these was deducted from their pay.[39] This surely means that only a small part of the money that was theoretically due was actually paid over. It is these considerations that led Nicolet to assert that booty must have been the chief appeal of military service.[40]

It may be suggested that the meagerness of military pay during the second century BC helps to explain the general lack of enthusiasm for the campaigns in Spain, where no easy victory and rich booty could be expected. At the same time the foregoing observations provide us with a plausible background for Gaius Gracchus' *lex militaris*, which provided that legionaries were to be supplied with clothing free of charge.[41] Although it would certainly be wrong to interpret this law as an attempt to alleviate an acute shortage of military manpower, its contents do suggest that service in the army was widely regarded as unattractive. Interestingly, Plutarch notes that "the poor, when they found themselves forced off the land, became more and more unwilling to offer themselves for military service" (*T. Gracc.* 8.3). Even if this generalizing passage cannot be accepted at face value, it remains plausible that impoverished peasants were often as eager to avoid military service as many of their better-off neighbors.

In short, while the high census figures for 124 and 114 BC are entirely incompatible with theories of population decline, the relatively low figures for the period 160–130 BC can be explained by assuming that a significant number of country-dwelling citizens became increasingly reluctant to serve in the legions and correspondingly eager to avoid registration by the censors.

5   The Property Qualification for Military Service

Before the threads of the foregoing discussion can be pulled together, we must also address the thorny issue of the property qualification of the fifth class. As is well known, republican Rome long stuck to the principle that only those citizens owning a certain amount of property could be called up for military service (except in emergencies). There are, however, clear indications that the threshold for military service did not remain constant during the third and second centuries BC. One important clue is that Livy, who claims to describe the system of *classes* introduced by Servius Tullius, gives the rating of the fifth class as 11,000 *asses*, whereas Polybius gives it as 400 drachmae, which is generally interpreted as representing 4,000 *asses*. Although these figures may seem straightforward, their interpretation is complicated by the fact that Rome adopted a new standard for its bronze coinage during the Second Punic War. At the outbreak of the war the bronze coinage consisted of so-called "heavy" *asses* that were coined on a weight standard of ten Roman ounces.

After 217 BC this standard was lowered several times until stability was restored in 212 or 211 BC. From then on we find a new system based on a light (so-called "sextantal") *as* of two Roman ounces. This means that at least two interpretations of the reduction of the census of the fifth class can be defended. The first of these is that both Livy and Polybius refer to the light *asses* that were used after 212/1 BC. On this interpretation the threshold for military service was reduced by roughly 64 percent. Alternatively, Livy's figure may be interpreted as representing 1,100 "heavy" *asses* (weighing 11,000 ounces). According to this reading the *census* of the fifth class was reduced by a mere 27 percent in terms of bronze.[42] Whichever of these readings is correct, there can be little doubt that the aim of this reduction was to increase the pool of potential recruits that could be fielded against Hannibal.

A far more difficult question is whether there was a further reduction in the mid-second century BC. The main evidence for this second adjustment is two passages from Gellius and Nonius, both of which define the *proletarii* as those whose property was worth less than 1,500 *asses* (A. Gellius 16.10.10, Nonius 228 L). In addition to this there is a problematic passage in the manuscript of Cicero's *De Republica* (2.40): although the original text appears to have given 1,100 (heavy?) *asses* as the rating of the fifth class, the late antique corrector of the manuscript is thought to have changed this to 1,500 *asses*. An important argument against interpreting these scanty sources as evidence for a second reduction is that none of them unambiguously refers to the second century BC. Yet there is one clue that points to this period. After defining *proletarii* as the poorest citizens whose declared *census* was less than 1,500 *asses*, Gellius goes on to explain that the term *capite censi* was used to denote those whose property was worth no more than 375 *asses*. It is generally agreed that this distinction is due to a mistake, and that the terms *proletarii* and *capite censi* referred to the same group of people. If this is the case, it becomes possible to speculate that Gellius may have misread a reference to the *census* rating of the fifth class being 375 *sestertii*, the exact equivalent of 1,500 *asses*. It would then follow that the *census* rating of 1,500 *asses* belongs to the period after 141/0 BC, when the *sestertius* became the normal official unit of reckoning of the Roman state. In terms of silver coinage the reduction of 4,000 (sextantal) *asses* to 375 sesterces would have been equal to a reduction from 400 to 94 denarii.[43] In practical terms this would have meant that henceforth the ownership of a hut and a garden sufficed to make a Roman citizen liable for legionary service.[44]

In view of the paucity and poor quality of the evidence, this reconstruction remains to a large extent conjectural. Yet, as long as no one has come up with a more convincing explanation of the two figures of 375 and 1,500 *asses*, we must at least reckon with the possibility that the census rating of the fifth class was reduced to a very low sum after Polybius wrote Book VI (c. 150 BC). Can we be more precise than this? In a well-argued article on the historical development of the Roman census ratings Dominic Rathbone suggested that the new rating of 1,500 *asses* was introduced simultaneously with the numismatic reform of 141/0 BC. A major weakness of this theory is that the putative reduction of 141/0 BC did not lead to more adult male citizens being registered in the census of 136/5 BC. Even though the censors were expected to register all adult male citizens, it is widely agreed that those belonging to the five *classes* were registered more efficiently than the proletarians (for the obvious reason that the latter were not liable for legionary service). The expansion of the fifth class, implied by the alleged lowering of the threshold for military service, should therefore have reduced the number of adult male citizens not registered by the censors. Yet the census figure for 136/5 BC is almost 10,000 lower than that for 142/1 BC.

In an influential study that was published in 1949 the Italian ancient historian Emilio Gabba argued that the threshold for military service must have been lowered in the early 120s BC. In formulating this theory he started from the assumption that the Roman census figures were to be interpreted as comprising only those Roman citizens having sufficient property to qualify for military service. In other words, Gabba held that these figures did not comprise the no doubt numerous proletarians. His next step was to interpret the sudden jump in the census figures after 131/0 BC as an indication that the census rating of the fifth class was reduced between 131/0 BC and 125/4 BC. Since this reduction must have taken place before the dramatic date of Cicero's *De Re Publica* (129 BC), he concluded that the census rating of 1,500 *asses* was introduced either in 130 BC or in 129 BC.[45]

During the second half of the twentieth century many scholars have criticized this ingenious theory on the grounds that some ancient sources use the term *capite censi* as a synonym for proletarians, and that the mere existence of this expression proves that the censors were in fact expected to register those adult male citizens whose assets fell short of the property qualification for military service.[46] Since this counterargument seemed decisive, Gabba's date for the second reduction has generally been abandoned. There are, however, some grounds for thinking that Gabba's critics have dismissed his explanation for the high census figures of 125/4 BC and 115/4 BC too easily. Of course, there can be no doubt that the surviving evidence works against the idea that the censors were expected to register *assidui* only. However, even if in theory all adult male citizens were to be registered, it seems clear that the names of many proletarians were not recorded (cf. above). For this reason the idea that the introduction of a lower threshold for military service resulted in a more efficient registration of formerly proletarian citizens retains much of its original plausibility. The only serious rival explanation for the census figures of 125/4 BC and 115/4 BC is Brunt's theory that the partial implementation of the Gracchan land reforms between 131 and 129 BC reduced the number of unregistered proletarians.[47] However, even if there may be much truth in this theory, it seems far-fetched to suppose that the assignations carried out under the *lex Sempronia agraria* of 133 BC prompted some 75,000 formerly unregistered citizens to register themselves at the census of 125/4 BC. In brief, even though one of the premises of Gabba's reading of the census figures is clearly wrong, he may well have been right to date the second lowering of the census rating of the fifth class to 130/29 BC.

Why, though, should the Roman government have thought it necessary to take such a step? Perhaps not surprisingly, many ancient historians have explained this downward adjustment as a symptom of demographic decline.[48] Against this interpretation it may be pointed out that the introduction of a lower census rating is equally compatible with a scenario of population growth: if the citizen population continued to expand during the period 168–130 BC and if this led to Roman citizens becoming poorer on average, the Roman government may have decided to lower the property requirement for military service in order to widen the basis for legionary recruitment. Moreover, the slow but steady decline in the census figures in the years 163–130 BC may well have given rise to the (erroneous) belief that the Roman citizen body had begun to shrink.[49] If this view was widely shared, it must have seemed all the more necessary to reduce the census rating of the fifth class so as to make a larger proportion of the adult male citizen population eligible for the call-up. In short, even if some politicians of the 140s and 130s BC seem to have thought that the number of Roman citizens was declining, the real problems may well have been under-registration and an increase in rural poverty that was partly the product of an ongoing process of population growth.

6 Epilogue

The principle aim of the foregoing discussion has been to show that there is no firm evidence to support the theory that Roman manpower resources were eroded by a demographic decline from the late 160s BC onwards. In fact, the few pieces of evidence we have are entirely compatible with the view that the demographic system of mid-republican Rome was characterized by a high fertility rate that more than offset the high mortality rate resulting from quasi-permanent warfare. As the census figures for the early decades of the second century demonstrate, the existence of this system made it possible for the Roman population to recover quickly from the losses suffered during the Hannibalic War. There are also indications that the number of Roman citizens continued to grow during the decades that followed. On the other hand, it seems clear that the continuing demographic expansion of this period was not accompanied by a corresponding increase in the amount of land available for cultivation by country-dwelling citizens. In this respect, there was a marked contrast with the period 200–170 BC, when many Roman citizens had benefited from colonial foundations and *assignationes viritanae*. The inevitable outcome of population growth without an expansion of the cultivable land was an increase in rural poverty.

Interestingly, the expansion of the citizen body was not reflected by the census figures for the period 163–130 BC. As we have just seen, it may well have been the slow but unmistakable downward trend in these figures that led some contemporary observers, including Tiberius Gracchus, to believe that the free citizen population was in decline. Part of the correct explanation may be that many poor citizens were reluctant to serve in the legions and correspondingly eager to avoid registration by the censors. At the same time there are grounds for thinking that the impoverishment of a growing proportion of the citizen population slowly eroded the number of *assidui*. Since potential legionaries are likely to have been registered more efficiently than their proletarian fellow citizens, this development must have decreased the number of citizens whose names were recorded by the censors. An interesting implication of this reconstruction is that any lowering of the threshold for military service was bound to reduce the rate of under-registration. It may tentatively be suggested that this causal connection helps to explain the abrupt rise in the census figures after 131/0 BC. Partial confirmation seems to be provided by Gaius Gracchus' *lex militaris*, which strongly suggests that the Roman legions of the 120s BC comprised a significant number of very poor citizens.

If these findings are correct, Gabba was right to suggest that the Roman legions had become heavily "proletarianized" some considerable time before Marius appeared on the scene. On the other hand he was almost certainly wrong to interpret this trend as the result of a steady demographic decline. More probably the gradual proletarianization of the legions was caused by a continuous demographic expansion that reduced an ever-growing number of Roman citizens to poverty during the second half of the second century BC.

NOTES

1   Brunt 1987, 418–20 and 425.
2   Brunt 1987, 674.
3   Rawson 1971, 15.
4   Brunt 1987, 77.
5   Brunt 1987, 625–7.
6   Cornell 1995, 354.
7   Hopkins 1978, 33.
8   Rich 1983, 292.
9   Hopkins 1978, 35.
10   Crawford 1996, 118.
11   Lo Cascio 1991/1994.
12   Toynbee 1965, 424–37.
13   Brunt 1987, 547.
14   For example Brunt 1987; Lo Cascio 1999b.
15   Rich 1983, 323.
16   For example Toynbee 1965; Hopkins 1978; Brunt 1987; Cornell 1996.
17   De Ligt (forthcoming).
18   Rich 1983.
19   Hopkins 1978, 29–30.
20   Rosenstein 2004, 26–52.
21   Rosenstein 2004, 85.
22   For further discussion see Connolly 1989, 152–5, and Keppie 1998, 34–5.
23   Shaw 1987.
24   De Ligt 2004, 749.
25   Rathbone 1981, 18–19.
26   Rich 1983, 296 n.44.
27   Evans 1991; Rosenstein 2004, 93–8.
28   Erdkamp 1998, 266–7.
29   Sallares 2002, 250–1.
30   Rosenstein 2004, 141–69.
31   Hopkins 1978.
32   De Ligt 2004 745–7.
33   For example Rich 1983, 293–4 and Brunt 1987, 21–5.

34 Lo Cascio 1994 and 1999b.
35 Scheidel 1996, 167–8.
36 Beloch 1886, 351; Toynbee 1965, 471.
37 Rich 1983, 317.
38 Rathbone 1993.
39 Gabba 1976, 9–10; Brunt 1987, 405.
40 Nicolet 1980, 117.
41 Rich 1983, 318–19.
42 For example Lo Cascio 1988, 293; Rathbone 1993, 144.
43 Rathbone 1993, 142 and 144.
44 Rich 1983, 298; Brunt 1987, 405–6.
45 Gabba 1976, 7–8.
46 For example Brunt 1987, 22–3.
47 Brunt 1987, 79.
48 For example Gabba 1976, 9.
49 De Ligt 2004, 751–3.

BIBLIOGRAPHY

Beloch, K. 1886. *Die Bevölkerung der griechisch-römischen Welt.* Leipzig.

Brunt, P. A. 1987². *Italian Manpower, 225 BC–AD 14.* Oxford.

Connolly, P. 1989. "The Roman army in the age of Polybius," in J. Hackett (ed.), *Warfare in the Ancient World.* London, 149–68.

Cornell, T. 1995. *The Beginnings of Rome. Italy and Rome from the Bronze Age to the Punic Wars, c. 1000–264 BC.* London.

—— 1996. "Hannibal's legacy," in T. Cornell et al. (eds.), *The Second Punic War. A Re-appraisal.* London, 97–113.

Crawford, M. 1974. *Roman Republican Coinage.* Cambridge.

—— (ed.). 1996. *Roman Statutes,* vol. I. London.

De Ligt, L. 2004. "Poverty and demography: The case of the Gracchan land reforms," *Mnemosyne* 57: 725–57.

De Ligt, L. Forthcoming. "The economy: Agrarian change during the second century BC," in N. Rosenstein and Robert Morstein-Marx (eds.), *A Companion to the Roman Republic.* Oxford.

Erdkamp, P. 1998. *Hunger and the Sword. Warfare and Food Supply in Roman Republican Warfare (264–30 BC).* Amsterdam.

Evans, J. 1988. "Resistance at home: The evasion of military service in Italy during the second century BC," in T. Yuge and M. Doi (eds.), *Forms of Control and Subordination in Antiquity.* Tokyo, 121–40.

—— 1991. *War, Women and Children in Ancient Rome.* London.

Gabba, E. 1976. *Republican Rome. The Army and the Allies.* Oxford.

Hopkins, K. 1978. *Conquerors and Slaves.* Cambridge.

Ilari, V. 1974. *Gli italici nelle strutture militari romane.* Milan.

Keppie, L. 1998². *The Making of the Roman Army. From Republic to Empire.* London.

Lo Cascio, E. 1988. "Ancora sui censi minimi delle classi cinque 'Serviane,'" *Athenaeum* 76: 273–302.

—— 1991/1994. "I *togati* della 'formula togatorum,'" *Annuali dell'Istituto Italiano per gli Studi Storici* 12: 309–28.

—— 1994. "The size of the Roman population: Beloch and the meaning of the Augustan census figures," *JRS* 84: 23–40.

—— 1999a. "The population of Roman Italy in town and country," in J. Bintliff and K. Sbonias (eds.), *Reconstructing Past Population Trends in Mediterranean Europe (3000 BC–AD 1800)*. Oxford, 161–71.

—— 1999b. "Populazione e risorse agricole nell'Italia del II secolo a.C.," in D. Vera (ed.), *Demografia, Sistemi Agrari, Regimi Alimentari nel Mondo Antico*. Bari, 217–45.

—— 2001. "Recruitment and the size of the Roman population from the third to first century BCE," in W. Scheidel (ed.), *Debating Roman Demography*. Leiden, 111–38.

—— 2004. "Il rapporto uomini-terra nel paesaggio dell'Italia romana," *Index* 33: 1–15.

Morley, N. 2001. "The transformation of Italy, 225–28 BC. *JRS* 91: 50–62.

Nicolet, C. 1978. "Le stipendium des alliés italiens avant la guerre sociale," *PBSR* 46: 1–11. Repr. in *Censeurs et publicains. Économie et fiscalité dans la Rome antique*. Paris 2000, 93–103.

—— 1980. *The World of the Citizen in Republican Rome*. Berkeley.

Rathbone, D. 1981. "The development of agriculture in the Ager Cosanus during the Roman Republic. Problems of evidence and interpretation," *JRS* 71: 10–23.

—— 1993. "The census qualification of the *assidui* and the *prima classis*," in H. Sancisi-Weerdenburg et al. (eds.), *De Agricultura. In Memoriam Pieter Willem de Neeve (1945–1990)*. Amsterdam, 121–52.

Rawson, E. 1971. "The literary sources for the pre-Marian army," *PBSR* 26: 13–31.

Rich, J. 1983. "The supposed Roman manpower shortage of the later second century BC," *Historia* 32: 287–331.

Rosenstein, N. 2002. "Marriage and manpower in the Hannibalic War: *Assidui, proletarii* and Livy 24.18.7–8," *Historia* 51: 163–91.

—— 2004. *Rome at War. Farms, Families and Death in the Middle Republic*. Chapel Hill.

Roth, J. 1994. "The size and organization of the imperial legion," *Historia* 43: 346–62.

Sallares, R. 2002. *Malaria and Rome. A History of Malaria in Ancient Italy*. Oxford.

Salmon, E. T. 1982. *The Making of Roman Italy*. London.

Scheidel, W. 1996. *Measuring Sex, Age and Death in the Roman Empire. Explorations in Ancient Demography*. Ann Arbor.

—— 2004. "Human mobility in Roman Italy, I: The free population," *JRS* 94: 1–26.

Shaw, B. D. 1987. "The age of Roman girls at marriage: Some reconsiderations," *JRS* 77: 30–46.

Toynbee, A. 1965. *Hannibal's Legacy. The Hannibalic War's Effect on Roman Life*. London.

Wulff Alonso, F. 1991. *Romanos e itálicos en la Baja República. Estudios sobre sus relaciones entre la Segunda Guerra Púnica y la Guerra Social (201–91 a.C.)*. Brussels.

FURTHER READING

In recent years a growing number of scholars have expressed dissatisfaction with the standard view that the Roman citizen body (and the free population of Italy as a whole) declined or stabilized during the mid-second century BC. Initially, the main challenge came from a number of archaeologists, whose contributions to the debate are summarized in my contribution to the *Blackwell Companion to the Roman Republic*. More recently, ancient historians have come up with new (and often mutually exclusive) interpretations not only of Polybius' manpower figures but also of the census figures of the last two centuries BC. See e.g. Lo Cascio 1994 and 1999; Scheidel 1996, 167–168 and 2004; Morley 2001; De Ligt 2004. This has also led to re-interpretations of the literary evidence concerning the "manpower crisis" that allegedly lay behind the Gracchan land reforms.

On the size of legions during the last two centuries of the republic, see Roth 1994. Cf. Keppie 1998, for the view that the size of the post-Marian legion was c. 5,000 rather than c. 6,000. Although Brunt 1987 is lucid on the *formula togatorum*, Ilari 1974 offers a more detailed discussion of this topic. On the financial obligations of the allies see Nicolet 1978. Cf. also Wulff Alonso 1991, for a general discussion of their contribution to the Roman war effort and on the officers commanding allied units.

On the effects on warfare on the agrarian economy, both during the Hannibalic war and in the second century BC see the revisionist accounts of Erdkamp 1998 and Rosenstein 2004.

The best recent discussions of the census rating of the fifth class are Lo Cascio 1988 and Rathbone 1993. There is, however, a large body of earlier literature, from which I single out Toynbee 1965; Crawford 1974; Gabba 1976, 2–10; and Rich 1983. A closely related topic is the number of *proletarii* at the time of the Hannibalic War and during the second century BC, on which widely divergent views have been expressed by Rich 1983; Brunt 1987; and Rosenstein 2002.

CHAPTER EIGHT

Military Command, Political Power, and the Republican Elite

Nathan Rosenstein

1 Introduction

At Rome under the republic, as in most societies throughout the ancient Mediterranean, the wealthy and well-born ruled. After the fall of the monarchy c. 509 (all dates BC), members of the Roman aristocracy – comprising the senators, numbering 300 down to Sulla's reforms in 81 and 600 thereafter, their close male relatives, and other men of comparable economic and social status who aspired to a leading role in the city's public affairs – competed among themselves to gain election to a limited number of public offices. The winners enjoyed substantial power over the lives of their countrymen and others during their year in office and a lifetime of honor and influence thereafter. The arbiters of this competition were the citizens of Rome who, meeting in the assemblies of the centuries or the tribes, selected among the several contenders every year. Because the duties of several of these offices (particularly the highest, the two consuls elected annually as heads of state and often one or more of the praetors who ranked just below them), included leading the republic's armies, politics powerfully affected Roman warfare. At no time did a cadre of professional officers command the city's armed forces. Rather, just as military service was incumbent upon every male citizen, an obligation embedded at the very core of what it meant to be a Roman citizen, so, too, was military command simply a facet of political leadership, part of what it meant to be a Roman aristocrat and the fruit of electoral success.

But warfare bulked equally large in republican politics. Constant military pressure between the early fifth and the mid-fourth centuries had threatened the city's very existence, and the imperatives of survival forced Roman society to change in critical ways. Among the most important was the inception or acceleration of an ethos among the city's elite of service to the republic and its citizens. For any aristocrat what matter most are honor, rank, and preeminence among his or her peers, and for the aristocracy of the Roman Republic these derived almost exclusively from action on behalf of their community. And because throughout these years of crisis the greatest benefits that one could bestow on one's fellow citizens were those that contributed to success in the wars that ensured the city's survival, that ethos was highly martial. Although the Roman historian Sallust lived centuries later, long after Rome had become a great power, his description of Rome in the republic's early years captures this spirit well:

> But it is amazing to recall how much the state grew in a brief time once it had gained its liberty, so passionate was the desire for glory (*cupido gloriae*) that arose among them. To begin with, as soon as the young men were ready for war, they learned the practice of soldiering through hard work in camp, and they took their pleasure in weapons and war horses rather than in whores and feasting. So no toil was unfamiliar to such men, no place was rough or steep, no armed enemy formidable. Courage (*virtus*) conquered all. Rather they waged their greatest struggle among themselves over glory. Each man rushed to strike an enemy, mount a wall, to make himself conspicuous in the doing of such a deed. These things they accounted as riches, this was a fine reputation (*bona fama*), this was great nobility. They were eager for praise (*laus*), but open-handed with their money. They wanted immense glory but honorable wealth. (Sallust, *Cat.* 7.3–6)

Courage (*virtus*) on the battlefield brought glory (*gloria*), praise (*laus*), and renown (*fama*) and these in turn were the foundation for a political career throughout much of the republic. Although achievements in the civilian sphere were not inconsequential in the calculus of political success, it is fair to say that from the early third to the early first centuries, an aristocrat could not hope to compete for public office without having first proven himself on the battlefield.[1] The voters who selected among the contenders for public office, after all, constituted the soldiers of Rome; they were often choosing the man who would lead many of them to war. And throughout his life, the success an aristocrat achieved in those wars heavily influenced his prospects for further electoral success, a fact that held true even down to the end of the republic. Warfare affected political competition at Rome just as much as politics did war – if not more so.

2   Courage and the Aristocratic Ethos

Source problems bedevil our understanding of events and developments during the early and much of the middle republic, from the late sixth century to the late third. Not until the early and middle years of the second century do our sources allow us to gain an impression of political culture sufficiently detailed to permit scattered bits of earlier evidence and information drawn from later authors to be worked into a general picture of the period from c. 300 to c. 100. Our principal informant for conditions in this era is Polybius, a Greek aristocrat from Achaea deported to Rome as a hostage in 167 where he lived for many years on terms of familiarity with members of some of the leading Roman political families of the day. Polybius wrote an insightful and highly regarded history of his times in order to explain to his countrymen how Rome had come to dominate the Mediterranean world. Large parts of this work survive, and what Polybius has to say about the character of the Romans reveals much about the value system that animated the republican elite of this era. Polybius regarded courage as "nearly the most essential virtue in any state, but particularly so at Rome" (31.29.1) and stressed to his readers that the Romans had many ways of inculcating in their young men a desire to win a reputation for valor. As one example, he described in a well-known passage (6.53.1–54.1) their custom whenever a famous man died: masks of not only the deceased but all his ancestors were paraded to the forum worn by men dressed in the robes and preceded by the symbols of the offices each ancestor had held. The son of the deceased or other close male relative eulogized him, emphasizing his achievements, and then similar speeches were made for each of the ancestors.[2] The result, Polybius writes, was that, "young men are thus inspired to undergo every suffering on behalf of the public welfare for the sake of gaining the glory that attends brave men" (6.54.3).

Unspoken but unmistakable here is the presumption that those who won a reputation for valor would go on to hold the offices and achieve the victories celebrated in the obsequies Polybius describes. The result was an intense pressure on young aristocrats at the very least not to fall short of the courage expected of them. The son of the Elder Cato lost his sword during the battle of Pydna in 168, and rather than suffer this shame threw himself into the fighting along with a number of comrades in a frantic attempt to recover his weapon (found ultimately, we are told, under a pile of enemy corpses: Plutarch, *Cato Mai.* 20.7–8). But far better that simply not falling short was to achieve some striking feat of arms. Marcus Claudius Marcellus (cos. 222 etc.) won a great name for himself as a young man when he saved his brother's life during a battle (Plutarch, *Marc.* 2.1–2); and P. Cornelius Scipio Aemilianus about a century later made his mark when in his thirties he defeated and killed an enemy soldier in a duel in Spain (Livy, *Per.* 48; Appian, *Iber.* 53). Such feats, Polybius notes, brought renown first in the praise generals bestowed in speeches before their armies and then in the decorations they awarded: headless spears, medallions, and various crowns such as the civic (*corona civica*) made of oak leaves for saving a fellow citizen's life or the mural crown of gold (*corona muralis*) for being first to scale an enemy's wall (Polybius 6.39.1–11). Soldiers gained these decorations not simply for braving the ordinary dangers of combat but for extraordinary courage above and beyond the call of duty. To win the civic crown required not simply saving another citizen's life; a Roman had to slay the enemy threatening him without yielding ground in the fight (A. Gellius 6.5.13). Likewise a soldier despoiled an enemy only after having killed him in a man-to-man encounter (A. Gellius 2.11.3). These decorations testified to the risks one had run on behalf of one's fellow citizens; spoils hung outside a victor's doorway announced his courage to all who had not been there to witness it. And the connection between the valor and service to the republic that such trophies demonstrated and subsequent success in the political arena is unmistakably clear. In the aftermath of Rome's great disaster at Cannae in 216 a special supplementary selection of senators was undertaken to replace the many who had died there and in previous defeats against Hannibal. The magistrate empowered to do the choosing, Marcus Fabius Buteo, announced that he would select first those who had held various minor offices and then, "those who had spoils taken from the enemy on display in their homes or who had been decorated for saving the life of a citizen in combat" (Livy 23.23.5–6). Patently in Fabius' view those who had demonstrated exceptional courage in battle were those worthy to assume a leading role in the political life of the community. The voters regularly agreed. Marcellus' bravery lifted him to the office of *curule aedile*; the reputation Gaius Marius gained as a soldier won him unanimous election to one of the first offices on his rise up the political ladder (Sallust, *Jug.* 63.3–4, compare Plutarch, *Marius* 3.2–4.1); and Scipio's duel and other feats in Spain and Africa helped elevate him to a consulship at an extraordinarily early age (Appian, *Pun.* 112).[3]

Young aristocrats spent long years at war. According to Polybius, no one at Rome could run for public office until he had completed ten years of military service (6.19.5), a requirement that was probably long-standing by the mid-second century. Most of those years would have been spent in the cavalry.[4] Rome drew its mounted soldiers from the wealthiest segment of its citizenry, thought to be those who in the second century possessed property worth more than 1,000,000 *asses* (about 62,500 pounds of bronze).[5] We happen to know from Polybius that in 225 they numbered probably around 23,000 out of 283,000 citizens able to bear arms.[6] However, the Romans distinguished two different categories of cavalry, those who provided their own horses (*equites equis suis*) and a smaller, select group of 1,800 whose horses were furnished at public expense (*equites equo publico*). The former were introduced c. 403 (Livy 5.7.13); the latter were a holdover from an earlier stage in the Roman army's development. By the second century if not earlier *equites equo publico* constituted a social and political – but not a military – elite. Their members were chosen by the censors for enrollment in one of the eighteen equestrian centuries that, until the middle of the third century, voted in a privileged position in the assembly of the centuries. Membership was a mark of honor reserved for members of the Senate (at least until 123) and other aristocrats. But otherwise *equites equo publico* and *equites equis suis* were mixed indiscriminately among the 300 cavalrymen who served with each Roman legion.

But whether they served with their own or a public horse, members of the republic's upper class formed the republic's cavalry because it was more honorable to serve there than in the infantry. Their superior status within the army reflected their social position in civilian life. That superiority is clear in Polybius' description of their duties in camp, in their higher rates of pay, the larger donatives they collected at triumphs, and the bigger allotments of land they received when colonies were founded. The wealthy also served in the cavalry because it was more expensive to do so: cavalrymen employed three mounts and were attended by two slaves on campaign.[7] Social and economic factors thus differentiated the military service owed by aristocrats from that required of ordinary citizens. But cavalry service entailed a political benefit as well because, as Polybius emphasizes, decorations for valor were awarded "to those who in skirmishes and other similar actions, where there is no need to endanger themselves in individual combat, willingly and deliberately put themselves in such situations" (6.39.4). Cavalry combat and the cavalry's role in military operations generally offered many opportunities to display bravery of this sort, far more than service as an infantryman, and hence more chances to exhibit the courage that would help pave the way for future electoral success. Interestingly, until the Hannibalic War Roman cavalrymen fought without the benefit of effective defensive armor, probably because of the greater freedom of movement and comfort that the absence of heavy armor allowed. However one consequence – if not a cause – of this preference was the greater likelihood of sustaining wounds, and honorable scars – those on the front of the body – were a visible symbol of one's courage. They unmistakably demonstrated sacrifice on behalf of one's countrymen, and hence their display was tantamount to a claim to political authority like the one Marcus Servilius Pulex Geminus (cos. 202) made in 167 when in seeking to sway an assembly he tore off his toga and pointed to his scars, describing where and when he had received each one (Livy 45.39.16–17).

3   Warfare and the First Steps in a Political Career

During this period of cavalry service, young aristocrats became eligible to seek election to the office of military tribune (*tribunus militum*).[8] Every legion had six. They were its junior officers and performed a variety of duties under the overall command of a magistrate who possessed *imperium* (see below). The six tribunes together selected the recruits for their legion during a levy and administered the military oath to them; they enforced discipline and supervised various activities like the layout and fortification of a marching camp and the organization of its sentries; and they saw to the general welfare of their troops. Although a legion comprised 30 maniples along with ten squadrons of ten cavalrymen and 1,200 light armed *velites*, nothing indicates that charge of a specific group of maniples, squadrons, or *velites* rested with each tribune. Rather, the tribunes were general offices, and there appears to have been no permanent division of responsibility among them. Pairs of tribunes did exercise overall command of their legion by turns for a month at a time, and each pair probably alternated command on a daily basis. Possibly, too, the tribune whose turn it was to take charge of his legion on the day of a battle exercised tactical control during combat in the absence of the general. Otherwise we do not know that particular tribunes regularly led specific components of their legions in battle. However, from the frequent reports of the deaths of military tribunes it is clear that their duties could bring them into close contact with the enemy – into the "killing zone" – along with the legionaries.[9] But tribunes could also undertake a variety of other duties – leading independent detachments or scouting, for example.

The assembly of the tribes elected the 24 military tribunes who served in the four legions allotted to the two consuls each year. Of those chosen, according to Polybius, 14 had to have at least five years' service and the others ten (6.19.1–2). This regulation seems to have been introduced not long before Polybius came to Rome; we know of tribunes in the third century who were much younger men. When Rome fielded more than four legions, as was frequently the case beginning with the outbreak of the Hannibalic War, tribunes known as *rufuli* were appointed by their commanders for the additional legions. When consular legions were kept in the field beyond a magistrate's year in office, their tribunes likewise were usually continued in their posts as *rufuli* until the legions were disbanded. While most tribunes were young aristocrats just starting out on a political career, this was not inevitably the case. Because their duties could sometimes entail substantial responsibilities in the second century, more seasoned aristocrats not uncommonly held these posts. Cato the Elder, for example, was elected military tribune in 191, despite having already been consul and celebrated a triumph four years earlier (Cicero, *Sen.* 32).[10] Gradually, however, the practice developed of giving such senior figures the rank of legate (*legatus*). The Senate appointed a legate on the recommendation of the magistrate under whom he would serve. Because legates were generally older, more experienced men, they formed what might be termed an army's senior officers, although it is not clear that there was ever a formal system of ranks during the middle republic. Legates were often delegated important independent commands by their magistrates. So Titus Quinctius Flamininus had his brother Lucius appointed legate when he was consul in 198 and given charge of a fleet to conduct what were virtually independent naval operations against King Philip during the Second Macedonian War. Legates might also serve as military advisers to magistrates, as Scipio Africanus famously did for his brother Lucius Cornelius Scipio when the latter was consul in 190, in order that Africanus might direct the campaign that would ultimately conquer King Antiochus the Great of Syria.

There were other officers as well. Roman armies were not constituted entirely of citizen legions. Contingents of allies (*socii*) fought alongside them, and their numbers equaled and often exceeded those of the legionaries. Allied troops were organized into two "wings" (*alae*), each of which was commanded by three prefects (*praefecti*) who were Roman citizens and probably three from the allies.[11] In either case, these officers, like the military tribunes, were drawn from the upper classes of either Rome or the allied communities. Little is known about their duties, but they were probably similar to those of the tribunes. Rome's naval forces in the third century, at least down to the Hannibalic War, were under the charge of a pair of magistrates known as *duumviri navales* ("the two naval men"). They, like the military tribunes, were elected by the assembly of the tribes and served under the overall command of the consuls. Their duties seem mainly to have been connected with coastal defense, since when major naval operations were in prospect, magistrates of consular or praetorian rank or legates conducted them, and it is unclear whether *duumviri* were elected every year or only as the occasion demanded. Finally, each magistrate commanding an army would have a quaestor serving under him. The assembly of the tribes elected quaestors, and their duties were primarily administrative. They kept records of the army's disbursements and income and saw to the legionaries' pay and the collection and distribution of their rations. But their duties might also entail military command in the absence or incapacity of the commander. In 119, the quaestor Marcus Annius organized a counter-attack against a force of Scordisci who had invaded Macedon and twice defeated them after the praetor under whom he was serving had fallen in battle.[12]

At the end of his ten-year period of military service, at around 28, an aristocrat would begin his political career, standing for election to a sequence of public offices, the *cursus honorum*, that would culminate, if he was successful at every stage, with tenure of the consulship or, for a very few, the censorship. Yet despite the era's constant wars and the importance of gaining a reputation for valor, most of the offices he would seek on his way to a consulship were civilian in character. The quaestorship, the first of these, might involve duties connected with a military campaign but more often did not. The activities of the four aediles and ten tribunes of the *plebs* elected each year in the tribal assembly were confined to the city of Rome. Even the praetors were more usually administrators or presiding officers at judicial tribunals than generals. When it came time to elect the consuls who regularly did lead Rome's armies to war in this era, therefore, the candidates who (like those seeking the praetorship) came before the voters in the assembly of the centuries presented a much wider spectrum of experience and achievements than simply what they had gained on the battlefield, and accomplishments there went into the scales alongside other, less bellicose services to the republic when merit was being weighed. The duties of aediles included, among other things, the provision of games to honor the gods (and not coincidentally entertain the public), and voters could often be mindful of their splendor when an aedile later stood for the consulship. Likewise the stance a tribune of the *plebs* took in defense of the interests of the people and the laws he promulgated in pursuance thereof might heavily affect the public's perception of his worthiness for higher office. Equally important were actions undertaken in a private capacity on behalf of individuals: service as a patron, especially as an advocate in the law courts. The support of other aristocrats, particularly senior figures, also went into the mix. Above all, lineage mattered. The ranks of the republic's consuls were filled mostly with the descendants of consuls, particularly their sons and grandsons, whose ancestors' services to the republic and its citizens the voters regularly remembered and rewarded. The highest political offices were not closed to outsiders, but they faced an uphill battle in the face of this preference for the scions of eminent families. To characterize the republic's aristocracy as a "warrior elite" as is sometimes done therefore misleads. In the constant rivalry for public office that was the lifeblood of republican politics, a reputation for courage gained on the battlefield unquestionably meant much, particularly to a young man just starting out up the *cursus honorum*, but many other things did too. Ultimately, services to the Roman people – collectively and individually, one's own and one's ancestors' – were what the voters rewarded; these and an ethos that put commitment to serving the republic above all else. Service in war was simply one element among many, albeit a very large one.

4   Command

Consequently, the magistrates who led Rome's armies to war might or might not have displayed any special aptitude for generalship prior to their election. Those praetors who had celebrated triumphs for victories won in that office unquestionably gained an advantage in their pursuit of a consulship, and most of them were successful. But as already noted, praetors did not usually conduct major military operations; that was the job of the consuls. So former praetors rarely came before the voters with anything more than a presumption of competence as a general. Nor did anything like the formal training a modern military officer receives exist. Young aristocrats during their ten years with the legions might have the opportunity to observe their general go about his duties, particularly if they were among the group of young men attached to the commander's retinue, his "tent-mates" (*contubernales*). Such instruction was very much in keeping with the norms of civilian life, where aristocratic education was a matter of observing one's elders, particularly one's father and his friends, imitating their actions, and absorbing their precepts. The military tribunate afforded actual experience in command, but it is not known for how many years a young man might hold this post, or if it was even obligatory. Toward the latter part of the second century, as Roman aristocrats became increasingly conversant with Greek culture, Hellenistic military handbooks seem to have become a source of military knowledge, although how regularly and systematically they were utilized we do not know. Certainly, the historian Sallust could portray Marius, on his election to the consulship in 107, contrasting his long, practical experience of war with the ignorance of his aristocratic rivals, who when they became consuls had to get their knowledge from books (Sallust, *Jug.* 85.11–12). But this may reflect contemporary political polemic more than reality.

Still, the fact remains that the consuls and praetors who led Rome's armies were not usually experienced generals, and – even more striking – laws were in place that kept it so. Beginning in 342, repetition of the consulship was limited: first to once every ten years and then c. 151 forbidden altogether. Exceptions are known and explanations can be offered, but the restriction itself seems on the face of it to conflict with the demands of military effectiveness. Had not generals who won victories demonstrated a superior aptitude for command? Why then place armies in the hands of someone with little or no prior experience instead of someone who had proven he could get the job done? Yet even in the crisis of the Hannibalic War, the Senate never sought to suspend competition for the consulate in order to place the republic's best generals in charge of the war (although it did then and subsequently often keep successful generals in their provinces for a year or two beyond their year in office as proconsuls or *propraetors* ["acting consuls" or "acting praetors"], but this practice was mainly a response to the limited number of regular annual magistrates the Senate could deploy for the tasks at hand each year rather than a means of ensuring competence in command). Indeed, the practice of assigning the conduct of specific military operations by lot made the question of which consul or praetor got to lead a particular war a matter of chance. Perhaps most curiously of all, generals who *lost* battles were not only not punished for those failures but went on to win political success in equal measure with their aristocratic peers. Some even led Roman armies once again.[13]

The explanation for this odd state of affairs lies in the interplay among the demands of politics, ideology, and war. Honor and glory were paramount for every aristocrat, and these could only be acquired through service to the Roman people. Because command of the wars that vanquished Rome's enemies, protected the city, and enlarged its hegemony represented the greatest services to the state, the magistracies that bestowed it were the source of the greatest glory and so were eagerly, even desperately, sought since family luster never guaranteed preeminence at Rome. Aristocrats in each generation had to validate their claim to a place among the republic's elite by equaling or surpassing the honor and achievements of their ancestors. Hence great danger lay in the monopolization of high office by a single figure or small clique, for the anger and resentment of those excluded from magistracies could engender bitterness, political strife, and possibly even civil war. Conflict over access to honor – in the form of the plebeians' demand for access to the consulship and other offices – had once already rent the republic during the Struggle of the Orders. Only timely compromise in the face of grave military threats had forestalled its destruction. Political concord therefore required that military efficiency yield to the needs of aristocratic cohesion. Although it might seem inevitable that a city so often at war would naturally seek to ensure that generals of proven ability led its armies, particularly when many of the voters who elected the consuls would serve as soldiers under them, at Rome this was not typically the case. Opportunities to hold the consulship and win glory and honor through leadership in war instead circulated widely among the aristocracy, even though this meant debarring by statute Rome's best generals from repeated command.

Religious beliefs and the nature of combat itself helped sustain this primacy of political over military necessity. In the minds of the Romans, their republic's prosperity and success stemmed fundamentally from the relationship between themselves and their heavenly protectors, the *pax deorum* (the "peace of the gods"). They thought of themselves not as the cleverest or the strongest people but unquestionably the most religious (Cicero, *Nat. Deo.* 2.8, *Har.* 19). Thus military victory was ultimately the product of effective religious ritual: as long as the apparatus of the public cult was operating properly, success on the battlefield would follow. Conversely, military defeat signaled that some religious error had occurred, usually unnoticed but occasionally willful. Generals, particularly consuls, had important religious responsibilities, but their duties were mechanical. Anyone could perform the rituals provided he knew the proper procedures and followed them scrupulously, which made it possible for many different men to assume the consulship. Victory did not depend on some special favor or blessing that the gods had bestowed upon a particular individual. Although from time to time such notions surfaced, they never attained general currency.

Similarly, ideas about what won their wars helped sustain confidence that the practice of changing consuls every year did not undermine Roman military power. Victory was usually the result of one or more set-piece battles whose outcomes depended much more on the discipline, determination, and valor of the legionaries and allied troops than on the tactical or strategic skills of their commanders. Soldiers had to maintain good order and cohesion within their maniples under the enormous pressure of hand-to-hand combat, moving forward into the zone of direct contact with the enemy, fighting effectively, and falling back to allow fresh men to take their places without disrupting the ranks and files of their formations. The maniple as a whole had to be able to move up into or withdraw from the front line without falling into disorder, being driven back, and so routed. When the Romans lost battles, the tendency was to blame the soldiers. After the defeat at the Trebia River in 218, where Hannibal had clearly out-generaled the Roman commander, the Senate, Polybius informs us, attributed the defeat to their soldiers' lack of training (3.106.5). And following the disaster at Cannae two years later, when Hannibal's tactical skills had again crushed the Romans, the Senate shipped the survivors off to Sicily for the duration where they were visited with every variety of indignity and punishment, while their commander, Varro, was thanked for "not having despaired of the state" (Livy 22.61.14, 23.25.7–8, 24.18.9, 25.7.3–4, 27.11.14).

Consequently, because the outcome of battle was thought to depend mainly on the favor of the gods and the quality of their soldiers, the Romans did not have to believe that any particular commander made a unique, essential contribution to securing victory. The importance of a specific leader could be de-emphasized. Generals of course had a wide range of practical responsibilities. They had to levy troops when new legions were required, train them, move them to the theater of war (*provincia*), organize the logistics that supported the army, obtain and evaluate intelligence, find the enemy, bring him to battle and, if all went well, win. But little of this required highly specialized knowledge or training beyond what might have been absorbed during any aristocrat's early service in the ranks. Many of the practices were undoubtedly so well established as to be common knowledge. The Roman order of battle, for example, seems to have varied little if at all over the course of more than two centuries. Writings also may have existed setting out how things were to be done. Polybius' famous descriptions of the levying and organization of a Roman army and of the layout of a marching camp appear to have been drawn from a handbook for military tribunes. Similar crutches may well have existed for commanders, therefore.[14] Other practices were simple in the extreme: when a commander wished to assemble his troops in his *provincia*, for example, he had them swear an oath to be at a particular place by a particular day and then left it up to them to make their own way there.

Combat itself rarely involved a high degree of maneuver or coordination of various arms, so that the degree to which success or failure depended upon "command and control" by a general was limited. It was essential to know when and how to move fresh maniples or allied cohorts up into the front line and withdraw weary ones, but the military tribunes and centurions will have played a vital role in passing this information to their commander and in executing his orders. Otherwise, victory depended mainly on the efforts of the soldiers. Hence a general's efforts to furnish a model for his men were far more critical: urging them on, letting himself be seen near the front lines sharing their danger, and presenting an image of the courage and determination that they would need to bear up under the extreme pressure of hand-to-hand combat. But displaying valor was well within the capacity of any aristocrat who had spent his young manhood serving in the cavalry and earning a reputation for courage and self-sacrifice. The belief that a general's moral character was what really counted in the heat of battle in turn constituted a vital part of the ideological underpinning for the practice of distributing military command and opportunities to win honor and glory widely among the republic's political elite.

Apart from battle, generals were responsible for conducting relations with foreign and allied peoples within their *provinciae*, and the parameters within which they operated were quite broad. Diplomacy was formally the domain of the Senate, but the Senate allowed magistrates in the field a great deal of latitude to make war or peace and otherwise act as they saw fit, particularly as the republic's military operations took its armies farther and farther from Italy, inhibiting rapid communication between Rome and the frontiers.[15] But even within Italy the Senate's primary concerns in its diplomatic dealings were less practical than moral: to uphold the majesty of the Roman people; to protect Rome's friends; and to punish severely those who harmed them or failed to show proper respect to Rome. The details mattered little, and serious conflict between the Senate and a magistrate over the execution of policy was rare. Yet when it occurred, the extraordinarily broad powers a magistrate possessed in his *provincia*, embodied in the *imperium* and *auspicia* (the power to command and the right to consult the gods) bestowed upon him by his election and the ceremonies surrounding his entry into office, made it difficult for the Senate to enforce its will. In the main however, smooth relations between the Senate and its generals were the rule rather than the exception because these depended less upon a general carrying out explicit instructions than on acting in accord with a shared sense of what the interests of Rome required. And this moral consensus on the republic's dignity and the deference to it expected of others was the common possession of every Roman aristocrat, which again made it possible to entrust the implementation of foreign policy to any one of them.

5   Military Laurels and Political Power

After their year in office, generals returned to Rome, except for those the Senate made proconsuls or *propraetors*, whose commands usually continued for an additional year or two. Commanders who had won an important victory would convene the Senate outside the *pomerium* (the ritual boundary of the city, not coterminous with the urban area) to request a triumph. Here politics might intrude on military and diplomatic concerns. Ideally, a victory worthy of a triumph had resulted in the complete pacification of the *provincia* and the end of the war. But matters were not always clear cut, and opposition sometimes arose from rivals and enemies within the Senate. Not every claimant was awarded his triumph.[16] Those who did received a formal vote from the assembly of the centuries allowing them to march their armies into the city (weapons were otherwise forbidden within the *pomerium*) in a procession both solemn and boisterous. Booty was on display and often pictures of key moments in the war or models of cities captured, helpfully labeled. The general followed in a chariot wearing a richly embroidered toga (the *toga picta*), his face painted red (for reasons not really understood), with a slave standing behind holding a laurel wreath over his head and repeating, "Remember you are human." His most eminent captives (who would later be put to death) preceded him, his children rode with him, and his army followed. The procession ended at the temple of Jupiter Greatest and Best, the protector of the city, on the Capitoline Hill where the general offered sacrifice in thanks for victory (Plutarch, *Aem.* 32.1–35.4; Pliny, *Nat.* 33.111–12; Epictetus, *Disc.* 3.24.85). The construction of temples in fulfillment of vows to particular gods for victories or other monuments often followed. Generals decorated them and sometimes other public buildings with art looted from conquered cities or sometimes paintings depicting their campaigns. Booty also adorned their houses – weapons and other spoils taken from the enemy – which remained in place even when the house changed owners. All this helped to secure for a general's achievement a lasting place in the public's collective memory.

A triumph proclaimed unmistakably that an aristocrat's victory had bestowed a great benefit upon the Roman people, thereby staking his claim to great honor, and honor was a key to political power. It implicitly but powerfully demanded deference. Those who had rendered extraordinary service to the republic were men of great authority (*auctoritas*) whose advice was difficult if not impossible to ignore.[17] Who knew better what the interests of the Roman people were than one who had so well served them in the past? As Publius Cornelius Scipio Nasica once said, chastising an unruly assembly, "Quite, please, Citizens, for I know better than you what is good for the republic" (Valerius Max. 3.7.3). Occasionally, however, the benefit that a victory conferred was so great and the honor that accrued so enormous that the resultant *auctoritas* threatened to disrupt political equilibrium within the aristocracy. Refusing a triumph was out of the question, for that would have been to neglect to thank the gods. But thereafter such men often faced determined opposition from the rest of the senators who feared their collective authority would be overwhelmed. For Scipio Africanus, for example, following his conquest of Hannibal at Zama in 202 to end the Second Punic War, for Marius after defeating the Germans at Aquae Sextae and Vercellae at the close of the second century, and a few others, the consequences of their victories both enlarged and at the same time set limits on their political power.

6   The Late Republic

The relationship between war, the aristocracy, and politics that prevailed during Rome's rise to empire, from the late fourth through the end of the second century continued in many respects unchanged into the first. Military victory still represented a source of enormous symbolic capital within the political economy of the republic (as well as of enormous wealth for some generals who enriched themselves from booty), and opportunities to command continued to be eagerly sought. But important changes within aristocratic culture, the character of political competition, and in the position of the republic itself combined to alter the role war played in the lives of aristocrats and in politics during the last 50 years of the republic. Most importantly, the requirement of ten years military service before a young man could stand for public office fell into abeyance. Julius Caesar (born 100) is the first politician we know of who did not fulfill it, so the change probably occurred sometime early in the first century, perhaps in connection with another, the decision to abolish the citizen cavalry during the Social War of 91–89.[18] This crisis, when many of Rome's Italian allies revolted, compelled the Senate to devote all available manpower to meeting it. Effective foreign cavalrymen could be hired; legionaries could not, and so men who would otherwise have served on horseback fought in the infantry instead. But the key question is not why the citizen cavalry was suspended at this time but why it was never reinstated when the crisis had passed.

The answer lies in broader changes taking place within aristocratic culture and politics during the latter part of the second and the early first centuries that diminished the value of a reputation for martial valor that military service, and cavalry service in particular, had helped young aristocrats obtain. During this period widespread poverty and landlessness came to occupy center-stage in republican politics. Legislation and other efforts to protect the rights of the people, alleviate their distress, and check the abuses of the Senate came to seem as great a service to the republic as striking down an enemy on the battlefield – if not more so. At the same time, an increasing familiarity with Greek rhetorical theory and technique dramatically increased the level of skill, and thus of training, required to speak effectively in favor of or against such measures.[19] Greater benefit accrued to a young man setting out on a political career from spending the time required to gain the oratorical mastery needed to shine as a public speaker than from a reputation for courage on the battlefield. And by this point, too, foreign threats began to seem far less urgent. The Social War was the last serious challenge Roman supremacy faced, and consequently the value of martial prowess, while always respected, counted for less in the political currency of the age. Because cavalry service (and war generally) no longer served an important role in the structure of aristocratic politics, it could be allowed to go by the boards.

This is not to say that aristocrats ceased to play a military role. They continued to officer the legions, and many a young aristocrat sought the cachet of martial glory by serving a few years as a junior officer or as one of a general's "tent mates." No professional officer corps developed at this point or for long thereafter. A class of officers, often termed *viri militares* ("military men"), is sometimes described as such, but although they served lengthy terms as military tribunes or more usually legates, they were members of the republic's upper class, and their aims were entirely consonant with traditional aristocratic goals, that is, to win election to high office, serve the state, and gain honor thereby. They simply pursued these ends by the traditional means of long years at war rather than the brief terms others served. They were often men of equestrian rather than senatorial origins, or if the latter, their forebears had usually remained in the lower ranks of that body. Or they came from families that had formerly formed the ruling classes of Rome's Italian allies. Following the Social War, these cities had lost their independence and been incorporated into the republic. Their leading families now enjoyed citizenship and so had to compete for office and honor in the much larger Roman political arena. The scions of such families either lacked the economic resources or more often the political connections required for a first class rhetorical education at Rome. Hence war offered them the means to make a name for themselves and so open the way to political advancement.[20]

The aristocracy's great fear of a single figure or small group gaining unassailable control over the republic through overwhelming prestige and authority remained, yet the nature of the military challenges facing Rome over its last century were tending in precisely this direction. The city's wars were becoming more difficult and more complex, requiring much greater command of the skills of military leadership as well as, at times, an ability to implement a much broader strategy than was possible under a system of annually rotated commands. Thus the public demanded that Scipio

Aemilianus be placed in command first of Rome's final war with Carthage and later its war with the Spanish city of Numantia despite the laws that ought to have prevented his election to these consulships in 146 and 134. In response to the grave crisis ushered in by the destruction of two Roman armies at Arausio 30 years later in 105, the public likewise insisted on reelecting Marius to four successive consulships plus a fifth as a reward for his victories. Even his enemies were forced to admit the necessity of these steps and the fact that Marius' achievements had saved the state. The anarchy at sea a generation later and then the intractable Mithradatic War necessitated in the public's mind placing extraordinary military commands in the hands of Pompey the Great in 68 and 67. The wars that the Romans fought first with their Italian allies and then against one another in the civil wars that raged from 88–87 and again in 83–81 (and in Spain down to 73) were waged for such high stakes – the very existence of Rome's hegemony in Italy in the first case and the lives of the leaders on each side and control of the state in the second – that considerations of aristocratic comity had to yield to military necessity. In the end, Pompey's victories in both the civil and foreign wars of the republic's last generation allowed him to rise to unprecedented heights of glory, prestige, political power, and wealth. To compete with him for eminence and authority would require wars and victories on a similarly vast scale, and this was precisely what Caesar set out to achieve. This is not the place to detail the story of the cooperation and later the clash between these two men or the determined efforts on the part of their peers to resist their domination. But the link between the benefits that victorious wars bestowed upon the Roman people and the political stature of the men who achieved them remained as close as ever. It was left to Caesar's adoptive son Augustus to use it to subvert the collective rule of the aristocracy and lay the foundations for monarchy by accumulating so many victories and so much glory as to be able to claim services to Rome so great as to make his authority unchallengeable.

NOTES

1   Rosenstein 2006.
2   Flower 1996.
3   Astin 1967, 62–3.
4   McCall 2002.
5   Nicolet 1966, 63–6.
6   Poly. 2.24.14–16, from the earlier Roman historian Fabius Pictor: Eutropius 3.5; Orosius 4.13.6–7. Interpretation is controversial: Brunt 1971, 44–7; *contra* Lo Cascio 1999, 166–9. See also De Ligt (in this volume).
7   Gelzer 1969, 7–8.
8   Suolahti 1955, 29–57.
9   Harris 1979, 39–40.
10 Astin 1978, 56–9.
11 Suolahti 1955, 200.
12 Quaestors: Erdkamp 1998, 103–4; Annius: Kallet-Marx 1995, 38.

13   Rosenstein 1993, 313–38; id. 1995, 43–75; id. 1990.
14   Rawson 1971, 13–15; Campbell 1987, 13–29; Goldsworthy 1996, 116–70 on the duties of generals in battle.
15   Eckstein 1987.
16   In some cases, generals received a lesser honor, the *ovatio* or "ovation" in which he entered the city on foot and without his soldiers. And in rare cases, a general denied a triumph could celebrate one privately, on the Alban Mount.
17   Galinski 1996, 10–20.
18   McCall 2002, 100–36.
19   David 2006.
20   De Blois 2000, 11–30.

BIBLIOGRAPHY

Astin, A. E. 1967. *Scipio Aemilianus*. Oxford.
—— 1978. *Cato the Censor*. Oxford.
Brunt, P. 1971. *Italian Manpower*. Oxford.
Campbell, B. 1987. "Teach yourself how to be a general," *JRS* 77: 13–29.
David, J.-M. 2006. "Rhetoric and public life," in Rosenstein and Morstein-Marx.
De Blois, L. 2000. "Army and society in the late Roman republic: Professionalism and the role of the military middle cadre," in G. Alföldi, B. Dobson, and W. Eck (eds.), *Kaiser, Heer und Gesellschaft in der Römischen Kaiserzeit*. Stuttgart, 11–30.
Eckstein, A. 1987. *Senate and General: Individual Decision Making and Roman Foreign Relations*. Berkeley.
Erdkamp, P. 1998. *Hunger and the Sword, Warfare and Food Supply in Roman Republican Wars (264–30 BC)*. Amsterdam.
Flower, H. 1996. *Ancestor Masks and Aristocratic Power in Roman Culture*. Oxford.
Galinski, K. 1996. *Augustan Culture*. Princeton.
Gelzer, M. 1969. *The Roman Nobility*. Oxford.
Goldsworthy, A. 1996. *The Roman Army at War 100 BC–AD 200*. Oxford.
Harris, W. V. 1979. *War and Imperialism in Republican Rome*. Oxford.
Hölkeskamp, K.-J. 1993. "Conquest, competition and consensus: Roman expansion in Italy and the rise of the *Nobilitas*," *Historia* 42: 12–39.
Kallet-Marx, R. 1995. *Hegemony to Empire*. Berkeley.
Lo Cascio, E. 1999. "The population of Roman Italy in town and country" in J. Bintliff and K. Sbonias (eds.), *Reconstructing Past Population Trends in Mediterranean Europe (3000 BC–AD 1800)*. Oxford, 166–9.
McCall, J. 2002. *The Cavalry of the Roman Republic*. London.
McDonnell, M. 2006. *Roman Manliness. Virtus and the Roman Republic*. Cambridge.
Nicolet, C. 1966. *L'Ordre équestre à l'époque républicaine*. Paris.
Raaflaub, K. 1996. "Born to be wolves? Origins of Roman imperialism," in R. W. Wallace and E. M. Harris (eds.), *Transitions to Empire. Essays in Greco-Roman History, 360–146 BC. In Honor of E. Badian*. Norman. 273–314.
Rawson, E. 1971. "The literary sources of the pre-Marian army," *PBSR* 39: 13–15. (= *Roman Culture and Society: Collected Papers of Elizabeth Rawson*. Oxford 1991, 34–57.)
Rosenstein, N. 1990. *Imperatores Victi: Military Defeat and Aristocratic Competition in the Middle and Late Republic*. Berkeley.

—— 1993. "Competition and crisis in mid-republican Rome," *Phoenix* 47: 313–38.

—— 1995. "Sorting out the lot in republican Rome," *AJP* 116: 43–75.

—— 2006. "Aristocratic values," in Rosenstein and Morstein-Marx.

——, and R. Morstein-Marx. 2006. *Blackwell Companion to the Roman Republic*. Oxford.

Suolahti, J. 1955. *The Junior Officers of the Roman Army in the Republican Period*. Helsinki.

FURTHER READING

Harris 1979 is fundamental on war, politics, and the aristocratic ethos during the middle republic; see also recently Rosenstein 2006 and on *virtus*, McDonnel 2006. On cavalry service see McCall 2002, and on military tribunes and other junior officers Suolahti 1955. On the ways in which war affected political competition and in particular how the needs of the latter could prevail over the exigencies of the former see Rosenstein 1990, 1993, 1995. On relations between the Senate and commanders in the field, see Eckstein 1987. Campbell 1987 focuses mainly on the lack of formal training in military command among imperial aristocrats, but has much light to shed on conditions under the republic; Goldsworthy 1996 discusses extensively the responsibilities of generals in the late republic and imperial periods. On the *viri militares*: De Blois 2000, and on the growing importance of rhetoric and other forms of aristocratic endeavor in the late republic, David 2006 and McCall 2002. On the origins of the ethos of service among the aristocracy during the early republic, see Hölkeskamp 1993, 12–39, and Raaflaub 1996, 273–314.

CHAPTER NINE

Colonization, Land Distribution, and Veteran Settlement

Will Broadhead

One of the most immediate fruits of the great success of the Roman army under the republic was the acquisition of *ager publicus*, land confiscated from defeated enemies and made the property of the Roman people. How the Romans chose to exploit this land has long been recognized as a key to their successful conquest of the Italian peninsula and of much of the Mediterranean world. Appian, looking back from the second century AD, described the range of uses to which the territorial acquisitions of the republican period were put: "The Romans gradually conquered Italy and regularly confiscated some of the land and either founded colonies or settled their own citizens on individual lots in the territory of existing cities. They regarded these settlements as garrisons" (*B. Civ.* 1.7, trans. Crawford 1992). In other words, upon the confiscation of land, the Senate and people decided by formal legislation the use to which the newly acquired *ager publicus* would be put. Some was given over to colonization, to the creation of new towns whose new inhabitants would be assigned plots of land in the associated territory. Other stretches of land were set aside for division and distribution to individual settlers, often referred to by modern scholars as viritane settlement (*ager viritim divisus*). In the same passage, Appian goes on to describe a third category of land which was not specifically assigned at all and could be used by anyone, though subject to laws *de modo agrorum*, which restricted the amount of use allowed to any one individual. Our interest here is in the first two, which together constitute one of the most important products of and subsequent contributors to Roman military might in the republican period.

The colonization and distribution of land was an important aspect of Roman policy from the fourth century right down to the age of Augustus. Within that larger space of time, we can usefully identify two major phases of activity. The first runs from the beginning of Rome's dominance of central Italy in the fourth century to the middle decades of the second century. This first phase follows closely the strategic concerns of the Roman state as it successfully conquered all of Italy south of the Alps. The settlements of this period are easily consistent with Cicero's well-known description of traditional Roman colonies as *propugnacula imperii*, "bulwarks of empire" (*Agr.* 2.73). Colonization and land distribution from the later second century to the age of Augustus constitutes a second, distinct phase of the phenomenon. In this later period, colonization was less immediately strategic in nature, increasingly involved land acquired through means other than traditional conquest and confiscation, and revealed as its primary function the serving as an outlet for the urban poor or reward for time-served legionaries rather than the creation of garrisons on the frontiers of the empire.

1 Colonization and Viritane Settlement 338 to 169 BC

Rome's settlement with the Latins in 338 BC marks the point from which we can begin to speak of a distinctly Roman phenomenon of colonization. The Romans had participated in colonial projects before that date, but only as one of the several member states of the Latin League who contributed to communal foundations at some 14 sites in and around Latium. From 338, the Romans were the dominant force in central Italy; they waged war on their own terms; and they alone determined the way in which the territorial fruits of victory were exploited. Before long, a basic model had emerged, one that would serve the Romans extremely well throughout the following century and a half, the period that witnessed their conquest of central and southern Italy, their defense of the peninsula against Hannibal's invasion, and their subsequent conquest of the Po Valley.

The basic model included three different forms of state-organized settlement on newly acquired *ager publicus*: the Latin colony, the colony of Roman citizens, and viritane settlement on territory not associated with a particular urban foundation. Behind all three was a basic similarity of purpose: the projection of power into still hostile regions, the consolidation of control in recently subjected regions, and the provision of a reliable supply of manpower. On the ground, however, differences between the three would have been obvious, and are worth looking at in turn now.

The 28 Latin colonies founded by Rome served as garrisons on the front lines of Roman expansion in Italy, their form and status determined by that role. Latin colonies were established on sites beyond Roman territory, frequently in areas still hostile to Rome at the time of their foundation (e.g. Placentia and Cremona were almost immediately overrun by Gauls after their foundation in 218: Polybius 3.40.3ff.). The new foundations had to be easily defensible and able to respond quickly and efficiently to external threats. Probably for this reason the colonies were reasonably large and theoretically autonomous city-states. Between them, Livy and Polybius preserve numbers of original colonists for a dozen of the Latin colonies, with a low of 2,500 at Cales and Luceria (Livy 8.16.13–14, 9.26.1–5) and a high of 6,000 at Alba Fucens, Placentia, and Cremona (Livy 10.1.1; Polybius 3.40.3–5). An average of 3,500–4,000 adult males is reasonable for those whose size is not preserved. The new community created for these colonists was under certain significant obligations to Rome but was in most regards entirely self-governing, the production of their own coinage by some colonies usually cited as merely the most tangible manifestation of their sovereignty.[1]

The process of foundation will have been broadly similar for the majority of republican colonization, centered on the formal act of *deductio*. Following deliberation in the Senate as to the details of location, size, and status of a proposed colony, a law was formally passed by the *concilium plebis* assigning to the colony whatever plot of *ager publicus* had been chosen (e.g. Livy 8.16.14: Cales). A committee of three men, the *tresviri coloniae deducendae*, was then appointed to oversee the implementation of the project (e.g. Livy 9.28.8; 10.21.9; 34.53.2; 37.46.10). The *tresviri* began by recruiting the required number of colonists at Rome, though the colonists themselves were drawn from both citizens and non-Romans, before formally leading the colonial party out to the chosen site. Polybius' account of the foundation of Placentia and Cremona in 218 suggests that in some cases the *tresviri* would go out ahead of the colonists to secure the site and then order the colonists to present themselves there within a certain number of days (3.40.3–5). Once arrived at the site of the future colony, the committee proceeded to lay out the boundaries of the colony's territory and of its urban center, in the process dividing both the urban and the rural land into plots to be assigned to colonists. Allotments in Latin colonies could be quite large, necessary for the self-sufficiency of the new community, and were, where we know the details, distributed according to military rank: at Thurii Copia in 193 the 3,000 *pedites* received 20 *iugera* each (1 *iugerum* = 0.25 ha), the 300 *equites* 40 (Livy 35.9.7–9; cf. Vibo Valentia at Livy 35.40.5). The final step was the implementation by the *tresviri* of the colonial charter, establishing the constitutional framework for the colony's future self-government, and the installation of the new community's local Senate and first elected officials.[2]

There would have followed several years of construction as the colony built the physical spaces required for the role it would now play. Thanks to extensive excavations of the second half of the twentieth century at the sites of Fregellae, Alba Fucens, Cosa, and Paestum, we have a reasonably reflective sample of archaeological remains of Latin colonies.[3] The least surprising feature common to them all is impressive fortification. Cosa's city wall, for example, was built in the first years of the colony's life, its dimensions showing how serious fortification was taken: it is 2–2½ meters thick and over 9 meters high in places, with polygonal masonry facades and rubble fill in a circuit of 1,400 meters that follows the contours of the hilltop and encloses an area of 33 acres. At Paestum, where the Latin colony of 273 was founded on the site of the originally Greek, then Lucanian town of Poseidonia, the colonists appear to have extended and further fortified the existing wall circuit, resulting in one of the most impressive surviving ancient fortifications in Italy: 5 kilometers of limestone blocks laid out in two curtain walls with earth fill (5–7 meters thick) and 28 towers along the way.

Once fortified, and thus able to begin carrying out their primary role as garrisons, the Latin colonies set about gradually adding public buildings to their urban centers. The basic plan across our sample of sites is similar, beginning with a rectangular forum at or near the center of the urban street grid. Around the forum in each case was a similar catalogue of structures: temple, Senate-house (*curia*) and assembly-place (*comitium*), *basilica*, and structures relating to retail activity. In other words, the colonies unsurprisingly equipped themselves with a central space that reminds most scholars of Rome itself. In the case of colonies founded *ex novo*, this tendency to replicate Rome should not surprise us; it would be more surprising if the new towns had arranged their public space according to a plan unfamiliar to them. In the case of a colony like Paestum, however, which occupied a pre-existing city and could conceivably have made use of buildings already in place, the colonists nevertheless went to great lengths to impose the typically Roman town plan. A large forum (about 200×60 meters) was opened up in the heart of the site with a *curia-comitium* complex on the long north side and a market-building (*macellum*) on the south, to which a *basilica* was later added. The most obvious political structure of the Greco-Lucanian city, the circular *ekklesiasterion*, was backfilled within a few years of the arrival of the Latin colony. Frequently cited in this context is a passage of Aulus Gellius, in which Gellius distinguishes *municipia* from colonies, saying "the colonies convey the impression of being miniatures and reproductions of Rome herself" (*NA* 16.13.9). The appeal to Gellius is of course chronologically inappropriate; his *coloniae* are those of the later second century AD which carried the title as a mark of prestige, not because they were the product of a colonial *deductio* from Rome. Furthermore, some scholars have recently stressed diversity over conformity amongst the Latin colonies and have pointed to centrifugal elements of colonial life that might have outweighed the centripetal pull of Rome.[4] We should certainly not oversimplify the situation by imagining all Rome's Latin colonies as "miniature Romes"; within decades of their original foundations, many of the colonies were on trajectories determined by their local circumstances as much as, if not more than, by their relationship to Rome. What is important for our purposes here is to note that the Latin colonies of this early period were large, well fortified communities fully equipped with the constitutional and physical apparatus of self-government.

The second type of colony founded by Rome in the same period is variously called the citizen, maritime, or Roman (as opposed to Latin) colony. Between 338 and 184 BC, the Romans established some 20 such colonies, each distinct from the Latin colonies in three important and related ways. First, settlers in these colonies retained, or took on, full Roman citizenship. The colonies were not autonomous new city-states, but rather extensions of Rome itself, the earliest examples actually contiguous with Roman territory. Second, they were much smaller affairs. In the six cases for which a figure is transmitted by Livy, the number is always 300 families (8.21.11; 34.45.1), a size consistent with the archaeological record of the colonial fortifications at Ostia and Minturnae, to take two examples, each enclosing an area of about five acres. And third, all citizen colonies founded down to the second century were located on the coast, hence Livy's references to settlers in these colonies as *coloni maritimi* (27.38.3; 36.3.4). It is tempting to link this last characteristic in particular with the observation that Rome was slow to develop a serious navy and to interpret the maritime colonies as coastguard garrisons intended as a substitute for naval defense. They certainly will have contributed to such a defense, but also seem to have been intended for other roles as well: the original colony at Minturnae, for example, sat precisely on the spot where the via Appia crossed the Liris River on its way to Capua. It is also of course important to note that a full nine colonies of Latin status were also established on or near the coast before the second century. It would seem therefore that their proximity to the main block of Roman territory in Latium was the main factor determining the status of the citizen colony.

The strategic importance of these Latin and citizen colonies to the Roman conquest of Italy between the fourth and early second centuries was immense. The settlements might incidentally have served other social and economic purposes, but their primary purpose was to help the Romans conquer and defend new territory. The example of Rome's long-running conflict with the Samnites from the 340s to the 260s should suffice to illustrate the role of an often aggressive colonial policy in Roman military undertakings. Through the founding of well-placed colonies, and the construction of military roads through them, the Romans succeeded in surrounding, subduing, and ultimately breaking the Samnites' hold on much of southern Italy. After the initial hostilities of the late 340s, the Romans sought to establish themselves in northern Campania with a Latin colony at Cales in 334. Cales was followed by the citizen colony at Tarracina in 329 and the Latin colony at Fregellae, on the Samnite side of the Liris River, in 328. This latter is often considered the *casus belli* of the Second Samnite War, the name conventionally given to the hostilities that lasted on and off from 327 to 304. After recovering from their disastrous defeat at the Caudine Forks, the Romans again took the offensive, this time crossing to the Adriatic side of the peninsula, seizing the crucially strategic site of Luceria and establishing there in 316 another Latin colony. Once they had gained the upper hand, the Romans quickly established two further pairs of Latin colonies, at Saticula and Suessa Aurunca in 313 and at Pontiae and Interamna Lirenas in 312, simultaneously reinforcing the original pair of Cales and Fregellae. Rome now had Samnium surrounded by colonial garrisons: five Latin colonies and one citizen colony pushing the Samnites out of northern Campania, a Latin colony on the island of Pontiae to protect seaborne communication, and a further Latin colony penning the Samnites in from the east at Luceria. A Latin colony at Venusia in 291 placed a wedge between the Samnite Hirpini and their Lucanian allies, before a final pair of Latin colonies in the Samnite heartland, at Beneventum in 268 and Aesernia in 263, broke the collective strength of the Samnites once and for all.[5] The strategic importance of the colonies showed also on the defensive during Hannibal's invasion of Italy in 218–203. Not only did all the Latin colonies remain loyal to Rome throughout those trying years; but several came face to face with Hannibal's considerable forces and managed to hold out (e.g. Fregellae in 211: Livy 26.9.3–11). In perhaps the most frequently cited passage on the nature of early Roman colonization, Cicero, looking back from a time when settlements had taken on a very different role, reminds his audience of the traditional role of the colonies:

> Is every place of such a kind that it should not matter to the republic whether a colony is founded there or not? Or are there some locations that call for a colony and others that clearly prohibit a colony? On this issue, just as on every other aspect of the republic,

it is worth remembering the careful practice of our ancestors, who so established colonies as a defense against danger that the colonies seemed less towns of Italy and more bulwarks of empire. (Cicero, *Agr.* 2.73)

On the level of the individual colonist, participation in a colonial foundation was considered a *militia*, a form of military service that could be an alternative to, or overlap with traditional service in the legions. Many indicators point to a Roman view of their colonists as practically on active duty. Livy's many references to colonization consistently employ the language of the military: e.g. colonists are frequently distinguished by military rank (*pedites, equites*, and *centuriones* at Aquileia: 40.34.2–3). Furthermore, as noted above, the allotment of land in Latin colonies was carried out according to military rank, with *equites* and centurions receiving considerably larger plots than *pedites*, thereby creating an instant social hierarchy, one based on military criteria. Life in the citizen colonies would perhaps have felt even more like active duty. That a colonist's presence in his maritime colony was itself considered a form of military service is implied by the exemption from traditional legionary service (*vacatio militiae*) applied to all such colonies down to the Hannibalic War (Livy 27.38.1–5). It is also possible that the prohibition that prevented any maritime colonist from being away from the colony for more than 30 nights, known from the time of Hannibal's presence in Italy, might have operated in some form or other as a normal regulation.

In this context, it is worth revisiting what has traditionally been considered the juridically privileged position of the Latin colonists. The conventional view begins with the observation that a Roman citizen who enrolled in a Latin colony exchanged his Roman citizenship for that of the new colony, thereby taking on, from Rome's perspective, the Latin status. In return for this juridical "sacrifice," Rome granted the Latin colonists certain privileges in their relationship with Rome, known as the Latin rights and thought to include intermarriage (*conubium*), intercommerce (*commercium*), and the right to migrate to Rome and resume full Roman citizenship (the so-called *ius migrandi*). There are several problems with the conventional emphasis of these rights, not least the strong probability that many settlers in Latin colonies were in fact not originally Roman citizens. More important for our purposes here is the misleading assumption of a right to migrate to Rome, in effect to abandon the colony. The relevant evidence is minimal, coming from one passage of Livy, in which he records that in 177 BC "the law granted to the Latins that those of them who should leave behind in their hometown an offspring of their own could become Roman citizens" by migrating to Rome and registering in the census there (41.8.9). The conventional view has been that before the second century Latin colonists could return to Rome freely and that Livy's reference of 177 is relevant to a later restriction of that free movement, requiring the colonists to leave a son behind in the colony. What is more likely is that the law, exactly as Livy records it, was part of the original foundation charters of the Latin colonies from the start. In other words, far from enjoying the privilege of emigrating from their colony whenever they wished, Latin colonists were explicitly prohibited from leaving the colony unless they could guarantee its continued manpower by leaving behind a son.[6]

The prohibition of emigration from colonies in fact goes to the heart of the question of the nature of Rome's colonial projects between the late fourth and early second centuries. If the colonies were successfully to carry out their primary role as *propugnacula imperii*, they needed more than impressive fortifications; they needed reliable manpower. Rome's attitude toward the manpower of her theoretically autonomous Latin colonies emerges clearly from two episodes recorded by Livy. The first relates to the colonies at Placentia and Cremona, who in 206 sent delegates to the Senate at Rome complaining that many of their colonists had abandoned the colonies for fear of the continuing hostility of neighboring Gauls (Livy 28.11.10–11). Rome responded with a consular edict ordering the citizens of Placentia and Cremona to return to the colony. When this edict proved ineffective, more direct executive action was taken by the consul Sextus Aelius, who "spent almost the whole year compelling (*cogendis*) the people of Cremona and Placentia to return to the colonies from which they had been scattered by the dangers of war" (32.26.3). The second episode relates to the group of 12 Latin colonies who claimed, in 209, that they were demographically exhausted and could no longer provide men for the fight against Hannibal (27.9.7–14). The Roman response was to condemn the 12 as criminally traitorous and, five years later, when the war was going considerably better for Rome, to punish them by forcing them to contribute twice as many men, to pay an extra tax, and to conduct future local censuses under much closer scrutiny from Rome (29.15.1–15). The two episodes encapsulate the Roman perception of colonial participation as a *militia*: the colonies were equivalent to standing armies, their citizens under obligation to remain "on guard" in the colony itself and, in the case of the Latin colonies, to present themselves when called for service in the Roman legions.

The third category of use to which *ager publicus* was traditionally put was that of viritane settlement, wherein individual settlers were assigned plots of land in a particular territory without the accompanying construction of a fortified town or the creation of an organized, self-governing community. These essentially rural communities might eventually support the evolution of a local administrative or market center (a *conciliabulum* or *forum*), but their urban center was theoretically the city of Rome itself. The sources record several examples of this type of settlement from as far back as the distribution of the *ager Veientanus* in 393 to the distribution of the *ager Ligustinus et Gallicus* in the Po Valley in 173 (Livy 5.30.8; 42.4.3–4). In a few instances we know the size of the plots assigned (e.g. in the settlement of 173 citizens received ten *iugera* and Latins three); but in no case do we know the number of assignees involved, making it impossible to judge the scale of the phenomenon with any precision. In most cases, the decision by the Senate to use *ager publicus* for viritane settlement rather than a colonial foundation seems to have been based on the security of the land in question and its proximity to Rome. Such, at any rate, is one interpretation of the vocal but ultimately ineffectual senatorial resistance to Flaminius' proposal as tribune in 232 to distribute the *ager Gallicus* between Ravenna and Sena Gallica: the land was far from Rome and far from securely pacified (Polybius 2.21.7–9; Cicero, *Sen.* 11).

According to Polybius, senatorial opposition to the viritane distribution of 232 was not caused by its distance from Rome but by its perception as an act of demagoguery by Flaminius: Polybius calls it a "popular policy" and "the first step in the demoralization of the Roman populace" (2.21.8). Such a sentiment sounds more like a reflection of the concerns of Polybius' Roman friends of the later second century than of the reality of the later third. This aspect of land distribution would develop more clearly in due course. In the meantime, it is worth considering viritane settlement as another side to the strategic use of *ager publicus* so evident in the colonial foundations of the period. The rural communities resulting from viritane settlement can hardly be called *propugnacula imperii*, but can be linked to another essential strategic concern of the rapidly expanding Roman state: manpower. In an age when the property qualification for service in the legions was very much a significant factor, the distribution of land to citizens (to the landless, or to the adult younger sons of families with small-holdings elsewhere) would obviously have increased the number of eligible recruits. The sentiment is reflected in a passage of Livy, expressly relevant to colonization as a whole but particularly appropriate to viritane settlement: colonists are described as having been sent out from Rome "to settle on land captured in war in order that they might increase their offspring" (27.9.11: *stirpis augendae causa*).

One example of viritane settlement from this early period stands out from the others, and brings us back to a more immediately military context, namely the settlement of Scipio's veterans of the Hannibalic War on land in the Italian south. Livy records the Senate's decision of 201 to distribute land in Samnium and Apulia to soldiers who had been fighting under Scipio at the end of the war. The land was to be distributed according to military seniority: two *iugera* of land for every year of service in Spain or Africa (Livy 31.4.1–3; 31.49.5). It is possible that the number of soldiers who thus qualified was as high as 40,000.[7] What is especially worth noting is that this settlement represents an early, and for the moment isolated, example of a phenomenon that would become a central feature of Roman agrarian policy in the first century BC: the distribution of land specifically to time-served soldiers.

The model of colonization outlined above – larger Latin colonies as frontier bulwarks, smaller citizen colonies as garrisons closer to Rome, and viritane settlement as a means of increasing manpower – was employed by the Roman Senate with little variation for the century and a half from 338 BC to the second century. In the first decade and a half of the second century, however, there began to emerge indications that the original model of colonization was under strain. The Latin colony of Copia, for example, was founded in 193 with a smaller number of colonists than its territory could actually have supported, while in 189 only one of two proposed Latin colonies in the Po Valley was successfully established, at Bononia (Livy 35.9.7–9; 37.47.2; 37.57.7). In 194, eight traditional maritime colonies were founded at various points around the coasts of southern Italy; by 186, two of the eight had been abandoned by their colonists (Livy 34.45.1–5; 39.23.3). Whatever the reason for the apparent difficulties of these years, the Romans responded by experimenting with a new type of colony, like traditional Latin colonies in size and distance from Rome, but with the significant difference that colonists would have full Roman citizenship. The first certain examples of the new-style citizen colony were those at Mutina and Parma in 183, each with 2,000 colonists (Livy 39.55.6–8).[8] At least five of the new-style citizen colonies were founded between 183 and 177, while at the most only two traditional

Latin colonies were ever founded again, one of them, at Aquileia in 181, might just as easily have been of the new Roman variety. According to Livy, there was a debate in the Senate as to whether Aquileia was to be of Latin or Roman status (39.55.5). If Livy had also recorded the arguments on either side, we might be able to say why the Romans eventually ceased to found Latin colonies altogether. Without those details, we are limited to speculation.

Though no more Latin colonies would be founded after 180 BC, those that had been founded up to that date of course continued to exist and to play an important role. It is worth looking briefly here at their later history as it relates to the issue of manpower in the second century and to later, more immediate strategic concerns. After the case of the 12 colonies' refusal of manpower in 209 and their punishment in 204 (see above), the role of the Latin colonies as suppliers of manpower again appeared on the Senate's agenda in the early decades of the second century. On two occasions, in 187 and again in 177, embassies from all the Latin colonies appeared in Rome to report that their citizens, some through an elaborate fraud and others quite openly, had left their colonies along with their families, in clear violation of the prohibition against emigration without leaving a son behind. At issue was the colonies' ability to continue supplying manpower. Rome's response to the recurring problem of colonial emigration in these years was to force the emigrant Latins, many thousands of whom had taken up residence at Rome, to return to their original colonies (Livy 39.3.4–6; 41.8.6–12).[9] In addition to these measures, the Roman Senate on at least seven occasions in these years recruited *supplementa*, reinforcements of sometimes several thousand new colonists, and sent them out to colonies that had complained of thinning populations. Rather than lower the number of men each colony was required to contribute, Rome consistently opted for reinforcement and forced repatriation. The Senate had been willing to experiment with some aspects of colonization in these years; but their view of the Latin colonies as bulwarks of empire and sources of manpower had not changed.

As the second century progressed, many of the Latin colonies had developed into much more than single-purpose fortified garrisons, a development that began to put a strain on their relationship with a Roman Senate that expected them all to con-tinue to play the role of *propugnacula imperii*. Fregellae is the most obvious case.[10] Founded in 328 with a clear strategic purpose that had served the Romans well in conflict with the Samnites and later with Hannibal, Fregellae by the second century had developed into a regional center of economic and political importance. Located on vital lines of communication, the colony was home to an important market and had attracted large numbers of immigrants from surrounding areas (Strabo 5.3.10; Livy 41.8.8). According to Strabo, Fregellae once held several of its neighboring cities as dependencies (5.3.10). Representatives from the colony also appear at Rome leading delegations (Livy 27.10.3; Cic., *Brutus* 170). For reasons that remain obscure, relations between Fregellae and Rome broke down and ended in a violent clash in 125 BC. The subsequent destruction of the colony is recorded by our sources in the briefest of notices (Livy, *Per.* 60). It is possible that Fregellae was not alone among the Latin colonies in somehow chafing at Roman oversight. We can only wonder what tensions Livy might have recorded in that part of his narrative that is lost to us. However widespread disaffection might or might not have been in 125, the rest of the Latin colonies remained notably loyal to Rome into the first century. In the first year of Rome's war against the allied states of Italy in 91, the colonies stood by Rome, once again showing their immediate strategic importance. Only the colony at Venusia joined the rebels; it did so in the second year of the war and probably because it was isolated in rebel territory.[11] To reward their loyalty, and of course also to remove any incentive to following Venusia in joining the rebels, Rome granted full citizenship to the Latin colonies, which then began their transformation into the *municipia* of the new Italy.

Turning back to the early second century, it was not only the traditional Latin colonies that ceased to be founded. After the supplement sent to Aquileia in 169, we hear of no other colonial projects of any kind for almost 50 years. The silence is possibly to be explained by the loss of Livy's narrative of these years, our most reliable guide to colonial activity. There are, however, plenty of reasons to believe the cessation of any record of colonial activity in these years actually reflects the reality of Roman policy in the middle decades of the second century. Following the resumption of military activity in the Po Valley and the successful conquest of that region in the early decades of the second century, the immediate strategic motives for colonization no longer existed. With Italy south of the Alps now firmly under Roman control, there was no longer a need for the *propugnacula imperii* that had played so important a role in Roman expansion of the previous century and a half; and as for colonization outside Italy, opposition to the concept was strong in the mid-second century and would only slowly subside.[12]

2 Colonization and Settlement in the Late Republic

When serious efforts toward colonization and individual settlement re-emerged in the closing decades of the second century, the nature of the phenomenon had clearly changed. Certain members of the Roman elite, by no means a majority, began from the 120s BC to display a new attitude toward the role of colonization. Coming fast on the heels of Tiberius Gracchus' agrarian reforms, colonization in these years became a tool for the satisfaction of social and political needs, its traditional strategic function, though never absent, beginning to fade from view.

Of this new strain of colonization, Gaius Gracchus' proposed colonies are the first examples about which we are reasonably well informed. As part of his wide-ranging and popular legislative program of 123–122 BC, Gaius proposed the foundation of three new colonies, Neptunia (Tarentum) and Minervia (Scolacium) in the south of Italy and Junonia at the site of Carthage in Africa (Velleius Pat. 2.7.7; Plutarch, *C. Gracc.* 8–11). Not surprisingly, there was strong senatorial opposition to these plans, as there was to most of Gaius' program, with the proposed settlement at Carthage provoking the strongest reaction. The fact that the site was overseas did not sit well with many Romans, who were apparently not yet comfortable with the idea of planting Roman communities outside the Italian peninsula. In the end, that part of the plan was abandoned when the law providing for the colony was repealed. Rather than putting a stop to the two other Gracchan colonies, the senatorial opposition adopted a strategy that reveals much about the changed role of colonization in the life of the city-state. In a situation Plutarch expressly compares to comedy, the senators attempted to undermine Gaius' popularity by competing openly with him for the favor of the people. Gaius had promised his supporters three colonies; M. Livius Drusus and his senatorial supporters promised them 12. There is no evidence any of Drusus' proposed colonies were ever actually founded. Strategic concerns in the empire played little part in the colonial proposals of these years. Colonies had instead become a useful weapon in the political arsenal of the competitive aristocracy within Rome.

According to Velleius Paterculus, the nature of Roman colonization changed fundamentally after the (otherwise unattested) foundation of Eporedia in 100: "It would be difficult to mention any colony founded after this date, except the military colonies" (1.15.5). His use of the term *coloniae militares* is misleading since, as we have seen, Roman colonization was from the start a "military" phenomenon, with very clear strategic objectives from the fourth to the second century. Nevertheless, there is certainly a case for following Velleius in considering the colonial projects of the first century to be qualitatively different from all that had gone before and in linking that difference with the Roman soldiery. The form of state-organized land distribution that dominates the history of the first century is after all the veteran settlement, the allotment of land specifically to time-served legionary soldiers, either in a colony or as part of a viritane settlement. In every case such settlements were facilitated, directly or indirectly, by the generals under whom those soldiers had served – Marius, Sulla, Pompey, Caesar, and the triumvirs – often in the face of stiff opposition from the conservative senatorial elite. As has long been recognized, land distribution thus played a central role in the shift of legionary loyalty from the Senate and the state to the series of individual military dynasts whose extraordinary careers culminated in the return to monarchy.[13]

One further feature of the first century BC context that contributed directly to the distinctive nature of colonization in these years was the availability of land. By the end of the second century BC there was precious little *ager publicus* left in Italy that could be used for distributions of any kind. The large tracts of land confiscated during Rome's original conquest of the peninsula and those deriving from the punishments and conquests of the early second century had by now already been put to use. The privatization of post-Gracchan small-holdings by the *lex Thoria* of 111 BC yet further reduced the amount of publicly held land that might have been available for redistribution. There were two significant consequences of this situation. First, any colony founded on *ager publicus* would have to be founded outside Italy, a concept with which many of the Roman elite had been uncomfortable as recently as 122 BC. And second, any colony founded in Italy would have to be founded on land newly acquired either by forceful confiscation or by purchase. Confiscation by force had always been the method by which Rome had acquired *ager publicus* in Italy; the difference in most of the first century cases is that the dispossessed were actually Roman citizens.

This final wave of republican land distribution begins with Marius and his efforts, with the help of the tribune Saturninus, to win land grants for his time-served soldiers in

103 and 100. The settlements proposed in those years are often unnecessarily associated with Marius' abolition in 107 of the property qualification for service in the legions, on the apparent view that it was the newly eligible pauper-soldiers of 107 who were in need of land by 103 and 100. Even without the new phenomenon of landless volunteers, there would have been plenty of veterans in 103 whose need for some kind of livelihood after discharge was pressing: men who had only barely satisfied the already minimal property qualification of the late second century, or men whose long service abroad with Marius had left their original holdings in ruins or in the hands of another. At any rate, in 103 Marius teamed up with the popular tribune L. Appuleius Saturninus to push through a law providing land for the veterans of his African campaigns (*De vir. ill.* 73). Optimate opposition to the settlement of veterans in 103 was strong. It was only through popular agitation in the form of stone throwing that the law was passed. Marius and Saturninus teamed up again in 100 with the aim this time of providing land to the veterans of Marius' German campaigns; but when Saturninus' propensity for political violence looked like becoming too serious a liability, Marius abandoned him. It seems likely that Marius was able to secure the second round of land grants nonetheless.[14] Marius had thus shown the way for the dynasts of the next century. If necessary with the threat or reality of political violence, an unusually successful general could obtain a grant of land for his own veterans even in the face of strong senatorial opposition. From the perspective of the potential volunteer, legionary service under such a general will also have taken on a whole new attraction once the link between service and land grants had so clearly been made.

On his return to Rome in 82 BC, Sulla followed Marius' precedent of personally seeing to the settlement of his veterans, but did so from a quite different position. With the power of the dictatorship granted him by the *lex Valeria*, he took a number of steps to secure his victory and pave the way for his package of reforms. At least 500 prominent individuals from among his opponents he targeted for proscription. Any Italian city that had supported Marius and Cinna, of which there were many in Etruria and Samnium especially, he subjected to severe punishments and confiscations of land. And on this land he settled his now numerous veterans, perhaps as many as 80,000.[15] Unprecedented was the fact that Sulla founded colonies and distributed land across Italy without reference to the Senate, a practice in which he would soon be followed by Caesar, the triumvirs, and Octavian.

Sulla's veteran settlements sometimes come across as rewards to the soldiers for their service to him. He would certainly have had to depend on his troops' personal loyalty during the civil war, when he was officially an enemy of the state; and there is some indication that material rewards for loyalty were promised by Sulla and expected by his men (e.g. Appian, *B. Civ.* 1.57). On the ground, however, Sulla's veteran colonies in Italy actually had much in common with the *propugnacula imperii* of traditional Roman colonization. Appian states that Sulla settled his soldiers in the towns that had opposed him "so that he might have strongholds to control Italy" and elsewhere describes the veterans as a force that might quickly be mobilized if necessary (*B. Civ.* 1.96, 104). Like their colonial counterparts in the fourth and third centuries, Sulla's colonial veterans remained in effect on active duty in their new homes, both in their policing role over the potentially hostile native populations with whom they now shared "double communities" all over Italy (see Cicero, *Sull.* 62 for tension at Pompeii), and in their role as manpower in reserve for the defense of the Sullan regime whenever called. What is more, it appears that many of the Sullan veterans never managed to make ends meet, with the result that by 63 BC there was a significant pool of such veterans eager to join other contingents of the destitute in support of Cataline (Sallust, *Cat.* 16.4; 28.4).

The post-Sullan period saw little in the way of fresh distributions until the agrarian legislation of Julius Caesar in 59 BC, one of whose principal purposes was to provide land for Pompey's veterans. As far back as 70, the Senate had agreed to set aside land for soldiers who had fought with Pompey in Spain; but no distributions had taken place. In 62, Pompey had returned from his eastern campaigns with another wave of veterans and another request that the Senate provide land for their settlement; but the Senate was firm in its opposition: proposals to distribute land in 63 and in 60 came to nothing. In desperation Pompey was driven into the political alliance with Crassus and Caesar that brought the latter to the consulship for 59 and into a position to push through legislation for Pompey's veterans. Pompey now had his friendly consul; but even so, the threat of armed violence from his still landless soldiers was necessary to see the legislation through (Plutarch, *Pomp.* 48; Cassius Dio 38.5.4; Appian, *B. Civ.* 2.10).[16] The resulting distributions provided allotments to perhaps 25,000 of Pompey's veterans and as many as 20,000 poor civilians (Suetonius, *Jul.* 20).

The agrarian law of 59 established Caesar's credentials both as a general who would look after his veterans and as a Gracchan-style leader eager to provide for the urban poor. It also revealed his willingness to circumvent the traditional role of the Senate in deciding the fate of *ager publicus*. All these features reappeared as part of Caesar's own agrarian policy during his dictatorship. Like Sulla before him, Caesar founded colonies and settled veterans through his dictatorial authority, thereby avoiding the kind of public charade that had surrounded the passage of his law of 59. Unlike Sulla, however, Caesar was careful to avoid causing too much turmoil in Italy through confiscations and the imposition of veteran garrisons (Appian, *B. Civ.* 2.94).

Though it is difficult to compile a complete list of Caesar's colonial activity, we know enough to say that it was extensive, with many settlements in the provinces as well as in Italy, and diverse in nature, providing land both for his Gallic veterans and for the civilian poor. More than any of his predecessors, Caesar showed himself willing to settle colonies in overseas provinces, a willingness probably to be linked to the limited amount of *ager publicus* remaining in Italy, his desire to avoid Sullan-style confiscations, and his open acceptance of the concept of settling Roman citizens at such a distance from Rome. Suetonius claims Caesar settled 80,000 colonists in the provinces (Suetonius, *Jul.* 42). Of these, perhaps 10,000 were veterans of his own legions, perhaps another 10,000 were veterans of Pompey's defeated legions, settled at various colonies in Gaul, Africa, and Spain.[17] The remainder, a full 60,000 (if we include Pompey's veterans, 70,000 if not), were drawn from the urban *proletarii* of Rome for Gracchan-style settlement in the provinces for social and economic reasons. Caesar's colonial plans thus included settlements like Urso in Spain, whose full title, Colonia Genetiva Julia Urbanorum, identifies it as a colony for the urban *plebs*, and whose foundation charter allows for the holding of public office by freed-men, and Carthage and Corinth, both of whose foundations seem to have been guided by commercial considerations (*FIRA* i², no. 21; Strabo 8.6.23). In Italy, by con-trast, Caesar distributed land to veterans only, even these in small number: perhaps only 20,000 men, who had nothing like the impact of Sulla's settlements of 82–81. He appears to have kept to the sentiment Appian records him expressing to his soldiers in 47: that he would provide his soldiers with public land or even his own land rather than confiscating land as Sulla had and planting veterans alongside bitter and hateful original owners (*B. Civ.* 2.94). At any rate, most of Caesar's veterans who were settled in the early 40s were soon recalled to service with one or other of the triumvirs in the aftermath of Caesar's assassination.

Caesar had made these arrangements for the settlement of his Gallic veterans before his death. The settlement of his many recruits from the years after 49, however, was a problem left for the triumvirs. Antony, Lepidus, and Octavian addressed the issue at their famous conference at Bononia in 43, with the war against Brutus and Cassius on the horizon (Appian, *B. Civ.* 4.3):

> they would spur their troops on to win the rewards of victory in the war . . . especially by granting them eighteen Italian towns where they could settle. These towns, which were remarkable for their wealth and fine lands and houses, they intended to allocate to the army . . . like a substitute for plunder taken on enemy soil.

Following their victory at Philippi in 42, it was Octavian who returned to Italy with the task of delivering on the pre-war promise (Appian, *B. Civ.* 5.3). He began the expropriation of land from the 18 cities in early 41; by summer of that year, some 46,000 time-served Caesarian soldiers were settling in to their new Italian homes.[18]

The triumviral settlement is perhaps the best one with which to conclude as it encapsulates better than any other example from the first century the many ways in which the institution of colonization and land distribution had completely transformed from the traditional model of the fourth and third centuries BC. Traditional colon-ization began with *ager publicus*, land confiscated from Rome's defeated enemies or rebellious allies. The land expropriated by the triumvirs for the settlement of 41 was nothing of the kind. The 18 towns chosen for confiscations were Roman towns, whose Roman citizens would suffer from the arbitrary judgment of the triumvirs. The towns had committed no crime, displayed no particular disloyalty; they were chosen simply for their wealth and the quality of their fields and houses. There was little the affected could do except make their way to Rome to appeal to Octavian for exemption (Vergilius, *Ecl.* 1). The purpose of the settlements was also in stark contrast to the traditional model. Early colonies were *propugnacula imperii* with clear strategic purposes, their inhabitants engaged in a form of military service by their very presence and by their continued obligations to the local community and to Rome. The 18 towns whose land was distributed to veterans in 41 were offered as a reward, dangled before the soldiers as payment for what consequently amounted to mercenary service under the triumvirs.

Most reflective of the wider developments of the late republic, however, was the authority by virtue of which the triumvirs effected the settlement of their veterans after Philippi. In late 43, after the conference at Bononia and with their senatorial opponents fearfully awaiting news of the proscription list drawn up at that meeting, Antony, Lepidus, and Octavian made their way to Rome where, with their armed supporters visible on all sides, a law of the tribune Titius, passed on the spot, made them *tresviri reipublicae constituendae* (Appian, *B. Civ.* 4.7). With the powers granted them by the *lex Titia*, the triumvirs were able to carry out their veteran settlement two years later without any reference to the Senate whatsoever. This was a far cry from the senatorial control of colonization that had been the norm from the fourth to the early second century. That control of this most consequential aspect of Roman military activity had been gradually eroding since the Gracchi first challenged it in the later second century. By 43, a meeting of three tenuously allied military dynasts on a small island in the middle of a river outside Bononia had more control over land distribution than Cicero's Senate at Rome. The Senate and people of Rome would never again have the control over colonization that Cicero had optimistically encouraged them not to cede to Rullus in 63 (*Agr.* 2).

NOTES

1   See also Erdkamp (in this volume).
2   See Salmon 1969, 13–28 for a general account of the foundation process, including details of the survey and division of land at the colonial site.
3   See further reading below for publication details.
4   See, for example, the opposing views of Mouritsen and Coarelli on the use of colonial *fora* as formalized voting spaces in imitation of the *saepta* at Rome: Mouritsen 2004, 37–67; Coarelli 2005, 23–30. See also Torelli 1999, 43–88 for a speculative argument that the colonists at Paestum organized the sacred topography of the colony in imitation of Rome.
5   For a full narrative of colonization and conquest in this period, see Salmon 1969, 55–111. For the close link between colonial foundations and road construction, see Coarelli 1988, 35–48.
6   For the full argument, see Broadhead 2001, 69–89.
7   Brunt 1971, 70, n.1.
8   It is possible Pisaurum and Potentia, founded in 184, were the first of the new citizen colonies; but Livy is silent on their status.
9   For a fuller account of internal migration and its impact on Rome and the colonies in the second century, see Broadhead 2004, 315–35.
10   See Coarelli and Monti 1998.
11   Crawford 1992, 142.
12   Crawford 1992, 94–106.
13   Brunt 1988, 240–80, is fundamental. See now also De Blois (in this volume).
14   On the settlement of Marius' veterans, see Brunt 1988, 278–80. Crawford 1992, 126–7 suggests Marius, before turning on Saturninus, obtained a promise from the Senate that his men would receive their land.
15   See Brunt 1971, 300–12 for details and for the estimate of 80,000.
16   Brunt 1971, 312–19; Crawford 1989, 179–90.
17   Brunt 1971, 255–9, 319–26, and 589–601 for a list of provincial colonies; Keppie 1983, esp. 49–58. See also Rawson 1994, 424–67.
18   Keppie 1983, 58–69.

BIBLIOGRAPHY

Broadhead, W. 2001. "Rome's migration policy and the so-called *ius migrandi*," *Cahiers Glotz* 12 (2001) 69–89.

—— 2004. "Rome and the mobility of the Latins: Problems of control," in *La mobilité des personnes en Mediterranée, de l'antiquité à l'époque moderne*. Paris, 315–35.

Brown, F. E., E. H. Richardson, and L. Richardson Jr. 1993. *Cosa III. The Buildings of the Forum. Colony, Municipium, and Village*. Rome.

Brunt, P. 1971. *Italian Manpower 225 BC–AD 14*. Oxford.

—— 1988. "The army and the land in the Roman revolution," in P. Brunt, *The Fall of the Roman Republic*. Oxford, 240–80.

Coarelli, C., and P. G. Monti (eds.) 1998. *Fregellae 1. Le fonti, la storia, il territorio*. Rome.

Coarelli, F. 1988. "Colonizzazione romana e viabilità," *Dialoghi di Archeologia* 6: 35–48.

—— (ed.). 1989. *Minturnae*. Rome.

—— 2005. "Pits and fora: A reply to Henrik Mouritsen," *PBSR* 73: 23–30.

Cornell, T. 1995. *The Beginnings of Rome. Italy and Rome from the Bronze Age to the Punic Wars (c. 1000–264 BC)*. London.

Crawford, M. H. 1989. "The lex Iulia agraria," *Athenaeum* 67: 179–90.

—— 1992². *The Roman Republic*. London.

De Ruyt, F. 1982. *Alba Fucens 3*. Brussels.

Keppie, L. 1983. *Colonisation and Veteran Settlement in Italy 47–14 BC*. London.

Meiggs, R. 1973². *Roman Ostia*. Oxford.

Mertens, J. 1969. *Alba Fucens 1–2*. Brussels.

Mouritsen, H. 2004. "Pits and politics: Interpreting colonial fora in republican Italy," *PBSR* 72: 37–67.

Pedley, J. 1990. *Paestum. Greeks and Romans in Southern Italy*. London.

Rawson, E. 1994. "Caesar: Civil war and dictatorship," in *CAH²* 9, 424–67.

Salmon, E. T. 1969. *Roman Colonization under the Republic*. London.

Torelli, M. 1999. *Tota Italia. Essays in the Cultural Formation of Roman Italy*. Oxford.

FURTHER READING

General: Salmon 1969 remains an interesting and full account of the colonization, though dated on certain details; Brunt 1971 is fundamental; Cornell 1995 and Crawford 1992 for the role of colonization in wider historical developments of the period. On the history and archaeology of individual Latin and citizen colonies: Coarelli and Monti 1998 on Fregellae; Mertens 1969 and de Ruyt 1982 on Alba Fucens; Brown et al. 1993 on Cosa; Pedley 1990 on Paestum; Meiggs 1973 on Ostia; Coarelli 1989 on Minturnae. On veteran settlement and the first century BC: Brunt 1988 remains an essential starting point; Keppie 1983 through the use of the epigraphic record, among other things, greatly clarifies the picture of settlement in Italy.

CHAPTER TEN

Army and General in the Late Roman Republic

Lukas de Blois

1 Introduction

In the first century BC large crowds in Rome and in the armies became involved in political quarrels of the ruling Roman elite, either as cheering partisans in popular assemblies and combatants in street-fighting, or as soldiers doing service in the armed forces during civil wars. These crowds have often been interpreted as more or less automatically operating extensions of quarreling leaders, which would wrongly reduce the history of the late Roman Republic to a story about its ruling upper class. Late republican armies, on which we concentrate in this chapter, have been characterized as personal retinues of their leaders and Marius has been blamed for this. From BC 107 he admitted proletarian volunteers to the armed forces and in doing so he reputedly created the late republican *Heeresgefolgschaft*. Soldiers who did not have any property to fall back on after retirement demanded land, booty, and donatives from their generals and became tools in the hands of military leaders who could give such things to them. In a recently published *History of Rome* we read that after Marius' military reforms

> soldiers would tend to turn professional and become ever more closely bound to their leaders, from whom they would expect everything – pay, booty, distributions of gifts at the times of triumphs, and plots of land when colonial allocations were being made. An *esprit de corps* would develop. The republican national army was replaced by the armies of Marius, Sulla, Pompey, and, above all, Caesar. These were armies that were totally devoted to their leaders.[1]

Large crowds are not and were not, however, machines that can be switched on and off at will by superior leaders, and devotion to leadership can be very dependent on material well-being, military successes, and other factors; it is not a fixed, permanent element. Large-scale collective actions must be well organized and require leaders who have a good cause, have knowledge and understanding of either urban or military masses, and are acceptable as their spokesmen. Such actions also require a clever handling of henchmen and middle cadres, who are trusted by craftsmen and proletarians in cities or by soldiers in army camps.[2] Furthermore, Rome was not a tribal stateless society ruled by great chiefs, each of them having their own personal groups of followers. The Roman Republic had magistrates, laws, *comitia*, and a Senate, the authority of each of which was generally acknowledged among Roman citizens.

The question that will be discussed in this chapter is: how could competing leaders who wanted to use their armies as weapons in civil strife swing the moods of the soldiers to their side? The hypothesis is that such leaders had to take into account in each case a different interplay of several factors: collective and individual interests of soldiers and officers, their cohesiveness as a group, their self-esteem based on past *res gestae*, their degree of alienation from Roman republican state organs, the value of the leader's cause and his formal position. Besides, leaders had to be persuasive, just like politicians in popular assemblies in Rome. In a handful of cases we will see that successful leaders knew how to manipulate the military middle cadre, which could in turn heavily influence the soldiers.

2   State, Army, and Middle Cadre

Important basic concepts are the Roman republican state, late republican Roman armies, and their military middle cadre. These concepts will be dealt with first.

Firstly, the state. According to Martin van Creveld, a state is an abstract entity which can be neither seen, nor heard, nor touched; the state, being separate from both its members and its rulers, is a corporation in the sense that it possesses a legal *persona* of its own, which means that it has rights and duties and may engage in various activities *as if* it were a real individual. The points where the state differs from other corporations are, firstly, the fact that it authorizes them all but is itself authorized or recognized solely by others of its kind; secondly, that certain functions are reserved for it alone; and, thirdly, that it exercises those functions over a certain territory inside which its jurisdiction is both exclusive and all-embracing. The most important of those functions is the monopoly of violence. In tribal societies such things do not exist. Such societies are characterized by the predominance of family-structures, tribal custom, private wars, patronage, reciprocity, and the absence of an abstract authority of any kind. There may be some government, but not a state.[3] Was the late Roman Republic a state? Maybe not completely so in Van Creveld's sense, because it was not yet a completely abstract entity, but it was certainly more than a tribal pre-state society. The Roman Republic had a territory, *nobiles* had far more authority when acting as lawful magistrates of the Roman people, *leges* were more than just tribal custom, and – above all – the Roman Republic had a monopoly on large-scale violence, such as war.[4] After the disastrous private war of the *gens Fabia* against Veii, in 479–477 BC, there were no more such private enterprises in Roman republican history. Or should we characterize Caesar's conquest of Gaul as a private war? A difficult question, but anyhow his attack on tribes in Gallia Comata was launched when he was a lawful proconsul of the Gauls and Illyricum, and on a pretext which was constructed as a valid *casus belli*. So at least Caesar felt the need to do this, instead of just marching in on his own right, as if he were a Viking chief or another Ariovistus. There is a parallel phenomenon from Roman internal history. In a Roman late-republican context leaders of collective actions had much more credibility among masses if they had a strong formal position, for example as a lawful magistrate. In his book on popular leadership and collective behavior in the late Roman Republic Paul Vanderbroeck rightly observes:

> Characteristically, popular leadership in Rome was by definition a formal leadership. The higher level leaders who were involved in collective behaviour all held a magistracy. In this we discover a distinctive Roman modality which distinguishes the Roman Republic.[5]

Secondly, the army. According to Lawrence Keppie, the Roman army of the early and middle republic was its citizenry under arms led into battle by its elected magistrates. He adds, however,

> yet to describe the army as a militia is to understate its capacity and misunderstand the attitude of mind of its leaders and individual members. Discipline and training were its hallmarks; the care with which the camp was laid out reveals no ordinary grouping of amateur warriors. The Romans adopted professional attitudes to warfare long before the army had professional institutions.[6]

Could we say this about *the* Romans, all of them? In my view most Roman armies were rather heterogeneous and consisted of a core of seasoned troops, with inexperienced recruits added to it. In Livy's *Ab urbe condita* 42.32–34 there is a story about the *dilectus* of the army that was to fight the Macedonian king Perseus in 171 BC. In 42.32 Livy tells us that the consuls assembled an army with the utmost care. One of them mobilized veteran soldiers and former centurions as well as young recruits. Many experienced men and veteran centurions volunteered, because they had seen that the men who had fought the Macedonians or the Seleucid king Antiochus III had become rich. There were so many old centurions that some of them could not be placed into their former rank, which caused a fierce reaction among the candidates, who approached the tribunes of the *plebs* and in this way received what they wanted.[7] Livy puts a revealing speech into the mouth of one of them, Spurius Ligustinus, who explains that after his initial obligatory six years as a soldier in Macedonia he volunteered to serve in Greece, Spain, Asia Minor, and probably elsewhere for a further 16 years, and obtained many military decorations. He became a centurion in 195 BC, under Marcus Porcius Cato in Spain, and rose to higher ranks within the centurionate afterwards. In 171 BC Ligustinus wished to ensure that he would be appointed to a post appropriate to his experience and status.

Livy's story probably reflects common practice: any Roman commanding magistrate would like to have as many volunteering seasoned soldiers, centurions, and officers in his army as he could assemble. This is implied in Livy 32.9.1 (198 BC):

The consul Titus Quinctius, when he had conducted his levy in such a way as to select generally soldiers of tried courage who had served in Spain or Africa, and was hastening his departure for his province, was detained by reports of prodigies and by their expiation. (*Consulem T. Quinctium ita habito dilectu, ut eos fere legeret, qui in Hispania aut Africa meruissent, spectatae virtutis milites, properantem in provinciam prodigia nuntiata atque eorum procuratio Romae tenuerunt.*)

Sallust tells us in *B. Jug.* 84.2 that – on the eve of his Numidian campaign in 107 BC – Marius carefully selected seasoned volunteers from among the *Nomen Latinum* and the allies, most of whom were known to him from earlier campaigns or hearsay. In *B. Jug.* 86.2 we read that Marius also opened the ranks of his army to volunteers of Roman stock:

He himself [i.e. Marius] in the meantime enrolled soldiers, not according to the *classes* in the manner of our forefathers [i.e. enrollment based on property qualifications], but allowing anyone to volunteer, for the most part the proletariat. (*Ipse interea milites scribere, non more maiorum neque ex classibus, sed ut lubido quoiusque erat, capite censos plerosque* [mostly proletarians, not all of them!].)

Marius' mules, as his soldiers were called, did not constitute a professional mercenary army, but they became nearly as good as professionals by experiencing one military campaign after the other, either in Northern Africa, against the Numidians, or against invading Germanic tribes in Southern Gaul and the Po Valley.

One more example. According to Appian, *B. Civ.* 2.34, in January 49 at the start of the second civil war the Senate – wrongly thinking that Caesar's army would be slow in arriving from Gaul – directed Pompey to assemble 130,000 Italian soldiers, *chiefly veterans who had experience in war*. However, their initiative came too late. Caesar rashly came down upon them and Pompey could not assemble this huge army and had to make do with some hastily levied troops.

From 88 BC most military campaigns became longer and had to be fought in far-off lands. The soldiers in the armies that were involved in such campaigns came to be known by the name of their commanders (*Sullani, Fimbriani*) and by the numbers and symbols of their military units, for example of the legions in which they continuously served.[8] Legions and auxiliary units came to represent something like a home to the soldiers serving in their ranks. Living together for many years and doing things together in a series of military campaigns welded such groups of soldiers together into cohesive blocks that are referred to as such in the works of contemporary and later authors. Such armies were more homogeneous than the forces in which Ligustinus and his companions had served. New levies, which during the first century BC kept being recruited in traditional *dilectus*, and had to come up against such experienced homogeneous military blocks, were no match for them. The emergency levies of the Marians who fought Sulla in 83–82 BC in Italy, and those of Domitius Ahenobarbus and other Pompeian generals who commanded hastily levied recruits who were to withstand Caesar's veteran army in Italy in January 49 BC had no chance of winning the struggle.[9] In 63 BC Catiline and his lieutenant Manlius, an experienced officer from Sulla's army, had at their disposal some old Sullan veterans, but as most of his other soldiers were poorly armed recruits they lost the battle at Pistoria against the seasoned troops of the Pompeian general Petreius (Sallust, *B. Jug.* 56–60). In *Familiares* 10.24.3f. Munatius Plancus, one of the combatants in the civil wars of 44–43 BC, wrote to Cicero that the armies that were commanded by Decimus Brutus (one of the opponents of Caesar and the succeeding *Caesariani*) and himself were large, but almost worthless, because they consisted of miserable recruits who would have to confront armies which had a nucleus of Caesarean veterans who from 58 to 50 BC had conquered the Gauls, and who, from 49 onwards, had successfully fought a series of civil wars. Ancient authors such as Cicero (e.g. *Tusc.* 2 (16) 38) and Appian (e.g. *B. Civ.* 3.69) were aware of the good fighting qualities of veteran troops, especially if they were led by experienced commanders and officers, and they knew the much inferior military value of newly recruited soldiers who were commanded by senatorial nobles who had spent most of their life and career in Rome.[10]

It was not only the soldiers of the armies that fought in prolonged campaigns in far-off lands who became near-professionals; so did their middle cadre officers, such as military tribunes, *praefecti* of auxiliary units, centurions, and *primipili*. In his own times Ligustinus cannot have been a sole exception. Many centurions and kindred officers who served in auxiliary units must have become near-professionals during successive wars in the third and second centuries BC. In the course of the first century BC a similar process of professionalization took place among the higher middle cadre of tribunes, prefects, and other staff (for example the commanding generals' *comites*). In the first decades of the first century BC such officers and staff of commanding generals were still largely recruited from among young senatorial nobles and young members of traditional land-owning equestrian families which stood in close contact with the senatorial upper class. The Roman armies of the Social War and the campaigns of Sulla and Pompey still had at their disposal many noble senatorial officers and *comites*, most of whom were young scions of senatorial families, amateur gentlemen who still had to participate in a number of military campaigns in order to be eligible for the *cursus honorum*, and they hence became reasonably trained through this practical military activity.[11] In Polybius 6.19 we read that young nobles even had to do ten campaigns before they could enter the *cursus honorum*, but it is a matter of doubt whether this was still the rule in the first century BC. Maybe a smaller number would do. In this age – and even earlier, during the later second century BC – young nobles had probably begun to refrain from the usual long period of military service. Participation in actual military activities by older senators must have been waning too. In the first century BC they started to prefer the post of a legate to that of the military tribunate. Sallust offers a more negative interpretation. In *B. Jug.* 8.1 he remarks:

> At that time there were a great many in our army, both new men and nobles, who cared more for riches than for virtue and self-respect; they were intriguers at home, influential with our allies, rather notorious than respected. (*Ea tempestate in exercitu nostro fuere complures novi atque nobiles, quibus divitiae bono honestoque potiores erant, factiosi domi, potentes apud socios, clari magis quam honesti.*)

"Novi" and "potentes apud socios" indeed. Decades ago Suolahti established that young knights and young scions of the Italian gentry, members of leading municipal families, took over a good deal of the positions within army staffs, the military tribunate, and comparable functions. They became near-professional officers who settled for the best career available to them and who were not so closely tied to the ruling senatorial families. Caesar went a step further in this development to a semi-professional military middle cadre. During the eight to ten years of his campaigns in Transalpine Gaul – according to Cassius Dio 44.43.2 an exceptionally long period for one commanding magistrate – Caesar turned his army into a first class near-professional fighting unit, led by some 660 centurions who spent their lives in the army and by military tribunes, prefects, *legati*, and other members of the commander's staff, who were mainly knights, Italians, members of rather humble senatorial families, provincial Romans or even Celtic noblemen, not *nobiles* from the nucleus of the governing senatorial oligarchy. They became well-trained officers who were able to win Caesar's battles. Together with some Caesarean senators, *equites*, and henchmen who organized Caesar's supplies, money, and information – people like the banker Oppius and Balbus, a *domi nobilis* from Gades in Spain – they formed the group of Caesarean *satellites* which looms large in some of Cicero's letters and in 44 BC took over the Roman state after their leader had been assassinated.[12]

Through a few case-studies we will try to establish which were the interacting factors that gave generals the opportunity to use their armies in civil strife and what was the role and importance of the near-professional military middle cadre.

3 Sulla

The first case that will be discussed is Sulla's march on Rome and its aftermath, 88–87 BC.[13] In 88 BC a difficult war in Italy, the Social War, was almost over. This war had started in 91 BC as a rebellion of some Italian allies who felt frustrated by their subordination under Roman dominance and by the high-handed demeanor of Roman magistrates. The rebellious allies were after equal rights in the distribution of land and an equal share in the spoils of empire. Some allies wanted to receive Roman citizenship, whereas other allies wished to have a state of their own. The Romans were only able to quell the rebellion after they had promised to give Roman citizenship to allies who gave up fighting, which some of them did. The Social War produced a crop of new military specialists within the governing elite and in the social layers just underneath, and it led to a deterioration of civic mentality. Soldiers became accustomed to civil war in Italy and to fighting against former Italian allies, once their comrades in arms. It was then that an ambitious king of Pontus, Mithridates VI, tried to expand into neighboring regions of Asia Minor, which were dominated by the Roman Republic and its client states. The Senate appointed the consul Lucius Cornelius Sulla, one of the most successful commanders in the Social War, as commander against Mithridates, using a perfectly normal procedure. His political enemies, however, supported by some dissatisfied nobles, *equites*, Italian gentry, and poor town-dwellers in Rome, saw to it that the popular assembly (*concilium plebis*) defied the Senate by appointing Marius, the old conqueror of the Numidians and the Germans, and like Sulla one of Rome's commanders in the Social War. This happened in a rather tense political atmosphere. According to Appian (*B. Civ.* 1.55–56) problems arose in 88 about the distribution of new Italian citizens, who had received their new civil status at the end of the Social War, among the 35 *tribus*, the voting units in the tribal assembly. Sulpicius, a tribune of the *plebs*, wanted to distribute them among all 35 tribes, thus giving them a fair share in decision-making, but many old Roman citizens opposed his proposals and fought the new Italian citizens in the Forum. The consuls, Quintus Pompeius and Lucius Sulla, proclaimed a vacation of several days and postponed the day of voting to calm down the crowds, but Sulpicius and his gang forced them to annul the vacation. In the ensuing riots the son of Quintus Pompeius, who was Sulla's son-in-law, was killed, but both consuls escaped, whereupon Sulpicius enacted his law about the new citizens, and had Marius chosen commander of the war against Mithridates in place of Sulla. Appian is suggesting that everything was done for Marius' sake. Normally Appian's *Bella Civilia* is one of our better sources, based on good information in earlier works now largely lost to us, but this is probably exaggerated. In *B. Civ.* 1.57 Appian relates:

> When Sulla heard of this he resolved to decide the question by war and called the army [i.e. the army that was encamped at Nola in Campania, which was to march against Mithridates under Sulla's command]. The soldiers were eager for the war against Mithridates because it promised much plunder, and they feared that Marius would enlist other soldiers instead of themselves. Sulla spoke of the indignity put upon them by Sulpicius and Marius, and while he did not openly allude to anything else – for he did not dare as yet to mention this sort of war – he urged them to be ready to obey his orders. They understood what he meant, and as they feared lest they should miss the campaign, they uttered boldly what Sulla had in mind and told him to be of good courage, and to lead them to Rome. Sulla was overjoyed and led six legions thither forthwith; but all his superior officers, except one quaestor, left him and fled to the city, because they would not submit to the idea of leading an army against their country. Envoys met him on the road and asked him why he was marching with armed forces against his own country. "To deliver her from tyrants," he replied.

Livy's epitomator (*Per.* 77) and Velleius Paterculus 2.18–19 give the story in abbreviated form mentioning Sulpicius' role and accentuating Sulla's initiative, as did Plutarch, *Marius* 35.6. In *Sulla* 8.4–9.1 and *Marius* 35.4f. Plutarch tells us that Sulpicius had the command transferred to Marius and subsequently sent military tribunes to Sulla's army-camp at Nola with instructions to take over the army and conduct it to Marius. When Sulla turned up at Nola, however, his soldiers, when they learned what had happened, slew these military tribunes, in return for which Marius and his partisans in Rome began slaying the friends of Sulla and plundering their property. So we cannot be sure that Marius really had the intention of leaving Sulla's soldiers behind, but probably they themselves thought he would. Sulla marched on Rome, and there it came to fierce street fighting against Marian town-dwellers, who had little chance against Sulla's well-armed seasoned troops. Sulla took a few precautions and marched to the East, leaving some of his soldiers at Nola, probably to their disappointment. They were approached by Sulla's opponent Cinna, consul in 87 and a friend of Marius. Like Marius he had been driven from Rome by the Sullans. Now he tried to return and take control in the capital. According to Velleius Paterculus 2.20.4 he first bribed the centurions and military tribunes and then approached the private soldiers with promises of generous gifts:

> Cinna was then received by the army at Nola, after corrupting first the centurions and tribunes and then even the private soldiers with promises of largesse. (*Tum Cinna corruptis primo centurionibus ac tribunis, mox etiam spe largitionis militibus, ab eo exercitu, qui circa Nolam erat, receptus est.*)

Appian gives more credit, however, to Cinna's oratory for this turn of events; his powers of persuasion convinced the troops to side with him (*B. Civ.* 1.65–66), but he tells us in the same passage what was Cinna's strongest argument: he was a lawful consul. Probably Cinna prepared his decisive oratorical performance by well-targeted actions among the middle cadre and the soldiery of this army, which had been left aside by Sulla and so did not have strong feelings of adherence to the Sullan cause any more. In the end Cinna seized power in Italy and recalled Marius from exile. Marius became consul for a seventh time and died early in 86. Cinna was murdered in 84. Sulla beat the Pontic forces in Greece, profited by successes gained by Marian troops, which fought Mithridates in Asia Minor, came to an agreement with the Pontic king, and returned to Italy in 84–83. His army had to smooth the way for him a second time, because in 87 his Marian enemies had seized power in Rome and Italy. When Sulla landed in Italy, young Pompey came to his support with an army of volunteers who had fought under Pompey's father during the Social War and undoubtedly felt attracted to Sulla's successes. Furthermore, many senatorial nobles flocked to Sulla's standards, thus giving him an air of legitimacy (Livy, *Per.* 85.4f.).

Which interacting factors gave Sulla and Cinna the opportunity to use their armies as weapons in civil strife? What conclusions are to be drawn from this *casus*? First of all, after having been together during a difficult war, the Social War, Sulla's soldiery had developed a common identity. Secondly, Sulla had the charisma of military fame, and a good cause, because – although being a lawful consul – he had been offended and unjustly relieved of his command against Mithridates. Thirdly, his soldiers and officers had a collective interest: they were about to lose a good opportunity to enrich themselves in the gorgeous East, and they must have felt that their achievements in the Social War entitled them to a better treatment.

Nonetheless Sulla's higher officers and staff almost completely deserted him: except for one quaestor they all left him; their adherence to the existing system was too strong. Most of Sulla's staff still were young nobles or knights who had strong ties with the senatorial aristocracy. We may surmise that his centurions, however, stayed with him.

Sulla's army was not a slavishly obedient retinue. Sulla had to persuade them with a clever speech and make sure that his soldiers would march on Rome with him; troops that he had left behind at Nola when he departed to the East went over to the other side when another lawful consul, the Marian partisan Cinna, approached them. Decisive to them were the strong formal position of Cinna, their collective interests, and feelings of disappointment about the way Sulla had robbed them of the opportunity to gain booty and donatives. The case of Cinna reveals another factor: the importance of the middle cadre, which was approached earlier than the soldiers. Both Sulla and Cinna had to be persuasive. Like politicians in popular assemblies, they could not simply ask the soldiers to do what they wanted them to do, but they had to use their rhetorical skills to persuade them.[14]

4   The Fimbrians

A second case study. The civil disturbances of 88–87 BC had some consequences in the East. Despite Sulla's successes against Pontic troops and their allies in Greece and the unexpected death of Marius, Cinna determined to send his own men to the East to destroy Mithridates, restore Roman control in Asia Minor, and eventually fight the Sullan forces. Cinna's colleague, the *consul suffectus* L. Valerius Flaccus, who had taken Marius' place after the latter had died, was dispatched to Asia Minor with only two legions, however, Sulla's forces being much stronger. Flaccus wisely avoided battles against Sulla, but he did not know how to handle his own army, in which Sullan sympathies and fears of Sulla's much bigger army had become strong, and was murdered by his own men, who then went to Asia Minor under the command of C. Flavius Fimbria, and fought Mithridates to a standstill. In *Mithr.* 59f. Appian tells us that Fimbria's troops began to incline towards Sulla again after the latter had come to an agreement with Mithridates. Fimbria, an avaricious villain, but a loyal Marian, tried in vain to prevent his men from deserting him. He lost his life and Sulla took over his army, which he left behind to keep an eye on Mithridates when he himself returned to Italy to fight another round of civil war against the Marians. The Fimbrians, as they became known, probably joined Murena in his abortive campaign against Mithridates in 83–82 and after eight years they served in the army of Lucullus, who had to fight another prolonged war against the Pontic king (74–67 BC). In Asia Minor the Fimbrians earned a reputation of rapacity. When Lucullus took over the command in 74 he took strict measures against the hoodlums of Fimbria's army, but after some years he had to cope with a few cases of rapacity and unruliness, which were nourished and activated, particularly among the Fimbrians, by Publius Clodius, Lucullus' brother-in-law and one of his officers, who started his career as a demagogue in this army. The Fimbrians and other soldiers listened to him, because they believed that the veterans of Pompey's campaigns in the Iberian peninsula had received much more after a struggle that had been far less hard and because it was generally assumed that Lucullus had been lining his own pocket at the soldiers' expense. Besides, Lucullus was about to lose his formal authority, as his successor was on his way to take over command.[15]

Which conclusions can be drawn from this case study? First of all, a military command could become very unstable in a formally and morally questionable situation (should soldiers fight Sulla, a former consul, who had gained great fame and successes against an enemy of the Roman people?). There were collective and individual material interests at stake. The Fimbrians developed a group identity and enriched themselves shamelessly. Such a military group, welded together by a common past of this type, could be a great nuisance to even a greatly successful and lawful commander such as Lucullus had been; as soon as they had the impression that they received too little and their commander too much, this commander seemed to lose his formal position, and a demagogic officer like Clodius stirred their discontent. This case study does not show any kind of *Heeresgefolgschaft*, but an interplay of formal arguments, material interests, demagoguery by leading officers, and strong collective identities of groups of soldiers.

5   Caesar

A third case study, about Caesar's army. Like Sulla in 88, in January 49 Caesar could pose as a great and victorious general. He had added Gallia Comata to the provinces that he had received in 59, i.e. Cisalpine Gaul (the Po Valley), Transalpine Gaul (Southern France), and Illyricum (part of Slovenia/Croatia), and he had been the first Roman to cross the Rhine into Germany and the Channel to invade Britain. His soldiers, officers, and other aides had every reason to be grateful to Caesar. The military had suffered serious losses, but the survivors had been enriched,[16] and quite a few of Caesar's other aides had gained the opportunity to become wealthy and influential, particularly clever people like Balbus and Oppius (see above). Caesar was acceptable to many other Romans too. He was a *popularis*, and a very successful orator, but he was not a destructive revolutionary such as Catiline had been.

Nonetheless even Caesar had to make sure that the soldiers of his thirteenth legion, the only one that was with him at the Rubicon, shared his views before he could venture to start civil war and launch a quick attack on the Pompeian forces in Italy. Pompey was already assembling a sizeable army and the Caesarean tribunes of the *plebs*, Mark Antony and Cassius, had been pushing the conflict to breaking-point by continuously interceding in favor of Caesar, against Pompey and the die-hard optimates in the Senate.[17] The two tribunes of the *plebs* had consequently been driven from the Senate's house and the Roman Forum by the enraged optimates and had escaped to the north, to Caesar's army. In *B. Civ.* 1.7 Caesar tells us that in a speech to his troops he commemorated all the acts of injustice that his enemies in Rome had committed against him, in spite of his great victories, and against the two Caesarean tribunes of the *plebs*. The soldiers of the thirteenth legion then shouted that they were prepared to avenge the wrongs done to Caesar and the tribunes. Only then did Caesar summon his other troops and invade Italy, as he himself admits (Caesar, *B. Civ.* 1.7–8). The newly enrolled soldiers of the Pompeians were no match for Caesar's veteran troops and succumbed quickly. Pompey escaped to the Balkans and tried to rebuild his forces there. In the meantime Caesar eliminated Pompeian forces in Spain and took Massilia, which had opted for the Pompeian cause. Caesar subsequently crossed the Adriatic Sea, although the Pompeian fleet was very strong there, beat Pompey in 48 at Pharsalus and got rid of remaining Pompeian armies and their allies in a series of difficult campaigns from 47 to 45. In his last year, 45–44, Caesar was the unchallenged dictator of the Roman Empire. He rewarded his allies well; some of them were given the opportunity to make careers for themselves in Rome, while others were appointed to lucrative officer's positions or were made governors of provinces. As was indicated above, Caesar turned his army into a first class near-professional fighting unit, led and administered by experienced centurions, military tribunes, prefects, *legati*, and other members of the commander's staff, who were mainly knights, Italians, members of rather humble senatorial families, provincial Romans, or even Celtic noblemen. To them were added a handful of Caesarean senators, and a group of *equites* and henchmen who organized Caesar's supplies, money, and information. Among Caesar's officers and middle cadre were not so many young scions of politically independent senatorial families. A staff like this was more dependent on the successes of their master, Caesar, than earlier groups of *comites* and officers had been.

There are indications that Caesar purposefully used his officers and centurions to influence others, employing them as intermediaries in a demagogic game. In the tense situation on the eve of the battle against the German chief Ariovistus in Gaul (57 BC) he talked to his officers and centurions first and then, using them as go-betweens, tried to change the mood of the soldiers, in which aim he was successful (Caesar, *B. Gal.* 1.40–41; Cassius Dio 38.35.3 and 38.47.1). Caesar knew the value of his middle cadre and consequently enriched them greatly. In 49 BC he could borrow enough money from his officers and centurions to grant his soldiers a bonus (Caesar, *B. Civ.* 1.39.3f.). On several occasions in his own writings Caesar explicitly mentions the centurions as a separate category, for example in lists of casualties, in accounts of courageous acts, or in reports of consultations (*B. Gal.* 1.40.1; *B. Civ.* 3.53; 3.71.1; 3.91.1ff.). Caesar's officers sat at separate tables at the banquets that he organized in his provinces. Suetonius (*Jul.* 48) tells us that in Gaul Caesar had dinner served in two large rooms, one for his officers and Greek friends and one for Roman citizens and some important provincials. Caesar is also known to have reprimanded a military tribune of the tenth legion, Avienus, for having filled an entire ship with his own booty and war spoils when he was on his way to Africa in 46 (*B. Afr.* 54). Caesar also manipulated his opponents' officers. In 49 in Spain he sent some of his own men to the Pompeian camp. Although we do not know exactly whom they were to approach, we do have an indirect indication. Appian tells us that Petreius, one of the Pompeian commanders in Spain, had some of the Caesarean agents put to death and also killed one of his own officers who had tried to stop him (Appian, *B. Civ.* 2.43).

However, even Caesar had to cope with mutinies every time he overburdened his troops or did not put into effect the promises that he had made.[18] In 57 Caesar faced his first near-mutiny at Vesontio – on the eve of the battle against Ariovistus – which he was able to quell with the help of his centurions, whom he had convinced first. In 49 BC Caesar faced a second mutiny, at Placentia in the Po Valley, among veteran troops that he had sent ahead, while he himself was besieging Massilia. The men involved in the mutiny had numerous grievances. They had been short of food and other supplies during recent campaigns and expected similar conditions in the future. They had not been paid their salaries, they had not been given their promised bonuses, nor had they been allowed to plunder. They had served continuously for years and had suffered heavy losses. They were now marching to Brundisium and more wars in the East. In response to these factors, they mutinied, demanding back pay and promised *donativa*. Some soldiers demanded discharge as well. Others used the mutiny merely as a bargaining ploy; they wanted to continue serving but knew their value to Caesar and were taking advantage of his precarious position to obtain more money and concessions. They also may have been encouraged by Caesar's continuously problematic position within the republican system and its governing elite. Caesar was able to put down this mutiny because he had the support of sufficient other seasoned troops. Another serious mutiny took place in 47, for comparable reasons. Soldiers who were encamped in Campania began causing trouble by plundering various cities. Antony vainly tried to pacify them. Chrissanthos convincingly argues that Caesar had to meet their demands and could not punish the ringleaders, because he did not have an army at hand with which to force his men to obey his orders. The mutiny of 47 was far more serious than has generally been recognized and was not quelled with the ease often assumed. While the civil war was still raging, nine of Caesar's ten veteran legions, his best troops, mutinied. In the end he could only take five of those legions to Africa, supplemented by five legions of recruits. Caesar discharged the four remaining legions and rewarded them with money and land, as they had demanded. The legions which continued to serve eventually received increased financial rewards. All the men had their grievances addressed by Caesar, who, in the end, was unable to impose his will on them. The mutiny of 47 may very well have been a success for the participating soldiers.[19]

What do these mutiny stories reveal about Caesar's army of the Gauls? Years of continuous fighting had given them a strong sense of unity and a keen understanding of their own interests. They had become well aware of their value to Caesar during civil war and were not afraid to express their feelings and present demands to Caesar. In this army there was no trace of any automatic *Heeresgefolgschaft*. Instead, Caesar's apparatus of soldiers, officers, and other aides became the dominant force in Roman politics, both under Caesar and even more after Caesar had been murdered. Caesarean officers and centurions saw to it that the dictator's *acta* remained in force and that veterans continued to be settled, and repeatedly tried to reconcile quarreling Caesarean leaders, such as Mark Antony and Caesar's adoptive son Octavian, in order to safeguard their own individual and collective interests. Caesar's henchmen and assistants retained their positions and influence, as Cicero observes in his letters. Contemporary and other ancient writers were aware that the *caesariani* – as they were called – formed an independent block in politics. Caesar's old soldiers were not easily impressed by noble magistrates or senatorial viewpoints. In *B. Civ.* 3.76 Appian tells us that after the battle of Mutina (43 BC), where a senatorial army under Octavian and the two consuls of the year, Hirtius and Pansa, beat Mark Antony, a mortally wounded consul Pansa advised Octavian to take over his veterans and the new levies. Hirtius had already died on the battlefield. Pansa warned Octavian of the possible awe of the inexperienced recruits for the Senate, and indeed Octavian failed to win them over to his side. Their allegiance to the Caesarean cause was rather weak and their loyalty to the existing republican system too strong.[20]

Octavian proved himself to be one of the most cunning manipulators of the military middle cadre. Already in March and April 44 BC, and more so in the autumn of that eventful year, he was successful in winning over military tribunes and centurions of the Caesarean armies, enough to get many Caesarean veterans and a few legions to his side, which turned out to be of great consequence to his career. Quintessential in his maneuvering were two things: Caesar's name – Octavian became Gaius Iulius Caesar Octavianus through Caesar's will – and the financial support of Caesar's henchmen, people such as Balbus and Oppius, which gave Octavian the means to promise handsome bonuses to Caesar's veterans, and to influence the middle cadre of his opponents; he was always able to promise more than they could, and – in Caesarean eyes – as Caesar's son he seemed to have a good cause, revenge against Caesar's murderers and the preservation of the dictator's *acta*.[21]

6   Conclusions

The three case studies given above clearly show that late republican Roman armies were no slavish retinues of powerful magnates. The post-Marian armies were not automatically *clientelae* of leaders who were to enrich them; the interaction between army and leader was dependent on a number of interplaying factors, and the attitude of one army differed from the mood of another one. Officers and soldiers had a keen eye for personal qualities, merits, formal positions, and good or bad causes of competing generals and knew how to safeguard or promote their common and individual interests. Much depended upon the degree of professionalism, cohesiveness, and common past of groups of soldiers. Newly enrolled recruits were more easily overawed by famous leaders and had less self-esteem than veteran armies, which had more insight into their generals' dependency upon them and better knew how to force their leaders to give them what they wanted. The position of the generals' staff and their military middle cadre, consisting of centurions, prefects, and military tribunes, was important. They were the intermediaries between leaders and soldiers and could influence the lower ranks. Leaders who wanted to use their armies in civil strife knew this and tried to win over their staff and military middle cadre first and the soldiers afterwards. Another important factor was closeness to or alienation from the traditional republican system and the governing senatorial elite. Sulla's higher officers, consisting of members of noble ruling families and knights who had strong ties with the governing elite, left him as soon as they saw that he was marching on Rome. Only one quaestor stayed with him. Caesar's staff, officers, and centurions – who were not so closely linked to the governing elite – stayed with him in the civil war; only one of his lieutenants left him. Last but not least, all three cases indicate that leaders had to be persuasive in words and deeds: Sulla and Caesar were, but in the end Fimbria was not and went down.

NOTES

Translations into English of ancient texts were taken from Loeb editions, unless indicated otherwise.

1　Le Glay, Voisin, and Le Bohec 2001, 114. On Marius' new way of recruiting new soldiers see Gabba 1976, 13–19. Cf. Lintott 1994, 92: "He (i.e. Marius) also included in this levy the property-less *capite censi* – a move criticized by later historians, on the ground that it filled the army with unprincipled men who were ideal material for aspirants to dictatorial power."

2　In a different context Peter Brunt briefly remarks that in revolutionary times centurions were the natural spokesmen and leaders of the troops, but in my view the middle cadre is broader and includes tribunes and prefects. See Brunt 1988, 274.

3　Van Creveld 1999, 1–7, esp. 1f. On debates and discussions about the Roman republican state see Hölkeskamp 2004.

4　The common opinion about the Roman Republic is that it was an oligarchy, in which a handful of noble families had the upper hand. Fergus Millar, on the other hand, emphasizes the importance of the popular assembly and of good orators who could change the opinion of assembled crowds. See Millar 1998, 197–226. The importance of the popular assembly, being the *populus* that chose the magistrates, is also emphasized by Hölkeskamp 2004, 82.

5　Vanderbroeck 1987, 34.

6　Keppie 1984, 55.

7　De Blois 2000, 11–13.

8　See Sallust, *Cat.* 11.4; 16.4; 37.6 (old Sullans); Plutarch, *Luc.* 7.1–2 (Fimbrians). See Harmand 1967, 231–43; MacMullen 1984, 440–56.

9　On the civil war in Italy in 83–82 BC see Lovano 2002, 114–35. On the fighting in Italy early in 49 BC see Caesar, *B. Civ.* 1.8–30; Suetonius, *Jul.* 34; Appian, *B. Civ.* 2.30–39; Keppie 1984, 103ff.; Rawson 1994, 424.

10　De Blois 2000, 11–15.

11　De Blois 2000, 15f.

12　On Caesar's staff see Harmand 1967, 7, 148, 290–8, 331–41, 355f., 360ff., 375ff., 407, 425, 435ff.; Gruen 1995, 112–19, esp. 116–18. On its role in politics from March 44 BC see Cicero, *Att.* 14.5.2; 14.6.1f.; 14.9.2; 14.10.1f.; 14.13.6; 14.17.6. Cf. Cassius Dio 44.34. In *Att.* 14.5.2 Cicero says: *sed vides magistratus, si quidem illi magistratus, vides tamen tyranni satellites in imperiis, vides eiusdem exercitus, vides in latere veteranos, quae sunt euripista omnia.* See De Blois 1994, 335–39; De Blois 2000, 20–8. On Balbus and Oppius see Cicero, *Att.* 14.5.1; Tacitus, *Ann.* 12.60; Cassius Dio 48.32.2; cf. Wiseman 1971, 209ff., no. 137; Alföldi 1976, 31–42. On Caesar's "apparatus" see Syme 1966, 61–96; Gruen 1995, 112–19; and Gotter 1996, 21–41.

13　On Sulla see Keaveney 1982; Christ 2002.

14　Cf. Millar 1998, 226, about politics in the city of Rome. Lovano 2002, 36f., emphasizes Cinna's rhetorical skill in winning over the army at Nola.

15　Livy, *Per.* 98; Velleius Paterculus 2.33; Plutarch, *Luc.*, esp. 7 and 30–5. Cassius Dio 36.14 calls them "Valerians," after their original commander Valerius Flaccus, who had been killed by his own troops. On the Fimbrians see Lovano 2002, 98f.; De Blois 1992, 111; De Blois 2000, 19.

16　Caesar enriched them even more at the end of the civil war (Suetonius, *Jul.* 38), which must have contributed to the cohesiveness and awareness of common interests, which his officers and soldiers were shown to have after Caesar had been murdered in March 44. See De Blois 2000, 20f.

17　De Blois 2000, 19f. On Pompey's mobilization see Caesar, *B. Civ.* 1.3.2; Appian, *B. Civ.* 2.32 and 34. On the filibustering which the Caesarean tribunes of the *plebs* put into practice and the flight of the tribunes see Livy, *Per.* 109; Appian, *B. Civ.* 2.27 and 33;

Plutarch, *Caes.* 30f. See Raaflaub 1974, 152ff. On Caesar in general see Gelzer 1968. On Caesar's "apparatus" and the careers they could make thanks to Caesar see above, note 12 and De Blois 1992, 112.

18   On the mutinies of 49 and 47 BC see Appian, *B. Civ.* 2.47 and 92–94; Livy, *Per.* 113; Cassius Dio 41.26.1ff. and 42.52f.; Plutarch, *Caes.* 51.2ff. On mutinies against Caesar see De Blois 2000, 20; Chrissanthos 2001, esp. 67–9, 71–5.

19   This is the opinion of Chrissanthos 2001, 71–5, whom I am quoting and following here.

20   On the political role of Caesar's followers after their master had been murdered at the Ides of March 44 BC see above, note 12.

21   See De Blois 2000, 26–30. In the end Octavian won the civil wars, which raged from 44–30 BC, and became sole ruler. In 27 BC he received the title Augustus and became the first emperor; the days of Republican rule were over.

BIBLIOGRAPHY

Alföldi, A. 1976. *Oktavians Aufstieg zur Macht.* Bonn.

Blois, L. de. 1992. "Roman officers and politics. The manipulation of the military middle cadre in the period 44–36 BC," *Laverna* 3: 104–28.

——— 1994. "Sueton, Aug. 46 und die Manipulation des mittleren Militärkaders als politisches Instrument," *Historia* 43: 324–45.

——— 2000. "Army and society in the late Roman Republic: Professionalism and the role of the military middle cadre," in G. Alföldy, B. Dobson, and W. Eck (eds.), *Kaiser, Heer und Gesellschaft in der Römischen Kaiserzeit.* Stuttgart, 11–31.

Brunt, P. A. 1988. *The Fall of the Roman Republic and Related Essays.* Oxford.

Chrissanthos, S. G. 2001. "Caesar and the mutiny of 47 BC," *JRS* 91: 63–75.

Christ, K. 2002. *Sulla. Eine römische Karriere.* Munich.

Gabba, E. 1976. *Republican Rome. The Army and the Allies.* Oxford. (Translated from the Italian edition: *Esercito e società nella tarda Repubblica Romana.* Rome 1973.)

Gelzer, M. 1968. *Caesar: Politician and Statesman.* Oxford. (Original: *Caesar. Der Politiker und Staatsmann.* Wiesbaden 1960.)

Gotter, U. 1996. *Der Diktator ist tod! Politik in Rom zwischen den Iden des März und der Begründung des Zweiten Triumvirats.* Stuttgart.

Gruen, E. S. 1995². *The Last Generation of the Roman Republic.* Berkeley.

Harmand, J. 1967. *L'armée et le soldat à Rome de 107 à 50 av. n.è.* Paris.

Hölkeskamp, K.-J. 2004. *Rekonstruktionen einer Republik. Die politische Kultur des antiken Rom und die Forschung der letzten Jahrzehnte.* Munich.

Keaveney, A. 1982. *Sulla: The Last Republican.* London.

Keppie, L. 1984. *The Making of the Roman Army.* London.

Le Glay, M., J.-L. Voisin, and Y. Le Bohec. 2001². *A History of Rome.* Oxford. (Original: *Histoire romaine,* Paris 1994².)

Lintott, A. W. 1994. "Political history, 146–95 BC," in *CAH* 9. Cambridge, 40–103.

Lovano, M. 2002. *The Age of Cinna: Crucible of Late Republican Rome.* Stuttgart.

MacMullen, R. 1984. "The legion as a society," *Historia* 33: 440–56.

Millar, F. G. B. 1998. *The Crowd in Rome in the Late Republic.* Ann Arbor.

Raaflaub, K. A. 1974. *Dignitatis contentio. Studien zur Motivation und politischen Taktik im Bürgerkrieg zwischen Caesar und Pompeius.* Munich.

Rawson, E. 1994. "Caesar. Civil war and dictatorship," in *CAH* 9. Cambridge, 424–67.

Suolahti, J. 1955. *The Junior Officers of the Roman Army in the Republican Period*. Helsinki.

Syme, R. 1966[6]. *The Roman Revolution*. Oxford.

Van Creveld, M. 1999. *The Rise and Decline of the State*. Cambridge.

Vanderbroeck, P. J. J. 1987. *Popular Leadership and Collective Behavior in the Late Roman Republic (c. 80–50 BC)*. Amsterdam.

Wiseman, T. P. 1971. *New Men in the Roman Senate, 139 BC–AD 14*. Oxford.

FURTHER READING

In general: De Blois 2000, 11–31; Gruen 1995; Keppie 1984. On Sulla, the first case-study: Keaveney 1982 and Christ 2002. On the period of Cinna and the Fimbrians: Lovano 2002. On Caesar and his aftermath: De Blois 1992, 104–28; Gelzer 1968; Gotter 1996; Chrissanthos 2001, 63–75.

PART III

The Empire
(Actium to Adrianople)

CHAPTER ELEVEN

The Augustan Reform and the Structure of the Imperial Army

Kate Gilliver

The army of the early Roman Empire is probably the most extensively studied and certainly the best known of any period in Roman history. It is also the one most widely known to different audiences, through the archaeological evidence that remains from its permanent bases throughout the empire and the propaganda monuments in Rome and elsewhere, and from its depiction in movies and displays by "living history" societies. In spite of the considerable amount of surviving evidence, or perhaps because of the nature of that evidence and the way it is presented for modern consumption, it is easy to forget that the Roman army continued to evolve and develop throughout the imperial period. The uniformed, homogenous fighting force illustrated on monuments such as Trajan's Column is a product of imperial propaganda and this image has been encouraged by modern misconceptions that a professional standing army such as Rome had must have been similar to later professional armies. The period covered by this chapter sees the evolution of the army from one without permanent existence but which was regularly involved in campaigns and fighting, and indeed whose very existence resulted from the republican tradition of annual warfare and the political ambitions of their commanders, to one that was a permanent army of occupation throughout the provinces, concerned particularly with internal security and frontier defense, but only occasionally becoming involved in the large-scale campaigns of conquest that were the norm for the armies of the republic. As the permanent units of the imperial army became settled in their provincial bases and drew increasingly on local recruitment to maintain their numbers, the army became regionalized. A legion stationed on the Rhine frontier in the second century AD was a rather different unit from a legion stationed in Syria, not only in terms of the racial and cultural identity of the legionaries, but also, of necessity given the different terrain and enemies, in equipment and fighting styles. The structure of the imperial army was a highly flexible one that evolved in response to the changing political and military requirements of the imperial period, and the foundations of one of the world's first standing armies were laid by Rome's first emperor, Augustus.

1 The Establishment of a Professional Army

In 31 BC in the aftermath of Actium, Octavian held under his control not only the combined legions of his own and Antony's armies, totaling some 60 legions of probably varying strength, but also the fleet that had won his decisive victory for him, numbering some 400 or so ships, and the unrecorded numbers of allied units that had contributed to the armies of the triumviral period. These numbers needed to be reduced: an over-large army was financially unsustainable, would be impossible to employ usefully, and posed a threat to political and social stability. Romans saw the existence of large armies loyal to individual generals rather than the state as a major factor contributing to the civil strife of the late republic; they were also clear evidence of political crisis (Cassius Dio 52.27). If Augustus wanted to stabilize the state and build public confidence in his new regime, he needed to show that the crisis was over. A massive reduction in the legions would help to do this, as well as appease the soldiers themselves, many of whom had enlisted or been conscripted to fight for individuals in civil war and were eager to be discharged with an appropriate reward. Whether reducing the size of the army would have provided any reassurance to the Senate as to the nature of Augustus' regime is another matter, but the *princeps* himself considered it important enough to give it considerable prominence in his *Res Gestae*. The inscription begins with an extremely brief and partisan account of Augustus' rise to power, a bald statement concerning the extent of his campaigns and conquests, and then, the first action of the newly self-appointed *princeps* to be recorded is that of the half a million men under arms he discharged 300,000 of them with the reward of land grants or cash bonuses (*Res Gestae* 3).

In order to retain his position as Rome's sole leader and prevent a recurrence of the civil wars and political instability that had brought an end to the republic, Augustus needed not only to maintain firm control of the army, but to change its whole relationship with the Roman state. The military reforms he undertook served to remove soldiers from the active involvement in politics that they had enjoyed during the last century of the republic and the triumviral period, and aimed to break the ties of loyalty to individual generals and expectation of reward that had made a major contribution to the end of the republic; instead the army's loyalties were directed towards the emperor and members of the imperial family rather than to their own commanders. The citizen militia of the early and middle republic was already evolving into a more professional army by 31 BC, but Augustus accelerated that process by establishing a standing army with permanent units of citizen legions and non-citizen auxiliaries. The army was based in the provinces and on the frontiers; with the exception of the Urban Cohorts and Praetorian Guard, no military units were stationed in Italy, which had suffered so much during the wars of the first century BC, and Italian society swiftly became demilitarized. Whilst many of Augustus' military "reforms" were little more than the regularization of changes that had been taking place in the late republic, others were radical in the context of a generally conservative society that placed great emphasis on ancestral traditions.

By the late republic the legions, which had originally been raised on an annual basis to wage war in Italy, were serving for continuous periods, sometimes for many years, in provinces throughout the Mediterranean. That length of service could vary enormously. The two legions raised by Valerius Flaccus in 86 BC for the campaign against Mithridates were still serving when Pompey took over the command nearly 20 years later, whilst the three legions of Metellus Creticus involved in operations against pirates may have served for only three years, from 68–65 before being returned to Italy and discharged. The rewards of service could be equally inconsistent with some legions being settled on land, such as Saturninus' settlement of Marius' veterans (Appian, *B. Civ.* 1.29) and Sulla's displacement of Italian farmers to settle his civil war veterans, whilst other legions received no substantial reward when their service was completed. The potential reward on discharge was one of the principal factors that encouraged the loyalty of soldiers to their generals rather than to the Roman state, and contributed to the civil wars that ended the republic. By establishing fixed rewards which were available only after completion of an established minimum length of service, Augustus was able to break the financial dependence of soldiers on their generals and some of the ties of loyalty. This might seem an obvious solution, and, after the establishment of the *aerarium militare* in AD 6 to finance the settlement of veterans, an appropriate one since the new taxes inevitably had a greater effect on the elite who had so steadfastly refused to reward veterans in the late republic, but we should not be too critical of the senate for failing to take such steps earlier. In spite of the growing tendency in the last century of the republic for some citizens to see the army as a profession and the decreasing importance of any kind of property qualification for legionary service, there had remained a strong belief in the idea of a Rome whose military superiority lay in the traditions of a citizen militia drawn on the property-owning classes who served in the legions when necessity demanded. The creation of an army of long-service professionals recruited regardless of social, and sometimes citizen, status signaled an end to this central feature of the Roman Republic, and even though it was merely the next logical step in the evolution of the Roman army, Augustus drew on republican precedents in establishing his imperial army.

After the mass settlement of veterans following Actium, Augustus retained in service 28 of the legions that had been in existence in 31 BC, drawn from both his own and Antony's armies. Although the number of legions fluctuated over the next two and a half centuries as units were destroyed, disbanded for dishonorable behavior or raised for campaigns, the total number of legions, and indeed overall size of the army, did not change fundamentally from that established by Augustus, as indicated by Cassius Dio's valuable summary of legionary comings and goings (Cassius Dio 55.23–24). Tacitus (*Ann.* 4.5) stated that the number of auxiliaries approximately equaled that of the legionaries, but opted not to provide a list of all the units and their stations because there were so many; military strength in the early imperial period was around 300,000, about half of whom were legionaries and half auxiliaries. In setting the length of legionary service, Augustus drew on the traditional requirement that a citizen be available for up to 16 campaigns, or 20 in times of national emergency (Polybius 6.19) and set service at 16 years plus four in reserve. Dio records this in 13 BC (Cassius Dio 54.25), but it is likely that since Actium there had been an expectation that soldiers would serve for this length of time. In AD 5, this was increased to 20 plus five in reserve; whatever the distinction was between ordinary soldiers and those in reserve, it seems to have been dropped fairly soon afterwards and all legionaries and auxiliaries served for 25 years. Conscription through the *dilectus* remained an option but although there are occasional references to levies, such as during the Pannonian revolt or in the aftermath of the Varian disaster, or the occasional levy of non-citizen troops in the provinces, the vast majority of recruits were volunteers.[1]

Augustus did not raise military pay which had been doubled to 225 *denarii* a year by Caesar (Suetonius, *Jul.* 26), but soldiers were now guaranteed a regular income for a fixed period of time, followed by a guaranteed discharge bonus. At first the reward for veterans came in the form of a land grant, following the precedents of the late republic and triumviral periods, and continuing, though in a different form, the long established link between land ownership and military service. Augustus went to great efforts to avoid the confiscations that had provided for veteran settlement in the unsettled decades at the end of the republic. Such redistributions of land were associated with civil strife and political dominance such as Sulla's dictatorship or the triumvirate, in which the then Octavian had been responsible for the deeply unpopular confiscations in Italy following Philippi (Appian, *B. Civ.* 5.19; Suetonius, *Aug.* 13; Vergilius, *Ecl.*). As Augustus, he ensured that in both Italy and the provinces the lands assigned to the veterans were purchased, not confiscated, and he publicized in his *Res Gestae* not only the extraordinarily large sums he personally committed to this task (a total of 860,000,000 sesterces for the large-scale settlements of 30 and 14 BC), but also the boast that he was the first and only person to have paid for such lands, another clear sign that the political and military crises of the late republic had been resolved. The size of the allotments is not known, though it is estimated that they may have been up to 50 *iugera* (14.7 ha) for ordinary legionaries, sufficient to provide for a family and produce a surplus, and more for former centurions and tribunes.[2] Military colonies were set up throughout the empire, and 28 were established in Italy (*Res Gestae* 28). However, Augustus was unable to sustain this kind of expenditure and there was a limit to the amount of available land, especially in Italy, so increasingly the discharge bonus was paid in cash rather than land. These pay-outs, recorded in the *Res Gestae*, amounted to 400,000,000 sesterces and were made in 7, 6, 4, 3, and 2 BC (*Res Gestae* 16). The soldiers receiving these cash bonuses on retirement had been recruited in the 20s BC, had not fought in civil wars, and had only ever sworn an oath of allegiance to Augustus, who was by now so well established in power that he could afford to divert from republican traditions, and perhaps be less generous to his soldiers. The evidence of the *Res Gestae* suggests that by the end of the first century BC a cash bonus on discharge had become the norm, and this is confirmed by Cassius Dio who records that at the same time that military service was increased to 25 years in AD 5, the bonus was set at 12,000 sesterces, a sum equivalent to over 13 years' pay. To finance the retirement benefits of 4,000–5,000 men a year, Augustus established the *aerarium militare*, the military treasury, in AD 6, which he set up with a donation of 170,000,000 sesterces from his own funds (*Res Gestae* 17). The treasury's income was derived from the introduction of new taxes, a 1 percent tax on sales at auction and a 5 percent inheritance tax. Whether auxiliaries also received such retirement payments is uncertain, but probably unlikely; from the time of Claudius, however, they automatically received Roman citizenship after their 25 years' service. With the establishment of fixed lengths of service and retirement benefits, and a dedicated treasury to finance the latter, it is apparent that by the beginning of the first century AD, the Roman army was now a professional force; whereas in the republic the ideal was of the citizen soldier, now Augustus even separated his soldiers from the ordinary people in the theater (Suetonius, *Aug.* 44).

Augustus ensured the loyalty of his new professional army through these financial arrangements, and through other means. The *sacramentum* or oath of allegiance, had originally been sworn by legionaries who undertook to obey the consuls or their generals for the course of the campaign, and generals in the late republic had drawn on this to encourage great loyalty from their armies as the oath was sworn to them personally (Plutarch, *Sulla* 27); Augustus took this one stage further by requiring all those under arms to swear allegiance to him personally, rather than to their unit commanders or provincial governors, and this was repeated annually (Tacitus, *Hist.* 1.55). At some point in the early empire, the *imago* was adopted as an additional military standard by both legions and auxiliary units; this standard was one which carried the image of the emperor (who also appeared on the coinage in which they were paid) and served to identify the unit with their emperor and commander-in-chief; the *imago* was closely associated with the unit's standards which were considered sacred and housed in a *sacellum* in the *principia* or headquarters building when the unit was in garrison. The Rhine legions first expressed their change of allegiance from Galba to their provincial governor Vitellius by stoning or destroying the *imagines* of Galba (Tacitus, *Hist.* 1.55). Various legal advantages were bestowed on soldiers, though to facilitate the swift movement of troops and their separation from civilian life, they were forbidden to contract legal marriages, another factor highlighting the difference between the republican army and the professional army of the principate.[3]

The commanders and senior officers of all military units owed their positions to the patronage of the emperor, though it is uncertain whether or not centurions were also appointed directly by the emperor. Officers of senatorial and equestrian status owed future career promotions and magistracies to the emperor's patronage whilst centurions were probably encouraged in their loyalty by rates of pay that were vastly superior to those of ordinary legionaries, and by the status and future career opportunities in imperial service that the most senior centurions could attain.[4] The loyalty of tribunes, prefects, and legates could contribute to the loyalty of those under their command, but ordinary soldiers were very aware of their own oaths of allegiance; there were no serious military threats to Augustus' power and given the chaotic last decades of the republic and almost constant civil war, he did a remarkable job of taking firm control of Rome's armies and establishing the armed forces that would maintain the *pax Romana* for several centuries.

2 The Army of the Principate

Much of the Roman army with which we are familiar from the narratives of Tacitus and Trajan's Column was not fundamentally different from that of the late republic; Augustus did not undertake substantial tactical reforms to the units that emerged from the civil wars, but he did regularize them and formally adopt some of the developments that had been occurring in the first century BC. And most significantly, for the first time in her history, military units were permanently stationed in Rome.

The legions

The "life" of legions in the late republic had been becoming increasingly prolonged in response to civil wars and the demands of garrisoning a growing empire, even though the tradition still persisted that legions were raised for specific campaigns and disbanded on conclusion of those campaigns, however long that might be, but the 28 legions that Augustus retained after Actium now became permanent units. Some of those legions, such as VII Claudia, VIII Augusta, and X Gemina (previously Equestris) could trace their existence back to the start of Caesar's governorship of Gaul in 59 BC or even earlier; others such as V Alaudae and VI Ferrata were raised by Caesar in preparation for impending civil war. But the majority of the legions of the Augustan period were established in the triumviral period; legion XXII Deiotariana began its existence as a levy of local troops in the army of Deiotarus, the king of Galatia, and was incorporated into the Roman army in the early 20s BC.[5] Legions were raised by later emperors usually in preparation for military campaigns or to replace legions that had been destroyed or disbanded (Vespasian's two legions, IV and XVI Flavia Firma replaced Legions IV Macedonica and XVI Gallica which were cashiered after their disgraceful conduct during AD 69 [Tacitus, *Hist.* 4.57–62], and probably included soldiers from the disbanded units). Legions I and II Adiutrix ("Helper") consisted of sailors from the fleets based at Misenum and Ravenna respectively and were raised during the civil wars of AD 68–9, indicating the potential of the military units stationed permanently in Italy. In the same way as under the republic, each legion was identified by its number, though because of the confused origins of the imperial legions in the armies of Antony and Octavian several of the numbers were repeated. Later emperors made little effort to avoid repetition of numbers since titles had become as important a means of identifying individual legions.

Legionary titles had begun to be adopted in the late republic, probably partly to distinguish between legions with the same numeral in different armies, but perhaps also because of the increasing length of legions' "lives" and a growing association of soldiers with a particular legion, encouraging *esprit de corps*. Titles were usually adopted or awarded to reflect service in a certain area or province, such as I Germanica and

IX Hispana, with a particular god, such as XV Apollinaris, with an identifying feature, or from some action, such as V Alaudae ("the larks"), VI Ferrata ("the ironclads"), XII Fulminata ("the thunderbolt"), and XXI Rapax ("grasping"). Legions raised during the imperial period were given their titles by the emperor who raised them and these sometimes included the emperor's name, such as IV and XVI Flavia Firma, II Traiana Fortis, and XXX Ulpia Victrix, but not always; Gaius raised two legions named after the deity Fortuna Primigenia (XV and XXII Primigenia), Nero raised I Italica, and Marcus Aurelius II and III Italica, whilst Septimius Severus raised I, II, and III Parthica for his campaigns in the East, their names a statement of intent. In addition to their names, legions might be granted honors by the emperor in recognition of either valorous conduct in war or for conspicuous loyalty. Legions XX and XIV Gemina were awarded battle honors, the ancient equivalent of a unit citation, during the early occupation of Britain, almost certainly for their involvement in the crushing of the Boudiccan revolt (Valeria Victrix and Martia Victrix respectively), whilst legions VII and XI were granted the titles Claudia Pia Fidelis (Claudian, loyal and faithful) by Claudius for their refusal to march against their emperor with Scribonianus in AD 42. Such official recognitions of loyalty were granted with increasing regularity towards the latter half of the second century AD, and especially during the political and military crises of the third century. Legion V Macedonica became Pia Constans (loyal and constant) or Pia Fidelis for loyalty to Commodus (*CIL* 3.905), and by the reign of Gallienus had received seven grants of Pia Fidelis (*RE* 12 [1925] 1580). Such honors were a clear indication of the vital importance of the relationship between the emperor and his soldiers.

The legions of the early empire were in size and organization not substantially different from those familiar from the commentaries of Caesar. In spite of Caesar's detailed descriptions of campaigns, the historical narratives of the early principate and a wealth of archaeological and epigraphic evidence, there are still aspects of legionary organization that are ill-understood. In each legion, which consisted of about 5,000 infantry, the smallest tactical unit was the century, which contained 80 men and was commanded by a centurion, assisted by his second in command, the *optio*, a standard-bearer (*signifer*), and a *tesserarius*, the officer in charge of the watchword. Whether on campaign or in garrison, the century lived together in a line of tents or barrack rooms, with a larger space at one end of the line for the centurion's quarters, and perhaps those of the century's other officers too. Legionaries identified themselves closely with their century, frequently including that information in their epitaphs, along with the name of their legion. Six centuries made up a cohort of 480 men, and a legion contained ten cohorts, so in theory such a legion would have contained 4,800 infantrymen. A small force of 120 cavalry was included in each legion, though their duties were probably restricted primarily to scouting and communications since the majority of cavalry were provided by the auxiliary units. However, whilst cohorts two to ten of the legion seem to have followed this general organizational pattern, the first cohort of the legion was different. Literary evidence indicates that the first cohort was divided into five centuries rather than six, but that these centuries were double strength (Ps.-Hyginus 3; Vegetius 2.6), giving a first cohort of 800, and a total legionary strength of 5,120. This milliary first cohort is reflected in archaeological evidence from some legionary fortresses, most notably Inchtuthil in Scotland. Other sites, including Caerleon, Chester, and perhaps Lambaesis and Neuss, had the space to accommodate an enlarged first cohort, but the archaeology is unclear and interpretations problematic, making it difficult to draw definite conclusions about how typical this organization was. The enlarged legionary first cohort may have been a temporary feature of the first century AD, and it may have been limited to some legions heavily involved in campaigning.[6]

By the late republic the tradition of tribunes commanding legions in pairs on a rotating basis (Polybius 6.34) had been largely superseded and generals appointed colleagues and clients, usually of senatorial status, as legates commanding one or more legions. Augustus regularized this development and from early in his reign to that of Septimius Severus nearly every legion was commanded by a *legatus Augusti pro praetore*, a senator who had held the relatively senior magistracy of praetor in Rome and who was appointed to his command personally by the emperor. The legate would have been in his early 40s, and although there were no fixed rules of tenure, the standard period of command seems to have been about three years. The legate was assisted by six military tribunes, which again continued the republican practice in a moderated form; all were undertaking military service before embarking on public careers either as senators or equestrians, a requirement that had its origins in republican practice (Polybius 20.19). One of the tribunes, the *tribunus laticlavius*, was a man of around 20 years old, about to embark on a senatorial career; the remaining five, the *tribuni angusticlavii*, were equestrians and probably older than their senatorial colleague since they would already have commanded an auxiliary cohort and may have held municipal magistracies previously. There is no direct evidence to support the view that equestrian tribunes were primarily concerned with the legion's administration, and given their previous military experience, it seems very likely that all the tribunes undertook a range of military duties.[7] The senatorial tribune was nominally second in command of the legion, a position owed entirely to his social status, but the third in command was a career soldier, the *praefectus castrorum* or prefect of the camp, who held equestrian status. The position seems to be an Augustan innovation and its creation is likely to be related to the establishment of permanent forts to house the new standing army. The camp prefect's role included the administration of the fort or camp when the army was on campaign, and supply and logistics (Vegetius 2.42), duties that had been performed by the tribunes and probably the quaestor in the republican army (Polybius 6.26).[8] Under Augustus, the *praefectus castrorum* seems to have been a former military tribune or *primus pilus*, senior centurion in a legion, and epigraphic evidence indicates that by about the reign of Claudius the *praefectus castrorum* was usually a former *primus pilus*. Each of the legions stationed in Egypt was commanded by its *praefectus castrorum*, to accommodate Augustus' concerns about the presence of senators in that province. However, it was not until the third century AD that equestrian prefects began to be appointed to legionary commands more commonly.

Ranking below the tribunes and *praefectus castrorum*, were the centurions; there were 59 in each legion, and they formed the backbone of the legion. Each centurion was responsible for the 80 men under his command and he led them on campaign, as in the republic, from the front. Promotion to centurion under the republic was dependent on experience and bravery, though patronage helped as well (Livy 42.34); the standing army of the empire required such attributes too, and others such as literacy, a quality that seems to have been required for most promotions from the rank of *miles gregarius* or ordinary soldier (*BGU* 423 = Campbell #10; P. Mich. 466 = Campbell #36). Centurions were appointed from several different sources: from the junior officers in the legion (the *principales*), probably after 10 to 15 years' service; from the ranks of the Praetorian Guard in Rome; and the direct appointment to centurion of men of sufficient social status, often from provincial *municipia*, or sometimes from those of equestrian status, though the unrepresentative nature of the epigraphic evidence makes it difficult to determine the proportions of centurions from each source. L. Decrius Longinus, for example, was appointed centurion through the influence of his senatorial patron (*AE* 1913, 215) and the Younger Pliny acquired an appointment to centurion for a client with no prior military experience (*Epist.* 6.25), whilst others were appointed *ex equite Romano* (*ILS* 2654–2656). Centurions do not seem to have been automatically discharged after 25 years' service and some are recorded as in service at quite an advanced age; for centurions the standing army meant literally a career for life, a rather different situation from the republic when the average age of centurions was probably considerably lower (Spurius Ligustinus was promoted to centurion after less than three years of campaigning, and was presumably in his 20s [Livy 42.34], whilst centurions of 70 [*ILS* 2653] and even 80 years old [*ILS* 2658] are recorded in the imperial period). Centurions provided not only the military experience that many of the elite officers lacked, but also continuity of practice and personnel, vital in a system in which the tribunes and legates held office usually for no more than three years.[9]

Centurions gave their name to their century, but they and their centuries were also known by the position of their century in the legion as a whole, which followed republican tradition. In each cohort the centurions and their centuries were titled *pilus prior*, *pilus posterior*, *princeps prior*, *princeps posterior*, *hastatus prior*, and *hastatus posterior*. In the first cohort with its five centuries, there was only one *pilus* centurion, the *primus pilus* who was the senior centurion in the legion, a post which conferred equestrian status and might have led to promotion to a tribunate of one of the units stationed in Rome or appointment as *praefectus castrorum*. A small number of men held the position for a second time, *primus pilus bis*, which was normally followed by appointment to more senior positions on the equestrian career ladder (*ILS* 1364, 1379, 1385). The centurions in the first cohort were known collectively as the *primi ordines*, and their elevated status and experience is reflected in their frequent inclusion in the general's council of war (*consilium*), though some historians have argued that the *primi ordines* also included the senior centurion in each cohort, the *pilus prior*.[10] The relative status of the remaining centurions in the legion has been the subject of considerable debate and the issue is probably irresolvable. Vegetius describes a highly complex hierarchy in which when promoted, a soldier is positioned in the tenth cohort and has to work his way up to the first cohort through a series of promotions (Vegetius 2.21); this may have involved moving up century by century in each cohort, so it would take 59 steps to reach the position of *primus pilus*, or more simply, moving up cohort by cohort, taking ten steps to becoming chief centurion. Alternatively, apart from the *primi ordines* (whoever they were), there may have been no substantial difference in rank and status between the different centurions, centuries, and cohorts.[11]

It has recently been suggested that the *pilus prior* in each legionary cohort was the cohort commander, the *primus pilus* in the case of the first cohort.[12] The argument is based on the seemingly logical premise that since the cohort was the principal tactical unit below the legion it had to have a commander in order to operate effectively on the battlefield. However, the republican legion had no permanent commander and there is no reason to suppose that cohorts of the imperial legion had to have one. Vegetius states that tribunes or *praepositi* (officers appointed by the legionary commander) were responsible for the individual cohorts (Vegetius 2.12); he may be getting confused with the commanders of auxiliary cohorts, but there is no evidence for centurions commanding legionary cohorts. Legionary legates may simply have appointed tribunes or others of appropriate social status, senatorial or equestrian, on an ad hoc basis to command individual or groups of legionary cohorts on campaigns.

Below the centurions was a myriad of other positions which conferred privileges on the soldiers who held them, and who were known as *principales* and *immunes*. The main difference between the two categories seems to have been that the former had been promoted to a position such as *optio*, standard-bearer, or *tesserarius* which brought with it higher pay, whereas the *immunes* held minor positions, frequently of an administrative nature, whose primary benefit was immunity from fatigues (P. Mich. 466 = Campbell #36; *Dig.* 50.6.7). The *Digest* provides an extensive list of *immunes* ranging from medical orderlies through a whole range of craftsmen, to those engaged in secretarial work, whilst Vegetius' list of *principales* includes *optiones*, standard-bearers, eagle-bearers, and the like, but also surveyors and trumpeters, whom the *Digest* lists as *immunes*, suggesting some overlap or confusion (Vegetius 2.7). It is entirely possible that *immunes* were appointed as necessary and that there was no "standard" list of *immunes* that were appointed in every legion. Whilst appointment as an *immunis* might have been possible for a significant percentage of ordinary soldiers, the proportion appointed as *principales* who might have hopes for eventual promotion to the centurionate was extremely small.[13]

Legionaries were armed with full panoply, equipped for fighting in close quarters combat, and are most frequently depicted in armor and a helmet, carrying a large shield (*scutum*), javelin (*pilum*), and short sword (*gladius*), at least in the early imperial period. Small groups of legionaries are sometimes described as *leves cohortes* (light cohorts, Tacitus, *Ann.* 4.25), but the sources fail to indicate whether they were equipped differently, or were simply operating without much in the way of supplies, camping gear etc. that might weigh them down. However, it is clear that the uniform image of the imperial legionary wearing segmented armor that we are familiar with from Trajan's Column is an ideal; sculptures from tombstones and provincial monuments such as Adamklissi depict legionaries with a range of different armor and weapons, and in some legions some of the soldiers were equipped differently from others. Arrian's two legions for his proposed engagement with the Alan cavalry in AD 135 were divided into two groups; the first four ranks were armed with one type of pike or spear (*kontos*) whilst the rear four carried a different spear (*lonkhē*) (*acies contra Alanos* 16–18). The latter may have been similar to the *lancea* with which some of the legionaries in Legion II Parthica were equipped in the early third century AD, when it was stationed at Apamea in Syria.[14] These variations in equipment were not necessarily permanent and were a response to local military conditions and the particular threats being faced; such changes indicate that the Roman army was able to accommodate change, and flexibility and variation of roles could occur both within legions and through the employment of other types of unit.

Auxiliary and other units

Auxiliary units have long been regarded as supplementary to the legions, the support that their name suggests. The non-citizen status of auxiliaries, at least in the early empire, estimates of their pay relative to that of legionaries, the attitude of the principal source for early imperial history, Tacitus, and the experiences and prejudices of modern imperialistic powers have led many historians to view auxiliaries as second rate units of lesser value militarily than the legions. However, this is not necessarily the view now held, and auxiliary units would perhaps more accurately be considered as complementary to the legions: well-trained and reliable troops who could fight in the line of battle along with legionaries, as well as providing the diversity of forces vital to Rome's military success, in the form of cavalry, camel riders, slingers, archers, and the skirmishing troops that had been lost to the legions with the manipular system. Auxiliary units were initially raised from Rome's provinces and were identified by their tribal or geographic origin, but gradually, local recruitment where the units were stationed diluted much of their ethnic identity, and in the second century AD citizens were serving in auxiliary units as well as legions. There is considerable evidence relating to the size and organization of auxiliary units in the form of official strength reports for a variety of different cohorts stationed throughout the empire which reveals that reality was rather different from the "paper" strength of the units.[15] Units might be over or under their theoretical strength, and it is entirely likely that legions experienced similar fluctuations in numbers. The titles of an auxiliary unit provide valuable information about the origins of the unit, its size, the types of troops it contained, its status and, like the legions, the battle honors it had been awarded. Cohors I Lepidiana equitata civium Romanorum had been awarded a block grant of Roman citizenship for actions on campaign (*ILS* 2590), whilst the Ala Gallorum et Pannoniorum catafractata, as its name suggests, was a unit of heavily armed cavalry (*ILS* 2735). Like the legions, auxiliary units too received official recognition in their titles of the emperor who raised the unit, or for loyalty to a particular emperor.

The theoretical organization of auxiliary units reflected that of the legions and was probably based on it; units could be either quingenary (nominally 500 strong) or milliary (nominally 1,000 strong), and came in three basic types: infantry, cavalry, or a part-mounted unit containing infantry and a small cavalry force (Ps.-Hyginus 16, 26–28). A quingenary infantry cohort, like a normal legionary cohort, contained six centuries of 80 men; the milliary was the same strength as a legionary first cohort, but contained ten normal sized centuries. The quingenary part-mounted unit (the *cohors equitata*) had the infantry of a quingenary infantry cohort and 120 cavalry, whilst the milliary version had ten centuries of infantry and 240 cavalry; the cavalry were divided into *turmae* probably 32 strong. The *alae* or cavalry units contained either 16 or 24 *turmae*, thus containing 512 or 768 men. The milliary auxiliary unit seems to have been a slightly later development, the first recorded cases dating to the late 60s AD (Josephus, *B. Jud.* 3.67). The internal hierarchy of the cohorts again mirrored aspects of legionary organization, with each century including a centurion, *optio*, *signifer*, and *tesserarius*, whilst the *turma* was commanded by a decurion with an *optio* and a *vexillarius* as standard-bearer. Many of the same positions held by *immunes* in the legions are found in auxiliary units. In the early empire some auxiliary units were commanded by the tribal elite of the areas in which they had been raised but this seems to have become less common during the first century AD – perhaps because of the cases of commanders such as Arminius (Velleius Pat. 2.118) and Julius Civilis (Tacitus, *Hist.* 4.16) who turned their military skills and knowledge of Roman military procedure against their masters – though the practice was not dropped entirely. However, with the tendency to local recruitment once units were put into permanent garrison, such associations would have been less relevant, and at least some of the former tribal elite of the increasingly Romanized provinces were probably following equestrian careers and commanding other auxiliary units. Other auxiliary units were commanded by experienced legionary centurions or former *primi pili*. As the equestrian career structure began to take shape in the first century AD, however, the majority of these commands were held by equestrian prefects, often as their very first experience of military service. Once the equestrian *tres militiae* had been established by the mid-first century AD, after the prefecture of an auxiliary cohort, equestrians proceeded to a legionary tribunate, and subsequently became prefect of an *ala*.[16]

The wide range of fighting styles employed by auxiliaries is illustrated in literary and sculptural evidence, and by the descriptive unit titles, though the precise details are often uncertain. Though mail armor, oval shield, and the long *spatha* sword are popularly considered to be usual for auxiliary infantry, contrasting with the segmented armor and *gladius* of the legionaries, equipment varied enormously and concepts of "standard" equipment for auxiliaries should be employed cautiously.[17] Some auxiliary units were equipped to stand in the front line of battle along with legionaries, such as the Batavians and Tungrians at Mons Graupius (Tacitus, *Agric.* 36) and they were probably equipped with the panoply mentioned above, but the historical sources refer to a wide range of different types of infantry, and how they differed from each other is not made clear. Josephus (*B. Jud.* 3.126) contrasts heavily armed infantry (ὁπλῖται/"hoplites") with other presumably "lighter" infantry (πεζοί/*pezoi*) whilst elsewhere "light" infantry are referred to as ψιλοί (*psiloi*) (Appian, *B. Civ.* 2.46; 5.113; Josephus *B. Jud.* 3.116; Cassius Dio 62.12.3, contrasting the ὁπλῖται and ψιλοι of the Britons and Romans) and γυμνῆτες (*gymnētes*, literally "naked"; Appian, *B. Civ.* 3.24 who notes that the army in Macedonia in 44 BC contained legions, cavalry, ψιλοί, and γυμνῆτες). Roman authors refer to "light" units as *levis armatura* and *expeditae cohortes*.[18] Though it would be reasonable to suppose that γυμνῆτες were even more lightly armed than ψιλοί, the differences between these types of "light" troops are unclear, and both Greek and Roman authors of the Roman period are often too unspecific in their use of vocabulary to draw any useful conclusions about the equipment and nature of these troops. It is clear though that there was considerable variation in the type of equipment employed by auxiliary units and allied forces, some of which were very lightly armed and presumably highly mobile. When first raised, auxiliary units would very probably have fought in their "native" style but it is impossible to know to what extent local recruitment led to the homogenization of fighting style and Romanization of units that some historians have suggested as the reason for the introduction of new non-citizen units in the first and second centuries AD, the *numeri*.[19]

Numeri are often regarded as "irregular" units, but that is only because they lacked the more standard organization that legions and auxiliaries had. The units were raised in many of the same areas that were providing auxiliary units, notably Britain, North Africa, and the East (largely in the form of Palmyrene archers), and in addition to archers included cavalry, infantry, spearmen, and possibly slingers and stone-throwers (the clubmen illustrated on Trajan's Column [scenes 94–96] may represent another type of *numerus*). Unit size varied from about 100 to 1,000 and many were commanded by a legionary centurion; the *numeri* were used on campaign and as garrisons in small frontier forts and fortlets. These were not the only "irregular" troops serving in the Roman army; the "paper" army of Pseudo-Hyginus' manual on the fortification of camps includes a number of *nationes*, ethnic units which are clearly different from the auxiliary units and may be precursors to the *numeri*, along with Moorish cavalry, Pannonian *veredarii* ("light" cavalry, though with the exception of the heavily armed cataphracts and *clibanarii*, distinctions between different types of cavalry unit are highly problematic), *symmacharii* ("allied" troops of some indeterminate kind), and some camel riders who do not seem to have been attached to an auxiliary unit (Ps.-Hyginus 19, 29–30). Because of its nature, the manual's imaginary army contains a vast range of troop types for illustrative purposes. It does not, however, mention local levies and troops provided by local client kings and allies for the course of a campaign. Arrian's army for his proposed engagement with the Alan cavalry in AD 135 included allied infantry from Armenia Minor and Trapezus and spearmen from Colchis and Rhizus (*ektaxis* 7), whilst Corbulo had raised local levies of Iberians for his Armenian campaigns (Tacitus, *Ann.* 4.47). Such troops could provide additional numbers to Roman armies and valuable local knowledge of terrain and the enemy, but were probably not as well trained and effective on campaign as the permanent units of legions, *auxilia*, and *numeri*.[20]

The military units described above were all stationed in the provinces; until the reign of Septimius Severus (AD 193–211) when Legion II Parthica was garrisoned at Albano only 20 kilometers from Rome, the only military units stationed in Italy were the Rome cohorts raised by Augustus, and the fleet. In the early principate the two legions garrisoned in Illyricum (VII and XI Claudia Pia Fidelis) could have provided forces in case of a military emergency in Italy, though Scribonianus showed that potentially they were as much a threat to the emperor's security as a safeguard.

By the third century AD concerns about *libertas* and republican ideals would have been irrelevant, but Augustus was initially cautious about garrisoning forces in Rome, something which was entirely untraditional and, like over-sized armies, synonymous with political crisis and civil war. Augustus established three different types of units for Rome: the *vigiles*, the urban cohorts, and the Praetorian Guard. Of these only the latter went on campaign and fought; the others were concerned primarily with issues of control and public order (Cassius Dio 55.26; Tacitus, *Ann.* 6.11), as indeed were the Praetorians when necessary, but their principal function was the protection of the emperor and imperial household.[21] All had the military organization of cohorts with centurions and other junior officers, tribunes and a commanding prefect, or, in the case of the urban cohorts, the senatorial city prefect. The command structure and promotions between the Rome units and those stationed in the provinces indicates that these cohorts were regarded as a part of the regular army.

The most significant of these units was of course the Praetorian Guard which followed the republican tradition of a guard for the general's headquarters or *praetorium*. As commander of all Rome's forces, Augustus established his guard at his headquarters, Rome, but units also accompanied the emperor or members of the imperial family when on campaign (Tacitus, *Ann.* 1.24; Ps.-Hyginus 6–10). There is some uncertainty about the size of the guard; the original nine cohorts may have been quingenary but fluctuated in number and size during the first century AD so that by the reign of Domitian there were probably ten milliary cohorts. Augustus sensibly restricted the number garrisoned in Rome to three to lessen the blow to republican tradition that Rome be free of soldiers, and it was the Praetorian prefect Sejanus who famously under Tiberius concentrated the guards' cohorts in one camp in Rome, an overt statement about the nature of imperial rule that Augustus in his guise as the restorer of the republic could not have afforded. The political role of the guard was far greater than their military importance and they should not be regarded as elite troops, though unlike the legions, which became strongly provincialized through local recruitment, the guard recruited almost exclusively from Italians, their pay and discharge bonuses were vastly superior to that of legionaries, they received much more generous donatives, and only served for 16 years (Cassius Dio 43.11; 55.23; Suetonius, *Claud.* 10; Suetonius, *Nero* 10).

Whilst the armies of the republic were primarily campaigning armies, those of the principate spent far more time in garrison in permanent forts and fortresses than on campaign. The removal of units for campaigns elsewhere could disrupt frontier systems and internal security, and might not be very popular with locally recruited soldiers, so as an alternative, detachments of legions and auxiliary units were frequently deployed either individually or along with other detachments in the form of vexillations. The size of detachment from a unit depended on need: there appear to have been no standard sizes, though epigraphic and literary evidence indicates vexillations 1,000 or 2,000 strong from legions were fairly common (*CIL* X 5829; *CIL* VIII 2482; Tacitus, *Hist.* II.18). Vexillations were commanded by *praepositi*, often equestrian prefects of auxiliary units, former *primi pili*, or senators, including military tribunes (*CIL* XIV 3602; *CIL* XIV 3612), indicating the significant responsibility that might be placed on young men with comparatively little military experience. These vexillations indicate the considerable flexibility of the imperial army; they are recorded as early as the reign of Tiberius (*CIL* XIV 3602) and were used throughout the period, and may well represent the beginnings of the field armies of the later Roman Empire.

Conclusion

The army of the Roman imperial period was the western world's first standing army but it was still essentially an army of the ancient world in which appointments and promotions depended as much on social status and patronage as experience, ability at command, and soldiering. Augustus did not carry out radical reforms to the structure of the army but formalized many of the changes that had been taking place during the first century BC, and the army continued to evolve as it turned into a frontier army and faced varied and changing threats on the different frontiers. There remains doubt about the theoretical strength and internal organization of legions and auxiliary units, whilst papyrological and epigraphic evidence clearly indicates that whatever the theory, in practice units fluctuated considerably in strength and quite possibly in structure. The size and shape of the Roman army varied according to necessity, as did its equipment and fighting styles. Legions were not always equipped in the same way, and equipment might vary even within a legion, though not necessarily within all legions; these were variations that were necessary in an essentially frontier army. In addition to the permanent legions, auxiliary units, and *numeri*, other forces might be raised for campaigns from provinces, local tribes, and allied kings, and the newly established system of vexillations provided vital flexibility in the deployment and use of troops, indicating that in spite of its static nature, the Roman army retained the potential for a high degree of mobility and tactical flexibility.

NOTES

1 Brunt 1974, 90–115, reprinted 1990, 188–214.
2 Keppie 1983, esp. 122–7.
3 Soldiers' legal privileges are examined in detail by Campbell 1984, chapter 4, and soldiers' marriage has been the subject of a detailed study by Phang 2001, and is discussed by Scheidel in this volume. The legislation banning official marriage (*conubium*) could not of course prevent soldiers marrying unofficially and was probably not intended to do so.
4 Campbell 1984, 101–9. The rates of pay of centurions are not known, but were probably several times that of ordinary legionaries, whilst senior centurions might qualify for equestrian status on retirement.
5 Keppie 1984, 205–12 provides a useful summary of the Augustan legions, but the most comprehensive survey remains Ritterling 1924/5.
6 Breeze 1969, 50–5 suggests the enlarged first cohort contained administrative and specialist staff.
7 Webster 1981, 113 for the view that equestrian tribunes had mainly administrative duties.

8   Roth 1999, 258–9 for the quaestor's role in military supply and finance during the republic.

9   Contrary to previous views that the equestrian and senatorial officers were "amateurs" who relied entirely on the experience of their centurions, it is now generally accepted that their background and social status furnished these men with many of the qualities necessary for senior command (Goldsworthy 1996, 122–5).

10   For the composition and role of the *consilium* in the late republic and early empire, see Goldsworthy 1996, 131–3.

11   Von Domaszewski (1967) argued that each centurion within the legion had a different status but Vegetius' description notwithstanding, this is generally considered to have been too cumbersome a system. Webster 1981, 114 and Goldsworthy, 1996, 13–14 prefer a flat hierarchy, though the latter argues that the *pilus prior* of each cohort was one of the *primi ordines*; the evidence for this, however, is slim.

12   Goldsworthy 1996, 15–16.

13   Breeze 1974, 438–51.

14   Bally and Van Regen 1993, 24–6.

15   Hassall 1983 summarizes the information in the strength reports. The principal sources are: Ps.-Hyginus 16, 26–28; the strength reports of Coh XX Palmyrenorum (Fink *RMR* 47), Coh I Hispanorum Veterana (Fink *RMR* 63), Coh I Augusta Praetoria Lusitanorum Equitata (Fink *RMR* 64), and Coh I Tungrorum (P. Vindoland. 88.841).

16   Cheesman 1914, 90–101 traces the changing patterns of auxiliary command during the principate. Under Claudius the equestrian *tres militiae* was firmly established, with the legionary tribunate being the final of the three commands, but this order seems to have been fairly short-lived.

17   In response to Maxfield's contention (1986) that "*lorica segmentata* was available to auxiliary troops," Bishop and Coulston 1993, 206–9 argue strongly that whilst legionaries were not necessarily all equipped with segmented armor in the principate, auxiliaries were definitely not equipped with it, and that there were differences between "legionary" and "auxiliary" equipment. The evidence, both literary and archaeological, is inconclusive, but given the absence of segmented armor in sepulchral sculptures, it was probably not as prevalent amongst legionaries as the sculptures on the Columns of Trajan and Marcus Aurelius imply.

18   *Levis armatura* – Caesar, *B. Gal.* 2.10; 2.24; Tacitus, *Ann.* 2.8; 2.16 and *expeditae cohortes* – Caesar, *B. Civ.* 1.79; *B. Afr.* 11.3; Tacitus, *Agric.* 37; *Ann.* 1.50, 12.39.

19   Cheesman 1914, 90. Southern 1989 provides a comprehensive survey of scholarship on *numeri*, and the units themselves. However, fighting style is closely related to the type of equipment being employed and without significant changes in equipment, which would be difficult to see in the archaeological record, there is no reason to suppose that the way auxiliaries fought became any less appropriate to the circumstances.

20   The importance and significance of training to Roman military success is greatly stressed by both ancient and modern writers, though levels of training probably varied considerably between units and provinces even with the move to a standing army. Levels of fitness and training were certainly nowhere near that of more modern armies; Rome's great advantage in training was that in relative terms, in the early imperial period her armies were better trained than any others. Watson 1969, 31–53 describes Roman training methods.

21   Freis 1967; Baillie-Reynolds, 1926. The Julio-Claudian emperors also employed a personal bodyguard of German and Batavian warriors, Suetonius, *Aug.* 49; *Gaius* 43; Tacitus, *Ann.* 13.18; they were disbanded by Galba, Suetonius, *Galba* 12.

BIBLIOGRAPHY

Baillie-Reynolds, P. K. 1926. *The Vigiles of Imperial Rome.* Oxford.

Bally, J. C. and W. van Regen. 1993. *Apamea in Syria: The Winter Quarters of Legion II Parthica.* Brussels.

Bishop, M. C. and J. N. C. Coulston. 2006². *Roman Military Equipment.* Oxford.

Breeze, D. 1969. "The organisation of the legion: The first cohort and the *Equites Legionis,*" *JRS* 59: 50–5.

—— 1975. "The career structure below the centurionate during the principate," *ANRW* II.1, 435–51.

Brunt, P. A. 1974. "Conscription and volunteering in the Roman imperial army," *Scripta Classica Israelica* 1: 90–115 (repr. in *Roman Imperial Themes.* Oxford 1990, 188–214).

Campbell, J. B. 1984. *The Emperor and the Roman Army.* Oxford.

—— 1994. *The Roman Army. A Sourcebook.* London.

Cheesman, G. L. 1914. *The Auxilia of the Roman Imperial Army.* Oxford.

Domaszewski, A. von. 1967. *Die Rangordnung des römischen Heeres,* ed. B. Dobson. Cologne.

Feugere, M. 1993. *Les Armes des Romains.* Paris.

Fink, R. O. 1971. *Roman Military Records on Papyrus.* Cleveland.

Freis, H. 1967. *Die Cohortes Urbanae.* Cologne.

Frere, S. 1980. "Hyginus and the first cohort," *Britannia* 11: 51–60.

Gilliver, C. M. 1999. *The Roman Art of War.* Stroud.

Goldsworthy, A. 1996. *The Roman Army at War.* Oxford.

Hassall, M. W. C. 1983. "The internal planning of Roman auxiliary forts," in B. Hartley and J. Wacher (ed.), *Rome and her Northern Provinces.* Gloucester, 96–131.

Holder, P. A. 1980. *Studies in the Auxilia of the Roman Army from Augustus to Trajan.* Oxford.

Keppie, L. 1983. *Colonisation and Veteran Settlement in Italy.* London.

—— 1984. *The Making of the Roman Army.* London.

Le Bohec, M. and Wolff, C. (eds.). 2000. *Les légions de Rome sous le Haut-Empire.* Paris.

Maxfield, V. 1986. "Pre-Flavian forts and their garrisons," *Britannia* 17: 59–72.

Phang, S. E. 2001. *The Marriage of Roman Soldiers.* Leiden.

Ritterling, E. 1924/5. "Legio," in *RE* 12.1–12.2, 1186–829.

Roth, J. P. 1999. *The Logistics of the Roman Army at War.* Leiden.

Saddington, D. B. 1982. *The Development of Auxiliary Forces from Caesar to Vespasian.* Harare.

Southern, P. 1989. "The *numeri* of the Roman imperial army," *Britannia* 20: 81–140.

Watson, G. R. 1969. *The Roman Soldier.* London.

Webster, G. 1981. *The Roman Imperial Army.* London.

FURTHER READING

A valuable survey of the establishment of the army of the early principate is provided by Keppie 1984, and the structure of the imperial army is discussed in detail by Goldsworthy 1996, whilst Breeze 1969, 50–5 and Frere 1980, 51–60 consider some of the minutiae of legionary organization. The most detailed study of individual legions remains Ritterling 1924/5, much of which is now accessible in English translation on the RomanArmy.com website, though the conference proceedings Le Bohec and Wolff 2000 update Ritterling's work. Saddington 1982 traces the establishment of the non-citizen units, and Holder 1980 provides a valuable analysis of the disposition of auxiliary units throughout the empire. Dobson's revised edition of Von Domaszewski 1967 outlines the complex rank structure of the imperial army, and a more accessible study of junior grades can be found in Breeze 1975, 435–51. Feugere 1993 and Bishop and Coulston 2006 provide the most comprehensive studies of arms and armor, the latter including a valuable appendix on the issue of "legionary" and "auxiliary" equipment, and more recent articles on equipment can be found in the *Journal of Roman Military Equipment Studies*, edited by M. Bishop. Key papyrological documents relating to the Roman army including auxiliary unit organization are collected in Fink 1971 some of which, along with many other papyri and inscriptions, are translated by Campbell 1994.

CHAPTER TWELVE

Classes. The Evolution of the Roman Imperial Fleets

D. B. Saddington

1 Introduction

Like the ancient Israelis, who felt concern for those "who went down to the sea in ships" (Ps 107.23), the Romans, especially by comparison with the Greeks, have often been regarded as reluctant seafarers. Before the Battle of Actium Plutarch (*Ant.* 64) has a centurion adjure Antony, as Shakespeare puts it, not to "fight by sea; Trust not to rotten planks." But the Romans had a port in the city and put a ship's prow on their early coins. They developed Ostia at the mouth of the Tiber, had to defend the long coasts of Italy, and became a Mediterranean power. Eventually they controlled countries bordering the Atlantic and rivers like the Rhine, the Danube, and the Nile. *Classes* or fleets became a standard part of the armed forces of the Roman Empire.

However, they did not establish a "navy" as distinct from the army. In fact, just as there was no Roman army as such, but only separate groups of legions in different areas under commanders independent of each other, so, on an even more ad hoc basis than with the different *exercitus* of the provinces, fleets were commissioned for particular needs. They were not assigned to separate "admirals," but came under the command of the ex-consul or ex-praetor in charge of the relevant provincial *exercitus*. But in the late republican period small squadrons might be assigned to *praefecti*, sometimes not of senatorial, but equestrian status. Only exceptionally were freedmen given command and this was done in order to take advantage of their desperately needed naval expertise. The specifically "naval" complement on board was drawn from the non-Romans in the empire. An inscription from the island of Cos (*IGRR* 1.843) illustrates the position on a typical warship in detail. It records A. Terentius Varro, the *presbeutes* or *legatus* in charge (in the First Mithridatic War of 84–82 BC), as "leading the whole fleet," Eudamos (a Greek) as *nauarchos* (navarch) in command of the squadron, and specifies the other officers as a *trierarchos*, the captain, a *kybernetes*

(Lat. *gubernator*), the helmsman or pilot, a *keleustes* (Lat. *celeusta*), the rowing officer, a *proreus* (Lat. *proreta*), the officer in the bow, a *pentacontarchos,* apparently a junior officer, an *iatros* (Lat. *medicus*), a doctor, and at least 20 *epibatae* or marines. The inscription breaks off before the oarsmen, *eretai* (Lat. *remiges*) are mentioned (if in fact they were).

2   Shipping and Infrastructure

The basic warship was a long, narrow galley propelled by oarsmen (and fitted with sails for easier movement when not actually engaged). The prow ended in an armored point for ramming enemy vessels. Ramming was in fact the standard mode of attack in ancient naval warfare. Before ramming, attempts might be made to weaken the crew of the enemy by shooting at them with arrows or by discharging artillery at the ship or trying to set it on fire. A special maneuver requiring great skill was to row parallel to the enemy craft close enough to shear its oars off. It was regarded as specially characteristic of the Romans to board enemy ships, engaging their crews in hand-to-hand battle, the marines involved being legionaries or specialized auxiliaries.

Smaller ships had one, two, or three banks of oars, being called monoremes, biremes, and triremes respectively. But bigger ones were also built, fours (quadriremes), fives (quinqueremes), sixes (hexaremes), and even larger. The warship par excellence was the trireme, which was perfected by the Athenians in the fifth and fourth centuries BC. A replica of one, the *Olympias,* was built in the 1980s. It was c. 37 meters long and 6 meters wide, with a crew of 170 rowers and 30 others. On a calm sea it could reach a speed of eight knots.

The Romans called a warship a *nauis longa,* a "long ship," to distinguish it from the *nauis oneraria* or merchantman. In the republican period they built the larger vessels characteristic of the Hellenistic period. These survived into the imperial period: the fleet at Misenum had quadriremes, quinqueremes, and even a six, the *Ops.* But then smaller ships dominated, especially triremes and biremes. The latter were called liburnians after the people of that name in Dalmatia, who had developed a fast galley for piratical raids. Their main advantages were speed and maneuverability. They might be cataphract or aphract, decked or undecked. Most seem to have had rams (*rostra,* hence the phrase *naues rostratae*). Some were fitted with *turres* (turrets) on the forecastle from which missiles could be discharged. A ship was distinguished by its *parasemum* or *insigne,* its figurehead. The *aplustre* on the stern-post was usually ornamented. Most had a shrine where the Tutela or protecting deity was worshipped. The most commonly cited representations of Roman warships are on the Praeneste Relief (from Palestrina) in the Vatican Museum and those on Trajan's Column. They are often portrayed on coins, but in a highly stylized form.[1]

Warships were given names. They might derive from the religious sphere, including personifications, like the hexareme *Ops* ("Plenty") noted above, or from the emperor, like Augusta, or from victories, like Dacicus, or from mythical beings, like those in Virgil's (*Aen.* 5.114ff.) description of the naval contest at the funeral games for Anchises: an apparent quinquereme is called *Centaurus,* the triremes *Chimaera* and *Scylla,* and a liburnian *Pristis* (a sea-monster).

Plate 12.1   Bireme depicted on Trajan's Column, Rome. The emperor disembarks after having crossed the Adriatic. Alinari Archives – Florence

Warships were accompanied by *nauigia minora*, lesser craft, especially *scaphae*, long boats or skiffs, and scouting vessels.

Since only a few passengers could be accommodated on a warship, large numbers of troops were generally conveyed, often under escort, in *naues onerariae* or transports. Special vessels were designed for the transport of the cavalry's horses, the *hippagones* (horses can be seen disembarking in Scene 34 on Trajan's Column).

Plate 12.2 Roman bireme, depicted on a relief from the Temple of Fortuna Primigenia in Praeneste. © 2003. Photo Scala, Florence/Fotografica Foglia

The construction of a war fleet demanded a large amount of raw materials, especially wood. That favored was the silver fir (*abies alba*), which was seasoned after felling. But, especially when invasion fleets were being built in remote territories, unseasoned wood might have had to be used. Ships built from it moved more slowly. There were many other essential materials, such as metal for nails, armoring, etc., pitch, resin, flax for sails and ropes, and much else.

Ancient warships were designed for short spurts at maximum speed. But food and a large amount of water had to be taken on board to prevent exhaustion and dehydration in the crew: at Actium Antony's rowers used their drinking water in an attempt to quench the flames after their ships had been set alight (Cassius Dio 50.34). After a battle in 36 BC Agrippa was advised not to pursue the defeated too long so as not to exhaust his rowers (Appian, *B. Civ.* 5.108). If at all possible a war fleet would put in to land at night to rest and to replenish supplies. It has been calculated that a warship could not spend more than four days in continuous sailing.

Invasion fleets might be built in undeveloped areas on beaches or rivers, but normally the facilities of a harbor were used. In the early empire the classic form of harbor that came to be favored consisted of moles going into the sea with an artificial island built between them to break the force of the waves at the entrance (for construction methods cf. Vitruvius 5.12). When Pliny the Younger was invited to sit on

Trajan's *consilium* or Advisory Council at his villa at Centum Cellae (Civitavecchia) in Etruria he observed a harbor being constructed there (*Epist.* 6.31). Of the two moles the left had been reinforced while the right was still under construction. The artificial island in the center was being raised on a foundation of huge rocks. They were held in place by their own weight and formed into a rampart ("agger"). Piles or piers were surmounted onto the rocks: the island itself was to be laid above them. Rutilius Namatianus (*Red.* 1.239ff.) adds that there was an inner pentagonal basin.

As noted below, Octavian had built ships at Rhegium and Agrippa had built the Portus Julius near Cumae. Octavian had also had fleets built on the Tyrrhenian and the Adriatic coasts of Italy, as Caesar (Appian, *B. Civ.* 2.41) had done before him. As Augustus, Octavian decided to place permanent harbors in those seas, at Ravenna and Misenum. The latter site (still Miseno) was at the northern end of the Bay of Naples. Virgil (*Aen.* 6.162ff.; 233ff.) alerted his readers to its importance by describing the tomb Aeneas built there for the hero Misenus. It consisted of an inner harbor, now the Mare Morto, connected to an outer harbor by a narrow channel over which a wooden bridge was built. The naval headquarters was called the *castra* or camp: the fellow-townsman and heir of a *scriba* of the fleet who died on duty at Ephesus had him recorded there (*ILS* 2888). The small town at the site grew rapidly as many veterans from the fleet settled there and it was eventually raised to the status of a colony.

Ravenna was situated in a swampy area with many lagoons. Augustus had the site connected to the Po by a canal, the Fossa Augusta. He had an inner harbor constructed with a new suburb adjacent to it, called Classis, the current S. Apollinare in Classe. The headquarters was called the *castra*: a second-century papyrus (*CPL* 193) records a soldier from a quinquereme in the fleet having a transaction ratified there, "aktoum kastris klasses praitoriai Rabennatous" (Latin, but written in Greek lettering). Ravenna had been made a *municipium* in 49 BC. Rather anomalously its "mayor" or chief executive had the title of *magister* (*ILS* 6665). It became an important ship-building center: an early tombstone there (*ILS* 7725) records the death of a citizen who was a "faber naualis" or shipwright and he is shown building a ship.

3 The Late Republic

During the Civil War and the Second Triumvirate that succeeded it (47–31 BC), major battles were fought all over the Mediterranean area. This involved huge logistical problems connected with troop transfers, and the need to protect convoys with warships. An urgent problem was the securing of grain for the capital as rival dynasts attempted to cut off or facilitate the imports as it suited their purposes. The two most decisive engagements may be briefly considered. The first was fought off Sicily, between Octavian, Caesar's adopted son, and Sex. Pompeius Magnus Pius (as he came to style himself), the son of Pompey the Great. In 46 and 45 he had won some successes against the Caesarians in Spain and had been saluted Imperator, an acclamation entitling him to a triumph. In 43 the Senate put him in command of the fleet and the sea-shore of Italy. His title on coins was "praefectus classis et orae maritimae ex s(enatus) c(onsulto)" (*BMCRR* 2.560ff. [7ff.] = *RRC* 1.520 [511]).

It is not known how his authority on the coast was defined in detail, or what land forces he had at his disposal, but his main duty would have been to secure the corn supply to the capital (which later he found it politic to interrupt). He expanded his fleet by enlisting refugees and fugitives, many of them slaves. As admirals ("praefecti classium") he used freedmen of his father's, especially (Cn. Pompeius) Menas (an abbreviation of Menodorus) and (Cn. Pompeius) Menecrates. They had presumably been of service in the *Bellum Piraticum* of 63.

The navy of Sex. Pompeius was superior to that of Octavian. His crews were better trained and his ships better built. In an initial engagement in 42 he defeated a close associate of Octavian, his legate Q. Salvidienus Rufus (Appian, *B. Civ.* 4.85). Sling-shots from the battle survive, hailing Rufus as imperator, "Q. SAL(uidienus) IM(perator)" (*CIL* 10.8337).

In 38 Octavian proceeded to build new fleets at Rome and at Ravenna in the Adriatic (Appian, *B. Civ.* 5.80). In 37 he received 120 ships from Mark Antony which his sister Octavia, then Antony's wife, supplemented with ten further craft which were combined merchantmen – warships, called "phaseloi trieritikoi" by Appian (*B. Civ.* 5.95) and "myoparones" by Plutarch (*Ant.* 35).

But the major preparations were left to M. Vipsanius Agrippa, his long-time colleague, who was consul in 37. He did this in a new harbor, the Portus Julius, formed by joining the Lucrine and Avernian lakes on the coast of Campania near Cumae (Cuma): Virgil (*Georg.* 2.161–4) described the works. Agrippa was able to use the forests of the area for timber (Strabo 5.4, 5, 245). He levied soldiers and trained sailors (Vell. 2.79), at first on practice benches put up on the land (Cassius Dio 48.51). Octavian had manumitted 20,000 slaves "ad remum" (Suetonius, *Aug.* 16; Cassius Dio 48.49). Agrippa introduced modifications to the warships' armaments. He developed a powerful grapnel ("harpago") which could be fired from a catapult. It had a claw at one end and ropes at the other with which to draw the enemy vessel in. He also put high towers at both ends of the warships (Appian, *B. Civ.* 5.118; 106).

Social dissonance began to manifest itself in Sex. Pompeius' navy. His senatorial colleagues took umbrage at the prominence of his freedmen admirals. He had given Menas charge of his forces in Sardinia and Corsica: Cassius Dio (48.45) says he acted like a governor (governing was a preserve of the senatorial order). Eventually, and this for the second time, Menas deserted to Octavian with a flotilla of 60 ships (Appian, *B. Civ.* 5.78; Orosius 6.18, 21). At this date Octavian's key supporters were men of questionable social status (like Salvidienus Rufus, Agrippa, and T. Statilius Taurus; at Actium, however, Taurus was assigned land forces). He accepted Menas with alacrity, bestowing not only "freedom of birth" but even equestrian status on him (Cassius Dio 48.45): Suetonius (*Aug.* 74) says Menas was the only freedman ever admitted to Octavian's table, but this of course was in this unsettled period.

In 36 Octavian set sail from Puteoli (Pozzuoli). The number of ships in his fleet – it included liburnians – had been reduced from 130 to 102 due to the death of many oarsmen during the winter, a rare reference to disease in the crowded warships of the time. He suffered further disaster in a storm.

Octavian owed his victory at Naulochus to Agrippa. He awarded him the rare naval garland, the "corona classica" (Velleius Pat. 2.81), which Virgil (*Aen.* 8.683f.) singled out and which appeared on coins (*RIC* 1.107f. [29; 32]; cf. 77 [170]). The Tenth Legion bore the title of Fretensis, "Of the Straits of Messina," surely gained on this occasion.

But the main concern of the time was the impending conflict with Antony, who was based in Egypt. He started building ships, and one of his agents, who had the title of prefect, M. Turullius, was censured for cutting down sacred groves for timber. Octavian got kudos after Actium by having him executed (Valerius Max. 1.1.19). By 32 Antony had concentrated his land and sea forces in Greece round the Gulf of Corinth. He issued a series of coins with the names of his praetorian cohorts and legions on the reverse and on the obverse a galley with a standard on its prow. On a series of denarii three of the legions have *cognomina*, one, the XVIIth, that of Classica (*BMCRR* 2.526ff. [cxvff.] = *RRC* 539 [544]).

He was short of rowers: his trierarchs impressed men from all available sources in the area, including youngsters (Plutarch, *Ant.* 62). He was also troubled by defections and disease among the men (Cassius Dio 50.12; 15). Even though he burnt some of his ships, they were still undermanned in the battle (Plutarch, *Ant.* 64f.).

The final engagement took place at Actium (Aktion) at the entrance to the Ambracian Gulf in northwest Greece (Plutarch, *Ant.* 66ff.). Antony had assembled a fleet of 500 warships and a land army of 100,000 (i.e., some 20 legions) and 12,000 cavalry. Most of his ships appear to have been triremes, but he had larger vessels, up to eights and tens. Many had been provided with extra plating against ramming (Cassius Dio 50.32). He included an Egyptian squadron of 60 ships in his battle line. This was under the command of Cleopatra, who called her flagship the *Antonias*. Against the advice of his *gubernatores* he loaded sails onto the ships. Twenty thousand legionary infantry (four legions) and 2,000 archers were put on board.

Octavian was content with 400 ships, 80,000 infantry (i.e., 16 legions), and 12,000 cavalry: both sides had to be prepared for a land rather than a sea clash. The ancient sources for the battles are very sparse, but several authors seem to place emphasis on liburnians in Octavian's fleet. Horace wrote a poem celebrating Maecenas sailing in one among the high bulwarks of the other ships ("ibis liburnis inter alta nauium/ amice, propugnacula" – Epod. 1,1f.). Vegetius (4.33) ascribed Octavian's victory to his liburnians. In fact, there was a persistent tradition that his fleet contained swifter, more easily maneuverable vessels than Antony's (Plutarch, *Ant.* 62). He put his friends or political advisers in "hyperetica," "auxiliary boats" (Cassius Dio 50.31 – smaller than Maecenas' liburnian?).

Exploits by subordinate commanders have been recorded. When Antony fled the battle one of the liburnians that gave chase was that of Eurycles the Spartan, whose father, "a pirate," had been executed by Antony (Plutarch, *Ant.* 67): he was granted Roman citizenship. In a skirmish just before the main battle, Tarcondimotus of Cilicia – the stronghold of the pirates in Pompey's day – who called himself Philantonius (*RPC* 1.3871) on his coins, was killed. Whether there were other auxiliaries involved at Actium besides Antony's archers, his Egyptian squadron, and Tarcondimotus' Cilicians and, on Octavian's side, Eurycles' Spartans, is not known. Many of the recent recruits in Antony's legions were provincials from the East.

Octavian naturally drew the maximum propaganda benefit from his victory. A large monument was erected on the site of his base camp and dedicated to Neptune and

Mars for peace gained by land and sea. It was decorated with rams taken from the
ships captured from Antony.[2] Many of Antony's ships were burnt, but some were
sent to Forum Julii (Fréjus) in Transalpine Gaul (Tacitus, *Ann.* 4.5).

Further prows from Antony's fleet were displayed in Octavian's triumph in Rome:
Propertius (2.1.34, but cf. his dark reference [15, 44] to the bones of Romans being
swirled round in the sea of Actium) records them coursing down the Sacred Way
(the route of a triumph – "Actiaque in Sacra currere rostra Via"). They were attached
to the new Rostra on the podium of the Temple of the Deified Caesar in the Forum
(Cassius Dio 51.19), no doubt recalling those affixed to the original Rostra in the
Forum from the ships of the Antiates whom Rome had defeated in 338 BC.

4 Augustus

Two wars under Augustus involved large fleets. The first was that assigned to the
prefect of Egypt, Aelius Gallus, in 24 BC. He had an army of 10,000 (i.e., two legions)
and many auxiliaries (of which 1,500 are named) and built warships ("makra ploia"),
not less than 80 biremes ("dikrota"), triremes, and other light boats ("phaseloi"),
and 130 transports. Strabo (16.4.23.780) criticized him for building a fleet while
the Arabs did not have one, and for the time he wasted in so doing. His remit was
to invade Arabia across the Red Sea. An intriguing papyrus fragment (P. Oxy. 2820)
seems to imply that he (if not an earlier governor) had incorporated ships from
Cleopatra's navy into the fleet.

Drusus the Elder acquired an even larger fleet for his expedition in Germany east
of the Rhine. It was also used for exploration (and intimidation): as Augustus said
"classis mea," "my fleet," sailed as far north as the land of the Cimbrians (that is,
Jutland, *Res Gestae* 26.4). After Drusus' death Tiberius continued his combined land
and naval incursions, as did Germanicus, who built a fleet of 1,000 ships in AD 16
(Tacitus, *Ann.* 2.6): it is not certain whether the otherwise unknown Anteius, who
was placed in charge of the fleet, had the title of "praefectus classis." Harbors used
during these German wars have been recorded by archaeologists, most notably one
at Haltern on the Lippe where there is a block of eight wooden ship sheds suitable
for boats the size of liburnians.

Such fleets were not standing fleets stationed in the areas concerned on a permanent basis, but were specifically constructed for a particular war. As such they may
be labeled "invasion fleets."

5 The Italian Fleets

Augustus' enduring contribution to the Roman navy was the stationing of permanent
fleets in Italian waters. A possible precursor of this was his sending part of Antony's
fleet after Actium to Forum Julii, which he raised to the status of a colony, including
Classica in its title. It is possible that Sex. Aulienus (*ILS* 2688), a distinguished equestrian officer and *duovir* or "mayor" of Forum Julii, who is called a "praef(ectus)

classis," commanded it, but its subsequent history is unknown. The Roman army contained several atypical auxiliary regiments, in which Roman citizens served, called *cohortes classicae*. They must have been formed from its personnel: certainly some of the earliest members of the cohorts gave their *origo* as Forum Julii. The considerations which led Augustus to base permanent fleets off Italy are not known. Tacitus (*Ann.* 4.5) merely lists "duae classes, Misenum apud et Rauennam" in his catalogue of the armed forces of the empire, while Suetonius (*Aug.* 49) says they were to protect the Italian seas. They were hardly intended to protect troop convoys, as the legions were increasingly being stationed on the frontiers and piracy, although not fully suppressed, was controllable.

Augustus' action may not have been a complete innovation. In the later 60s BC there was a fleet large enough to be assigned to a consul in Ostia (Cicero, *Leg. Man.* 33) and after his defeat of the pirates Pompey (who had been assigned all "available" ships against them) proposed that a fleet be based off Italy as a deterrent against piracy (and that sufficient financing for it be voted – Cicero, *Flacc.* 30). L. Staius Murcus, who had governed Syria in 44, was given command of the fleet and supervision of the sea the next year ("qui classi et custodiae maris praefuerat" [Velleius Pat. 2.72]). Sextus Pompeius (whom Murcus had joined) seems to have acceded to a similar position. Appian (*B. Civ.* 4.84) says he took command of all the ships he could find in Italian harbors and Dio (46.40) says "the navy," "to nautikon," was assigned to him. If pressed, this language could imply remnants of an official fleet off Italy in the late republican period.

The size of the fleets stationed at Misenum and Ravenna is not known. Deductions have been made from the fact that Nero and his successors in the Year of the Four Emperors (68–69) created up to three legions (i.e., 15–18,000 men) from them. But at the same time new recruits were being drafted into the fleets: Tacitus (*Hist.* 3.50) names Dalmatians being sent to the Ravennate fleet.

The fleets were put to differing uses. Their deterrent effect upon piracy was important – Augustus claimed to have made shipping safe. On one occasion the crew of an Alexandrian corn vessel poured libations to him, proclaiming that they lived, and sailed, through him (Suetonius, *Aug.* 98). In Alexandria itself he was worshipped as "epibaterios," the one on board (Philo, *Leg.* 151).

There appear to have been groups of sailors in Rome from an early date. Initially they seem to have been housed in the barracks of the Praetorian Guard (Josephus, *Ant. Jud.* 19.253). Later there was a Castra Misenatium near the Colosseum and close to the training school for gladiators and its armory and a Castra Ravennatium across the Tiber. Their skills were used at public entertainments. In particular they set up the awning in the amphitheater (*HA, Comm.* 15.6).

Naturally they were used politically. Sometimes covert operations were assigned to them rather than to the Praetorian Guard. This was notoriously the case when Nero murdered his mother Agrippina the Younger in 62. He entrusted the deed to a freedman of his,[3] Anicetus (Tacitus, *Ann.* 14.3), whom he had appointed prefect of the Misene fleet. His chief assistants were a trierarch Herculeius and a "centurio classicus," Obaritus (it may be noted that during the Pisonian Conspiracy in 65 an attempt was made to suborn a navarch of the fleet, Volusius Proculus – Tacitus, *Ann.* 15.51).

The groups of sailors mentioned above were not used for exploration, which was undertaken, if at all, by the invasion or provincial fleets. Nor were they involved in large-scale transport of men and supplies (until the second half of the second century AD: cf. *AE* 1956, 124).

Nevertheless, as Suetonius suggested, their function was basically military. It seems best to regard them as part of the immediate forces available to the emperor. This is clearly indicated by their title of Praetoria, which they had acquired by Domitian if not before. Like the lesser urban forces in Rome, they were an adjunct to the Praetorian Guard to be used when operation by sea was the most convenient approach.

6   Personnel

The "admiral" or prefect of a fleet was initially either an imperial freedman – the emperors used freedmen in other high-ranking posts as well – or a member of the equestrian order. From the Flavian period onwards only those who had gone through the *militia equestris* were appointed. Such was Pliny the Elder, who had a distinguished career not only in the army but in financial administration as a procurator. His nephew, Pliny the Younger (*Epist.* 6.16; 20), described his death while prefect at Misenum (where "classem imperio regebat"). When Pliny the Elder observed the cloud forming during the eruption of Vesuvius in 79, he decided to investigate and ordered that a liburnian be prepared for him to cross the bay. When he received information about the increasing scale of the disaster he ordered other vessels to be prepared, quadriremes. Although hot ash and pumice stone were falling on his boat, he ordered the *gubernator* to continue making for the area of danger. However, he was eventually asphyxiated. In later times it was not unusual for the prefect of the Misene fleet to go on to become prefect of the Praetorian Guard.

The most senior officers below the prefect were the navarchs, trierarchs, and centurions. Their relationship is obscure. The titles of the first two were inherited from Hellenistic navies. They are distinguished on an inscription (*AE* 1925, 93) to Mindius Marcellus, "praefectus classis" under Octavian at Naulochus. A navarch is usually regarded as superior to a trierarch. This is suggested by their order on a diploma of 71 (*RMD* 205) which was issued to "nauarchis et trierarchis et remigibus" of the Ravennate fleet. The standing of a navarch is also implied in the list of witnesses to a diploma of 54 (*CIL* 16.3): the *beneficiarius* or special assistant of a navarch is placed above those of military tribunes. One approach has been to regard navarchs as commanders of larger vessels than those under trierarchs. But it seems clear that they commanded squadrons or other sections in a fleet, while trierarchs commanded single vessels (of any size). Some career patterns show promotion from trierarch to navarch (*ILS* 2846; cf. 2852, an "archigybernes" promoted to navarch). Later there was a post of "nauarchus princeps": one (*ILS* 2842) was adlected among the duovirs or "mayors" of an Italian *municipium*. Another (*ILS* 2847) was promoted to a primipilate in a legion.

Navarchs and trierarchs could be of peregrine status as late as the third century: Ulpian (*Dig.* 37.13, 1) expressed the opinion that even so, by military law, they could

Plate 12.3 Part of a fresco in the Casa dei Vetii at Pompeii, showing two Roman warships engaged in a *naumachia*. Museo Nazionale, Naples. © 1999. Photo Scala, Florence

make wills that were valid. "Centurion" is a term from the land army. Centurions on warships came initially from the legions. (In 56 BC, during the Gallic War, D. Brutus had put specially picked legionaries onto his ships – Caesar, *B. Gal.* 3.7–16.) The ships were under centurions, who were obviously superior to the captains and were in control of operations. A "centurio classicus" is known (*ILS* 2231), but he was "centurio legion(is) XXXXI Augusti Caesaris" and therefore served during the Second Triumvirate. Those on the diplomas – they appear from AD 70 onwards – were of course peregrine; a Thracian on *CIL* 16.12, an Illyrian on *RMD* 204, a Pannonian on *RMD* 205, and a Dalmatian on *CIL* 16.14. *Centurion* was becoming a standard term in the navy, but was applied not to men transferred from the legions, but to promoted peregrines analogous to the centurions of auxiliary regiments. For the early use of "land" terminology in the fleets see also the Illyrian who described himself as a "mil(es) de lib(urna) Triton(is) 7 (=centuria) M. Vetti," "soldier from the liburnian *Triton* of the century of M. Vettius" (*ILS* 2826). A common formula was to call one's ship a century as a Dalmatian did when he said he was "of the century of the trireme *Minerva*," "centur. triere Minerua" (*ILS* 2838). In fact, recruits to the fleet seem to have been drafted straight into a century rather than assigned to a ship (P. Mich 8.490f).

Like all armed forces those of Rome were very conscious of status. In 52 a governor of Egypt felt it necessary to lay down the law; he stated the position unequivocally – members of the fleet were not entitled to the same privileges as auxiliaries or legionaries (P. Fouad 1.21; cf. P. Yale 1528 = *FIRA* 3.171): they were called "hoi ek tou eretikou" or "hē ton kopelaton," those of the oar. The first fleet diploma used the term "remiges" but interestingly the actual recipient was called a "gregalis" (a "land" term: *caligatus* and *manipularis* appear on inscriptions). The usual term, however, was *miles*. This was not just a polite convention, but a legal status, as Ulpian stated in the *Digest* (37.13.1 – "in classibus omnes remiges et nautae milites sunt"). However, the generic *miles* was generally replaced by *classicus* in contexts where it was important to distinguish sea from land soldiers. The term first occurs on a diploma under Domitian (*CIL* 16.32 of 86). But literary authors seem to prefer the form *classiarius* to *classicus*.

As far as the status of ordinary men in the fleet is concerned, Claudius took an important decision to give legal privileges to those who had served in the fleets (the period of service was fixed at a minimum of 26 years). He did this by formal decree (a *constitutio*) which was inscribed in bronze and duly displayed in a prominent position in Rome itself. The recipient could get an extract copied onto a folded piece of bronze, attested to by seven witnesses (the normal practice). This is usually called a military diploma.[4] Basically the beneficiary received Roman citizenship for himself and his family. The first extant fleet diploma (*ILS* 1986 = *CIL* 16.1) was issued to "trierarchis et remigibus qui militauerunt in classe quae est Miseni." It was made out for a "gregalis" (an army term), an ordinary rating, who was a Bessan (a Thracian people). It may be noted that not only the ordinary oarsmen but captains as well (*trierarchi*) received citizenship: accordingly some, if not all, of them were also of peregrine status. The diploma names the prefect of the fleet under whom they served, an imperial freedman, Ti. Julius Augusti lib(ertus) Optatus.

The question arises whether, besides the oarsmen and the sailors, there was a separate category of marine in the imperial navy. There appear to be occasional references to them. When staging a mock naval battle with 30 "naues rostratae" in Rome in 2 BC, Augustus deployed not only "remiges" but also one thousand "homines" or "men": "men," because, since they were gladiators or slaves, one could not apply the honorable term *milites* to them.[5]

The practice in actual sea-battles is difficult to ascertain since so few occurred in the early principate. However, there was a minor engagement during the Batavian Revolt of 69 when men from the Classis Germanica, feigning incompetence, defected: the *remiges* were in fact themselves Batavians (Tacitus, *Hist.* 4.16). They frustrated the operations of the "nautae." These were probably specialists from the south, like the *gubernator* from Elaea in Asia (Çandarli) and the *proreta* or bow officer from Alexandria buried in Cologne (Colonia Agrippinensis, *ILS* 2828; 2827). There were also "propugnatores" or marines on board. Whether they came from the legions or the auxilia is uncertain. Similarly those who some months later "discharged light weapons" from the Roman fleet of Petilius Cerialis against that of Civilis were presumably also drawn from the land army (Tacitus, *Hist.* 5.23). Somewhat earlier in the year gladiators were used as "propugnatores" in a battle on the Po in "liburnicae," presumably from the Classis Ravennas (Tacitus, *Hist.* 2.35).

But it seems clear that Augustus did not create a category of *epibatae* or marines as such for the fleet. Presumably, if serious engagements occurred as in the cases just discussed, commanders would have to turn to the land forces for actual fighters. This is not to say that fleet personnel received no military training. "Armorum custodes" or superintendents of armories formed a regular rank and recruits for the fleet bought weapons on enlistment (P. Mich 8.467f.).

7   The Provincial Fleets

Large fleets continued to operate away from Italy under Augustus, but these were "invasion fleets." Eventually smaller fleets were stationed permanently in the provinces.

The northern fleets

A Classis Germanica is mentioned for the first time in 69 (Tacitus, *Hist.* 1.58) and a Classis Britannica in 70 (4.79). The first diploma issued to either fleet was *RMD* 216 of 98. It was made out for "classicis qui militant sub eodem [i.e., Imp. Traiano Aug. – Trajan was governing Germania Inferior at the time] praef(ecto) L. Calpurnio Sabino." If the men's 26 years of service is deducted from the date of issue, their recruitment can be placed immediately after the Batavian Revolt, in 72. However, various considerations, including the availability of warships for Domitius Corbulo's naval operations against the Chaucans in 47 (Tacitus, *Ann.* 11.18) and the extent of the preparations for the invasion of Britain, suggest that the German and the British fleets go back to Claudius.

The headquarters of the German fleet was on a branch of the Rhine at Alteburg 3 kilometers south of Cologne (Colonia Agrippinensis) (although the site itself may have been used earlier by land forces). As noted above some of its rowers were Batavians and Julius Burdo, "Germanicae classis praefectus" (Tacitus, *Hist.* 1.58), could well have been a Batavian, like the Batavian noblemen commanding auxiliary regiments in the area. However, the "nautae" in the fleet were probably professionals from elsewhere.

The main base of the Classis Britannica was at Boulogne (Gesoriacum, later Bononia) in Gallia Belgica. In the second century the fleet had a second headquarters in Britain, at Dover (Dubris). Local involvement with repairing or building ships may be indicated by a dedication (*RIB* 91) at Chichester (Noviomagus Regnorum), which some regard as a possible landing place for a division of the invading fleet. With the authorization of the local king, already enfranchised, Ti. Claudius Cogidubnus, a guild of "fabri" set up a temple to Neptune and Minerva (the goddess of craftsmen). Does the choice of Neptune indicate that they employed their skills by sea as well as on land? Agricola made full use of the fleet in his campaigns in the north under Domitian (Tacitus, *Agr.* 24f.). With him in the lead boat it advanced northwards in conjunction with the land forces. "Pedes equesque et nauticus miles," the legions, the cavalry (i.e., auxiliaries) and the rowers and *nautae*, were housed in the same camps. The fleet is said to have inspired terror in the British. A bizarre incident occurred during the campaigns. A newly recruited auxiliary unit, the Coh. Usiporum (Tacitus, *Agr.* 28; they came from a people east of the Rhine), mutinied. It seized three liburnians for the return to Germany and compelled the *gubernatores* on them to act as their helmsmen. As the normal strength of a cohort was 500, this would imply that they calculated more than 150 men to a liburnian (assuming that the regiment was at full strength). After his final victory at Mons Graupius Agricola used the fleet for exploration: the "praefectus classis" was ordered to circumnavigate Britain (Tacitus, *Agr.* 38; cf. 10). He was assigned "uires," "a force," presumably land soldiers, as marines. Plutarch (*Def. Or.* 410a; 419e) mentions a friend of his, Demetrius of Tarsus, in Cilicia, a literary critic, who went on an official "mission to remote islands." Presumably he was on board and presumably he was the Scribonius Demetrius who made a dedication (in Greek) to Ocean at York (Eburacum, the northern legionary headquarters at the time) (*ILS* 8861 = *RIB* 662f.). The distinguished jurist Javolenus Priscus served as *iuridicus* or senior legal officer under Agricola. One of the cases he heard involved a trierarch and an *archigybernus*, Seius Saturninus, who had given his son the evocative cognomen of Oceanus (*Dig.* 36.1.48 [46]). That the British fleet at this date had such a senior official in it implies that it was of considerable size.

The Danube

During his Illyrian campaigns prior to the battle of Actium Octavian deployed an invasion fleet on the Danube (Cassius Dio 49.37).

The later fleet there that gave refuge to the Sueban chieftain, Vannius (Tacitus, *Ann.* 12.30), in 50 was presumably the Classis Pannonica. It may be asked whether it is attested on a fragmentary diploma found near Zagreb (*CIL* 16.17 of 71) issued to a Pannonian. Since he had served for 26 years (rather than the 25 of auxiliaries) he must have been a member of a fleet. It could have been an Italian or any provincial fleet, but the context is entirely Illyrican which suggests that it was the Pannonian. If so, subtracting 26 from 71, the fleet could have been in existence in 45, five years before the Vannian incident. Its main base was probably at Taurunum (Zemun), at the mouth of the Sava in the Danube.

The Classis Moesica patrolled the Lower Danube. It is named on a diploma of 92 (*CIL* 16.37), with the title of Flavia, which was also borne by the Pannonica. Ninety-two minus 26 gives 56, a date under Nero. The names of two harbors on the Danube probably reflect some of the different types of boats it used. Ratiaria (Archer in Bulgaria) derives from *ratis* (*OLD* svv.), a raft (propelled by oars) as well as a type of flat skiff, with which pontoons could be built for river crossings. (There was a "ratis," the *Minerva*, at Misenum – *AE* 1964, 103). Sexaginta Prista (Rusé) reflects the *pristis* (*OLD* 1c), a type of *lembus*, a fast vessel used for reconnaissance, but also for transporting troops: *lembi* were so used by Julian in crossing the Danube in 361 (Ammianus Marc. 21.9).

In the second century a group of Roman citizens settled at a "uicus classicorum," a village of men from the fleet, under an official with the title of *magister*, at Halmyris (Murighiol) (*AE* 1988, 986ff.).

Fleets in the East

When Nero turned the kingdom of Pontus into a province, he took over the royal fleet to patrol the Black Sea as the Classis Pontica. Josephus (*B. Jud.* 2.367) says it comprised 40 ships. Its main port was Trapezus (Trabzon). The navarch, a Roman citizen, C. Numisius S[p. f.] Qui(rina) Primus (*ILS* 2824), who was priest of Augustus and *duovir* at nearby Sinope (Sinop), must have belonged to an earlier fleet: Agrippa had used its facilities in 14 BC during his expedition to the kingdom of Bosporus (the Straits of Kerch; Cassius Dio 54.24).

The Classis Syriaca is first heard of on a diploma of 119.[6] Subtracting 26 years brings it down to 93. Its main base was at Seleucia Pieria (Kaboussié): in 75 an artificial tunnel and a canal to divert a river clogging the harbor were built there. Only legionaries and auxiliaries were involved (*AE* 1983, 927). The fleet is not mentioned, which seems strange if it had been in existence by that date. Detachments of the Misene fleet were also stationed at Seleucia. An interesting papyrus of 166 (*FIRA* 3.132 = *CPL* 120) records the purchase of a boy slave, "natione Transfluminianum," i.e., from across the Euphrates, by an *optio* or deputy-centurion from a trireme, the Tigris, and a *miles* of the same ship. The guarantor was a "manipularius" or ordinary rating from another trireme: as he was illiterate, a "suboptio" acted for him. The rank of three of the witnesses, all from triremes, is stated: another "suboptio," a centurion, and a "bucinator" or trumpeter. The proceedings were conducted in Latin "in castris hibernis uexillationis clas(sis) pr(aetoriae) Misenatium." But the "misthotes quintanos Meisinaton," the contractor for the poll tax involved, added his attestation in Greek.

The Egyptian fleet

The Classis Alexandrina seems to be attested under Gaius Caligula (Philo, *Flacc.* 163). Its rowers were referred to by the governor of Egypt under Nero. *Classici* were discharged from it in 86 (*CIL* 16.32), again pointing to its existence under Nero (86 − 26 = 60). During the Jewish Revolt of 70 Titus used "makra ploia" (Josephus, *B. Jud.* 4.659) to convey troops up the Nile.

A former masseur of Tiberius and Claudius, an imperial freedman, Ti. Julius Xanthus (*ILS* 2816), was a sub-prefect. A prefect in the second century, possibly during the Jewish Revolt under Trajan, L. Valerius Proculus (*ILS* 1341), was at the same time put in charge of the *potamophylacia* (cf. *B. Alex.* 13), a guard on the Nile responsible for the collection of customs: he eventually became prefect of Egypt.

A Classis Nova Libyca, the New African fleet (*ILS* 1119), is only known from a dedication by one of its trierarchs to a senatorial patron (*ILS* 1118) of his whom Lucius Verus and Marcus Antonius had appointed to deal with pressing problems in the corn supply.

Fleet personnel might be used in non-naval contexts. In the large expeditionary force described by Ps.-Hyginus a detachment of *classici*, protected by cavalry, was used for road-building (*Mun. Castr.* 24). Men from the Classis Germanica worked in the quarries in the Brohltal near Bonn (*CIL* 13.7719) and a vexillation of the British fleet worked on Hadrian's Wall (*RIB* 1340; 1944f.). In the Antonine period "classici milites" were involved in the construction of a tunnel at Saldae (Bejaia) in Africa (*ILS* 5795).

8 Conclusion

To the Romans, the military meant the legions, brigades of Roman citizens commanded by senior senators. They realized that these needed supplementation, but organized the cavalry and light-armed troops they employed as "auxiliaries," or supplementary troops, in *alae* and cohorts commanded by prefects of equestrian origin. Warships were even more peripheral. Permanent fleets were only established later. Like the auxiliaries the crews were of peregrine extraction and also commanded by equestrian prefects.

However, they were soon assimilated to Roman army patterns with a complicated series of ranks. They used Latin and were adept in the application of Roman legal procedures in their financial dealings. They tended to cling to their peregrine names, sometimes quoting them after their new Latin names (using the "qui et" formula). But their tombstones were Roman.

The emperors recognized their worth. After a quarter of a century of service (but ancient life expectancy was low) they were made full Roman citizens. Some returned as men of prominence to their home villages, others settled near their bases. The veteran *classiarius* was fully integrated into Roman society.

NOTES

1 The sculptures are reproduced in the edition of Vegetius by Baatz and Bockius 1997, esp. 59, fig. 7; 52, fig. 3; and in Reddé 1986 (between pp. 662 and 665), figures 38, 45–47. For those on coins, cf. Höckmann 1997, 213ff.; Orna-Ornstein 1995, 179ff.

2 Suetonius, *Aug.* 18. For the badly mutilated inscription on the monument cf. *AE* 1937, 114. Murray and Petsas 1989, 137ff. has counted the number and size of the sockets for the rams displayed and deduced that Octavian recovered some 330 to 350 ships, pointing to the very heavy losses suffered by Antony.

3 The ship carrying Agrippina was to be struck by a *liburnica*. It had been tampered with to facilitate it sinking. It was apparently a *camara* (Suetonius, *Nero* 34, 2), which was a light vessel incorporating a covering such as was used by pirates on Pontus (Strabo 11.2, 12, 495; Tacitus, *Hist.* 3.47.3).

4 For fleet diplomas cf. Forni 1986; Pferdehirt 2002, 56ff.; for the early witnesses Saddington 1997, 157ff.; Saddington 2004.

5 *Res Gestae* 23. According to Tacitus, *Ann.* 12.56 in a similar spectacle on the Fucine Lake in central Italy, Claudius deployed 18,000 "men whom he had armed," i.e., gladiators, on triremes and quadriremes propelled by the strength of *remiges* and the skill of *gubernatores*. To prevent escape the fleet was surrounded by rafts on which some of the praetorian guard (including its cavalry) stood guard and deployed artillery. The rest of the lake was occupied by *classiarii* in *tectis nauibus*, i.e., boats from which marines could operate. If so, were such persons supplied by a land force? (Whether the *milites* from the Classis Rauennas buried at the lake [*CIL* 9.3891; *ILS* 2825] belong to this event or not is uncertain.) For *hoplitai* and *toxotai* on ships of Trajan cf. Cassius Dio 68.26.2.

6 Eck, Macdonald, and Pangerl 2002, 427. This item needs to be added to Saddington 2001, 581 and 583.

BIBLIOGRAPHY

Baatz, D., and R. Bockius. 1997. *Vegetius und die römische Flotte*. Mainz.

Bounegru, O., and M. Zahariade. 1996. *Les forces navales du Bas Danube et de la Mer Noire*. Oxford.

Casson, L. 1971. *Ships and Seamanship in the Ancient World*. Princeton.

Eck, W., D. Macdonald, and A. Pangerl. 2002. "Neue Diplome für das Heer der Provinz Syrien," *Chiron* 32: 427–35.

Forni, G. 1986. "I diplomi militari dei classiari," in W. Eck and H. Wolff (eds.), *Heer und Integrationspolitik*. Cologne, 293–321 = Mavors V (Stuttgart 1992) 419–49.

Höckmann, O. 1997. "The Liburnian," *International Journal of Nautical Archaeology* 26: 192–216.

Kienast, D. 1966. *Untersuchungen zu den Kriegsflotten der römischen Kaiserzeit*. Bonn.

Konen, H. C. 2000. *Classis Germanica. Die römische Rheinflotte im 1.–3. Jahrhundert n.Chr.* St. Katharinen.

Lehmann-Hartleben, K. 1923. *Die antiken Hafenanlagen des Mittelmeeres*. Leipzig.

Mason, D. J. P. 2003. *Roman Britain and the Roman Navy*. Stroud.

Murray, W. M., and P. M. Petsas. 1989. "Octavian's campsite memorial for the Actian War," *TAPhS* 79: 1989, 1–172.

Ormerod, H. A. 1924. *Piracy in the Ancient World*. Liverpool.

Orna-Ornstein, J. 1995. "Ships on Roman coins," *OJA* 14: 179–200.

Panciera, S. 1956. "Liburna," *Epigraphica* 18: 130–56.

Pferdehirt, B. 2002. *Die Rolle des Militärs für den sozialen Aufstieg in der römischen Kaiserzeit*. Mainz.

Rankov, B. 1995. "Fleets of the early Roman Empire," in R. Gardiner and J. Morrison (eds.), *The Age of the Galley*. London, 78–85.

Reddé, M. 1986. *Mare Nostrum. Les infrastructures, le dispositif et l'histoire de la marine militaire sous l'Empire romain*. Rome.

—— 2000. "Les Marins," in G. Alföldy, B. Dobson, and W. Eck (eds.), *Kaiser, Heer und Gesellschaft in der Römischen Kaiserzeit. Fs. E. Birley*. Stuttgart, 179–89.

Saddington, D. B. 1990. "The origin and nature of the German and British fleets," *Britannia* 21: 223–32.

—— 1991. "The origin and character of the provincial fleets," *Limes* 15: 397–9.

—— 1997. "The witnessing of pre- and early Flavian military diplomas and discharge diplomas and discharge procedures in the Roman army," *Epigraphica* 59: 157–72.

—— 1998. "*Praefecti classis, orae maritimae* and *ripae*," *Jarbuch des römisch-germanischen Zentralmuseums Mainz* 35: 299–313.

—— 2001. "The Roman naval presence in the East," *Archäologisches Korrespondenzblatt* 31: 581–6.

—— 2004. "Local witnesses on an early Flavian military diploma," *Epigraphica* 66: 75–9.

Spaul, J. 2002. *Classes Imperii Romani*. Andover.

Starr, C. G. 1960². *The Roman Imperial Navy*. Cambridge.

Throckmorton, P. 1972. "Romans on the sea," in G. F. Bass (ed.), *A History of Seafaring Based on Underwater Archaeology*. London, 65–86.

Torr, C. 1894. *Ancient Ships*. Cambridge.

CHAPTER THIRTEEN

Battle, Tactics, and the Emergence of the *Limites* in the West

James Thorne

By the end of the reign of Augustus (31 BC–AD 14) the most vigorous era of Roman expansion had come to an end. That this occurred as the republic gave way to the principate was no coincidence.[1] The new monarchs of Rome could not afford to hand out armies of ten or a dozen legions to ambitious aristocrats. To do so would have been to invite a return of the chaos of the civil wars which had wracked the state for nearly a hundred years before the battle of Actium (31 BC), and of which the anarchy following Nero's death (AD 68) provided an unpleasant centennial reminder. Nor was it often safe for an emperor to leave Rome and command his armies in person: Claudius, for example, though desperately needing the glory of conquering Britain, spent no more than 16 days there – entering Colchester with praetorian troops and elephants to crown "his" achievement. The slowdown in Roman expansion was also partly determined by conditions in the periphery: it had always relied on the co-option of local elites whose assets Rome could threaten, and areas like Germany and northern Britain lacked these, or were "not worth" conquering. However, this was not true of all areas, and it became less true of Germany as the centuries progressed.

Rome retained an aggressive attitude to its neighbors, and maintained, despite the limitations described, almost constant mid-level warfare throughout our period; for example the campaigns of the imperial princes, Drusus, Tiberius, Germanicus, and later the Emperor Domitian in Germany. There was also occasional major warfare in the West, for example Trajan's Dacian Wars (AD 101–6) which involved elements of no less than 13 legions. When I turn, later in the chapter, to the development of the *limites*, the so-called "fixed frontiers" of the empire, it will be important to bear in mind that these do not imply any kind of defensive mentality: the Roman Empire, even in the second century, was not "under siege." An effort to protect the empire efficiently did not imply a loss of interest in conquest; on the contrary, an investment in defensive infrastructure in one sector could free up troops for offensives elsewhere. To use a crude metaphor, the Roman did not put down his sword when he picked up his shield.

1   The Soldiers' Battle

Battle dynamics

Even the fullest accounts of battle we find in Tacitus and Cassius Dio are highly summarized, and often focus on the actions of the commanders, only describing the actions of troops in terms of the highest groupings: typically whole legions, or forces of several *alae* or cohorts. What is never described is combat at the level of its atom: the typical soldier. When enlisted men are picked out for special mention, they have always done something exceptional, be it courageous or dastardly.

Understanding Roman combat at what we might call the "atomic level" cannot be the preserve of the social historian alone. For although ancient historiography tends to gloss over the battle experience in terms of its execution at the sharp end (and to be fair, the blood, excrement, and adrenalin of one battle would always very much resemble any other), to a Vespasian or a Corbulo an understanding of the physics and the psychology of the armed clash was a vital accoutrement. If we want to understand them, we need it too.

The sources being what they are, we must proceed by inference.[2] We know that opposing troops were often "in contact" for several hours, either because the source gives an indication of when the battle started and finished, or because there is some kind of "internal clock," in other words the time taken for a certain maneuver to take place: for example, in AD 69, Cerialis' legions were in contact with Civilis' Germans the whole time in which the route for Cerialis' flank attack was being discovered and the cavalry were moving round it; furthermore we know the main fighting went on until it was nearly dark (Tacitus, *Hist.* 5.19).

Troops taking casualties can only be cut or shot down en masse if they are trapped, or by faster pursuers. If there is room to move away, the threat of further destruction will quickly compel them to do so: either they will break ranks and flee, or if their discipline is good enough and the threat sufficiently moderate (or a combination of both) they will move back more or less in formation to a perceived "safety distance," at which they feel able to stand their ground. It is important to note that what discipline allows is this possibility of recoiling to the safety distance rather than plain routing; it does not mean disciplined troops fight indefinitely (or even very long) like automata at close quarters, because, as Colonel Armand du Picq said, in a nineteenth-century account of Roman warfare that is still worth reading, "you cannot suppress the flesh."[3] Discipline may also mean a reduction of the subjective safety distance, "safety" always being a relative term on a battlefield in any case.

The idea of the safety distance helps to explain how contact could be sustained for such long periods, between opponents who were after all very fearsomely equipped, without the near annihilation of even the victorious side. A reconstruction of a Dacian *falx* (war-scythe), for example, indicates that it could penetrate 1.2 millimeters of mild steel plate and inflict a wound 40 millimeters long, 38 millimeters deep, and up to 6 millimeters wide on the tissue beneath.[4] It is clear that Roman troops and their opponents did not stand toe-to-toe and hammer at each other for hours on end. Rather, being in contact meant being for most of the time at the safety distance, a range at which missiles could cause relatively light casualties (and it is here that the troops' discipline helps subjectively to determine what rate of casualties is "light," and therefore what distance is "safe"). Bold individuals or small groups might make dashes forward leading to flurries of hand-to-hand fighting lasting seconds rather than minutes. Such dashes would sometimes draw a broader section of the line forward, leading to a wider but equally brief flurry of intimate fighting. After a few seconds, though, a combination of fear, the physical exhaustion of fighting for their lives, and possibly the death of the bolder spirits, would cause one side or both to recoil back to the safety distance.

If the troops who had made the rush recoiled, both sides would then be roughly where they had started. If the troops who had been rushed recoiled as well or instead, the result would be a slight gaining of ground by the troops who had taken the initiative. A number of such rushes and recoils could result in the more confident side "pushing back" their opponents. It is important to understand that such "pushing" is meant figuratively, or at least psychologically. Troops were not involved in a kind of rugby scrum, or shield to shield shoving match any more than a modern armored division "pushes" back the enemy with the hulls of their tanks – but note the figure of speech persists.

We see further evidence of the importance of the safety distance, and the ability to move back to it, in the disastrous moral effect of being simultaneously attacked from the front and flank and/or especially rear. Ancient units fought several (often many) ranks deep. If the men had been fearless automata, they could simply have turned their rear ranks around and fought two enemies at once, prevailing over both if they were superior. In reality, such a predicament pinned the unit, denying it on the one hand the psychological safety net of recoil and on the other the opportunity to follow up against a wavering foe. A major physical disadvantage to being sandwiched was that the shield could only be directed against missiles coming from one direction, and the shields of men behind one offered no protection from long-range missiles, which would arrive on a plummeting trajectory.

Equipment and tactical roles

The imperial army fielded a host of troop types, using a vast array of different weapons and armor, but the main distinction was between the legions and the auxiliaries. The legions are often termed heavy infantry, which is accurate, but their excellent protective equipment combined with a generous scale of hand tools (saws, picks, chains) means that "combat engineers" would also be an apt description. This is certainly the role we as often as not find them in; an apt combination with the artillery they manned, which meant that very few strongholds were able to resist their assault, a subject we will come to later.

The javelin (*pilum*) was a very effective weapon. At around 1.7 kilograms, it was roughly the weight of a modern house-brick, and reconstructed versions with an elongated pyramidal head easily penetrated all but the most impractically heavy shields.[5] The metal shank was thin enough to follow the point through, and long enough (60–90 cm) to propel the point into the body of the unfortunate recipient before the ash haft came up against the shield, even if this was held at arms length.

The same experiments suggest that the maximum range of the javelin was about 30 meters, which would not give much time to throw it against a charging enemy. Nonetheless, against a compact body of men it would be hard to miss, and the effect of a volley of javelins would be very shocking – especially if followed up seconds later by legionaries springing forward with not just swords, but also shields: we hear legionaries exhorted to batter and knock over opponents with these "defensive" items (Tacitus, *Hist.* 4.29; *Ann.* 14.36). The main drawback of the javelin was that it required a run-up, or at least a step back, to achieve a decent range. This was not always possible: Tacitus notes that fighting in marshes against the Cherusci the legionaries could not use their javelins properly because their legs were in the water (*Ann.* 1.64). Similarly, when defending walls, where space may have been confined, a special and now somewhat mysterious type (*pilum muralium*) seems to have been used, along with improvised pikes (*ferratae sudes*) (Tacitus, *Ann.* 4.48; *Hist.* 4.29).

The legionaries were well equipped with artillery: a figure of around 60 machines per legion is found in both Josephus (*Jewish War* 3.166) and Vegetius (2.25). The machines were of various sizes: Trajan's Column shows both man-portable bolt-throwers (*manuballistae, cheiroballistrae*) and those mounted on a mule-drawn carriage (*carroballistae*) (Scenes 65–66). Range and accuracy were impressive: at Hod Hill in Dorset, a hill-fort probably captured by Legio II Augusta in AD 43, 17 bolt-heads have been found, still embedded in the chalk where they struck. Eleven had hit Hut 37 (dubbed by archaeologists the "Chieftan's Hut"), landing in a ten-meter circle, including four that landed in a three-meter circle, all from an estimated range of 170 meters. Of the six other shots it is likely that some at least were initial ranging shots, from which the firers corrected their aim. A reconstructed *cheiroballistra* has achieved similar results.[6] Although crucial in sieges and assaults, artillery was used in field battles too: at Cremona in AD 69, an "enormous ballista," of the Fifteenth Legion threw "huge" stones at the Flavian army; only by disguising themselves with the shields of fallen Vitellian troops did two bold individuals put it out of action, by cutting the twisted cord springs which provided its torsion (Tacitus, *Hist.* 3.25) – a key vulnerability of such machines.

We have seen so far that the legionaries had plenty of firepower; they were also well protected, but a consequence of this was that they were relatively slow, except when they marched with fighting order only (*expeditus*) – but then they might find themselves at a loss for their assault equipment (Tacitus, *Hist.* 2.45). When rapid mobility was needed it was more common to call upon the auxiliaries, with an array of cavalry and light infantry (missile) troops. Even the auxiliaries who were equipped to fight as "heavy infantry," for example cohorts of spearmen, were "light" compared to the legions, because they did not carry artillery or the same quantity of tools. As a consequence, we often hear of auxiliaries being sent ahead of the legions

(Tacitus, *Ann.* 1.51, *Hist.* 2.17 and 3.18; proposed by Antonius Primus, Tacitus, *Hist.* 3.2), and sometimes the fighting was over by the time the legionaries arrived: indeed, Ostorius Scapula campaigned against the Iceni and Ceangi using just auxiliaries in the late 40s, calling on the legions only when he moved into Wales in 49 (*Ann.* 12.31–32).

"Light infantry" have generally managed the somewhat conflicting demands of high operational mobility and high fighting power by being missile troops. Fighting at a distance they could dispense with some armor, and their weapons were light, particularly in the case of slingers. Archers (*sagittarii*), both foot and mounted, feature prominently in Tacitus' account of Germanicus' campaign against the Cherusci (*Ann.* 2.9–17), in which we also see the common shortcoming of missile troops – inability to face a hand-to-hand attack by heavier troops (in this case by Arminius, from whom they have to be rescued by other auxiliary infantry [2.17]); similarly, Poppaeus Sabinus' archers were able to inflict casualties with impunity at long range on Thracian rebels, but had to fall back on a supporting Sugambrian cohort when the tribesmen made a sudden charge (*Ann.* 4.47; Sabinus triumphed in AD 26).

Slings were light enough for anyone to carry in addition to their other weapons, and troops who were solely thus equipped (*funditores*) would clearly be the fastest moving and most agile of all infantry. Any small object could technically be fired from a sling, alleviating ammunition shortages, but lead bullets were preferred. These have been found to fly with greater range, accuracy, and hitting power than stones, because the denser material gives them a higher ballistic co-efficient (roughly the ratio of mass to surface area, which creates drag). Sling bullets could be rapidly fabricated, even during combat, as the desperate defenders of Velsen (probably the Flevum of Tacitus, *Ann.* 4.72–74, attacked by the Frisians in AD 28) knew: lead, which melts at only 328°C, was poured into holes in the sand made with a finger – the impression of which can still be seen, preserved in a number of bullets found there by archaeologists.[7] Although the weapon seems rudimentary, its effect was not to be despised: we often hear of contingents of slingers being picked out for special missions (*Ann.* 2.20, 13.39), and according to Onasander's first-century-AD treatise, *The General* (19), the sling was more deadly than the bow or the javelin. The "effective" range, in other words that useful in battle, is not the same thing as the maximum range of a weapon. Two hundred yards is given as the practice range for both slings and arrows by Vegetius (2.23), perhaps because he thought of it as the optimal tactical range.[8]

Such lightly armed troops, as well as the semi-naked club-wielding auxiliaries of Trajan's Column (Scene 38) were well suited for the swimming maneuvers of which we quite often hear (e.g. Vitellius' Germans at the Po in AD 69, Tacitus, *Hist.* 2.35; Agricola's swimming cavalry at Anglesey, *Agr.* 18). Light troops have always exploited their ability to use terrain deadly or inaccessible to others; taking bodily to the water was the example of this par excellence.

Cavalry performed such a vital role in scouting that ancient armies would have brought them along for that purpose alone, but they also had their uses on the battlefield. Horse archers did not need supports in the same way as the foot archers we have already mentioned: they could always make their escape if their tormented targets tried to charge them (indeed, the Romans themselves faced this frustration in trying to deal with desert tribesmen like those of Tacfarinas). Cavalry units were used for "shock" action as well, but it is important to stress that horses will not physically charge into formed infantry, because they perceive the unit as a solid object. Occasionally a charging horse might be killed at the last moment, and achieve what no living horse will dare, but on the whole cavalry units had to stop before steady footmen. Hence the importance of the long spear, which enabled the rider to outreach his opponent in the ensuing fencing. From the reign of Trajan on, we hear of units armed with the *kontos*, a heavy two-handed lance, and from the second-century onwards cataphracts and *clibanarii* – lancers with scale or plate armor completely covering both horse and rider – become more common. As noted, cavalry cannot ride over infantry, but it is certainly plausible that the combined noise, speed, and glittering appearance of a charge by these troops would cause their opponents to turn and run, presenting the cavalry with an opportunity for a massacre. Onasander stresses the fearsome effect that any troops could produce with ferocious shouting and dazzling weapons – "the terrible lightning flash of war" (*The General* 28–29) – but armored cavalry were ideally suited for this sort of psychological warfare.

After the battle, cavalry played perhaps their most decisive role: pursuit. A victor with a preponderance of cavalry would be able to pursue and slaughter the fleeing enemy (in Tacitus, *Ann.* 5.18, a cavalry pursuit was expected, but nightfall curtailed it; Trajan's Column, Scene 64 shows a Dacian rearguard battling with African auxiliary horsemen, and Scenes 142–3 show Roman cavalry in pursuit). Conversely, if a defeated army had more horsemen, it might be able to mitigate the disaster somewhat by checking the victors' pursuit.

2   The General's Battle

The general's role

Tacitus had a very clear (if perhaps rather dogmatic) idea of the duties of a good general. When Titus, the emperor-to-be, entered enemy territory, "his troops advanced in strict order, he scouted exhaustively, and was ever-ready for battle" (*Hist.* 5.1). Whereas Vitellius betrayed his "military ignorance" by being "without foresight, un-acquainted with the proper order of march, the use of scouts, and the limits within which a general should hurry on a campaign or delay it." (*Hist.* 3.56)

Leading by example on the march and in physical labor was also important. Onasander (42), stresses this, and we also see it in Tacitus' rather similar portraits of both Titus (*Hist.* 5.1) and Corbulo (*Ann.* 13.35). The latter, in an Armenian winter which froze the sentries to death, "lightly clad, with head uncovered, was continually with his men on the march, amid their labours; he had praise for the brave, comfort for the feeble, and was a good example to all."

It is noticeable that these skills and qualities (to which expertise in feeding the army and denying the enemy food could be added – according to Vegetius (3.3), "the main and principle aim in war") relate to activities *around* rather than *on* the battlefield. The Romans recognized that the general could do much to shape the conditions under which battle would be fought, up to and including battle dispositions and battle-plan (see below) but once he had delivered his harangue,[9] and the fighting had started, there was much less he could do. This is borne out by Onasander's *General*, of which only a tiny portion describes what to do during combat itself. That is not to say there was *no* battlefield role for the general; indeed, unlike Greek commanders down to Alexander the Great, who had often fought in the front rank once they had issued their orders, Roman war-chiefs even in the republic had stood back and attempted to "manage" the battle in a rudimentary way.

To do this, continuing a development of the later republic, it was common practice for the general to hold a reserve (*subsidium*) either to relieve exhausted troops, to follow up a success, or "*ad improvisa*" (to meet unexpected contingencies) (Tacitus, *Hist.* 5.16). At "The Castors" in 69, Otho's generals Celsus and Paulinus kept with them a thousand praetorian and auxiliary horsemen as their reserve, about 7–9 percent of their whole force (Tacitus, *Hist.* 2.24). The use of reserves, Tacitus says, is one of the things the Germans had learnt from the Romans by Arminius' time (*Ann.* 2.45).

In order to manage the battle, the general should ride up and down the line, "to show himself to those in danger, praise the brave, threaten the cowardly, encourage the lazy, fill up gaps, transpose a company if necessary, bring aid to the wearied, anticipate the crisis, the hour and the outcome" (Onasander 33). Whilst the general would not fight in the front rank as a matter of course, he might find himself there if he personally intervened in a crisis, and this was not frowned upon. M. Licinius Crassus, in command against the Bastarnae in 29 or 28 BC personally killed his enemy counterpart, King Deldo (Cassius Dio 51.24). The general might legitimately use force to stem the flight of his own troops: Antonius Primus, portrayed by Tacitus along similar lines to the ideal general of Onasander, ran a fleeing standard-bearer through with a spear, then picked up the standard himself and turned it back towards the enemy (*Hist.* 3.17).

Grand tactics: dispositions and plan

Two basic formulae for field battles can be discerned from the sources: the straightforward offensive battle, often including a Roman attack on the enemy flank or rear, and the dummy-defensive battle, in which the Romans received the charge of an over-confident opponent before counterattacking.

Onasander (22) recommends the detachment of a force to march round behind the enemy during the night: this should then emerge the next morning once the battle has begun, and fall upon the enemy rear. That this was (1) not an innovation of the imperial period, and (2) it had the potential to go badly wrong, is shown by Julius Caesar's attempt to send troops under Labienus to envelop the Helvetii in 58 BC: after Caesar's scouts misidentified Labienus' men as the enemy, the two

Roman commanders were left facing each other whilst the Helvetii slipped away (*B. Gal.* 1.21–2). A worse danger still was that, if the attacker timed it badly, his separate forces could be defeated one at a time by his intended victim. This happened to L. Apronius in Germany in 28 AD, when he disastrously mishandled an attempt to envelop the army of the Frisii (Tacitus, *Ann.* 4.73), leading to the loss of more than 1,300 of his men.

That such a risky tactic continued to be used is testimony to its potential pay-off, which was indeed large. Obviously the ambitious form of the maneuver, featuring a more or less prolonged night march exacerbated potential communications problems. On the other hand, a much less far flung envelopment with fast troops could work very well indeed: Cerialis' troops enveloped Civilis' Germans in 69 with two *alae* despatched after the battle was already well advanced. Their appearance in the enemy rear, which was made evident by a great shout, cracked the German morale and electrified Cerialis' legions, who then charged the Germans' front (*Hist.* 5.18).

It may only be by chance, but we do not tend to hear of such envelopments in the British campaigns. Mons Graupius was a straightforward frontal attack, and Suetonius Paulinus' battle with Boudicca was a dummy defense.

Mons Graupius (AD 84), of which we have a relatively detailed account (Tacitus, *Agr.* 35–37) was unusual in one respect: the auxiliaries alone made up the first line (unusual but not unique: Cerialis adopted the same deployment in the battle just mentioned). Otherwise it exemplifies several of the features of Roman tactics which we have discussed: the holding back of a reserve, usually of cavalry, in this case four *alae*, "against the sudden emergencies of war" (*ad subita belli*); also the use of cavalry to hammer home the victory: there is no reason to suppose that before the pursuit began the Britons had lost many more men than the 360 Romans who were killed, but by the end of it, Tacitus claims, there were 10,000 British dead.

Suetonius Paulinus had used what was perhaps a more common deployment against Boudicca (AD 62): legionary troops in the center (the Fourteenth and part of the Twentieth legions), auxiliary infantry on either side of them, and on the far wings, the cavalry.[10] On this occasion, confident of victory (rather undermining Roman claims to have been seriously outnumbered) the Romans received the charge of the Britons in place, before, javelins thrown, delivering a charge of their own which swept Boudicca's men before it. The impression which Tacitus gives is of a battle decided very swiftly, perhaps in much less than an hour, which gave way to a prolonged pursuit and massacre of the British troops and camp followers, whose escape was impeded by the carts they had parked behind their initial position. About 400 Romans were lost.

3   On the March

Disposing the troops carefully on the march is one of Tacitus' hallmarks of a good general (*Hist.* 3.56 and 5.1), and according to Vegetius (3.6), military experts considered the march to be more dangerous than battle, as the troops could be complacent, and might not be fully armed. It was on the march, due to poor organization, not just a difficult environment, that Varus' three-legion force was destroyed in AD 9 (Cassius Dio 56.19–22).

The best descriptions of orders of march come from eastern wars, which are not properly within the scope of this chapter,[11] but as far as we are told, practice in the West was not very different: the baggage should go in the middle, and there should be a vanguard and rearguard comprised of both infantry and cavalry (Vegetius 3.6). One hazard of marching was the extension of the column (*agmen*) over a long distance, hampering communication and effectively rendering various parts of the army unable to assist each other. To counteract this, the Romans sometimes marched in parallel columns, which grouped the army more tightly overall, although at the cost of some lateral dispersion. For example, Agricola formed three columns to advance into Scotland, wary of "enemy numbers and their superior knowledge of the country" (Tacitus, *Agr.* 26), and in AD 14 Germanicus made what we might call an "advance to contact" ("ready to march or fight," Tacitus, *Ann.* 1.51), illustrating that there was no neat division between battle and march formations. In this case he used a screen of cavalry and auxiliary infantry up front, with the four legions in a diamond, implying that the First (front) and Twentieth (rear) legions cannot have been on quite the same route as the Twenty-first (left flank) and Fifth (right flank); further auxiliaries covered the rear. (Julius Caesar, too, had marched semi-deployed as he neared the forces of the Bellovaci in 51 BC – in the so-called *agmen quadratum*, or "square column," with three legions forward and one back, *B. Gal.* 8.8.) Yet parallel march columns must have been slow and difficult to coordinate effectively under ancient conditions, only becoming standard practice in Napoleonic warfare, when road networks were usually denser, and detailed maps were becoming available for many areas, and the system of "divisions" (in the technical sense) was developed to exploit this.[12]

To find detailed (which does not necessarily mean accurate) accounts of Roman operational march speeds, we have to go back to the republic and Caesar, and his response to the sudden attacks on the scattered winter-quarters of his legions shortly after October 29, 54 BC (Julian).[13] He tells us that he sent messengers to P. Crassus, 25 Roman miles (38 km) away at about the "eleventh hour" (4.20 pm),[14] with orders that his legion should move out at midnight and march to Caesar (*B. Gal.* 7.46). Crassus marched all night, and his outriders reached Caesar by about the third hour (9.55 am) of the following day. Caesar himself then left with other troops, and advanced 20 miles (30 km) (*B. Gal.* 7.47).

This picture of what Roman republican infantry might have been capable of conforms to the rather less detailed picture we get from the principate. In the civil war of AD 69 in one case, a march of 16 miles with full kit was not necessarily unusual, but Celsus and Paullinus warned it would leave troops wearied and vulnerable to the opposition, which had marched only four (Tacitus, *Ann.* 2.40). Shortly after, on the other hand, a force of six Vitellian legions marched 30 miles (45 km) and then fought (and lost) the battle of Cremona during the night (Tacitus, *Ann.* 3.21–22). The longest "march" of which we hear was that of L. Caesennius Paetus away from Armenia in AD 62: 40 miles. However, this retreat was not much more organized than a flight, with casualties being left behind, and presumably therefore much equipment also (Tacitus, *Ann.* 15.16).

4 Clothing

Much of the evidence for military clothing is problematic. Tombstones, such as that of the centurion M. Caelius,[15] lost in the Varian disaster of AD 9, presumably show men in their best uniforms, as they would have appeared on parade, or battle. As such they often give quite good detail for weapons, armor and decorations but they give us no idea of how men would have been attired for marching and fatigues like sentry duty, especially in northern winters. The same problem arises with Trajan's Column, which may seek to present the troops as splendidly as possible, at the expense of veristic realism. In any case, the clothing required for a summer campaign in Dacia would hardly have been adequate for a German or Cumbrian winter.

Nonetheless, there is some evidence for heavier clothing being worn in colder climes, some of it preserved by the same inclement conditions that made it necessary. At the fort of Vindolanda, a few thousand meters behind Hadrian's wall, for example, water-logged contexts have turned up heavy socks and leather boots.[16] A sensitive reading of the literary evidence, too, can help us: in AD 69, A. Caecina Alienus marched into Italy in command of troops from Germany as part of the Vitellian faction. His dress included trousers (*bracae*) and a parti-colored cloak (*sagulum versicolore*) rather than the *paludimentum*, the traditional cloak of the general (Livy 41.10 and 45.39). This made a bad impression on the citizens in the towns north of the Po, according to Tacitus (*Hist.* 2.20), and it is hard to say that Tacitus did not share their distaste for what had for a long time been thought of as "barbarian dress." In 69 BC Cicero had raised an eyebrow at exactly these items, worn in Rome by an Allobrogan embassy (*pro Font.* 33, which describes the Gauls as *sagati*, "cloaked," and *bracati* "trousered"). Yet Caecina presumably did not dress with the intention of alienating his country-men, or provoking a Tacitean sneer; rather the Roman army in Britain and Germany wore appropriate costume for the climate, and when Caecina crossed the Alps in late winter he was no exception. This reminds us too that cultural change in the Roman Empire was no one-way process by which the conquered were "Romanized," but a process of convergence to which not just the famous literature of the Greeks, but also the material culture of northern Europe made its contribution.

5 Assaults on Fortified Places

The assault techniques of the late republic, described in some detail by Caesar, seem to have been continued by the imperial army. The key was to gain physical possession of the enemy ramparts, and this meant selected assault troops first approaching under missile fire, and then scaling them at sword-point. The attackers had a number of counters to the defenders' missiles. The first was their own fire support: the Roman artillery, archers, and slingers would return fire, their aim being, if not to kill defend-ing marksmen, then at least to force them to take cover, thus preventing them from firing at the assault troops (Vegetius 4.21, Tacitus, *Ann.* 13.39). Second, there were a number of protective measures: here the large shield of the legionary came into its own. The "tortoise" (*testudo*) was not an exclusively Roman tactic (German and Gallic use: Tacitus, *Hist.* 4.23; Caesar, *B. Gal.* 2.6), but the curve of the legionary shield would help it interlock with others, and its rectangular shape meant fewer gaps. Note also that whilst he eschewed greaves for the sake of mobility, the legionary did not skimp on protection from above, as the neck guard of his helmet and the generous shoulder protection of his body armor (*lorica*) show. Collective protection was also used in the form of portable sheds, screens, and galleries (*plutei, vineae, crates*) made from wicker-work, and/or covered with hides. The legionaries had the tools to knock these up over night, and they provided valuable cover from both fire and view whilst the men worked within enemy range. Much assault work was physical laboring: building an earthwork (*moles* or *agger*) which could either offer the fire support troops a more commanding platform, or be a ramp for the assault troops on to the defenses themselves. Ladders were a more rapid, but more tenuous alternative. In the Vitellians' failed attempt on Placentia in AD 69 there were also attempts to undermine the walls, and to smash the gate (Tacitus, *Hist.* 2.20–22).

Incendiary missiles were popular with both sides in sieges, either to set fire to the town, or to the besiegers' works, in various forms including hot sling bullets. If it was impossible or too time consuming to break into a structure, an attempt could be made to burn the defenders out, and this was actually done to the Capitol during the Flavian capture of Rome in AD 69. Clearly plenty of fire-fighting gear would feature in the inventory of a well-equipped defender. Finally, improvisation was necessarily very much to the fore, especially for the defender: a heavy object like a mill-stone could crush troops below, even if protected by a *testudo*; dead bodies were also put to good use, as well as on at least one occasion a ballista itself being thrown down (Tacitus, *Hist.* 3.27–29).

It is important to be clear that there was no neat divide between "field battles" on the one hand, and assaults on fortified places on the other. Roman troops, especially but not only when fighting each other, often fought on battlefields where substantial improvements had been made to the defensive advantages of the pre-existing terrain. Campaigning in mountainous North Wales in 51, for example, Ostorius Scapula's men faced the Ordovices "dug in" behind a small river with precipitate banks. Here and there the Britons had piled up ramparts of rocks, from behind which they were getting the better of the Romans using missiles – until the legionaries formed *testudo* and quickly closed with and routed the defenders (Tacitus, *Ann.* 12.35). Germanicus, faced with a similar situation by the Cherusci used his slingers and artillery to strip their rampart (*Ann.* 2.20) – another favourite "siege" technique. Conversely, even the most formidable "towns" the Romans took by storm in the West were hardly in the same league as fortresses and cities of the eastern Mediterranean, where military engineering was already over a millennium old.

6   The Emergence of the *Limites*

Function: what were the limites *for?*

The security of the Roman Empire in the first and second centuries was based on a strategy of "mobile defense." In contrast to "fixed defense," where the defenders spread their forces uniformly across the area to be defended and wait to be attacked, mobile defense envisages the concentration of strong reserves which will move against any intruder and are prepared to fight offensively at the tactical level. Under almost any conditions, ancient or modern, fixed defense is an inferior strategy, because it enables even a relatively weak attacker to gain local superiority against the dispersed posts of the defender, nibbling him away with impunity, a possibility which mobile defense largely eliminates, always seeking to confront the attacker with the defender's main force.

The marching time from Rome to Cologne was 67 days, and to Antioch 124 days, with messengers able to travel no more than six or seven times faster. In other words, compared to the size of the empire, strategic mobility was very low. This meant that at an empire-wide level some forward basing of reserves was necessary. Basing the empire's some 300,000 troops together at Rome would have been just as absurd as distributing them uniformly, one every 20 meters, round the 4,000 mile frontier: potential enemies both great and small would be able to emerge, strike, and then withdraw before Roman troops had been notified, let alone reached the scene. So it was at regional level that we see strong strike forces concentrated. Whether the Romans had a "Grand Strategy" (Luttwak's much-debated term)[17] very much depends on how one defines it. Isaac, who has severely criticized Luttwak finds it hard to believe that imperial forces were disposed according to "modern" strategic principles. As he puts it, if the Romans understood all the subtleties of strategy, "they kept quiet about it," in other words no surviving articulations on strategy survive.[18] Yet this is not quite true. Tacitus, for one, was able to talk explicitly in terms of mobile defense at a strategic level. In his well-known description of the army's dispositions in AD 14 (*Ann.* 4.5), he says: "But our main strength (*praecipuum robur*) was the eight legions on the Rhine, as a reserve (*subsidium*) against both the Germans and the Gauls." In the same passage, he speaks of the two legions stationed in Dalmatia as "backing up" the other four on the Danube, but also able to move swiftly to Italy if "assistance at short notice" (*auxilium repentinum*) was needed there. This is a strategy of mobile defense, if anything is.

Strange as it may at first seem, the "fixed frontiers" which emerged under the principate were precisely intended to facilitate mobile defense. So far we have only spoken of central reserves, but mobile defense cannot dispense with perimeter forces entirely. These, the other main component of the system, act as a kind of sensor, providing the surveillance without which the mobile reserves cannot be directed against threats. From a military point of view, the structures on the *limites* were designed to: (1) maximize the effectiveness of surveillance and signal communication; (2) offer a degree of protection from low-intensity threats to the troops manning them, in order that their numerical strength could be minimized, thus freeing up further troops to be held in reserve. Hadrian's Wall did not provide an effective fighting platform to defend against an attacking army, but, as Luttwak has pointed out, a patrol walking the parapet could not be casually set upon in the dark in the same way as if they had been patrolling a simple track at ground level; (3) deter medium-level threats like the mounted raiders of north Africa. These would have had to breach the wall/fill in the ditch at their entry point, which could then be guarded, helping to trap the intruders and negate their key strength: their elusiveness. High-level threats (full-scale invasions) would take time to develop, and could hopefully be detected and defeated *beyond* the *limites* by Roman main forces.

Surveillance on Hadrian's Wall was carried out by no more than 3,000 troops accommodated at small forts one Roman mile apart. Evenly spaced between each of these "mile-castles," two observation turrets were provided. Local reserves were provided in three forts beyond the wall and 16 on it, numbering probably 5,500 cavalry and 10,000 infantry, whilst the legions at York and Chester, some seven to nine days easy march away, must also be considered available to this sector. These forces make some 30,000 in all, of which 90 percent were mobile reserves at some level – an impressive economy of force, and a very necessary one, given that the empire spent most of our period teetering under the burden of military pay.

Tacitus' description of the Rhine garrison as centrally located against *both* Gauls and Germans illustrates another very important point: the "frontiers" where Roman surveillance forces were stationed, and sometimes main forces happened to be garrisoned, were not the "edge" of Roman territory in the sense of modern frontiers. In its sense of "the right to command," Roman *imperium* was considered to extend over the whole world, and Suetonius is probably stating the official line when he says that the invasion of 43 was required because Britain was "in revolt" (*Claud.* 17). Consequently, in practice, Roman sovereignty faded gradually with distance, rather than stopping at a delimited "frontier." The Rhine and Danube were not chosen as defensive boundaries. Rather troops were sited there for economy of maintenance, the personnel alone of each legion eating 7.5 tonnes of food per day, and water transport costing only a fraction as much as overland supply. Thus in Britain too, the major legionary bases of Kingsholm (Gloucester), York, and Chester were all located on navigable rivers (Severn, Ouse, Dee).

The development of the limites

These then were the principles on which the *limites* operated, which is not to say the system sprang into life fully formed. If the latter is what the opponents of "Grand Strategy" refute, then they are indeed attacking an Aunt Sally. The system had antecedents in Roman field campaigning, from which its evolution in Germany can be clearly traced.

First, as we have begun to see, military engineering had long been used in "open" warfare at a tactical level. A classic example is that when Caesar drew up for battle against the Belgae in 57 BC, he dug ditches on his flanks and provided them with *castella* for his artillery (*B. Gal.* 2.8). The development we see in the early principate is digging being taken to the "operational" level, if we may call it that, with Blaesus' engineering war against Tacfarinas:

> Since Tacfarinas' army was no match in fighting strength, but much superior in making raids, he attacked using many small groups of soldiers, avoided direct contact, and set up ambuscades . . . [but] Blaesus established forts (*castella*) and armed outposts (*munitiones*) in strategic places, penned the enemy in and harassed them on all fronts,

because whichever way they turned, there was part of the Roman army in front of them, on the flanks, and often in the rear. (Tacitus, *Ann.* 3.74)

Because Blaesus' outposts were fortified, they could do with smaller garrisons. At the same time, he hounded the Africans with three mobile columns. In the contemporary campaigns in Germany, we frequently hear of the importance of roads and causeways which the Romans had built to facilitate troop movements: in AD 16 for example, Germanicus spent time fortifying the area between Fort Aliso and the Rhine "with new earthworks and *limites*," here meaning "boundary tracks" (Tacitus, *Ann.* 2.7).

The second antecedent from field campaigning, was the centuries-old employment of lines of pickets in advance of the main body. This role belonged to so-called *exploratores*: when the army was on the march they would scout the terrain ahead, trying to locate the enemy, prevent ambushes, blind the enemy by driving in his own scouts, and find routes;[19] mounted *exploratores* beckon Trajan onwards in Scene 37 of the Column. When the main force was stationary, the *exploratores* would still be deployed, but on these occasions in standing patrols (Tacitus, *Hist.* 3.15). This must be what Caesar, camped outside Cenabum in 52 BC, meant when he tells us that *exploratores* informed him in the middle of the night that the populace were moving silently out of the town (*B. Gal.* 7.11); Vercingetorix' *exploratores*, posted all along the bank of the Allier, "lest the Romans build a bridge and cross over" (*B. Gal.* 7.35), must have been standing patrols too. Their role was not to fight against Caesar themselves, but to cue the main Gallic forces forward to the appropriate spot, which shows that mobile defense was quite widely understood in the first century BC, even if not described in such terms.

It is easy to see how such arrangements could lead to the later built-up *limites*. In Upper Germany, Domitian, in his war against the Chatti (83 AD), advanced a system of *limites* on a front of 120 miles (Frontinus, *Stratagems* 1.3.10). It had no structures as far as we are told, but did involve the clearance of vegetation to facilitate surveillance, which in turn implies that troops were stationed on it at least for a short time, in order to carry the surveillance out. Dozens of *castella* of Domitianic or Trajanic date housed auxiliary cohorts and *alae* in reserve (as later on at Hadrian's Wall) with the main reserves for the sector consisting of two legions at Mainz, and one each at Strasburg and Windisch. In the early second century, perhaps under Trajan, wooden watchtowers appeared for the first time on the stretch between the Rhine and Danube,[20] but it is only in Hadrian's reign that a barrier element, an oak palisade, was added alongside the patrol track which ran in front of the towers. In the middle of the century the (now probably decrepit) wooden towers were replaced with stone towers, and at or after the beginning of the third century the final change was implemented: in Upper Germany a ditch was dug between the fence and the towers, and in Raetia the fence was replaced with a 3-meter-high wall.[21] The construction of watchtowers (which would also have facilitated lateral signaling) would have been a very obvious thing to do once troops with the basic function of *exploratores* became static for even a few days. However, we should remember that once the towers were built, their existence is not evidence that they were occupied permanently: for long periods they may have been visited only by patrols, or manned in times of heightened alert.

As in Germany, the *limites* in Britain developed incrementally. A number of posts, linked by the lateral Stanegate road, appeared in the 30 years before Hadrian's Wall proper was built in the 120s, although this, admittedly, did represent a massive and coherent augmentation of the infrastructure. Still, great caution should be exercised in interpreting the comment of the *Historia Augusta* (*Hadr.* 11), that "Hadrian first built the wall for eighty miles through Britain, in order to divide the Romans from the Barbarians." Since this was probably written in the fourth century, when the empire truly was under siege, it may well misconstrue the intentions of the optimistic rulers of Rome in what Gibbon called its "most prosperous condition."

7   Conclusion

There was much continuity from the army that Caesar knew to that of Trajan: much more so than from Polybius to Caesar, despite the equivalent chronological gap. The built-up *limites*, for instance, were not a conceptual departure from earlier thinking, but rather a practical implementation of it under new political circumstances. The most significant development was the incorporation of more cavalry and specialized infantry into the regular Roman army, as auxiliaries, rather than the often fickle allied contingents of the republic. We would expect this new availability of more reliable light troops and cavalry to afford Roman commanders increased tactical finesse, and in the campaigns of, for example, Germanicus, Vespasian, and Agricola, this is what we seem to see.

NOTES

1   Cornell 1993 convincingly makes this point.
2   This section is largely based on ideas from Sabin 2000, although Sabin's article uses mainly republican evidence.
3   Du Picq 1987, 69.
4   Sim 2000, 40.
5   This type, well known in the republic, is also found in Britain in the later first century AD, and particularly at Oberaden in Germany. Reconstructions were tested for penetration of 11 mm three-ply wood. Connolly 2000, 45–6.
6   Wilkins 1995, upon which this discussion has drawn.
7   Bosman 1995, 99–104.
8   Brudenell 2002, 67.
9   Pre-battle speeches by commanders receive a deal of attention from ancient historians, who were after all engaged in a literary endeavor, and perhaps exaggerate the importance of the harangues because of the opportunity they afford to dramatize the character of the protagonists and build a crescendo towards the armed clash. Their content is often of doubtful authenticity at best.
10 Similar to that of Furius Camillus against Tacfarinas in 1 BC (Tacitus, *Ann.* 2.52).
11 They are: Josephus 3.115–126 (Vespasian's advance on Galilee) and Arrian.

12 Clausewitz 1993, 375–9; Crone 1978, 85–123.
13 *B. Gal.* 23–6. Caesar sailed from Britain when "the equinox [23rd September] was at hand," then marched to Amiens and held a council, which taken together would have consumed a week. Sabinus and Cotta then marched to Aduatuca (160 statute miles as the crow flies), which must have taken a fortnight. The uprising began "about fifteen days later," for 36 days in all.
14 All further distances in miles use the Roman mile (1.5 km). Time of day calculations are based on sunrise and sunset times from Brown 2006, 223:

1st November, Amiens (50°N)			
Sunrise	Sunset	Length of day	Length of Roman hour
6.49am	4.37pm	9hrs 48'	41'30"

15 In the Rheinisches Landesmuseum in Bonn. Photograph widely published, e.g. in Lendon 2005, 249.
16 Birley 2002, 103, 142.
17 Luttwak 1976. The "Grand Strategy" of the title has perhaps been taken to be more inflammatory than the very sensible contents of the book. Still, the "Luttwak" debate persists: for an up-to-date summary and intervention see Whittaker 2004, chapter 2 and Wheeler (in this volume).
18 Isaac 1990, 373.
19 Superb survey in Austin and Rankov 1995, chapter 3.
20 A chain of watchtowers is also depicted on Trajan's Column (Scenes 1–2), presumably representing installations on the Dacian sector before the first war started in AD 101. The towers have a wooden viewing gallery around the upper storey, and are displaying (signal?) torches.
21 Rabold, Schallmayer, and Thiel 2000, 13–17.

BIBLIOGRAPHY

Austin, N. J. E., and N. B. Rankov. 1995. *Exploratio. Military and Political Intelligence in the Roman World.* London.

Birley, A. 2002. *Garrison Life at Vindolanda. A Band of Brothers.* Stroud.

Bishop, M. C., and J. C. N. Coulston. 1993. *Roman Military Equipment from the Punic Wars to the Fall of Rome.* London.

Bosman, A. V. A. J. 1995. "Pouring lead in the pouring rain: Making lead slingshot under battle conditions," *JRMES* 6: 99–104.

Brown, T. (ed.). 2006. *Brown's Nautical Almanac 2006.* Glasgow.

Brudenell, F. 2002. "*Fundis sagittisque*: Roman military archery from the republic to the second century AD," in P. R. Hill (ed.), *Polybius to Vegetius: Essays on the Roman Army and Hadrian's Wall Presented to Brian Dobson.* Oxford.

Clausewitz, C. 1993 [1832]. *On War*, trans. M. Howard and P. Paret. London.

Coarelli, F. 2000. *The Column of Trajan.* Rome.

Connolly, P. 2000. "The reconstruction and use of weaponry in the second century BC," *JRMES* 11: 43–6.

Cornell, T. J. 1993. "The end of Roman imperial expansion," in J. Rich and G. Shipley (eds.), *War and Society in the Roman World*. London, 139–70.

Crone, G. R. 1978⁵. *Maps and their Makers. An Introduction to the History of Cartography*. Folkestone.

Du Picq, A. 1987 [1880]. *Battle Studies*, trans. T. R. Phillips (ed.) *Roots of Strategy*, vol. 2. Harrisburg.

Feugère, M. 2002. *Weapons of the Romans*. Stroud.

Gilliver, C. M. 1999. *The Roman Art of War*. Stroud.

Goldsworthy, A. K. 1996. *The Roman Army at War*. Oxford.

Isaac, B. 1990. *The Limits of Empire*. Oxford.

Keegan, J. 1987. *The Mask of Command*. London.

Lendon, J. 2005. *Soldiers and Ghosts. A History of Battle in Antiquity*. London.

Luttwak, E. 1976. *The Grand Strategy of the Roman Empire*. London.

Rabold, B., E. Schallmayer, and A. Thiel. 2000. *Der Limes: die Deutsche Limes-Strasse vom Rhein bis zur Donau*. Stuttgart.

Sabin, P. 2000. "The face of Roman battle," *JRS* 90: 1–17.

Sim, D. 2000. "The making and testing of a *falx* also known as the Dacian battle scythe," *JRMES* 11: 37–41.

Whittaker, C. R. 1994. *Frontiers of the Roman Empire. A Social and Economic Study*. London.

—— 2004. *Rome and its Frontiers: The Dynamics of Empire*. London.

Wilkins, A. 1995. "Reconstructing the *cheiroballistra*," *JRMES* 6: 5–60.

FURTHER READING

In addition to the works mentioned in the footnotes, the following works are recommended. Both Goldsworthy 1996 and Gilliver 1999 are both excellent on "how it was done." Whittaker 1994 is still useful in addition to his more recent book. Chapter 1 of Keegan 1987, although dealing primarily with Alexander the Great, is seminal on leadership in ancient battle. More detail on equipment can be found in either Feugère 2002 or Bishop and Coulston 1993. Finally, Trajan's Column contains a wealth of evidence untouched on here: Coarelli 2000 provides comprehensive, large plates.

CHAPTER FOURTEEN

The Army and the *Limes* in the East

Everett L. Wheeler

1 Scholarly Approaches

Geography

The East as a monolithic geographical concept and military theater is an illusion. From a Roman perspective, anything beyond the Adriatic was "the East," but this chapter must draw a line at the Bosphorus and forsake the Balkans. Even the phrase, "Euphrates frontier," a conventional symbolic term, inaccurately denotes troops stationed at Pityus in northern Colchis, Singara in eastern Mesopotamia, and Aela on the Gulf of Aqaba, not to mention Egypt. Taken most literally, the Euphrates could be a border only from Cappadocian Dascusa, where the Euphrates' northern and southern branches merge, to Syrian Sura downstream, where (before the Parthian War of 161–166 and subsequent Severan extension of Roman outposts to Ana and Krifrin below Dura-Europos) the Roman border abandoned the river for the Syrian Desert. But even in this stretch of the upper and middle Euphrates Roman bridge-heads controlled the crossings: Tomisa, near Melitene and on the *east* bank, belonged to Cappadocia; Zeugma, joined to Apamea across the river, had a *chora* (a city's non-urban territory) extending even farther east; likewise the *chora* of Samosata in Commagene, only c. 30 miles northwest of Edessa and a more significant crossing than often supposed, probably already included territory east of the river, as in the late empire; and after the capture of Dura-Europos (165), Romans held both banks of the Euphrates upstream. Further, as Sophene (southwestern Armenia) was under indirect Roman control and Osrhoene often belonged to the Roman clientele, the middle Euphrates as a border has little meaning before the Parthian War of 161–166 and almost none after Septimius Severus' creation of the provinces Osrhoene and Mesopotamia (195–199). The Euphrates as a border belongs to a Parthian desideratum in negotiations with Rome, but not a point ever conceded. Even Augustus' directive to maintain the empire within its current limits (Tacitus, *Ann.* 1.11.4) does not mention the Rhine, Danube, and Euphrates.

Unlike the West, where Rome expanded into un-urbanized, less explored territory of tribes at a lower stage of societal development in Gaul, Germany, the northern Balkans, and Britain, the East featured major cities and states with Hellenized or semi-Hellenized ruling classes and established lines of communication. A Seleucid road system already existed in Syria. Besides, mass armies had crisscrossed the so-called Fertile Crescent for nearly 2,000 years before the Romans arrived. Lucullus and Pompey had little difficulty finding their way around either north or south of the Taurus and even east of the Euphrates. Roman expansion in the East did not enter *terra incognita* in the same way as in the West.

But just as the West subdivides into different frontiers in Britain, the Rhine, and the Danube, the East features northern and southern theaters. The northern embraced the southern and eastern Black Sea (including the Bosporan Kingdom of the eastern Crimea), Anatolia, the Caucasus, northern Mesopotamia, and northern Syria. A southern theater, to which Egypt was appended, stretched from southern Syria through Phoenicia and Judaea to Nabataean Arabia. Syria, never a geographical entity, represents the dichotomy, as the upper Orontes Valley with Antioch (part of modern Turkey) and the Cyrrhestice relate to Anatolia more than to the Hauran and desert climes to the south. Drawing a solid line between the two theaters is impossible. Janus-like Syria belonged to both.

The degree of external threat also distinguished the two theaters. Before the late empire, a southern threat from the Arabian Peninsula was inconceivable and the desert between Roman territory and the lower Euphrates precluded movement of mass armies. Eastern invaders had to follow the Euphrates upstream to Syria or the Tigris River into northeastern Mesopotamia before veering off westward toward Nisibis and the relatively well-watered approach north of the Chabur River and its tributaries. Armenia, open on the southeast from Media Atropatene, offered access to either northern or central Anatolia.

Victor Chapot's epic comprehensive history of the Roman army in the East from Pompey to Heraclius (*La frontière de l'Euphrate*, 1907) treated both the northern and southern theaters. But an explosion of archaeological activity in Israel and Jordan following the 1967 Arab–Israeli War has produced an emphasis on the southern theater not justified from a broader perspective of the army and Roman strategic interests. Hence a current tendency to define the Roman East as largely the Semitic world of Syria and the southern theater, thereby ignoring the archaeologically less explored and more epigraphically impoverished areas of eastern Anatolia and northern Mesopotamia. Rome and Parthia, however, never went to war over Arabia or Judaea. Characterizing the East as a "desert frontier" comparable to north Africa also illustrates the point: the northern theater was not a desert. Emergency surveys and rescue excavations along the upper Euphrates and the upper Tigris in the wake of Turkish dam projects have revived some archaeological interest in the northern theater, although major sites have been (or will be) lost (e.g. Samosata, Zeugma, Tigranocerta), and national work (e.g. the Georgians at Pityus and Mtskheta, the Armenians at Artaxata) remains known essentially only to specialists. Even some frontier specialists display ignorance of the cultural and political contexts of Armenia and the Iranian world, to which the northern theater belonged. As Rome entered the East via Anatolia, restoring balance to northern and southern perspectives of the eastern army is merited. Regrettably, the East's southern appendage, Egypt with its treasure-trove of documentary evidence, better fits discussion of socio-economic aspects and logistics than a chapter on political, strategic, and tactical affairs. Egypt must be sacrificed.

Methodology

Since 1976, debate has raged about Roman grand strategy. Was there centralized planning for deployment and use of the army? Did the empire have definite borders designed for defense? Did the central government dictate policies on specific frontiers? To what extent, if at all, did the Romans use military intelligence and maps? Or, did a Roman state, run by amateurs and lacking a bureaucracy, survive for centuries by chance and haphazard reaction to events without any sense of foreign policy, never being pro-active, and bumbling in geographical ignorance? The debate, of which the origins partially lie in interpretation of the East's southern theater, is as much about differing methodological and ideological approaches to the sources and which evidence to emphasize as about the evidence per se, although the anti-strategy school continues to screech the loudest in what has become a dialogue of the deaf. A new evaluation of the debate from a pro-strategy perspective is warranted, but only an impression of the issues must suffice here. The issue of Roman strategy remains an open question.

Armies as the coercive branch of government assigned to carry out policy (both domestic and foreign) by force or the threat of force have responsibility for both external and internal security. One branch of the anti-strategy school denies any external threat from Parthians, Sasanid Persians, and Saracens. Hence the army functioned as a force of occupation to exploit, abuse, and suppress populations; prolific banditry required dispersal of forces often billeted in cities; and forts guarded roads but not territory; Romans did not think defensively and, poised always for offensive operations, sought only glory for individual emperors and booty for the soldiers. As it is currently fashionable in some circles to think "empire" a dirty word and that all empires represent injustice to the conquered (victimology), it is easy to see how some (by no means all) scholars of the southern theater could formulate such views from the evidence for southern Syria, Judaea, and Arabia. But outlaws, like death and taxes, are perennial and few would argue that the Roman army should be equated with the Boy Scouts. Denying a Roman perception of threat from powerful Iranian empires, "the enemy" in wars and diplomatic crises occurring at least once in every generation through the fourth century, marginalizes a large amount of evidence and suggests the absence of a Roman foreign policy. Likewise the view assumes that maintenance of internal security did not involve strategy, that an army cannot serve two functions, and that offensive operations in non-Roman territory, if termed glory-seeking by sources hostile to the emperors involved or the operations themselves, must be solely adventurism devoid of any strategic or rational function. This branch of the anti-strategy school seeks to generalize a view of the East's southern theater to the northern and the empire as a whole.

Another branch of the anti-strategy school primitivizes Roman government in much the same way as efforts (now generally refuted) once attempted to primitivize the ancient economy. Genuflections to the new gospel of cultural anthropology and the so-called "new archaeology" (often theorizing itself into irrelevancy) and a supposed superiority of socio-economic interpretations are combined with an essentially 1960s style of anti-military sentiment. This branch masquerades behind an allegiance (rarely acknowledged) to the methodology of the French *Annales* school of historiography, although this branch of the anti-strategy school also has obvious ideological roots elsewhere. Selective literalist and reductionist views of the sources (when convenient) are a favorite technique, as is an assertion that Roman propaganda proclaiming a borderless, universal empire is to be equated with policy in practice on frontiers. But primitivizing the army, the most bureaucratized and best documented branch of Roman government, marches in step with a self-imposed blindness: the primitivists' narrow conception of strategy as an unalterable blueprint administered through constant micro-management from the center. Any event apparently varying from this hypothesized blueprint becomes an excuse to cry "no strategy," just as Roman failures are attributed to a lack of military intelligence, premised on military intelligence as an ideal practice functioning perfectly. And of course, as no maps useful for large-scale planning have survived, geo-political calculations must have been impossible. On these criteria, no government – ancient or modern – could practice strategy. Indeed, just as one branch of the anti-strategy school has its roots in the southern theater of the East, major exponents of the primitivizing branch began their fascination with frontier studies in North Africa – with a single legion the least military of all frontiers and lacking an external threat comparable to Parthians, Germans, or Sarmatians.

Strategy evolves as a function of historical experience, present circumstances, geography, available means, and human calculation. As a human product, strategy is fallible but also malleable as situations change. Or should the Roman genius for adaptation also be denied? For present purposes, the army in the East will be presented as directed by guiding principles of policy, conditioned by the past and modified by changing circumstances.[1]

2   Prelude

Pompey's arrangements of the East at the conclusion of the Mithridatic wars (89–63 BC) began Rome's permanent military commitment. In the north, Bithynia, bequeathed to Rome (74 BC), merged with much of the old Pontic kingdom as a new Bithynia-Pontus and a "Pontic road" extended the via Egnatia from Byzantium into Anatolia via Nicomedia to Nicopolis (Pürk) in Armenia Minor. In the south, Pompey's annexation of Syria (64 BC), the Seleucid Empire's surviving fragment, created the first Roman province in the Semitic Near East. Syria would constitute only the major cities of the coast and the Orontes River Valley with the Greek cities of the non-contiguous area of the Decapolis (mainly east of the Jordan River) appended.

Direct Roman rule involved only a distorted S-shaped chain of provinces (Bithynia-Pontus, Asia, Cilicia, Syria) with a military commitment reduced from Pompey's 12 legions to only four (two each in Cilicia and Syria) or possibly five (one in Bithynia-Pontus?). Permanent legionary camps for these 20,000–30,000(?) troops are unknown. Indirect Roman control through client-kings, however, not only filled gaps around the regular provinces, but also presented a block of Roman influence and (in theory at least) Rome-protected territory running from the Crimea along the Caucasus' south side through Armenia, Osrhoene, and the Syrian desert to the Arabia peninsula. The Mithridatic wars shifted Rome's eastern frontier from the Aegean coast to the Euphrates and beyond, although as typical in late republican unrestrained imperialism, large bites of new territory still required organizational and pacifying digestion.

Rome's eastward advancement collided with the westward ambitions of Iranian Parthia, a multi-ethnic empire, whose Arsacid dynasty had replaced Seleucid control between Mesopotamia and India. Thus began a rivalry of Mediterranean and Iranian powers over seven centuries that would yield the Near East to fresh Arabian blood heated with Muslim enthusiasm. Initial contact came in 95 BC (or 92 BC), when Cornelius Sulla, then propraetor of Cilicia, encountered a Parthian embassy in Cappadocia. No formal *foedus* (treaty) with the Parthians came from Sulla, Lucullus, or Pompey. Nor was the Euphrates established as a border. Pompey set the empire's Mesopotamian border at the obscure Oruros some 50 (or 250) miles from Zeugma (Pliny, *Nat. Hist.* 6.120). Parthia, after 31 BC the only true state bordering Roman territory and not a client-kingdom, approximated Rome's own capabilities and became the prime focus of Rome's foreign and military policy in the East for the next 250 years.

Further, Pompey established Rome's right to name Armenian kings, when he permitted Tigranes II (a descendant of Artaxias I) to retain his crown (66 BC). After all, Rome's recognition of Armenian independence (188 BC) had created that state. Sophene, however, annexed by Tigranes c. 93 BC, was added to Cappadocia (64 BC). Armenia became the chief bone of contention between Rome and Parthia from Augustus on, the cause – directly or indirectly – of nearly all wars and crises. Roman sources (Parthian sources scarcely exist) never explicitly explain Parthian claims to Armenia in particular (cf. Tacitus, *Ann.* 6.31.1). Tigranes II, however, fathered sons by a Parthian wife and his offspring (both male and female) married Arsacids. Parthia probably had dynastic claims to Armenia, especially as Roman candidates with suitable Artaxiad blood eventually represented genealogical gymnastics. Pro-Parthian and pro-Roman factions within the fiercely independent Armenian nobility aggravated the situation.

3 Augustus and the Julio-Claudians

Augustus (31 BC–AD 14), in setting military dispositions in the East, lacked the luxury of a tabula rasa. Like any new monarch, Augustus had to deal with a present produced by the past. The generation between Syria's annexation (64 BC) and the end of the Roman civil wars at Actium (31 BC) had witnessed dramatic events that shaped future attitudes about the army's role in the East. Sandwiched between Crassus' debacle at Carrhae (53 BC) and M. Antonius' disaster in Media Atropatene (36 BC) lay Parthian operations in Syria (51–50 BC), a Parthian occupation of Syria (40–39 BC) in conjunction with the Pompeian Q. Labienus' raid across Anatolia into Caria, and evident Parthian sympathies in Judaea, Commagene, and Arabia. Pharnaces' attempt to revive his father's Pontic empire (49–47 BC) further demonstrated that the north was no more secure than the south. Indeed the Bosporans had no taste for another Mithridatic scion as king like Mithridates of Pergamum, Caesar's choice for the Bosporan throne, who died (46 BC) trying to claim it. Augustus had much to ponder.

Carrhae, etched beside Allia, Cannae, Teutoburg Forest, and Adrianople in the hall of fame of Roman defeats, clearly demonstrated Parthian military capability: no easy victories beyond the Euphrates. Whether Carrhae ignited a "military revolution" will be addressed later. But seven legions, including some legionary *signa*, were essentially lost. Osrhoene returned to Parthian allegiance and Rome, the new master of the East, seemed a "paper tiger," as the Parthian prince Pacorus rummaged through northern Syria with a force large enough to besiege Antioch. The joint Pompeian–Parthian invasion of 40 BC certainly had to impress. More *signa* became Parthian prizes, and Labienus launched an Anatolian blitzkrieg, while the Parthian Pacorus took control of Syria and received homage from the Nabataeans. Labienus' offensive, however, petered out in Caria and the Antonian general Ventidius Bassus with minimal forces managed two Parthian victories north of the Taurus (39 BC), before the decisive contest at Mt. Gindarus (38 BC) in the Cyrrhestice ended Pacorus' life and Parthian activity in Syria.

Like Crassus, M. Antonius' grandiose plans for Parthian conquest sought to exploit a change of kings in Parthia. His bungled foray into Media Atropatene (36 BC), followed by an annexation of Armenia (34–33 BC), cost two of his 16 legions and alienated the Armenians. In 31 BC Antonius probably had 23 legions, of which 19 went to Actium and four were in Cyrenaica. As earlier, civil war denuded the East of Roman troops, but fortune smiled. A Parthian pretender (Tiridates) temporarily ousted Phraates IV in 31 BC. Little wonder that Octavian headed for Syria in 30 BC after securing Egypt.

Augustus' policy in the East prevailed until the Parthian War of 55–63 demonstrated its inadequacies and stimulated changes under the Flavians and Trajan. Legionary assignments reflected policy. A common view of a peaceful Augustan disposition in the East should be modified to opportunism. The Parthian situation remained volatile during the 20s BC. Aelius Gallus' failed Arabian expedition (26–25 or 25–24 BC) attempted to probe Parthia's southern flank, just as M. Antonius had tried a northern approach. Gallus' campaign coincided with another attempt of Tiridates (26 BC) to oust Phraates IV. The famous Augustan settlement of 20 BC did not involve a treaty (*foedus*) with stipulations about Armenia, a border at the Euphrates, and delivering four sons of Phraates IV as hostages (an event of 11 or 10 BC). Rather, Phraates IV traded Augustus' recognition of his legitimacy (Tiridates still lurked in Syria) for surrender of the *signa* of Crassus and Decidius Saxa (the Syrian governor killed in 40 BC) and some Roman prisoners of war. Augustus' propaganda machine subsequently grossly exaggerated the recovered *signa* into a brilliant Parthian victory.

The numerous twists and subtleties of Roman–Parthian relations cannot be pursued here. From the Roman perspective, friendship (*amicitia*) existed with Parthia, but dynastic succession represented the Arsacids' Achilles heel. Parthian kings often sought Roman recognition of their legitimacy (e.g. Phraataces/Phraates V, 2 AD). The bevy of Arsacid princes in Rome could threaten Parthian stability, if an emperor and/or discontented Iranian nobles wished to raise a rival. Parthia, the sleeping giant, seemed docile in the period from Augustus to Claudius, but Rome carefully avoided direct prodding. Diplomacy to defuse crises was supported by the threat of military force.

Likewise the Armenian situation, tortuous in its developments, was clear: Armenia was a Roman client, whose king Rome had to approve. Candidates acceptable to the Armenian nobility, however, and with at least a few drops of Artaxiad blood in their veins proved increasingly rare. Armenia became the chessboard, where Rome and Parthia played out their rivalry usually with minimal direct confrontation. Yet less noticed in scholarship were Augustus' efforts to retain Media Atropatene, with which Armenia disputed a border. Augustus entertained the prospect of a northern encirclement of Parthia. The adventurous Artabanus II's rise to the Atropatenean and later the Parthian throne (11–38) put Media Atropatene permanently in Parthian hands.

Tiberius' management of the crisis of 35–37 illustrates Augustan policy. When Artabanus II enthroned his son in Armenia at the death (c. 34) of Artaxias III, installed by Germanicus (18), Tiberius prompted Pharasmanes I of Iberia to take action in Armenia, while one, and later a second, Parthian pretender attempted to unseat Artabanus. Pharasmanes set up his brother Mithridates in Artaxata (35) and in the following year, aided by Alan allies, defeated a Parthian army. Meanwhile, L. Vitellius, appointed the Syrian governor in 35 to manage the situation locally, threatened an invasion and compelled Artabanus to accept the *fait accompli* in Armenia. If yet another Rome-sponsored pretender in Parthia failed, the threat of Roman military force from Syria decided the crisis and a client-king had done the messy work without loss of Roman blood.

But how was the army initially deployed in the East? For the period between Augustus and Nero permanent legionary camps, except in Egypt, are unknown. Throughout Augustus' reign (and the first century generally) legions were still mobile, dispatched as whole units when needed. *Vexillationes* (detachments from legions as expeditionary forces) became common only in the second half of the first century. Egypt, Augustus' personal possession, initially had, besides auxilia, three legions (XXII Deiotariana, III Cyrenaica, and one unknown) at Alexandria, Babylon (Old Cairo), and probably Thebes. By 23 (if not earlier) the *ignota legio* was transferred elsewhere (Syria?) and by 38 at the latest the two permanent Egyptian legions camped at Nicopolis, just outside Alexandria.

Syria's garrison, initially three legions, probably rose to four in Augustus' reign: III Gallica, VI Ferrata, X Fretensis, and XII Fulminata. Only X Fretensis' deployment at Cyrrhus in 18 is certain. Raphanea, at the crossroads of the Orontes River Valley with the route passing from Emesa to the Phoenician coast, is another possible site. Camps at or near major cities (Zeugma, Antioch, Tyre) remain purely speculation. Indeed Philo of Alexandria (*Leg.* 207; cf. 259) implies a substantial part of the Syrian army lay on the Euphrates by Tiberius' reign.

Besides external foes, internal security was a concern. Just as the double legionary camp at Egyptian Nicopolis suggests a response to Greek–Jewish strife in Alexandria, Raphanea overlooked Ituraea to the southeast, a hot bed of banditry, as was the Cyrrhestice. But much of the southern theater – still under client-kings (e.g. Emesa, Arabia) – escaped direct Roman control. Turbulent local politics and resentment to taxation after Herod the Great's death (4 BC) brought the annexation (AD 6) of Judaea and Samaria as perhaps the empire's first procuratorial province: an equestrian governor at Caesarea with auxilia. In severe situations the Judaean governor could call on the Syrian governor with his legions for help, but unruly tribes in the southern Taurus also occasionally directed a Syrian governor's attention northward.

A mere six legions (Syria and Egypt) for the East cannot be correct. The annexation of Galatia (25 BC) required one (perhaps two) legions there for a time. Under Augustus legions frequently moved and the eventual four Syria legions did not serve exclusively in Syria. Wars on the lower Danube and in Pannonia required manpower from the East, and Thrace and the lower Danube were still considered part of the East in this period. A Danube–Euphrates nexus was already in operation. Later, Danubian legions (IV Scythia, V Macedonica, VII Claudia, VIII Augusta) did some eastern service. Indeed the armies that Tiberius (20 BC), Gaius Caesar (AD 2), and Germanicus (18) took to Armenia were not Syrian forces.

Much northern territory also remained under client-kings (Commagene, Armenia Minor, Cappadocia, Pontus). A scheme to unite the eastern Black Sea coast from the Bosporan Kingdom through Colchis to the Iris River in Pontus collapsed with the death of Polemo I (8 BC), while he was fighting natives east of the Maeotis (Sea of Azov). Hence the Bosporan Kingdom escaped incorporation with Pontus and remained an independent client until its demise in the fourth century. Pythodoris, Polemon I's widow, retained rule of Pontus and subsequently wed the powerful Archelaus of Cappadocia (36 BC–AD 17), whose domains also included Armenia Minor and Rough Cilicia. Tiberius ended Archelaus' virtual lordship of the upper Euphrates, when he deposed him (17) – whether for his old age or intrigues in Armenia – and converted Cappadocia to a procuratorial province on the eve of Germanicus' mission to the East.

4 Collapse and Reorganization: The Northern Theater

Augustan policy, effective for nearly three-quarters of a century, collapsed in the Parthian War of 55–63. "Nero lost Armenia," as Festus tersely stated (*Brev.* 20). The coincidence of Iberian court intrigues c. 51 against their kinsman Mithridates and a rejuvenated Parthia under Vologaeses I (c. 51–78) resulted in the Arsacid Tiridates' occupation of the Armenian throne by 54. Domitius Corbulo could conquer (58) and re-conquer Armenia (63), but Rome's well of candidates with traces of Artaxiad blood in their veins had run dry after Tigranes VI (59–61) proved unreliable. Rome could prevail militarily but not politically. Nero's festive coronation of Tiridates I at Rome (66) disguised a lost cause: Rome would crown Armenian kings but henceforth of Arsacid lineage. Again, Rome and Parthia sealed an agreement, although not a treaty (*foedus*).

The Parthian War of 55–63 exposed structural shortcomings in Augustus' eastern arrangements, which assumed a weak Parthia. A now aggressive Parthia and the loss of Armenia drastically changed the strategic situation. Hitherto the Syrian governor with four legions held responsibility for the entire eastern front, but the collapse of the Armenian situation in 51–54 demonstrated the inadequacies of a governor in Antioch to monitor affairs north of the Taurus, observe the middle Euphrates, and maintain order in Syria. Only after 66, when Rome re-thought its eastern deployments, does *limes* in the sense of an organized defensive disposition have meaning. Developments to 251 in the northern and southern theaters will be treated separately.

In 66, troops were already in motion for a Caucasian campaign. Caucasian Albania (east of Iberia), a client since Pompey's conquest (65 BC), was conspicuously absent from the Roman war effort and may have sheltered at times the Arsacid Tiridates, Corbulo's opponent. Albania's absence left a hole in Rome's plan to encircle the new Parthian Armenia with a string of forts and clients and presented the unwelcome prospect of Arsacid access to Sarmatian mercenaries. If Nero's execution of the concept came to naught, Vespasian (69–79) strengthened the fortifications of the Iberian capital Mtskheta in 75 and before 96 a centurion of the XII Fulminata (now a Cappadocian legion) left a record of his presence (possibly a diplomatic mission?) under Domitian in southwestern Albania. By 114 Trajan had secured Albanian loyalty for his Parthian War (114–117) and appointed a king for the Albani, who remained Roman clients until the Sasanid conquest in 251. Roman troops were never stationed in Albania, nor in Iberia until operations under Valens (370s).

A supposed Sarmatian threat from north of the Caucasus is a scholarly fiction. The Alans served as Iberian allies in Armenia (35–36) and the Alan inroad of 135, which the historian Arrian (Flavius Arrianus) as Cappadocian governor deterred from Roman territory, came at Iberian instigation and cannot be divorced from Pharasmanes II's feud with Hadrian. An Alan raid(s) of c. 75 into Media and Armenia originated east of the Caspian and exposed a Parthian northeastern frontier problem, perhaps connected with a Hyrcanian revolt (late 50s–?). A similar raid of the Dahae occurred c. 53.

The defensive disposition of Anatolia, devoid of legions (although not auxiliary units) since some point under Augustus, demanded change after 66. Loss of the Armenian buffer left the entire upper Euphrates and access to central Anatolia defenseless against potential Parthian hostilities. With legions active in Armenia (55–63) the lack of development in central and northeastern Anatolia exposed the now inadequate system of client-kings. Rome annexed Pontus in 64, Armenia Minor in 72, and possibly contemplated adding the Bosporan Kingdom, whose failure to protect Chersonesus on the western Crimean coast against the Scythians c. 62 required action from the Moesian governor. By 76 three-quarters of Anatolia were united as a gigantic consular province, the Galatia-Cappadocia complex administered from Ancyra. The XII Fulminata moved from Syria to Cappadocian Melitene in 70 and by 76 a new legion, XVI Flavia Firma, was at Satala, whose strategic significance emerged in Corbulo's campaigns. Legions on the upper Euphrates in combination with the clients Iberia and Albania enveloped Arsacid Armenia on the north and west.

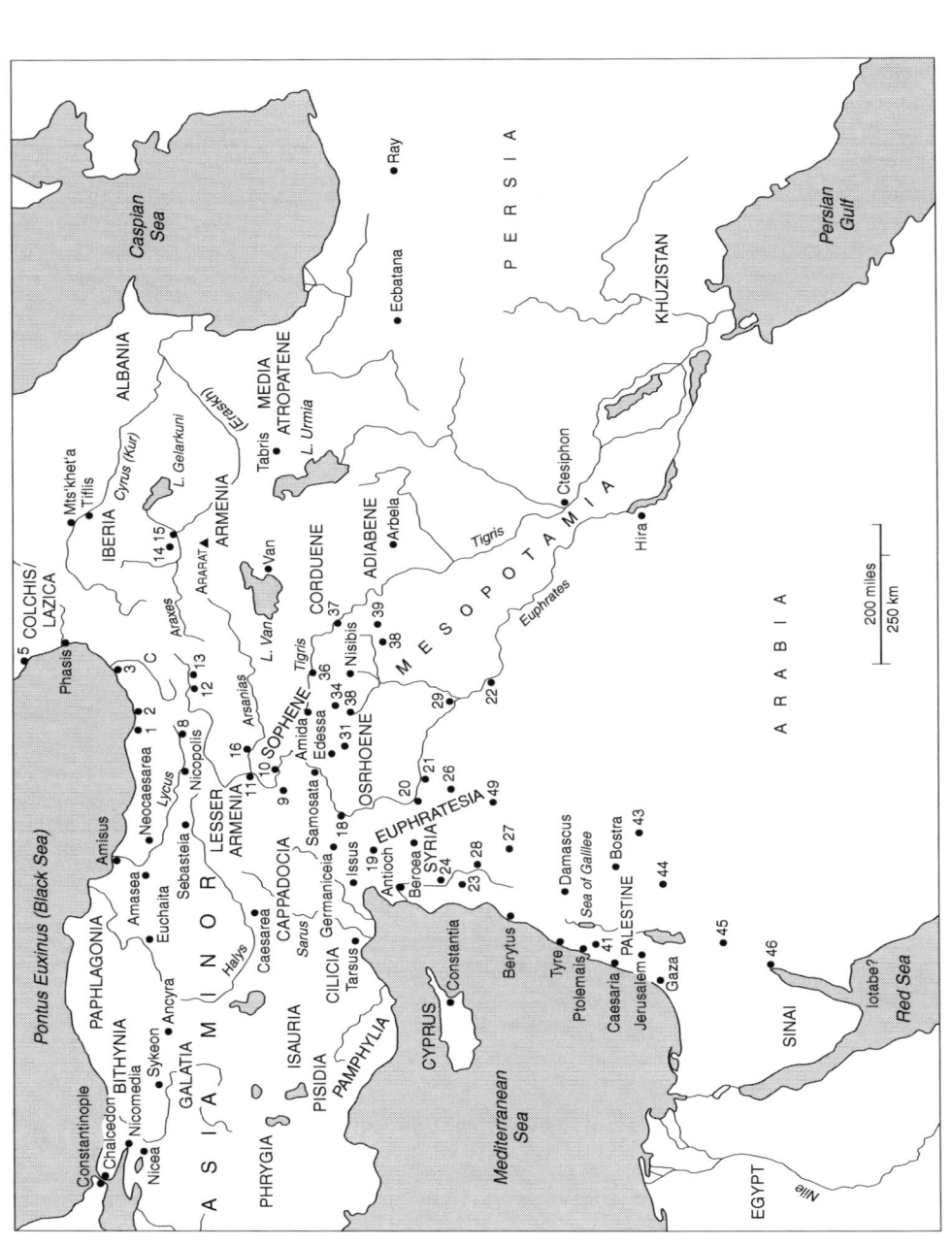

Map 14.1 Roman East: Southern Theater.

Source: Greatrex, G., and S. Lieu (eds.), *The Roman Eastern Frontier and the Persian Wars, Part II, AD 363–630: A Narrative Sourcebook*, London

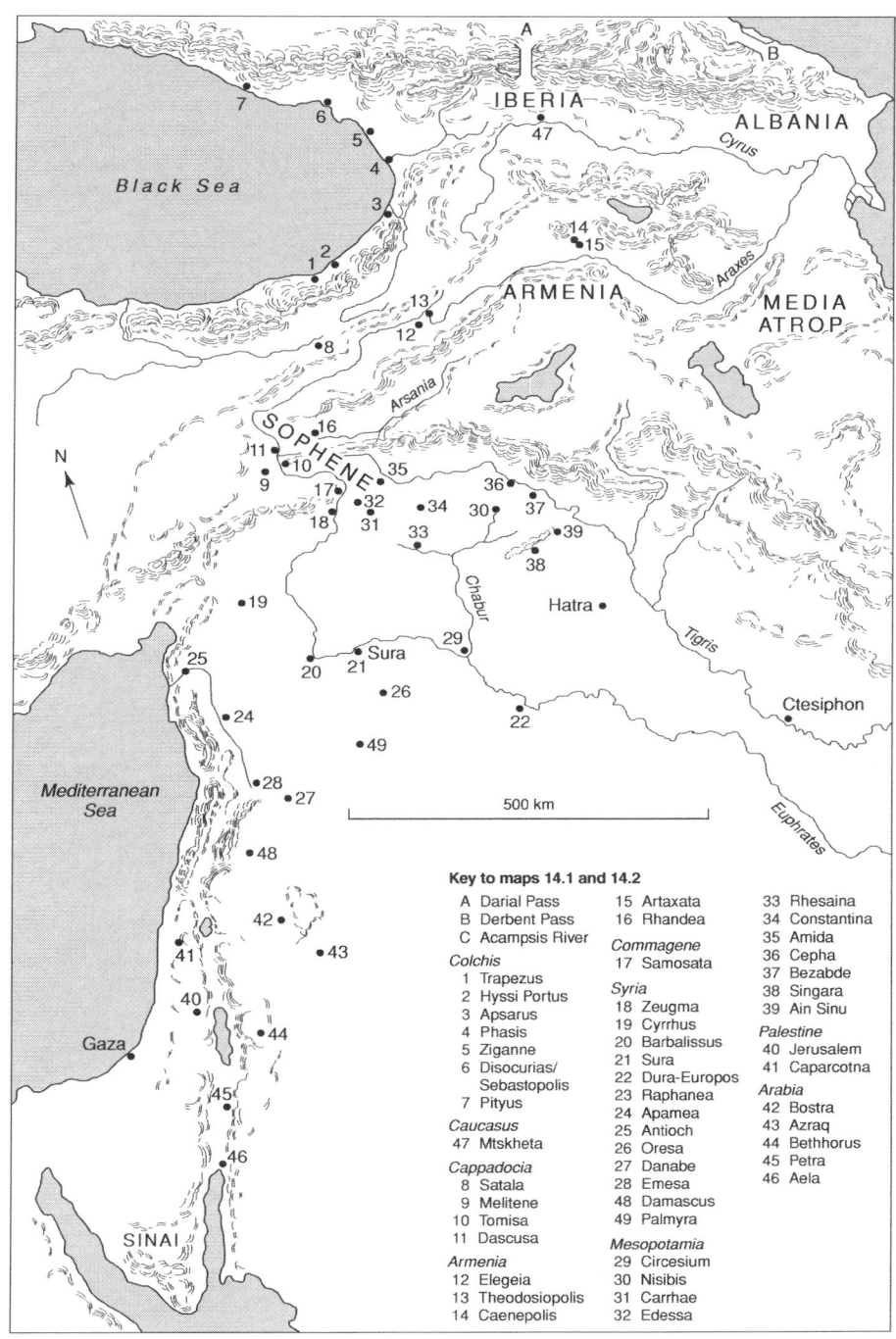

Key to maps 14.1 and 14.2

A Darial Pass
B Derbent Pass
C Acampsis River

Colchis
1 Trapezus
2 Hyssi Portus
3 Apsarus
4 Phasis
5 Ziganne
6 Disocurias/
Sebastopolis
7 Pityus

Caucasus
47 Mtskheta

Cappadocia
8 Satala
9 Melitene
10 Tomisa
11 Dascusa

Armenia
12 Elegeia
13 Theodosiopolis
14 Caenepolis

15 Artaxata
16 Rhandea

Commagene
17 Samosata

Syria
18 Zeugma
19 Cyrrhus
20 Barbalissus
21 Sura
22 Dura-Europos
23 Raphanea
24 Apamea
25 Antioch
26 Oresa
27 Danabe
28 Emesa
48 Damascus
49 Palmyra

Mesopotamia
29 Circesium
30 Nisibis
31 Carrhae
32 Edessa

33 Rhesaina
34 Constantina
35 Amida
36 Cepha
37 Bezabde
38 Singara
39 Ain Sinu

Palestine
40 Jerusalem
41 Caparcotna

Arabia
42 Bostra
43 Azraq
44 Bethhorus
45 Petra
46 Aela

Map 14.2 Roman East: Northern Theater.
Source: Kennedy, D. (ed.) 1996. *The Roman Army in the East*, Ann Arbor

Corbulo had opened a supply route from the upper Euphrates over the Pontic Alps to the port of Trapezus, which, however, lacked a good harbor until Hadrian built one. In wartime, Trapezus became a major logistical base (e.g. during Statius Priscus' reconquest of Armenia, 163), when a *praepositus orae gentium Ponti Polemoniaci* took charge of supply operations. At a later date the logistical base of the Cappadocian army moved east to Hyssi Portus, whence Satala could be reached by a less arduous pass than the Zigana, although the fertile plains around the Roman colony at Nicopolis and elsewhere in central Anatolia also provided a "breadbasket." Grain from the Bosporan Kingdom did not exclusively feed the Cappadocian army.

As usual, a *limes* road linking all legionary and auxiliary camps ran from Trapezus to Satala to Melitene and across the Taurus to Samosata, where it joined the Syrian road system. A major Flavian achievement, however, was an extensive road network, subsequently repaired and expanded under later emperors, connecting the Danubian legions with the Euphrates. Ancyra emerged as major hub. This Danube–Euphrates nexus, rudimentary under Augustus, paved the way for transfers of whole legions and *vexillationes* in the second and third centuries, whether going east against the Parthians or west against Dacians, Quadi, and Sarmatians.

The annexation of Pontus and the addition of legions to the upper Euphrates gave the Black Sea new prominence. A Pontic fleet based at Trapezus, Sinope, and Amastris policed the northern Anatolian coast and neutralized Colchian pirates. Colchis as part of Pontus also became Roman territory with troops at the coastal sites of Hyssi Portus, Apsarus, Phasis, Dioscurias/Sebastopolis, and occasionally Trapezus (detachments of XII Fulminata, XV Apollinaris), where a second-century mint produced bronze coins to pay troops at Pityus and the other Colchian garrisons. Tribal chieftains as client-kings controlled the interior. Josephus' claim (*BJ* 2.366–67) that a fleet of 40 ships and 3,000 troops patrolled the Black Sea in 66 more probably reflects a Flavian disposition. Under Antonius Pius (138–161) or certainly under the Severi, Pityus, c. 60 kilometers northwest of Dioscurias, became the new terminus of the empire with a garrison from the XV Apollinaris through the late 250s. Yet the militarization of eastern Anatolia did not alter Rome's assignment for Crimean affairs. The western Crimea remained the concern of the governor of Moesia Inferior, while the governor of Bithynia retained supervision of the Bosporan Kingdom and the rest of the Crimea. A Cappadocian governor's province stopped at Dioscurias (later Pityus).

Trajan's Parthian War (114–117), which envisioned the annexation of Armenia and extension of the empire to the lower Tigris, briefly (114–116) saw the union of Cappadocia, Armenia Minor (both detached from Galatia c. 111), and Armenia Maior as a single province. But revolts throughout Mesopotamia and Armenia forced Trajan to yield (116) a part of Armenia to the Arsacid Vologaeses, son of Sanatruces. Under Hadrian (117–138) Cappadocia, including Armenia Minor, Colchis, and most of Pontus Polemoniacus, assumed the size it would retain as a military command through the fourth century. Caesarea, with an important imperial mint, was the capital. With two legions and numerous auxilia, Cappadocia as a consular province ranked second among imperial eastern commands only to Syria. A Cappadocian governor held responsibility for the eastern Black Sea, the Caucasian kingdoms, and – not least – observation of Armenia. Sophene remained independent of the Armenian king and under the Cappadocian governor's eye, although not formally a Roman possession. In the realignment of legions under Hadrian, XII Fulminata retained Melitene, but at Satala XV Apollinaris (in Egypt c. 107–c. 117) replaced XVI Flavia Firma, which moved to Samosata. A third legion may have been added to Cappadocia under Antoninus Pius, if Sedatius Severianus' apparent loss of a legion at Elegeia (161) accounts for the disappearance of IX Hispana.

The aftermath of the Parthian War of 161–166 saw detachments of the Cappadocian legions at Vagharshapat (Caenepolis), the new Armenian capital c. 20 miles north-west of Artaxata, apparently to bolster the rule of Sohaemus of Emesa, whom Statius Priscus installed (164). A peacetime legionary presence in Armenia marked a change in policy, probably reflecting Parthian weakness after its defeat in 166 and a reassertion of Roman prerogatives, especially given Sohaemus' thin Arsacid credentials. Hitherto only auxiliaries had been permitted (e.g., support for Mithridates the Iberian's rule 41–51 under Claudius). The Cappadocian *vexillatio* in Armenia ceased in Commodus' reign (180–192). Caracalla (211–217) planned to annex Armenia as part of his grandiose eastern designs, but Tiridates II, son of the unnamed Armenian king deposed c. 214, gained the Armenian throne through Macrinus' treaty of Nisibis (218) with the Parthians.

Besides detachments in Armenia, the Cappadocian legions were thinly stretched after 166. XV Apollinaris had detachments at Pityus and Trapezus (as did XII Fulminata) and sent a *vexillatio* to the Marcomannic wars, where XII Fulminata also served in whole or part. Policing the extensive road network of the province should also be noted. Yet the Cappadocian legions remained apolitical, abstaining from Avidius Cassius' revolt (175) and from support of Pescennius Niger against Septimius Severus in 193–194.

In neither the northern nor the southern theater did Rome attempt to construct a *limes* in the sense of a continuous fortified barrier. As Victor Chapot recognized over a century ago, the East had an open frontier, in which natural barriers (rivers, mountains, deserts) dispensed with the need for extensive fortifications. An open frontier in the East is hardly a new discovery of recent commentators on (or deniers of) Roman strategy. Only major invasion routes, river crossings, and other strategic points required fortifications, as confirmed for the Cappadocian army in the *Notitia Dignitatum* (395/400). Cappadocian units in this document closely correspond to those in Arrian's army against the Alans and thus illustrate the relative stability of the Cappadocian garrison over two centuries. Nevertheless, the placement of units, so far as sites can be identified – and some sites escaped Ptolemy's *Geography* – reveals a deployment closely tied to the Euphrates, which bears little resemblance to political reality before 251, when Sophene was unofficially under Roman control, after 299, when Sophene consisted of five satrapies (*gentes*) of Roman *foederati*, or after the Roman–Sasanid partition of Armenia in 387, when northwestern Armenia became the sole remnant of a pro-Roman Armenia Maior, which at some point c. 390–420s was annexed as Armenia Interior. The deployment of the *Notitia* may therefore reflect the period of Sasanid control of Sophene and Armenia Maior 251–299 with some alterations from the reigns of Valens and Theodosius I. Most glaring is the omission of any unit at the Tomisa crossing, the most important ford of the Euphrates north of the Taurus. The legionary base at Melitene does not guard the ford directly.

The northern theater also had interior frontiers. Disturbances in Isauria, like Cilicia, an elastic term for the south-central Taurus region from southern Pisidia to Rough Cilicia, repeatedly popped up like an irritating pimple. Isaurian brigandage by the mid-fourth century became a festering sore (revolts 367–369, 375) requiring a permanent command. The *Notitia* records a *comes per Isauriam* with two legions (I–II Isaura). Even the *Historia Augusta* (*Tyr. Trig.* 26.6) recognized Isauria as an internal *limes*. Likewise the Sanni/Tzanni in the rough terrain between Trapezus and the upper Acampsis River became an internal *limes*.

5   Reorganization and Expansion: The Southern Theater

If the southern theater remained relatively untouched by the Parthian War of 55–63, its legions were not. All four Syrian legions served at some point north of the Taurus, and Corbulo (Syrian governor, 60–63) had to fortify the Euphrates against a threatened Parthian invasion (61–62). Three Danubian legions, V Macedonica, IV Scythica (subsequently a Syrian legion), and XV Apollinaris reinforced the eastern legions. Yet the Armenian crown scarcely touched Tiridates I's head, when a Jewish revolt, destined to last until 70, erupted in 66. Various rebel strongholds in the south (e.g. Masada) fell only some years later. Vespasian's bid for the purple in 69 disrupted the war effort, as did the dispatch of 13,000 troops to support the Flavian cause. In the end, Judaea became a praetorian province with the X Fretensis in garrison at Jerusalem. Fifth Macedonica and XV Apollinaris returned to the Danube.

Judaea, with lairs infamous for banditry on nearly all its borders and a turbulent populace, retained its explosive potential. Although it is not clear that the bloody Jewish revolts in Mesopotamia, Cyrenaica, Egypt, and Cyprus 116–117 also touched Palestine, Lucius Quietus, whom Trajan charged with suppressing the revolt in Mesopotamia, curiously appears as the Judaean governor by 117. Perhaps Judaea had already become a consular province – confirmed, if milestones of 120 on the Caparcota–Sepphoris road in Galilee indicate work of II Traiana. Hadrian's conversion of Jerusalem into Aelia Capitolina offended Jewish sensibilities and sparked the Bar Kokhba revolt in 132, which dragged on to perhaps 136. A legion (XXII Deiotariana?) was lost and reinforcements had to be called in from Syria, Arabia, Cappadocia (at least a *vexillatio* of XII Fulminata), and as far off as the Danube (X Gemina). Judaea now became the consular province Syria Palestina with X Fretensis at Aelia Capitolina and VI Ferrata at Caparcotna (Legio, Maximianoupolis) in the north. The last major war of Romans and Jews was over, although not the problem of brigandage. Debate continues over an internal *limes* west of the Dead Sea on the edge of the Negev.

When the dust from the First Jewish War had settled, Vespasian (69–79) began a reorganization of the southern theater, where (as in the northern) an open frontier would be the norm. In 72 Antiochus IV of Commagene, suspected of Parthian intrigues, was deposed and sent off to Sparta, but annexation of Commagene involved a minor *bellum Commagenicum* into 73. Commagene was added to Syria with III Gallica at the important Euphrates crossing and former royal residence of Samosata. Fourth Scythica continued its camp (since 66) at Zeugma, the customs post for traffic into the empire from northern Mesopotamia and a major staging area (the field "At Meydarı" northwest of the Zeugma acropolis) for western legions marching to Parthian/Sasanid wars. Its legate often assumed the role of acting governor of Syria in the absence or death of the regular governor.

With the loss of the X Fretensis to Judaea, the Syrian garrison was reduced to three legions, but Flavian emphasis was clearly on defense of the Euphrates (Samosata, Zeugma). Only VI Ferrata at Raphanea in the south monitored internal affairs. Much of the southern theater, however, still remained under client-kings. Despite the lack of an explicit statement in literary sources, the sequence of events indicates policy. The age of client-kings west of the Euphrates was over; kingdoms would be annexed as the reigning kings died off. Emesa quietly passed into the empire in the late 70s(?), and the scattered kingdoms of the Herodians Agrippa II and Aristobulus of Chalcis were absorbed in the early 90s. Thus in 106, when Rabbel II of Nabataean Arabia expired, the Syrian governor Cornelius Palma occupied Arabia with the VI Ferrata, aided by the Egyptian III Cyrenaica, which would eventually become this praetorian province's legion based at Bostra. A *limes* road connected Bostra with the port Aela on the Gulf of Aqaba, the famous via Traiana, and part of the Decapolis was transferred to Arabia from Syria. Trajan merely continued Flavian policy. A connection of Arabia's annexation (106) with the Parthian war (114–117) is fanciful.

In northern Syria, legionary detachments in the mid 70s improved the harbor at Seleucia Pieria, west of Antioch, and dug canals to facilitate movements of goods from the coast to the Syrian capital. A Syrian fleet, first attested under Hadrian, probably had a Flavian origin. In the Parthian War of 114–117, Trajan directly benefited from Flavian improvements, as Cyrrhus became a major staging site of troops and supplies. Elsewhere, Ulpius Traianus (Syrian governor 73–78), credited with an obscure Parthian victory, built roads – particularly one connecting Palmyra via Oresa and Rasafa with the Euphrates at Sura or Callinicum. Trajan's road reflects this desert city's integration into Roman Syria. An obscure desert outpost under Parthian control in the 40s BC, a Roman protectorate in 18 AD, Palmyra experienced a meteoric rise in the second century, when Palmyrenes protected the caravan trade and policed the eastern fringes of the southern theater besides part of Egypt.

How far down the Euphrates Roman control extended in the 70s is unclear – Dura-Europos was still Parthian – but titles like *curator ripae superioris et inferioris* and *praefectus ripae fluminis Euphratis* suggest that by Domitian's reign (81–96) the Euphrates, navigable only from Samosata downstream, was acquiring an administrative and logistical unity. In the third century the Roman commander at Dura-Europos was a *dux ripae*.

Trajan's annexation of Armenia and Mesopotamia (114–117) exploited the Flavian substructure established in both the southern and northern theaters. In the end, Rome retained few of Trajan's conquests. Osrhoene returned to client-king status and Sophene remained under Cappadocian purview without direct control. Indeed necessity prompted Hadrian's abandonment of Trajan's conquests. Despite Lucius Quietus' efforts to restore Roman gains in Mesopotamia, the planned renewal of offensive operations in 117 did not materialize and the Danube, denuded of troops for Parthian operations and ablaze with Dacian and Sarmatian unrest 117–118, demanded attention.

A reshuffling of legions after Trajan's Parthian War produced the disposition that would last until reorganization under Diocletian. In Cappadocia XVI Flavia Firma abandoned Satala for Syrian Samosata. Its replacement was XV Apollinaris, transferred from Carnuntum to Egypt c. 107 to replace III Cyrenaica (then active in Arabia). Twelfth Fulminata remained at Melitene in Cappadocia, just as IV Scythica continued at Syrian Zeugma. Third Gallica moved from Samosata to Raphanea. To Arabian Bostra III Cyrenaica returned after numerous shifts of assignment. Sixth Ferrata at Caparcotna and X Fretensis were the Judaean legions. Second Traiana eventually became the sole Egyptian legion after the apparent loss of XXII Deiotariana in the Bar Kokhba revolt (132–136). This Antonine deployment reveals an even split of four legions for frontier defense in Cappadocia and northern Syria and four for internal security in southern Syria, Syria Palestina (Judaea), and Arabia.

Vologaeses IV's surprise offensive of spring 161 delivered a blow not seen since the invasion of Labienus and Pacorus in 40 BC. Armenia was lost for two years (161–163), Osrhoene had a pro-Parthian ruler for two (162–164), and the Syrian border as far as Sura became a battle zone for three (161–164). Parts of Syria may actually have been under Parthian control, before the Roman counterattack (165–166) took the war to Ctesiphon and Media. Dura-Europos, captured in 165, advanced Roman control of the Euphrates far downstream and Nisibis possibly also received a garrison of Syrian troops (cf. Cassius Dio 75.1.2–3).

A generation later, Septimius Severus (193–211) brought profound changes. In an effort to limit the potential of Syrian governors for usurpations, Severus divided Syria into two provinces. From one perspective, the division only formalized Syria's geographical diversity. South of a line running from Arados on the coast to the Euphrates lay the new Syria Phoenice with a single legion: III Gallica at Raphenea; to the north Syria Coele retained its two legions at Samosata and Zeugma, but also included the Euphrates down to Dura-Europos, where detachments of XVI Flavia and IV Scythia occasionally appear. Further, two Parthian campaigns (195, 197–199) resulted in the annexation of Osrhoene (except a reduced kingdom of Edessa) and Mesopotamia. The new provinces became (like Egypt) imperial praefectures. Three new legions were raised, I–III Parthica, of which II Parthica became the emperor's personal reserve stationed at Albinum north of Rome, but during eastern tours under Caracalla and Macrinus (215–218), Severus Alexander (231–233), and Gordian III (242–244) it wintered at Apamea in the Orontes Valley. First Parthica was assigned to Singara on the southern slopes of Jebel Sinjar ridge and within marching distance of the middle Tigris. A location for III Parthica is unknown: Rhesaina and Nisibis are possibilities. Carrhae and Nisibis obtained colonial status. Severus justified his annexations: Mesopotamia provided a defensive bulwark (*probole*) for Syria (Cassius Dio 75.3.2). Events of the fourth century rather than the third validated his strategy, for after Sapor I's raids of 252–53 and 260 Roman–Sasanid conflicts focused on Mesopotamia.

A new *limes* in the sense of a continuous fortified frontier from the Euphrates up the Chabur River with an overland extension along the Jebel Sinjar ridge to the Tigris cannot be proved. The Chabur–Jebel Sinjar line was, like the Euphrates earlier, an open but not unguarded frontier. Diocletian (284–305) first anchored this line with a fort at Circesium, where the Chabur empties into the Euphrates, but Severan outposts of auxiliary detachments (attested in documentary sources) policed the lower Chabur. At the opposite end of the line, besides the I Parthica at Singara, an auxiliary fort c. 30 kilometers east of Singara at Ain Sinu guarded a pass over the Jebel Sinjar. A recently discovered auxiliary fort at Qubur al Bid (east-southeast of Nisibis) may be the castra Maurorum of literary sources. By 235 Hatra, the desert city besieged in vain by Trajan and Septimius Severus, had allied with Rome and housed perhaps a *vexillatio* of I Parthica and the cohort IX Maurorum Gordiana, before Sapor I captured it by treachery in spring 240. It thus seems erroneous to claim that a Chabur–Jebel Sinjar line did not exist and that defense of Mesopotamia in the third and fourth centuries was solely dependent on fortified cities. In the fourth century the area east of Nisibis was even more strongly held (e.g. a fort at Bezabde on the Tigris northeast of Nisibis). If Septimius Severus' annexation of Mesopotamia initially rendered the legions of Cappadocia and Syria Coele on the Euphrates superfluous frontier forces, such was no longer the case after 251 when the Sasanids held both Armenia Maior and Sophene.

6   Transition to the Late Empire

Four significant dates mark the final two centuries covered in this chapter: 218, 299, 363, and 387. Artabanus IV's victory at Nisibis (217) erased a century of Roman dominance over the Parthians. The treaty of Nisibis (218) restored an Arsacid (Tiridates II) to Armenia, compelled Rome to pay Parthia reparations, and (most significantly) forced Rome to recognize for the first time Parthia's equality of status in a genuine *foedus aequum*. Nisibis initiated a string of Roman defeats in the East that, despite the change of dynasties in Ctesiphon (226) from Arsacids to Sasanids, continued until Odaenathus, the Palmyrene prince entrusted with eastern defense after Sapor I's capture of Valerian (260), stemmed the tide. A decade later, Aurelian snuffed out Palmyra's pretensions of imperial glory that extended this desert city's rule from Egypt to southern Anatolia, and restored Roman authority in the East's southern theater. Likewise in the north, Galerius' victory over the Sasanid Narses (293–302) reversed Sasanid ambitions in Armenia and Iberia and restored Sophene, lost in 251, as well as Nisibis and northeastern Mesopotamia, perhaps lost in 293, to Roman control in another treaty of Nisibis (299). Julian's disastrous Persian expedition produced yet another Nisibis treaty (363), whereby Rome lost Nisibis and eastern Mesopotamia permanently and gave Sapor II (309–379) a free hand in Armenia against the last of the Arsacids, although the five satrapies (*gentes*) of Sophene remained Roman. The territory gained in 299 and lost in 363 was not identical. Valens' efforts (370–378) to preserve a pro-Roman Armenia and Iberia led to partitions of Iberia (370) and Armenia. The latter partition, formalized under Theodosius I (387), surrendered three-quarters of the land to Persian hegemony. A reorganization of the northern frontier followed in the 420s after the death of the last Arsacid ruler of

Roman western Armenia c. 390. The Persian sector became a province (Persarmenia) under a marzpan after the Sasanids deposed the last Arsacid king in 428.

7   Transition: The Southern Theater

The Sasanid wars of 251–261 mark the initial stage of the transition to the late empire in the East. Sapor I's conquest of Armenia and the Caucasian kingdoms of Iberia and Albania in 251 fulfilled a long-standing Sasanid ambition to eradicate the last vestiges of the Armenian branch of the Arsacid dynasty, from which Ardashir I had seized the Parthian throne (226). Whatever Philip the Arab had negotiated with Sapor in 244 about Armenia was now irrelevant and Sapor's raid up the Euphrates in 252–253 punished alleged Roman perfidy. A second raid of 260 netted the emperor Valerian near Edessa. The poverty of the sources and the near chaos of the mid-third century, which witnessed numerous usurpers and barbarian invasions across the Danube and via the Black Sea, precludes precise knowledge of individual eastern legions. Sapor I's defeat of a Roman army of 60,000 at Barbalissus (252) facilitated the capture of Antioch and the legionary bases at Raphanea and Zeugma, before he advanced into Cilicia and southern Commagene. Antioch fell again in 260, when Sapor also captured the legionary base at Samosata and the Cappadocian capital Caesarea and plundered as far as Iconium. Dura-Europos, a Persian victim in 252, was subsequently recovered only to be recaptured in 256. Henceforth Rome was content to control the Euphrates only down to its confluence with the Chabur.

Rome's military disarray 252–260 is clear from the role of Odaenathus in ending the Persian threat, possibly counterattacking as far as Ctesiphon (261?) and holding the title *corrector totius Orientis*. Palmyra's rapid rise to military prominence, a late second- and third-century phenomenon, filled the vacuum of Roman power in the East in the 260s. Zenobia's ephemeral Palmyrene Empire (270–272) proved no match for Aurelian's army of Danubian forces in 272–273, although the III Cyrenaica's camp at Bostra fell to the Palmyrenes and Egyptian forces stoutly resisted before defeat.

The destruction of Palmyra left a gigantic hole in Rome's security arrangements in the southern theater, including Egypt, for Palmyra had not only policed caravan routes but also buffered the southern theater against various Arab tribes now generally called Saracens and consolidating into more cohesive entities than Bedouin bands of brigands. Piracy in the Red Sea increased in the second century and by the mid-third century desert tribes on the southern and western fringes of Egypt were also troublesome – trends that continued into the fourth century. Rome had done little to improve security in Arabia and Syria Phoenice since the Severan era: reliance on Palmyra had relieved the need to do so. But times changed.

Traditionally Diocletian (284–305) is credited with reorganizing eastern defenses. His fort at Circesium at the confluence of the Chabur and the Euphrates became the node of a new expanded road system tying the Euphrates to the port of Aela on the Gulf of Aqaba and featuring the strata Diocletiana, connecting Palmyra with Damascus, where the creation of an arms factory emphasized that city's increased importance. New legions were raised (at the new smaller size of c. 1,000 men) and additional forts constructed in Arabia. Tenth Fretensis abandoned Jerusalem for Aela and the new IV Martia manned c. 300 a new fort at Betthorus (el-Lejjûn) to guard the southern Moab east of the Dead Sea. A nearly identically designed fort at Adrou (Udruh) c. 15 kilometers east of Petra, also built c. 300, certainly housed a legion in the fourth century – possibly VI Ferrata, formerly at Caparcotna in Syria Palestina, although no evidence from Adrou supports VI Ferrata's presence. This legion is missing in the *Notitia.*

Nevertheless, a much discussed inscription from a fort at the Azraq oasis (Amatha, c. 50 km east of Philadelphia/Amman) at the western end of the Wadi Sirhan has now been re-dated from Diocletian to Aurelian. Hence legionary road-building attested in the Azraq text occurred a generation earlier and the newly raised I Illyricorum, which Diocletian stationed at Palmyra (now assigned to Syria Phoenice), came east with Aurelian. Further, other legionary shifts may be earlier than Diocletian. Sixteenth Flavia and IV Scythica, whose bases at Samosata and Zeugma had been razed by Sapor I in 260 and 252–253 respectively, moved much farther east: XVI Flavia to Sura on the Euphrates and IV Scythica to Oresa (Tayibe), where the road from Palmyra forks north to Sura and east to Circesium. Third Gallica similarly abandoned Raphanea for Danaba, an obscure site c. 60 kilometers southeast of Emesa and just north of the Damascus–Palmyra highway. Thus Diocletian's efforts no longer appear to fill a generation-long void in Roman control of the southern theater.

Clearly Diocletian's measures in southern Syria and Arabia reflected a problem other than internal security. Indeed Diocletian waged war on the Saracens (identity uncertain) in 290. Valens in the 370s would make further improvements. Internal security primarily characterized Roman military dispositions in the southern theater during its initial 250 years, but an external threat from Arab tribal confederations emerged by the later third century. These confederations, combining groups both within and outside Rome's borders, henceforth added a significant variable to the strategic situation. Diocletian's alliance with one confederation, the Lakhmids, proved workable for three-quarters of the fourth century. Yet the revolt of the Saracen queen Mavia (377–378) raised havoc from Syria Phoenice to the Sinai and hindered Valens' ability to deal with the Gothic crisis on the lower Danube that led to Adrianople (378). Another Saracen revolt probably belongs to 383.

The often heated debate about the character of the Arabian frontier – a microcosm of the Roman grand strategy controversy – has focused on frontier defense (strategy) vs internal security (no strategy), as if the two concepts were incompatible, and at times becomes mired in discussions of transhumance (a scholarly obsession in the 1980s): the relationship between settled populations and nomads. As recently demonstrated, however, transhumance flourished well within Arabia's borders and cannot be adduced as exclusively an external threat. Yet the *Notitia* certainly depicts deployment for frontier defense, despite hairsplitting scholarly arguments that forts somehow guard roads but not territory. Given the growing power of Arab confederations transcending Roman borders, the key to the puzzle of Roman Arabia from the mid-third century on was not the lack of strategy but the wrong strategy – the need for another Palmyra, which Roman experiments with various confederations never successfully filled. Over time barbarian pressure on the lower Danube and efforts against the Sasanids, besides the loss of manpower at Adrianople, funneled manpower and money elsewhere, while the Saracen confederations expanded northward despite the continued presence of Roman forces. Sasanid use of Arab confederations mirrored that of Rome. By the seventh century both parties, exhausted by mutual struggles, were caught napping and underestimated a southern threat, although the eventual Arab conquerors can by no means be equated with transhumant Bedouins. The southern theater never changed its character: an economically valuable area with severe security problems and a distraction from the international power plays farther north.[2]

8   Transition: The Northern Theater

The waves of barbarian inroads beginning around 250 on the lower Danube extended into the mid 270s and lashed the northern and western coasts of Anatolia. An abortive Sasanid strike on Armenia Minor, however, probably in coordination with Sapor's thrust up the Euphrates in 252, captured the legionary base at Satala and prefaced the Gothic raids, which in the mid 250s plunged into north-central Cappadocia. The emperor Tacitus (275–276) halted a Gothic (Herulian?) foray through Pontus, Galatia, and Cappadocia only at the Cilician border. A victory (275/276–279/280) of the Bosporan king Teiranes cut off further raids at their source. The Cappadocian legions, although poised to face Armenia, must have had some role in these events. But Goths were not the only problem. The Borani, probably a Sarmatian tribe in connivance with a Bosporan usurper, unsuccessfully attacked Pityus in northern Colchis, manned by a *vexillatio* of XV Apollinaris (254). Four years later they returned to capture Pityus as well as Trapezus, then a transit site for troops moving to the Euphrates for Valerian's projected confrontation with Sapor. The Borani's sea-borne raids attest that a Pontic fleet, shifted into the Propontis (175) after raids of the Costoboci and also probably active in the Severan siege of Byzantium (194–195), had disappeared from the northern Anatolian and the Colchian coasts. Moreover, the Borani in 258 faced no opposition between Pityus and Trapezus from earlier known garrisons at Dioscurias/Sebastopolis, Phasis, and Apsarus. Apparently, Rome had abandoned central Colchis by the 250s as a result of needs for manpower against Sapor. Thus the rise of the Lazi in this area (henceforth Lazica) as an independent kingdom. These raids of the Borani and the Goths prompted Diocletian to station the newly formed I Pontica at Trapezus.

As in earlier periods, the issue of Armenia and Roman opportunism during Sasanid dynastic strife or northeastern frontier problems prompted Roman–Persian conflicts. Carus' promenade down to Ctesiphon (283) may have had its greater significance in regaining Nisibis and eastern Mesopotamia. Diocletian exploited Sasanid weakness c. 287 to restore an Arsacid to the rule of at least part of Armenia. This Tiridates III/IV may or may not be the Tiridates the Great, Armenia's first Christian king, whose death c. 330 set in motion the series of Roman–Sasanid clashes from c. 337 resulting in the treaty of 363 and Rome's permanent loss of Nisibis. The Roman–Persian partition of Armenia (387) only temporarily resolved the centuries-old Armenian problem, for Armenia remained a cockpit of Roman–Iranian rivalry until the Muslim conquests.

Shifts in deployments and the raising of new legions responded to these changing political developments. The eastern section of the *Notitia Dignitatum* of c. 395 (or 400/401, as recently argued from Egyptian evidence) provides the best guide, although the *Notitia* reflects the army reforms of Diocletian and Constantine and other modifications of the fourth century. A detailed discussion of these reforms follows in the next chapter, but a few notes are relevant.

Diocletian's divorce of civil from military authority in provincial administration placed provincial armies (eventually called *limitanei*) under a *dux*: hence, e.g., a *dux Syriae et Euphratensis, dux Osrhoenae, dux Mesopotamiae*, and *dux Armeniae* (formerly Cappadocia). Division of the central mobile army (*comitatenses*) between Constantine I's sons (c. 337) created various army groups under either an Augustus' direct command or a *magister militum peditum* or *equitum*. By 365 (*Cod. Theod.* 8.1.10) legions of the ducal commands selected for elevation to the mobile reserves were called *pseudocomitatenses*. Theodosius I created (379–380) three regional (supra-provincial) commands for the eastern half of the empire: *magistri militum* of the East, Thrace, and Illyricum, each with its own mobile reserve force. These three *magistri militum* held equal rank with the two *magistri militum praesentales*, who each commanded a central reserve army. The *magister militum per Orientem* held supervision of the entire eastern front from Armenia to Egypt. None of these reserve armies had permanent bases, although it is notable that when the emperor was in Constantinople (only from the late fourth century a regular imperial residence), the "armies at court" (*praesentales*) usually camped at Hebdomon seven miles east of the city.

Changes from earlier deployments are most evident in Osrhoene and Mesopotamia, a war zone c. 337–363. Three new (Diocletianic?) Parthica legions are attested, IV–VI, of which two belong to Osrhoene. Fourth Parthica manned Diocletian's new fort at Circesium and III Parthica, at Rhesaina or Nisibis under Septimius Severus, moved to Apadna (uncertain location), if a *lacuna* in the *Notitia* is correctly restored. At Amida (Diyarbakir) V Parthica garrisoned a fort, which Constantius II as Caesar in the 320s had established. This legion, destroyed in Sapor II's siege of Amida (359), was not reconstituted. Valens refortified Amida at some point 367–375 during his military interventions in Armenia, but the *Notitia* no longer lists it. Sapor II's attacks on Mesopotamia in 360 show that I Parthica held its original Severan post at Singara, supported by I Flavia, while Bezabde on the Tigris northeast of Nisibis was defended by II Parthica, II Armeniaca, and II Flavia. After Sapor's capture of both these sites, the defenders were slaughtered or enslaved. Whether whole units or only detachments of these legions were present is unclear, for I Parthica reappears at Constantia (Tella), a site fortified by Constantius II (340s) on the road between Edessa and Nisibis, and the *Notitia* has II Parthica at Cepha (c. 100 km down the Tigris from Amida and c. 75 km north-northeast of Nisibis). The new postings of I and II Parthica reflect the situation after the 363 Nisibis treaty. Some conjecture that VI Parthica, among the *pseudocomitatenses* of the *magister militum per Orientem*, had earlier posted at Cepha. Second Armeniaca, however, later served with VI Parthica in the same army of *pseudocomitatenses*, as did I Armeniaca, a veteran unit of Julian's 363 Persian campaign and active in Isauria in 382. The legions I–II Flavia (Constantinian?) vanished from the East, unless they are the I–II Flavia gemina in the *pseudocomitatenses* of the *magister militum per Thracias*. The 12 legions (whether *limitanei, comitatenses,* or *pseudocomitatenses*), which Valens sent to southern Iberia in 370, and the force of unspecified size dispatched into Armenia the same year, cannot be identified in detail.

The Armenian (Cappadocian) command remained stable (XII Fulminata at Melitene, XV Apollinaris at Satala) except for the addition of I Pontica at Trapezus. Probably late under Constantius II (337–361) a new auxiliary fort replaced an earlier Domitianic *castellum* north of the confluence of the Euphrates' two branches at Pagnik Öreni in the Dascusa area, and remained occupied into the early fifth century. A remodeling of the fort (under Valens?) perhaps responded to Sapor II's raid through Sophene in the mid 360s, which brushed the banks of the upper Euphrates. With the partition of Armenia in 387 and the discontinuation of a western Arsacid monarchy after c. 390, the Roman frontier shifted far to the east. Theodosiopolis (Erzerum), built in the 420s, replaced Satala as the chief northern legionary post of the Armenian ducate. References to XV Apollinaris vanish after the *Notitia*.

Intriguing, however, is the situation in the Colchian sector of the Armenian ducate. The fort at Apsarus near the mouth of the Acampsis River was rebuilt at a new site (4th c.?). It approximates the size of Diocletian's fort at Arabian Bethhorus. This remarkably well preserved fort (in its medieval manifestation), significant through the seventh century, is absent from the *Notitia*, unless perhaps it is the New Camp (Caene Parembole, *ND., Or.* 38.35), a suitable name for a new fort replacing an old one in the same area. In northern Colchis, Pityus, rebuilt in the late third/early fourth century, became a bastion of Roman power in Abkhazia through the sixth century. Dioscurias/Sebastopolis possibly was briefly renamed Valentia. Both these sites had garrisons of auxilia with epithets betraying Theodosian origins. Approximately 60 kilometers southeast of "Valentia," a cohort raised by Valens manned Ziganne/Ziganeas (Gudava) at the mouth of the Ziganis (Okumi) River. The interest of Valens and Theodosius I in this area corresponds to the late fourth-century's sharp increase of Roman imports (especially weapons) in the hinterland of these forts to the tribes of Apsiles and Abasgi, Roman clients since the early second century, who controlled the Kodori River Valley leading to the Clukor Pass, an old trade route for Sarmatians north of the Caucasus with the Dioscurias emporium. Explanations for Rome's attempt to arm these tribes omit a new development in Ciscaucasia at this time – the Huns.

Already at the Tanais (Don) River by c. 370, the Huns devastated the territory of the Alans as far south as the Terek River 370–375. The Huns, of course, triggered the Gothic crisis on the lower Danube that led to Adrianople (378) and the destruction of much (the mobile element at least) of the eastern Roman army. But in 395 the Huns broke through the central Caucasus and ravaged through Cappadocia and Armenia into northern Syria and Sasanid domains, when many eastern forces had not yet returned from Theodosius I's 394 campaign against Arbogast. Arcadius' minister Eutropius finally mustered sufficient forces to repel them in 398. The Hun inroad of 395–398 initiated a new phase in the Roman East – a threat to both Romans and Sasanids that offered potential for common action as well as intrigues and ambitions, but also stimulated new interests in control of Armenia and the Caucasus. In the end, the terrible Hunnic monsters of the North proved less dangerous than the sleeping Arab giants of the South.

9   Tactical Developments in the East

Romans – and some modern historians – conjured up bizarre images of a mystical East: corrupt discipline, inferior eastern soldiers, and a Roman "RMA" (revolution in military affairs) after Carrhae. Like other frontiers, the East placed its own special demands on the army, but the myths have less substance and the adaptations are less dramatic than often supposed.

The image of the corrupting East, where soldiers served comfortably in rich cities and shunned rigorous duties for voluptuous pleasures, owed much to classical Greek views of effeminate Persians, late Seleucid excess, climatological theories of eastern inferiority, and Roman propaganda, which portrayed new emperors or newly appointed eastern commanders stiffening lax discipline. This "topos" features prominently in Corbulo's Armenian campaigns (55–63) beside L. Verus' Parthian War (161–166) and is implied for Crassus' defeat at Carrhae (53 BC) and the conflict of the Syrian governor Calpurnius Piso with Germanicus (18–19). Ammianus Marcellinus even makes a "Corbulo" of Ursicinus (*magister equitum Orientis*, 349–355, *magister peditum Orientis*, 357–359). In reality, the Syrian capital Antioch with its suburb Daphne, notorious for sensuous delights, was never a legionary base. Lengthier training for eastern legions than the one-year norm cannot be proved. Western legions and *vexillationes* dispatched for eastern operations only supplemented local manpower. Such reinforcements do not imply inferior eastern troops, who also marched west to fight on the Danube or occasionally bolstered Dacia's defense. Decorations for distinguished service to eastern legionaries and transfers of centurions from eastern to western legions attest the capability of eastern forces.

As peacetime armies (ancient and modern) rarely maintain full "paper strength," a crisis or war could initiate recruitment, and Romans were always searching for "a few good men." Positing eastern legions over four centuries (first–fourth) as an outside army of occupation is unjustified, especially after c. 100 when Italy ceased to furnish the majority of legionaries. Local recruitment became the norm in the East as elsewhere and almost from the beginning. Either A. Gabinius (proconsul of Syria, 57–55 BC) and/or Licinius Crassus (proconsul of Syria, 54–53 BC) increased the Syrian army from two to eight legions for projected Parthian expeditions and M. Antonius possibly had 16 legions for his Parthian War (36 BC). Such increases of manpower must have tapped local resources with grants of citizenship upon enrollment although not exclusively, as Crassus also recruited in Italy. Eastern recruitment extended as far as Cyrenaica (Parthian crisis, late 54) and Arabia (Parthian War, 161–166), although veteran colonies (e.g. Berytus-Heliopolis) also provided Italian stock. Epigraphical poverty precludes a full appreciation. Corbulo (55–56), however, focused on Galatia and Cappadocia. The mountain peoples of the Taurus were particularly targeted: Diocletian's I Pontica was probably raised in Isauria.

Besides individual legionaries, native peoples contributed auxilia or perhaps formed the core of legions bearing ethnic names. Amyntas' army, when Galatia was annexed (25 BC), certainly produced XXII Deiotariana and possibly also part of III Cyrenaica. By the later fourth century the *magister militum* of the East's *pseudocomitatenses* included I–II Armeniaca and the Transtigritani. The Sanni/Tzanni southeast of Trapezus supplied a legion for Julian's Persian expedition (363) besides a cohort in the Egyptian Thebaid. Annexations of client-kingdoms often incorporated established units as auxilia, to which non-native commanders were assigned. Pontus (64) yielded a fleet and Arabia (106) produced at minimum six *cohortes equitatae*. Commagene contributed about six cohorts and an *ala*. Syria's numerous units read like a list of cities: Antioch, Apamea, Tyre, Damascus, Emesa, Palmyra, and Sura. Palestine offered multiple units from Ituraea and a few from Caesarea. Anatolia was a rich source for legionaries and auxilia (Galatia, Paphlagonia, Phrygia, Cilicia) and Thrace, considered part of the East, became a major recruiting ground for both cavalry and infantry. Even units from the Bosporan Kingdom appear, although populous Egypt with only a few units of Thebans seems (as often) exceptional. Under the Severi (193–235) Osrhoene supplied auxilia and the so-called Transtigris area, acquired in 299, contributed units of Cordueni, Assyrians, and Zabdeni. Parthian units in the *Notitia* may actually be Armenians (Arsacids), although at least five *alae* and one cohort of Parthians are known for the early empire. Caucasian cavalry is also represented: two units of Iberians and one of the Abasgi from northern Colchis. The *Notitia* simply calls some units *indigenae* (natives).

Eastern auxilia, like those raised in the West, served throughout the empire. Local recruitment diluted a unit's original ethnic content over time, but many units remained in the East. Syrian units, for example, served in Britain or Mauretania Tingitana but also in Palestine, Egypt, Cappadocia, or even in Syria. Vespasian (69–79) and Trajan (98–117) increased auxiliary cohorts of Roman citizens (units of volunteers often commanded by a tribune rather than a prefect) in the East, where a higher proportion of such to native (non-citizen) units and a greater number of citizens in non-citizen units are attested – perhaps a sign of higher professionalism in these units.[3]

The East, however, did have peculiarities. The relative scarcity of water, especially in desert areas, encouraged use of camels. Corbulo's dash from Syria (62) to relieve Caesennius Paetus, trapped by the Parthians at Armenian Rhandea, featured the first attested Roman use of camels as pack-animals. Within another century the Ps.-Hyginus (*Mun. Castr.* 29) could foresee camels on the Danubian frontier (possibly during Marcus Aurelius' Marcomannic wars); camel bones appear in second- and third-century contexts in Pannonia Inferior. A *turma* or two of camel-riders (*dromedarii*) occur in some *cohortes equitatae* in Syria, Arabia, and Egypt. Trajan established the first regular camel unit, Ala I Ulpia dromedariorum Palmyrenorum; the *Notitia* attests three such *alae* of Diocletianic origin in Egypt. Their limited battlefield utility explains the slight number of dromedary units, although dromedaries operated throughout the southern theater as escorts, couriers, patrols, and in various police functions. The governor of Arabia supplemented his *equites singulares* with a guard of dromedaries.

Dromedaries directly reflect the southern theater's needs, but other Eastern tactical peculiarities (e.g. archers, cavalry, cataphracts, phalangical infantry formation) only seem a response to Iranian opponents (Parthia, Sasanid Persia) and a legacy of Carrhae. A distinction should be drawn between what is eastern per se, what belongs to empire-wide tactical trends, and what constitutes a reaction to Iranian warfare. Herodotus' exaggerated contrast of differing eastern and western styles of warfare in the Persian wars of the fifth century BC pictured Greek infantry's superiority to Persian cavalry. The East was "horse country": the name Cappadocia derived from the Persian for "land of beautiful horses"; Sophene and Armenia were horse-breeding areas and Median breeds were thought the best. The East's vast expanses flavored mobile warfare and a fluid style of battle with missiles. If Alexander's conquests asserted a role for heavy infantry in the East, generalship and superior skill in combined arms forged victory, not an Herodotean superiority of the spear to the bow. Seleucid and Pontic armies of the Hellenistic period retained a phalangical base, but both reverted over time to an Achaemenid Persian multi-ethnic force featuring native specialties. After all, Eumenes II of Pergamum's cavalry, not Scipio Asiaticus' legions, proved the decisive factor in Seleucid defeat at Magnesia (190 BC).

Parthian expansion reinforced the mobile trends of eastern warfare. Parthians, like the Achaemenid Persians, shared a heritage of Iranian nomadic warfare with their Scythian and Sarmatian cousins of Central Asia and southern Russia. By the mid-third century BC, when Parthia with other Seleucid Upper Satrapies revolted, the Parthians were a sedentary people with a capital at Nisa and an Iranian script of their own. Parthians were by no means half-civilized barbarians only slightly removed from the tribes of Central Asia. Proper evaluation of the Parthian war machine, however, suffers from a lack of sources. The Arsacid King of Kings ruled a feudal empire without a standing army and centralized logistic support. Nobles served as cataphracts (fully armored mounted pikemen) with levies of retainers, the famous Parthian horse archers, and possibly some infantry. Reinforcements (generally also mounted) could be summoned or hired from Central Asia and tribes north of the Caucasus, although Parthians, like the Sasanids, faced northern frontier problems east of the Caspian. Hyrcania, subject to separatist urges, and the northern frontier fostered pretenders, especially after Ctesiphon in southern Mesopotamia became the capital. Persis in southern Iran, the Sasanid homeland, was perhaps also troublesome.

Strategically, the Parthians, like the Sasanids in the late third and fourth centuries, generally shunned sustained defense of Mesopotamia when Romans invaded. Ctesiphon would be sacrificed to siege (if the Romans got that far), but the Iranian heartland preserved, as Roman expeditions exhausted their offensive impetus by the time they reached lower Mesopotamia, and their extended line of communications through territory not sufficiently pacified exposed them to revolts and counterattacks. Trajan's failure to retain Mesopotamia (115–117) provides the paradigm, as does Julian's march to Ctesiphon (363). Stout resistance to Roman offensives, as in the case of Vologaeses IV, when L. Verus' armies had to fight their way through Osrhoene and down the Euphrates to Ctesiphon and into Media (164–166), or possibly Ardashir I in Rome's first confrontation with the Sasanids in Severus Alexander's obscure Persian War (232), are exceptions (unless Ardashir benefited from Roman incompetence). Yet Septimius Severus' extension of Roman Mesopotamia to the middle Tigris (199) and Caracalla's campaign into Media (216) aroused Parthian reaction. Evidence is emerging of a Parthian *limes* in northeastern Mesopotamia. The Sasanids, administratively more centralized than the Parthians, formally organized defense of their territory, although they lacked a standing army until Chosroes I Anushirwan (531–579). But such matters belong to late Roman events. Despite some operations in Media, Roman campaigns beyond Mesopotamia into the Iranian heartland were never attempted.

Parthian tactics can be evaluated from only two battles: Roman accounts of Carrhae (53 BC: Plutarch, *Crass.* 22–31; Dio 40.21.2–27; cf. 40.14.3–15) and Tacitus' highly rhetorical version of Parthians in Armenia battling the Iberians and their Sarmatian allies in 36 (*Ann.* 6.35–36). How typical Surena's tactics against Crassus at Carrhae were is difficult to assess. Parthian pack-animals loaded with supplies of arrows ensured Parthian horse archers the capability of a high volume of fire over an extended period, and Parthian fire was effective against closely packed legionaries. Horse archers loosened close formations or lured counterattacks, so that the charge of cataphracts could be effective. A collision of cataphracts against massed infantry generally never occurred, for either the infantry panicked and fled or the cataphracts (or their horses) refused to smash themselves into an apparently solid wall. Parthian infantry was absent at Carrhae. Massive numbers of Parthian infantry occur only in the so-called Syriac *Chronicle of Arbela* (probably a modern forgery). Curiously, however, the only ancient scene of field combat between Romans and Parthians, depicted on the helmet (Antonine date) of a Roman auxiliary buried in southern Syria, shows three Roman infantrymen and a mounted *contarius* (pikeman) surrounded by five Parthian infantrymen and two mounted (non-cataphract) spearmen. Perhaps Parthians employed infantry more than literary sources suggest.

In any case, the tactical problem for the Romans, as with any army of predominantly heavy infantry opposing a cavalry/missiles-oriented force, is to fix the enemy and to negate his mobility, so that the infantry can do its job. Carrhae demonstrated the effectiveness of Parthian horse archers, but Surena also outgeneraled Crassus. In fairness, Crassus suspended his initial offensive in 54 BC and forsook strategic surprise to await additional (and much needed) cavalry. Roman Gallic cavalry, however, proved ineffective (at least at Carrhae) against the Parthian combination of horse archers and cataphracts. Romans had seen cataphracts before – at Magnesia (190 BC) and Tigranocerta (69 BC) – and had successfully dealt with them. Indeed the Parthian military model extended to Armenia besides Iberia and Albania, where Pompey would have also encountered it. Cataphracts at Carrhae were hardly a tactical surprise. Ventidius Bassus' success against the Parthians (39–38 BC) came from using slingers, whose range outdistanced Parthian archers and occupying higher ground, which compelled cataphract charges uphill. Later, it was known that Roman catapults and ballistas outranged Parthian archers (Tacitus, *Ann.* 15.9.1), although such artillery was not very mobile.

Julius Caesar's plans for Parthian conquest called for 16 legions and an advance through mountainous Armenia to avoid the cavalry-friendly plains (by no means a desert as Roman sources for Carrhae imply) of northern Mesopotamia. M. Antonius' attempt (36 BC) to execute Caesar's plans included an Armenian approach, 16 legions, numerous slingers, and 10,000 Gallic and Spanish cavalry, but Antonius still could not force the enemy to engage in a major field battle, became bogged down in an unsuccessful siege, and eventually found himself overextended and exposed to excessive harassment in retreat. The Parthian strategy of trading territory for time is again evident. The approach to Parthia via Media Atropatene proved not an easy nut to crack. Antonius blamed his debacle on an inferiority of cavalry and archers.

Roman failures to fix the Parthians and essentially to be fixed themselves may lie behind the defeat of Sedatius Severianus, the Cappadocian governor killed with perhaps the loss of a legion in the plain of Elegeia, when he reacted to the Parthian invasion of Armenia (161). Likewise, if we may read between the lines of Julius Africanus' military advice in the *Cesti* (c. 231) to Severus Alexander before his Persian War, Macrinus' defeat at Nisibis (217) in the last major battle of Romans and Parthians involved a Roman army (as at Carrhae) pinned down by superior missile fire and with infantry ineffective against cataphracts.

The absence of sufficiently detailed descriptions of Roman–Persian field battles preclude assessment of Sasanid tactics c. 226–c. 400. Cataphracts figure prominently in commemorative reliefs of Sasanid victories, although Procopius omits cataphracts in Sasanid armies of the Justinianic era. By the fourth century the Sasanids had reintroduced elephants on the battlefield, not seen since the Hellenistic era and perhaps reflecting conflicts with the Kushan on the northeastern frontier. Elephants terrorized horses, provided mobile archery platforms, and had the potential to smash through infantry, if their charge took the right direction. Whether Sasanid elephants exceeded Hellenistic pachyderm effectiveness (often intimidating but a tactical liability in practice) cannot be said. Parthians also had elephants, although their Arsacid employment in battle is unattested. Vologaeses I, riding an elephant, paraded about Caesennius Paetus' army, which had just surrendered to him at Rhandea (62), unless this detail amounts to rhetorical Roman "orientalism."

Certainly, Carrhae had its effects on Roman military thinking, but a "military revolution" can hardly be postulated. Parthian cavalry and archers had to be dealt with. Ventidius Bassus found the solution in slingers and superior positioning, although M. Antonius' slingers and additional cavalry could not overcome failures of strategy and execution. Indeed Carrhae only became prominent after Augustus' Parthian agreement of 20 BC, when the emperor's propaganda machine glorified the return of the *signa* of Crassus and Decidius Saxa (and erroneously those of M. Antonius) in one of the greatest "non-events" of Roman history.

Structurally, Crassus' defeat produced no major reforms. Eastern recruitment of horse archers largely belongs to the Flavians (69–96), Trajan, and later. Augustus and the Julio-Claudians relied on client-kings to supply them. Hadrian (117–138), however, first decreed training in the specific techniques of Armenian and Parthian horse archers. But not all archers were mounted: numerous auxiliary cohorts of foot archers served and the *Notitia* (*Or.* 7.56) records a whole legion of archers, I Isaura sagittaria, although new legions of the late empire, often at only c. 1,000 men, approximated the size of a milliary cohort of the early empire.

Mounted pikemen (*contarii*) first appear in Vespasian's army in the Jewish War (66–70) and perhaps originated in Corbulo's Armenian–Parthian campaigns (55–63). But the first such unit, Ala I Ulpia contariorum, was Trajanic and the first unit of cataphracts (fully armored *contarii*), Ala I Gallorum et Pannoniorum cataphracta, became Hadrian's creation. The impetus for such units came from fighting Sarmatian cataphracts (e.g. Rhoxolani) on the lower Danube and had nothing to do with Parthians. A proliferation of cataphract units began in the third and fourth centuries, when they did respond to Sasanid practices. Tactically and strategically, Corbulo's campaigns exceed Carrhae's significance. Indeed milliary *alae* and cohorts, doubling the conventional size of c. 500 men, originated in the East with Corbulo. The Flavians multiplied milliary auxiliary units throughout the empire.

Eastern topography and ethnic traditions favored an emphasis on cavalry and archery, to which the Romans had to adapt. If the *Notitia* and epigraphical records point to a particular concentration of cavalry and archer units in the East, such cannot be directly connected with Carrhae or Iranian warfare, but must be assessed against empire-wide tactical trends, with which the tactical style of Parthians and Persians coincided. Syrian recruits accounted for about half of all archers in the Roman army, but not all of them served in the East. The Parthian units of the Augustan age – for obvious security reasons – were sent elsewhere (e.g. the Rhine). Indeed the ratio of infantry to cavalry units overall in the Roman army remained at 3:1 in the fourth century, before the age of the mounted archer seen in Procopius began, but the ratio had been as high as 10:1 in earlier centuries. A proliferation of mounted units from the mid-third century on is clear.

Nevertheless, numbers of units hardly tell the true story. Rome's elimination and absorption of rival states meant that clashes of heavy infantry in formal pitched battles became less frequent, except when Roman armies fought each other in civil wars. In general, barbarians of both East and West avoided open confrontations of concentrated masses and preferred exploiting space and terrain. A Roman inferiority (numerical as well as qualitative) in cavalry and light infantry, clear since the Second Punic War (218–202 BC), accounts for Rome's reliance on allies to supply such troops and eventually for the creation of auxilia. A trend toward increased use of cavalry, light infantry, and missiles in combination with heavy infantry (combined arms, in other words) emerged in the West (Spain, North Africa, Gaul) long before Carrhae. Conditions in the East only reinforced a trend already in evidence, which would continue into the late empire. The business of empire (frontier surveillance, internal policing, etc.) required mobility, speed, flexibility, smaller units, and open formations rather than massed heavy infantry.

A fragment of Arrian's *Alanica* (*Acies contra Alanos*), detailing his proposed disposition of the Cappadocian army against Alan cataphracts in 135, offers the most detailed description of Roman tactical deployment for a field battle between Caesar's works and Ammianus Marcellinus. Arrian deploys the XV Apollinaris and a *vexillatio* of the XII Fulminata in a phalangical formation eight ranks deep, of which the front four ranks have *conti* (more probably *hastae* than *pila*) and the rear four ranks use *lanceae* (javelins). The auxilia on flanking hilltops mirror the legionary disposition: infantry in front with javelin men or archers behind. Foot archers stand in the legions' rear, and behind this are placed artillery, backed up by horse archers. Arrian aimed to thwart the Alans' charge with firepower, using the legions as a defensive bulwark (*probole*), which subsequently would provide a base for retreat of the cavalry and auxilia in a cautious pursuit, if the Alans counterattacked.

Efforts to discount Arrian's tactics as his own innovation or an eastern peculiarity are erroneous. Crassus at Carrhae (53 BC) and M. Antonius against the Parthians (36 BC) resorted to the phalangical formation of a field *testudo*; Caesar likewise used a phalangical deployment in North Africa at Ruspina (46 BC). Pompeius at Pharsalus (48 BC) deployed his legions phalangically (perhaps ten deep) against Caesar. Sparing legionaries in combat at the expense of auxilia coincided with increasing use of phalangical deployment (e.g. Agricola at Mons Graupius, 84).

In fact, Arrian's deployment and tactics indicate future trends. Third-century inscriptions of the II Parthica (based at Albinum near Rome and not an "eastern" legion), which wintered at Syrian Apamea on several occasions (215–218, 231–233, 242–244), attest its legionaries as *phalangarii* and *lanciarii* – the dual functions within Arrian's legions in the *Acies*. The duality of *phalangarii/lancarii* may foreshadow the development by the fourth century of front-rankers more heavily armored (*armati*) than the javelin men behind them (*scutati*). At the Battle of Issus (194) the Severan legions attacking Pescennius Niger's Syrian army advanced in a rolling *probole* to protect their missile-shooters, while the Severan cavalry secretly circled Niger's flank to attack his rear. A similar offensive use of the phalangical legion occurred in Aurelian's clash with the Palmyrenes at Daphne (272), and Julius Africanus' commentary on Macrinus' defeat at Nisibis further suggests the Romans in a phalangical formation against the Parthians. Clearly by the fourth century (Ammianus, Vegetius), Roman heavy infantry in formal pitched battles assumed a phalangical formation, which by the sixth and seventh centuries was called *syskouton* or *fulcum*.

Efforts to discern a distinctive Roman way of war in the East are misguided. Carrhae produced no structural changes in the army. Roman needs for better and more cavalry, light infantry, and missiles were already evident in the West before Crassus met his fate. Neither cataphracts nor phalangical heavy infantry were initially direct responses to Iranian warfare. Rather, conditions in the East reinforced existing tactical trends. Reaction to Parthians may really have come only with Trajan and Hadrian. In the East, Roman absorption of native skills in cavalry and archery reflected local conditions. Rome, as often, adapted to circumstances.[4]

NOTES

1   As the strategy debate now attracts commentators from all quarters, citations will be limited to major players. The pro-strategy school, which (contrary to a common perception) is not necessarily a defense of Luttwak 1976, the spark igniting the powder keg, is represented by Ferrill 1991; Wheeler 1993, 7–41, 215–40 (a detailed response to Whittaker 1989 and Isaac 1990: see inf.); Nicasie 1997, 455–60; and Howard-Johnston 1995, 157–226, esp. 182 n.56; note also Parker 2000, n.2 inf. Lee 1993 and Zuckerman 1998, 108–28, esp. 112–24, seem to accept Roman strategy for the late but not the early empire. A middle position might also be assigned to Austin and Rankov 1995. Bachrach 2002, 313–57, expanding on Wheeler 1993, presents a case for the continuity of Roman and Carolingian strategy.

The anti-strategy school is spearheaded by Whittaker 1989, expanded to include the East in 1994, and 2004 (republication of scattered papers), and Isaac 1990 (a 1992 edition adds only additional bibliography on the southern theater). Shaw 1999, 133–69, offers a remarkably pure example of *Annaliste* historiography, mixed with an attitude toward war and violence characteristic of the Vietnam-War era and a very selective choice of historical examples to show alleged trends; his implication that members of the pro-strategy school simply do not understand the problems of the sources strikes a new low in the debate. Mattern 1999 represents a slightly different effort at primitivizing Romans, rejecting any practical strategy and limiting the Roman mentality of ruling an empire to concepts such as honor and revenge, with various bizarre interpretations and occasional misinformation. The attempt of Young 2001 to deny a role for economic motivations and trade in Roman foreign policy has little to do with the strategy debate and ignores eastern trade in the northern theater.

2   The ancient sources (translated with commentary) for the eastern frontier 226–630 are collected by Dodgeon and Lieu 1991, and Greatrex and Lieu 2002. Azraq text: Christol and Lenoir 2001, 163–78, followed by Kennedy 2004, 60 no. 2; for contrasting views of late Roman Arabia, see Parker 2000, 367–88 and Graf 2002, 153–60.

3   Myths about eastern and Syrian legions are demolished in Wheeler 1996, 229–76; on recruitment in the East: Cheesman 1914; Kennedy 1989, 235–46; Russell 1995, 67–133; Graf 1994, 265–311; Anatolia: Mitchell 1993, I, 136–41; citizen cohorts: Saddington 2002, 879–82.

4   General assessments of Roman tactical development in the East: Coulston 1986, 59–75; Wheeler 1997, 575–9; *dromedarii*: Dabrowa 1991, 364–6; milliary cohorts/*alae*; Kennedy 1985, 181–5; Parthian battle scene: Abdul-Hak 1954–5, 162–88, Pl. VII; missiles: Wheeler 2001, 169–84; empire-wide trends and the phalangical legion: Wheeler 2004a, 309–58, and 2004b, 147–75; *armati/scutati*: Janniard 2004, 389–95.

BIBLIOGRAPHY

Abdul-Hak, S. 1954–5. "Rapport préliminaire sur les objets provenant de la nécropole romaine située de Nawa (Hauran)," *Les Annales Archéologiques de Syrie* 4–5: 162–88.

Austin, N., and N. Rankov. 1995. *Exploratio: Military and Political Intelligence in the Roman World*. London.

Bachrach, B. 2002. "Charlemagne and the Carolingian general staff," *Journal of Military History* 66: 313–57.

Bowersock, G. W. 1983. *Roman Arabia*. Cambridge, MA.

Butcher, K. 2003. *Roman Syria and the Near East*. London.

Chapot, V. 1907. *La frontière de l'Euphrate de Pompée à la conquête arabe*. Paris.

Cheesman, G. 1914. *The Auxilia of the Roman Army*. Oxford.

Christol, M., and M. Lenoir. 2001. "Qasr el-Azraq et la reconquête de l'Orient par Aurélien," *Syria* 78: 163–78.

Coulston, J. 1986. "Roman, Parthian and Sassanid tactical developments," in Freeman and Kennedy, 59–75.

Dabrowa, E. 1991. "*Dromedarii* in the Roman army: A note," in Maxfield and Dobson, 364–6.

—— (ed.). 1994. *The Roman and Byzantine Army in the East*. Krakow.

Dodgeon, M., and S. Lieu (eds.). 1991. *The Roman Eastern Frontier and the Persian Wars (AD 226–363): A Documentary History*. London.

Ferrill, A. 1991. *Roman Imperial Grand Strategy*. Lanham.

Freeman, P., and D. Kennedy (eds.). 1986. *The Defence of the Roman and Byzantine East.* Oxford.

Freeman, P., J. Bennett, Z. T. Fiema, and B. Hoffmann (eds.). 2002. *Limes XVIII.* Oxford.

French, D., and C. Lightfoot (eds.). 1989. *The Eastern Frontier of the Roman Empire.* Oxford.

Gebhardt, A. 2002. *Imperiale Politik und provinziale Entwicklung. Untersuchungen zu Verhältnis von Kaiser, Heer und Städten im Syrien der vorseverischen Zeit.* Berlin.

Graf, D. 1994. "The Nabataean army and the *cohortes Ulpiae Petraeorum,*" in Dabrowa 1994, 265–311.

—— 2002. "Nomads and the Arabian frontier: The epigraphic perspective," in Freeman et al., 153–60.

Greatrex, G., and S. Lieu (eds.) 2002. *The Roman Eastern Frontier and the Persian Wars, Part II, AD 363–630: A Narrative Sourcebook.* London.

Gregory, S. 1995–6. *Roman Military Architecture on the Eastern Frontier,* 3 vols. Amsterdam.

Groenman-van Waateringe, W., B. L. van Beek, W. J. H. Willems, and S. L. Wynia (eds.). 1997. *Roman Frontier Studies 1995.* Oxford.

Gudea, N. (ed.). 1999. *Roman Frontier Studies XVII/1997.* Zalau.

Howard-Johnston, J. 1995. "The two great powers in late antiquity: A comparison," in A. Cameron (ed.), *The Byzantine and Early Islamic Near East,* III: *States, Resources and Armies.* Princeton, 157–226.

Isaac, B. 1990. *The Limits of Empire: The Roman Army in the East.* Oxford.

Janniard, S. 2004. "*Armati, scutati* et la catégorisation des troupes dans l'Antiquité tardive," in Le Bohec and Wolff, 389–95.

Kennedy, D. 1985. "The construction of a vexillation from the army of Syria and the origin of *alae milliariae,*" *ZPE* 61: 181–5.

—— 1989. "The military contribution of Syria to the Roman imperial army," in French and Lightfoot, 235–46.

—— (ed.). 1996. *The Roman Army in the East.* Ann Arbor.

—— 2004². *The Roman Army in Jordan.* London.

—— and D. Riley. 1990. *Rome's Desert Frontier from the* Air. London.

Le Bohec, Y., and C. Wolff (eds.). 2000–3. *Les Légions de Rome sous le Haut-Empire,* 3 vols. Paris.

——, and ——. (eds.). 2004. *L'armée romaine de Dioclétien à Valentinien I.* Paris.

Lee, A. 1993. *Information and Frontiers: Roman Foreign Relations in Late Antiquity.* Cambridge.

Luttwak, E. 1976. *The Grand Strategy of the Roman Empire.* Baltimore.

Magie, D. 1950. *Roman Rule in Asia Minor.* Princeton.

Mattern, S. 1999. *Rome and the Enemy. Imperial Strategy in the Principate.* Berkeley.

Maxfield, V., and M. Dobson (eds.) 1991. *Roman Frontier Studies 1989.* Exeter.

Millar, F. 1993. *The Roman Near East 31 BC–AD 337.* Cambridge, MA.

Mitchell, S. 1993. *Anatolia: Land, Men, and Gods in Asia Minor,* 2 vols. Oxford.

Mitford, T. 1980. "Cappadocia and Armenia Minor: Historical setting of the *limes,*" *ANRW* II.7.2: 1164–228.

Nicasie, M. 1997. "The borders of the Roman empire in the fourth century," in W. Groenman-van Waateringe et al., 455–60.

Parker, S. T. 2000. "The defence of Palestine and Transjordan from Diocletian to Heraclius," in L. Stager, J. Greene, and M. Coogan (eds.), *The Archaeology of Jordan and Beyond: Essays in Honor of James A. Sauer.* Winona Lake, IN, 367–88.

Russell, J. 1995. "A Roman military diploma from Rough Cilicia," *BJ* 195: 67–133.

Saddington, D. 2002. "The Roman *auxilia* in the east – different from the west?" in Freeman et al., 879–82.

Sartre, M. 1991. *L'Orient romaine: Provinces et sociétés provinciales en Méditerranée orientale d'Auguste aux Sévères (31 av. J.C.–235 ap. J.C.)*. Paris.

—— 2005. *The Middle East under Rome*, trans. C. Porter and E. Rawlings. Cambridge, MA.

Shaw, B. 1999. "War and violence," in G. Bowersock, P. Brown, and O. Grabar (eds.), *Late Antiquity: A Guide to the Postclassical World*. Cambridge, MA, 133–69.

Speidel, M. P. 1977. "The Roman army in Arabia," *ANRW* II.8, 687–730.

Syme, R. 1995. *Anatolica: Studies in Strabo*. Oxford.

Wagner, J. 1985. *Die Römer an Euphrat und Tigris, Antike Welt* 16 (*Sondernummer*).

Wheeler, E. L. 1993. "Methodological limits and the mirage of Roman strategy," *Journal of Military History* 57: 7–41, 215–40.

—— 1996. "The laxity of Syrian legions," in Kennedy, 229–76.

—— 1997. "Why the Romans can't defeat the Parthians: Julius Africanus and the strategy of magic," in Groenman-van Waateringe et al., 575–9.

—— 1999. "From Pityus to Zeugma: The northern sector of the eastern frontier 1983–1996," in Gudea, 215–29.

—— 2001. "Firepower: Missile weapons and the 'face of battle,'" in E. Dabrowa, *Roman Military Studies, Electrum* 5: 169–84.

—— 2004a. "The late Roman legion as phalanx, Part I," in Le Bohec and Wolff, 309–58.

—— 2004b. "The late Roman legion as phalanx, Part II," *Revue des Études Militaires Anciennes* 1: 147–75.

Whittaker, C. R. 1989. *Les frontiers de l'empire romain*. Paris.

—— 1994. *Frontiers of the Roman Empire: A Social and Economic Study*. Baltimore.

—— 2004. *Rome and its Frontiers*. London.

Young, G. 2001. *Rome's Eastern Trade: International Commerce and Imperial Policy, 31 BC–AD 305*. London.

Ziegler, K.-H. 1964. *Die Beziehungen zwischen Rom und dem Partherreich*. Wiesbaden.

Zuckerman, C. 1998. "Sur le dispositif frontalier en Arménie, le *limes* et son evolution, sous le Bas-Empire," *Historia* 47: 108–28.

FURTHER READING

On the Euphrates as a frontier see Chapot 1907; for general surveys of the East (not primarily army studies), see Sartre 1991; cf. 2005; northern theater: Wagner 1985; Wheeler 1999; Anatolia: Magie 1950; Syme 1995; Galatia: Mitchell 1993; Cappadocia: Mitford 1980.

The southern theater is richly surveyed but poorly indexed in Millar 1993, and (with problematic views of the army) in Isaac 1990; forts: Kennedy and Riley 1990; Gregory 1995–6 (not definitive for the northern theater); Syria: Gebhardt 2002; Butcher 2003; Arabia: Bowersock 1983; Speidel 1977.

CHAPTER FIFTEEN

Strategy and Army Structure between Septimius Severus and Constantine the Great

Karl Strobel

1 The New Army of Diocletian and Constantine, Fact and Fiction

In the traditional view of the development of the Roman army into late antiquity, it is assumed that the "old army" of the principate declined during the third century and collapsed in its later half. The new army of late antiquity is considered a reaction to and a result of the "crisis of the third century." Gallienus is supposed to have been the great reformer of the Roman army who removed men of senatorial rank from the army and opened the way to power for professional officers of low social and cultural status. Diocletian, conservative in his strategic ideas, is thought to have replaced the principle of quality by that of mere quantity. The old discipline was lost during the third century. The legions and units along the frontiers, the *limitanei*, had minor or even no military value being a peasant militia tied down to the cultivation of their fields and to hereditary service in the garrisons. The mobile field army is often thought to be a creation of Constantine I. Cavalry supposedly gained dominance over the infantry, and the growing barbarization of frontier legions and elite units of the field army is thought to be a characteristic factor under Diocletian and Constantine. However, such widespread assumptions are no longer valid, nor is the traditional picture of the "crisis of the third century." It is necessary to cast a glance towards the military innovations under Diocletian and Constantine I first, because they often serve as the starting point for reconstructing the military history of the third century.

A "new Roman army" of late antiquity is often postulated to have emerged out of the reforms of Diocletian and Constantine I. However, their reforms were not completely innovative and should be considered as the result of a long and gradually evolving process of change which had already started in the second century AD. Diocletian built his military policy on the experiences, developments, and changes of the third century. After his victory over Licinius in 324, Constantine established the organization and order of the army of the fourth and fifth century AD, based on earlier measures which had existed in his army since 312 AD. It is an open question whether the formal division between the *Limitanei* and the units of the field armies, the *Comitatenses*, was created under Diocletian or Constantine. We should suppose an evolutionary process gradually developing during the third century AD. However, infantry continued to dominate numerically and to form the basis of tactics in the fourth century. There was no dramatic increase in the number of soldiers. Approximately 330,000–350,000 professional soldiers, or roughly 400,000 including the navy, can be reasonably estimated under the Severan emperors and a number of about 400,000 increasing to about 435,000 men under Diocletian. Johannes Lydos (*Mens.* 1, 27) gives the following numbers, based on the authorized strength of the units in his sources: 435,266 men in total, including 45,562 men of the navy. The total increased to about 450,000 men under Constantine I. The increasing number of cavalry in the third and early fourth century AD caused changes in supply and training.

The frontier armies were no militia, no armed farmers stationed in the camps along the frontiers. The *limitanei* were professional and well-trained army units well into the sixth century AD that were garrisoned in the frontier zones. It was forbidden by law for the soldiers "who get their arms and supplies from the state" to work in the fields or to herd animals even in 458 AD (*Cod. Just.* 12.35.15). The units of the frontier provinces developed into the late antique frontier armies in a continuous process, although many provinces were divided, new units established, and the military command definitively separated from the civil administration during the Diocletian's reorganization. The systematic deployment of frontier troops was a result of the tetrarchic frontier policy. The number of legions was enlarged (up to at least 67) so that normally two legions were stationed in an armed province. However, the new legions were only the size of the former legionary fighting-vexillations: the old legions were permanently split into several parts.[1] The term *vexillatio* was already used in 293 AD to characterize cavalry units in opposition to the infantry legion.

In a polemic passage, Zosimus (2.34) contrasts the measures of Diocletian and Constantine: "the frontiers of the Roman empire were everywhere studded with cities and forts and towers . . . and the whole army was stationed along them. . . . But Constantine ruined this defensive system by withdrawing the majority of the troops from the frontiers, and stationing them in cities which did not require protection." This statement is neither true for Diocletian nor Constantine. Constantine withdrew troops from the frontiers primarily for the civil wars. After the tetrarchy was established in 293, each of the two Augusti and two Caesares had his own field army. At the same time the frontier garrisons were strengthened, the density of the line of fortifications along the frontiers increased, and garrisons were established at important points in the rear of the frontier zones. Many of the units in the frontier zones were divided into smaller sub-units to garrison the newly built or rebuilt fortifications. They had to secure everyday life against small-scale attacks and plundering, defend the strongholds, and build a psychological barrier for potential aggressors. Large-scale warfare was now a matter of the field armies, which could be strengthened whenever necessary by a concentration of frontier units. The military policy of Diocletian shows a double strategy: first, strong and very mobile field-armies under direct imperial command concentrated in the rear of each of the important frontier regions where imperial residences were now established (Trier, Mediolanum, Aquileia, Sirmium, Serdica, Thessalonike, Nikomedeia, and Antiochia); and second, the defense of the frontiers was systematically strengthened to stabilize and revitalize the frontier zones, where the military command was separated from the office of the governor and became an organization of its own. Diocletian reorganized and re-established the traditional frontier defense, in special areas increased in depth, and he combined this policy with the ongoing development of the field army of late antiquity. His policy was no conservative reaction to the development in the second half of the third century; it was a consequent policy to gain stability and security concerning domestic and military affairs. Parallel to his construction of the system of the tetrarchy, Diocletian tried to summarize the historical experiences of the third century in his military policy and to give answers to the obvious problems of the monarchy and military security. Thus, two different levels of command, organization of supply, and military administration were now finally established, one for the army in the garrisons of the frontier zones and one for the field armies. The splitting up of the frontier armies made the administrative and logistic infrastructure even more complex. New lines of communication and logistics had to be built for the areas of concentration of the field armies. However, this process was already of great importance in the later third century AD.

The tetrarchic *sacer comitatus*, the field armies of the Augusti and Caesares, is often underestimated and misunderstood in size, structure, and importance. Under Diocletian and his co-rulers, the Roman policy shows in some way a revival of the "Augustan" attitude. Forts were built to provide bases beyond the direct frontier lines for Roman offensive campaigns against the neighboring people. Far-reaching campaigns were led not only in the East, but also beyond Rhine and Danube to restore a deep glacis in front of the Roman frontier. A good example for the career of a soldier serving in the field armies of the tetrarchs is Aurelius Gaius (*AE* 1981, 777 = *SEG* 1116; Drew-Bear 1981). He started as *eques legionis*, then served as *lanciarius* in a legion and was promoted to several posts of *optio*. He served in an impressive number of provinces and fought several times in campaigns, once in Carpia, four times in Sarmatia, twice in Gothia, and in the areas beyond Rhine and Upper Danube.

2   The Development of the Imperial Field Army

The most important innovation of the third century was the emergence, over a long period of time, of the permanent field army. Imperial escort and field armies had always existed when the emperors went to war, especially under Domitian, Trajan, and Marcus Aurelius. The accompanying praetorian prefect played a central role in the general staff or in the imperial chief command. This position led to the throne Macrinus in 217, Iulius Philippus in 244, Florianus in 276, and Carus in 282. The imperial escort and field army of Septimius Severus was organized in 193 for his march on Rome and followed the emperor to the east to defeat Pescennius Niger. It fought in the First Parthian War, against Clodius Albinus, and again in the East in the Second Parthian War. It ceased to exist when the imperial family returned to Rome in 202 AD. The imperial field army of Severus Alexander was formed in 231/232, fought in the Persian War, followed the emperor to the Rhine in 233/234, and gave support to the proclamation of Maximinus in 235. Similar armies were organized or taken over by the predecessors of Maximinus, by Gordian III, Philippus Arabs, and Decius.

The era of Valerian and Gallienus was a major step in the development towards late Roman army structures. Several long-standing, organized imperial field armies came into being: for example, the imperial field army of Valerian 253–260 and of Gallienus 254–268, a field army stationed in Northern Italy since 260 against the threat of an invasion by Postumus, a field army in the East under the command of Odaenathus, the viceroy of the eastern part of the empire since 262 AD, and in the years 256–258 a field army under the formal command of the Caesar Valerianus Junior on the Danube (Sirmium/Viminacium) which probably provided the military power for the usurpation of Ingenuus in 259 AD. After the murder of Gallienus in 268, his imperial field army became the core of the military power of Claudius II and later of Aurelian. Valerian's and Gallienus' imperial field army was continued by their successors without interruption and provided the foundation for the development during the tetrarchy.

Legionary vexillations were brought to the Rhine in 255/56 by Valerian coming from the East and by Gallienus coming from the Danube. Vexillations of the legions from Britain and Germany, together with auxiliary vexillations, were brought to the East in Valerian's field army in 258; surviving troops were led by the Macriani against Gallienus in 261 and later stationed in Sirmium (*ILS* 546). These vexillations were units in their own right, having their own recruitment and being filled up several times to reach necessary battle strength. It is very probable that such legionary vexillations had no special sub-units for training recruits and that the services behind the lines and administrative services, an important part of the normal legionary garrison, were missing too. Hence, these vexillations were units of a new type of under-strength battle- or *vexillatio*-legions, but were called *legio* without a differentiation from their former mother-units. This seems to be the characteristic development of the long existing field armies of the third century. There is evidence that a special system of recruitment and of recruit training was established for the field armies, a system independent from the mother units of the vexillations. In 235, Maximinus, a high equestrian officer and very popular in the field army of Severus Alexander, was commander of the recruit corps of the emperor's field army on the Rhine, in which numerous recruits were trained to fill up the vexillations and legions. After his successful insurrection he organized special training corps for the youth of the cities of Italy recruited in two levies, the *Iuventus Nova Italica Sua* of the *dilectus prior* and *posterior* (cf. *InscrAq* 2892a.b, 2893a.b).

The field armies of the third century and the tetrarchy were always attached to the emperors, to the Augusti and Caesares. Regional field armies as in the mid-fourth century AD (in Gaul, Illyricum, and the East) did not exist in addition to the imperial field armies. They were only temporarily organized to deal with warfare on the frontiers or in civil war. The imperial field army became the core of the military power of the emperors and its body of officers was the military elite of the empire, but also a possible threat to the emperor himself. Anyone in charge of a field army was a potential usurper possessing the powerful influence of a potential *capax imperii*. Examples are Postumus in 260, and Aureolus, the commander of the field army stationed in Mediolanum in 268. The existence of the so-called Gallic Empire of Postumus and his successors made a permanent army necessary in Northern Italy until 274 AD to oppose this threat to the "central" emperor. Aquileia was the second important place of garrison for parts of this field army protecting Italy and Rome against barbarian incursions and attacks in civil wars.

Maximian, Diocletian, Constantius I, and Galerius fought their wars and their expeditionary campaigns with field armies formed in the tradition of the later third century, consisting of guard units (infantry and mounted troops), *vexillatio*-legions, and cavalry corps and brigades. Additionally ethnic units, especially of Germanic origin, were organized in growing number. The long-standing legionary vexillations were not re-incorporated into their original mother-units by Diocletian, as is often argued, but developed now finally into separate units.

The term *sacer comitatus* for the imperial field army was already used in late Severan times. It is attested on the gravestone of the eagle-standard bearer of Legio XXX Ulpia Victrix from Ankyra under Caracalla or Elagabal (*CIL* III 6764) and in the treatise *De re militari* of the jurist Aemilius Macer during the reign of Severus Alexander (*Dig.* 49.16.13.3). That gravestone also demonstrates that the legionary eagle followed a large combat vexillation, thus really representing the whole legion. There was an early trend towards the de facto separation between the legions and their vexillations in the field armies. The disappearance of the leading function of the primipilate, which lost its role in the organization of the vexillation of the field army, should be seen in this context.

3 Army Command and Officers

A major problem is the widespread opinion based on Aurelius Victor, that Gallienus had forbidden in a formal edict that senators could be officers and commanders.[2] This edict is a fiction of Aurelius Victor exaggerating the anti-senatorial policy of Gallienus. The real background is the trend towards replacing the senatorial officers, legionary commanders, and governors of military provinces with equestrian officers and officials which had already started in the reign of Septimius Severus. The legion's senatorial *tribunus laticlavius* is only attested until 249 AD. Since Domitian, equestrian officers had been in charge of extraordinary commands, even of whole army corps. Moreover, Egypt had provided the model of equestrian governors and legionary commanders since Augustus. The navy always had equestrian commanders. However, since 193, all usurpers coming to power outside Rome had to form an administrative and military staff and to appoint extraordinary military commanders or to replace specific personal in a very short time. They took officials and officers from the military staff of their legions and provinces. This must have made the rise of equestrian officials or officers to the highest positions and the promotion of soldiers and subaltern officers more rapid.

When Septimius Severus began his march against Rome, an equestrian officer was appointed quartermaster-general, *praepositus annonae*, and the equestrian officer and procurator L. Valerius Valerianus[3] got the command of the cavalry corps of the imperial field army, the first attested in our sources, which he commanded successfully against Pescennius Niger. Under Commodus, he had been *praepositus equitum gentium peregrinarum*, commander of a cavalry corps of foreign mercenaries. In 195 AD, he became commander-in-chief of the army in the conquered Northern Mesopotamia where an equestrian procurator, Iulius Pacatianus, was appointed governor.

When Severus ordered the organization of three new legions in 195/6 – in the official version for a war of conquest against the Parthian Empire, but in reality to strengthen his force for a war against Clodius Albinus – they got the corresponding names I, II, and III Parthica. During winter 196/7, the Parthians launched their counterattack to profit from the Roman civil war (Cassius Dio 76[75]9.1); the new legions I and III Parthica were sent to the East. Pacatianus became the equestrian commander probably of I Parthica. Legio III Parthica had an equestrian commander too. In 198, the new province of Mesopotamia was created and was given an equestrian governor, and the two legions now stationed in this province maintained their equestrian command. Severus followed the Augustan model of Egypt. Pacatianus later became *praefectus vexillationum per orientem*, commander of the vexillation corps brought to the East for Caracalla's Parthian War, in 215, and equestrian governor of Mesopotamia in 216/17 AD.

The Legio II Parthica, stationed by Severus in Castra Albana near Rome to strengthen the emperor's military force in Italy, was under the command of an equestrian *praefectus legionis* too. The inscriptions of the legion from Apameia attest an *exactus librarii legati legionis* in 118 AD and a *librarius officii legati legionis* and a *strator legati legionis* during the Parthian campaign of Severus Alexander (*AE* 1993, 1587; *AE* 1993, 1586). However, Severus' command structure in this case consisted of an equestrian prefect acting *vice legati*, instead of a legionary legat (*ILS* 1356), so that the formal structure of the new legion in Italy was unchanged.

Severus had decided against a senatorial command of the new legions and provinces. The general trend of commanding equestrian officers in the legions, *praefecti agentes vice legati legionis*, and of equestrian governors *agentes vice praesidis*, acting instead of *legati propraetore* of praetorian or consular rank, is increasingly attested from the mid-third century AD onwards. The equestrian camp prefects were already titled *praefecti legionis* and when important parts of the legion were on campaign, forming one or even several vexillations under their own commanders, the remaining parts of the legions in the garrisons may have been from time to time only under the command of the camp prefect, acting *vice legati legionis*. This means that there was no formal abandonment of the senatorial command. The last consular legatus *propraetore* is attested in 270 in Moesia Inferior (*CIL* 3.14460); in Britain, the entire traditional hierarchy was still unchanged in 257/8 AD (*RIB* 334). A good example of these changes is M. Simplicinius Genialis, equestrian governor *agens vice praesidis* of the praetorian province of Raetia and commander of Legio III Italica, who defeated the Semnoni/

Iouthungi in a pitched battle in April 260, commanding a field army made up of his provincial army, units from Upper Germany, and a provincial militia. The trend to appoint equestrian "substitutes" in the provincial government and legionary command probably also increased because of problems in the relationship between senatorial legionary legates and equestrian *praepositi* of legionary vexillations or between equestrian commanders of regional army corps or parts of the field armies and senatorial governors in the provinces.

Field armies which had existed for a long time or which were organized with some long-term perspective made it necessary to have a long-serving staff of officers. The officers of the field army were professional, permanently-serving officers, and this trend must have been dominant at least since 253 AD. A new corps of permanent serving officers of equestrian rank and a corps of centurions and non-commissioned officers of the field army emerged and became part of the regular structure of the army. For the professional higher staff of officers and subaltern officers, a special corps or *collegium*, the *protectores*, developed before the mid-third century AD. Commanders of army corps and vexillations were appointed out of this corps. At the end of the third century, the corps of the *protectores* became a sort of staff academy opening middle- and upper-level careers in the army for centurions, non-commissioned officers, and especially for sons of veterans. The career of such a professional officer is documented in a fragmentary inscription from Mauretania (*AE* 1954, 135); he advanced from the decurionate of Ala Parthorum to the centurionate of Legio III Augusta, thereafter he became *centurio et protector* in the Legio IV Flavia and then *primipilaris protector*, both posts in the field army, and *primipilus II protector* in the general staff of two Augusti, obviously Valerian and Gallienus. The second category of *protectores*, being personal guards, appeared earlier in the third century, when *protectores* of provincial governors and of the praetorian prefects are attested. Later the Equites Singulares Augusti sometimes got the title *protectores domini nostri* or *Augusti nostri*. For higher officers, the honorific title *protector* first appeared for the tribunes of the praetorian cohorts. From the time of Valerian and Gallienus onwards, equestrian legionary commanders, governors or *duces* and *praepositi*, commanders of army corps and vexillations, often had the title protector. However, *protectores Augusti*, not equestrian *praepositi*, could also command a corps of combined legionary and auxiliary vexillations from several provinces. Since the time of Claudius II, *protectores ducenarii* had been a special rank commanding vexillations and cavalry corps. In 284, Diocletian was the powerful chief of the *collegium protectorum* and of the imperial guards and was proclaimed emperor by the Eastern field army.

4 Gallienus and the Rise of Cavalry in the Third Century

An important development during the reign of Septimius Severus was the rise of heavy armored cavalry in the Roman army caused by the major challenge of the confrontation with the Parthian and then Sassanid Empire in the East, where heavy armored cavalry with long spears, the *clibanarii*, was a dangerous shock force. The Roman army introduced cavalry with the *contus*, a heavy spear of 3 meters to 5 meters in length in the time of Trajan. The first attested unit of *cataphractarii*,[4] the heavy armored cavalry imitating Parthian tradition, is the Ala Gallorum et Pannoniorum in the time of Hadrian. The introduction of fully armored heavy cavalry with long lances was surely a consequence of Trajan's Parthian War. During Severan times, especially at the time of the Second Parthian War of Septimius Severus, of Caracalla's campaign, and of Severus Alexander's Persian War, the fully armored heavy cavalry of the Roman army was finally properly organized. The Roman *cataphractarii* had special long armor (Heliodoros, *Aith.* 9.15) and helmets, big round shields, long swords and lances (*contus*), one or two additional horses and a pack horse, all with the necessary grooms (one or two *calones*). However, no horse armor was used by the Roman heavy cavalry. The cataphracts were only a small number of specialized cavalrymen and their effectiveness was most evident in combined arms' combat, especially in combination with mounted archers. Mounted archers with heavy armor became part of the Roman field armies in the East especially after the defeat of Palmyra in 272 AD; *equites sagittarii clibanarii* are attested in the late Roman army. In earlier times, the Roman army had used the famous Palmyrenean and other oriental mounted archers.

However, cataphracts were not only serving in special units. On the Arch of Galerius and on the Arch of Constantine, the emperor's guard, the Equites Singulares Augusti, now called *protectores Augusti*, were armed as cataphracts. At an unknown date in the later third century, small groups of cataphracts were also introduced in other mounted units to be used in combined arms combat. For example, cataphracts are known in the Ala II Dromedariorum in Egypt in 300 AD (P. Panop. Beatty 2, l.27–31). Officers and under-officers were fighting in the front rank of the cavalry by the time of high empire, leading the three files of the *turma*; the same is attested from the fourth century to 600 AD, when each file of Maurikos' cavalry unit was ten men deep and led by an officer, a sub-officer, or a *dekarches* or *decanus*. They were equipped, probably from the later third century onwards, with heavy armor; the *duplicarii* and *sesquiplicarii* were now called *catafractarii*, and the decurions were wearing cataphract armor too. The late Roman Ala was also organized in battle in *turmae* with files of ten men led by the *decurio* and the two subaltern *catafractarii*. In principle, the order of the *turma* of the early and high empire was unchanged into the fourth century AD: 30 horsemen, two non-commissioned officers (*duplicarius*, *sesquiplicarius*), and the *decurio*, each of them leading a file of ten men in combat or maneuver, the first having three, the second and third two horses, the spare horses being led by grooms (Fink 1971, no. 1.2; Ps.-Hyginus, *Mun. Castr.* 16).

Since the Parthian War of Lucius Verus and the Danubian wars of Marcus Aurelius the general importance of cavalry had been steadily rising. The cavalry units formed by Septimius Severus are mentioned above. But Arrian's Ektaxis against the Alani shows that the legionary cavalrymen and the Equites Singulares of the governor with their centurions and decurions and a selected guard of legionary infantrymen (*lanciarii*), the *protectores*, formed the escort of the commanding general which was also employed as tactical reserve during battles (Arrian, *Ekt.* 22–23). Septimius Severus doubled the imperial horse guard, the Equites Singulares Augusti, and the praetorian horse. The cavalry of the guards now consisted of 4,400 men. Mounted archers were always part of the Equites Singulares Augusti. In the late third century, the Equites Singulares Augusti following the emperor in the field army became the *protectores Domini nostri*. The praetorian horse in the field army was separated from the praetorian infantry and now called *equites promoti Dom(i)nici*. Under these names, both elite troops entered the late Roman army forming the highest-ranking units of the elite cavalry. The legionary cavalry, equally separated and organized in special cavalry corps, received the title *equites promoti* too, indicating that they were an elite cavalry. A third category of *equites promoti* was created under Diocletian, the units of *equites promoti indigenae*, equipped and trained as heavy cavalry, but recruited among the local or regional population and partly consisting of armored archers. The legionary cavalry consisted of very well trained, heavy-armored horsemen (*equites loricati*, mounted legionaries), who were very effective in fighting in formation. Hadrian's speech in Lambaesis emphasized the fighting quality of *equites legionis*. At the same time, the legionary horsemen were an important source of future centurions and decurions (*dekarches*) for mounted auxiliary units. Centurions of the legionary horse were even used as commanders of mounted units. On campaign, they served as the army commander's special guard. In the Jewish War or in Arrian's campaign against the Alani, the legionary horsemen of all legions formed a special elite and reserve cavalry corps following the commanding general (Josephus, *B. Jud.* 5, 47–49; Arrian, *Ekt.* 4–6; 22). The legionary horsemen, organized in *turmae*, were brigaded together with the Equites Singulares. The *turma* had a centurion as commander, an *optio* and a *vexillarius* as standard-bearers. Each file of ten men was led by one of them. The centurions and *principales* of the legionary horse were called *supernumerarii*, because they were not included in the number of the officers and non-commissioned officers of the ten legionary cohorts. The same is true for all the legionary horsemen. The traditional legionary cavalry consisted of 120 men, made up of four *turmae*, with four centurions and eight file-leading under-officers; in sum 132 men and officers (a turma having 32 men and under-officers and one centurion). The men were listed in the legionary cohorts, but encamped separately from the *contubernia* of the *centuriae*.[5]

For his Parthian campaign, Caracalla organized a special corps of legionary horsemen, *equites extraordinarii*, and put them under the command of the equestrian commander of Legio II Parthica, the escort legion of the emperor. These horsemen were by definition outside the regular organization of a legion. These *equites extraordinarii* should be seen as additional horsemen serving in the legions. The rise in number of the legionary cavalry should be attributed to the time of Septimius Severus and Caracalla and not later. It is probable that the new legions I, II, and III Parthica got a larger cavalry force first. A cavalry component of its own would fit very well into the preparation for fighting on the eastern frontier, and II Parthica, stationed in Italy, had no mounted auxiliary unit serving as a cavalry component at all.

It was the theory of E. Ritterling that Gallienus created the Roman cavalry army, the "Schlachtenreiterei," and that his "Kavalleriereform" separated the mounted corps from the provincial armies and their original units, especially the legions.[6] The number of legionary horsemen given by Vegetius was taken as a proof of this reform.

Large cavalry corps, consisting of various forces, always escorted the emperors on campaign in the third century AD. For his Parthian campaign, Caracalla had added mounted Moorish *foederati*, famous javelin-throwers, and specialists in cavalry tactics for mountainous areas (Cassius Dio 78 [79] 32, 1), and mounted Germanic and Gothic *foederati*. The Moorish mounted javelin-throwers had already been used by Trajan in great numbers. Ethnic troops of Mauretanian *foederati* were part of the army of Alexander Severus in the Persian and Germanic wars and escorted Maximinus Thrax to Italy in 238 AD (Herodian, 8.1.3; Zosimus 1.15.1; Zonaras 126.7). The *equites Dalmatae* were an elite cavalry force who played an important part in the murder of Gallienus in 268 and later fought successfully under Claudius II (Zosimus 1.40.2; 1.43.2; *HA, Gall.* 14.4.9). Zosimus (1.52.3–4) mentions the Dalmatian and Moorish horsemen in Aurelian's battle force at Emesa against the superior cavalry of Palmyra. The Dalmatian horsemen seem to have been recruited under Gallienus to strengthen his field army in 260 AD. The grooms of the cavalry of the field armies must have been very numerous and well-trained horsemen. At an unknown date, probably as an ad hoc measure, some of the grooms were organized into fighting units of different sizes as *stablesiani* (*numeri, cunei*, or *vexillationes stablesianorum*) to strengthen the heavy cavalry.

There is no doubt that a large cavalry corps escorting the emperor or operating as a mobile advance army was the elite core of Gallienus' field army (Zosimus 1.40.1; Zonaras 143.10–26, esp. 143.14.21; 145.11–12; 147.4–149.5). Federate cavalry and new special cavalry formations were added to the mounted auxiliaries and to the legionary cavalry vexillations, whose strength was probably that of an *ala qingenaria*. This cavalry corps developed a corporate identity (Zosimus 1.45.2 under Claudius II.; Zonaras 147.28; *HA, Aurel.* 18.1). In 268, the later emperor Claudius II was in charge of the cavalry corps of the imperial field army and Aurelian was second in command, and both played an active role in the murder of Gallienus. Aurelian, who became commander of the cavalry corps of the field army under Claudius II, seems to have abolished this high command, which brought a certain risk to the security of the emperor. In particular, the high command of the mobile core of the imperial field army with its cavalry corps, the elite troops of the imperial army, had made officers *capax imperii*.

5   The Development of the Roman Infantry

The infantry legion remained the basic military instrument of the Roman army in the third century AD. Tactics and drill were based on the *contubernium* of eight men and half-*contubernium* of four men, forming marching columns of four men or battle formations of twice four ranks (eight lines deep), as demonstrated in Arrian's array against the Alans. This system was established some time after Vespasian's Jewish War and before the time of Hadrian.[7] The basic system of four/eight men continued into Byzantine times, as is attested in the Strategikon of Pseudo-Maurikios c. 580/ 600 AD. An innovation in the use of the legion, or more accurately of the *vexillatio*-legion, in the field armies of the later third century was the organization of a legionary infantry reserve, which was named *triarii* after the republican legionary unit.

The necessity of having javelin throwers, archers, and slingers directly combined with the first combat lines of heavy armored legionary infantry to gain greater long-distance effectiveness had already developed in the second half of the second century AD (Cassius Dio 75[74]7.2.4; 76[75]6.6). A new differentiation of arms developed within the legions. Light-armed legionaries already appeared on the Arch of Septimius Severus in Rome. The new dominating role of spears and lances in fighting, characteristic arms of late antiquity, started early. By the time of Hadrian's rule one group of legionaries was equipped with the *pilum*, the other with *lanceae*. Arrian[8] described his battle order against the Alani as a Roman variation of the Hellenistic phalanx: a dense phalanx out of the first four lines of infantry using the *pila*-like pikes against the armored cavalry of the Alani; the lines in the rear had to throw the *lanceae*, heavy javelins with projector-belt, which were a weapon of the auxiliaries and imperial guards, of the *speculatores* and special elite units selected from the legions in the first century AD (Josephus, *B. Jud.* 3.120; 5.47; Suetonius, *Claud.* 35.1; *Galba* 18.1). Phalanx-like formations were always an option in the Roman tactical doctrine and became the dominating formation of the late Roman and Byzantine heavy infantry. In preparation for his Parthian campaign, Caracalla ordered the army to be trained in the Macedonian phalanx tactic and selected 16,000 men to fight in a phalanx-like formation (Cassius Dio 78[77]7.1–2; 18.1; Herodian 4.8.2; 4.10.3). The intention was without doubt to protect the lines against Parthian cavalry attacks, and not because of Caracalla's wish to imitate Alexander the Great. Most likely the legions' first combat lines were trained to act as a phalanx as attested in Arrian's Ektaxis. Severus Alexander did the same in his Persian War when the *phalangiarii* of six legions were formed into a phalanx (*HA, Sev. Alex.* 50.4).

The gravestones of soldiers of the Legio II Parthica in Apameia show important changes in the structure of the legions in the early third century. A trainer in the use of the *lanceae*, the *discens lanciarum*, a trainer in the use of longer spears to build a phalanx, the *discens phalangiarum*, and a *lanciarius* in the rank of an *immunis* are attested; one gravestone shows a soldier with the *lancea*. In the late third century AD, partly mounted units of *lanciarii* drawn from the legions were attested in the imperial field army. Legionary helmets of the late second century AD of the Niedermörmter and Niederbieber types were constructed for soldiers fighting in closed, phalanx-like formations that remained close even when using swords. The Niedermörmter type gave the maximum protection, but allowed only a small range of movement to the body. Fighters had to be in an upright position in closed formation; throwing *pilum* or javelins became difficult and the sword had to be used downwards and directly forward. The Niederbieber type gave maximal protection too; only eyes, mouth, and nose are uncovered, but the neck protection made it much easier to move the body. Both types restricted the view forwards. Sextus Iulius Africanus attests complaints because of the immobility of the head covered by contemporary helmets.[9]

6 Recruitment

An ever-growing number of recruits came from veteran families, especially for non-commissioned officers and the centurionate, and they were earmarked to be moved into higher-ranking positions. People coming from military society, developed in the garrison provinces, had already become the backbone of the army in the second century AD. Now the new areas of army concentration in the interior of the empire, primarily in Northern Italy, made a new organization and administration of recruitment necessary for the units of the imperial field army, many of which had been without contact with their mother units since 254 AD. Since the installation of the Legio II Parthica near Rome at the end of the second century AD, Italy had become more important for recruitment. Maximinus Thrax tried to introduce a new systematic recruitment drawing on the youth of the Italian cities, especially in the north. In the first half of the third century AD, most of the known soldiers of Legio II Parthica, being the escort legion of the emperors on campaign, came from Thrace (half of all the soldiers in this legion!), Italy, and Pannonia. When the power of the central empire was restricted to Italy, Africa, and the area from Raetia/Noricum to the Aegean between 260 and 274 – the eastern part of the empire was restricted to the recruitment for its own troops – "Illyricum" (Noricum/Upper Pannonia to Moesia) and Thrace became the main recruitment areas of the imperial army and the units stationed there provided soldiers and officers for transfer and promotion into the imperial field army. Therefore, the *decennia* after 260 saw the rise of "Illyrian" officers and soldiers to the highest posts and even to the imperial throne (Claudius II, Aurelian, Probus, Diocletian, Maximian, Constantius I, Galerius).

7   The Question of Barbarization

The increasing assimilation of the regular auxiliary forces to the legions since the late first century, which reached its peak in the later second century, had made the tactical distinction between the two categories of troops obsolete at the end of second century AD. This caused problems in the provision of light armor or special arms and fighting tactics for combat using combined arms. Foreign forces, having their own internal organization, were fighting as *foederati* and took over the previous responsibilities of the regular auxiliaries. The rise of mercenaries and foreign elite troops, especially *foederati* from Germanic peoples incorporated into the Roman forefront of the empire, was one of the characteristic developments of the third century. The intensified fighting and the heavy losses in several civil wars and in periods of epidemic disease caused an increasing need for already well-trained fighters in the third century AD. Usurpers, who had at hand only that part of the legions remaining in the camps of the provinces they controlled and often also several corps of vexillations, had to reinforce their troops in a very short time to prepare them for fighting against other Roman troops. It was increasingly necessary to obtain ready-trained soldiers, although Vegetius later argued that it would be cheaper to train his own men rather than hiring foreigners (Vegetius 1.28). Marcus Aurelius had already recruited slaves, gladiators, and robber bands from Dalmatia and Dardania and a great number of Germanic mercenaries from beyond the frontiers during the preparation of the planned offensive war on the middle Danube in 169 AD when heavy losses were caused by the Antonine plague. Under Commodus, a cavalry unit of foreign mercenaries (*equites gentium peregrinarum*) is attested. *Gothi gentiles*, probably hired by Septimius Severus for his Second Parthian War, were serving in the province Arabia in 208 AD. Caracalla formed a mounted guard of federate Scythian, in other words Gothic, and Germanic tribesmen, called *leones*, "Lions." Partly mounted "barbaric" mercenaries of a *numerus Orientalium* are attested in Egypt in 203. In 251, several mercenary horsemen were serving in the Cohors XX Palmyrenorum at Dura Europos, and *salarati peregrini*, foreign mercenaries, serving in a unit of *peregrini cataphractarii*, of foreign heavy-mailed horsemen, were known in Egypt in 267 (P. Oxy. 41.2951). Foreigners, either captives of war or deserters, were also organized in regular *numeri* of the army. Caracalla added forces of Germanic people from north of the Danube, including Gothic tribes-men, to his field army on the Danube and brought them to the East for his Parthian campaign. Gordian III had Germanic and Gothic forces for his Persian campaign, which were specifically mentioned in the annals of Shapur I. Valerian brought Germanic forces to the East in 258 AD and Parthian mercenaries fought as heavy armored horse-men (cataphracts) in the Germanic campaigns of Severus Alexander. Maximinus Thrax had Parthian cataphracts, being mercenaries, deserters, or prisoners of war conscripted into the army, and in 238 a large force of Germanic cavalry, Gothic *foederati* or, more accurately mercenaries obviously hired during his Danubian war, followed him to Italy. However, foreign federate forces and hired or mobilized *symmarchiarii*, fellow-combatants, always fought in the wars of the empire. The Dacian and Parthian wars of Trajan provide excellent examples. Only our knowledge of such phenomena is fragmentary.

During the tetrarchy, foreign units became a regular part of the elite corps of the field armies. An elite unit of Marcomannic cavalry, *vexillatio equitum Marcomannorum*, is known in Egypt in 286; it had been brought there by Probus in 279. The oldest and highest ranking of these elite units, the Cornuti and Brachiati and the Petulantes and Celtae, providing infantry and cavalry (*auxilia* and *vexillationes palatinae*), were organized by Constantius I from tribesmen of Schleswig, Jütland, and Denmark. In 312 AD, the army of Constantine I was partly raised from prisoners of war settled or kept in Gaul; these units developed into an important part of the Auxilia Palatina. In the late Roman army, however, the majority of soldiers were of Roman provincial origin, and barbarian influences on tactics, equipment, and organization appear to have been very limited too.[10]

8 Equipment and Logistics

There were no centralized reforms of Roman army equipment, as changes usually developed regionally and in response to particular fighting situations. The *lorica segmentata* was no longer used after the later third century AD. Heavy armed soldiers had scale, mail, and lamellar body armor, both for mounted troops and infantry. The legionary *pilum* and the *scutum* vanished in the third century too. Large oval and round shields and several categories of spears, lances, darts, and javelins had been in use since the early third century. The equipment of all regular troops, legions and *auxilia*, was now similar and all these troops could be used in the same way. The old distinction between legions and *auxilia* was no longer relevant. From the second century AD onwards, a sword with long blades, the spatha, replaced the gladius and was used for slashing and thrusting in infantry combat. The legionary helmet changed to the Weisenau-Niedermörmter type in the later second and early third century and also to the Buck and Niederbieber type, which represented the peak in the development of Roman helmets, which was introduced in the later second century AD.[11] Legions and auxiliaries, infantry and cavalry used this type of helmet in the East and West until a total change in the late third century when it was replaced by the more open faced "Spangenhelm" and the "Kammhelm" of the Deir-el-Medineh and Intercisa types. The new types were influenced by Persian and Sarmatian models but were Roman constructions. Their production was much less complicated and more convenient for mass production in big public workshops, which developed at the end of the third century AD. The helmet of the Niedermörmter type in the Sammlung Axel Guttmann was found together with a spatha, a long dagger with a scabbard and a *dolabra*, pioneer-axe, with sheath, representing the equipment of a legionary of the early third century AD. In addition to these, the legionary soldiers were using long-shafted spears and javelins.

The logistics and the supply of the Roman army, of field armies and garrisons, worked very well in the third century, serving all the needs of men and horses and allowing extraordinary mobility in terms of unbelievable speed in marching and easy transfer of army forces. This is remarkable because the number of campaigns against foreign enemies and in civil war had drastically increased since 249 AD and the existence of the field armies created new needs and made new structures necessary. The supply of the army was based in the third century AD on the resources of taxes in kind, on compulsory purchase, on special levies, and on the free market. At least since the Severan emperors wheat had been given to the soldiers by the state without any reduction in their pay. Private entrepreneurs were given contracts by the governors for transportation or delivery of goods and private merchants had to sell goods at prices fixed by the state or by the officials of the provincial or military administration. The widespread opinion that the *annona militaris* as an ordinary tax in kind was introduced in Severan times must be rejected. The use of the term *annona* in the context of supply had increased since the beginning of the third century AD, especially for the supply of marching troops or for campaigns. This was organized by the provincial governors. Such special levies or *annona* had become an additional impost in the early third century, but seems to have been deductible from ordinary taxes. *Annona* became the *terminus technicus* for temporary extraordinary levies. Only from Diocletian onwards did the *annona*, tax in kind on land, exist and it was used for the remuneration in kind of the army, of officials, of public workshops, and also for the supply of the army, the imperial court, and the population in the great cities. The reforms of Diocletian and Constantine I fundamentally changed the organization and administration of army supply.[12] In time of civil war, requisition and contribution could be used to punish the enemies' supporters or to obtain urgently needed supplies. However, usurpers as well as ruling emperors had to take care to gain loyalty and not to loose sympathy. Thus, requisition and quartering had to be handled carefully. The events of 238 demonstrate that an emperor and his army depended on the supply provided by the cities and their city-government. Requisitions were only a temporary burden and had minor long lasting effects. Only in those areas where army movements were numerous did real problems emerge.

9 Conclusion

The battle performance of the Roman armies in the third and fourth centuries was not significantly worse than that of their early imperial counterparts. The dominant strategy remained the ability to move quickly and effectively inside and beyond the frontiers and to defeat enemies in pitched battles, combined with having the highest standard of technical equipment, engineering, and professional drill. The army in the third century did not act like a marauding band and there was no antagonism between the army and civilians. The often-repeated theory of an increasing militarization of the Roman Empire, of society, and administration ("militarized bureaucracy") in the third century must be rejected. The Roman army of the third century AD demonstrated its impressive abilities in combat especially in civil wars and was able to defeat every foreign enemy. A disaster such as happened in 251 at Abritus had occurred in earlier times as well – for example the *Clades Variana* in 9 AD or the disaster of M. Claudius Fronto in 170 AD. The so-called "Limesfall" of 260 AD is often cited as evidence of a military crisis of the third century AD. But the *limes* between the Rhine and upper Danube had already been weakened before 259 AD when troops and vexillations were withdrawn to become field armies, and especially in 253 when Valerian marched against the usurper Aemilianus. In 262, the zone between the Rhine and the Iller became the frontier zone between the usurper Postumus and Gallienus, a zone of no direct interest to either party. The "Obergermanisch-raetische Limes" vanished because troops were no longer deployed and the Romanized population left the area.

Under Septimius Severus and Caracalla, several measures of reorganization, but no so-called Severan army reform, can be seen. Many changes emerged out of the historical situation since the time of Severus Alexander, especially in the reigns of Valerian and Gallienus and under Aurelian. The reorganization of the empire by Diocletian brought important changes, but also continuity. Neither Diocletian nor Constantine created the late Roman field army. It developed from the later second century AD onwards. The navy and its regional formations, the medical services, intelligence service, and an efficient military administration continued to exist on several levels. There was no dramatic change forced by the so-called "crisis of the third century." The relevant developments had already started in the first half of the second century and increased in the Danubian wars of Marcus Aurelius and in the first half of Septimius Severus' reign. The real starting point of the late Roman army was the reorganization of the military forces of the empire by Constantine I after his victory over Licinius in 324. The organization and equipment of the infantry units were the result of a long process of change and adjustment. In the legionary vexillations of the earlier field army, cohorts had not had the same structure and tasks as the regular legion. The tactical sub-units of the vexillations were *centuria*-like administrative subdivisions and the *contubernium* fixed the place of a soldier in the vexillations in the second century, when the cohort lost its role as the basic tactical unit in combat too. The last legionary cohorts are mentioned in 312 AD. The administration and logistics of the imperial field army became part of the central administration. In the third century and especially in its second half the trend towards a more centralized administration and a higher level of administrative organization increased to mobilize all the resources to cover the expenses and needs of war. The following tetrarchic and Constantinian reorganization of the empire consequently led to the development of a pre-modern civil bureaucracy.

NOTES

1   See Legio II Traiana in Egypt. One part remained in the camp of the legion in Nicopolis near Alexandria (province Iovia), but a vexillation of its *equites promoti*, the new title of the *equites legionis*, was stationed in Middle Egypt (province Herculia; P. Columb. 7.188; 320 AD; a centurion of the vexillation under the command of a *praepositus* and seven colleagues in the centurionate are attested). This vexillation had at least eight turmae, about 264 horsemen and officers. Two vexillations of the legion, one unit of its *lanciarii*, and a second vexillation of its *equites promoti* (also called *equites promoti secundiani* of Legio II Traiana; P. Grenf. 2, 74; 302 AD), all under the command of *praepositi*, were stationed in Upper Egypt (province Thebais) in 300 AD (P. Panop. Beatty 2.l. 180sq.). Both vexillations of *equites promoti* had very probably together the size of a traditional Ala quingenaria consisting of 16 turmae (512 horsemen and non-commissioned officers and 16 decurions).

2   Aur. Vict. Caes. 33, 34 *senatum militia vetuit et adire exercitum*. Aurelius Victor, *Caes.* 37.6 pretends that the Senate would have been able to regain the lost military commands under Tacitus, the "emperor of the Senate," but did not use the chance; this is an obvious fiction. For the whole discussion, see Le Bohec 2004.

3   Cf. Cassius Dio 75 (74) 7, 4.8; *AE* 1985, 829; Speidel 1992, 321–26; Lehmann and Holum 2000, 37–41 no. 4.

4   Cf. Harl 1996. The famous graffito from Dura Europos shows a Parthian, not a Roman heavy armored horseman (Harl l.c. 623sq.). See also Speidel 1992, 406–13; James 2004, 113–14, with the corrections by Harl's study. *Clibanarii* is the Persian name for this cavalry, not a special type to be distinguished from the *cataphractarii*, a *terminus technicus* first attested in the third century BC. The famous horse armor in Dura Europos has to be considered as Roman booty.

5   See also Ps.-Hyginus, *Mun. Castr.* 4 (not *vexillarii* of legionary vexillations). In the discussion of the size of the imperial legion, Roth 1994 argued for a standard legion of 4,800 men in the first century and for an expanded legion (first cohort of double strength) of 5,280 men in the second century. The *centuria* encamped in one barrack numbered 80 men in ten contubernia (cf. Ps.-Hyginus, *Mun. Castr.* 1). However, Ps.-Hyginus attested that the legionary cohort numbers in total 600 men (*Mun. Castr.* 5), thus a number of 6,000 men for the legion. Against Roth, Ps.-Hyginus clearly does not speak of *calones* or slaves in this number. The expanded legion had 54 centuries of 80 infantrymen, four centuries of 160 men and the first *centuria* of 320 men commanded by the *primuspilus* in the first cohort (later divided into two separate double-strength *centuriae*). We must

add 60 (or 59) centurions and 60 (or 59) *optiones centuriarum* and 132 *equites* (horsemen, under-officers, and *centuriones supernumerarii*), in sum 5,532 men and officers, and the people not encamped in the *centuriae*-barracks: *principales* and *officiales*, the medical staff, and some special craftsmen and engineers. Septimius Severus completed the assimilation not only of the centurions, but also of the *principales* to equestrian rank. It is impossible that these men of higher pay and rank encamped together with the common soldiers in the barracks. All together, the full strength of a legion of the second century numbered about 6,000 men, horsemen, officers, and non-commissioned officers.

6   Ritterling 1903; cf. Keyes 1915; De Blois 1976, 26–30. Considering the sources, Bleckmann 1992, 226–37, 255–60 argues convincingly. Cf. in general also Strobel 1999.

7   Josephus, *B. Jud.* 3.124; 5.48 marching in closed columns of six men, continuing the republican system of drill based on six men. For the tactical function of the system based on four men in marching order, see Arrian, *Ekt.* 4–6, in combat line of eight ranks = twice four ranks, Arrian, *Ekt.* 15–18.

8   Arrian, *Ekt.* 16–17 (*kontos* means *pilum*). Important for the changes in the legions are the gravestones of the soldiers especially of Legio II Parthica in the army camp at Apameia dating from Caracalla to 252 AD; cf. Balty 1987, 1988; Balty and van Rengen 1993; van Rengen 2000, 407–10; Ricci 2000, 397–406; especially *AE* 1993, 1588; Balty and van Rengen 1993, 18; *AE* 1993, 1574; 1575; 1573 (relief); Balty 1988, 101.

9   Kestroi 1, 1, 50–52.78–80.

10 See also Whitby (in this volume).

11 Junkelmann 2000, 83–5, 85–7, 90–2; Junkelmann 2000, no. 800 (p. 143–53) with no. 801–3.

12 Cf. Mitthof 2001, esp. 31sq. for the basic supply of frontier and field armies (so-called *annona militaris*).

BIBLIOGRAPHY

Balty, J.-C. 1987. "Apamée (1986). Nouvelles données sur l'armée romaine d'Orient et les raids sassanides du milieu de IIIe siècle," *CRAI*: 213–41.

—— 1988. "Apamea in Syria in the second and third centuries AD," *JRS* 58: 97–104.

——, and W. van Rengen. 1993. *Apamea in Syria. The Winter Quarters of Legio II Parthica. Roman Gravestones from the Military Cemetery.* Brussels.

Bleckmann, B. 1992. *Die Reichskrise des III. Jahrhunderts in der spätantiken und byzantinischen Geschichtsschreibung.* Munich.

Blois, L. de. 1976. *The Policy of the Emperor Gallienus.* Leiden.

Coulston, J. C. N. 1990. "Later Roman armour," *JRMES* 1: 139–60.

Drew-Bear, T. 1981. "Les voyages d'Aurélius Gaius, soldat de Dioclétien," in *La géographie administrative et politique d'Alexandre à Mahomet.* Strasburg, 93–141.

Eadie, J. W. 1967. "The development of the Roman mailed cavalry," *JRS* 57: 161–73.

Grosse, R. 1920. *Römische Militärgeschichte von Gallienus bis zum Beginn der byzantinischen Themenverfassung.* Berlin (repr. New York 1975).

Harl, O. 1996. "Die Kataphraktarier im römischen Heer. Panegyrik und Realität," *JRGZ* 43: 627.

Hoffmann, D. 1969. *Das spätrömische Bewegungsheer und die Notitia Dignitatum,* 2 vols. Düsseldorf.

Isaac, B. 1998. "The meaning of the terms *limes* and *limitanei*," in B. Isaac, *The Near East under Roman Rule*. Leiden, 345–87.

James, S. 2004. *The Excavations at Dura-Europos. Final Reports 7*. Ann Arbor.

Junkelmann, M. 2000. *Römische Helme. Sammlung Axel Guttmann*. Band VIII, H. Born (ed.). Mainz.

Keyes, C. 1915. *The Rise of Equites in the Third Century of the Roman Empire*. Princeton (new edn. Ann Arbor 1985).

Kissel, T. 1995. *Untersuchungen zur Logistik des römischen Heeres in den Provinzen des griechischen Ostens (27 v. Chr.–235 n. Chr.)*. St. Katharinen.

Le Bohec, Y. 2004. Gallien et l'encadrement senatorial de l'armée romaine, *REMA* 1: 123–32.

——, and C. Wolff (ed.). 2000. *Les légions de Rome sous le Haut-Empire*, 2 vols. Paris.

——, and C. Wolff (ed.). 2004. *L'armée romaine de Dioclétien à Valentinien Ier*. Paris.

Lehmann, C. M., and K. G. Holum. 2000. *The Greek and Latin Inscriptions of Caesarea Maritima*. Boston.

Levin, A. 2001. "Kastron Mefaa, the Equites Promoti Indigenae and the creation of a late Roman frontier," *LA* 51: 293–304.

Mitthof, F. 2001. *Annona militaris. Die Heeresversorgung im spätantiken Ägypten. Ein Beitrag zur Reichs- und Verwaltungsgeschichtedes Römischen Reiches im 3. bis 6. Jh. n. Chr.* Florence.

Nicasie, M. J. 1998. *Twilight of Empire. The Roman Army from the Reign of Diocletian until the Battle of Adrianopel*. Amsterdam.

Negin, A. E. 1998. "Sarmatian cataphracts as prototypes for Roman equites cataphractarii," *JRMES* 9: 65–75.

Palme, B. 2004. "Die römische Armee von Diokletian bis Valentinian I.: Die papyrologische Evidenz," in Le Bohec 2004, 101–15.

Remesal Rodríguez, R. 1997. *Heeresversorgung und die wirtschaftlichen Beziehungen zwischen der Baetica und Germanien*. Stuttgart.

Rengen, W. van. 2000. "La IIe Légion Parthique à Apamée," in Le Bohec and Wolff 2000, 407–10.

Ricci, C. 2000. "Legio II Parthica. Una messa punto," in Le Bohec and Wolff, 397–406.

Richardot, P. 1998. *La fin de l'armée romaine (284–476)*. Paris.

Ritterling, E. 1903. "Zum römischen Heerwesen des ausgehenden 3. Jahrhunderts," in *Festschrift O. Hirschfeld*. Berlin, 345–9.

Roth, J. 1994. "The size and organization of the Roman imperial legion," *Historia* 43: 346–62.

—— 1999. *The Logistics of the Roman Army at War (264 BC–AD 235)*. Leiden.

Speidel, M. P. 1974. "Stablesiani. The raising of new cavalry units during the crisis of the Roman Empire," *Chiron* 4: 541–6.

—— 1992. *Roman Army Studies II*. Stuttgart.

—— 1996. "Raising new units for the late Roman army: Auxilia Palatina," *Dumbarton Oaks Papers* 50: 163–70.

—— 1998. "The stratarches of legio VI Ferrata and the employment of camp prefects as vexillation commanders," *ZPE* 120: 226–33.

—— 2000. "Who fought in the front?" in G. Alföldy, B. Dobson, and W. Eck (ed.), *Kaiser, Heer und Gesellschaft in der Römischen Kaiserzeit. Gedenkschrift E. Birley*. Stuttgart, 473–82.

—— 2004. "The four earliest Auxilia Palatina," *REMA* 1: 132–46.

Strobel, K. 1993. *Das Imperium Romanum im "3. Jahrhundert."* Stuttgart.

—— 1999. "Pseudophänomene der römischen Militär- und Provinzgeschichte am Beispiel des 'Falles' des obergermanisch-rätischen Limes. Neue Ansätze zu einer Geschichte der Jahrzehnte nach 253 n.Chr. an Rhein und oberer Donau," in *Roman Frontier Studies XVII*. Zalau, 9–33.

Wheeler, E. L. 2004a. "The legion as phalanx in the late empire. Part I," in Le Bohec and Wolff 2004, 309–58.

—— 2004b. "The legion as phalanx in the late empire, Part II," *REMA* 1: 147–75.

Zuckerman, C. 1993. "Les barbares romains: au sujet de l'origine des auxilia tétrarchiques," in F. Vallet and M. Kazanski (ed.), *L'armée romaine et les barbares*. Paris, 17–20.

FURTHER READING

On the army of Diocletian and Constantine, see Grosse 1920; Coulston 1990; Hoffmann 1969; Isaac 1998; Le Bohec and Wolff 2004; Nicasie 1998; Palme 2004; Richardot 1998; Speidel 1996, 2004; Zuckermann 1993. On the senatorial army command, in particular Speidel 1998; De Blois 1976. On the development of the cavalry: Eadie 1967; Levin 2001; Negin 1998; Speidel 1974, 2000. Infantry: Wheeler 2004a and b. Logistics and equipment have recently been discussed by Roth 1999; Mitthof 2001; also Kissel 1995; Remesal 1997.

CHAPTER SIXTEEN

Military Documents, Languages, and Literacy

Sara Elise Phang

1 Introduction

How did the Roman army maintain control over some 400,000 (at maximum) personnel, especially given their long terms of service and their frequent mobility? "Personnel management" and control were achieved not just through (for example) severe punishment for desertion, but through a relatively sophisticated system of documents, proof of the close association of literacy and power.

The army clerks produced documentation concerning recruitment, daily tasks and long-term missions, the giving and confirmation of orders, furlough, and annual reports on the composition of units. These records show a high degree of uniformity over space and time. The bureaucracy required literate clerks and propagated a documentary culture. However, the degree of modernity of the military bureaucracy has often been overestimated, as I will argue.[1] This chapter will cover documents pertaining to military personnel management during the principate, not financial accounts or documentation concerning discharge privileges and *praemia*.

Our evidence comes from various findspots around the empire and from different periods: the main finds are wooden writing tablets from Vindolanda (and a few from Carlisle) near Hadrian's Wall in northern England, dating to the turn of the second century AD; ostraca from Bu Njem or Gholaia, a small frontier outpost in the Libyan desert occupied in the early third century AD; papyri from Dura-Europos on the River Euphrates, occupied by the Cohors XX Palmyrenorum milliaria equitata sagittaria, an unit of Palmyrene archers in the early to mid-third century AD; and ostraca from Mons Claudianus, an imperial stone quarry in the Eastern Desert of Egypt. Individual papyri and ostraka from Roman Egypt also attest military records.[2]

2 Writing Materials

Roman military records employed papyrus, ostraca, and wooden tablets as writing materials. Papyrus is made from the papyrus reed, *Cyperus papyrus*, native to and raised in the Nile Delta in Egypt. Making papyrus required peeling the thick triangular stalks and slicing the pith into thin strips, which are laid in crossing layers and pounded or pressed to unite them into a paper-like sheet which when dry was smoothed and written on with ink.[3] Perhaps the army made its own papyrus instead of paying the rather high price on the commercial market (two obols for a single sheet, P. Oxy. 14.1654). Soldiers are assigned to making papyrus in one document (*ad chartan confici[endam]*, *RMR* 10 = Campbell 184).

Ostraka – potsherds – varied in shape and size, and offered a light-colored, often curved but smooth writing surface at no cost. Most were written on directly with ink, some inscribed with a point. No medium seems to be more "casual" than another – though one assumes that the most formal documents, the *pridiana*, were always written up more carefully on papyrus, and extensive records pertaining to daily administration might be kept on ostraka, such as O. Amst. 8.

At Vindolanda, thin sheets of wood (1–3 mm thick) were written on directly with ink across or sometimes with the grain, sometimes folded or bound together with string through holes and notches in the wood. This processing indicates a formal quality to the tablets. They were not merely wood scraps. *Tabulae ceratae*, wood tablets on which the writer used a stylus to scratch letters in a layer of wax, were reusable but much more expensive. Cost and availability of material seems to favor the use of papyrus and ostraca in Egypt and at Bu Njem and Dura, as in these arid regions wood was scarce and expensive. At Vindolanda (and probably throughout the North) wood was plentifully available, whereas papyrus was "difficult and expensive to obtain"[4] from the East. Wood (non-waxed) tablets were also known in the South, where lime-wood was used (Herodian 1.17.1; Cassius Dio 72 [73] 8.2).

To write on papyrus, ostraka, and tablets, personnel used reed or metal-nibbed pens and ink made from soot, gum, and water. The clerks may have learned a standard Latin script, using a mixture of capitals (usually for headings only, though the Feriale Duranum and *RMR* 64 are exceptional in containing larger amounts of capital text) and cursive. Capital headings are not universal even in so official a document as the *pridianum* (as P. Brooklyn 24 is interpreted).

3 The Enlistment Process

Paperwork began to follow the imperial Roman soldier from his enlistment onward, which had two stages: an examination (*probatio*) of eligibility and fitness to serve, performed by the governor's staff, and enrollment in an actual military unit.[5]

In *probatio*, prospective recruits seem to have had to prove their legal status (free birth and free status were required; Roman citizenship was required in the praetorians and legions). In AD 92 one T. Flavius Longus declared that he was of free birth and able to serve in a legion (Campbell). Recruits underwent a cursory medical examination, their height being measured (*Acta Maximiliani* 1.1–5 = Campbell 5) and their eyesight probably being checked (a weaver with weak eyesight is dismissed, P. Oxy. 39 = Campbell 6). The *probatio* was probably routine and brief. The later Roman military writer Vegetius is idealizing when he states that in the past only recruits six Roman feet tall were accepted (*Epit.* 1.5.1–3), or that recruits from cities (1.3.1–5) and "dishonorable" professions (1.7.1) should not be accepted. The modern speculation that all recruits needed letters of recommendation (*litterae commendaticiae*) is also idealized. Examples of these letters are extant, e.g. *Sel. Pap.* I 122 = *CPL* 249 or P. Berol. XI 649 = *CPL* 257), but in early second-century Egypt, Claudius Terentianus complained that he could not get into the unit of his choice without bribery: *hic a[ut]em sene ae[re ni]hil fiet neque epistulae commendaticiae nihil val<eb>unt nesi si qui sibi aiutaveret* (P. Mich. 8.468 = Campbell 43). "Nothing happens here without money, and letters of recommendation are of no use unless someone helps himself."

The Roman jurists' works excerpted in the *Digest* show merely that slaves, convicts, and even those whose free/slave status was in doubt could not enlist. But proving status might be difficult in a society in which "identification papers" (such as birth certificates or registrations) were not routine.[6] Pliny informs Trajan that several slaves had infiltrated the recruits (*Epist.* 10.29). The document *CPL* 102 in which T. Flavius Longus declares that he is freeborn and a Roman citizen and has the right to serve in a legion, may represent a challenge made some time after his enlistment, as he gives military comrades as his guarantors.

Pliny's letter and Trajan's reply (*Epist.* 10.29–30) shed light on the documentation of recruitment. Pliny (*Epist.* 10.29) inquires how several slaves should be punished for infiltrating the recruits. The slaves have taken the military oath but have not yet been entered in the rolls (*ita nondum distributi in numeros erant*). In *Epist.* 10.30 Trajan replies to Pliny that the slaves, who have not yet been assigned to individual units' rolls (*per numeros distributi sunt*), may be punished if they joined voluntarily, otherwise those who submitted them should be punished.

We may compare *Dig.* 29.1.42 (Ulpian, *Edict* 45), discussing when soldiers become legally able to use the military will. Ulpian defines *tirones* as those yet to be entered in the rolls (*debent etiam in numeros referri*), though they may have taken the oath and be traveling to their unit; until they are entered in the rolls, they cannot make a military will. The process is also illustrated by Pliny's agreement to obtain Suetonius a transfer if he has not yet been entered on the rolls of the unit he originally sought (*Epist.* 3.8, *neque enim adhuc nomen in numeros relatum est*).

In normal cases, the governor authorized a letter to be sent to the unit, listing and describing the *tirones probati* to be enrolled. *RMR* 87 = Campbell 9 is a copy of such a letter, from 103 AD, in which the prefect of Egypt, C. Minicius Italus, sends six approved recruits (*tirones sexs probatos a me*) to the commander of coh. III Ituraeorum at Oxyrhynchus to be entered in the lists (*in numeros referri*) on a given date. They are listed by name, age, and distinguishing marks (scars). The date on which they were entered on the lists became part of their permanent identification.

These actual rolls (*numeri* or *matriculae*) of personnel may be represented by the document *RMR* 1, a Dura roster of *Coh. XX Pal.* organized according to centuries and *turmae*, and many other rosters. Within these, individuals are listed by seniority (year of enlistment in consular dating). The individual's *nomina*, his unit (legion, cohort or *ala*), his century or *turma*, and his date of enlistment formed his military identification, though in practice some of these elements are often omitted: according to R. O. Fink, "the combination of two names only, century or *turma*, and date of enlistment served surprisingly well to distinguish one man from another." However, in some documents this formula is abbreviated: only a single or two names appear per individual. The Roman cognomen and Greek patronymic may be used to denote an individual. Even in what seem to be official rosters, the full *nomina*, filiation, tribe, city of origin, and consular date of enlistment appear, for example in *CPL* 109 = Daris 14. *Nomina*, *origo* and date appear in *CPL* 129 = Daris 16, but other rosters contain only *duo nomina* and not always the date. Abbreviation to a single name is frequent in small unit records and in Dura rosters after the *Constitutio Antoniniana* of 212 AD, which conferred the Roman citizenship and the nomen Aurelius on all new citizens.[7] However, rolls of personnel continued to be kept, now called *matriculae* by Vegetius (1.26.4; 2.5; 2.7).

4   Modernity of Bureaucracy

A modernizing view of documentation is common in modern scholars of the Roman army. Harris acknowledges that the Roman army was "almost modern in its love of documentation" and Stauner is impressed by the uniformity of the documentation from one branch of the service to another (not just legions, but also *auxilia* and vexillations) and from Northen Britain to Dura-Europos, over time from the first century AD to the mid-third. However, Stauner also emphasizes "documentary pragmatism," in which documents also reflect the local needs, situations, and competences of the personnel (e.g. documents in Greek).[8]

What does a modern bureaucracy look like? The organizing principles of a modern professional bureaucracy are highly abstract: individuals are known by identification numbers. Files are organized by alphabetization, Christian Era consecutive dates, or docket numbers, and documents are titled and numbered in such a way that the structure of the bureaucracy can be reconstructed from them.

Many of these features are poorly developed or absent in the Roman army. Our typology of Roman military documents remains relatively uncertain, as it would not in a modern system. *Ancient* titles or categories for specific types of military documents below *numeri* and *pridianum* (and possibly *renuntium*) are unknown. Fink remarks on the lack of "a very extensive or exact technical vocabulary to designate particular categories of military records." Probably most documents were not meant to be read by others than the military clerks who were familiar with them. *Breves* or "notes" are a general term for documents. Rufinus in *Against Jerome* 2.36 and Isidore of Seville, *Origines* 1.24.1 regard *brevicula* as rosters. It is possible that a day book was kept by the unit, called *acta diurna* or *biblion ephemeron* in Appian, *B. Civ.* 5.46.

Modern authors often assume that each soldier was assigned a personal dossier or file on enlistment, containing all documentation pertaining to his service (his initial *probatio*, his long-term posts, requests for and grants of *commeatus*, disciplinary episodes, sickness, transfers to other units, promotions, and discharge). A discrete dossier makes access to information and transfer of information to other authorities much easier. But no individual dossier has actually been found. It is likely that when information was needed or requested concerning an individual, the clerks consulted general documents and made extracts or copies, such as P. Oxy. 1022 appears to be: a copy of the original letter dispatching *probati* to a cohort, authenticated by the *cornicularius* (head clerk) of the cohort. Clerks also made various topical lists of individuals of a certain rank or of several individuals' missions over time – the latter showing the lack of individual dossiers, since several persons' records over time appear on one document. *P.Gen. Lat. I recto* iii–iv (*RMR* 10) is a list of several soldiers detached for outside duties over time, *ad frumentum, ad humos confodiendos, ad chartam confici[endam], ad moneta* ("to the granaries, to dredging harbors, to making papyrus, to the mint"). It was probably compiled from duty rosters and morning reports, as Fink suggests *ad loc.*

Various other lists of types of individuals survive, for example *RMR* 21, which is a list of legionary *principales*. These lists suggest that clerks were frequently requested to make extracts from the master rolls, which in turn were frequently updated. Numerous annotations (dashes and dots) in the margins of the Dura rosters suggest purposes of this sort that remain cryptic, though the most plausible explanation is that personnel's departures from and return to the base were marked.

Recommendation letters do not refer to dossiers or details of performance that would be found in personnel records; they stress the subject's moral qualities. This omission is not solely an effect of literary *litterae commendaticiae* such as in Pliny's *Letters*. Recommendation letters also survive on papyrus and tablets, but they show the same conventional moral generalizations and lack of technical detail.[9]

The "identification" of each soldier (*nomina*, filiation, tribe, *origo*, date of enlistment in consular dating) cannot be equated with a modern ID number, which is abstract. It is essentially an address, which could be used in abbreviated form to address a letter, and a formal description of status, found in honorific inscriptions and in epitaphs. This form of identification is socially embedded, hence it can be abbreviated. Furthermore, the names of the *centuriae* or *turmae* changed as centurions died, were promoted, transferred, or discharged, which must have required constant updating of identifications in documents. The consular dating system of the Roman period must have required either memorization or a list, though emperors often held the consulship repeatedly. In Egypt consecutive years of a reign appear.

Another un-modern feature is that military and civilian documents may be mingled. This is most apparent in the finds from the Vindolanda *praetorium*, in which drafts at least of the prefect Cerialis' letters and administrative documents are mingled with possible household accounts. Even when the context is clearly military, most military documents do not seem produced according to standard forms, though some chits are produced en masse to be filled in. Standard elements appear for instance in the morning reports at Dura, but the order of these in the document varies, suggesting the lack of a full-length exemplar to be copied. The *renuntia* at Vindolanda do suggest copying of an exemplar, but feature a grammatical error (*debunt* for *debent*) that is unlikely to have originated at Roman elite levels of command.

A relative lack of sophistication (both good and bad: professional systematization and jargon) may be due to the fact that most of these clerical grades in the principate were temporary posts held by men who might be promoted to tactical posts and centurion. Their identity remained "soldier" – though literacy, as a mark of elite status, was prized. This contrasts with later Roman bureaucratic professionalism, analyzed by C. M. Kelly: later Roman emperors voiced frustration with professional bureaucratic obfuscation.[10]

We do not know how long the military unit archives were maintained for discharged soldiers to refer to should they need to confirm status; the military *diplomata* records were archived separately at Rome. Records going back 16 years in the Praetorian Guard, 20 to 25 years in the legions and *auxilia*, and 28 in the fleet were a minimum necessity. *Diplomata*, inscribed on bronze tablets, were issued to discharged personnel (other than legionaries and *vigiles*) to confer and confirm privileges of Roman citizenship (if applicable), the right to marry, and citizenship for one's children (before 140 AD). They are published separately from military papyri, in *CIL* 16 and the series edited by Margaret M. Roxan, though some papyrus copies of diplomas are known.

General duty rosters, guard duty rosters, and reports

The most day-to-day task of the bureaucracy was to record the daily tasks assigned to personnel and to confirm their fulfillment of these. Various duty rosters survive. The most famous is *RMR* 9 of the Legio III Cyrenaica, from Egypt AD 90–96, dated by its use of *Domitianus* for October. This document assigns 36 (extant) individuals to routine duties over a period of ten days. It takes a highly compressed tabular form, combining the set of individuals (far left column), with the set of the ten days (top row) and inserting the assignments in the resulting grid. Elsewhere a clerk might draw up a separate document for each day as a list of the personnel's tasks on that day. The tabular form is attested only once elsewhere in O. Claud. 308. Tasks in *RMR* 9 include *ornatus Heli*, tending the gear of the centurion Helius; *ballio*, usually translated as "baths fatigue," feeding furnaces; various guard stations around the camp; *scoparius*, "sweeper"; and *ad stercus*, cleaning latrines or mucking horses' stalls. Many have no assignment, and there is no indication of how many hours were to be spent at any task.[11]

The Bu Njem ostraca duty rosters (one per day) show that individuals might be assigned to punishment (*ad virgas*, O. Bu Njem 2 or *ad carcere(m)*, O. Bu Njem 8). Sick individuals are also listed. These ostraca also show that certain individuals (probable *immunes*) were listed as not assigned to duties, while the rest were "checked off," *reliqui repungen(tur)*.

Guard duty rosters such as *RMR* 12, 15–17, 19 (from Dura) or O. Amst. 8. show that such a roster might be organized by the sites to which personnel were assigned. O. Amst. 8 features a list of watchmen (*scopelarii*) assigned to "upper" (*ano*) and "lower" (*kato*) posts, in a specific regular pattern. Clarysse and Sijpesteijn speculate whether these refer to levels of a watch tower or to geographical locations in this region of Egypt.

Confirmation that the day's tasks had been carried out or stations held also might require writing. Polybius 6.34–35 describes the procedure of passing the watchwords used to confirm that all guards were at their posts during the four watches of the night. Harris expresses skepticism that all guards needed to be literate to understand the process. Watchwords appear in the documents, both in guard documents and given with the day's orders in the Dura morning reports. At Vindolanda, a specific type of document, highly formulaic, attested that orders had been fulfilled. These tablets are called *renuntia* by modern scholars from the formula *renuntium [unit] omnes ad loca qui debunt et impedimenta renuntiarunt optiones et curatores detulit [name] optio [centuriae]*, surviving in full as Tab. Vindol. 3.574.

Morning reports

Fink emphasizes the importance of general reports of the collective units to the higher-order command of the army: "the organization exists so that the commanding general will not have to deal entirely with single persons. In order to secure this result, the records of persons must be digested into records of legions, cohorts, and *alae* which will enable the responsible authorities to manipulate large numbers of men as units." The unit reports, especially the daily morning reports at Dura (*RMR* 47–57) and the at least once-yearly *pridiana*, appear somewhat more formal.

The morning reports feature:

date (day and month)
total number of all personnel
separate statements of numbers of centurions and sub-officers, number of *dromedarii*
    and their officers, number of *equites* and their decurions
full official name of unit, its commander
daily watchword
departures of personnel
return of personnel
announcement of orders of the day and other items
oath of obedience
names and ranks of personnel performing *excubatio ad signa* (ritual guarding of the
    standards)

The morning report represents a higher level of organization. Daily duties on base, such as those in *RMR* 9, were not listed in the Dura morning reports or *acta diurna* (Marichal, *ChLA* 7 p. 29). Longer-term missions may be cited, as are ritual duties, such as the *excubatio ad signa* and *supplicationes*. The detail of the duty roster will have been understood in *ad omnem tesseram parati erimus* ("we are ready for all orders"). This omission represents not just hierarchical scaling of detail, a modern concern, but Roman ideas of propriety, as the morning report (e.g. *RMR* 47) is rather formal, representing a formal ceremony, the military version of *salutatio* (as Marichal notes). To list duties such as *ad stercus* would be unfitting. The morning reports thus have a ritual or expressive as well as instrumental function.[12]

5   Interim Reports and *Pridiana* of Units

The *pridianum*, a yearly strength report showing the total number, accessions, and losses of personnel, is the only document the specific formal title of which is attested. The *pridianum* also represents a higher level of organization and scaling of detail, but the degree of detail varies somewhat from one extant example to another.

The discussion of the *pridianum* has suffered most from the fragmentary state of the documents – demonstrating the recursive nature of papyrology, in which missing portions of stereotyped documents can be restored from extant parts of similar documents – and from the desire of modern authors for systematization. It would be agreeable to imagine that the *pridianum* was issued at the same time all over the empire, and that it was uniform in format, but this does not appear to be the case. The *pridianum* was typically issued once a year, on December 31, abbreviated from *pridie Kalendas Ianuarias*, but in Egypt a *pridianum*-type document appeared twice yearly, once on December 31 and once on August 30, since the Egyptian administrative year traditionally began on August 29.[13]

Summary of structure of ideal pridianum

Not every surviving document shows all of these categories.

Pridianum
Name and titles of unit
Date (day, month and year)
Location of unit headquarters and date of its arrival there
Commander full *nomina*, filiation, tribe and *origo*; title; date of his *militia* and name
   of his predecessor

Total number of personnel (*summa m(ilitum) perf(ecta)*)
Numbers of centurions/decurions, cavalry and infantry

Accessions to personnel since last report
Returns
Promotions and transfers in
Recruits *probati* by the governor
Gross accessions (*summa accesserunt*)
Net strength (*reliqui numero puro*)

Losses
Deaths
Discharges of *causarii*
Transfers out
Gross losses (*summa decesserunt*)
Net strength (*reliqui numero puro*)

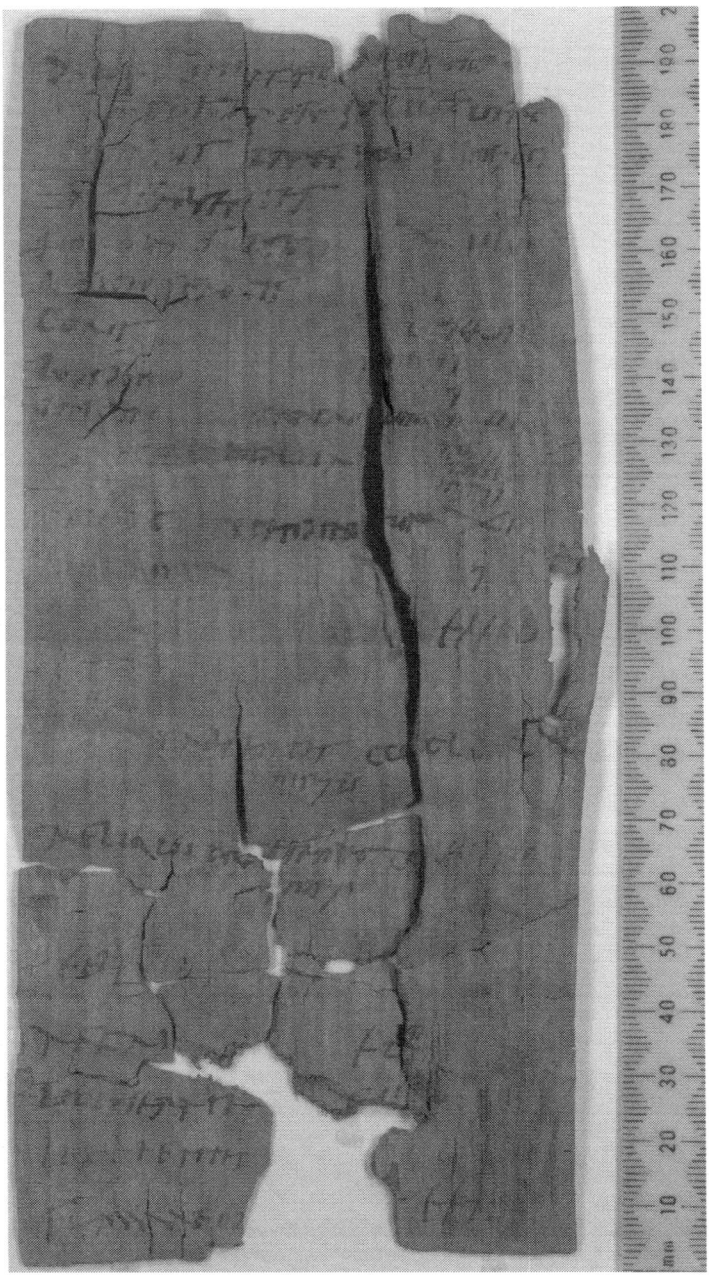

Plate 16.1   Strength report of Coh. I Tungrorum at Vindolanda near Hadrian's Wall in Britain, c. 92–97 AD. Similar to pridiana (Tab. Vind. 2.154). Reproduced by permission of The British Museum and the Centre for the Study of Ancient Documents, University of Oxford

The four *pridiana* or *pridianum*-type documents that are extant are not uniform; the degree of detail varies. *ChLA* 501 is not convenient for comparison, as only the top block survives (stating *pridianum detulit*, possibly an interim report). In *RMR* 63, though the factual detail about causes of losses and absences is extensive, no names of individuals are given, only numbers, below the rank of the commanding officer. In *RMR* 64 officers, new recruits (*tirones probati*), and transfers are listed by name and century, but the section that would list losses and absences is not preserved. P. Brooklyn 24 preserves details of the causes of accessions and losses, but the names of individuals are not given.

Thus the scaling of information is not followed strictly. The compilers of some *pridiana* or strength reports may have been requested to provide a greater amount of detail (*RMR* 63 lists deaths by drowning, brigands, and combat, and gives details of absent personnel's missions) for specific circumstances. *RMR* 63 (from Stobi c. 106 AD; how it came to Egypt is unclear) may have been drawn up in connection with Trajan's Dacian wars.

Stauner draws attention to the formal and highly legible layout of the *pridianum*: headings may be written in capitals as opposed to cursive, and more words are spelled out in full than is usual in other documents. Information is grouped into distinct blocks, and number totals are clearly visible. Someone unfamiliar with the unit would be able to read the document at a glance. Though Stauner does not speculate on the intended readers, the governor (when not also the legate of the legion) is a possible candidate, or even the emperor, at least ideally. Suetonius, *Aug.* 101.6 (cf. Cassius Dio 56.33) reports that Augustus on his death left a statement of how many troops were stationed in different parts of the empire, *quantum militibus sub signis ubique esset. HA, Sev. Alex.* 21.6 claims that

> [Alexander Severus] knew all about his soldiers, wherever he might be; even in his bedchamber he had records containing the number of the troops and the length of each man's service (*breves et numerum et tempora militantum continentes*), and when he was alone he constantly went over their accounts (*rationes*), their rosters (*numerum*), their several ranks, and their pay, in order that he might be thoroughly familiar with every detail.

But the impression from the actual documents is that only the *pridianum* was intended to be read by superiors not familiar with the daily administration of the unit. Alexander Severus, an emperor idealized by the *Historia Augusta*, cannot be regarded as usual, whereas *quantum militibus sub signis ubique esset* is a fair description of the level of information that the *pridiana* comprised.

Uncertainty remains as to whether certain strength reports are *pridiana*, and it is possible that *pridiana* were compiled from interim reports (e.g. Tab. Vindol. 2.154 or *RMR* 58). To state that interim reports were issued at the end of every month (Fink's category "Monthly Summaries," *RMR* 58 and 59) is too positive. Interim reports may have been requested and issued on an ad hoc basis, perhaps in preparation for or as a result of a campaign. Tab. Vindol. 2.154 (Campbell 182), issued on May 18, not at the end of the month, may be one of these.[14]

6 *Immunes* and Their Status

Certain *milites* were *immunes*, exempted from regular daily duties because of their occupational specialties as artisans, engineers, or clerks. Tarruntienus Paternus in *Dig.* 50.6.7 offers a long, though by no means exhaustive, list of specialties. The *librarii*, and thus presumably the other clerks, are among the *immunes*, usually regarded as "exempted from fatigues." Too much has been made of Julius Apollinarius the *librarius*' boast that "as a *principalis* [junior officer] I walk about doing nothing" (P. Mich. 8.465) and that "while others have been breaking stones all day . . . up until today I have suffered none of this" (P. Mich. 8.466, March 26, 107 AD). He was spared from cutting stones in the desert heat of Bostra in the new *provincia Arabia*. But we cannot assume that the *Schreibsoldaten*, as Stauner terms them, were desk-bound bureaucrats, their "acquaintance with drill or with the enemy . . . pleasantly remote," as MacMullen claims in *Soldier and Civilian*. This claim is inaccurate for "clerks" of the first two centuries AD. They were "soldiers first of all" and their promotions in the principate show that they might be expected to go on to combat duties: "the 'rule' seems to have been to try to ensure that prospective centurions were trained in both sides of army life, the military and the administrative," according to David J. Breeze. *Librarii* and other clerks might be promoted to *optio*, *signifer*, and centurion, which involved tactical duties in combat, so probably though they were exempted from the heavier and degrading fatigues, they received combat training and were expected to keep fit. In the early third century, the clerical grades begin to be promoted on a separate track, not including tactical posts or centurion.[15]

A great deal of travel (on foot or riding) was expected of "administrative" personnel, and it might involve danger, being attacked by "bandits" or insurgents. Soldiers were allowed and indeed required – Tacitus, *Ann.* 11.18 – to be armed. We suppose that this kind of travel maintained the military *habitus* (armed appearance and fitness) of the administrative personnel.

The social and economic status of the clerks seems to be relatively high, both before their enlistment and inside the army. They were recruited from the literate class, as both Vegetius, *Epit.* 2.19 and the letters of Julius Apollinarius show. He and his family, and some other soldiers who appear in the papyri letters (e.g. Apion in *BGU* 423, a recruit to the fleet) seem to belong to the Greco-Egyptian "middle class" which secured at least an elementary education (*grammatikê*) for their sons. Apion writes to his father Epimachus that he hopes for promotion because of his education, which his father encouraged.

Furthermore, at Lambaesis c. 198–211, the clerical grades of the Legio III Augusta formed a *collegium* or voluntary association (*ILS* 9100 = Stauner no. 499) which required new members to contribute 1,000 denarii to a common sum from which bounties of 800 denarii were paid to honorably discharged members, in addition to official imperial discharge *praemia*. This was no small sum because ordinary legionaries between 197–211 may have received 450 denarii a year and *principales* who were *sesquiplicarii* (including some of the clerks) 675, *duplicarii* 900. The soldier promoted to *librarius* or other clerical grade after some years of legionary service could have saved the money. However, a literate recruit promoted at once to *librarius* at Lambaesis would need family wealth or a loan, which he no doubt expected to repay from the bribery that is sometimes attested.

This *collegium* inscription is our most detailed single testimony as to the ranking of the clerical grades: the *cornicularius* (chief clerk) headed the department (*officium*), followed by the *actarius*, then by 22 *librarii* and 21 *exacti*. The organization of the clerical grades is surveyed by Stauner. He de-emphasizes the fact that many of these were intermediate and temporary posts during the principate, which explains something of both the relative lack of system and the relative lack of rhetoric and jargon: the "clerk" remained relatively unprofessionalized, since he would hopefully be promoted to other positions. This flexibility makes it hard to reconstruct the extent of bureaucracy that was assigned to sub-units, though tribunes and *praefecti castrorum* seem to have been given *cornicularii* and a few *librarii*. At Gholaia, a *librarius* was for a time in charge of the entire detachment and probably had to prepare all documents. It has been suggested that each century had its *librarius*, but other personnel, *optiones* and *signiferi*, whose duties were partially tactical, routinely produced documents as well.

It is unlikely that any one clerical grade prepared only one type of document (e.g. only morning reports) or level of comprehensiveness (only *pridiana*). The *commentariensis* may have written up daily proceedings, an *acta diurna* or *ephemeris*. *Actuarii* in the later empire were associated with fiscal administration and delivered pay or rations, and as a result were denounced as avaricious and dishonest, see for example Aurelius Victor, *Caes.* 33.13. But *librarius* is an unspecialized term; the specialties in *Dig.* 50.6.7 (Paternus) are not official titles. Stauner's suggestion that *exacti* redacted the daily documents produced by the *librarii* into periodical documents may be too tidy. *Exceptores* or *notarii* specialized in taking shorthand. However, clerks were frequently dispatched on military or civilian assignments that required a general competence.[16]

7 *Commeatus*[17]

Roman elite writers recommended that *commeatus* or furlough be difficult to obtain. Too many men on leave was a sign of poor discipline (e.g. Sallust, *Jug.* 44.5), whereas a good commander restricted *commeatus* (e.g. Suetonius, *Aug.* 24.1; *HA*, *Hadr.* 10.3). Vegetius 2.19 says,

> *quando quis commeatum acceperit vel quot dierum, adnotatur in brevibus. Tunc etiam difficile commeatus dabitur nisi causis iustissimis adprobatis.*

> It used to be recorded in the records whenever someone received furlough and for how many days. Then *commeatus* was also given sparingly and only for the most justified reasons.

This is counseled also by *Dig.* 49.16.12.1 (Macer, citing Paternus). Tacitus, *Hist.* 1.46 sketches a dismal picture of soldiers' bribery of centurions in order to obtain *commeatus*. As a result the soldiers resorted to extra-military and extra-legal sources of income, and manpower was depleted.

> A fourth of the troops were scattered on leave or loitering in the very camps, for which they paid bribes to their centurions; nor was there any limit to the extent or the type of money-grubbing they resorted to, as they obtained the price of their furloughs through brigandage, pillage or servile tasks.

Tacitus claims that the resulting impoverishment of the soldiers made them politically unreliable, likely to support usurpers (Livy 43.14.7 claims that some commanders granted leave to ingratiate themselves, *per ambitionem*). Tacitus 1.46 adds that in 69 Otho agreed to pay the centurions the bribe which had become customary. However, that bribery persisted is implied by *HA Hadr.* 10.3 in which Hadrian represses the obtaining of *commeatus* by "unjust means," *iniuste*. In the later empire emperors ruled that no officer below a certain rank should grant *commeatus* (*Cod. Theod.* 7.12.1 Constantine, 323 AD and *CTh* 7.1.2 Constantius) or grant *commeatus* to more than 30 men at a time (*Cod. Just.* 12.37.16.2 Anastasius).

The exaction of a bribe for *commeatus* or exemption from *munera* is also alluded to at Tacitus, *Ann.* 1.17. In the documentary sources a fee is possibly attested in P. Mich. III 203. Soldiers speak of the difficulty of obtaining *commeatus*, e.g. Julius Apollinarius promises to visit his parents "directly if the governor should give me *commeatus*" in P. Mich. 8.466. In P. Oxy. 14.1666 = *Sel. Pap.* 1.149, from the third century AD, a father writes to his brother that he and his son, a legionary transferred to a cohort, wanted to visit him but the boy was not granted sufficient *commeatus* by the prefect. The *Sortes Astrampsychi* (P. Oxy. 1477) are a numerological oracle in Greek from the turn of the third century AD, in which questions numbered 12 to 102, usually about life events, were each matched with ten possible answers. Question 78 was "am I to obtain furlough?" Nine answers are preserved for it; of these five are positive, three negative, and one states "you will obtain the money slowly." If the lost answer was negative, getting *commeatus* would seem a fifty-fifty probability, but bribery for *commeatus* may still have been the rule.

The Vindolanda tablets show that *commeatus* was there requested in a formal and formulaic petition (Tab. Vindol. 2.166–177, esp. 167–169, 171–172, from 97/102–3 AD), employing the formula *rogo, domine, dignum me habeas cui des commeatum*: "I beseech, my lord, that you hold me a worthy person to whom to grant leave." *Domine* appears to be a formal term of address to superiors in the army (and to superiors in general, used by Pliny to the emperor Trajan in Pliny, *Epist.* book 10). An application for furlough is also found in *ChLA* 11.467, a petition that subserviently addresses the superior as *humanitas tua*.

Once *commeatus* was granted, the individuals on leave (like those absent on expeditions or work missions) were probably entered in the morning reports and other lists, and in Egypt a passport or chit was given to the soldier on leave, e.g. O. Florida 1: "You have ten day's *commeatus*, Ammonas; you have ten days' *commeatus* and two days to return." Oddly enough the specific dates are not given on this ostracon and perhaps it was not used. Ten days' leave is specified in *ChLA* 11.467 (from 152 AD) and one day in *SB* 6.9272.

The specification of the dates of *commeatus* will have been used to determine when absence without leave became actionable. The jurists in the *Digest* (*Dig.* 49.16) do

Plate 16.2 Fragment of petition for leave (Tab. Vind. 2.168). Reproduced by permission of The British Museum and the Centre for the Study of Ancient Documents, University of Oxford

not state a specific length of time, but take into account individual circumstances, both hardships of the journey and personal circumstances (*Dig.* 49.16.3.7; 3.12; 4.15; 5.5; 14.pr). A degree of bureaucratic consciousness appears in Paul (*Dig.* 49.16.14.pr) who rules that in proving that he was unavoidably delayed, the soldier should show the duration of his journey, when he set out, and how many days he was late, proving that he not set out so late that he could not be expected to arrive on time.

From other sources, causes of delay might include travel in bad weather (in the Vindolanda tablets Octavius complains about the state of the roads, *dum viae male sunt*, Tab. Vindol. 2.343), travel in dangerous parts of the empire (mountainous areas were likely to be brigand-infested; on the way to Saldae the legionary architect Nonius Datus was attacked by bandits, *CIL* 8.2728 = Campbell 204), and travel by sea (the apostle Paul's ship was stranded at Malta for three months, Acts 28:11). A commander who jumped to conclusions concerning a soldier's failure to return promptly from *commeatus* features in a moral tract on the evils of anger (Seneca, *ira* 1.18.3–5).

These are reasons, besides corruption and the ideal of *disciplina*, why *commeatus* was not to be granted too often: the inefficiency of transport and communications in the empire made it too easy for soldiers to overstay their leave. The system may already have been strained by soldiers' extensive travel on military duties. Fragmentary documents have been discovered that seem to address the problem of excessive *commeatus* and soldiers away from the standards (*ChLA* 10.500; possibly P. Dura 55 = *RMR* 90).

8   Literacy and Literate Culture

In the late republic, some remarkable efforts seem to have been made to propagandize Roman civil war armies with written material, starting with Caesar and Nasica in the African War (Cassius Dio 43.5; [Caesar] *B. Afr.* 32). Octavian distributed *biblia* to Antony's soldiers in 44 (Appian, *B. Civ.* 3.7.44). The Caesarians fired leaflets into Brutus' camp before the second battle of Philippi (Cassius Dio 47.48.1). Antony had leaflets attached to arrows and fired into Octavian's camp outside Alexandria in 30, and Octavian read them to the soldiers (Cassius Dio 51.10.2–3). These measures do not prove that all soldiers could read. Presumably literate comrades read aloud to the illiterate. The *Perusinae glandes* from the same period, lead sling-bullets inscribed with obscene insults in Latin directed at the commanders, may have been inscribed by the soldiers themselves. Harris suggests that "legionary soldiers must very commonly have been fully literate or semi-literate," but expresses greater doubts about the *auxilia*, in which many men, especially in the West, must have been illiterate. In P. Hamb. 39, a collection of receipts for hay money written by cavalry auxiliaries in Egypt in 179 AD, two-thirds of the cavalrymen cannot write for themselves (in Greek, no doubt their native language). The comrades who were literate wrote for those who were illiterate or slow writers, so that the latter could at least participate in the use of documents and thus in a literate culture.

However, the military man who sought to rise in the army needed to be literate and even to acquire culture. In the principate, there is no instance of an illiterate military clerk like the village secretary (*komogrammateus*) Petaus in P. Petaus 121, who could barely write the formula he used to subscribe documents; he was assisted by his brother Theon and by scribes. As a military man ascended the ranks, he needed to be familiar with elite literate and literary culture, at least in the polite phrasing of administrative letters to peers and superiors (e.g. the "letter of Cerialis," Tab.Vindol. 2.225), since a persistent prejudice among the senatorial and equestrian aristocracy was that military men were uncultured. The *litterae commendaticiae* of *beneficiarius* Aurelius Archelaus to Julius Domitius, tribune of the legion, concerning his friend Theon (P. Oxy. 32 = *Sel. Pap.* 1.122) strives for a literary effect.[18]

9 Romanization

The modern impression that Latin was the official and exclusive language of the Roman army is unrealistic, as J. N. Adams's work on bilingualism in the Roman Empire shows. In the Hellenized east, everyone above a minimum social level spoke Greek. Soldiers' names are almost always Roman or Greek (Hellenized eastern names appear), and in the East, their private letters are usually in Greek. It is likely that personnel also spoke Greek (or possibly other native languages in ethnic units) in the Roman army in the East, except for some Latin words or phrases in formal, bureaucratic, or ritual contexts. In the northwest, the native languages were not competitive with Latin in this way. Furthermore, many soldiers of eastern origin were scarcely literate in Greek; they could not be expected to write Latin.

In Egypt, some of the documents of small units are written in Greek or in mixtures of Greek and Latin. In O. Amst. 8, col. 4 the guards are numbered with Latin ordinal numbers in Greek script (*prima, sekonda, tertia, korta* = *quarta*) and with Latin numerals I, II, III, IV, though the rest of the document is in Greek. In O. Claud. 2.320 the numerals assigning the order of duties to individuals are Roman

(I, III, IIII, etc.) but the date is given in Greek form. In the Mons Claudianus ostraka, which are mostly in Greek, even a series of Latin passwords are written in Greek letters: *signen Martis* (O. Claud. 320), *Phortouna* (321), *Ouiktori* (322), *Mineroua* (323), *Pake* (328), *Pietatis* (329), *Saloutis eimperat(oris)* (331). Adams concludes that "there was no rigid adherence to a policy of using Latin for public documentation in the Roman army." Allowing low-status clerks to write in Greek or Greek script suggests, Adams says, "low rates of literacy and the shortage of learned scribes capable of doing a job properly," at least at small posts in the East.[19]

Adams suggests that Latin was "the language of power," used in the Hellenophone milieu to stress in limited contexts the authority and rituals of the Roman army. Military titles of units and individuals appear in Latin. Watchwords were given in Latin, as seen above for Mons Claudianus, and at Dura Latin *signa* also appear in the morning reports, for example *RMR* 47 line 2, *Mercuris*; *RMR* 50, *Securitatis*. Dates are in Latin, as probably were oaths such as the annual *sacramentum* or the daily oath of obedience (*quod imperatum fuerit faciemus et ad omnem tesseram parati erimus*). Tactical commands may have been given in Latin, going by Maurice's *Strategikon*, a seventh-century Byzantine tactical manual (12.14).

Latin was also the language of the more formal documents of the army. Clerks recruited as literate in Greek (there is no sign that Julius Apollinarius of P. Mich. 8.465–66 knows Latin) will have learned to write documentary formulae in Latin. Soldiers who were Roman citizens also had to employ legal documents in Latin for their private affairs. The military *diplomata* were written in Latin (though Greek translations on papyrus exist). Latin was also the language of epigraphy, a declaration of institutional affiliation and of social status. Military Latin documents and epigraphy show largely correct spelling and grammar. These are of course highly formulaic Latin, suppressing everyday speech patterns. Centurions and clerks represent a Latin-literate elite. That Latin was consciously a "language of power" is suggested by the legionary's addressing the gardener in Latin in Apuleius, *Met.* 9.39, though the scene is set in a Greek-speaking milieu. The soldier's employing the language of authority was a statement of power, a (from Lucius the ass's viewpoint) *superbo ac adrogante sermone* ("with arrogant and high-handed speech"), even if a somewhat useless one since his addressee might not know it.[20]

In conclusion, the Roman military bureaucracy shows a high degree of flexibility and attests the seeds of the bureaucratic mentality: that the commander should have knowledge and control over his forces; that efficiency and fair treatment are promoted by the keeping of records; that individuals can verify their status and secure justice by referring to the archives (as in *CPL* 102). A greater degree of rationalization might have become too rigid given the high mobility of administrative personnel.

NOTES

1 I thank Alan K. Bowman for reading this chapter prior to publication. Literacy and power: Bowman 1994a, at 119; see also Bowman and Woolf 1994, introduction 1–16. Uniformity and documentary culture: Stauner 2004, 210–15.

2   On these particular sites' documents, see also Bowman 1994a and b (rev. edn. 1998);
    Rebuffat 2000; Maxfield 2003.

3   On writing materials in social context, Bagnall 1995, 9–16; Cribiore 2001, 147–59. Price:
    Harris 1989, 195.

4   Bowman 1998, 15; cf. Bowman 1994a, 113.

5   Recruitment: Gilliam 1957, 207–16 = 1986, 163–72; Watson 1969, 37–44; Watson 1974,
    493–507 at 496; Davies 1989, 3–30; Stauner 2004, 36–9. Bribery possibly required:
    Alston 1995, 136.

6   Slaves banned from military service: *Dig.* 49.16.11 Marcian. Criminals: *Dig.*
    49.16.4.1–7. Deserters: *Dig.* 49.16.4.9 Arrius Menander. Status in dispute: *Dig.* 49.16.8
    Ulpian. Lack of documents: Gardner 1986.

7   Identification: Gilliam 1957, 165; Stauner 2004, 36; Fink 1971, 5 (quoted). Abbreviation
    of onomastic formula: Bagnall 1976, 12ff.

8   Harris 1989, 217. Posner 1972, 4–5 (on the Roman army, 201–3) expresses caution.
    "Documentary pragmatism," Stauner 2004, 207, 208.

9   Lack of titles: Fink 1971, 2; Stauner 2004, 18–19. Dossier assumed: Davies 1989, 26;
    Stauner 2004, 61: "eine Akte über jeden Soldaten mit allen personal- und dienstrele-
    vanten Informationen."

10 Lack of an exemplar: Fink 1971, 180. *Debunt* for *debent* in *T. Vindol. renuntium* formula:
    Adams 1995, 86–134 at 131. Clerks as soldiers: see section on *immunes* in this chapter.
    Later empire: Kelly 1994, 161–76. On military diplomas, Eck and Wolff 1986; Phang
    2001, chapter 2; Wilkes 2003.

11 O. Claud. 308 discussed by Stauner 2004, 26–8. On *RMR* 9; Davies 1974, 299–338
    = 1989, 48–51; Watson 1974, 500–2.

12 *Renuntium*: Bowman 1998, 38–9. "The organization exists": Fink 1971, 179. Morning
    report: Stauner 2004, 73ff; Watson 1974, 500 suggests that the *pridiana* were compiled
    from them. Formal or "high" genres of Latin literature exclude "sordid" terms. Reporting
    sick, deceased, etc. would not fit the ceremonial and morale-raising military *salutatio*.
    New accessions (*tirones probati*) might be listed, inserted from the governor's letter such
    as *RMR* 87.

13 *ChLA* XI 501 (48–52 AD), first part of a *pridianum detulit*. *RMR* 63 = Hunt 1925,
    265–72 = *CPL* 112 = Fink 1958, 102–116 = Gilliam 1962, 747–56 = 1986, 263–72 =
    ChLA 3.219. *Pridianum* of coh. I Hispanorum veterana at Stobi in 105/6. *Pridianum*
    appears in l.24. *RMR* 64 = *BGU* 2.696 = *Sel. Pap.* 2.401 = *CPL* 118 = Fink 1942, 61–3
    = Lewis and Reinhold 1990, 148 p. 478–9 (trans.). *Pridianum* of coh. I Augusta praet-
    oria Lusitanorum equitata at Contrapollonospolis Maior in 156. *Pridianum* appears in
    first line.
        P. Brooklyn 24 (215 AD) = Thomas and Davies 1977, 50–61 = Lewis and Reinhold
    1990, 148 p. 475–6 (trans.). Document of a Cohors quingenaria equitata in Egypt. On
    the dates of issue of *pridiana*, Stauner 2004, 108–10.

14 Bowman and Thomas 1991, 62–73; Bowman and Thomas 1994, 32–5.

15 *Immunes*: Watson 1965, 45–55; cf. O. Bu Njem duty rosters discussed above.
    Schreibsoldaten, Stauner 2004, 117, vs. MacMullen 1963, 72; Breeze 1974, 245–92, quote,
    270, separate track, 290. That *immunes* were still combat soldiers is emphasized also by
    Speidel 2001, 59.

16 Social and economic status of recruits: Cribiore 2001, 245–6; Stauner 2004, 116–17
    and 427; organization of clerical grades, Harris 1989, 218; Stauner 2004, 137, 140–1,
    149–52.

17   *Commeatus*: Bagnall 1976, introd. and O. Florida 1; Speidel 1985, 283–93; Bowman
      1998, 39–40, 107–8; Wesch-Klein 2000. Wesch-Klein emphasizes the later empire's laws,
      463–5. The *Sortes Astrampsychi*: Bagnall 1976, 20 n.40; Browne 1974.
18   Propaganda efforts: Harris 1989, 253 n.413. *Glandes*: Hallett 1977, 151–71. Legionaries
      vs auxiliaries: Harris 1989, 254; sub-literate use of documents, also Bowman 1991, 119–31,
      shallow literacy, 126; also by Hopkins 1991, 138. Petaus: Cribiore 2001, 172. Shorthand
      is found in some Vindolanda tablets, Tab. Vindol. 2, 122–6.
19   "Official language": Adams 2003, 599. O. Amst. 8 is discussed by Clarysse and Sijpesteijn
      1988, 71–96; Mons Claudianus by Adams 2003, 394–5. "No rigid adherence": Adams
      2003, 602; "low rates," 634.
20   Latin-using families in Roman Egypt are rare, the best known case Claudius Terentianus
      the young recruit and his "father" Claudius Tiberianus in P. Mich. VIII 467–472, discussed
      by Adams 2003, 593–4, who suggests that Tiberianus was an Italian veteran, as Terentianus'
      Latin is nonstandard and shows Greek influences. Language of power: Adams 2003, 299,
      406. Documents and legal instruments: Adams 2003, 562–3. Correctness: Adams 1999
      and 1995. Apuleius: Adams 2003, 383, cf. 608.

BIBLIOGRAPHY

Adams, J. N. 1995. "The language of the Vindolanda writing-tablets: An interim report,"
    JRS 85: 86–134.
—— 1999. "The poets of Bu Njem: Language, culture, and the centurionate," *JRS* 89: 109–34.
—— 2003. *Bilingualism and the Latin Language*. Cambridge.
Alföldy, G., B. Dobson, and W. Eck. 2000. *Kaiser, Heer, und Gesellschaft in der römischen
    Kaiserzeit: Gedenkschrift für Eric Birley*. Stuttgart.
Alston, R. 1995. *Soldier and Society in Roman Egypt*. New York.
Bagnall, R. S. 1976. *The Florida Ostraka (O. Florida): Documents from the Roman Army in
    Upper Egypt*. Durham, NC.
—— 1995. *Reading Papyri, Writing Ancient History*. London.
—— and D. Rathbone. 2005. *Checklist of Editions of Greek, Latin, Demotic, and Coptic Papyri,
    Ostraca and Tablets*, at http://scriptorium.lib.duke.edu/papyrus/texts/clist.html
Bowman, A. K. 1991. "Literacy in the Roman empire: Mass and mode," in J. H. Humphrey
    (ed.), *Literacy in the Roman World*. Ann Arbor, MI, 119–31.
—— 1994a. "The Roman imperial army: Letters and literacy on the northern frontier," in
    Bowman and Woolf, 109–25.
—— 1994b. *Life and Letters on the Roman Frontier: Vindolanda and Its People*. New York
    (rev. edn. 1998).
——, and J. D. Thomas. 1991. "A military strength report from Vindolanda," *JRS* 81: 62–73.
——, and ——. 1994. *The Vindolanda Writing-Tablets* II. London.
——, and G. Woolf (eds.). 1994. *Literacy and Power in the Ancient World*. Cambridge.
Breeze, D. J. 1974. "The organisation of the career structure of the *immunes* and *principales*
    of the Roman army," *BJ* 174: 245–92.
Browne, G. M. 1974. *The Papyri of the Sortes Astrampsychi*. Meisenheim am Glan.
Campbell, B. 1994. *The Roman Army, 31 BC–AD 337: A Sourcebook*. London.
Clarysse, W., and P. J. Sijpesteijn. 1988. "A military roster on a vase in Amsterdam," *AncSoc*
    19: 71–96.

Cribiore, R. 2001. *Gymnastics of the Mind: Greek Education in Hellenistic and Roman Egypt.* Princeton.

Davies, R. W. 1969. "Joining the Roman army," *BJ* 169: 208–32 = 1989b, 3–30.

—— 1974. "The daily life of the Roman soldier under the Principate," *ANRW* 2.1, 299–338 = 1989, 33–70.

—— 1989. *Service in the Roman Army.* New York.

Eck, W., and H. Wolff (eds.). 1986. *Heer und Integrationspolitik: Die römischen Militärdiplome als historische Quelle.* Cologne.

Fink, R. O. 1942. "Mommsen's Pridianum," *AJP* 63: 61–3.

—— 1958. "Hunt's *Pridianum*: British Museum papyrus 2851," *JRS* 48: 102–16.

—— 1971. *Roman Military Records on Papyrus.* Cleveland, OH.

Gardner, J. F. 1986. "Proofs of status in the Roman world," *BICS* 33: 1–14.

Gilliam, J. F. 1957. "Enrollment in the Roman imperial army," *Eos* 48: 207–16 = 1986, 163–72.

—— 1962. "The Moesian 'pridianum,'" *Hommages à Albert Grenier.* Brussels, 747–56 = 1986, 263–72.

—— 1986. *Roman Army Papers.* Amsterdam.

Hallett, J. P. 1977. "*Perusinae glandes* and the changing image of Augustus," *AJAH* 2: 151–71.

Harris, W. V. 1989. *Ancient Literacy.* Cambridge, MA.

Hopkins, K. 1991. "Conquest by book," in J. H. Humphrey (ed.), *Literacy in the Roman World.* Ann Arbor, 133–58.

Hunt, A. S. 1925. "Register of a cohort in Moesia," H. I. Bell (ed.), *Raccolta di scriti in onore di Giacomo Lumbroso.* Milan, 265–72.

Kelly, C. M. 1994. "Later Roman bureaucracy: Going through the files," in Bowman and Woolf, 161–76.

Lewis, N., and M. Reinhold. 1990. *Roman Civilization: Selected Readings*, vol. II, *The Empire.* New York.

MacMullen, R. 1963. *Soldier and Civilian in the Later Roman Empire.* Cambridge, MA.

Maxfield, V. 2003. "Ostraca and the Roman army in the Eastern Desert," in J. J. Wilkes (ed.), *Documenting the Roman Army: Essays in Honour of Margaret Roxan.* London, 153–74.

Phang, S. 2001. *The Marriage of Roman Soldiers, 13 BC–AD 235: Law and Family in the Imperial Army.* Leiden.

Posner, E. 1972. *Archives in the Ancient World.* Cambridge, MA.

Rebuffat, R. 2000. "L'armée romaine à Gholaia," in Alföldy, Dobson, and Eck, 227–59.

Speidel, M. A. 2001. "Specialisation and promotion in the Roman imperial army," in L. de Blois, *Administration, Prosopography, and Appointment Policies in the Roman Empire.* Amsterdam, 50–61.

Speidel, M. P. 1985. "Furlough in the Roman army," *YCS* 28 (1985), 283–93.

Stauner, K. 2004. *Das offizielle Schriftwesen des römischen Heeres von Augustus bis Gallienus (27 v.Chr.–268 n.Chr.).* Bonn.

Thomas, J. D., and R. W. Davies. 1977. "A new military strength report on papyrus," *JRS* 67: 50–61.

Watson, G. R. 1965. "Immunis librarius," in M. G. Jarrett and B. Dobson (eds.), *Britain and Rome: Essays Presented to Eric Birley.* Kendal, 45–55.

—— 1969. *The Roman Soldier.* Ithaca, NY.

—— 1974. "Documentation in the Roman army," *ANRW* 2.1, 493–507.

Wesch-Klein, G. 2000. "*Commeatus id est tempus, quo ire, redire quis possit*: Zur Gewährung von Urlaub im römischen Heer," in Alföldy, Dobson, and Eck, 459–71.

Wilkes, J. J. (ed.). 2003. *Documenting the Roman Army: Essays in Honour of Margaret Roxan.* London, 153–74.

FURTHER READING

A list of editions of papyri and ostraca is found in Bagnall et al. 2004. Collections in English: Campbell 1994; Lewis and Reinhold 1990. Online Databases: Vindolanda Tablets Online, featuring Tab. Vindol. 118–573, is maintained at Oxford: http://vindolanda.csad.ox.ac.uk/. This site features scanned images of tablets, transcriptions, translations, commentary, and notes, as well as search functions, indexes, and bibliography. The editors view the database as the definitive version of Tab. Vindol. For papyri and ostraca in Latin and Greek, the Duke Data Bank of Documentary Papyri is accessed through the Perseus Project website: http://www.perseus.tufts.edu. O. Bu Njem, O. Claud., O. Florida, *BGU*, P. Mich., and P. Brook are accessible. Translation, commentary, and images are not included in most DDBDP documents. APIS, or Advanced Papyrological Information System, links the DDBDP and other on-line collections at Columbia, Princeton, Yale, the University of California at Berkeley, the University of Chicago, the University of Michigan at Ann Arbor, the University of Toronto, and others. It is located at: http://www.columbia.edu/cu/lweb/projects/digital/apis/

CHAPTER SEVENTEEN

Finances and Costs of the Roman Army

Peter Herz

1 Introduction

Even before the development of costly modern weaponry, armies were expensive. This means that pre-industrial societies, including the Roman Empire, had to spend a significant amount of state revenue on the maintenance of their armies. Before we can examine the financial costs of the Roman army, we must first clarify its role in Roman society.

In terms of its organizational structure, and criteria for recruitment, the Roman military was a direct reflection of Roman society. The recruitment of young men into the Roman army was not only based on their bodily capacity to perform military service, still a prerequisite for military service today, but also on their social and legal status. It was social criteria, and not military prowess, which finally determined the unit to which each man was assigned. It was only in times of crisis – when there was an urgent need for recruits – that the Romans deviated from the rules of social status. Slaves were not usually considered appropriate for use in war (Cf. Pliny, *Epist.* 10.29–30). They were only pressed into military service in the event of an extreme shortage in manpower, but they were freed from slavery first, and only ever served in the navy.

The recruits were generally between 18 and 20 years old, though there were significant exceptions. One soldier from the Arabian people the Ituraioi (today the Golan region on the Israeli–Syrian border) was recruited around the age of 40. This was probably the result of a forced recruiting action in his homeland, which was intended to reduce unrest and avoid the possibility of a rebellion. Given the average life-expectancy, the length of service for simple soldiers was very long.[1] A legionary performed an average service of 20 years and an additional five years as a reserve in the camp. An auxiliary soldier, or a soldier in the fleet, usually had to serve at least 25 years before he was discharged. The members of the Praetorian Guard served with the emperor for only 16 years, and were presented with interesting job opportunities upon discharge. The true career soldiers (*centuriones*), who for the most part had begun in the lower ranks, would usually remain in active service as long as they were bodily fit and could fulfill their duties. See for example the career of the *centurio* Petronius Fortuinatus, who served 46 years as a *centurio*, and in this capacity served with at least 15 legions throughout the empire (*CIL* 8.217 = *ILS* 2658).

2   Life in the Army

Even in peacetime soldiers took pains to keep themselves as prepared as possible. Apart from obligatory guard duty in the camp, by the emperor, or the standards, soldiers spent a large part of their time doing simple camp chores (cleaning the camp and the latrines, procuring firewood and water, feeding animals and stable work), and looking after their arms and equipment. Many soldiers were occupied with external tasks, such as guarding state depots, or escorting transports. Some worked as couriers, and others accompanied high ranking officers and officials. Soldiers performed police duties at border crossings and major road intersections, they worked in quarries, cleared forests, made roads and bridges, manufactured roof tiles, and worked in the administration of their units. Specialists, such as surveyors, helped with the measurement of land and the planning of extra infrastructure, such as canals, tunnels, aqueducts etc. In border zones which lacked sufficient civil institutions, officers fulfilled the roles of state authority (*centurio regionarius, praefectus gentis*).

While a *centurio* in a fixed legionary camp had a living quarters of about 100 square meters, common soldiers were housed together in groups of eight (*contubernium*) either in a tent or a small room with bunk beds and no more than four square meters of living space. The regular watch duties, hard weapons training, frequent engagement in the hardest of physical work, and the iron discipline, enforced by a brutal system of penalties, are all factors that would cause a modern army major recruitment problems, but it seems that the Roman army usually had no problem finding sufficient soldiers.

So what was it that brought a young man to volunteer for service under these less than attractive conditions? The explanation for many young soldiers should be relatively simple: life outside the army was not much better. Many recruits came from circumstances which were just as brutal and deprived as those in the army, but in contrast to a military life, they could not look forward to regular meals, pay, and free medical treatment from an army doctor.[2] If a soldier survived his active service period, for which he had a 50 percent chance in peacetime, and was honorably discharged from the army, there were considerable rewards. Members of the auxiliaries or the navy had a good chance of receiving Roman citizenship upon their discharge, and natural Roman citizens could hope for a substantial cash settlement. Many soldiers came from poor country families which lived permanently on a minimum subsistence, and for them military service represented a good alternative, in spite of its harsh requirements. Another significant percentage of the soldiers must have come from families in which there was a military tradition. Many recruits were the sons of former soldiers, born out of illegal relationships in the settlement around the encampment where their fathers served (birthplace: *castris*), or came from colonies of veterans with their corresponding military traditions (Cf. *CIL* 3.14507 from *Viminacium*). The Roman army always paid attention to the origins of its recruits, as the entries in later legal texts make very clear. For instance, preference was given to young men from the countryside who were already accustomed to hard physical work, and who were valued as tough and easier to discipline.[3]

In normal circumstances, the standing army of 30 legions in the imperial period would require between 7,500 and 10,000 new soldiers each year in order to maintain its fighting strength. The loss of soldiers must have corresponded to current military operations. Thus in September of AD 117 in Egypt, the *cohors I Lusitanorum equitata* received 126 young recruits from Asia Minor in order to make up for casualties incurred in the ongoing campaign against the rebellious Jews. These replacements equaled about 25 percent of the normal strength of the entire unit (*RMR* 74). In the period of crisis under Marcus Aurelius (161–180), the establishment of two completely new legions (*legio II* and *III Italica*), the effects of a devastating plague, and the high losses troops suffered in an on-going war on the Danube must have increased recruitment to at least 50,000 for a few years.

3   Pay

The social differences in Roman society affected not only the distribution of soldiers and officers in the various divisions of the army, but also their pay. The level of pay was more dependant on the social status of a unit than it was on their function or the difficulty of their actual tasks. Thus in the early imperial period a foot soldier in a auxiliary unit probably earned one sixth the pay of a legionary (750 to 900 *sestertii* a year). Each of the 120 cavalrymen in a legion received one sixth more than soldiers serving with the legionary infantry (900 to 1,050 *sestertii* a year). Similarly, service with the praetorians resulted in a comparable increase in salary.[4]

The differences amongst the officers were even more striking: a simple *centurio* in a legion earned 13,500 *sestertii* a year under Augustus, or 18 times the pay of a simple soldier. A centurion of the first cohort, however, received 27,000 *sestertii*, and the highest centurion of the legion, the *primus pilus*, earned 54,000 *sestertii* yearly, 72 times the pay of the humble *miles legionarius*. The officers of the first cohort received preferential treatments, because they were the most experienced officers in the legion and were required to undertake numerous special assignments.

This blatantly uneven rate of pay was not changed in later salary adjustments, but was intentionally preserved, and under the emperor Maximinus Thrax (235–238) the nominal salary of the *primus pilus* was set at 432,000 *sestertii*. The exceptionally good pay of the *centuriones* in relation to that of the simple soldiers is not merely a sign of their importance in the army, but was also maintained by all of the emperors from Augustus onwards. In contrast to the majority of equestrian and senatorial officers, who were often nothing more than amateurs, long serving *centuriones* were military specialists on whose professional competence and loyalty both the safety of the emperor and the success of the Roman military machine was based.

Until the great restructuring of the Roman army under Septimius Severus (193–211) it is necessary to distinguish between the nominal salary and what was actually paid. This is confirmed by a preserved account for individual soldiers from AD 81. Here, the pay in denarii was calculated in drachmae, which was the normal currency of Egypt:

P.Gen.Lat. 1 recto I (AD 81)

Q.Iulius Proculus, born in Damascus	
Received the first payment in the 3rd year of the emperor,	247½ drachmae
minus expenses:	
hay money	10 drachmae
for food	80 drachmae
shoes, socks	12 drachmae
camp saturnalia	20 drachmae
——	60 drachmae
total given out	182 drachmae
difference deposited	65½ drachmae
previous balance	136 drachmae
new balance	201½ drachmae
Received the second payment in the same year,	247½ drachmae
expenses:	
hay money	10 drachmae
food	80 drachmae
shoes, socks	12 drachmae
for the standards	4 drachmae
total expenses	106 drachmae
difference deposited	141½ drachmae
previous balance	201½ drachmae
new balance	343 drachmae
Received the third payment in the same year,	247½ drachmae
expenses:	
hay money	10 drachmae
food	80 drachmae
shoes, socks	12 drachmae
clothing	145½ drachmae
total expenses	247½ drachmae
new total balance	343 drachmae
Rennius Innocens (probably the name of the military clerk responsible for the correctness of the account)	
C. Valerius Germanus, born in Tyre	
Received the first payment of the 3rd year of the emperor,	247½ drachmae
expenses:	
hay money	10 drachmae
food	80 drachmae

P.Gen.Lat. 1 recto I (AD 81)

shoes, socks	12 drachmae
camp saturnalia	20 drachmae
clothing	100 drachmae
total expenses	222 drachmae
difference deposited	25½ drachmae
previous balance	21 drachmae
new balance	46½ drachmae
Received the second payment in the same year,	247½ drachmae
expenses:	
hay	10 drachmae
food	80 drachmae
shoes, socks	12 drachmae
for the standards	4 drachmae.
total expenses	106 drachmae
difference deposited	141½ drachmae
previous balance	46½ drachmae
new balance	188 drachmae
Received the third payment in the same year,	247½ drachmae
expenses:	
hay	10 drachmae
food	80 drachmae
shoes, socks	12 drachmae
clothing	145½ drachmae
previous balance	188 drachmae
[the papyrus breaks off here.]	

From this evidence we must assume that an account was kept for each soldier within his unit. The standard-bearer (*signifer*) of each company must have been responsible for these lists. In the *turma*, the *summus curator* oversaw this task. We should also assume the existence of a central office which administered the salary lists for the entire unit (the *legio* in the case of citizen soldiers, the *cohors* or *ala* for auxiliaries). The scribes needed for this work probably came from the first cohort of the legion, which contained twice the usual number of men compared to the other nine cohorts (around 1,000 instead of 500), due to the fact that it included many of the administrative positions of the entire unit.[5]

Recruits received a payment to cover travel to their future posts (*viaticum*), the remainder of which would be paid into their accounts upon their arrival, and subsequently administered by the standard-bearer or accountant of their *centuria* (*RMR* 74). Basic foodstuffs (grain, oil, cheap wine or vinegar, pulse, and salt) as well as personal equipment (weapons, clothes, shoes) were procured directly by the state, and subsequent deductions were made from the soldiers' accounts.[6] Indeed, the state could obtain foodstuffs such as grain from sources that were directly controlled by the state itself, acquired either in the form of a direct tax or as harvests from state land. In many parts of the empire, taxes corresponded to a percentage quota (10 percent [*decuma*] or 12.5 percent [*octava*] of the harvest). State domains were worked by farmers who delivered about one-third of their crop as a natural payment to the state.[7]

For this reason the Roman government could set a fictional market price at which the use of such produce by soldiers could be calculated. If the state's direct resources were insufficient to cover the needs of the military, it was always possible for the state to bypass normal market rules and buy grain and other goods on the open market at a fixed price (*coemptio*). The same system was employed for hay (used by the pack animals of a unit). This last expense would be considered one of the fuel costs of an army today, and not placed on the shoulders of the soldiers themselves.

The sizeable deductions for clothes, shoes, socks, and leggings, meant that a substantial amount of cash remained under the control of the state as well, since the state had the corresponding clothing and shoes produced by civilian craftsmen in a monopoly (Hunt's *Pridianum* mentions soldiers on their way to Gaul. See *RMR* 63 with a complete status report of the *cohors I Hispanorum Veterana quingenaria* in Stobi). In case of the second soldier cited above, Gaius Valerius Germanus, the Roman state deducted a total of $281^{1}/_{2}$ drachmae for clothing, more than a third of his yearly salary.

It is not possible to say conclusively whether it was always cheaper for a soldier to have procured his own clothing. If he was stationed in a province with a good textile economy, then it would have been easy, but in many of the remote border garrisons there cannot have been sufficient clothing available for purchase in the private sector. The Roman state, or its representatives, not only influenced the cost of the products with large orders, but also assured some uniformity in appearance and quality. Exactly what garments the soldiers received for these deductions is unclear. They probably received new tunics at regular intervals, perhaps also a thick coat and additional blankets for their sleeping quarters. Clothing of a better standard, or additional garments, had to be purchased by the soldier himself at his own expense.

Who covered the cost of equipment not attached to individual soldiers is unclear. For instance, we know about a state order of blankets for a military hospital in Cappadocia which was supposed to be completed in Egypt (*BGU* 7.1564). In this instance, we must assume that the Roman state picked up the bill.

The state acquisitioning system for the clothing of soldiers (*vestis militaris*) is better known in the late antique period.[8] Thus we know from Diocletian's Edict of Maximum Prices that certain pieces of clothing were designated with the term "*militaris.*"[9] On top of this, the *Historia Augusta* gives us a certain overview of what high-ranking officers could expect from the state in the way of equipment (certainly exaggerated, but still very informative: *HA Claudius* 14.2–16; *Aurelianus* 12.1–2). The total sum of 240 drachmae per year for food is certainly a generous estimate, as it seems to be only for basic foodstuffs. It is possible to deduce from this that the state deductions for provisions were usually higher than their cost, and that the state normally made a profit. In other words, as a general rule of thumb, about two-thirds of the gross income of the soldiers was kept back.

The money that was kept back from the salary was administered within the *legio* by the *officium* of the *primus pilus*,[10] and in auxiliary units probably by a *centurio*. These officers organized the acquisition of the necessary provisions, in a manner dependent on local conditions. Units stationed in less serviceable border provinces were sometimes required to order provisions from great distances. Individual shipments could be provided by private concerns: "*Ala Veterana Gallica, turma* of Donacianus, Serenus, *procurator*, to the hay contractors. I received hay for fellow-members of my *turma* for the month of June and I have paid the freight myself and they total thirty cavalrymen for you [makes no sense]. [Written in the] Consulate[ship] of Catullinus and Afer" (*RMR* 80). In regions with large imperial domains, it was probably possible to obtain deliveries directly through the imperial administration: "[. . .] Sarapion, the cavalryman afore mentioned, to Trethonius, imperial *oeconomos*. I have been measured out by you my grain of the preceding year, the [–th?] for two months. Total, two artabas. [I, *turma* (?)] of Taurinus Melas, cavalryman, have written for him" (*RMR* 79).

We know from inscriptions that the supplies of the *legio III Augusta* in north Africa were organized by the equestrian *procurator* of the *regio Thevestina*, who had an *officium* with imperial slaves and freedmen at his disposal for this purpose.[11] In this special case it seems that the *procurator* was also responsible for the payment of the salaries of the legion as well. His *officium* consisted of imperial *liberti* and *vernae*, whose services under the titles *tabularius legionis III Augustae* (*AE* 1956, 123), *adiutor tabularius legionis III Augustae* (*CIL* 8.4272 and 4273 = 18553), *dispensator legionis III Augustae* (*AE* 1969/70,664), and *arkarius legionis III Augustae* (*CIL* 8.3289 + p. 1741) provide a glimpse into the range of their duties. While a *tabularius*, together with his helper (*adiutor*), usually did the job of an accountant, the *ark(c)arius* looked after the cash itself. The distributor (*dispensator*) was responsible for the payments to the troops, being the equivalent of the legion's *primus pilus*.

It appears that soldiers who wished to could also refuse the delivery of certain provisions, and receive the corresponding cash instead: "Pricus Paulus, cavalryman, *turma* of Herminus, to Apollos, *cibariator*. I have received from you the value of lentils, salt, and vinegar 4 denarii, 8 obols. Year 3, Tybi 3. I wrote (?)" (*RMR* 78, 15). Soldiers who found themselves on the way to longer external duties could also receive the cash value of the provisions which they would normally get in the camp in order to provide for themselves while away: "Aelius Capiton, cavalryman of the *ala Gallica, turma* of Optatianus, to Iulius Serenus, *summus curator*. I have received from you my hay allowance for the nineteenth year of the Aurelii Antoninus and Commodus, the Lords Emperors, in advance (since I am) leaving for Scenae Megalae, *denarii* 25, in full. Year 19 of the Aurelii Antoninus and Commodus, Caesars and Lords, Tybi 20 (January 15, 179)" (*RMR* 76, Col. III 20–26).

One reason why this system of deductions from the Roman state was maintained so long was that it reduced the state's need for cash, as a smaller percentage of the soldiers' salaries actually had to be paid out. It is completely unknown whether or not officers had such salary deductions as well. Additionally, a significant proportion of the net salary remained in the camp coffers, where a large amount of cash could be collected. After the rebellion in AD 89 of Saturninus, governor of upper Germany under Domitian, a regulation was established that only 1,000 *sestertii* per soldier had to be present in camp treasuries (Suetonius, *Dom.* 7.3).

Unfortunately, we do not know what happened to the remaining (excess) money. It has been suggested that it probably went over to the *procurator* of the province, who was responsible for regulating the deductions from the soldiers' nominal pay, who then moved the money to other places. In any case, we may suspect that the correct procedure for such a sum would have been meticulously followed. It is difficult to explain why the two soldiers in the text above had so little money in their accounts to begin with; perhaps they had only just begun their service and had not yet saved much.

The actual money for salaries was administered by the respective *procurator* in the region where the soldiers were stationed. He was also responsible for setting the regular deductions in nominal salaries, and the use of the money that was held back. Theoretically, the Roman state could check up on the financial conditions of individual soldiers, provided the necessary documents had not been lost by a troop. This suggests a well-documented process. The civil administrator of the upper Egyptian district of Panopolis, who was responsible for the acquisitions of military units stationed in his district, sent, upon demand, the documents (*matricula*) of these units to his superiors (P. Panop. Beatty 1.72 ff. in the month of *Thoth*). Shortly afterwards he received an order to reclaim salary from certain named soldiers who had been paid too much: another letter delivered by transmission of the Strategus of the Thinite nome, Mecheir 9th.

> Aurelius Isidorus, Procurator of the Lower Thebaid, to Apolinarius, Strategus of the Panopolite nome, greeting. Demand, on the order of my lord the Governor of the Thebaid, Julius Athenodorus, . . . from each of the following, . . . and Ammonius, cataphractarii, Peteesis, decurio, Sarapion, summus, Isidorus the accountant and . . . (? Amm)onius, private soldiers, serving in the Ala II Herculia Dromedariorum under the command of Eudaemon, Prefect, 3,000 denarii, making a total in all of 2 myriads and 1,000 atticae . . . and credit the amount to the Imperial revenues, and report to my office. I bid you farewell, for many years. (P. Panop. Beatty 2.27ff. in the month of *Tybi*)

For a long time it was worthwhile for the Roman state to limit the operational costs of the military with manipulations and a strict policy of payments.[12] In the almost 200 years between Augustus and the end of the second century there was only one rise in pay: the introduction of a fourth *stipendium* under Domitian. The avalanche of expenses began under Septimius Severus (the first doubling of salaries) and reached a highpoint under Maximinus Thrax (235–238), with a final doubling of the previous basic salary. The legionary under Domitian received 1,200 *sestertii* as basic salary, which would rise to 7,200 *sestertii* by the year 235. Because the system of deducting certain costs from soldiers' salaries was eliminated under Septimius Severus, the years 193–235 saw not only an increase in the payment of actual salary of almost 500 percent, but also a corresponding increase in the state's expenses. This demand was made up for by the systematic debasement of the precious metal content of the coinage, and increased taxes on the civilian population.[13]

4 Expenses Structure

The Roman army's financial costs can be divided into one-time expenses and regular expenditure.

One-time expenses

This category included the creation of completely new units, and the replacement of equipment that was completely lost. In such cases, private producers undertook to manufacture equipment for many thousands of soldiers in a relatively short period of time. This included weapons, clothes, shoes, leather tents, and cooking utensils, as well as vehicles.[14] The acquisition of the draft animals and other mounts must have been centralized. In the imperial period, new legions were always set up in Italy, where they could take advantage of the well-established Italian industries.

More problematic is the production of individual weapons. There is evidence that some weapons were the property of individual soldiers, and that they marked them with signs of their ownership. We can imagine a system where the state looked after the initial provision of weapons, which, amongst other things, assured a certain uniformity and quality in the equipment.[15] The state handed over the weapons to individual soldiers and deducted the cost in their bills. Thus the accounts of young soldiers were burdened with a large deficit, which could only be paid off after a few years.

Regular expenditure

The costs of paying the soldiers

We can assume that the area in which an army was stationed had to pay the salary of the troops. In some provinces this would not have been a major problem. The riches of Egypt produced such a significant income that the Egyptian army could be financed easily, without impairing the other functions of the remaining tax revenue. A similar situation existed in North Africa and Spain. Troops concentrated on the eastern borders (Syria, Cappadocia, Arabia, Iudaea-Palaestina) could also be funded by the tax revenues of wealthy Syria and Asia Minor.

The financing of troops based on the Rhine and Danube was significantly more problematic. While the main needs of the first two centuries AD could be met by payments in kind, the large border armies still required a lot of money to cover salaries. The early imperial troop concentrations along the Rhine, with a total of eight legions, a fleet, and numerous auxiliary troops, must have been very expensive, as the economic potential of this region was largely undeveloped.

One can assume that the running costs of these troops were met by the taxes from the entire Gallic area. Thus the soldiers were financed by taxes from the provinces Belgica, Aquitania, and Gallia Lugdunensis, and perhaps also the southern French province Gallia Narbonensis. The man responsible for this problem was the highest financial administrator of Gaul (*procurator Galliarum*) stationed in Lugudunum (Lyon), who had a special account, the *fiscus Gallicus*, at his disposal. Taxes from the three central and northern Gallic provinces flowed into this account, which was used for the salary and provision of the region's army. The fact that the Gallic provincial account was already set up in the early imperial period is a sign of the financial significance of this area. Added to this was the establishment of a mint in Lyon, which covered the need for cash. Without taking account of the higher salaries of officers, and the lower ones of the auxiliaries, we can estimate a yearly requirement of 60 million *sestertii* for the salary of this army.

In the advanced imperial period, the financial administrator of Belgica and the two Germanies (*procurator Belgicae et duarum Germaniarum*) was responsible for the payment and provisioning of both the German border armies. Even for these massively reduced armies (four legions) the tax-income in these provinces was probably not enough to cover their costs. This deficit had to be made up by the contributions of the rich civilian province Belgica.

Expenses for provisions

A soldier received a basic monthly allowance of 3.5 bushels of un-milled grain (7.5 kg for each bushel of grain), plus a payment of olive oil, wine or wine-vinegar, and salt. With about 6,000 men in each legion, we can estimate a total requirement of 252,000 bushels of wheat; or, with a total strength of 80,000 men for the entire army along the Rhine, 3.36 million bushels or 25.2 million kg (25,200 tons) of wheat.

The replacement of weapons and equipment

It has been shown that many Roman military camps included workshops and specialized troops who could undertake small repairs of weapons and equipment, such as shields and saddles. They could also produce weapons (arrowheads, slingshots, and spears) but probably only in small numbers, and larger requirements had to be provided by the private sector. Thus we know that the great material loss of the year AD 15 had to be replaced by special production of the civilian population of Gaul. In that year two legions returning through tidal marshes were surprised by the tide and were barely able to escape with the lives of the soldiers (Tacitus, *Ann.* 1.70).

It seems that the Roman army always took into account the possibility of local production. For Britannia there is evidence that one large production site was kept under military control (See the inscription *RIB* 156 = *CIL* 7.49 = *ILS* 2429). In other areas, where it was possible to turn to the civilian sector, it seems that much production was delegated to civilians.[16] One veteran from Mainz is known to have described himself as a sword dealer (*negotiator gladiarius*), but it is not clear whether he organized the supply of swords to the troops, or merely obtained expensive or special weapons for officers and wealthy soldiers (*CIL* 13.6677 = *ILS* 2474).

Replacements for the cavalry

A very plausible calculation by Ann Hyland is based on the assumption that a cavalry horse in the Roman army lasted an average of four years before it had to be replaced. Hyland's example, the Roman army in Britain, had roughly 12,700 cavalry horses and replacement requirements of about 3,175 mounts per year.[17] Thus one can estimate that there were between 30,000 and 40,000 horses throughout the empire which would need to be replaced each year. If we assume a flat price of 125 denarii (500 *sestertii*) for each horse, and assume an average of 35,000 remounts per year, then we arrive at the yearly sum of 17.5 million *sestertii*. Moreover, these are estimates based on peacetime conditions, and do not take military campaigns into consideration, which must have drastically increased the demands for replacement horses.

It must be assumed that the number of horses on hand within all of the mounted units (*legiones, alae, cohortes equitatae*) was always kept at such a level that some replacements could always be provided. This was due to the fact that military horses required basic training before they could be employed. Transport capacity is more problematic. I am very skeptical of the idea that all of the draft animals necessary for a complete decampment, especially in the case of the legions, were kept in perpetual readiness. Given the reserved use of the *legiones* from the middle of the second century onwards, it seems more likely that camps only had sufficient animal capacity for the deployment in a *vexillatio milliaria*, and that excess requirements for transport would have to be taken from the civilian population. (Cf. P. Oxy. 3602–5 [November 215] for the working of the system. P. Oxy. 3109 [253/56], on the other hand, shows that plough-oxen from Egypt were requested for service in Syria. Plough oxen were usually not used for military transport. The papyrus illustrates the preparatory work of the administration to distribute the burden of the on-coming Parthian campaign among the population of Egypt.)[18]

The definitive work on the acquisition of cavalry mounts has already been produced by R. Davies.[19] The necessary horses would first be tested (*probatio*) on behalf of the governor, the supreme commander of the provincial army, and then handed over to the army. The test was usually performed by professional members of staff. Finally, each horse would be transferred to its unit, with the name of its future rider already stated in the record of transfer (*RMR* 83). The standard sum of 125 denarii per horse given by Davies was based on a known deposit provided by each rider. Should the horse be lost or injured to the point that it was no longer fit for service due to the carelessness of its rider, this deposit would be kept back and used to provide a replacement.[20] The amount could probably be taken from the account of the soldier, or be deducted the next time he was paid. The total deposit for a normal cavalry regiment of about 500 men (*ala quingenaria*) and about 560 horses was the considerable sum of 70,000 denarii. The rules for officers are completely unknown. We do not know if the state provided their horses, or if they had to buy them at their own expense.

The true cost of horses may well have been more than 125 denarii. While this part of the acquisition process is comparatively well documented, other areas still require significant clarification. While we know, for instance, of imperial studs in Cappadocia in late antiquity,[21] the existence of similar organizational systems earlier on cannot be demonstrated.

While Davies has proved the existence of state-owned stud farms in Britannia,[22] it seems that the bulk of military horses in the imperial period were raised by private concerns and sold to the army. The details of this trade are unclear. We do not know whether or not there were middle men, state purchasers of horses, what modified the prices (e.g. the open market, or a price set by the state), or even which administrators were responsible. The most likely model was that horses were purchased from private entrepreneurs by military agents and after passing the *probatio* were taken by the military. Certificates from the test, documents of transfer, and the receipts of purchase were then presented by the vendors to an office of the *procurator* responsible for the *provincia*, and money was paid out.

The care of horses and pack animals

The daily minimum requirement for an ancient military horse was about ten kilograms of hay and between one and three kilograms of barley, with the amount of grain varying significantly depending on the horse's workload. On top of this there was a large requirement for straw (3 kg per day). Thus a simple cavalry regiment (*ala*) with about 560 horses used between 560 and 1,680 kilograms of barley, and 5,600 kilograms of hay each year, or between 204.4 and 613.2 tons of barley and 2,044 tons of hay a year. The need for fodder and hay must have been met by deliveries from the local populations.[23]

The needs of pack and draft animals of the unit was almost larger, but must have fluctuated depending on the level of preparedness. The cost of procuring vehicles is entirely unknown. The initial purchases must have been covered by the state, but it is uncertain if this holds true for replacements.

One expense, which can be a heavy burden on modern armies and their states, was completely lacking in the Roman period. There was no expensive pension system for retired soldiers – whose expectations were met in the form of the discharge-*donativum* – and also no legal claims on the state by the widows and orphans of active soldiers or veterans. Until the reign of Septimius Severus, soldiers under the rank of *centurio* could not legitimately marry, and thus, legally at least, had no wives or children who could expect state care.[24] The children were considered illegitimate until they were officially acknowledged by their father, when he had become a *veteranus*, and were therefore not entitled to inherit. The claim to the *donativum* that occurred upon a soldier's discharge was connected to the living soldier and therefore could not be handed down to his heirs. Should a potential veteran die before his official discharge, his chances for a *donativum* were completely lost. So while the loss of Varus' three experienced legions to the Germans in the Teutoburger forest in the year AD 9 was both a human and political tragedy, it was also something of a blessing to the strained finances of the empire.

It is at best unclear whether or not, and in what circumstances, a soldier rendered unfit for duty prior to the end of his normal period of service was legally eligible for financial compensation. Soldiers who became severely ill, or who had to leave the service due to wounds they had sustained all fall into this category. While the official and honorable discharge due to the inability to serve (*missio causaria*) seems to be mainly concerned with securing the soldier's legal privileges, it actually had no immediate financial consequences in the point of view of the Roman state. If the Roman state paid out anything in these cases, then it was more like an honorable act (*beneficium*) than a legal obligation. Thus the problem of expensive post-military expenses solved themselves. In spite of this advantage, the state's guarantee of regular discharge payments seems to have been a major political problem in all periods, and to assure these payments a single account was set up. For a long time, Augustus paid the discharge-*donativa* out of his own pocket (because he wanted to underscore his special connection to his soldiers), but towards the end of his reign his reduced financial circumstances meant that he was no longer able to make such generous payments, and a special military fund (*aerarium militare*) was established. This fund was replenished, for the most part, by a 5 percent inheritance tax, which even Roman citizens in Italy had to pay. The money was intended exclusively for the care of veterans. The actual military expenses (equipment and salary) were hereafter covered by the proper state treasury (*aerarium populi Romani*).[25] As a rule, it seems that emperors usually paid the discharge (and the bestowal of the *donativa*) personally to veterans from units of the capital city, and thus continued to underline their personal concern for their soldiers. For this reason these soldiers described themselves afterwards as veterans of the emperor (*veteranus Augusti*). The dishonorable discharge of the whole praetorian guard in June 193 (Cassius Dio 70.1.1.), because they had failed to prevent the murder of Pertinax, meant that the Roman state saved a remarkable amount of money which the new emperor Septimius Severus was able to use in a period of tight state finances. The soldiers were confronted with this news during a meeting where they had expected the new emperor to announce exactly how much money they would receive on the occasion of his inauguration.

In financially tight times, the official discharge of veterans, and with it the payment of their *donativa*, was intentionally delayed by many years, so that the state's financial burden would be "naturally" reduced by the death of many of the soldiers. This policy lead to unrest amongst the armies of the Rhine and Danube between the reigns of Augustus and Tiberius, as these armies possessed a large number of veterans who had already been waiting years for their long overdue discharge (Tacitus, *Ann.* 1.17.1–3).

There are indications that the commander of each unit possessed a single fund which could be used for expenses incurred representing the unit in public. It was probably this fund that was drawn on to pay for the guest gifts (*xenia*), which the commander of one unit gave to a representative of the Parthian great king, who was on his way to the emperor and had passed through the garrison.[26]

"Marius Maximus (Governor of the province of Syria Coele) to the tribunes and prefects and commanders of the units, greetings. I have attached that which I have written to Minicius Martialis, the *procurator* of our emperors, so that you should be aware of it. I hope that you are well.
Copy:
See that you also take care for the expenses of the units, which Goces, the messenger of the Parthians, who has sent to our lord, the most brave emperor, passes through, such that the habitual guest-gift may be presented to him. Write to me, what you have to spend in each unit."
(The names of the five garrisoned cities through which the Parthian messenger has passed on his voyage follow: Gazica, Appadana, Du[r]a, Ed[da]na, Bi[blada].)

In this case, the commanders of the units put up the necessary money for the guest gift. The expenses for the entertainment and lodgings of the messenger and his followers were paid by the commanders from the treasuries of the units. These expenses were then reimbursed out of the corresponding account by the governor. It remains unclear whether this took the form of a cash payment or if the amount was simply credited to the account of the unit. Such official embassies were certainly not cheap, even if they did not meet the cost level of the state visit of the Armenian king Tiridates to Nero. King Tiridates traveled by land through Asia Minor and probably all the way through the Balkans to Rome, a journey of at least nine months. He was accompanied by a train of many thousands of people, who cost the Roman state 800,000 *sestertii* each day (Cassius Dio 63.2.2).

A substantial amount of money was also necessary for the cults of the Roman military. The Feriale Duranum, the official calendar of festivals for a *cohors* in the Syrian camp at Dura Europos, shows that there were at least 50 official feast days at which sacrificial animals (usually cattle) would be slaughtered (*RMR* 117) or at which a sacrifice with wine and incense would be performed (*RMR* 47ff.). On top of these, the morning sacrifice, which had to be performed daily by the commanding officer, also incurred costs.[27] We have a minimum of 50 animals (oxen and cows), which were regularly slaughtered each year. On top of this there was the cost of the incense and wine used in the supplications and the regular morning offering.

We do not know if the regular deductions of 12 drachmae "for the standards" was sufficient for this. It was probably expected that the commanding officer paid some of these costs himself. These are the expenses for a unit of auxiliary soldiers, the expenses of the legions and troops in Rome must have been higher.

5   The Empire and the Expenses

So far we have mostly considered the expenses which the Roman military generated, and these were certainly the largest item in the budget of the Roman state. This would be very one-sided if we did not also consider the function of the Roman army. If we wish to calculate the gross national product, as in a modern political economy, we must also enquire as to the economic effect of the Roman army in general. The value of the political stability and the military security which the army's existence guaranteed both internally and externally is hard to put in hard financial terms.

But this is only one side of the coin. At the same time, the Roman army represented the largest organized and qualified work-force that was present throughout the empire; and the emperor alone controlled it. The general economic value of the infrastructure that the military provided must have been enormous. They made streets, bridges, ports, and aqueducts, especially in the border provinces, and on top of this there was state production in quarries and tile factories run by soldiers, and the use of military engineers on civilian constructions (*CIL* 8.2728 = *ILS* 5795; Pliny, *Epist.* 10.41.3). The costs saved by having the military build its own housing and defensive installations (camps), have yet to be studied, but such expenses are major components in modern military budgets, as they are now produced by civilian contractors.

Many of the expenses which burden the military states of today did not yet exist in the Roman period. There was no additional pay for soldiers who were deployed on the front. The additional costs for the board and lodging of deployed soldiers were the problem of the citizens and treasuries of the various communities through which the soldiers marched, and not a burden on the treasury of the state.[28] Soldiers on the march received an official document (*diploma*), either from their home units or the authority commanding them, which gave them the right to demand board and lodging from civilians at all times.[29] A large part of the transportation costs of a deployment were also shifted onto the civil population who were expected to provide the necessary pack and draft animals, wagons and workers, at best for only nominal compensation.[30] The cost of delivering supplies to the troops was also born by the provinces where they were stationed. Such burdens had long been part of the regular taxes and were added to the tax bill.[31]

In any event, the state of current research is very far from being decisive. As of now, we can at best only guess at the real costs, but not reproduce an actual budget.

NOTES

1   For the average life expectancy see Scheidel 1996 and his contribution to this volume. On recruitment and training, Wesch-Klein (in this volume).
2   Wilmanns 1995; Davies 1969c; Davies 1970.
3   Davies 1969a.
4   Speidel 1992.
5   Breeze 1969.
6   For the supply of weapons and armor see Coulston 1998.
7   On this system, Kehoe 1988.
8   Jones 1964, 433f.
9   Giacchero 1974.
10 Mocsy 1966.
11 Christol 1990, with additional material from other regions.
12 I follow here the numbers presented by Speidel 1992.
13 Harl 1996.
14 For an introduction to this subject see Herz 2002.
15 For the system in Judaea before the Bar Kochba-War, see Cassius Dio 69.12.2 and Herz 2005.
16 Herz 2005.
17 Hyland 1990, 89.
18 Published by Schubert 2001.
19 Davies 1969b.
20 Davies 1969b, 164.
21 Cameron 1976, 7f.
22 Davies 1969b, 167f.
23 Hyland 1990, 91f.; Dixon and Southern 1992; Stoll 2001, 443–51.
24 Cf. Phang 2001.
25 For its work see Herz 2003.
26 Chaumont 1986.
27 Stoll 1995.
28 Mitchell 1976; Herrmann 1990.
29 Kolb 2000, 109–17.
30 Mitchell 1976.
31 Lintott 1993, 70–80.

BIBLIOGRAPHY

Breeze, D. J. 1969. "The organization of the legion: The first cohort and the *equites legionis*," *JRS* 59: 50–5.

Cameron, A. 1976. *Circus factions. Blues and Greens at Rome and Byzantium*. Oxford.

Campbell, B. 1994. *The Roman Army, 31 BC–AD 337. A Sourcebook*. London.

Chaumont, M. L. 1986. "Un document méconnu concernant l'envoi d'un ambassadeur parthe vers Septime Sévère (P. Dura 60 B)," *Historia* 36: 422–47.

Christol, M. 1990. "Ti. Claudius Proculus Cornelianus, procurateur de le région de Théveste," in *L'Africa Romana VII*. Sassari, 893–904.

Coulston, J. C. N. 1998. "How to arm a Roman soldier," in M. M. Austin, J. D. Harries, and C. J. Smith (eds.), Modus Operandi. *How the Ancient World Worked*. London, 167–90.

Davies, R. 1969a. "Joining the Roman army," *BJ* 169: 208–32.

—— 1969b. "The supply of animals to the Roman army and the remount system," *Latomus* 28: 429–59.

—— 1969c. "The *medici* of the Roman armed services," *Epigraphische Studien* 8: 83–9.

—— 1970. "The Roman military medical service," *Saalburg Jahrbuch* 27: 84–104.

Dixon, K. P., and P. Southern. 1992. *The Roman Cavalry from the First to the Third Century AD*. London.

Erdkamp, P. (ed.). 2002. *The Roman Army and the Economy*. Amsterdam.

Giacchero, M. 1974. *Edictum Diocletiani et collegarum de pretiis rerum venalium in integrum fere restitutum e Latinis Graecisque fragmentis. I. Edictum*. Genoa.

Harl, K. 1996. *Coinage and Roman Economy 300 BC to AD 700*. Baltimore.

Herrmann, P. 1990. *Hilferufe aus römischen Provinzen. Ein Aspekt der Krise des römischen Reiches im 3. Jhdt. n.Chr.* Hamburg.

Herz, P. 1999. "Der centurio supernumerarius und die annona militaris," *Laverna* 10: 165–84.

—— 2002. "Die Versorgung der römischen Armee. Strukturelle Überlegungen," in Erdkamp, 19–46.

—— 2003. "Die Arbeitsweise der staatlichen Finanzverwaltung in der Kaiserzeit," in G. Urso (ed.), *Moneta, mercanti, banchieri. I precedenti greci e romani dell'Euro, Atti del convegno internazionale Cividale del Friuli 26–28 settembre 2002*. Milan, 167–84.

—— 2005. "Der römische Staat und die Wirtschaft. Staatliche Eingriffe in das Wirtschaftsleben (Kontrolle von Ressourcen)," in M. Polfer (ed.), *Artisanat et économie romaine. Italie et provinces occidentales de l'Empire. Colloque international Erpeldange 14–16 octobre 2004*. Montagnac, 17–30.

Hyland, A. 1990. Equus. *The Horse in Roman Times*. London.

Jones, A. H. M. 1964. *The Later Roman Empire. A Social, Economic and Administrative Survey*. Oxford.

Kehoe, D. P. 1988. *The Economics of Agriculture on Roman Imperial Estates in North Africa*. Göttingen.

Kolb, A. 2000. *Transport und Nachrichtentransfer im Römischen Reich*. Berlin.

Lintott, A. 1993. Imperium Romanum. *Politics and Administration*. London.

Mann, J. C. 1983. *Legionary Recruitment and Veteran Settlement during the Principate*. London.

Mitchell, S. 1976. "Requisitioned transport in the Roman Empire. A new inscription from Pisidia," *JRS* 66: 106–31.

Mócsy, A. 1966. "Das Lustrum Primipili und die Annona Militaris," *Germania* 44: 312–26.

Phang, S. E. 2001. *The Marriage of Roman Soldiers (13 BC–AD 235). Law and Family in the Imperial Army.* Leiden.

Scheidel, W. 1996. *Measuring Sex, Age and Death in the Roman Empire.* Ann Arbor.

Schubert, P. 2001. *A Yale Payrus (P. Yale III 137) in the Beinecke Rare Book and Manuscript Library III.* Oakville.

Speidel, M. A. 1992. "Roman army pay scales," *JRS* 82: 87–106.

Stoll, O. 1995. *Excubatio ad signa. Die Wache bei den Fahnen in der römischen Armee und andere Beiträge zur kulturgeschichtlichen und historischen Bedeutung eines militärischen Symbols.* St. Katharinen.

—— 2001. *Römisches Heer und Gesellschaft. Gesammelte Beiträge 1991–1999.* Stuttgart.

Wilmanns, J. C. 1995. *Der Sanitätsdienst im römischen Reich. Eine sozialgeschichtliche Studie zum römischen Militärsanitätswesen neben einer Prosopographie des Sanitätspersonals.* Hildesheim.

FURTHER READING

A book that covers all aspects of the logistic and the financing of the Roman army and fleet does not yet exist. Important aspects are covered by the contributions to Erdkamp 2002. Important for the recruitment of Roman soldiers are Mann 1983 and Davies 1969a. For a model of the development of the salaries under the empire, see Speidel 1992. For the connections between supplying and financing the Roman army and the general administration of the empire cf. Herz 1999 and 2002. Many important sources in translation may be consulted in the collections by Fink (= *RMR*) and Campbell 1994.

CHAPTER EIGHTEEN

War- and Peacetime Logistics: Supplying Imperial Armies in East and West

Peter Kehne

1 Sources

In the index of probably the most prominent sourcebook on the Roman army, Campbell's 1994 publication entitled *The Roman Army 31 BC–AD 337*, we look in vain for entries on logistics, military diet, army supplies etcetera. Obviously Campbell's Roman army could do without any food and fodder. The same goes for his *Selected Readings* in *Greek and Roman Military Writers*. However, if we look again much more closely, there is some source material with logistical relevance hidden in both of these publications, so his omissions are not due to the scarcity of ancient sources.

As far as we know, no ancient monograph about military logistics was ever written – at least none has come down to us. Of course ancient military writers knew about the significance of ensuring sufficient supplies, which they counted among the abilities required of every good general (Xenophon, *Cyr.* 6.2.25ff.; *Anab.* 2.6.8; Onasander 6.14; Tacitus, *Agric.* 19.4). *Poliorketiká*, treatises on siege warfare, advised that fortified positions should be provisioned with adequate supplies (Aen. Tact. 10.3; 10.12; 40.8; Campbell 2004, no. 221). Furthermore, the often rhetorical handbooks on military matters dealt with the right place for the baggage train in a marching formation (Onasander 6.6; Vegetius, *Epit.* 3.6.13f.), "the convoying of army suppliers by land and sea" (Onasander 6.14), with precautions on foraging expeditions against undisciplined plunder (Onasander 10.7–8), the advantages of pillaging enemy country, "for loss of resources and shortage of crops reduce war, while surplus increases it" (Onasander 6.11, 12), or with the need of sparing it, if the army intended to encamp there. Whenever possible, a general "should lead his army over as soon as possible . . . ; for from hostile country he will obtain abundant provisions . . ."

(Onos. 6.13; cf. Livy 34.9.12 with Cato the Elder's, principally propagandistic, maxim: *bellum se ipsum alet*).

Vegetius in his "Handbook on Military Affairs" (*Epit.* 3.1–3) dedicated entire chapters, or at least parts of them, to matters of provisioning; and there he also set out basic principles of military logistics:

> Most often shortage, rather than battle, consumes an army and more cruel than the sword is starvation. . . . In every expedition the one and most powerful weapon is, that you have sufficient food but lack of it destroys the enemy. Therefore, before war is begun, there ought to be sound calculation of supplies and expenses in order that fodder, corn and the rest of the provisions customarily demanded from the provincials are exacted in time and, always in more ample quantities than sufficient, stored in places best-fortified and situated opportune for warfare. (*Epit.* 3.3.1, 3; cf. Frontinus, *Strat.* 4.7.1 referring to Caesar, *B. Civ.* 1.72; cf. also Appian, *Iber.* 87 and Tacitus, *Ann.* 15.16.1).

In the Roman civil and military offices and archives there must have been a bulk of documents including, for example, plans of organization, statistics, records, letters, edicts, orders, receipts, and contracts concerning the office of the *praefectus annonae*, those of the *praefecti vehiculorum*, the corn supply of Italy, and the food supply of every single troop. But only a few documents, found in Vindonissa, Vindolanda, Dura Europos, Egypt, and elsewhere are preserved on papyrus, wooden tablets, *ostraka*, terracotta etcetera – merely by chance and mostly in fragmentary form. So we know something about the pay of imperial soldiers and what they spent on food and equipment and a little bit about the logistical duties of soldiers collecting grain, fodder, wood, wine, clothing, horses etcetera (e.g. Campbell 1994, no. 180, 183–185, 236; Tab. Vindol. 2.180–184).[1] The use of soldiers for infrastructure measures as, for instance, road building is attested by hundreds of inscriptions. And besides this source of information the Latin and Greek works of imperial historians offer many details on Roman military logistics in the context of their war narratives. This logistical information from written sources is supplemented by archaeological research which produces evidence for supply bases, granaries and other store-buildings, for transport containers like vessels, *amphorae*, and barrels, as well as for relics of army diets.

2   Military Diet and Daily Needs

The Roman state provided for its soldiers basic needs, in other words water and food; the latter in the form of about 880 grams per day of unground wheat[2] which the soldiers themselves either cooked with salt and oil to make some kind of porridge (*puls*) or baked to make "military bread" (*panis militaris*), or double-baked to make hardtack (*buccelatum*). Furthermore they received up to about 620 grams of additional food, consisting of pulses or vegetables, fruits, nuts, small quantities of cheese, half a *libra* or c. 160 grams of meat, especially smoked or air-dried like bacon (*laridum*), or fish, about a half-pint of sour wine or vinegar (*acetum*), some olive-oil, and salt. "This must have been the standard food towards the cost of which a fixed amount was deduced from each pay instalment."[3] The imperial soldiers' iron ration, which had to last for a minimum of three days,[4] consisted of *laridum*, *buccelatum*, and *acetum* (*HA*, *Avid.* 5.3).

On special occasions, e.g. festivals, the soldiers were given roasted cattle, pigs, goats, real wine etcetera as extra rations. Other kinds of food, for example the inevitable fish-sauce (*garum*), could have been bought by the soldiers at their own expense in canteens, in hot food stalls (*popinae*) in the *canabae*, or from the many sutlers (*lixae*) usually following the troops.[5] Hunting and fishing contributed to the meals. In the legionary fortress of Chester, for example, the remains of hares, boars, red and roe deer, oxen, sheep, pigs, goats, chickens, ducks, geese, pheasants, swans, oysters, and mussels were excavated. Some of these goods had come a long way. In Britain there is evidence of wine from Gaul, Italy, and Greece, *terra sigillata* from Italy and Gaul, olives, olive-oil, and plums from Spain, to name but a few. To Vindonissa were sent oysters from Portugal and the English Cannel coast, wines from southern Italy and Sicily, and oil from Spain.[6]

The troops' animals needed large quantities of water, barley, hay, and straw daily. A horse consumes 2.5 kilograms of barley and 7 kilograms of hay a day, a mule between 1.5 and 2 kilograms of barley as well as 5–6 kilograms of hay, and an ox approximately 7 kilograms of barley as well as 11 kilograms of hay or green fodder.[7]

3 Organization of Peacetime Logistics: Supplying Armies in Border Provinces and on the March

The quantitative problem

Most scholars, in their standard books on the Roman army, did not dare to give concrete figures about the size of Roman imperial forces. In the last third of the second century prior to the reign of Septimius Severus, there were 30 legions, 12,000 soldiers in the capital and approximately 483 auxiliary units, of which 36 were *alae* or *cohortes miliariae*, inclusive of servants and understrength effectives, on average altogether perhaps 450,000 men; to be added to this figure are about 30,000 men in the two main Mediterranean fleets and several provincial flotillas. If these 480,000 soldiers, sailors, and others needed 880 grams of wheat plus 620 grams of other foodstuffs daily, those in charge of Roman military logistics were confronted with the problem of providing at least 423 metric tons of corn plus 298 metric tons of supplements per day, totaling roughly 154,395 tons of wheat and 108,770 tons of supplementary food each year. In addition to that were the 670 tons of barley and 1,100 tons of hay per day for the c. 110,000 horses[8] and c. 60,000 mules which added up to an additional annual need of 244,550 tons of barley and 401,500 tons of hay or green fodder to sustain only those animals in military services. The annual need of only the Roman army in Syria – 3 *legiones*, 19 *cohortes*, 8 *alae* plus 2,500 mariners, totaling 34,500 men, all servants excluded – is estimated at 8,176 tons of wheat for the men, i.e. 22.4 tons per day, and (excluding all pack animals) at 2,505 tons of barley for the horses, i.e. circa 6.9 tons per day.[9]

An average of 35,000 horses and perhaps almost the same number of pack animals had to be replaced year by year. During the same period of time hundreds of thousands of *pila*, hundreds of thousands of tons of wood, and tens of thousands of tons of leather were needed. The legionary fortress of Inchthuthil alone consumed approximately 16,100 cubic meters of wood, 366,000 *tegulae*, and 1.575 million iron nails. The annual requirements of only the Roman troops stationed in Britain were estimated at 530,000 bushels of corn, "the total produce of an area of 106,000 acres" (Davies 1971, 137 n.104). Efforts to cover these needs changed the landscapes and native societies of newly conquered provinces and had a deep and mainly stimulating impact on agriculture and regional economies.[10]

Normal practice under the principate

The system of mobilizing material resources to provision the Roman armies in the form of taxes in money and kind had not changed substantially since the days of the republic. The tax system was imposed on the new provinces of Gallia, Britannia, Germania, Raetia, Noricum, Pannonia, and Moesia. They were responsible for the corn supply of the legions and auxiliaries stationed along the Rhine, the Danube, the *Limes*, the Fosse Way, in Wales, and later along Hadrian's or the Antonine Wall.[11] In the East the expansion of the empire under Tiberius brought comparativly slight changes insofar as in addition to the three legions stationed in Syria three more were moved to guard the frontier zones of the new province Cappadocia added to the empire by annexation. For the East, Egypt and the areas north to the Black Sea remained the most important regions for corn supply.

For several reasons the Roman Empire never developed a uniform and universally applied military supply system: first, the dislocation of the armies from the time of Augustus onwards, mainly along the borders of the empire at the Euphrates, in the northwest, middle, and east of Europe; second, the often totally different economic conditions in these European frontier provinces in which the bulk of the legions and auxilliaries were stationed permanently and which could not produce the agricultural surplus necessary for maintaining their armies of occupation; third, the deep distrust of almost every Roman emperor of any concentration or centralization of vital imperial functions and powers in other hands than his own hindered, if not prevented, a general organization of military logistics, though "by the third century the Imperial government had a standardized administrative system in place for supplying its army both in peace and war"[12] which, in my opinion, was in fact more effectively but never completely standardized. So, on the one hand, the Roman government had to meet the logistical needs of the armed forces on an ad hoc basis, with a lot of improvisation but constant improvement of the implemented institutions, too. On the other hand, the non-generalized procedure guaranteed a certain degree of flexibility, which was quite necessary if they were to cope with the problems already mentioned and those set by the different theaters of war.

The cities and communities normally provided the nearby troops with food, fodder and other requirements. For this they "were indemnified by the imperial treasury, though sometimes at below the market price with the cities to bear the loss."

In addition to this *frumentum emptum*, the *tributum*, and the *coemptio* in kind came ad hoc levies of grain as well as of other supplies to be contributed by wealthy individuals from municipal elites.[13] If soldiers, as was quite common in the East, were not stationed in their own camps but in big towns such as Antiochia, the local population had to house and feed them at their own expense. This form of *hospitium*, as it was called, made providing supplies for the army much easier for the Roman government because it did not have to be bothered with organization and transportation. So, requisition or forced purchase of military supplies of all kinds was common and is well reflected in our sources (Campbell 1994, no. 235f., 238f.). Regarding the provisioning of leather there is direct evidence beyond doubt of a public tax-in-kind for military purpose as Drusus Maior imposed a *tributum* of ox-hides on the Frisians (Tacitus, *Ann.* 4.72.1: *in usus militares*; cf. Tab. Vindol. 2.343). Whether the same was valid for the supply of arms under the principate is much debated.[14] Until the third century the *a rationibus* might have been in charge of the supply of arms; during the later Roman Empire the weaponry system was at first under the control of the office of the *praefectus praetorio* and afterwards of the *magister officiorum*. And it had been organized down to the last detail by state officials who also supervised or even ran the *armamentaria* and *fabricae*. There is still some doubt concerning the responsibility of the *praefectus annonae* for the organization or coordination of the peacetime grain-supply to the armies.[15]

Under the principate the regional distribution of money and food to the army was administered by the province's *procurator Augusti* who, under the supervision of the *a rationibus* in the imperial office in Rome, also organized the shipment of grain, oil, or wine from other provinces. But primarily responsible were the provincial governors. They not only attached to the *procuratores* soldiers, *frumentarii* in the original meaning, who had the duty of buying or collecting grain, fodder etcetera. Sometimes governors had to intervene in person against mismanagement, malfunction, or corruption in the system of collecting and transporting provincial grain to the troops (Tacitus, *Agric.* 19.4). Obviously the units themselves were responsible for at least parts of their own supply with each legion's *primus pilus*, who had under his control the *centurio frumentarius*, in direct communication with the *procurator* and the *summi curatores* doing the same job in the auxiliaries. With the money given to the units they bought food and material from local traders; and they sent detachments of soldiers out to buy grain and equipment or to fetch it from depots. And it does not seem to be unusual for soldiers to travel half the Roman Empire as is attested by the so-called Hunt's *Pridianum*, a frequently cited fragmentary day-by-day strength report of the Cohors I Hispanorum veterana stationed in the province of Moesia around 100 AD, which shows that some of its soldiers even went as far as Gaul to obtain clothing and smoked food (Fink, RMR 63 = Campbell 1994, no. 183).

The obligation to house and feed traveling soldiers on duty or whole units on the march was sometimes a great burden for smaller communities and caused much grievance – especially when soldiers, who were not on official military service and therefore not charged, did not pay for food and accommodation (*CIL* 3.12336 = Campbell 1994, no. 301; cf. Levick, no. 95). There was a great deal of complaining, mostly in vain, to the emperor or the governors, who were concerned but, though willing to redress (*OGIS* 609 = Campbell 1994, no. 299), often quite helpless in the end. To relieve the provincials at least from the private housing of soldiers passing through and the danger of forced billet (*OGIS* 609 = Campbell 1994, no. 299) villages ran public hostels. And the emperor Claudius "ordered that rest houses and official quarters should be constructed along the military roads" (Levick, no. 103).

Infrastructure of peacetime supply and transport systems

Roads, bridges, ports, ships, canals, river-dams, depots, and store houses were all part of the logistical infrastructure of the Roman supply system. Both military and civilian authorities, on the local and governmental level, provided the civil, military, and hydraulic engineering that was necessary for its construction, maintenance, restoration, and control (*Dig.* 1.16.7.1 = Campbell 1994, no. 193[16]). The governors assigned much of the task of supervision to the *beneficarii*.

In discussing the Roman military supply system Breeze put forward the question: "How were the supplies transported to the army?"; and he reviews the following four models: "1. the cities transported the goods requisitioned from them . . . ; 2. the cities employed contractors to transport the goods; 3. the army collected the goods from the point of origin; 4. the army employed contractors . . ." from which, for lack of source evidence, he only ruled out the last. In Egypt and other provinces the tax-in-kind was collected in regional depots. The transportation to these depots was the responsibility of the communities, but from there on the state was responsible for further transport, which was either undertaken by private entrepreneurs or by soldiers.[17]

Apart from the *cursus publicus*[18] all means of transport were used. Wherever possible waterborne transportation was preferred to overland transportation. A two-wheel mule-drawn cart could only move about 270 to 500 kilograms for a distance of 30 kilometers per day; a four-wheel cart had a capacity of 450 to 650 kilograms; two-wheel ox-drawn wagons moved about 363 to 500 kilograms over a daily maximum of 14 to 20 kilometers and a four-wheel wagon perhaps 430 to 650 kilograms over the same distance. Compared to these figures the loading capacities of even the smallest types of river-boats were very much higher; for example the flat-bottomed, 20–34 meters long and 3–4.5 meters broad Roman barge of the well attested Zwammerdam-type could in its smallest version carry approximately 35 metric tons, and in its biggest version up to 110 metric tons, almost reaching that of the bulbous riverboats, the *naves fluminales* pictured on Trajan's Column. So, rivers were made navigable as far as possible and quite often connected with each other by canals or by overland shuttle services. Even provincial fleets transported goods for the Roman army, and not only their own products like pottery and bricks (Konen 2002; Breeze 2000). Each fort had its own wooden or stone-built granary (*horreum*) which might have stored enough grain to sustain the unit stationed there for a whole year. In the hinterland, at strategically important or conveniently situated places on military roads, sea coasts, and rivers, some forts with extra grain capacity like Richborough, Usk,

South Shields, Benwell, Haltwhistle, Corbridge, Birrens, and Inchtuthil functioned permanently as supply depots.[19]

In order to avoid extensive abuses of the *cursus vehicularis*, which was to be provided by the provincials, their governors repeatedly had to enforce the official restrictions. Authorized were, inter alia, members of their own offices, soldiers passing through, military officials with valid warrants, and especially all personnel of the offices of the *procuratores*, who were responsible for the grain supply of the troops:

> The people of Sagalassus [sc. in *Pisidia*] must provide a service of ten carts and the same number of mules for the legitimate purposes of persons passing through, and receive from the users ten *asses* per *schoenus* [sc. Greek/Persian measure of length indicating "the distance that might be covered in an hour"] for each cart and four *asses* per *schoenus* for each mule. . . . However, the right to use these facilities shall not belong to everybody, but to the *procurator* . . . , a right to use them which extends to ten carts, or three mules in place of each cart . . . , for which they are to pay the fee established by me. Besides them, it shall belong to men on military service, and those who have a warrant, and those who travel from other provinces on military service on the following terms: . . . To those who are carrying grain or anything else of the kind for their own profit or use I wish nothing to be supplied. (Levick, no. 95)

Munera of providing ships, used as *naves frumentariae*, are emphasized in the *Digesta* (50.4.1.1; cf. 50.6.6.3ff.; 49.18.4 etc.).

Illegal requisition of transport facilities was noticed again and again. And, in case it happened to private persons, the one thing to do was following Epictetus' stoic advice: "If a requisition is taking place and a soldier takes (your mule), let it go, do not hold on to it, and do not complain. For if you do, you will get a beating and lose your mule all the same" (Campbell 1994, no. 298).

Trade and self supply

Several sources indicate the occurrence of private purchase or swap to enrich the often monotonous diet or to obtain in a cheap way articles for everyday use, like a pair of barber-shears (Campbell 1994, no. 186.13; Tab. Vindol. 2.180–184, 310). Individual soldiers bought food and other goods at private markets or from private traders. Though the use of the free market in supplying the armies is considered to have been quite limited, whole units were supplied with certain goods by *negotiatores* who sometimes had long-term sale contracts,[20] and it seems that soldiers were engaged in their own enterprises with grain, which they privately transported and traded to the army or otherwise (see Tab. Vindol. 2.343 and Levick, no. 95 cited above). The standing army of imperial times was also able to establish a quite effective system of self supply. Vast territories reserved for military use only, the *territorium* or *prata legionis*, were used for grazing cavalry horses and pack animals, raising horses and cattle such as cows, oxen, pigs, sheep, and goats, for lumbering, quarrying, and even farming. Part of the work was done by soldiers themselves, the rest by civilians or veterans to whom land was leased by the state.

Fundamental changes from the third century onwards: the new system of annona

During the political and economic crisis of the Roman Empire in the third century AD, and as a result of it, a new type of tax was created: the *annona militaris*. For the most part but not completely, this official tax-in-kind took the place of the soldiers' annual pay in money (*stipendium*), formerly given to them by the *aerarium* or the provincial *fiscus*, falling back upon the supplementary tax-in-kind system of former centuries and universalizing it throughout the empire. With it came an administrative apparatus of its own directed at the top by the *praefectus praetorio*. This new military tax did not only include the food allotment, the *annona* in the narrow sense, to civil servants and soldiers, but also fodder allowances, military clothing, and several other items of military equipment. The *actarius* or *actuarius* was in charge of both the state magazines storing the collected grain, foodstuff of all other kinds, and fodder in the provinces and the supply service of the single units for which he calculated and received the provisions from the official tax-collector, the *susceptor*.[21] But not even then had the *cursus publicus* been used for the transportation of military supplies; this is not attested until the fourth century.[22]

4 Organizing Wartime Logistics: Supplying Armies in the Field

Central planning

All logistical preparations for major wars started in Rome. After the emperor made his decision the *a rationibus* handled the finances for the forthcoming campaign, which involved the *a copiis militaribus* and on the provincial level the *procuratores Augusti*. The office of the *annonae* helped to plan, organize, and supervise the sometimes empire-wide collection and transportation of grain; and its *praefectus* presumably had to coordinate all supply efforts of overriding importance with the *a vehiculis* or the *praefecti vehiculorum*, including the distribution of food to armies on their well-scheduled march through Roman territories (cf. *ILS* 1455; *IGRR* 1.135). Of course eastern cities had to contribute and some of their wealthy citizens, like C. Iulius Severus of Ancyra, quite often took on the burden of supplying advancing troops (*OGIS* 544; cf. *AE* 1913.170). Requisitions were made frequently. And in the *Historia Augusta* the *vita* of Alexander Severus (45.2; cf. 47.1) cites an, even if faked, nevertheless highly illustrative, edict in which that emperor gave a list of all camping-places where his army was to be supplied. On another branch of the central administration the *ab epistulis* sent out demands for supplies to *civitates liberae* and *reges socii populi Romani* and recommended qualified officers or prefects for the special posts of a *curator copiarum exercitus* or a *praepositus annonae expeditionis*. All of these were extraordinary commands, limited in time and restricted to a single task. And at least until the third century everything happened on an ad hoc basis.[23]

During Domitian's Danubian wars Plotius Grypus, a *tribunus laticlavius*, was responsible for a part of the military *annona* and the provisioning of *stationes viarum* along the roads leading to the deployment zone (*Stat. Silv.* 4.9.17–19). In Trajan's Dacian War C. Caelius Martialis had the *copiarum cura* (*AE* 1934.2). The logistics of Lucius Verus' Parthian campaign were probably organized by the *comes Augusti*, L. Aurelius Nicomedes, a former *praefectus vehiculorum* who was then in charge of the *cura copiarum exercitus*, perhaps under the direct surveillance of that emperor in his strategic center at Antiochia (*ILS* 1740; Dio 71.2.2). During the same war the much honored M. Valerius Maximianus may have looked after the supplies from the Black Sea area; and in the first Marcommanic war he commanded at the same time a special cavalry unit and detachments of the fleets stationed in Ravenna, Misenum, and the English Channel in order to secure the shipment of military supplies to the armies in Pannonia on the Danube (*AE* 1956.124). Ti. Claudius Candidus functioned as a *praepositus copiarum expeditionis Germanicae secundae* in the second Marcomannic war (*ILS* 1140). On corps level some *primi pili* of the expeditionary forces were responsible for supplies.

Help from friends or allies: frumentum imperatum

Since the days of the republic it had become a common practice for foreign kings as allies and friends of the Roman people, *reges amici et socii populi Romani*, to be ordered to aid the Romans with troops and supplies during their wars. So, Herod the Great in 39 BC sustained a Roman army operating in Palestine with "a greater mass of provisions than anyone had hoped for, and also instructed those around Samaria . . . to bring down to Jericho grain, wine, oil, cattle and all other things in order that there should be no lack of supplies for the (Roman) soldiers for some days to come" (Josephus, *Ant. Jud.* 14.408); in 30 BC he supplied Octavian's army on its march to Egypt and back with water and all kind of provisions (Josephus, *B. Jud.* 1.395). In AD 54 and 63 the friendly kings of the East and in the neighborhood of Roman Syria received orders to obey and help Corbulo (Tacitus, *Ann.* 13.7.1; 13.8.2; 15.25.3; cf. 15.26.2; 12.12.2; *Hist.* 5.1.2); among them king Iulius Polemo of Pontus was responsible for the security of the Roman supply line running through his country from Trapezus into Armenia (Tacitus, *Ann.* 13.39.1).

Supply bases and army trains

Amphibious operations and overseas transport of military supplies are attested, for example, for the Augustan and Tiberian wars in Germany. Velleius Paterculus in his *Historia Romana* (2.106.3) mentioned the well-scheduled meeting of Tiberius' army and fleet shipping supplies over the North Sea into the Elbe. The same is reported by Tacitus (*Ann.* 1.60, 63, 70; 2.5ff.; *Agric.* 25.1) for Germanicus' campaigns in northern Germany in 15 and 16 AD and for Agricola's campaign in Scotland. To supervise the overseas supply lines in times of war *primi pili* were assigned to logistical duties in important harbors such as Aquileia; for Salona a *centurio frumentarius* is attested who, commanding *vexillationes* of the newly levied Legiones II and III, may have had a similar function (*ILS* 2287). In the East in the second half of the first century AD e.g. the Black Sea habor town of Trapezus became a major supply base for the operations in Armenia and later the naval base of the new Pontic fleet.

Riverborne provisioning is attested by historical reports, and epigraphical and archaeological evidence. During Trajan's Parthian War Aburnius Tuscianus, an equestrian officer, had to secure the supply lines on and along the Euphrates as a kind of *curator annonae bello Parthico ripae Euphratis* (*ILS* 9471; see 2709 for another *praefectus ripae fluminis Euphrati*). The importance of riverborne provisioning of campaigning armies in this area is also well attested for the expeditions of Septimius Severus and Julian (Dio 76.9.3–5; Amm. Marc. 23.3.9; 23.5.6). For the Danube the same is documented in the already mentioned inscription for Valerius Maximus. The excavations at Beckinghausen near the legion-fortress Oberaden and at Haltern-Hofestaat revealed at the River Lippe several so-called Uferkastelle with discharging-facilities. The fortress near Anreppen, built directly at the bank of the same river in the late autumn of 4 AD (Vell. 2.105.3), functioned as a supply base for Tiberius' operations in Germany in those years, and very probably much longer. It had a large magazine of approximately 3,808 square meters; in a specially restricted area of the *castra* at least five granaries of altogether about 2,370 square meters with a storage capacity of in the region of 2,370–2,844 cubic meters, sufficient for between 1,778 and 2,133 tons of wheat and therefore enough to sustain the above mentioned expeditionary forces of Tiberius for about 78 days. In the legionary fortress of Inchtuthil[24] at the River Tay archaeologists have found the remains of six wooden granaries; each of them measured roughly 41.5 × 12.8 m = 531.2 square meters, may have had a utilizable floor space of around 281 square meters and at least a capacity of 421 cubic meters for the storage of about 1,003 rations of wheat per man per year – all six totaling about 2,527 cubic meters with a capacity of about 6,018 wheat rations per man per year. More space was intentionally left for another two *horrea* that size, and a fortified, so-called stores compound nearby, too, provided enough space for a lot more magazines. Operational bases like this were established in all frontier zones at navigable rivers with the aim of sustaining armies in the field.

The expeditionary forces Tiberius led against the Germans beyond the River Weser in the autumn of 4 AD may have consisted of 3 legions, 3 *alae* of auxiliary cavalry and 9 auxiliary infantry cohorts, adding up to about 27,500 men of required or 25,000 men of effective strength, all *calones* included, plus 3,800 horses and at least 7,000 mules. Green fodder excluded, the daily need of a force that size came to roughly 25 tons of wheat, 7.5 tons of complementary food, 9.5 tons of barley for the horses, and 14 tons for the pack animals, totaling to transport requirements of 56 metric tons per day. Taking into account that all men and all animals carried their 17-day food ration themselves, this adding up to a volume of 952 tons, the army train still had the task of transporting 56 tons for each additional day. If every pack animal had a payload of a maximum of 135 kilograms for a minimum of 50 kilometers a day,[25] it, in addition to its own need of 35 kilograms of barley, could not have carried more than 100 kilograms of food for the army. So, the above estimated 4,000 mules could transport 400 tons, which meant a supply reserve for a week only and a total operational range of 24 days for the whole army. A mere multiplication of the number of pack animals was no proper solution to the problem, for all additional mules also had to be fed. Under normal conditions that was not too difficult, but dire straits were encountered when constant fighting, fast marches, or the country's barrenness prevented cavalry horses and pack animals from grazing or foraging green fodder. In those cases each horse had to carry another 9 kilograms of fodder per day and each mule another 6 kilograms, which increased the daily need of the whole army by 53 tons to a total of 109 tons and thereby automatically reduced the capacity of each pack to a payload of only 33 kilograms. The 4,000 mules could not have transported more than 132 tons of food for the army, thus limiting the latter's food reserve to not more than one-and-a-half days' worth. The logistical situation became even worse, for example on campaigns in the East, when the army had to carry not only its food but most of its daily need of water too. The consequence was an even more drastic reduction of the force's range of action. The logistical solution to this problem of supplying armies in the field was the starting of shuttle services. From the strategic base of Tiberius' army at Vetera its advanced supply depot at Anreppen was provisioned regularly via the rivers of the Rhine and Lippe. From this depot onwards wagon convoys transported food and equipment further east to a river depot at the Weser; and from there on again riverborne transport came into action shipping, rafting, or towing supplies to other river depots north or south, from which mule shuttle-transports finally reached the temporary camps of Tiberius' campaining army. In his German campaign of 10/9 BC Drusus the Elder used a small fort at Rödgen[26] in Hesse as an advanced tactical supply depot which could be reached and therefore provisioned via the rivers Lahn or Wetterau and by short overland transports. Archaeology has unearthed the remains of three wooden granaries with altogether approximately 3,457 square meters of ground floor and a capacity of 3,445 to 4,149 cubic meters for the storage of 2,584 to 3,112 tons of wheat, corresponding to 8,202 to 9,878 rations per man per year or grain for an army of three legions for half a year.

Living off the land: requisitioning, foraging, plundering

Where and whenever possible all resources of the enemy country were exploited through foraging, plundering, or requisitioning fodder, wood, water, and food for Rome's campaigning troops, which also tried to reduce the fighting ability of the enemy by pillaging his land. But in view of the figures given above for the daily needs of an expeditionary force, consisting of only three legions plus auxiliaries and train, sustaining armies off the land was, quite obviously, never easy, often impossible – especially in barren lands, deserts, or "barbarian" countries with undeveloped agriculture – and always dangerous: "Even in very fertile land at the right time of year, a large army exhausted quickly the land around it and was forced to send its foragers out further and further afield. (And) these small groups of men were always vulnerable to attack."[27] Especially while campaining in the East, in some regions water was seasonally scarce, and so Corbulo was in short supply of water and grain in Armenia until his army reached cultivated land and could forage (Tacitus, *Ann.* 14.24.1).

5 Conclusion: Roman Military Logistic Skills, the Way to Success?

Success in ancient and modern warfare was not and still is not due solely to the ability to put the biggest, best armed, organized, trained, disciplined, and commanded army into the field – if logistics failed, so did campaigns. In other words: it never depended on the will of Roman generals where, how, how fast, and with how many troops they could operate in Germany, Britain, Armenia, or Parthia, but on where, how, and how long they could supply their forces there. Storing enough food in strategic and operational bases, building and provisioning advanced supply depots, organizing and guarding shuttle-transports (cf. Tacitus, *Ann.* 13.39.1), advising regional and foreign friends or allies to collect and deliver supplies, advancing along routes which guaranteed a safe and steady water and food supply (cf. Tacitus, *Ann.* 15.12.1; 15.3.2), securing the harvest of a hostile country, capturing its supply depots – which meant preventing the enemy from carrying away or burning the first and from destroying the last – harming the enemy's logistics by pillaging, outmaneuvering enemy forces, and cutting off their supply lines meant victory – sometimes even without fighting.

NOTES

1 On the costs of the army, see Herz (in this volume). On logistical duties of soldiers Speidel 1996, 72ff.; Adams 1995; Birley 1997; Breeze 2000, 60f.; Whittaker 2002.

2 Calculations varied much: until the thorough analysis of Foxhall and Forbes modern experts used to estimate the daily corn ration of Roman soldiers at 3 pounds (e.g. Davies 1971, 123; Goldsworthy 1998, 291; Goldberg and Findlow 1984, 380); Foxhall and Forbes 1982, 73 and 56, calculated 895 grams, which corresponds quite well with the few quantitative data from ancient sources (two-thirds of an Attic *medimnos* which equals 35 liters or 4 Roman *modii* or c. 26.5 kilograms of wheat a month; see Erdkamp 1998, 27ff., 43ff.; cf. Manning 1975, 116; Kehne 2004, 139 and Erdkamp, in this volume) and arithmetical figures relating to the size of the Roman standard *centuria* of 10 *contubernia* with 8 men each (therefore 80 × 60 = 4,800 men in one legion) which was given one *modius* (= 8.75 l) of wheat a day, which made 10 *modii* per *centuria* and 600 per legion; cf. Roth 1999, 18–23, who therefore calculated 850 grams a day.

3 Davies 1971, 125; cf. Roth 1999, 24–53 and Webster 1985, 262f.

4 Josephus, *B. Jud.* 3.95. Following the testimonies of Cicero, *Tusc.* 2.37 and *HA, Sev. Alex.* 47.1 imperial infantrymen had to carry a ration to last half a month or even 17 days with them in their pack (*sarcina*). For the continuing discussion about the burdens Roman legionaries had to carry themselves see Veith 1928, 424f.; Roth 1999, 69ff.; Erdkamp 1998, 76ff.; Kehne 1999, 313 and Kehne 2004, 120 n.26.

5 Roth 1999, 93–101.

6 Davies 1971; cf. in Erdkamp 2002a, 244ff.

7 Roth 1999, 66f.; cf. Erdkamp (in this volume).

8   That is c. 200 per legion, 560 per *ala quingenaria*, 1,120 per *ala milliaria*, 132 per
     cohors equitata quingenaria, 264 per *cohors equitata milliaria*, 220 per *numerus* and up
     to 10 for each of all the other *cohortes* (cf. Herz 2002, 33f.).
9   Kissel 1995, 37, 394ff., fig. 5–8.
10   Cp. Birley 1981; Breeze 1984; 1990; Wierschowski 1984; 2002; Haynes 2002; cf. in
     Erdkamp 2002a, 6ff., 169ff., 345ff., 375ff.
11   For relations between logistic costs and Roman territorial gains in Britain see Goldberg
     and Findlow 1984, 366ff.
12   Roth 1999, 265.
13   Breeze 2000, 59; Erdkamp 2002b, 60ff; Birley, 59 (the quotation).
14   Wierschowski 2002, 276f. n.31; Kissel 1995, 178ff.
15   On *armamentaria* and *fabricae* see Kissel 1995, 191ff. and the literature in Kehne 2004,
     120 n.29, 142. On the responsibility of the *praefectus annonae* Erdkamp 2002b, 53f.
     with n.16; Roth 1999, 263f., cf. ibid. 240f.
16   Cf. Adams 1976, 11ff., 82ff.; Anderson 1992; Kissel 1995, 55ff., 67ff.; Roth 1999, 214ff.;
     Kissel 2002; Herz 2002, 31f.; Kolb 2000 and 2002; on storage see Rickman 1971; Gentry
     1976 and Manning 1975.
17   Breeze 2000, 60ff. Kolb 2000, 228ff., 237f., 240; cf. Kissel 1995, 45ff.
18   Kolb 2002, 163ff.
19   Land transport: Goldsworthy 1998, 293f.; Roth 1999, 211f.; Erdkamp 1998, 72. River
     transport: Konen 2000, 234ff. with fig. 31. Storage: Gentry 1976; Manning 1975; Rickman
     1971, 271ff.
20   Wierschowski 1984, 180ff.; 2001; 2002, 276f.; cf. Erdkamp 2002b, 65ff.
21   Who, in the later Roman Empire, took the place of the former *procurator*. For the role and
     the effect of the late antique *annona* as a tax-in-kind see among others van Berchem 1937;
     cf. Herz 1988, 181ff., 203ff.; Roth 1999, 265f.; the literature in Erdkamp 2002b, 47f.
     and Kehne 2004, 117f. with nn.12 and 14; and as a general study as well as an example
     for the various regional studies on the *annonae* in late antiquity especially Mitthoff 2001.
22   Kolb 2002, 165.
23   For all this and the following see Adams 1976, 220ff.; Kissel 1995, 131ff., 264ff., 271ff.;
     Roth 1999, 261ff.; Herz 2002, 24ff.; Erdkamp 2002b, 51ff., 61ff.
24   Pitts and Joseph 1985, 116ff. with several maps: fig. 2b, 24–7, 79–84; Manning 1975,
     108, cf. 110, tab. 3: each *horreum* had 140 × 40 = 5,600 *pedes quadrati*.
25   Roth 1999, 206f. gives modern proof for 135 to 160 kilometers per day; Goldsworthy
     1996, 293, tab. 5 estimates a payload of only 91 kilograms and a speed of 5 kilometers
     per hour; Erdkamp 1998, 72 calculates with a maximum payload of 100 kilograms per mule.
26   It only had c. 3.3 hectares: Manning 1975, 105; Rickman 1971, 239ff.
27   Goldsworthy 1998, 291.

BIBLIOGRAPHY

Adams, C. E. P. 1995. "Supplying the Roman army: O. Petr. 245," *ZPE* 109: 119–24.

Adams, J. P. 1976. *Logistics of the Roman Imperial Army. Major Campaigns in the First Three Centuries AD.* Diss. Yale.

Anderson, J. D. 1992. *Roman Military Supply in North-East England. An Analysis of and an Alternative to the Piercebridge Formula.* Oxford.

van Berchem, D. 1937. "L'annone militaire dans l'Empire romain au IIIe siècle," *Mémoires de la Société nationale des antiquaires de France* 10: 117–202.

Birley, A. R. 1981. "The economic effects of Roman frontier policy," in A. King and M. Henig (eds.), *The Roman West in the Third Century 1.* Oxford, 39–53.

—— 1997. "Supplying the Batavians at Vindolanda," in *Roman Frontier Studies 1995. Proceedings of the XVIth International Congress of Roman Frontier Studies.* Oxford, 273–80.

Breeze, D. J. 1984. "Demand and supply on the northern frontier," in R. Miket and C. Burgess (eds.), *Between and Beyond the Walls.* Edinburgh, 264–86 [and in Breeze and Dobson 1993, 526–52].

—— 1987/88. "The logistics of Agricola's final campaign," *Talanta* 18/19: 7–28 [and in Breeze and Dobson 1993, 574–95].

—— 1990. "The impact of the Roman army on the native peoples of North Britain," in *Akten des 14. Internationalen Limeskongresses 1986 in Carnuntum.* Vienna, 85–97 [and in Breeze and Dobson 1993, 596–608].

—— 2000. "Supplying the army," in G. Alföldy et al. (eds.), *Kaiser, Heer und Gesellschaft in der römischen Kaiserzeit. Gedenkschrift für E. Birley.* Stuttgart, 59–64.

Breeze, D. J., and B. Dobson. 1993. *Roman Officers and Frontiers.* Stuttgart.

Campbell, J. B. (ed.). 1994. *The Roman Army, 31 BC–AD 337. A Sourcebook.* London and New York.

—— (ed.). 2004. *Greek and Roman Military Writers. Selected Readings.* London and New York.

Davies, R. W. 1971. "The Roman military diet," *Britannia* 2: 122–42 [and in Davies, *Service in the Roman Army.* Edinburgh 1989, 187–206; 283–90].

Erdkamp, P. 1998. *Hunger and the Sword. Warfare and Food Supply in Roman Republican Wars (264–30 BC).* Amsterdam.

—— (ed.). 2002a. *The Roman Army and the Economy.* Amsterdam.

—— 2002b. "The corn supply of the Roman armies during the principate (27 BC–235 AD)," in Erdkamp, *The Roman Army and the Economy.* Amsterdam, 47–69.

Foxhall, L., and H. A. Forbes. 1982. "Sitometreia: The role of grain as a staple food in classical antiquity," *Chiron* 12: 41–90.

Gentry, A. 1976. *Roman Military Stone-built Granaries in Britain.* Oxford.

Goldberg, N. J., and F. J. Findlow. 1984. "A quantitative analysis of Roman military operations in Britain, circa AD 43 to 238," in R. B. Ferguson (ed.), *Warfare, Culture and Environment.* Orlando, 359–85.

Goldsworthy, A. K. 1998. *The Roman Army at War 100 BC–AD 200* (with a new preface). Oxford.

Haynes, I. 2002. "Britain's first information revolution. The Roman army and the transformation of economic life," in Erdkamp 2002a, 111–26.

Herz, P. 1988. *Studien zur römischen Wirtschaftsgesetzgebung. Die Lebensmittelversorgung.* Stuttgart.

—— 2002. "Die Logistik der kaiserzeitlichen Armee. Strukturelle Überlegungen," in Erdkamp 2002a, 19–46.

Kehne, P. 1999. "Logistik," in H. Sonnabend (ed.), *Mensch und Landschaft in der Antike. Lexikon der Historischen Geographie.* Stuttgart, 308–15.

—— 2004. "Zur Logistik des römischen Heeres von der mittleren Republik bis zum Ende der hohen Kaiserzeit (241 v. Chr.–235 n. Chr.): Forschungen und Tendenzen," *Militärgeschichtliche Zeitschrift* 63: 115–51.

Kissel, Th. 1995. *Untersuchungen zur Logistik des römischen Heeres in den Provinzen des griechischen Ostens (27 v. Chr.–235 n. Chr.).* St. Katharinen.

—— 2002. "Road-building as a munus publicum," in Erdkamp 2002a, 127–60.

Kolb, A. 2000. *Transport und Nachrichtentransfer im Römischen Reich.* Berlin.
—— 2002. "Army and transport," in Erdkamp 2002a, 161–6.
Konen, H. Cl. 2000. *Classis Germanica.* St. Katharinen.
—— 2002. "Die ökonomische Bedeutung der Provinzialflotten während der Zeit des Prinzipats," in Erdkamp 2002a, 309–42.
Levick, B. (ed.). 2000. *The Government of the Roman Empire. A Sourcebook* (2nd edn.). London.
MacMullen, R. 1984. "The Roman emperor's army costs," *Latomus* 43: 571–80.
Manning, W. H. 1975. "Roman military timber granaries in Britain," *Saalburg Jahrbuch* 32: 105–29.
Mitthoff, F. 2001. *Annona militaris. Die Heeresversorgung im spätantiken Ägypten.* Florence.
von Petrikovits, H. 1991. "Militärisches Nutzland in den Grenzprovinzen des römischen Reiches," in H. von Petrikovits, *Beiträge zur römischen Archäologie und Geschichte 2.* Cologne, 61–71.
Pitts, L. F., and J. K. St. Joseph. 1985. *Inchtuthil.* London.
Rickman, G. 1971. *Roman Granaries and Store Buildings.* Cambridge.
Roth, J. 1999. *The Logistics of the Roman Army at War (264 BC–AD 235).* Leiden.
—— 2000. "Logistics and the legion," in Y. Le Bohec and C. Wolff (eds.), *Les légions de Rome sous le Haut-Empire.* Lyon, 707–10.
Speidel, M. 1996. *Die römischen Schreibtafeln von Vindonissa.* Brugg.
Veith, G. 1928. "Die Zeit des Milizheeres," in J. Kromayer and G. Veith, *Heerwesen und Kriegführung der Griechen und Römer.* Munich [ND 1963], 254–469.
Webster, Gr. 1985. *The Roman Imperial Army of the First and Second Centuries AD.* 3rd edn., Totowa, NJ; with a new introduction by H. Elton, Norman 1998.
Whittaker, Ch. R. 2002. "Supplying the army. Evidence from Vindolanda," in Erdkamp 2002a, 204–34.
Wierschowski, L. 1984. *Heer und Wirtschaft. Das römische Heer der Prinzipatszeit als Wirtschaftsfaktor.* Bonn.
—— 2001. "Die römische Heeresversorgung im frühen Prinzipat," *Münstersche Beiträge zur antiken Handelsgeschichte* 20.2: 37–61.
—— 2002. "Das römische Heer und die ökonomische Entwicklung Germaniens in den ersten Jahrzehnten des 1. Jh.s," in Erdkamp 2002a, 264–92.

FURTHER READING

On the logistics of Roman republican and imperial armies at war the most substantial and comprehensive systematic studies of Erdkamp 1998 and Roth 1999 are basic. Erdkamp 2002a presents the most recent collection of (16) articles on the subject of supplying Roman armies in times of peace. Kehne 1999 views Roman army logistics in the context of ancient military logistics in its entirety. Kehne 2004 surveys the literature (until 2002) dealing with various aspects of Roman war- and peacetime logistics.

On the military diet, nutritional requirements, rations, quantities etc. see Davies 1971, Foxhall and Forbes 1982, Erdkamp 1998, 27–45, Roth 1999, 7–59; cf. the works cited in Kehne 2004, 118–19, 139–41. Veith 1928 discusses older theses on the individual soldier's burden; cf. Roth 1999, 71–7, Erdkamp 1998, 76–80, and Kehne 2004, 120 n.26.

Roth 1999, 236–41 is devoted to the sources of supplies in imperial times. Non-edible goods of military supply (weapons, wood, oil, leather, metal, bricks, roofing tiles or shingles, *terra sigillata* etc.) are dealt with by Kissel 1995, 177–237, Erdkamp 2002a, 235–63 and Herz 2002, 38; cf. Kehne 2004, 120 nn.29–30, 142, 146–7. On the supply of animals see

Roth 1999, 144–6, Kissel 1995, 234–7, Herz 2002, 33–7, and the literature in Kehne 2004, 145–6. Transportation of supplies to the armies and the operation and administration of the lines of supply are analyzed or described by Anderson 1992, Adams 1995, Erdkamp 1998, 46–83, Roth 1999, 189–214, 244–71, Breeze 2000, Kolb 2000, 2002, Erdkamp 2002a, 70–83, and Kehne 2004, 147. Roth 1999, 79–91 focuses on army trains.

For the on-going discussion, if the *annona militaris* was, without being named so, already established in the first century AD, see Kissel 1995, 120–42, Roth 1999, 240–3, 261–4, Wierschowski 2001, 2002, 271–82, Herz 2002, 39–43, Erdkamp 2002b, 51–5, Erdkamp 2002a, 80–2, 295–8, and Kehne 2004, 129–30. On the *annona militaris* during late antiquity see van Berchem 1937, Herz 1988, Mitthoff 2001, and the studies cited in Kehne 2004, 117–18, nn.10–14.

Economic factors of the Roman military supply system and its impacts are emphasized, e.g., by Birley 1981, Breeze 1990, Wierschowski 1984, 2002, Haynes 2002, and Erdkamp 2002a, 345–74, 382–6. On the relation of "command economy" and "private trade" in regard to military provisioning see furthermore the introduction to Erdkamp 2002a, 10–12. The article of Whittaker 2002 is devoted to the tablets of Vindolanda and other written sources giving evidence for the origins of military supplies. On the *territorium legionis* see von Petrikovits 1991 and the research cited in Kehne 2004, 126 n.62.

Adams 1976, as well as Kissel 1995, analyzes logistical preparations, infrastructures, ad hoc measures etc. of major campaigns in the East; cf. Kehne 2004, 132–4 for criticism of the latter. Erdkamp 1998, 122–40 and Roth 1999, 117–55, cf. 286–98 and 305, are fundamental on the strategy, techniques, and limitations of "living off the land." The importance of military logistics to warfare is stressed by Erdkamp 1998, 141–55 and Roth 1999, 279–328; cf. Kehne 2004, 115–16, 127–8.

The topic of the medical service of Rome's military forces and its logistical needs, omitted in this chapter, is treated, for example by Kissel 1995, 238–50 and the literature cited in Kehne 2004, 115 n.2; Roth 1999, 55–6 deals with the special aspect of the diet in military hospitals.

CHAPTER NINETEEN

The Roman Army
and Propaganda

Olivier Hekster

All Roman emperors waged war. If not in reality, certainly in the public perception. Roman leaders, in republic and empire, had to abide by a well-developed system of political values, in which military success, alongside and above other cardinal *virtutes*, was paramount. Inevitably, the message that all emperors broadcast was of their military capacity. Even an emperor such as Hadrian (117–138 AD), who gave up Roman territory, defined and indicated the limits of empire and – unlike most of his predecessors – avoided acceptance of the title *imperator* until subduing the threat to Rome of the Bar Kokhba revolt (132–135 AD), still displayed himself in cuirass on a substantial part of his coins, showed his hunting skills in imperial artwork, and continuously addressed the legions in reality and imagery. *Virtus*, manly courage and military daring, may not have been the most displayed imperial quality on imperial coins, but in combination with *providentia* (the foresight required to safeguard the state), militarily-related qualities comprised 25 percent of all imperial virtues as displayed on denarii between AD 69–238. Throughout the principate, also, emperors tended to start their letters to the Senate with the words: "I and the legions are in health." Roman subjects were aware of the military machine at imperial disposal. When the rhetorician Favorinus was reproached by friends for yielding to Hadrian in a matter of grammar though being in the right, he responded that the "most learned man is the one who has thirty legions." Emperors themselves, finally, realized the importance of the legions, and made sure that any statement of importance reached the soldiers. Thus, the *Senatus Consultum de Cn. Pisone patre* (*SCPP*), describing the senatorial proceedings against the alleged murderer of Germanicus (AD 20) explicitly states (line 173) that the degree should be set up, amongst other places, "in the winter quarters of each legion where the standards are kept."[1] The centrality of Roman armies, then, becomes clear from the continuous attempts of the emperor (or those around him) to broadcast the image of the princeps as successful war leader to the people of the Roman Empire at large, the soldiers in particular, and through the reception of that image by the diverse population of the realm. This chapter will focus on the distribution of, and to an extent reaction to, these public images. Before turning specific attention to the images disseminated of and to the armies, the question of whether this dissemination can be interpreted as "propaganda" must be addressed.

1   Imperial Images and Propaganda

As is often stated, the term propaganda originally referred to the affairs of the *Sacra Congregatio de Propaganda Fide*. This was a papal body which was founded in 1622 to "promote" obedience to key church doctrines. History since then has given the concept a multitude of connotations, which are expertly put forward elsewhere, as is the discussion on the application of the concept within the study of Roman imperial history. Much about "propaganda" is debated, but there seems to be common consent about the division into agitation propaganda – aimed at changing attitudes – and integration propaganda – aimed at reinforcing them. If anything, only the latter seems to be useful for describing Roman imperial practice. Recently, however, it has been argued that "propaganda" is too crude a term for a complex and multi-faceted phenomenon. It also easily implies associations to totalitarian states; associations that give political systems that are described as using "propaganda" a sinister and forbidding aspect. Yet, all of this does not render the term useless. Its application may need rethinking, and its definition clarifying, but to erase the notion from our theoretical framework entirely would result in losing all theories and explanations connected with it – an entire set of possibly useful tools. It is also questionable to what extent using alternative words is substantially different from using the term "propaganda" as such, when what is essentially meant is dissemination of ideas by people in power in a certain period, or whether side-stepping the question "by referring simply to the undoubted 'political themes' . . . rather than to 'propaganda' . . ." solves the problem.[2]

Setting aside the theoretical discussion for a while and returning to the ancient world, there seems to be at least one piece of evidence from the Roman Empire that, without qualification, fits the category "propaganda." It is the above mentioned *SCPP*. At first sight, it might seem a surprising example. Yet the inscription is "disseminating the model of behaviour which emphasised the position of the *domus Augusta* at the top of the social and political hierarchy." This decree of the Senate told an important story, which will have been new to most of its audience, expressing explicit values in the telling. The Senate "learned in particular from divus Aug. and Ti. Caesar Aug., its Principes" the virtues of "clemency, justice, and generosity of spirit" (lines 91–3). The *plebs* is praised "because it joined with the equestrian order in demonstrating its devotion towards our Princeps" (lines 155–6), whilst it is hoped that:

> all who were soldiers in the service of our Princeps will continue to manifest the same loyalty and devotion to the Imperial house, since they know that the safety of our empire depends on the protection of that House. (160–2)

Clearly, the position and behavior of the imperial family were presented as crucial to the empire as a whole. The virtues so explicitly put forward, constituted, furthermore, not some sort of common set. It therefore "follows that they were selected for advertisement because they sent a specific message about what it was that a specific emperor wanted his subjects to think about him." This value-laden document was, finally, deliberately disseminated. Not just amongst the soldiers, but:

> These decrees of the Senate, inscribed on bronze, should be set up in whatever place seems best to Tiberius Cae(sar) Aug., and likewise . . . in the most frequented city of each province and in the most frequented place in that city, and . . . in the winter quarters of each legion where the standards are kept. (169–73)

The image of a righteous imperial family is broadcast throughout the empire, alongside information on the vices of Cn. Piso, who tried to oppose them. The world was shown the image of the emperor that the Senate put forward. Whatever one may think of other pieces of evidence, this, at least, may count as propaganda. And it is noticeable that soldiers are an important group at whom this propaganda was directed.

Similarly, one can see a clear differentiation of messages in the coins of different denominations minted in the years AD 68–69 in which four different claimants for the throne loomed large. Galba aimed for provincial support in his gold and silver coins, but emphasized more urban themes in his bronzes. Otho, on the other hand, did not mint any bronzes at all, but tried to indulge the praetorians and senators instead. Vitellius, in his turn, did mint bronzes, proclaiming ANNONA AUGUSTI, CERES AUGUSTI, PAX AUGUSTI, and ROMA RENASCENS, whereas his silver and gold coins read, among other legends, CONCORDIA P(OPULI) R(OMANI) and CONCORDIA PRAETORIANORUM, PONT(IFEX) MAXIM(US). Vespasian (69–79), finally, on some rare coins combines the image of a victorious general with emphasis on the importance of the Moesian legions, which were instrumental in giving him the ultimate victory in the civil wars. Those coins, possibly samples from locally issued donatives (gifts of money to the soldiers at special occasions, such as the beginning of an emperor's reign), name the EXERCITUS MOESIC(US) and VICT(ORIA) AUG(USTI). Again, it seems that specific support groups were purposely targeted.[3] And again, soldiers were an important audience to reach. In some contexts, then, propaganda seems the right term to describe the distribution of imperial messages, though the necessary caveats should always be kept in mind.

2 Propagating Emperor and Army

The emperor and those surrounding him had various modes at their disposal through which to distribute the image of emperor and army to soldiers and the wider audience alike. Roughly, these can be divided into three categories. Firstly, the urban and artistic landscape of the empire, with special emphasis on the city of Rome. Secondly, actions and appearance which were directly linked to the figure of the emperor, such as titulature, acclamations, and ceremonies such as triumphs. Lastly, media which were transferred more easily from one individual to another, like coinage or literary works.

Monuments and sculptural art

Throughout her history, prominent Romans had adorned the city of Rome. Temples paid for by the spoils of war (*ex manubiis*) were constructed by victorious generals along the triumphal route through the city's center. Important families were responsible for the conservation of significant buildings. The arrival of emperors placed final responsibility for the upkeep of the city, both architectural and sculptural, in the hands of one individual. Buildings and sculptures reflected, if not directly what the emperor wanted, at least what people *believed* the emperor wanted. Imperial involvement stretched beyond that. Famously, Augustus (30 BC–AD 14) is supposed to have said of Rome that he "found it of mud-brick but left it of marble." Indeed, under Augustus Rome was transformed, to become a worthy seat of the new imperial family, emphasizing Augustus' ideology and dynasty. Later emperors followed suit.

Unsurprisingly, Rome was molded according to imperial preferences: harbors to guarantee food and (amphi)theaters or bathhouses to keep the *plebs* entertained; palaces to emphasize imperial superiority or (relatively) humble imperial residences to emphasize imperial modesty; omnipresent images of the emperor and his family. It is, then, telling for the centrality of the military that representations of armies and vanquished are near ubiquitous in Rome's urban and artistic landscape. The Imperial Fora, centerpieces of the emperors' self-fashioning and a dominant feature of ancient Rome, were ultimately victory monuments. Caesar's Forum was built following a vow to his mythical ancestress Venus Genetrix at the battle of Pharsalus and the Forum was dedicated on the last day of Caesar's great triumph of 46 BC. Augustus' Forum, with its central temple to Mars the Avenger, was built *ex manubiis* and housed the Parthian standards which were recovered in 20 BC, over 30 years after they had been lost at the battle of Carrhae (53 BC). The claim that it was built in reaction to a battlefield vow, to avenge the death of Caesar, though only reported (and probably conceived) in 17 BC, still betrays the importance of military motives in founding such a complex.[4]

More than either of these buildings, Vespasian's Templum Pacis emphasized the importance to the imperial family of military victory, and thus implicitly of the armies with which that victory was achieved. The Forum was begun after the capture of Jerusalem, which was extensively celebrated in a triumph (AD 71) that was somewhat delayed to make sure that Vespasian's son Titus, returned from the front, could share in it. Victory and peace were explicitly connected to the war in Judea:

> After these triumphs were over, and after the affairs of the Romans were settled on the surest foundations, Vespasian resolved to build a temple to Peace . . . he also displayed in it those golden vessels and instruments that were taken out of the Jewish temple, as signs of his glory.

The spoils of vanquished Judea were on display for anyone to see. These spoils, furthermore, supplied the money with which the Colosseum could be paid for – as an

Plate 19.1 Arch of Titus: relief depicting spoils from the temple of Jerusalem.
Photo: Olivier Hekster

inscription in bronze emphasized. Triumph and victory were further celebrated in Domitian's arch for Titus (after the latter's death), depicting in reliefs the great triumph of the Flavian dynasty, and the spoils taken out of the temple (Plate 19.1). The Flavian's military quality was, quite literally, set in stone.[5]

The Flavians only monumentalized the armies implicitly, perhaps in order not to overly emphasize the civil war through which Vespasian obtained power. In fact, the emperor's role in this war was underplayed, by portraying him as a reluctant contender and by stressing that during the fighting itself, Vespasian stayed in Alexandria. Cruelty and misbehavior of the troops was blamed on underlings. Trajan (98–117) had no such qualms. A military emperor par excellence, his forum emphasized him as omnipotent victor. The whole complex was a tribute to Trajan and his armies. Images of the conquered Dacians, of legionary standards, and of the victorious emperor were there for all to see. Again, the message that the forum was paid for *ex manubiis* was clearly displayed, in this case through inscriptions on the attics of the colonnades. Even the specific divisions that had fought the wars were named in further inscriptions. Finally, the famous column of Trajan shows in great narrative detail how the emperor, as a wise general, conducted the campaign, commanded the armies,

Plate 19.2   Arch of Constantine: Relief depicting part of the Great Trajanic Frieze.
Photo: Olivier Hekster

and defeated Rome's foes. There are descriptions of both Dacian wars that Trajan fought, with an image of Victory separating the two accounts. Rome's superiority over the barbarians is continuously stressed, with the emperor, repeatedly on show, as the uniting factor of the Roman forces. In the heart of Rome, Trajan built a show-case for his military prowess. Probably within the vicinity of the column, Trajan's personal leadership was, if possible, stressed even more on the Great Trajanic Frieze, a set of reliefs from an unknown monument (Plate 19.2). Here the emperor was shown personally leading the troops, overrunning the hapless Dacians. The reality of battle, in which Roman emperors directed from distance, was discarded for a new symbolic conception of imperial warfare. The image of the emperor as commander of the army needed to be spread.[6]

Fora were not the only monuments in Rome through which the image of emperor and army was disseminated. Following the example of Trajan's Column, the distinctly not militaristic Commodus (180–192) built a column to celebrate the martial achievements of his father Marcus Aurelius (161–180). In comparison to the earlier column, the emperor is even more the focus. He is the only fixed point, often shown isolated. Only very rarely is part of him blocked from view. He is the tallest figure at the center of action. Though again two campaigns (the Bellum Germanicum and the Bellum Sarmaticum) are separated by a Victory, the narrative is much more fragmented, focusing less on historical documentation and more on sending out the most powerful and most easy to comprehend image of the emperor and his troops. Equal focus is put on the emperor in the relief panels from a lost triumphal arch. They show the sequence of a successful campaign, from *profectio* to triumph. Interestingly enough, the connecting panels pay more attention to results of battle (allocution, a parade of prisoners, submission) than on the battle itself. The main message of the panels is that Marcus was a good commander – which was more important than the battle itself.[7]

As the Roman Empire continued, the position of the army became more and more openly accepted as the driving force behind imperial power. Septimius Severus' last words (193–211), as reported by Cassius Dio, are telling in this respect: "Rule together as brothers, enrich the soldiers, and forget about everybody else." It is no great surprise, then, that the great victory arch of Septimius Severus in the Forum Romanum, erected in AD 203, following Severus' Parthian triumph, paid much attention to the soldiers. Both the larger panels that adorn the arch and the underlying low relief bands show the main events of the great city conquests of the years 194–195 and 197–199. There is even less attention to narrative than in Marcus' Column. Only the main events – siege, battle, and *adlocutio* – are shown. Throughout imagery, soldiers and a group of officials are depicted as the core of the army as a fighting machine with the emperor as general at its head. At the bases of free-standing columns, large sculptures show Roman soldiers holding chained Parthian prisoners (Plates 19.3 and 19.4).[8]

Sculpture, like monuments, decorated Rome's streets. As with monuments, imperial busts and other sculpture projected the image of the armies, and the emperor as their commander-in-chief. The peculiar portraits of Severus' son Carcalla (211–217), for instance, which have often been interpreted as harsh and cruel, ought to be seen in line with his desire to present himself as a soldier. The iconography corresponds to the facial features of soldiers on the Great Trajanic Frieze, and the short cropped hair is likewise military in origin. Typically, also, Caracalla regularly is depicted wearing a military cloak. This type of imperial portrait became properly fashionable in the third century, the age of the so-called soldier emperors. Earlier busts and imperial statues had broadcast images of the emperor as victorious leader. The most famous example might be Augustus' heroic *prima porta* statue, depicting the first emperor as a heroic ageless leader, whose cuirass was decorated with the return of the Parthian standards, which were put on show in his Forum. Similar types of statues were made for almost all emperors, either during their reigns, or posthumously.[9]

Imperial busts and statues were not only on display in Rome. They were omnipresent, as the orator Fronto (*Ad M Caes*, 4.12.4) wrote to his pupil, the emperor Marcus Aurelius: "You know how in all money-changer's bureaux, booths, bookstalls, eaves, porches, windows, anywhere and everywhere there are likenesses of you exposed to view." Ubiquitous images showed the emperor as a leader of his armies. The message in the provinces must have been clear. Indeed, during a famous excavation of the site of Aphrodisias (Roman Asia Minor), a temple complex dedicated to Aphrodite and the Julio-Claudian emperors was discovered, the reliefs of which

Plate 19.3 Arch of Septimius Severus: Reliefs depicting the emperor on campaign. Photo: Olivier Hekster

betray the influence of such central militaristic imagery. For instance, Augustus is depicted alongside Victory, standing next to a trophy, with a bound captive sitting between them. The emperor's portrait follows the example of the *prima porta* statue. Even clearer examples are formed by reliefs showing the emperors Claudius (41–54) and Nero (54–68), who are, respectively, standing over the defeated body of Britannia and holding the slumping body of Armenia. Though in these types of images the role of the armies as such was rather underplayed, soldiers and their importance were propagated in monumental art and architecture outside the city of Rome. Good examples are Trajan's arch at Beneventum in Italy, the so-called Trophaeum Traiani from Adamclisi (Romania), or the arch of Septimius Severus in that emperor's home-town of Lepcis Magna (Lybia), all showing much the same imagery as Trajan's Column and Great Frieze or Septimius' arch in central Rome.[10]

"Personal propaganda"

Marcus Aurelius' panel reliefs clearly showed the importance of depicting the emperor always surrounded by spectators (Plate 19.5). Similarly, on-looking soldiers

Plate 19.4 Arch of Septimius Severus: column bases showing Romans with chained Parthians. Photo: Olivier Hekster

are dominant in the repetitious depictions of Trajan's and Marcus Aurelius' *contiones* on their columns and on the coinage of almost all emperors. The arch of Titus (79–81) celebrates the late emperor's triumph. Monumental art, in short, regularly stressed imperial "ceremonies" to emphasize military vigor. Such "ceremonies" were an important opportunity for emperors to establish themselves and their soldiers in the minds of their people. Most important were the triumphs. These were occasions for the emperor to march into Rome, accompanied by soldiers in full battle gear, defeated foes, and images of victorious campaigns.[11]

Unsurprisingly, triumphs became monopolized by the imperial family in the early empire. Unsurprisingly, also, emperors in general did their utmost to hold triumphs. It has already been mentioned that Vespasian's Jewish triumph was delayed to make sure that his son Titus could attend, and that the whole dynasty celebrated and commemorated the occasion. All triumphs were visual feasts: "Carried in triumph were spoils, captives and representations of mountains, rivers and battles." In fact, Caesar's famous "I came, I saw, I conquered (*veni, vidi, vici*)," became widely disseminated when Caesar broke with tradition and had only these words painted on the floats in his triumph. The spectacle could be gruesome, as when the cut off (and

Plate 19.5   Arch of Constantine (attic reliefs): Marcus Aurelius addressing troops.
Photo: Olivier Hekster

most likely decayed) head of the Dacian king Decebalus was put on parade in Trajan's triumph of AD 106. But it always showed the might of Rome and the emperor as glorious victor. Indeed, the importance of the triumph was such that a whole literary sub-genre of literature dealt with "fake triumphs"; the celebration of mock victories by "evil" emperors like Caligula, Nero, Domitian, and Commodus. Pride of place here must go to Caligula, who is said to have placed a line of soldiers on the shore of the Atlantic, then had them collect shells as "spoils from the Ocean," to finally compel the tallest of the Gauls "to dye their hair red . . . learn the language of the Germans and assume barbarian names."

Caligula's military reputation, predictably, did not grow as a result of his actions. Campaigns that really warranted triumphs, however, would almost inevitably give the emperor opportunity to add a victory title to their titulature, the honorary names with which they were officially addressed and which found their way to imperial coinage. These titles were fully linked to the person of the emperor, articulating the crucial role that military success played for Roman rule – repeated again and again when speaking of and to emperors. Thus, part of Trajan's titulature was *Traianus Optimus Augustus Germanicus Dacicus Parthicus*. And even though Hadrian's coins, from

AD 125 onwards, only showed Hadrianus Augustus, military names were included when people wrote to the emperor, or set up a dedication to him.[12]

Coinage or literary works

Monuments and sculpture did not, generally, travel on their own (though victorious commanders did regularly loot sculptural treasures, exhibiting them in their victory monuments). Triumphs and other forms of ceremony were only visible to those who were there to witness. Both, therefore, were limited as forms of propaganda. Other media, however, were bound in neither location nor time, thus forming near ideal vehicles of propaganda. Prime among these was coinage. Coins were widely disseminated. The discussion on how much they influenced public perception – and to what extent they were supposed to – is a heated one. Important contributions on the subject by a variety of authors over half a century have greatly improved our understanding of coinage in the ancient world, though consensus on the purpose of the images on coins seems impossible to reach. Still, it appears that central coinage reflected the ideological claims within individual reigns, and that these claims were different on coins of different values, displaying some sort of "audience control." Though it is impossible to say who exactly decided the imagery and legends on imperial coins, it seems inevitable that these decisions originated at the top and that coins, thus, propagated the ideological claims of the ruling regime. They had to display the emperor as he wished to be perceived.

It is, then, surely of importance that, apart from the earlier-mentioned 25 percent of militarily-related qualities displayed among imperial virtues, and the military titulature which accompanied almost all imperial portraits on coins, military busts were also regularly depicted. In fact, they form one of four loose groupings by which bust variants are distinguished, the others being civic, dynastic, and religious. These military busts, showing the emperor in cuirass, only started with Nero, became a truly separate type under Antoninus Pius (138–161), and were a dominant type in the third century, the age of the so-called soldier emperors, when imperial busts were similarly militaristic. But earlier coins had projected the image of the importance of the armies. The Flavians, for instance, whose emphasis on the war in Judea has already been discussed in light of the Templum Pacis, the Arch of Titus, and Vespasian's and Titus' triumph, emphasized similar themes in their coinage. Many coins showed Iudea Capta, depicting the conquered foe as totally defeated, with the conqueror as all powerful. The enemies are kneeling, sitting, or standing captives, naked and bound. Trophies and booty illustrate the victors' story. This motif, prominent among Flavian coinage, had already figured strongly in earlier conquerors' coinage, with only the enemies' identity changing. Likewise, Severus' Parthian triumphs, displayed in the sculpture of his arch, also made it onto his coinage. Captives seated under a trophy, Victoria crowning the emperor, proclaiming Virtuti Augusti, Mars or Victoria holding spear and prisoner, all illustrated the importance of the emperor's victories, for all the empire to see (cf. also the image of Augustus on the imperial reliefs of Aphrodisias, as described above). Even less convincing military displays could be depicted as victories. When the emperor Philip Arabs was forced to buy off invading Persians in AD 244, his coins presented this as the establishment of proper peace: Pax Fundata cum Persis.[13] The link to the emperor was easy to make. After all, it was his head which featured on the other side of the coin.

Coins were not the only medium that could be circulated easily. Despatches were sent by commanders to the Senate, from republican times onwards, to keep senators informed about campaigns. Emperors continued the practice as a matter of course until well into the third century. The information from these despatches could be widely disseminated, thus providing the emperors with another tool to propagate news of their importance and that of their armies. The traditional opening line, as mentioned at the beginning of this chapter, is emblematic: "If you are in good health, it is well. I and my army are in good health." Emperors could influence public interest in their despatches through dramatic effects. Thus, Caligula, after a rather uneventful campaign, only managed to:

> receive the surrender of Adminius, son of Cynobellinus king of the Britons, who had been banished by his father and had deserted to the Romans with a small force; yet as if the entire island had submitted to him, he sent a grandiloquent letter to Rome, commanding the couriers who brought it to ride in their carriage all the way to the Forum and the Senate, and not to deliver it to anyone except the consuls, in the temple of Mars the Avenger, before a full meeting of the Senate.

As it was forbidden for carriages to ride in the Forum at daytime, Caligula must have managed to catch the attention of many. Like his "fake triumph" however, the military action did not warrant the interest. Propaganda could not be wholly detached from facts.[14]

Real success was worth writing about. The tone was set by Augustus whose *Res Gestae*, an autobiography that was posthumously inscribed in front of his mausoleum, celebrated his military successes. Four main themes can be detected: 1) personal success, through listings of titles and triumphs; 2) the wars, especially the recovering of the standards, the extension of Roman territory, and emphasis that all wars had been just ones; 3) further domination, by listing client kings, embassies, and the hostages who foreign kings left in Rome; 4) peace established through military victory. These *Res Gestae Divi Augusti* were disseminated throughout the Roman Empire. Other emperors followed suit, with Vespasian writing memoirs about the Jewish War, Trajan commenting on his Dacian wars and Septimius Severus at least discussing the civil war in which he came to power in his autobiography. Historians and poets also praised the emperors' victories, triumphs and their bringing of peace, with Virgil, Horace, Statius, or Pliny the Younger only a few of the famous examples. But to what extent the writings of authors such as these can be considered propaganda is highly debatable, and goes beyond the scope of this chapter. Inscriptions made to honor the emperor are a different matter, and there seems to be a clearly propagandistic value in the one set up by senators for Marcus Aurelius who: "surpassed all the magnificent deeds of even the best of emperors preceding him, since he destroyed or disciplined extraordinarily warlike peoples" (*ILS* 374). Inscriptions like these (though perhaps not quite so grandiose) are found for many emperors and throughout Roman territory. The message traveled far.[15]

This short survey, then, illustrates that in the various media at imperial disposal it was mainly the emperor who was put forward. Demonstrating the military virtue and capacity of the ruler was one of the key aspects of imperial propaganda. This meant that the armies were put on display, particularly during the triumph, but also in the other "vehicles" of propaganda, such as monuments, sculpture, or texts. But even in one of the most "soldier friendly" of monuments, the arch of Septimius Severus at Rome, the prime purpose of the displayed soldiers seems to have been to represent the emperor as the general of this powerful fighting machine. Of course the survey is far from complete, and contradictory examples might be put forward. Yet in general terms, imperial propaganda cared much less about the armies than about the emperors commanding them.

3   Representing the Soldiers

To survive, emperors needed military support and focusing attention on imperial behavior did not mean that the soldiers were ignored. They were mostly in the background, as described above, but sometimes specific army units were explicitly used in propaganda. A coin from Vespasian's reign, naming the EXERCITUS MOESIC(US), has already been mentioned. It was probably part of donatives that were given to the troops themselves. When the soldiers were the prime audience, they could be lavishly praised. A similar situation occurred earlier, in the reign of Claudius, the successor to Caligula. Claudius came to the throne against senatorial wishes, because the praetorians (the only soldiers in Rome itself) proclaimed him the new head of the imperial household, and thus emperor. In return, high value coins of the first years of Claudius' rule openly honored the praetorians. The images on the coins even suggested that the emperor only ruled through the actions of the praetorians, members of which group are shown greeting the emperor, and whose camp and goddess feature on other coins. The accompanying text (PRAETORIANUS RECEPTUS) makes much the same point. A specific group of soldiers was given attention on the gold and silver coins that will have formed the prime (if certainly not only) form of military pay. Coins of lower denomination sent out a very different message. When Claudius boosted his reputation by conquering Britain (AD 43) (which as we have seen above was commemorated explicitly by the inhabitants of Aphrodisias), he was no longer *that* dependent on the praetorians, who figure less and less on his coins. Instead, the high-value coins with military themes celebrate the conquest of Britain – thus returning to the "normal" theme of imperial martial valor. Legions could, and were, presented in coinage, but this was not the norm.

There are, however, some indications that coinage was also used to target soldiers who were settled in the periphery of empire. Thus, an analysis of the bronze coins found at the *canabae legionis* at Nijmegen (the Netherlands) betrays the fact that new coins did not arrive at the edges of the empire in a continuous stream, but in larger quantities in a limited number of peak years. The distribution appears also to have been locally determined, with the military settlements along the Rhine as main recipients. Furthermore, the coins that were distributed seem to display homogeneous imagery. When, in other words, the troops needed payment, the coins that were minted showed the same images time and again. Thus, a revolt in Upper Germany in AD 89 was crushed by the legions in Lower Germany, who remained loyal to the Emperor Domitian. In return, they were allowed to call themselves *pia fidelis Domitiana* and the entire Rhine area was supplied with new coins in AD 90–91, nearly 50 percent of which depicted *virtus* (courage/bravery). Loyal soldiers were confronted with a message of courage, shortly after fighting for their emperor.

There were other ways to broadcast the importance of the armies to the soldiers. The naming of legions was one. Many emperors named legions after themselves, thus strengthening the link between army and emperor. At the same time, such a link clearly expressed the military valor of the emperor – anytime the legion fought this was reflected back (more even than in normal circumstances) to the emperor whose name it bore. Hence, Galba's only legion at the start of his fight for the throne in AD 68, was nicknamed Galbian, though that name disappeared altogether after Vespasian's victory in the civil wars. Clodius Macer, who at approximately the same time as Galba rebelled against Nero, called his two legions respectively Legio I Maciana and Legio II Augusta, and named them on his coins. In a similar vein, Augustus raised the Legio II, III, and VIII Augusta, Vespasian the Legio IV Flavia Felix and the Legio XVI Flavia Firma, and Trajan the Legio II Traiani, which is also mentioned on coins. Other examples could be added.[16]

The naming of legions aside, emperors put much effort into ensuring that their reputation amongst the soldiers was unproblematic. After all, showing the audience at large how heroic the ruler was or emphasizing to soldiers the importance of the armies would all be rather futile if the legions did not support their commander in chief. Praising troops on coinage or sculpture would be one way to please them. Winning victories and proving to be a competent general was another. Most important, though, was paying donatives and guaranteeing high and regular pay. Still other strategies could be employed to propagate the emperor's good reputation among soldiers. Doubtlessly, the multiple images of emperors in the army camps were of importance, not least the portraits on the military standards, which were highly potent symbols. The loss of standards was an enormous scandal, and returning them to Rome after a loss an important symbolic victory (which Augustus made good use of in 20 BC). Standards and the imperial portrait they bore were inseparable, creating a medium through which loyalty could be expressed that was unique to the soldiers. Thus, Tiberius, after the failed coup of his second-in-command Sejanus, explicitly rewarded the Syrian legions "because they alone had consecrated no image of Sejanus among their standards." Various rituals surrounding standards, such as the crowning of standards with roses in the summer, or celebrating the birthdays of specific standards, also strengthened the relationship between emperor and soldier.[17]

Better than the imperial image was imperial presence. Many emperors shared the hardships of their soldiers and then publicly emphasized that they had done so. This could obviously be done whilst on campaign, but those were not the only times when it occurred. Hadrian, whose traveling did not coincide with campaigning, visited an enormous number of army units throughout the realm, quite possibly to keep them happy notwithstanding the lack of military activity. The many coins depicting the provincial units of the army and Hadrian's addresses to them strengthen the point. It was already recognized in antiquity:

> Hadrian travelled through one province after another, visiting the various regions and cities and inspecting all the garrisons and forts. Some of these he removed to more desirable places, some he abolished, and he also established some new ones. He personally viewed and investigated absolutely everything . . . and he reformed and corrected in many cases practices and arrangements for living that had become too luxurious. He drilled the men for every kind of battle, honouring some and reproving others, and he taught them all what should be done. And in order that they should benefit from observing him, he everywhere led a rigorous life and either walked or rode on horseback on all occasions, never once at this period setting foot in either a chariot or a four-wheeled vehicle. He covered his head neither in hot weather nor in cold, but alike amid German snows and under scorching Egyptian suns he went about with his head bare. Thus, both by his example and by his precepts he so trained and disciplined the whole military force throughout the entire empire that even today the methods then introduced by him are the soldiers' law of campaigning. (Cassius Dio, 69.9.1–4)

Personal visibility was an important facet of Roman rule. It was the most direct way for an emperor to show interest. It is, therefore, relevant that emperors spent much of their time showing themselves to the soldiers.

There are some indications that imperial messages to the military could lead to stronger ties between ruler and soldiers. Thus, the support for Domitian amongst the Praetorians was such that after his death they forced the new emperor Nerva (96–98) to punish those who had killed their beloved emperor – even if Nerva preferred to describe him in negative terms. Then again, this may have had more to do with Domitian's increase of military pay than any imperial messages or behavior. Commodus, however, did not raise pay and did not engage in massive military campaigns. Still, his posthumous popularity amongst the troops was such that his successors revoked the damning of his memory that was enacted by the Senate instantly following Commodus' death – the only example in Roman history of such a revocation of *damnatio memoriae*. The emperor did increase the ease with which soldiers earned promotion, appointed his own officers, listened to the complaints of ordinary soldiers, and allowed a loosening of discipline, which were all ways to please the military. Of equal importance will have been his renaming of various legions (or perhaps even all) to *Commodiana*, and the general image of the emperor as divine victor, which seems to have been well received by the troops.[18]

Negative messages could also transmit the soldiers' value to their emperor. When, in AD 312, Constantine destroyed his opponent Maxentius, who had ruled the city of Rome and the surrounding area for six years, he expended substantial effort punishing two groups of soldiers: the Praetorian Guard and the so-called Equites Singulares (horse guards). Firstly, he disbanded these troops, which had been the traditional core of the Roman armies, and then destroyed the buildings that were related to them, such as their camps and graveyards. This behavior is difficult to understand until one realizes that exactly these two groups of soldiers had been fundamental as a base of power for Maxentius. The horse guards had even become so linked to the figure of Constantine's opponent that Constantine's victory arch depicts their rout on the relief that may show the death of Maxentius.[19] The dangers of supporting a loser were clear to all of Rome, but especially to the soldiers. Subjects had better obey their new emperor.

4 Conclusion

Throughout this chapter, attention has been on the different media though which the idea of the emperor as a great military leader, or the army as an important facet of an emperor's rule, could be (and was) disseminated. These different media sent out quite consistent images. The emperor was celebrated for his victories, with the defeated foe as an important focal point. If there was no obvious victory to celebrate, images of the emperor in military gear could still show his military valor. In this way, even the fairly non-militaristic Nero was depicted as a conquering hero by the people of Aphrodisias. If there was a proper victory, different media could be combined to strengthen the message. A clear example is the Judean victory over the Flavians: an actual triumph was commemorated through monuments, coinage, and texts, all accentuating connecting aspects of the success. In more general terms, the differences between the different media and their limitations notwithstanding (there was, for instance, much less space on coins than on the reliefs of triumphal arches), central imagery paid much attention to the emperor, some to specific legions, and no significant attention to individual soldiers. The names of those legions which had achieved particularly impressive victories were singled out – especially when an emperor was in need of military support. Individual soldiers could be reached by the attention that resulted from the personal presence of the emperor. Perhaps the best example stems from the reign of Hadrian:

> I am the one who was formerly very well known on the Pannonian shore,/ first in bravery among one thousand Batavians,/ the one who with Hadrian as judge was able across the vast / waters of the Danube to swim in full battle gear/ . . . (*CIL* 3.3676 = *ILS* 2558)

The soldier Soranus, who was the one to thus cross the Danube in AD 118, found the fact that the emperor was there to witness his feat sufficiently important to mention it on his epitaph. No medium was as direct as personal presence.

From a chronological point of view, it appears that soldiers were more openly celebrated in central imagery from the reign of Trajan onwards – though the limitations of surviving evidence and the fairly brief nature of this chapter prevent any clear conclusions or temporal demarcations. More than anything else, though, attention must be called to the fact that the military aspect was only one element of the multifaceted ideological claims that were disseminated through monuments, art, coinage, texts, and the public behavior of those in control of the Roman Empire. The armies formed an important part of imperial propaganda – both as subjects and audience. Yet, Roman ideology comprised of much more than military propaganda. There was more to Roman imperial representation than the Roman armies.

NOTES

1 Hölscher 2004, 17 on emperors and war images; Noreña 2001, table 3 gives a statistical analysis of the coins; on the Bar Kokhba revolt and Hadrian's acceptance of the title *imperator*, see Eck 1999, esp. 85–7; for Hadrian's hunting skills in imperial art, see Kleiner 1992, 251–3; addressing the troops: *CIL* 3.3676 (= *ILS* 2558); *CIL* 8.2532 and 18042 (= *ILS* 2487 and 9133–5); *RIC* II, p. 267 nos. 322–323. Senatorial letters: Dio 69.14.3; Favorinus: *HA, Hadr.* 15.13; Philostratus, *VS* 489. On the *SCPP* see especially Eck, Caballos, and Fernández 1996; Potter 1999, 71. The translation used here is the one given by Griffin 1997, 250–3.

2 In general on propaganda: Taithe and Thonton 1999, 1. In this context, it is impossible to overstate the importance of Syme 1939, 458: "Laws were not enough. The revolutionary leader had won power more through propaganda than through force of arms: some of his greatest triumphs had been achieved with but little shedding of blood." But cf. Hannestad 1988, 343. For an overview of the most recent discussion, see the various essays in Weber and Zimmermann 2003. "Referring to 'political themes' . . .": Howgego 1995, 71.

3 *SCPP*, "disseminating the model of behaviour . . .": Cooley 1998, 210; "follows that they were selected for advertisement . . .": Potter 1999, 71; imperial *virtutes*: Classen 1991, 20–2. Differentiation of messages on coins: Hekster 2003, 26–7, with appendices 1–2.

4 "Mud and marble": Suetonius, *Aug.* 29; Zanker 1988. Caesar's Forum: Appian, *B. Civ.* 2.68; Cassius Dio, 43.22.2. Augustus' Forum: *RGDA* 21.1; Rich 1998.

5 The passage on the triumph is Josephus, *B. Jud.* 7.158–62. On the Templum Pacis: Noreña 2003.

6 Vespasian's absence from civil war: Tacitus, *Hist.* 3.49; Levick 1999a, 67–8 with 227 n.7. Trajan's Forum paid for *ex manubiis*: Packer 2001, 190–1. Trajan's Column: Hannestad 1988, 154–67; Baumer, Hölscher, and Winkler 1991. Cf. Scheiper 1982. The Great Trajanic Frieze and the symbolism of warfare: Hölscher 2004, 6–7.

7 Column of Marcus Aurelius: Hannestad 1988, 236–44; Hölscher 2000. Panel reliefs: Scott Ryberg 1967.

8 The army as driving force: Birley (in this volume). Septimius' last words: Cassius Dio, 76.15.2. Septimius' arch: *LTUR* I, 103–5.

9 Caracalla as a soldier: Cassius Dio, 78.3.1–2; 78.9.1; 78.16.7; 78.24.1; Herodian, 4.4.7–8; 4.7.4–7, *HA, Caracalla*, 2.1; 2.3; 9.3; 11.5. On Caracalla's representation and imagery see Mennen 2006. Wearing a military cloak: Leander Touati 1991, 117. The Augustus *Prima Porta* statue: Kleiner 1992, 65–57.

10 Aphrodisias reliefs: Smith 1987, 101–4, 117–20.

11 On-looking soldiers: David 2000; Baumer, Hölscher, and Winkler 1991, 266, 268–70, 278–87. Military ceremony: Campbell 1984, 133–42.

12 Imperial monopoly on triumphs: Cassius Dio, 54.24.7–8, with Rich 1990, 202. Triumphs as visual feasts: Tacitus, *Ann.* 2.41.2 on Germanicus' triumph in AD 17. *Veni, vidi, vici*: Suetonius, *Caesar* 37.2 Decebalus: Dio 68.14.3; *Fasti Ostienses* AD 106. Fake triumphs; Caligula: Suetonius, *Cal.* 46–47; Nero: Suetonius, *Nero* 25; Cassius Dio, 62.20.1–6; Domitian: Tacitus, *Agric.* 39; Commodus: *HA, Comm.* 11.10–11. Titulature: Kneisl 1969, 89, 94.

13 For a good overview of the discussion on coins and ideology: Levick 1999b. On audience control: Hekster 2003. Military busts: King 1999, 131, 134. The conquered foe type: Cody 2003, 105–13, 123. Severan coins: e.g. *BMCRE* 5, 40 no. 118; 5, 139 no. 562; 5, 61 no. 252; 5, 62 no. 261; Mennen 2006. Philips Arabs: *RIC* 4, Philip I, no. 69.

14 Dispatches: Campbell 1984, 148–56. Traditional opening line: Cassius Dio, 69.14.3. Cf. 67.7.3; 68.29.1; 71.10.5; 77.18.2; 77.20.1; 78.27.3; 78.36.1; Suetonius, *Cal.* 44.2, 45.3; Herodian, 4.11.8; 7.2.8. Caligula catching attention: Suetonius, *Cal.* 44.2.

15 Four main themes in the *Res Gestae*: Campbell 1984, 151–2. Dissemination of the text: Elsner 1996. Other emperors and autobiography: Josephus, *Vita* 242, 358; Priscianus, 6.13; Millar 1964, 122, 141; Campbell 1984, 152–3.

16 Claudius and the differentiation of coinage: *RIC* 1², 122 nos. 11–12, 23–24, 123 no. 29; *RIC* 1², 122 nos., 19, 20, 25–26, 123 nos. 36–37; Hekster 2003, 27–9; Lummel 1991, 58–9. Coin differentiation at Nijmegen and along the Rhine: Kemmers 2006. Naming legions: Ando 2000, 314. Galbian nickname: Tacitus, *Hist.* 2.86.2; *AE* 1972, 203.

17 Tiberius and the Syrian legions: Suetonius, *Tib.* 48.2. Crowning standards: Pliny, *NH* 13.23; birthdays of standards: *ILS* 9125–9127. See further: Ando 2000, 261–2.

18 Hadrian's travels and the coins depicting provincial unity: Birley 2003, 426. Domitian's pay raise and Nerva's punishing of his assassins: Suetonius, *Dom.* 7, 22, 23. On Domitian's last years, including his relation with the legions, see especially Syme 1983. On Commodus and his posthumous reputation, Hekster 2002, 163–95, esp. 164–8 for his reputation among soldiers. Ways to please the military are set out by Tacitus, *Ann.* 2.55.

19 Hekster 1999, 736–7; 740–1; Speidel 1986, especially 254 n.5, 257–9, 260–2 pl. 1–3; Speidel 1988.

BIBLIOGRAPHY

Translations, unless indicated, are adapted from LCL.

Ando, C. 2000. *Imperial Ideology and Provincial Loyalty in the Roman Empire*. Berkeley.

Baumer, L. E., T. Hölscher, and L. Winkler. 1991. "Narrative Systematik und politisches Konzept in den Reliefs des Trajanssäule. Drie Fallstudien," *JDAI* 106: 261–95.

Beard, M. 2003. "The triumph of Flavius Josephus," in Boyle and Dominik, 543–58.

Birley, A. R. 2003. "Hadrian's travels," in De Blois et al., 425–41.

Blois, L. de, P. Erdkamp, O. Hekster, G. de Kleijn, and S. Mols. (eds.). 2003. *Representation and Perception of Roman Imperial Power*. Amsterdam.

Boyle, A. J., and W. J. Dominik (eds.). 2003. *Flavian Rome. Culture, Image, Text*. Leiden.

Campbell, J. B. 1984. *The Emperor and the Roman Army, 31 BC–AD 235*. Oxford.

—— 2002. *Warfare and Society in Imperial Rome, 31 BC–AD 280*. London.

Classen, C. J. 1991. "Virtutes Imperatoriae," *Arctos* 25: 17–39.

Cody, J. M. 2003. "Conquerors and conquered on Flavian coins," in Boyle and Dominik, 103–23.

Cooley, A. 1998. "The moralizing message of the *Senatus Consultum De Cn. Pisone Patre*," *Greece and Rome* 45: 199–212.

David, J.-M. 2000. "Les *contiones* militaires des colonnes trajane er aurélienne: les nécessités de l'adhésion," in Scheid and Huet, 213–26.

Eck, W. 1999. "The Bar Kokhba Revolt: The Roman point of view," *JRS* 89: 76–89.

——, A. Caballos, and F. Fernández. 1996. *Das Senatus Consultum De Cn. Pisone Patre*. Munich.

Elsner, J. 1996. "Inventing imperium: Texts and the propaganda of monuments in Augustan Rome," in J. Elsner (ed.), *Art and Text in Roman Culture*. Cambridge, 32–53.

Griffin, M. 1997. "The Senate's story," *JRS* 87: 249–63.

Hannestad, N. 1988. *Roman Art and Imperial Policy*. Aarhus.

Hekster, O. 1999. "The city of Rome and late imperial ideology: The tetrarchs, Maxentius and Constantine," *Mediterraneo Antico* 2: 717–48.

—— 2002. *Commodus. An Emperor at the Crossroads.* Amsterdam.

—— 2003. "Coins and messages: Audience targeting on coins of different denominations?" in De Blois et al., 20–35.

Hölscher, T. 2000. "Die Säule des Marcus Aurelius: Narrative Struktur und ideologische Botschaft," in Scheid and Huet, 89–105.

—— 2004. "Images of war in Greece and Rome: Between military practice, public memory, and cultural symbolism," *JRS* 94: 1–17.

Howgego, C. 1995. *Ancient History from Coins.* London.

Kemmers, F. 2006. *Coins for a legion. An analysis of the coin finds of the Augustan legionary fortress and Flavian* Canabae legionis *at Nijmegen.* Berlin.

King, C. 1999. "Roman portraiture: Images of power," in Paul and Ierardi, 123–36.

Kleiner, D. 1992. *Roman Sculpture.* New Haven.

Kneissl, P. 1969. *Die Siegestitulatur der römischen Kaiser. Untersuchungen zu den Siegerbeinamen des ersten und zweiten Jahrhunderts.* Göttingen.

Leander Touati, A. M. 1991. "Portrait and historical relief. Some remarks on the meaning of Caracalla's sole ruler portrait," in A. M. Leander Touati, E. Rystedt, and O. Wikander (eds.), *Munuscula Romana.* Stockholm, 117–31.

Levick, B. 1999a. *Vespasian.* London.

—— 1999b. "Messages on the Roman coinage: Types and inscriptions," in Paul and Ierardi, 41–60.

Lummel, P. 1991. *"Zielgruppen" römischer Staatskunst. Die Münzen der Kaiser Augustus bis Trajan und die trajanischen Staatsreliefs.* Munich.

Mennen, I. 2006. "The image of an emperor in trouble. Legitimation and representation of power by Caracalla," in L. de Blois, P. Funke, and J. Hahn (eds.), *Religion, Mentality, and Cultural Identity in the Roman World.* Leiden, 253–67.

Millar, F. G. B. 1964. *A Study of Cassius Dio.* Oxford.

Noreña, C. F. 2001. "The communication of the emperor's virtues," *JRS* 91: 146–68.

—— 2003. "Medium and message in Vespasian's *Templum Pacis*," *MAAR* 48: 25–43.

Packer, J. E. 2001. *The Forum of Trajan in Rome. A Study of the Monuments in Brief.* Berkeley.

Paul, G., and M. Ierardi (eds.). 1999. *Roman Coins and Public Life under the Empire. E. Togo Salmon Papers II.* Ann Arbor.

Potter, D. S. 1999. "Political theory in the *Senatus Consultum Pisonianum*," *AJP* 120: 65–88.

Rich, J. W. 1990. *Cassius Dio. The Augustan Settlement (Roman History 53–55.9).* Warminster.

—— 1998. "Augustus' Parthian honours, the temple of Mars Ultor and the arch in the Forum Romanum," *PBSR* 66: 71–128.

—— 2003. "Augustus, war and peace," in De Blois et al., 329–57.

Scheid, J., and V. Huet (eds.). 2000. *Autour de la colonne Aurélienne. Geste et image sur la colonne de Marc Aurèle à Rome.* Turnhout.

Scheiper, R. 1982. *Bildprogramma der römischen Kaiserzeit unter besonderer Berücksichtigung der Trajans-Saüle in Rom und korrespondierender Münzen.* Bonn.

Scott Ryberg, I. 1967. *Panel Reliefs of Marcus Aurelius.* New York.

Smith, R. R. R. 1987. "The imperial reliefs from the Sebasteion at Aphrodisias," *JRS* 77: 88–138.

Speidel, M. P. 1986. "Maxentius and his *Equites Singulares* in the battle at the Milvian bridge," *Classical Antiquity* 5: 253–62.

—— 1988. *Les prétoriens de Maxence.* Rome.

Syme, R. 1939. *The Roman Revolution.* Oxford.

—— 1983. "Domitian: The last years," *Chiron* 13: 121–46 (= *Roman Papers* IV, 1988, 252–77).

Taithe, B., and T. Thonton. 1999. "Propaganda: A misnomer of rhetoric and persuasion?" in B. Taithe and T. Thonton (eds.), *Propaganda. Political Rhetoric and Identity 1300–2000.* Thrupp, 1–27.

Weber, G., and M. Zimmermann. 2003. *Propaganda – Selbstdarstellung – Repräsentation im römischen Kaiserreich des 1. Jhs. n.Chr.* Stuttgart.

Zanker, P. 1988. *The Power of Image in the Age of Augustus.* Ann Arbor.

FURTHER READING

Anyone interested in the relationship between emperor and army, including the representational aspects of this relationship, should start with Campbell 1984, the finest treaty on the subject. Also of great interest is Campbell 2002, which looks at the impact of the army on Roman society as a whole, again with substantial attention to representation. For the relation between imperial art, monuments, and propaganda, Hannestad 1988 gives a thorough, though perhaps over-simplistic, overview. The role of ideology and representation for the functioning of the Roman Empire as a whole is wonderfully analyzed in Ando 2000, though this is a complex book that can only be appreciated with quite a lot of prior knowledge. For a much more fragmented approach to a similar theme, De Blois et al. 2003 forms a good starting point. A lot can be found in the various articles in De Blois' volume, especially (on army and representation) Rich 2003, which discusses how politics and propaganda can interact within one reign. Likewise, Rich 1998 analyzes how different media interacted to create and broadcast the "ideology" of a particular victory during the reign of one emperor. The most up-to-date discussion on the application of the term "propaganda" in Roman history is Weber and Zimmermann 2003 (in German). More information on Roman sculptural art (including the reliefs on arches, temples, and other monuments) can be found in Kleiner 1992. The book is excellently illustrated and supplies general introductions and further bibliography on all major (and any minor) monuments. For discussion of the role of coins in disseminating imperial propaganda, Levick 1999b is the most accessible starting point. On the Roman triumph, nothing competes with the actual description of the Flavian triumph in Josephus, *B. Jud.* 7.123–57, an actual eye-witness account, the importance of which is rightfully stressed in Beard 2003b – a short and lucid commentary on the passage.

CHAPTER TWENTY

The Army and the Urban Elite: A Competition for Power

Clifford Ando

1 Introduction

At some point in the 50s BCE., when Julius Caesar was operating in the foothills of the Alps, he ordered communities in the area to furnish supplies. One fortified *castellum*, or hilltop-fortress – the term designated settlements that in some respect fell short of Roman standards for autonomous political communities – preferred to rely upon the natural strength of its position and declined to obey the command. Brooking no such display of independence, Caesar ordered his men to heap wood against the town's gate and burn it down. To the Romans' amazement, the fire did the gates no damage. When the town later surrendered, having been surrounded by siege works, Caesar opted not for spectacular punishment, as he so often did, but inquired after the source of their nonflammable wood. Upon learning its name – *larignum*, or larch – the Romans gave the same name to the settlement, which found itself rapidly embroiled in a regional network of trade for its timber (Vitruvius 2.9.15–16).

The fate of Larignum brings to the fore several issues at the center of my topic. First, there is the obvious inequality between town and legion in their capacities for violence: had Caesar unleashed his soldiers, the history of Larignum would have ended that day. At the same time, the army needed towns, if not Larignum, then many like it, for soldiers were purveyors of violence, neither sowers of grain nor pressers of oil. Caesar could not afford Larignum's disobedience not because its supplies were unique or essential – he did not yet know about larch wood – but because other cities might have followed its example, and the cost, indeed, the danger involved in a regional rebellion more than justified the expenditure of time, effort, and resources in bringing Larignum to heel. Second, like many cities, Larignum joined the empire against its will, but its political and juridical integration ultimately led to complex social and economic ties between itself, its region, and the empire as whole. In choosing to pay its taxes and remain pacific, Larignum contributed to the well-being of the polity and, within very narrow bounds, found its voice in imperial politics. Finally, it was the power granted by knowledge and natural resources – a power not military, but strategic and economic – that impelled that process of integration, which even at the outset enabled Larignum to negotiate its fate with Caesar and cheat his army of itself as spoil.

2   Elites of Italy and Empire

The topic of this chapter might be understood in several ways. A great deal depends on whom we designate as the urban elite. (As we shall see, much also depends on how we understand "power.") If by "the urban elite," one understands the senatorial elite of the city of Rome, then we should unfold a tale of constitutional government – established as an outcome of murderous civil war, but constitutional nonetheless – gradually upended by its own army. That story is a traditional one, and its tellings have generally followed one or the other of two paths, each with its roots in classical historiography. The first concentrates on the ambitions of generals and magistrates, who in seeking to outdo their peers unwittingly abandon the safe solidarity of their class and sow the seeds of not only their own destruction, but that of the institutions that sustained their web of economic and political privilege. The second path pursues instead the soldiers themselves, who followed those generals and as citizens willingly bore arms against their own communities. In that tale, Rome the republic is undone by the very tools it had forged in the acquisition of empire; for the wealth of empire so corrupted the conduct of politics and culture of citizenship as to render the republic itself unsustainable.

But if we take "the urban elite" to denominate not, or not simply, the plutocrats of Italy, but the civic elites of the empire more generally, then we confront in this topic a twofold paradox. On the one hand, Rome and its armies ruled an empire, acquired for the most part by force of arms, and we would set ourselves a considerable burden to explain how even the elites of conquered territories might be conceived as competing for power with the soldiers of their suzerain. And on the other, writers both ancient and modern have traditionally construed the role of the army in provincial life at one or the other end of a single axis, as either a civilizing force in regions requiring Romanization, or a force itself to be corrupted by the seductive luxuries of city life. In neither of these latter models do cities' relations with the legions impinge on imperial politics, except perhaps by accident, and, if that were all the story, we should then be seeking here to understand a competition where none in fact existed.

These varied narratives might be pursued discretely, and with profit; but their separation can be sustained only by regarding as autonomous economic, social, and cultural interests that in political action, in history, were not so. In itself, this is neither surprising nor cause for alarm. That historians, even narrative historians, engage in reductive modeling – drawing forth certain factors and highlighting their operation, in light of *ceteris paribus* assumptions – is, of course, now well theorized and often acknowledged. Scholarship so produced is, like all scholarship, necessarily partial; but it is through such processes of reduction, modeling, and abstraction that we as historians are able to construct arguments and explanations, even simply to view problems, in light of our own interests and concerns. Viewed from this perspective, the narratives described above, well and often told, might now profitably be dissected and their constituent parts recombined, so that they are not so much rehearsed as reconstituted, to see what light they might shed upon each other.

3   Whose Power? Constitutionalism and its Discontents

We might begin by observing that each of the lines of research rehearsed above presumes a different definition of power: that of generals and soldiers, civic elites and cities themselves. We might therefore start by inquiring not into urban elites, but into power, and ask what sort of power was at issue in the contests embraced by this chapter. For the most part, we shall not be asking who had the greater capacity for violence, or which party had more regular recourse to it. Clearly the army did. But power might also be said to reside with those who ruled the army, those, in other words, who held or assigned the capacity to exercise legitimate social violence.

Describing power thus invites the asking of two related questions, about how governance was legitimated, and whose interests dominated in the development and deployment of particular principles of legitimation. The turn to theories of public law and political cultures – to the nature of magisterial power and power of communicative action – might seem to do two things, both problematic, whose articulation here will act as a warrant to be redeemed in what follows.

First, the turn to law and politics might encourage a concentration on institutions and communicative action, and hence distract attention from the role of violence, at Rome and in the provinces, in legitimating particular systems of governance and social arrangements more generally or, at the very least, in creating the space in which new principles of legitimation could be heard. For in both contexts the disruption and dislocation worked by Roman arms in the second and first centuries BCE substantially destroyed confidence in the institutions of government as well as the representations that had sustained them; and the emergence of a distinctive imperial political culture took place in this ground. Viewed in that light, the success of voices within that culture in redescribing power as an effect of constitutional arrangements was, quite simply, remarkable.

The second challenge to follow from taking what we might call the political turn issues from precisely those ancient theorists of power who described the army as a tool of government. For in their view, the army was not so much a competitor for power, but an instrument in its pursuit. We should furthermore be complicit in their project, so long as we uncritically maintain the theoretical distinction between force and power that they were at such pains to elaborate. That said, for long periods force played a remarkably subordinate role in imperial politics, and to explain why we might turn first to political theory.

In republican thought and practice, the power to command Roman citizens under arms belonged to properly-elected magistrates, and it was granted with both geographic and legal restrictions in one of two ways, by election to a traditional magistracy or by *lex*, by statute, conferring *ad hominem* what was literally an extraordinary command. (The *lex Manilia*, which conferred on Pompey the command against the pirates and which empowered him to command troops across traditional provincial boundaries, was one such law.) Clearly, then, there existed an intimate connection between the people as electorate and as soldiery, and the power of magistrates over soldiers could be construed as consciously conferred by the people in their one capacity over themselves in the other. This way of understanding the army in the structure of politics had a long life under the empire – the radical changes in the composition of the legions notwithstanding – and to it we shall return.

The more common way of theorizing the position of princeps bypasses the army and the electorate altogether, and views it instead as the result of negotiations between members of the governing class. In this tradition, best represented in book 53 of Cassius Dio and hallowed in modern commentaries on the *Res Gestae*, Augustus and the Senate strike a series of compromises – described as "settlements" – in which the emperor acquired legitimacy precisely by declining extraordinary magistracies and instead accepting within his one person an agglomeration of powers, each very precisely defined as analogous to that of some traditional office. And for what it is worth, the people and institutions of government at Rome do seem to have observed the rituals and protocols that concretized this understanding: they elected emperors to specific offices, often holding separate elections for the different offices, and passing statutes to confer the extraordinary powers that gradually accrued to their position.

Crucially, this construal of the emperor's station effected a radical transposition, removing from the legions the influence they had acquired under the triumvirate (however it be understood), and locating its legitimacy precisely in the operations of civil society. Its roots in the seeming lawlessness of the triumviral period should, however, be apparent; and its most important audiences were the legions and their commanders. By positing civilian corporate bodies as the final repositories of authority in the state, Augustus and his successors sought to persuade potential usurpers – and those that would support them – that neither assassination nor revolts would earn the throne. Guilty of murder or treason, the usurper would have to watch the Senate nominate and the people elect a man whose first official act would be gratefully to execute his benefactor. In Edward Gibbon's view, it was this constitutional "distance" between military and civilian authority that saved, as their proximity would later damn, the feeble or truculent men whom fate placed on the throne.

This strand in imperial ideology, too, had a long life. Its success, however limited, is visible in literature written under its presuppositions, in which the irruption of the army into the processes whereby imperial careers commenced or concluded is greeted with surprise, accepted with dismay, and denounced as treasonous. But the roots of imperial government in triumviral violence had only been disguised, and the most public of the veils whereby the emperor was conflated with the state was also the one most easily torn asunder, namely, the oath of loyalty that soldiers and civilians alike swore to the emperor's family and his person. So, for example, writing of events under Galba early in 69, Tacitus tell us that a few days after 1 January letters arrived from Pompeius Propinquus, a procurator in Belgica: their respect for their oath broken, the legions of Upper Germany were demanding another *imperator*, another emperor, but ceding the judgment regarding selection to the Senate and People of Rome, in order that their treason might be received more leniently. (*Hist.* 1.12.1)

Not for naught did Tacitus characterize the events of those years, and the death of Nero and accession of Galba in particular, as "having revealed a secret of empire, that an emperor could be made somewhere other than Rome" (*Hist.* 1.4.2; see also 2.76.4, Mucianus speaking to Vespasian, urging him to insurrection: "that an emperor can be made by an army Vitellius knows from his own example").

In suggesting that the legions of Upper Germany allowed the Senate and people to choose, Tacitus clearly adheres to the ideologically-motivated, constitutionalist construction of the emperor's station adumbrated above. What is more, it may well be that the legions and their commanders actually did so act, and similarly believed. But whatever the value of Tacitus' narrative in this case, this understanding of the place of the legions in imperial politics is misleading for several reasons, whether regarded in light of the emperor's relations with the soldiery or the economics of imperial rule, or even considered within the terms of Roman public law. In what follows, I consider first two ways of construing the letters of Pompeius Propinquus, as emblematic of ancient ways of understanding emperor and army in their mutual relations. Subsequent sections take up the situation of the army in more strictly economic theories of ancient politics, as well as the disappearance of the citizen-soldier and his vote from representations of government.

First, the language granted by Tacitus to the legions acknowledges two important facets of imperial politics. For what the legions requested was another *imperator* – another emperor, to be sure, but more precisely, another commander. In so designating the emperor, in historical narrative and otherwise, Romans pointed toward his primary function and principal historical inheritance, namely, that of commanding and winning in war. For in both constitutional and military terms, the princeps had succeeded and, indeed, superseded the chief magistrates of the republic. Under that regime, the overwhelming majority of grants of consular and praetorian *imperium* were exercised in war: on the Romans' own reckoning, their state had been at peace only twice between the foundation of the city and the reign of Augustus (Calpurnius Piso, *Ann.* fr. 9 Peter; Varro, *L.L.* 5.165; Livy 1.19.1–4). Bracketing for the moment the vast extent of the emperor's authority, what was novel about his position as it evolved under Augustus lay not in his holding of a command per se, nor in his acting through legates, but in his attempt to fulfill both civilian and military roles simultaneously. And in historical terms or, at least, through the lens of hindsight, one rationale for abrogating the mechanics of republican government had been precisely to hold on to the empire, to retain, in other words, the fruits that the greed and ambition of soldiers and generals had served to win but which they were ill-suited to nurture and retain (Velleius 2.89; Tacitus, *Ann.* 1.1.1; Appian, *B. Civ.* 1.1–24).

The second way to construe the legions' desire for another *imperator* places their request and its language in the context of the emperor's notionally personal relationship with his soldiers – with his *commilites*, with his "fellow-soldiers." Already under the republic, it had been customary for soldiers to express their esteem for particular commanders by acclaiming them as *imperatores*, in essence to (re)affirm as proven the claim to aristocratic virtue-*cum*-competence in war at least implicit, and probably always explicit, in the mere standing for election at Rome. The changes in military service in the late republic, combined with the changing nature of military commands, so cemented the ties between individual legions and their commanders as to facilitate, if they do not explain, their collaboration in the destruction of the republic as of their peers. The end of this process, by which citizens serving as soldiers came to view themselves as soldiers serving dynasts, is visible most famously in the discipline worked by Julius Caesar when he brought an obstreperous legion to heel by addressing its members not as his fellow soldiers, but as *Quirites*, "Citizens of Rome" (Suetonius, *Jul.* 70; Appian, *B. Civ.* 2.385–396).

The relationships forged between legions and commanders in the late republic must have varied in their bases; here it is sufficient to stress merely how many of those were extra-legal. That is to say, the relationships that mattered – those between specific legions and commanders, who together wreaked violence at Rome – could be, and often were described as the product of charismatic leadership or bribery or mutiny, or even some combination thereof: the soldiers, wanting land, supporting their commander in achieving some end in politics that conduced, *inter alia*, to the (re)distribution of land. Two features of contemporaneous and later representations of these events deserve scrutiny here, namely, the general failure of both politicians and political analysts to imagine the soldiery as an electorate, and the insistent desire of that soldiery for land; and I will return briefly to both in the next section.

For now, it suffices to stress the extent to which these relationships and their representations, too, had an afterlife in the principate. Emperors in that era persisted in construing their relationship with the army as a personal one or, rather, in publicizing that construal prominently among others. And in the differing economies of imperial political culture in general, and in the competition between principles of legitimation in particular, that personal relationship remained decidedly extra-constitutional, an important other to the place of senatorial privilege in the constitutionalist theories adumbrated above. What is more, it was precisely the personal aspect of that relationship that made it useful, to emperors and soldiers alike. For the emperor, the pressure of the army's superior power – power measured here by capacity for violence – enjoined the Senate to ask, where it might have required, that its voice should be heard in matters of state; likewise, the more an emperor directed the army's loyalty to his person rather than his office, the safer he might rest. Viewed in this light, the celebration in art and panegyric of emperors as *civilis*, as "civil" or respectful of the proprieties of civilian aristocratic society, suggested behaviors that had as opposites not simply despotism, but militarism as well.

Many of these issues receive precise and valuable articulation in the account of the death of Gaius and accession of Claudius preserved in book 19 of Josephus's *Jewish Antiquities*. Josephus was himself contemporary with these events; he must have become acquainted with many who lived through them in Rome itself; and he had access to significant sources that have since been lost. Several points relevant to this argument emerge from his narrative. The interests of the people, army, and Senate diverge: the senators are desirous of "freedom," a state in which their dignity is respected and their "slavery" to the emperors, ended (Josephus, *Ant. Jud.* 19.227); but the people and the soldiers in their different ways understand that freedom to consist largely in granting senators the opportunity to indulge their greed and involve the state in their petty rivalries. The formulation afforded the people urges that promoting Claudius would prevent a civil war, "such as occurred in the days of Pompey" (Josephus, *Ant. Jud.* 19.228). For their part, the soldiers twice canvas their options but conclude each time that democracy, whether inherently or in its Roman form, is insufficient to the burden of so great an empire (Josephus, *Ant. Jud.* 19.162, 225). Wanting, therefore, an emperor, they consider the possibility of "ceding the judgment regarding selection" to the Senate (the wording is that of Tacitus, above p. 000; but for the thought, see Josephus, *Ant. Jud.* 19.151, 249–250). But Josephus also makes the soldiers acutely aware that it is their obedience that grants power to emperors (Josephus, *Ant. Jud.* 19.42, 255); and from the gratitude thus created flow back money and prestige. Hence the conclusion, often attributed to legions here and elsewhere, that each might as well promote its own commander, as the surest route to riches (Josephus, *Ant. Jud.* 19.129, 151; formulated negatively by the Praetorian Guard at 19.163: "if one man should gain rulership over all, it would be altogether harmful to them not to have collaborated in establishing his rule").

If these strands in the narrative operate to one side of a constitutionalist construction of power in Roman society, others in the text both confirm it and explore its vulnerabilities. For though the assassins of Gaius rightly feared the anger of the populace and the soldiery, in the end they were killed not by the adherents of Gaius, but by his successor. So, when Claudius consulted his advisers about the chief assassin, Cassius Chaerea, they responded that "the deed seemed to them a splendid one, but they accused its perpetrator of disloyalty and they thought it would be just to inflict punishment upon him, as a deterrent for the future" (Josephus, *Ant. Jud.* 19.115, 268). And at one point when the contest between the Senate and Claudius might have seemed to hang in the balance, the Senate sent an embassy to Claudius in the camp. After its formal address was delivered, its members, Quintus Veranius and Sertorius Brocchus, tribunes of the *plebs*,

> fell to their knees and begged him on no account to hurl the city into war and evils, for they saw that Claudius was protected by a throng of soldiery and that the consuls were nothing in comparison to him. If he sought rulership, let him receive it as a gift from the Senate. For he would hold it more auspiciously and more felicitously if he obtained it not by force but with the goodwill of its givers. (Josephus, *Ant. Jud.* 19.234–235)

The tribunes thus concede that Claudius does not require their approval or that of their peers: an emperor might be made by agents other than the Senate. But they encourage him to seek it nevertheless; for like so many political representations, the attribution of authority to the Senate might and did have real and potent effects in the world.

Such constitutionalist understandings of the Roman principate speak to one sort of power, namely, that wielded by normative representations of legitimate government; and their flaws are most basely exposed by the exercise of force in moments of crisis. In other words, constitutional theorists and their ancient critics alike focus on the organs of imperial government at Rome, particularly – almost exclusively – insofar as they could be construed as developments upon public law of the late republic. The next section will explore some of the limitations of that view, as they pertain to our topic. But within those parameters, the contrast between republic and principate is stated most brutally and most elegantly by Tacitus, who substitutes for the formal language of the former, *SPQR, Senatus Populusque Romanus*, the new and violent *Senatus milesque et populus*, "The Senate, Army and People" of Rome (Tacitus, *Ann.* 1.7.2; see also *Ann.* 11.30.2: *populus et senatus et miles*).

4   Whose Power? The Army and the Land

To a Tacitus – to a Roman Senator, born to rule and bound by the limitations of ancient theories of empire – the strength of the army exposed the fragility of those representations by which Senate and emperor attempted its disestablishment. In suggesting that power was his to wield, because it had been the Senate's to give, those representations effectively disenfranchised the soldiery, both individually, by not providing any mechanism for citizen legionaries to vote, and collectively, by denying the army a role in the legitimation of emperors or offices. In presuming that power flows from the institutions of government at Rome, they also deny any role in politics to the provinces, except perhaps implicitly, as sources of revenue and arenas for aristocratic competition. But there are abundant reasons to regard with suspicion any model so conceived, of which the two most directly relevant here concern, first, the place of provincial elites in the political economy of the early empire and, second, the role of the army in maintaining their quiescence.

To highlight the connection between these issues, it is perhaps sufficient to point out that historians and politicians in the ancient world commonly represented the empire as pacified and described its armies as outward-looking. Situated almost exclusively in border provinces, those authors argued, the legions and auxiliaries existed primarily to protect the empire from its enemies without. (The impact of these accounts on modern studies of the army in provincial societies will be assessed briefly in the next section.) These portraits of the empire possess considerable rhetorical power – indeed, panegyrics to emperor and empire form a distinct category of extant imperial literature – and they played an important role in the creation of the Roman Empire's distinctive culture of loyalism. That said, their descriptions of the army and provinces occlude two issues in the history of that culture, consideration of which urges once again an examination of the empire's peculiar political economy. Those issues are, first, the need to understand the day-to-day functioning of an empire of perhaps 55 million people whose bureaucracy contained no more than several thousand individuals and, second, the role of spectacular violence in the reorientation of provincial subjectivities in the period of conquest and its aftermath.

Such consensus as now exists about the ambitions and limitations of Roman government – and that consensus is broad – views the stability of the empire not as an operation of laws, but as a function of economics and culture; and it locates the workings of government not only at Rome, but throughout the provinces. In short, having conquered any given society, Rome delivered its internal governance back into the hands of its land-owning elite, or select members thereof; and the agents of the empire collaborated with those individuals in designing regulations and institutions to sustain that oligarchy into the future. This system rested upon a convergence of interests that can be analyzed most transparently at the level of economics. Rome assessed taxes on any given region on the basis of its aggregate wealth and population and assigned to local governments the task of collecting those taxes; but it permitted those governments much latitude in distributing their burden, and many took advantage of that leeway to dispose it regressively. In return for being thus sustained in a position of social and economic privilege, local elites helped to suppress any currents that might have nurtured the realization of solidarity against Rome along broader regional or ethnic lines.

This model, rooted in Marxist historiography and sociology, can be variously elaborated. As here summarized, it presumes an alignment of material and political interests on the part of local elites that would require serious defense in itself. The reorientation of their political and cultural aspirations ran broader and deeper than mere financial calculus can explain. Beyond the shattering of structures and truths that Roman conquest will have worked in colonial contexts lie a set of procedures – communicative, economic, and material – whereby provincial elites learned, refashioned, and exploited the laws and culture of their rulers. In so doing, they came to describe their motivations in the language of honor – an imperial lingua franca in which one's ambitions for oneself, one's community, and the empire were understood to align. The performance of the scripts provided by imperial culture then took place in civic centers, amidst institutional and monumental structures, that Roman and local elites collaborated in creating and homogenizing.

All these issues this model leaves to one side. But it does respond in important ways to significant limitations of the constitutional model adumbrated above. In particular, it accomplishes three related goals: first, it embraces a far greater portion of the empire, in terms of both land and population, and in doing so resolves, at least in part, one historical puzzle, namely, how Roman rule over so vast a congeries of people was maintained, by so limited a bureaucracy and so small an army. Second, it locates the sources of power, and the processes whereby it was transferred, concentrated, and sustained, more intimately among the owners of wealth, the landed elites of the cities, towns, and villages of the empire. Third, its more catholic vision does not restrict our attention to moments of crisis, as though power were only contested when the throne itself was at stake.

At the same time, in expanding our vision from a focus on the governing elite of central Italy to the owners and rentiers of the provinces, we have once again written a history of the empire that omits its army – a consequence, in part, of fetishizing the concentration of wealth and commodification of labor as the primary forms of violence worked by humans upon their fellows. But whatever its cause, it must be acknowledged kindred to the way in which constitutionalist approaches write the army out of history, too. In that field, as we saw, the elision of the army could be understood as a strategic move within ancient politics, and not solely as an effect of some modern theory and its perspectival limitations. For it worked above all to the advantage of landed interests in Roman society, and it is in tracing the stages whereby soldiers ceased to be citizens and became mere instruments of force that we can bring these strands of our inquiry together.

The army of the Roman Republic was a militia: citizens subject to levy filled its ranks; they served for a season or a campaign and returned to civilian life. That service might be professionalized – and that such potential went unrealized in the early second century BCE – is illustrated by an anecdote in Livy. When in 171 the consuls Publius Licinius Crassus and Gaius Cassius Longinus conducted a levy "with greater care than at other times, Licinius enrolled many veterans and former centurions. Many gave their names voluntarily, since they saw that those who had served in the earlier Macedonian war or against Antiochus in Asia were now rich." But when in selecting centurions the military tribunes passed over men who had held that rank before, 23 ex-centurions, who had each also been *primus pilus*, appealed to the tribunes of the *plebs*. In Livy's narrative, they abandon their appeal when shamed by one of their peers, Spurius Ligustinus, who served on five campaigns over 22 years – twice enrolling as a volunteer – and was promoted to centurion four times (Livy 42.32–34).

Both practical and political considerations contributed over the next century to lengthen terms of military service. Roman armies fought further afield, often against rich and ancient kingdoms. Service under arms thus caused ever greater social and economic disruption in the lives of soldiers and their families, even as the quantity of spoils and booty available for distribution grew and grew. This influx of wealth had effects along two axes that concern us here. First, much of this new wealth remained in the hands of the elite, who through it came to possess more and more of the land of Italy, while those whose grip on the land was most tenuous were gradually dispossessed. Second, the Roman citizen body sought to restrict an increasing share of the spoils of empire for itself, against the claims of its Italian allies. The pressures created by the acquisition of empire found release in the first instance in two directions: in grants of land to veterans, effected by a variety of legislative means and often after considerable strife (regardless of means, the land had to come from somewhere); and in battles, political and military, that culminated in the Social War, fought between 90 and 88 BCE, which resulted in the extension of the franchise to all citizens of Italian municipalities.

Roman wars continued apace – Gaul and the entire eastern Mediterranean were conquered in less than 20 years – and their veterans continued to clamor for land. But the extension of the citizenship had rendered the large-scale redistribution of land still more fraught, since it would henceforth all have to be acquired from citizens, even as the concentration of wealth in Rome and its environs was distorting the market for land, grain, and all other goods. At the same time, the radical extension of the Roman community to the very borders of Italy effectively entailed the dissociation of citizenship from any meaningful exercise of the franchise. Soldiers thus came to be more and more dependent upon the political skill, even ruthlessness, of their commanders, even as they seem to have identified less and less with the common weal. The late republican army was thus itself a product of violence, and the fickleness of its soldiery a monument to failure, to the inability of its leaders to subordinate personal gain to some equitable system for the distribution of power and wealth. The veterans of the civil wars ultimately claimed some 130,000 parcels of land in Italy – a bloody and fitting resolution to a period of upheaval that, on a Roman understanding, had begun with agitation over land a century before.

The emperor Augustus brought an end to these difficulties by altering the terms of the conflict in two fundamental ways. Cassius Dio describes these changes as the product largely of a single reform in 13 BCE:

> He also arranged the years that citizens should serve in the army and the money they should receive when ending their service, instead of the land that they were always demanding. He did this so that the soldiers, having enrolled under agreed-upon terms, would no longer revolt for these reasons. . . . Among the soldiers these measures created neither pleasure nor anger at the time, because they neither obtained everything they desired nor lost it all, but in the rest of the population they created the hope of no longer being deprived of their possessions. (Cassius Dio 54.25.5–6)

These measures proved enormously expensive, and Augustus later extended the term of service to 20 years. He also created a system to finance the retirement bonuses, establishing a start-up fund of 170,000,000 sesterces from his own resources and an estate tax to maintain that fund into the future (*Res Gestae* 17.2; Cassius Dio 55.25.1–6). But the measures were worth that trouble. For under this system, soldiers could no longer expect financial rewards of whatever kind to follow upon any given campaign, no matter how successful; and the stability of the political system – and the emperor's own position within it – were immeasurably strengthened by the perception that Augustus had restored to humans "security in their persons and their property" (Velleius Pat. 2.89.4). He did this, crucially, by privileging the individual property rights of citizens over the nearly traditional claim of soldiers upon the state for homesteads upon their discharge. At the dawn of the principate, therefore, the army became in one crucial regard a public property, and its soldiers public servants. In ways both ideological and economic, Augustus thus subordinated the army to the civilians who notionally controlled its coffers, and rendered its power, in theory at least, an effect of collusion between propertied Romans and the imperial governing class.

5 Cities, Soldiers, and Civilians

If we should now seek to test the explanatory power of these models against our data for the actions and situation of the soldiers – their embeddedness within and effects upon social, economic, and political conduct in the provinces – we encounter almost immediately problems of evidence, ones occasionally crippling but often instructive.

The first model, the constitutionalist construal of power, speaks to the inner motivations of constituencies within Roman politics, and our knowledge of those motivations derives in large measure from writers in the same ideological position as the ones from whom our reconstruction of the theory derives. We can rely on normative representations by interested parties only so far. That said, it proves nothing that occasionally legions did revolt and impose their commanders on the empire. Usurpations were in fact quite rare before the Severan period: not for nothing did Gibbon lament that "posterity, who experienced the fatal effects of his maxims and example, justly considered [Severus] as the principal author of the decline of the Roman empire" (*History of the Decline and Fall* chapter 5, 1:148 Womersley). But how we should construe that inaction and whether we should attribute it to some regard for constitutional principle, are questions that cannot now be answered. For successors to the throne always justified their position by reference to multiple principles of legitimation, and habitually exploited all available mechanisms – legal, social, political, and religious – in appealing to their various constituencies. For their part, those constituencies and the individuals who composed them will no doubt have been susceptible to claims based on more than one such principle, in degrees that will have varied with their position.

To assess the second model, we must inquire more deeply into the place of the legions in their localities, and not least in the local, regional, and imperial economies. For the army consumed more than half of all government expenditure; its soldiers needed in excess of a hundred million kilograms of grains each year, and a vast quantity of materiel besides (cf. Ulpian "On the Praetor's Edict" bk. 17 fr. 584 = *Dig.* 50.16.27: "And, indeed, *tributum*, tribute [i.e., taxation], is named from intribution or from what is tributed to soldiers"). At the same time, soldiers and their pay constituted a significant engine in the circulation of coin and a principle mechanism in the monetization of local economies, particularly in the West. For soldiers received their pay and donatives in cash, and their savings and spending power were considerable: the Emperor Domitian forbade the uniting of two legions in a single camp and the depositing by soldiers of more than 1,000 sesterces in the legionary bank, "because Lucius Antonius [Saturninus] seemed to have taken confidence in his attempted usurpation from the total of such deposits in the winter quarters of two legions" (Suetonius, *Dom.* 7.3).

All this might seem to take us rather far from any "competition for power." But if the constitutionalist construal of power fails to account for violence – if, in other words, constitutionalists could not forever repress that other secret of empire, that an army can make an emperor – so, too, excessive concentration on ideological aspects of imperial Rome's political economy risks obscuring the divergent interests of the parties to the circulation of wealth that forms its especial index. For when once a student of the empire takes the army's on-going needs into account, the army becomes a competitor for precisely those resources that fueled the civilian economy, and which enabled its always imperfect transformation into an instrument of state.

But if we then turn to the legions themselves, and ask how they made Roman power and, indeed, their own interests immanent in provincial life, the evidence defies the abstraction of models, the more so, the more particular one's focus becomes.

There is first of all the problem that the legions were not evenly distributed throughout the provinces, but concentrated in those on the frontier. Although recently conquered territories were garrisoned, the Romans were consistent in expecting provinces to become quiescent and forces of occupation to become unnecessary. That said, legions in border provinces were understood to play a role in the interior, through the regular seconding of vexillations in support of police actions, as well as the imposition of spectacular violence in response to notionally irregular contingencies (see, e.g., Tacitus, *Ann.* 4.5.1: the eight legions on the Rhine were a guard "upon Germany and Gaul alike; Spain, recently conquered, was occupied by three legions"; see also Josephus, *B. Jud.* 2.365–377, where Agrippa, the King of Judaea, urges the Jews not to revolt, gesturing to the quiescence of provinces that had no garrison, but equally to the capacity of the legions to crush whatever rebellions might arise; and Cassius Dio 55.23.2–24.8). These depictions of the army as a frontier force have correlates in literary representations of life in the settled provinces, where the army – and almost Rome itself – casts no shadow, as also in modern scholarship, which has often followed those representations in locating the Roman army outside provincial life altogether.

The importance of this initial divergence, that in the placement of the legions, reaches in two directions. First, at an ideological level, the re-description of the army as an institution outside daily experience, and the removal of military service, as well as decisions regarding war and peace, from the socialization and conduct of citizenship set in motion radical changes in its understandings and applications (as, for that matter, in those of masculinity). In many respects, this represented a sea-change far greater than that suffered by traditional conceptions of aristocratic virtue. After all, military service of some kind remained a requirement for almost any senatorial career. It was only the ruin of self and state that, being restricted to the Caesars, was foreclosed to the paths of elite ambition. What is more, loss of autonomy in foreign policy – which meant, for all intents and purposes, loss of the freedom to make war – was in many respects the most widespread and invasive infringement upon self-rule practiced by Rome in the age of conquest. It is easily forgotten that communal membership will have entailed military service, for males, at least, in virtually every city and town of the Mediterranean world in the mid-second century BCE, and so not noticed that this was, on some vast scale, not so two centuries later. And though military recruitment in the provinces expanded rapidly in the principate, while that in Italy quickly fell from the extraordinary heights it had reached in the last decades of the republic, the overall percentage of the Mediterranean world's male population that had experience of warfare on behalf of its state fell dramatically, among both Romans and their subjects; and in this significant respect their experience of politics, and their relations to institutions of violence, gradually converged.

The second level at which to assess the divergent impact of the placement of legions is economic. At a very basic level, insofar as units of the army received (in modern terms) a disproportionate amount of government expenditure, and that in cash, they served as nodal points in the circulation of wealth. And by virtue of their housing of those units, the frontier provinces along the Rhine and Danube in particular must have siphoned off wealth from the pacified provinces of the Mediterranean basin. Of course, the overall scale of this transfer is hard to assess and harder to quantify. There remains considerable controversy over assumptions and hypotheses basic to the construction of any model of the imperial economy, not least over the rate of circulation of coin; the relative importance of taxes in cash and kind, as of regional, provincial, and imperial markets; the size of transfer payments between center and periphery; and even the rate of agricultural yields and acreage under cultivation in any given year. But while variation in the weight or value assigned these factors affects the degree of difference, it would not change the fact of a disproportion between provinces in income and outlay on the part of the imperial government.

This disproportion and its effects point to a second area in which significant differences emerged in provincial experience of Roman arms under the principate, and that is the influence of legionary camps upon the urban structures and conurbations in their vicinity. In the West, legionary camps were often built in places without significant pre-existing urban structures, and these, together with the unincorporated settlements that developed around them, gradually assumed the form and function of substantial Roman-style municipalities. This was so in spite of complex Roman understandings of military encampments, which saw them both as instantiating certain ideals regarding cities and civic structures on the one hand, and as an ideological other to civilian life and space on the other. Indeed, some camps came to compete with cities for precisely those resources that, in the Roman imagination, distinguished a political community from a mere gathering of individuals, namely, publicly-owned sources of wood, water, and pasture (see, e.g., *ILS* 2454–2455, setting off the *prata* of Legio IV Macedonica; see further *ILS* 5968, 5969). In the West, therefore, military camps often evolved into significant settlements in their own right, and as cities many flourish today, including (to use their modern names) Belgrade, Bonn, Budapest, Cologne, León, Mainz, Regensburg, Strasbourg, and Vienna.

A further constraint beyond these upon any attempt to generalize the competition for resources between the army and cities of the empire arises through consideration of the settlement of veterans. There patterns emerge that once again distinguish between regions and periods, but along lines that parallel neither the disposition of the legions and its economic effects, nor precisely those observable in the urbanization of camps and their *canabae*. First, under the triumvirs and early in the reign of Augustus, many veterans were settled in colonies en masse, on sites without prior Roman settlement. This was, according to Tacitus, ideal, but the practice of his own day was different, and in reflecting on events in the age of Nero he lamented the change.

> The veterans decommissioned and settled at Tarentum and Antium did not prevent the depopulation of those places, as many slipped away to the provinces in which they had completed their service. For being accustomed neither to take wives nor to care for children, they left behind homes empty of offspring. For no longer, as once, were entire legions settled, with tribunes and centurions and soldiers of the same unit together, so that by their unanimity and affection they might create a community. Rather, unknown to each other, from different maniples, without a leader, without mutual affection, as if from another race of humankind, they were gathered suddenly together, a number more than a colony. (Tacitus, *Ann.* 14.27.2–3)

The creation of veteran colonies *ex nihilo* slowed considerably after the reign of Augustus; and the preponderance of such colonies were located in the West, in regions recently conquered and, often, in locations from which a legionary camp was recently removed. But their importance in the history of provincial culture belies their number and restricted range, and so compels a number of questions that on current evidence defy adequate response. With whom did the interests of those colonies lie, and with whom their affection? When did a colony of veterans become, in its policies, politics, and legislation, city rather than army? In issuing both licit and illicit requests for services and supplies, did units and agents of the army respect the origin of military colonies?

The second feature of veteran settlement relevant here concerns not those settled en masse, but those who crafted lives for themselves in the towns and cities of the empire. The savings of soldiers at rank upon retirement must often have been sufficient to place them among the economic elite of at least medium-sized towns, and so to buy a place in the local *curia*. Of course, such rank lay within the aspirations only of centurions and their superiors, and, indeed, the distribution of like honors was occasionally used by generals in periods of social upheaval to break the solidarity of common soldiers with their officers. For instance, when pressed by demands for cash and land by the veterans of his war against Sextus Pompeius, Octavian hesitated, not wanting to spend the money or acquire the land to buy off 45 legions. When they grew restive,

> he said that he would lead them not into further civil wars, those having fortunately now stopped, but against the Illyrians and other barbarians races who were disturbing the hard-won peace, whence they could enrich themselves. But they said again that they would not serve until they received the rewards and honors of earlier campaigns. Octavian said that he was not withholding honors, but, having given many, he would offer still further crowns to the legions, and to the centurions and tribunes purple-bordered togas and curial rank in their hometowns. [In other words, Octavian offers equestrian rank within the Roman community and councilor's status at the municipal level, seemingly without giving the money normally required to hold either such rank.] While he was offering still further rewards of this kind, a tribune named Ofillius shouted that crowns and purple togas were trinkets for children, but the rewards for soldiers were land and money, and many cried out that he was right. Caesar descended the tribunal in anger, but others crowded around the tribune, praising him and insulting those who did not stand with him. Ofillius said that he was safe on his own, arguing as he was for such just causes. But having said that, he was nowhere to be found the next morning, and it was never known what had happened. (Appian, *B. Civ.* 5.530–533)

Under the principate, the presence of veterans on city councils is widely attested throughout the empire (see, e.g., *CIL* IX 1622; *ILS* 2227, 6619a; *AE* 1929, 173; 1938, 110; 1973, 361; Waddington 1969; 1984b; 1989, 2041, 2546). As with veteran colonies, so the presence elsewhere of veterans on city councils might complicate any easy separation of civilian and military interests in the analysis of political and economic conduct under the empire.

In point of fact, evidence for actual economic relations between soldiers and civilians, as between cities and legions, reveals a situation of enormous complexity. At a local level, in any given transaction, military interests might easily predominate. Gesturing toward the cause of that situation, namely, soldiers' monopoly on massive force, one might conclude that the army always carried the day, regardless whether its actions were legal or not; and, indeed, a great preponderance of our evidence attests attempts to correct or prevent abuses. But that same evidence can be read so as to tell a more complicated story, one in which the emperor, too, plays a role, negotiating demands and desires on many sides, not least his own. Consider one famous and remarkably complete text on illegal exactions, consisting of documentary protocols, a petition, an imperial response, and a partial record of proceedings involving the villagers of Skaptopara in Thrace, in modern Bulgaria, and the emperor Gordian III, from 238 CE. The opening lines of the petition read as follows:

(Address: ll. 8–11) To Emperor Caesar Marcus Antonius Gordianus Pius Felix Augustus, a petition from the villagers of Skaptopara, also known as the Greseitai.

(Preface: ll. 11–21) You had written often in your rescripts that in these most blessed and eternal times of yours, villages should be inhabited and flourish, and their inhabitants should not become refugees. For this is to the benefit of the health of humankind and the condition of your sacred treasury; wherefore we lay this legal petition before Your Divinity, praying that you look favorably upon us beseeching in this way.

(Exposition: ll. 21–73) We dwell and own property in the aforementioned village, which is well situated because it has a spring of hot water and lies between two army camps, which are in your province of Thrace. In the past, so long as the residents remained unharassed and secure in their property, they contributed their taxes and other imposts faultlessly. But when at times some people began to be arrogant and exercise violence, then the village began to decline.

A famous market is held two miles from our village. Those traveling for the sake of the market do not, however, stay in the place of the market for its full fifteen days, but leaving it, they come to our village and compel us to extend them hospitality and provide most other things for their reception free of charge.

In addition to these, soldiers dispatched elsewhere leave their proper routes and appear before us and likewise force us to provide them with hospitality and provisions, paying nothing whatsoever.

The governors of the province also stay with us, for the most part because of the hot spring, and your procurators come, too. Of necessity, we receive the authorities most hospitably, but, being unable to support the rest, we have appealed often to the governors of Thrace, who, following <your> divine regulations, have commanded that we should remain unharassed. For we made it clear that we could no longer remain but had it in mind to abandon our ancestral dwellings because of the violence of those coming among us.

For truly we have been reduced from many householders to very few.

For a time, the orders of the governors were effective and no one harassed us with demands for hospitality or provisions, but, as time has passed, again many people, despising our status, have dared to attack us. (*IGBulg* 659; *AE* 1994, 1552; Hauken 1998, no. 5)

At one level, the petition gestures to one area of immediate concern, to its parties as to us, and that is the multiplicity of imposts beyond taxes on their persons and property faced by residents of the empire – within certain geographic and other parameters, cities and villages had to provide goods and services on demand to agents of the government – as also to the potential for abuse within a system so designed. This was competition for resources at its most basic.

But at another level, in seeking help from the emperor the villagers place that competition directly within the sphere of imperial politics. For they remind Gordian that they do, *in extremis*, have a choice whether to pay their taxes, and in doing so supply him with the currency that enables his own uneasy control over the army. And emperors were indeed well acquainted with the phenomenon of tax flight, of individuals who abandoned their families, homes, and social network in response to oppression and taxation. The problem from an imperial perspective is analyzed with particular clarity by the Emperor Arcadius, when importuned by his wife Eudoxia to yield to the bishop Porphyry's request that he permit and even assist the destruction of the pagan temples in Gaza:

> The emperor, hearing her, became angry, saying, "I know that the city is full of idols, but it is well-disposed in the paying of taxes, contributing much. If, then, we frighten them suddenly, they will take flight and we will lose much revenue. But if it seems reasonable, let us afflict them bit by bit, depriving the idol-mad of honors and other political offices, and command that their temples be closed and no longer used. For when they are afflicted and constrained on every side, they will acknowledge the truth. But a sudden change is hard for subjects to bear." (Marcus Diaconus, *vita Porphyrii* 41)

The villagers at Skaptopara appealed to just this sensibility in their request, which follows upon the narrative of their troubles: "If we are weighed down, we will flee our homes and the treasury will suffer the greatest loss; therefore, receiving pity through your divine foresight and remaining in our homes, we will be able to supply the sacred tribute and the other contributions" (ll. 91–99). Thus did the finances of the least of villages, when aggregated with those of hundreds more, support the seat of power, and so might its leaders contest with governors and armies for the ear of the emperor himself.

6   Conclusion: Maximinus at Aquileia

I end before the gates of Aquileia, where travelers descending the Alps meet the via Annia and enter the network of roads that leads to Rome. There in 238 CE civil war was averted, through an exercise of economic power on the part of a city, in the face of an emperor and his army. Maximinus the Thracian had been acclaimed emperor by his army three years earlier, after he assassinated his predecessor, Severus Alexander; but the Senate did not recognize his elevation and eventually put forward its own candidates and attempted to field its own army. Maximinus marched on Italy, but without, one might say, divine foresight: he departed Sirmium in such haste that he neglected to send the customary advance notice requesting provision, and he had to gather it en route (Herodian 7.8.10–11). He encountered serious difficulty as soon as he reached Italy: the population of Emona had abandoned their city, burning whatever supplies they could not carry, and his army went hungry (Herodian 8.1.4–5). Aquileia therefore assumed even greater importance for the provisioning of his army, but its population closed their gates against him. Maximinus, unwilling, or perhaps unable, to advance without supplies, while leaving a large, hostile city as his back, undertook a siege. His army began to starve, murdered Maximinus and his son, and reconciled with the Senate and its emperor, Gordian III.

The events that encompassed the ruin of Maximinus, and the narratives by which we know them, thus subvert, even as they illustrate, those easy attempts to equate power with force, and to locate its origins in law, violence, or wealth, that lie at the heart of most construals of what Gibbon called "the system of imperial government." For if it was not the Senate but Aquileia that undid Maximinus, and not by force but flight, as it were, that it did so, neither did Aquileia choose its ruler. That power it ceded all the time: to the army when it chose Maximinus, to the Senate when it chose Gordian, and to the imperial system, when it accepted and with its money supported government by whatsoever Roman held the throne.

ACKNOWLEDGMENT

This chapter was prepared with the support of a Frederick Burkhardt Fellowship from the American Council of Learned Societies and the hospitality of the Huntington Library, San Marino, California. My thanks to both institutions for their aid.

BIBLIOGRAPHY

Alston, R. 1995. *Soldier and Society in Roman Egypt: A Social History*. New York.

Ando, C. 2000. *Imperial Ideology and Provincial Loyalty in the Roman Empire*. Berkeley.

Brunt, P. A. 1988. "The army and the land," in *Fall of the Roman Republic and Related Essays*. Oxford, 240–80.

—— 1990. "Did imperial Rome disarm her subjects?" in *Roman Imperial Themes*. Oxford, 255–66.

——, and J. M. Moore (eds.). 1967. *Res Gestae Divi Augusti. The Achievements of the Divine Augustus*. Oxford.

Campbell, J. B. 1984. *The Emperor and the Roman Army, 31 BC–AD 235*. Oxford.

—— 2002. "Power without limit: 'The Romans always win,'" in Chaniotis and Ducrey, 167–80.

Chaniotis, A., and P. Ducrey (eds.). 2002. *Army and Power in the Ancient World*. Stuttgart.

Ferrary, J.-L. 2001. "À propos des pouvoirs d'Auguste," *Cahiers Glotz* 12: 101–54.

Hauken, T. 1998. *Petition and Response. An Epigraphic Study of Petitions to Roman Emperors, 181–249*. Bergen.

Haynes, I. P. 2001. "The impact of auxiliary recruitment on provincial societies from Augustus to Caracalla," in L. de Blois (ed.), *Administration, Prosopography and Appointment Policies in the Roman Empire*. Amsterdam, 62–83.

Isaac, B. 2002. "Army and power in the Roman world: A response to Brian Campbell," in Chaniotis and Ducrey, 181–91.

Lendon, J. E. 1997. *Empire of Honour. The Art of Government in the Roman World*. Oxford.

MacAdam, H. I. 1995. "Cities, villages and veteran settlements: Roman administration of the Syrian Hawran," in D. Panzac (ed.), *Histoire économique et sociale de l'Empire Ottoman et de la Turquie, 1326–1960*. Paris, 641–52.

MacMullen, R. 1963. *Soldier and Civilian in the Later Roman Empire*. Cambridge.

Millar, F. 1977. *The Emperor in the Roman World*. Ithaca.

—— 2002a. "The Mediterranean and the Roman revolution," in Millar 2002b, 215–37.

—— 2002b. *Rome, the Greek World, and the East*. Vol. 1: *The Roman Republic and the Augustan Revolution*. Chapel Hill.

—— 2004. *Rome, the Greek World, and the East*. Vol. 2: *Government, Society, and Culture in the Roman Empire*. Chapel Hill.

Patterson, J. 1993. "Military organization and social change in the later Roman Republic," in J. Rich and G. Shipley (eds.), *War and Society in the Roman World*. New York, 92–112.

Pocock, J. G. A. 2003. *Barbarism and Religion*. Vol. 3. *The First Decline and Fall*. Cambridge.

Pollard, N. 2000. *Soldiers, Cities and Civilians in Roman Syria*. Ann Arbor.

Rowe, G. 2002. *Princes and Political Cultures*. Ann Arbor.

Ste. Croix, G. E. M. de. 1981. *The Class Struggle in the Ancient Greek World from the Archaic Age to the Arab Conquests*. Ithaca.

Wheeler, E. L. 1996. "The laxity of the Syrian legions," in D. L. Kennedy and D. Braund (eds.), *The Roman Army in the East*. Ann Arbor, 229–76.

Woolf, G. 1992. "Imperialism, empire and the integration of the Roman economy," *World Archaeology* 23: 283–93.

—— 1993. "Roman peace," in J. Rich and G. Shipley (eds.), *War and Society in the Roman World*. New York, 171–94.

FURTHER READING

Scholars have generally been disinclined to think hard about power in the Roman Empire, and perhaps in empires generally: they are, it seems, a self-explanatory political formation. Within certain conceptual limitations, however, questions of power and politics were central to ancient theories of empire, and particularly to investigations into the process whereby the freight of empire had impelled the end of the Roman Republic. Pocock 2003 offers a fascinating study of that literature. A more strictly historical inquiry into those topics may be found in Brunt 1988; Patterson 1993 treats the same period from a very different perspective. Campbell 1984 studies relations between emperors and armies.

Regarding the two theories of power discussed in this chapter, the constitutionalist tradition may be approached through Brunt and Moore 1967; Augustus' *Res Gestae* has now been subjected to searching inquiry by Ferrary 2001. Until quite recently, the provinces found themselves integrated into models of imperial politics in one of two ways, as participants in the imperial economy, or as contributors of senators to the imperial governing class. Woolf 1992 offers a brief survey of the former topic; de Ste. Croix 1981 is far the most sustained exposition. Where Rome is concerned, the study of a specifically imperial political culture at a level beyond prosopography has been inspired above all by the work of Fergus Millar: all the papers republished in *Rome, the Greek World, and the East* (vol. 1: 2002b; vol. 2: 2004) merit careful study, as does *Emperor in the Roman World* (1977). Works that build on his achievement include Lendon 1997, Ando 2000, and Rowe 2002.

In thinking about relations between cities and the army, it is tempting to separate events in war from times of peace. This is useful, up to a point. Millar, "The Mediterranean and the Roman revolution" (in Millar 2002a), asks the question how the provinces fared during the Roman civil wars. It is then tempting to write about relations between "soldiers and civilians" in ways that bracket violence, concentrating on such topics as cultural and economic exchange between army units and urban populations, on large-scale veterans settlements, or on social relations between veterans and civilians. Exemplary studies of this kind include Pollard 2000, and Wheeler 1996, both focusing on Antioch; as well as Haynes 2001 and MacAdam 1995, each writing about villages.

But the army dealt violence also in peacetime, in the form both of soldiers acting on their own initiative and of army units seconded to magistrates for the suppression of rebellion: on these topics, see Campbell 2002, Isaac 2002, and Woolf 1993. On the difficult question, "Did imperial Rome disarm her subjects?," which bears on the capacity of local populations to resist Romans and others, see Brunt's essay of that name, reprinted in Brunt 1990. And soldiers also acted in a wide range of official capacities and were undoubtedly the most commonly-seen agents of the government. On their presence in the provinces, see above all MacMullen 1963, a classic study, matched in its range of topics in the earlier period only by Alston 1995, which has a dramatically more restricted geographic scope.

CHAPTER TWENTY-ONE

Making Emperors.
Imperial Instrument or
Independent Force?

Anthony R. Birley

The republic fell not least because the ruling elite failed to solve the problem of paying the troops adequately and providing for the veterans. "Only a centralised despotism [that of Caesar] could tame Roman armies and remove them from politics; and it was as a despot – however much he might disguise despotism with republican catchwords – that Augustus, the adopted son of Julius, kept them tamed."[1] In a speech put into Caesar's mouth, supposedly delivered in 46 BC, Dio makes the dictator urge the senators

> not to fear the soldiers or regard them as anything but the custodians of my empire, which is yours as well. It is necessary for many reasons that they should be supported [i.e. paid]: but they will be supported for you, not against you. . . . This is why higher taxes than usual are being levied at the moment: to restrain the mutinous elements and deter those who have conquered from becoming mutinous by giving them an adequate living wage. (Cassius Dio 43.18.1–2)

No doubt the speech really reflected Dio's own views rather than anything actually said by Caesar. Dio had unhappy experiences of mutinous troops (see below).[2]

Caesar owed his position to legions hardened by years of fighting in Gaul and to the veterans, for whom he was determined to provide. He doubled legionary pay and began the settlement of many thousand veterans in new colonies. In the latter respect he was no different from Sulla, except that he declined to abdicate, which cost him his life. The events following the Ides of March showed that another Caesar could most readily gain the backing of the military. In summer 43 Caesar's 19-year-old heir marched on Rome with eight legions, seeking to be made consul (Cassius Dio 46.42.4–43.4). A delegation of 400 soldiers appeared before the Senate: when the senators temporized, one legionary fetched his sword, "touched it and said: 'If you will not give Caesar the consulship, this will'" (Appian, *B. Civ.* 3.12.88). He got his consulship and the men a donative of 2,500 denarii each, more than ten times their annual pay (Cassius Dio 46.46.1–7; Appian *B. Civ.* 3.13, 94) – this was the capital investment on which the principate was founded. But it was hard going for some time: there were still several rival warlords. In 41, the veterans were dissatisfied. They "gathered in Rome in large numbers," held an assembly on the Capitol and passed a resolution that they themselves should adjudicate between the feuding generals. The new Caesar's opponents made fun of this "senate in hob-nailed boots," *senatus caligatus* in Latin (Cassius Dio 48.12.1–3). He took them seriously.

He eventually achieved sole power and became Caesar Augustus. People were encouraged to forget the 20 years of anarchy. He paid the veterans off, settling them in 28 colonies in Italy and dozens more in the provinces, providing them with land and cash-grants (*Mon. Anc.* 3.3, 15.3, 16.1–2). Finally, to ensure future provision for veterans, in AD 6, in the face of strong opposition in the Senate, he set up a special fund, the *aerarium militare*, funded principally by a 5 percent inheritance tax, to be paid only by Roman citizens (*Mon. Anc.* 17.2; Cassius Dio 55.25.3; Suetonius, *Aug.* 49.2). By now a standing army had been created, with fixed terms of service, and it was stationed around the periphery of the empire, where it was given plenty of fighting against external enemies. For the elite in the Mediterranean heartland of the empire this was an admirable situation. For most of them the army had become invisible.[3]

All the same, Augustus now had the Praetorian Guard. Edward Gibbon's reflections on the army of the Caesars, and on this body in particular, are worth quoting:

The power of the sword is more sensibly felt in an extensive monarchy, than in a small community. It has been calculated by the ablest politicians, that no state, without being exhausted, can maintain above the hundredth part of its members in arms and idleness. . . . The advantage of military science and discipline cannot be exerted, unless a proper number of soldiers are united into one body, and actuated by one soul. With a handful of men, such a union would be ineffectual; with an unwieldy host it would be impracticable . . . there is no superiority of natural strength, which would enable one man to keep in constant subjection one hundred of his fellow-creatures; the tyrant of a small town . . . would soon discover that a hundred armed followers were a weak defence against ten thousand peasants or citizens; but a hundred thousand well-disciplined soldiers will command, with despotic sway, ten millions of subjects; and a body of ten or fifteen thousand guards will strike terror into the most numerous populace that ever crowded the streets of an immense capital. The praetorian bands, whose licentious fury was the first symptom and cause of the decline of the Roman empire, scarcely amounted to the last-named number. They derived their institution from Augustus. That crafty tyrant, sensible that laws might colour, but that arms alone could maintain, his usurped dominion, had gradually formed this powerful body of guards, in constant readiness to protect his person, to awe the senate, and either to prevent or to crush the first motions of rebellion. . . . Such formidable servants are always necessary, but sometimes fatal, to the throne of despotism.[4]

Augustus' last years tested the new military system almost to the limit. The Pannonian revolt and the disaster in the Teutoburg forest created enormous strains. Both man-power and money were lacking (Pliny, *Nat.* 7.149). At Augustus' death the legions were exhausted and anxious. Furthermore, shortly before he died he had evidently given the Guard, whose conditions of service were already greatly superior to that of the other troops, a massive pay rise, doubtless to ensure their loyalty to his suc-cessor.[5] This made the legionaries, who were in any case being denied discharge at the due term, all the more resentful (Tacitus, *Ann.* 1.17).

Suetonius cites Tiberius' explanation for his reluctance to accept the succession: his friends did not realize "what a monster the imperial power was" (Suetonius, *Tib.* 24.1). His "hesitation was caused by fear at the dangers threatening from all sides, so that he often used to say that he was holding a wolf by the ears, *ut saepe lupum se auribus tenere diceret*" (25.1). Brian Campbell tellingly applies the second remark to the emperor's situation vis-à-vis the army: "[Tiberius], who took his duties and responsibilities very seriously, could find no peace; if he let go the wolf might destroy him; to hold on required both courage and skill. The army was the most important problem with which every emperor had to deal."[6]

Discontented soldiers would on numerous occasions, with varying success, try to change their emperor. This first happened in AD 14. The Rhine and Illyricum armies mutinied, above all demanding a pay rise. As Suetonius puts it, the Rhine legions, "were even rejecting the *princeps* as not being appointed by themselves and with extreme force were urging Germanicus, their commanding officer at that time, to take over the state" (Suetonius, *Tib.* 25.2). Tacitus supplies much more detail. In Pannonia, after a few weeks, Drusus Caesar, Tiberius' son, helped by an eclipse of the moon, which unsettled the men, and the onset of winter, managed to suppress the mutiny of the three legions (Tacitus, *Ann.* 1.16–30). Meanwhile, on the Rhine, "from the same causes, the German legions were disrupted – all the more violently, given their greater numbers, and with high hopes that Germanicus Caesar would be unable to suffer the command (*imperium*) of another and would entrust himself to the legions, who would handle everything by their own force" (Tacitus, *Ann.* 1.31.1, translated by A. J. Woodman).

Germanicus successfully resisted. But the crisis was only averted after very ugly scenes; he then reinforced the legions' reluctant acceptance of Tiberius as emperor by lead-ing them against the Germans. According to Dio, "although [Germanicus] might have taken the imperial power on several occasions, with the agreement not only of the soldiers but of the people and the senate as well, he did not wish to have it" (Cassius Dio 57.18.8). What occasions other than in late summer 14 on the Rhine are meant is not clear. Tiberius clearly remained nervous at Germanicus' popularity until the latter's death; but he managed to avoid meeting the legions' demands.

Germanicus offers the first example of *recusatio imperii*, the "refus du pouvoir" of Jean Béranger's classic study.[7] This would later become an empty ritual: many "refusals" were by men who had primed the troops to acclaim them. Germanicus really had been under pressure from below. So too was the next man to refuse, L. Verginius Rufus in AD 68 and 69. Germanicus was loyal to the wishes of Augustus and to his adoptive father Tiberius, and had every expectation that he would eventually succeed Tiberius when the latter died. In 68 Verginius may simply have been too nervous, but he probably regarded his modest origins as an obstacle to acceptance by the elite. In April 69, the premium on noble birth as a qualification for imperial power had already sunk sharply, but by then he had missed the chance, and, as one who had been serving the losing candidate, Otho, was in an impossibly weak position.

Twenty-seven years after Germanicus' *recusatio* an emperor was indeed made by the army, following the chance discovery, by a soldier from the Praetorian Guard, of the terrified Claudius, hiding behind a curtain after Caligula's assassination. That is at any rate Suetonius' version (Suetonius, *Claud.* 10.2). There were variant accounts of what happened and why: some believe that Claudius was involved in the plot and had hoped or planned to succeed.[8] However this may be, Claudius clearly owed his accession to the Guard, and its men were richly rewarded. This was the first occasion when the Guard made an emperor. More would follow.

Claudius soon faced a counter-coup, launched by a leading conspirator against Caligula, L. Annius Vinicianus, in 42. Lacking an army himself, Vinicianus induced Camillus Scribonianus, governor of Dalmatia, the nearest military province to Rome, to proclaim himself emperor. But when Scribonianus announced his hope of restoring the free republic, his two legions deserted him (Cassius Dio 60.15.3), within four days, Suetonius says, but attributes their second thoughts to bad omens (Suetonius, *Claud.* 13.2). This time it was the general and his senatorial backers, not the soldiers, who had taken the initiative. There would be many such cases in the future, although usurpers, not least successful ones, tended to assert that they had had the power "forced on them" by the soldiers. More often a usurpation was motivated by the need for self-preservation or by naked ambition, and the troops had to be persuaded, or bribed, to acclaim their commander.

The proclamation of Galba in 68 was brought about by the actions of senators, not initiated by the soldiers. Self-preservation was probably his principal motive – besides, at his age he had nothing to lose – and he may even have been influenced by a supposed prophecy. Further, Vindex may have convinced Galba that he could rely on the army of Germany. What followed Galba's fall was to show that army actively seeking to create an emperor of their own. The Rhine legions "had been slow to desert Nero," and the Upper German commander, Verginius Rufus, "had not supported Galba straightaway" (Tacitus, *Hist.* 1.8.2). These men, confident in their strength, were unwilling to accept a new emperor chosen by others – not least by Julius Vindex, whom they had defeated. Twice they tried to force Verginius to accept their acclamation: straight after the death of Vindex; and shortly afterwards, when it was confirmed that Nero was dead (Plutarch, *Galba* 6.3, 10.2–3). The legions collected in Italy by Nero also made overtures to Verginius (Tacitus, *Hist.* 1.9.2). He was soon replaced by Galba, and in April 69, holding a second consulship granted by Otho, he was serving on Otho's staff. After Otho's defeat and suicide, his grieving soldiers "turned with threats and entreaties to Verginius, at one moment begging him to assume the imperial power, at another to undertake a mission to Valens and Caecina." Verginius "stole away through another door" (Plutarch, *Otho* 18.3–4; cf. Tacitus *Hist.* 2.51). A little later, when dining with Vitellius at Ticinum, he was nearly lynched by the latter's victorious soldiers, who thought he had been trying to have Vitellius murdered. Vitellius was sure of Verginius' innocence, but had difficulty in controlling men demanding the death of their own former general – whom they still admired, but "hated for having scorned their offer" (Tacitus, *Hist.* 2.68).

The legionary legate Fabius Valens, urging Vitellius "to take advantage of the enthusiasm of his army," added that "Verginius had done well to hesitate: from an equestrian family, with a nobody for his father, he would not have been equal to the task if he had received imperial power, and by refusing it he saved his own life." By contrast, the distinction of Vitellius' father in effect "thrust the rank of emperor on him and made it unsafe for him to remain a private citizen" (Tacitus, *Hist.* 1.52.4). If it had been "doubtful whether Verginius had really been unwilling" (Tacitus, *Hist.* 1.8.2, *an imperare noluisset dubium*),[9] he clearly insisted until his dying day that this had been the case and reiterated it for posterity with a self-composed epitaph: "Here lies Rufus, who once, when Vindex was defeated, claimed imperial power – not for himself, but for the fatherland," *Hic situs est Rufus, pulso qui Vindice quondam Imperium adseruit non sibi sed patriae*. Nine years after his death in 97, no one had troubled to have the tombstone erected, "although his glorious memory is spread all over the world," Pliny told a friend (Pliny, *Epist.* 6.10.4; the epitaph is quoted again in another letter, to a correspondent who had criticized Verginius, 9.19.1).

"Thirty years after his hour of glory" – during which he had withdrawn from public life – Verginius had been recalled, aged 83, to be consul for the third time, with the new emperor Nerva as his colleague. One may speculate that a reason for his selection was to set a signal. Nerva's position was very precarious: the honor indicated that army commanders who might be planning a coup would do well to follow Verginius' example. But Verginius slipped and broke his thigh when rehearsing his address of thanks and died after a protracted illness. "The crowning touch to his good fortune" was that the funeral oration was delivered by Tacitus, then consul, *laudator eloquentissimus* (Pliny, *Epist.* 2.1). The need to discourse on the events of 68–69 may well have given Tacitus the idea of writing about them at more length. Yet he chose to begin his *Histories* not with the fall of Nero but with January 1, 69. Hence he mentions Verginius' conduct in 68 and the behavior of his legions only in brief retrospective passages. Plutarch opens his *Life of Galba*, which fills in important details on the events of 68, with reflections on the horrors of military indiscipline, citing parallels from earlier times and quoting Plato: "a good general can do nothing unless his army is loyal and self-controlled," with stress on the lofty qualities required to inculcate obedience (Plutarch, *Galba* 1.3, quoting Plato's *Republic* 376C). "Many calamities, including those which befell the Romans after Nero's end, bear witness to this and show that there is nothing more dreadful in an empire than an army imbued with untrained and irrational impulses."

Tacitus clearly had a similar view. The *Histories* are filled with grim remarks about soldiers casting off discipline and taking the initiative. He could hardly have condoned Verginius' conduct in 68. Vindex had invited Galba to take power and "offer himself to a strong body – meaning the Galliae, which have 100,000 armed men and are able to arm thousands more – that was looking for a head" (Plutarch, *Galba* 4.3). Had Vindex had assurances from Verginius and Fonteius Capito that their combined forces, seven legions and the *auxilia*, which could have amounted to a figure of some 80,000 men, would support the rebellion? Verginius had certainly been conferring with Vindex at Vesontio – the natural point at which to join forces for a march on Rome – shortly before his legions "on their own initiative" attacked Vindex's Gallic levies (Cassius Dio 63.24.2; cf. Plutarch, *Galba* 6.4); and he certainly mourned the dead Vindex (Cassius Dio 63.25.1). Whatever Verginius had been planning, Tacitus would have had to reveal one clear fact: Verginius had been unable to control his own army, a cardinal sin in Tacitus' eyes. It was tactful to leap over these transactions.[10] Of course, to start with the beginning of a year was in the tradition of the old annalists, and the events of January 1, 69, first mentioned at *Hist.* 1.12, even though only treated in detail more than half way throughout the first book, triggered off so much.[11]

Only a few of the very numerous passages which show Tacitus' horror at the indiscipline of the soldiers can be cited here. First, there is the famous remark at the beginning of the work: "a secret of empire had been made common knowledge: that a *princeps* could be created elsewhere than at Rome" (Tacitus, *Hist.* 1.4.1). The "city soldiery (*miles urbanus*)," long loyal to the Caesars and feeling that they had been tricked into deserting Nero, resented Galba's failure to pay the promised donative and saw that they had been forestalled in his favor by the legions. They had been unsettled by their prefect Nymphidius Sabinus' abortive coup attempt and, not least, by Galba's statement, which Tacitus calls "honourable from the point of view of the state but dangerous to himself, that 'he chose soldiers, did not buy them'" (1.5.1–2). Rome was "full of unfamiliar troops . . . a vast material for revolution (*novis rebus*), but with no preference for any individual" (1.6.2). In particular, "the German armies were both anxious and angry, a very dangerous condition considering their great strength: they were arrogant because of their recent victory [against Vindex] and nervous at having favoured the wrong side [their attempt to raise Verginius to the throne]" (1.8.2).

Although Otho's coup was planned by him and his friends, not sparked off by a spontaneous rising by the Guard, nonetheless Tacitus writes of the men picked to organize Galba's assassination: "two common soldiers (*duo manipulares*) undertook to transfer the imperial power of the Roman People – and did transfer it" (1.25.1). As the coup proceeded and the Guard's armory was opened, "no tribune or centurion gave the order; each man was his own leader and instigator (*sibi quisque dux et instigator*)" (1.38.3). Once Galba and his newly adopted heir were dead, "everything was done on the initiative of the soldiers" (1.46.1). Dio's summary is worth comparing: "Everybody . . . hated [Otho] most of all because he had shown that the imperial power was for sale and had put the city in the hands of the boldest; also because he held senate and people in no esteem and, further, because he had persuaded the soldiers that they could both kill and create a Caesar" (Cassius Dio 64.9.1–2). Dio, who himself experienced military indiscipline at close hand (see below), shared the feelings of Plutarch and Tacitus. After the detailed account of Otho's coup, Tacitus returns to the events on the Rhine which had preceded it. The men there had been under strict discipline – but "discipline so sternly exercised in peace is dissolved by civil war." They were only too ready for another war, and confident of their strength (1.51.1–5).

The proclamation of Vitellius followed naturally from Verginius' *recusatio*. Dio's *epitomator* expresses it concisely: "the soldiers in the Germanies . . . , having failed to attain what they wanted under Rufus, sought to achieve it under some other man – and they succeeded. They put Aulus Vitellius, governor of Lower Germany, at their head, and revolted. All that they could see in him was his noble birth" (Cassius Dio [Xiphilinus] 64.4.1–2). Tacitus indicates that soon after Vitellius' arrival at Cologne, in late November 68, he was being urged to bid for the throne by two of the legionary legates, Caecina Alienus, recently put in charge of one of the Upper German legions (probably IV Macedonica), and Fabius Valens, who had been legate of the Lower German First legion (stationed at Bonn) for some time (Tacitus, *Hist.* 1.52.1ff.). Yet Tacitus takes pains to stress the initiative of the legions, "who made a secret compact with each other, into which the auxiliaries were admitted as well . . . and the auxiliaries joined them with even more eagerness than their own" (1.54.3).

On January 1 the four Lower German legions swore the oath to Galba, "though with much hesitation"; and some of the men from the First and Fifteenth threw stones at Galba's *imagines*. But the same day in Upper Germany the two legions at Mainz, IV Macedonica and XXII Primigenia, went much further, breaking the *imagines*, refusing to swear allegiance to Galba, and instead taking an oath to "the senate and people of Rome." The officers made no move to stop them and the commanding general, Hordeonius Flaccus, Verginius' successor, was too cowardly to intervene. The same evening the eagle-bearer of the Fourth brought the news to Vitellius, who reacted by issuing a despatch: his own troops "must either fight the rebels, or, if they preferred peace and concord, choose an emperor of their own" (1.55–56). The next day, January 2, Valens rode into Cologne with his legionary and auxiliary cavalry and saluted Vitellius as emperor. The Upper German army followed suit a day later. Although Tacitus does not say this, it is hard not to infer that Caecina had encouraged the men of the Mainz garrison to reject Galba.

As for Vespasian, there is no suggestion that his proclamation in July 69 was initiated from below. Certainly, Vitellius had soon become very unpopular, which made it easier for the men who managed it, Vespasian's son Titus, Mucianus, legate of Syria, and Tiberius Alexander, prefect of Egypt (Tacitus, *Hist.* 2.74–81). The latter started the ball rolling on July 1, getting his legions to swear allegiance to Vespasian, whose own troops in Judaea followed suit two days later without waiting for news from Syria. In Judaea "it was all done by the impetus of the soldiers" (Tacitus, *Hist.* 2.79). But the men had clearly been suitably primed, as Tacitus explicitly states of the Syrian army, "inflamed" by Mucianus' claim that "Vitellius intended to transfer the German legions to the lucrative and peaceful service in Syria, which those of Syria were to exchange for German winter-quarters with harsh climate and hard work" (2.80.3). After winning undisputed power, Vespasian treated the army with an iron hand and "lost no opportunity to improve discipline" (Suetonius, *Vesp.* 8.2–3). The elite must have heaved a sigh of relief.

His younger son Domitian, no doubt feeling insecure in his first years, gave the army a big pay rise, $33\frac{1}{3}$ percent, the first since Julius Caesar. Even so, there were numerous conspiracies against him, the most dangerous – until the one that succeeded in 96 – an attempted coup by an army commander. Twenty years after

Vitellius' putsch, to the very day, so it appears, the governor of Upper Germany, L. Antonius Saturninus, was proclaimed emperor by the two Mainz legions. But the sources are too meager – and too hostile to Saturninus – to indicate whether the legate or the legions were the driving force, let alone to have any true idea of Saturninus' motives.[12]

There were to be plenty of similar coups, successful and unsuccessful, over the next 200 years and more. But sources comparable to those for the Julio-Claudians and the years 68–9 are lacking, with a partial exception for the events of 192–197, until Julian's proclamation at Paris in 360. Domitian was finally murdered by a palace conspiracy. One of the Guard Prefects was privy to the plot, but the troops were not involved – and soon showed their anger. Nerva's position was precarious. In 97 the Guard mutinied and Domitian's murderers had to be sacrificed to them. Nerva's situation recalled that of Galba in 69. But he learned from Galba's fate and adopted, not a young aristocrat, but an army commander, the legate of Upper Germany. The nomination of Trajan has been called a "veiled coup," but there is no hint that he was urged on in advance by his soldiers. To be sure, the Guard may have hoped to raise another man to the purple.

Hadrian's succession in 117 was rushed through in a couple of days, with a claim that he had been adopted by the dying Trajan. Hadrian had to "ask the senate's forgiveness for not having allowed it the decision about his *imperium*: he had been saluted as *imperator* by the soldiers overhastily (*praepropere*), because the state could not be without an *imperator*" (*HA, Hadr.* 6.2). There is no sign of any attempted coup during his reign. Under Antoninus Pius, it is a surprise, two men conspired against him: Atilius Titianus and Priscianus (*HA, Ant. Pius* 7.3–4, cf. *Epit. de Caes.* 15.6). The former must be T. Atilius Rufus Titianus, *cos. ord.* in 127, whose names were erased in the *Fasti Ostienses*. Nothing whatever is known about his plot. The other man must be Cornelius Priscianus, who, as the *Fasti Ostienses* reveal, was condemned on September 15, 145: "judgment was made on Cornelius Priscianus in open session in the Senate, because he disturbed the province of Spain in hostile fashion." The circumstances are baffling: perhaps he had prepared a coup while governor of Hispania Tarraconensis. "After being accused of attempted usurpation, he committed suicide and the emperor did not allow an investigation into his conspiracy" (*HA, Ant. Pius* 7.4).[13]

It was 30 years before the next coup, by Avidius Cassius in 175. He claimed, in a letter to the people of Alexandria, "his paternal city," that he had been "elected by the most noble soldiers."[14] The sources are poor, but it seems probable that Avidius acted on a false report that Marcus Aurelius was dead, and persuaded his men to proclaim him. The Marcomannic wars under Marcus took a heavy toll and morale in the army clearly suffered. Desertion was rife under Commodus, apparently developing into a full-scale war in the western provinces. Meanwhile the army of Britain had had trouble on the frontier, perhaps the reason why Marcus sent there 5,500 of the 8,000 Sarmatians surrendered under the armistice of 175. In the early 180s the province was invaded by the northern peoples and "a general" even lost his life, starting what Dio called "the most serious war of Commodus' reign." It was ended by the governor Ulpius Marcellus in 184, when Commodus took the title Britannicus.

For reasons which remain obscure, the legions in Britain were soon seriously discontented. They tried twice to create an emperor. A fragment of Dio's *History* in the *Excerpta Vaticana* relates that "The soldiers in Britain chose the legionary legate Priscus as emperor, but he declined, saying that 'I am as much an emperor as you are soldiers'" (Cassius Dio 72.9.2a, from Petrus Patricius, *Exc. Vat.* 122). From its position in the *Excerpta* this must refer to an event between 177 and 189–190. A passage in the *Historia Augusta* points to the early 180s: "Commodus was called Britannicus by flatterers when the Britons even wanted to choose another emperor in opposition to him" (*Comm.* 8.4). The offer to Priscus can then be dated to 184. The *Historia Augusta* also transmits what was presumably the response to this abortive coup: the Guard Prefect Perennis replaced the legionary legates in Britain with equestrian commanders, a measure said to have led to his own overthrow, in 185 (*Comm.* 6.2). Another fragment of Dio gives more details: in an unparalleled example of indiscipline, the soldiers in Britain sent a force of 1,500 men from the British army to Rome, which demanded Perennis' head and was allowed to lynch him (Cassius Dio 72.9.2²).

Soon the British legions tried another coup, when a new governor, Pertinax, entered office in 185:

> He deterred the soldiers from all their revolt (*seditio*), although they wanted to make any man whatever emperor and especially Pertinax himself. . . . And he did indeed suppress the mutinies against himself in Britain, but came into huge danger, being almost killed in a mutiny of a legion – at any rate he was left among the dead. Of course, Pertinax punished this very severely. Finally, after this he sought to be excused from his legateship, saying that the legions were hostile to him because of his having upheld discipline. (*HA, Pert.* 3.6, 8–10, cf. Cassius Dio 73.4.1)

Commodus was eventually removed in a conspiracy masterminded by the Guard Prefect Aemilius Laetus. In the evening of December 31, 192, he was murdered through the agency of his chamberlain Eclectus and chief concubine Marcia. The soldiers were not involved. When the deed was done, Pertinax was informed: in spite of subsequent denials, he had surely been picked in advance as the new emperor. He left in secret for the camp of the Guard, where he told the praetorians that Commodus had died a natural death and that Laetus and Eclectus had "thrust the imperial power on him." He promised them a donative, 3,000 denarii a man. But the reaction was not enthusiastic. While he was waiting for the senators to attend a hastily summoned meeting, Commodus' elderly brother-in-law Claudius Pompeianus, Pertinax's former patron, arrived, "lamenting Commodus' death." Pertinax urged Pompeianus to take the throne, but he "saw that Pertinax was already invested with *imperium* by the soldiers, and refused." Addressing the Senate, Pertinax announced that he had been chosen emperor by the soldiers, then added: "I do not want the office and I shall resign it today, because of my age and poor health and the distressing situation." But the senators unanimously acclaimed him as emperor. After an uproar about the disposal of Commodus' corpse (the senators wanted to deny him burial), Pertinax expressed his thanks to the Senate, and also, especially, to Laetus. He then gave a tribune of the Guard the watchword, *militemus*, "let us serve." When on the next day Commodus' statues were overthrown and Pertinax gave them the same watchword, the Guard reacted unfavorably. On January 3, when the oath of loyalty was due, some praetorians attempted a coup, dragging a senator named Triarius Maternus into the camp. He managed to escape, "naked."

The praetorians continued to be discontented. Early in March while Pertinax was dealing with the food-supply at Ostia, they planned another coup, their candidate the consul Sosius Falco. Laetus was behind it, says Dio (Cassius Dio [Xiphilinus] 73.8.1–2); but it was nipped in the bud. The *Historia Augusta* does not name Laetus: Falco himself is said to have "plotted against Pertinax because he wanted to be emperor," but adds, "although many said that Falco was unaware that the imperial power was being prepared for him" (*Pert.* 10.1–7). On March 28 the blow fell: a few hundred soldiers attacked the palace and Pertinax was assassinated. This time the *epitome* of Dio does not name Laetus (73.10.1–3) but the *Historia Augusta* starts its detailed account with the statement that "a conspiracy against Pertinax was pre-pared by Laetus . . . and those whom Pertinax's integrity had offended," mention-ing that when Pertinax heard of the men's approach "he sent Laetus to meet them, but he avoided the soldiers and slipped through a portico with his head covered and went home" (*Pert.* 10.8–11.13). An important fact suggests that Pertinax's murder was a spontaneous act by mutinous soldiers: neither they nor Laetus had a can-didate for the throne ready. Pertinax left a reputation, deservedly or not, for having been forced to take the power and having dreaded it (*horror imperii*) (*HA, Pert.* 13.1, 15.8; Aurelius Victor, *Caes. Epit.* 18.1).

What followed his murder is notorious: the auction of the empire at the camp of the Guard. The two bidders were Pertinax's father-in-law Sulpicianus and Didius Julianus. Didius warned the Guard not to choose a man who would avenge Pertinax's death and promised that he would restore Commodus' good name. The *imperium* was knocked down to him when he offered them 25,000 sesterces a man, 5,000 more than Sulpicianus.

The news soon reached the provinces. On April 9 Septimius Severus was "pro-claimed emperor at Carnuntum, with many encouraging him, but against his own will, *repugnans*" (*HA, Sev.* 5.1). The word *repugnans* shows that he feigned *recu-satio* – but it was only a ritual. Among the "many encouraging him" may have been some legionaries, but there is no suggestion that they had taken the initiative. They were richly rewarded, even if they did not get what they demanded: the same sum as Octavian's men in 43 BC. Severus had to fight for almost four years to secure power. In the process he gave the army a large pay increase, the first since that of Domitian, and he greatly enlarged the garrison at Rome. The new Guard, now drawn from the Danubian legions, the other forces in the capital, the Urban Cohorts, the *vigiles*, and the Horse Guards, were all greatly increased in size; further, a newly formed legion, II Parthica, was stationed a few miles to the south. The pay rise and other privileges for the army may have been intended to improve recruitment, and the concentration of larger forces in and close to Rome may have been motivated by a perceived need for a mobile, central force. But these measures all helped to secure Severus' own power. His dying advice to his sons sums it up: "Do not disagree, give money to the soldiers, and despise everyone else" (Cassius Dio 76.15.2). Caracalla ignored the first few words but followed the rest: "he often used to say, 'No one ought to have money but me, so that I can give it to the soldiers'" (Cassius Dio 77.10.4).[15]

Caracalla's murder in 217, and the turbulent events of the next few years, marked the beginning of long period of upheaval, with numerous attempts at usurpation, far too many to detail here.[16] Severus Alexander's 13-year rule provided only a breathing space, but even then Dio had unhappy experiences. The Guard Prefect Ulpian was lynched by his own men in 223. Further, "many uprisings begun by many men, some of which caused great alarm, were suppressed." Then there was the rise of the new Persian kingdom, bad enough in itself,

> but the danger is rather the fact that some of our forces are joining [the Persian king] and others are refusing to defend themselves. They are so insolent and practise such unrestrained violence that those in Mesopotamia even dared to kill their commander Flavius Heracleo; and the praetorians blamed me, as well as Ulpian, because I had ruled the soldiers in Pannonia with a firm hand. (Cassius Dio 80.2.2–4.2)[17]

Alexander ignored the men's threats against Dio, indeed gave him a second consulship, for 229 – but when the praetorians reacted angrily again, the emperor advised Dio to hold office outside Rome, after which the old man left for his home town in Bithynia (80.5.1–3).

Alexander's murder and Maximinus' proclamation in March 235 are highlighted by the late chroniclers and by the *Historia Augusta* as a dreadful turning-point: the accession of a man who had started as a common soldier. A full account is provided by Herodian, although he dispenses with many details:[18]

> The soldiers decided to dispose of Alexander and proclaim Maximinus as emperor and Augustus, as being their fellow-soldier and tent-mate and appearing to be qualified for the present war by his experience and courage. Having assembled on the plain, fully armed as if for the usual training, when Maximinus approached to preside over them, they threw a purple imperial cloak on him and proclaimed him emperor – either he was unaware of what was being undertaken or he had planned it in secret. At first he refused and tore off the purple. But when they pressed him, threatening with drawn swords to kill him, he accepted the position, preferring to escape the immediate danger rather than a future one. (Herodian 6.8.5–6)

Did the soldiers really take the initiative? Herodian did not know: Maximinus might have "planned it in secret." He went through the *recusatio* ritual but "accepted the position" at sword's point.

Herodian ends with the year 238, which had more emperors in one year than ever before: Maximinus, Gordian I and II, Pupienus and Balbinus, and Gordian III. For the next half-century reliable information is lacking. The fullest source, the *Historia Augusta*, can here hardly be trusted at all, and the others, the Latins, principally Aurelius Victor, Eutropius, and the *Epitome de Caesaribus*, or the Greeks, Zosimus, Zonaras, and the Byzantine chroniclers, are brief, scrappy, and confused.

The deteriorating defenses of the empire produced many usurpations, some successful: the armies are often said to have proclaimed as emperors generals who had

had successes against external enemies. Zosimus reports this of Aemilianus in 253 (Zosimus 1.28) – who only lasted for a few weeks. Yet Victor simply says that he "seized supreme power after corrupting the soldiers" (Aurelius Victor, *Caes.* 31.1). The same Victor claimed that the so called "edict of Gallienus," debarring senators from military service, was motivated by his fear that "the imperial power would be transferred to the best of the nobles" (33.33–34). This clearly made no difference: Gallienus was deposed by one of his new equestrian commanders, Claudius (II), in a typical putsch, as the candidate of a junta of army commanders. As he was later alleged to be the ancestor of the house of Constantine, it was dressed up by the sources, including Victor: "The soldiers eagerly approved and praised the accession of Claudius, being compelled by the desperate state of affairs, almost against their natural inclinations, to make the right decisions" (Aurelius Victor, *Caes.* 34.1).

A curious fantasy seized the imagination of the Latin writers (most of all the author of the *Historia Augusta*): that after the murder of Aurelian in 275 there was an *interregnum* of six months, during which delegations from the armies and Senate conferred about the succession, outdoing each other in their self-restraint and modesty. The choice of Tacitus was hailed with delight by almost everyone, "because the senators (*proceres*) had recovered from the fierce soldiery the right to choose the emperor" (Aurelius Victor, *Caes.* 35.9–36.1). This supposed recovery did not last, Victor admits: with the murder of Probus in 282, "from this point on the power of the military increased and the Senate's *imperium* and right to create the *princeps* was snatched away – right up to our own time" (37.5).

Whether the Senate had ever had such a "right" is another matter. Writers who were themselves senators liked to claim this. But in effect the army had taken over the role of the sovereign Roman people. This was actually proclaimed by the orator Symmachus – for all that he privately considered the Senate to be "the better part of the human race" (Symmachus, *Epist.* 1.52) – when praising Valentinian I's appointment as emperor in 364: "The military senate (*castrensis senatus*) approved a man distinguished in war"; the army was "an electoral assembly entirely worthy of the principate of such a great empire" (*digna plane comitia tanti imperii principatu*) (Symmachus, *Relat.* 1.9). It might seem that they had recovered the ancient function of the *comitia centuriata*, the assembly of the Roman Republic under arms, but Valentinian had actually been selected by a group of senior officers, "the military senate"; they offered the army *comitia* a single candidate.

Later Roman rulers liked to claim that they had the *consensus militum* and if they had usurped the power, that they had been forced to accept it. A few years after Constantine I's proclamation at York on July 25, 306, a panegyrist claimed that "the soldiers threw the purple on your shoulders, in spite of your tears [for his father's death]" and that "you are even said to have tried to escape that passion of the army which was demanding you, unconquered emperor, and to have urged on your horse with your spurs" (*Pan. Lat.* 6[7].8.3) – the conventional *recusatio*. In Victor's view, "Constantine's mighty and passionate soul had been inspired since his boyhood with a burning desire to be emperor" (Aurelius Victor, *Caes.* 40.2). Julian and his friends worked hard to portray his acclamation at Paris early in 360 as having been forced on him by the soldiers, but there can be no doubt that he and his close advisers had staged it.[19]

Magnus Maximus, a defeated ruler, could be portrayed as a usurper who had seized power (*tyrannidem arripuisset*) ([Aurelius Victor] *Caes.* 47.7). But as he had been a fervent Catholic persecutor of heresy, Christian writers could express this more mildly: "he was created emperor by the army almost against his will" (Orosius 7.34.9); Maximus himself told Martin that "he had not taken the imperial power of his own accord but had defended with armed force the necessity of rule imposed on him by the soldiers in accordance with the divine will" (Sulpicius Severus, *Vita Martini* 20.3). By contrast the Greek writers were sure that Maximus was motivated by resentment that he had not achieved higher rank; and modern historians suspect that he may have been encouraged to depose Gratian by Theodosius.

As the situation of the empire became desperate, the armies did force the power on any candidate who might better defend them against external threat. The army of Britain, appalled by news of barbarian invasions on the continent, tried three times to find the right man in 406–7:

> The soldiers in Britain, having mutinied, elevated Marcus to the imperial throne, and obeyed him as the one controlling affairs there. But having removed him as not agreeing with their way of thinking, they led Gratianus into their midst and placing the purple robe and crown on him escorted him as their emperor. But being dissatisfied with him as well and having removed him four months later, they put him to death, giving the imperial power to Constantinus. (Zosimus 6.2.1–2)

Orosius omits Marcus but adds some detail:

> While they [the Alans, Suebi, and Vandals and many other peoples] were moving riotously through the Gauls, in the Britains Gratianus, a citizen of that island, was made a usurper and killed. In his place Constantinus, from the lowest soldiery, was chosen, solely on account of the hope in his name, without any deserving quality. (Orosius 7.40.4)

Sozomen stresses the last point: "The soldiers in Britain . . . elected Constantinus, thinking that because he had this name he would exercise the imperial power firmly [i.e. *constanter*]" (Sozomen, *Hist. Eccl.* 9.11.2). A passing mention in Jerome, in a letter written in 415, probably refers to the events of 406–7: he calls Britain "a province fertile in usurpers" (Hieronymus, *Epist.* 133.9; cf. Gildas, *De excidio* 4.3, who attributes the remark to Porphyry).[20]

The above is only a selection from what seems an endless series of army coups. In truth, it was astonishing that the first princeps survived more than 40 years after Actium, otherwise his four successors would never have lasted so long. But the Augustan system was inherently fragile and Nero's fall unleashed the whirlwind. Of course, the army was cosseted with material benefits and the army discipline so admired by Polybius was institutionalized. The adoptive emperors had a good run (96–180) but under Commodus things fell apart and became desperate in the third century. The reforms of Diocletian and Constantine failed to prevent repeated outbreaks and usurpations. Civil war destroyed the republic and eventually sunk the empire too, at least in the West.

NOTES

1 Stevens 1952, 373–8, repr. 1967, 20–30, at 378 (= 29). The classic account remains that of Syme 1939.
2 Millar 1964, 80f. concludes that "Dio's sentiments in the speech were applicable to any age, but perhaps particularly to that of Severus and Caracalla." Millar's dating of the time of composition of Dio's work is surely too early, see e.g. Barnes 1984, 240–55.
3 For the above and some of what follows see further Birley 1976 and 1981.
4 Gibbon 1776, chapter V: these remarks introduce his account of the "auction of the empire" in 193.
5 Watson 1969, 98. On army pay see more recently esp. Speidel 1992.
6 Campbell 1984, 417.
7 Béranger 1968; see further id. 1976, esp. 44f.
8 Thus e.g. Levick 1993, 35: "Circumstantial evidence suggests Claudius' complicity."
9 Reading *noluisset* with the *codex Laurentianus* rather than *voluisset*. An inscription presumably from one of Verginius' estates suggests that a slave forester of his assumed that he had accepted the acclamation, *CIL* V 5702 = *ILS* 982, between Mediolanum and the *lacus Larius: Iovi O.M. pro salute et victoria L. Vergini Rufi Pylades saltuar(ius) eius v.s.*
10 The view here put forward derives from the teaching (unpublished) of the late C. E. Stevens. From the very extensive literature note Hainsworth 1962; Shotter 1967 and 1975; Levick 1985. Wellesley 2000, gives a readable account of these events.
11 Syme 1958, 145, takes the latter view; the whole of that great work should also be consulted.
12 See Walser 1968, 500.
13 Titianus: *PIR²* A 1305; *FO²* 49. Priscianus: *FO²* 50; cf. E. Groag, *PIR²* C 1418; also Birley 1987, 91f.
14 *SB* 10295, conjecturally attributed to Avidius by Bowman 1970, 20–6; approved by Syme 1988, 695f. (pointing out that Avidius had presumably been born at Alexandria when his father Heliodorus, with his wife, was there with Hadrian in 130).
15 For an account of these years see Birley 1988, 81ff.
16 Note Dio 79.7.1–3: under Elagabalus, two attempted coups by named legionary legates in Syria, both of humble origin, but senators; and three others, too humble for Dio even to name.
17 These experiences surely colored Dio's depiction of several episodes in his *History*: see Zimmermann 1999, 80ff. Hence further reason to doubt Millar's (n.2) early dating of the work's composition; it was at any rate revised after Dio's second consulship.
18 On the exact location, the temporary "*Sicilia*" (i.e. imperial quarters) in the *vicus Britannorum* near Mainz, see Schumacher 2004, 1–10.
19 See now Bringmann 2004, 68ff.
20 For discussion of these usurpations see Birley 2005, 455–60.

BIBLIOGRAPHY

Barnes, T. D. 1984. "The composition of Cassius Dio's *Roman History*," *Phoenix* 38: 240–55.

—— 1998. *Ammianus Marcellinus and the Representation of Historical Reality*. Ithaca, NY.

Béranger, J. 1968. "Le refus du pouvoir," *Museum Helveticum* 5: 178 – 96 = id., *Principatus. Études de notions d'histoire politiques dans l'Antiquité gréco-romaine*. Geneva 1973, 165–80.

—— 1976. "L'idéologie impériale dans l'*Histoire Auguste*," *Bonner Historia-Augusta-Colloquium 1972/1974*. Bonn, 29–53.

Birley, A. R. 1976. "The third-century crisis in the Roman Empire," *Bulletin of the John Rylands University Library of Manchester* 58: 253–81.

—— 1981. "The economic effects of Roman frontier policy," in A. King and M. Henig (eds.), *The Roman West in the Third Century. Contributions from Archaeology and History*. Oxford, 39–53.

—— 1987². *Marcus Aurelius. A Biography*. London.

—— 1988². *The African Emperor Septimius Severus*. London.

—— 2005. *The Roman Government of Britain*. Oxford.

Bowman, A. K. 1970. "A letter of Avidius Cassius?" *JRS* 60: 20–6.

Bringmann, K. 2004. *Kaiser Julian. Der letzte heidnische Herrscher*. Darmstadt.

Campbell, J. B. 1984. *The Emperor and the Roman Army 31 BC–AD 235*. Oxford.

Chastagnol, A. 1994. *Histoire Auguste. Les empereurs romains des IIe et IIIe siècles*, Édition bilingue latin-français. Paris.

Flaig, E. 1992. *Den Kaiser Herausfordern. Die Usurpationen im Römischen Reich*. Frankfurt.

Gibbon, E. 1776. *The Decline and Fall of the Roman Empire*. London.

Griffin, M. T. 1987. *Nero. The End of a Dynasty*. London.

Hainsworth, J. B. 1962. "Verginius and Vindex," *Historia* 11: 86–96.

Levick, B. 1985. "L. Verginius Rufus and the four emperors," *Rheinisches Museum* 128: 318–46.

—— 1993. *Claudius*. London.

—— 1999²a. *Tiberius the Politician*. London.

—— 1999b. *Vespasian*. London.

Marasco, G. (ed.). 2003. *Greek and Roman Historiography in Late Antiquity, Fourth to Sixth Century AD*. Leiden.

Matthews, J. F. 1989. *The Roman Empire of Ammianus*. London.

Millar, F. 1964. *A Study of Cassius Dio*. Oxford.

Potter, D. S. 2004. *The Roman Empire at Bay AD 180–395*. London.

Schumacher, L. 2004. "Die *Sicilia* in Mainz-Bretzenheim. Zur Lokalisierung der Ermordung des Kaisers Severus Alexander," *Mainzer Zeitschrift* 99: 1–10.

Shotter, D. C. A. 1967. "Tacitus and Verginius Rufus," *Classical Quarterly* 17: 370–81.

—— 1975. "A time-table for the 'Bellum Neronis,'" *Historia* 24: 59–74.

Speidel, M. A. 1992. "Roman army pay scales," *JRS* 82: 87–106.

Stevens, C. E. 1952. "Crossing the Rubicon," *History Today* 2 (1952) 373–8, repr. in A. R. Birley (ed.), *Universal Rome*. Edinburgh 1967, 20–30.

Syme, R. 1939. *The Roman Revolution*. Oxford.

—— 1958. *Tacitus*. Oxford.

—— 1971. *Emperors and Biography. Studies in the Historia Augusta*. Oxford.

—— 1988. "Avidius Cassius: His rank, age, and quality," in *Roman Papers* V. Oxford, 689–701.

Walser, G. 1968. "Der Putsch des Saturninus gegen Domitian," in E. Schmid et al. (eds.), *Provincialia. Festschrift für Rudolf Laur-Belart*. Basel, 497–507.

Watson, G. R. 1969. *The Roman Soldier*. London.

Wellesley, K. 2000³. *The Year of the Four Emperors*. London.

Zimmermann, M. 1999. *Kaiser und Ereignis. Studien zum Geschichtswerk Herodians*. Munich.

Anthony R. Birley

FURTHER READING

The most directly relevant treatment is by Campbell 1984, esp. 365ff. For a sociological perspective on usurpations see Flaig 1992. Some narrative histories are worth consulting for particular episodes discussed in this chapter: for 60 BC–AD 14, Syme 1939; for the Julio-Claudians, Levick 1999 and 1993; Griffin 1987; for AD 68–69, Wellesley 2000; for the Flavians, Levick 1999; for the period covered by Tacitus and for his time of writing, Syme 1958, is full of valuable insights; for the second and early third centuries, Birley 1987 and 1988. Potter 2004 is a useful introduction to the later empire. There is a valuable analysis of the sources for AD 180–238 in Zimmermann 1999. See also Syme 1971. On the *Historia Augusta* the best edition, with introduction, translation, and commentary, is Chastagnol 1994. More detailed commentaries are appearing in the Budé edition, *Histoire Auguste*, Paris, in progress. Of the numerous studies of Ammianus Marcellinus see e.g. Matthews 1989 and Barnes 1998. See further Marasco 2003.

CHAPTER TWENTY-TWO

Military Camps, *Canabae*, and *Vici*. The Archaeological Evidence

Norbert Hanel

Military camps, which were established throughout the Roman Empire, and especially in the frontier provinces, are among the most impressive remains of the Roman army. Even if imposing ruins of only a few of them survive today, camps which are poorly preserved can still provide important evidence for how new territories were incorporated into the Imperium Romanum. Location, size, chronology, and garrison allow conclusions to be drawn about the process of occupation of a region. Furthermore camps can be indicators for confrontations within and outside the frontiers of the empire. Finally, together with other installations on the *limites*, they show the border-line of the Roman territory of domination and the changes to it over time.

Canabae and *vici* were closely associated with the military camps; they developed outside the fortifications and became an indispensable part of the garrisons in the principate. They demonstrate clearly the close cooperation between soldiers and sutlers, army suppliers, merchants, traders, and manufacturers.

1 The Development of Military Camps from the First to the Fourth Century

The demands of the expanding empire, and the foundation of new provinces and frontiers at the beginning of the principate, had repercussions on the organization of Roman military camps: theaters of war far away from Italy in northwest Spain, Germany, the Balkans, and the Danube provinces, in Syria, Egypt and North Africa, made the permanent stationing of Roman legions and allied auxiliary troops necessary in these

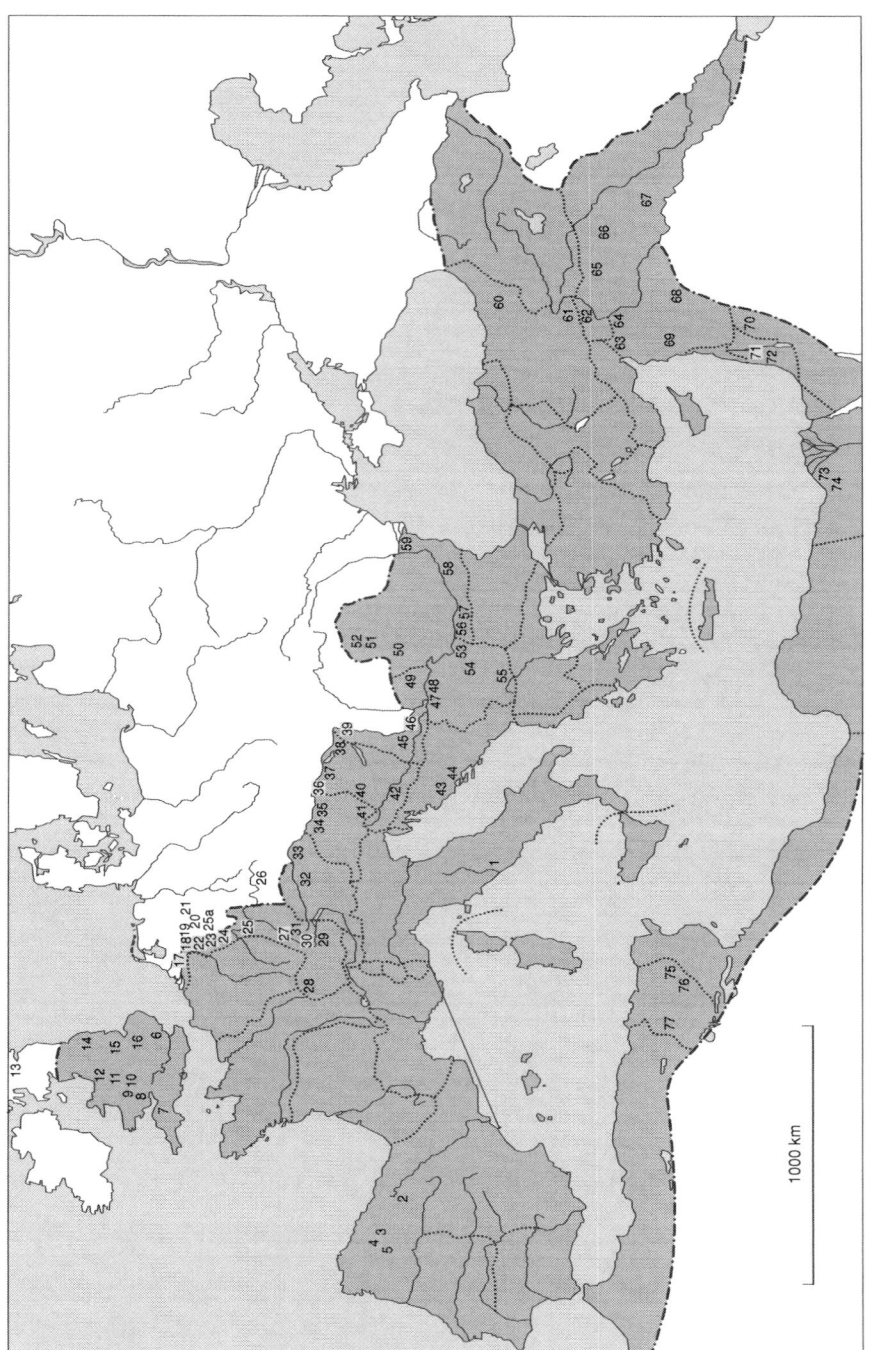

1000 km

Map 22.1   Legionary fortresses and camps with legionary troops in the Roman Empire from Augustus until the Tetrarchy (F. Daubner after H. v. Petrikovits, *Die Innenbauten römischer Legionslager während der Prinzipatszeit*, Opladen 1975, 27 f. Bild 1 with additions of the author/N. Hanel)

 1 Albano (Castra Albana) – I
 2 Herrera de Pisuerga (Pisoraca) – E
 3 León (castra legionis VII Geminae) – E
 4 Astorga (Asturica Augusta) – E
 5 Rosinos de Vidriales (Petavonium) – E
 6 Colchester (Camulodunum) – GB
 7 Exeter (Isca Dumnoniorum) – GB
 8 Caerleon (Isca Silurum) – GB
 9 Usk – GB
10 Gloucester (Glevum) – GB
11 Wroxeter (Viroconium) – GB
12 Chester (Deva) – GB
13 Inchtuthil (Victoria ?) – GB
14 York (Eboracum) – GB
15 Lincoln (Lindum) – GB
16 Longthorpe – GB
17 Nijmegen (Noviomagus) – NL
18 Xanten (Vetera castra) – D
19 Haltern – D
20 Oberaden – D
21 Anreppen – D
22 Neuss (Novaesium) – D
23 Köln (oppidum Ubiorum) – D
24 Bonn (Bonna) – D
25 Mainz (Moguntiacum) – D
25a Lahnau-Dorlar – D
26 Marktbreit – D
27 Strasbourg (Argentorate) – F
28 Mirebeau – F
29 Brugg/Windisch (Vindonissa) – CH
30 Dangstetten – D
31 Rottweil I (Arae Flaviae) – D
32 Augsburg (Augusta Vindelicorum) – D
33 Regensburg (castra Regina) – D
34 Lorch (Lauriacum) – A
35 Albing – A
36 Wien (Vindobona) – A
37 Bad Deutsch-Altenburg (Carnuntum) – A
38 Komáron/Szőny (Brigetio) – H

39 Budapest (Aquincum) – H
40 Ptuj (Poetovio) – SLO
41 Ločica – SLO
42 Sisak (Siscia) – HR
43 Šuplja Crkva (Burnum) – HR
44 Gardun bei Trilj (Tilurium) – HR
45 Osijek (Mursa) – HR
46 Sremska Mitrovice (Sirmium) – YU
47 Belgrad (Singidunum) – YU
48 Požarevak (Viminacium) – YU
49 Resiţa (Berzobis?) – RO
50 Near Hatseg (Sarmizegetusa) – RO
51 Alba Iulia (Apulum) – RO
52 Turda (Potaissa) – RO
53 Archar (Ratiaria) – BG
54 Niš (Naissus) – YU
55 Skopje (Scupi) – MK
56 Gigen (Oescus) – BG
57 Steklen (Novae) – BG
58 Silistra (Durostorum) – BG
59 Iglitsa (Troesimis) – RO
60 Sadak (Satala) – TR
61 Eski Malateja (Melitene) – TR
62 Samsat (Samosata) – TR
63 Cyrrhus – SYR
64 Belkis (Zeugma) – SYR
65 Tel Fakhariya (Resaina) – SYR
66 Beled Sinjar (Singara) – IRQ
67 Nusailin (Nisibis) – IRQ
68 Tadmar (Palmyra) – SYR
69 Rafnîyé – SYR
70 Bosra (Bostra) – SYR
71 Kefar ´Otnay (Caparcotna/legio) – IL
72 Jerusalem (Aelia Capitolina) – IL
73 Nikopolis (Alexandria) – ET
74 al Burdân – ET
75 Haïdra (Ammaedara) – TN
76 Tébessa (Theveste) – DZ
77 Tazoult-Lambèse (Lambaesis) – DZ

territories. In contrast to this, in Italy there were only a few military camps: in Augustan Rome, apart from the guard troops (*cohortes praetoriae*), only paramilitary units of the fire brigade (*cohortes vigilum*) and urban cohorts (*cohortes urbanae*) were stationed. Under Augustus' successor Tiberius the castra Praetoria were constructed for praetorians to the northeast in front of the town walls. In the rest of Italy larger military installations were restricted to two posts of the Praetorian fleet in Misenum (**I**) and Ravenna (**I**); marine units of unknown size were sent from these places to Rome and stationed there in two camps. The castra Misenatium, probably constructed in Flavian times, are supposed to have been situated on the slopes of the Mons Oppius in the vicinity of the *amphitheatrum flavium* (colosseum) and of *ludus magnus*. The position of the castra Ravennatium is not certain; they were presumably in the Transtiberim region. Under Septimius Severus the legionary fortress for the Legio II Parthica (castra Albana/Albano **1**) was added in the Colli Albani, southeast of the metropolis; the urban troops were reinforced and the riders of the guard (*equites singulares Augusti*) were equipped with another garrison close to their old camp on the Mons Caelius.[1]

The plan, structure, and internal buildings of the military camps in the principate have their roots in the (Roman) republic. A detailed description of a marching camp for two legions, cavalry, and units of allies from the second century is given by the Greek historian Polybius (6.26–36, 41–42). Many elements of the later military camps can already be recognized in the details he describes. Whereas the republican installations have only been analyzed insufficiently compared with those of the principate, we know plenty of camps of the latter period and from late antiquity. Despite the standardization of military architecture, each of these sites is unique as various factors – such as the size of the garrison, its function and external factors such as topography, contact with the enemy, drinking water resources etc. – had to be considered in the planning process.

Military camps of the early principate (especially under Augustus and Tiberius) often had a polygonal plan, with the line of defense being adapted to the topography for strategic reasons, but the internal structure followed an orthogonal scheme. In this initial phase of occupation the remains of Roman military camps speak for a more or less provisional construction; even in the permanent camps used for a longer period, the half timbered architecture predominated.[2] Indications for the mobility of the units come from some strategically important places (e.g. Haltern **16**, Vetera castra/Xanten **18**, Novaesium/Neuss **19**, Nida/Frankfurt am Main-Heddernheim **D**, Tenedo/Zurzach **CH**): in a relatively short period camps of various shapes and sizes were constructed and abandoned here. Only around the middle of the first century, with the consolidation of the frontiers, were permanent posts built to protect the freshly conquered territories. At the same time the long rectangular shape of the camps with rounded corners became common over the entire empire. Huge consequences resulted from the political events after the death of Nero. The destruction of all military places from the coast of the North Sea up to Mainz (**25**) during the Year of the Four Caesars on the one hand, and the subsequent conquest of the areas on the middle and upper Rhine and in North Raetia on the other hand, resulted in the reconstruction of the old camps and an extensive program of new building in the occupied territories. Whereas stone construction in military camps of the pre-Flavian period was restricted to a few legionary fortresses, and here especially to the central buildings, the massive stone construction technique gradually came to dominate in the other camps from the last third of the first century until the second century. In contrast to the western provinces, in the Eastern empire the Roman army could use an existing urban infrastructure; often troops were stationed directly in the towns or in their immediate vicinity (Zeugma/Belkis **64**, colonia Aelia Capitolina/ Jerusalem **72**, Bostra/Bosra **70**, Dura Europos/as-Sālihiya **SYR**).[3]

Consolidation and reinforcement of the frontier zones of the empire, as well as the new conquests under Trajan and Hadrian, resulted in the construction of Hadrian's Wall in Britain (from AD 122), the Upper German-Raetian *Limes*, and the Dacian *Limes*. In context with these measures numerous forts and smaller fortifications (mile castles, watch towers) came to exist, and these were integrated into the frontier systems. This process was repeated a few decades later under Antoninus Pius when the Antonine Wall was built in Britain (from AD 142) and the so-called Front *Limes* in Germania Superior (c. AD 150/160).

On the Danube, during the reign of Marcus Aurelius, the Marcomans overran the chain of forts and advanced to Upper Italy before they were eventually defeated. The reorganization of this stretch of *limes*, which hitherto had been protected exclusively by auxiliary troops, led to the construction of two permanent legionary fortresses in castra Regina/Regensburg (**33**) and Albing (**35**), and later at Lauricum/Enns-Lorch (**34**).

Internal political power struggles and external threats by hostile tribes in the third century also had repercussions on the military camps in the frontier zones. The reduction of troops in these provinces led to the abandonment of military posts and to architectural changes in the existing places. The reduction of troops only allowed a minimal protection of the installations; for that reason smaller forts were built in one corner of their predecessors partly using existing fortifications (Durnomagus/ Dormagen **D**, Kapersburg **D**, Abusina/Eining **D** etc.).[4] In various regions of the empire measures taken by the garrison to enforce the relatively weak camp defenses were recognized in archaeological excavations: at several camps it can be proven that one of the two passages of a gate or the whole gate had been blocked off by a new wall (e.g. Birdoswald **GB**, Vercovicium/Housesteads **GB**, South Shields **GB**, Legio VII Gemina/Léon **3**, Petavonium/Rosinos de Vidriales **5**, Holzhausen **D**, Miltenberg-Ost **D**, Osterburken **D**, Pfünz **D**, Tülln **A**, Răcari **RO**, Resculum/ Bologa **RO**) (Plate 22.1).

The smaller number of troops had an impact on the *vici* of the forts as well; some baths in forts, for instance, were reduced in size. The retreat of troops and emigration probably led to a shrinking population; at least temporarily the civil inhabitants moved into the forts for protection.

Already at the end of the third and especially in the fourth century civil settlements and military camps were fused to fortified towns. The fact that the purely civil population now also lived within massive fortifications makes a categorization of them into "military" and "civilian" difficult. In the eastern provinces troops were stationed in urban quarters using existing (ritual) buildings (cf. Luxor **ET**, Palmyra/Tadmar **68**). In the hinterland of the western empire hill forts of the native population were

Plate 22.1 León. Blocking of the eastern side gate (*porta principalis sinistra*) of the legionary fortress (V. García Marcos, León)

built on plateaus and mountain spurs in order to provide refuge; it is possible that later these fortified places were also used by the army.

An important military task was the control of traffic routes (long distance roads, passes, caravan routes, rivers, and large lakes) which were used by hostile tribes to access the territory of the empire. In order to protect these traffic routes, fortlets and *burgi* were constructed: in Severan times new forts and watch towers came into being, for instance on the Tripolitanian *limes* (Cydamus/Ghadames **LAR**, Gheriat al Garbia **LAR**, Gheriat-es Shergia **LAR**, Gholaia/Bu Njem **LAR**). Attacks of Germanic pirates made it necessary to fortify the Channel coast, probably by as early as the third century. Gradually the sections along the British coast and the Gallic Atlantic coast were defended by constructing strong forts and watch towers. An attempt was also made to protect the villas in the hinterland with so-called *burgi*. Finally, in the 60s and 70s of the third century hostile invasions caused the total withdraw of the Roman army from those territories of the empire which could not be held any longer (parts of Germania Superior and Raetia north of the Danube, Transdanubian Dacia).

After the devastating invasions of hostile tribes into Roman territory around the end of the third (tetrarchy) and the beginning of the fourth century (Constantinus I) a fundamental re-organization of the Roman army took place. Important innovations were the separation between a military and civilian command and, in the army, the separation between field army (*comitatenses*) and permanent frontier troops (*limitanei*). These reforms were accompanied by drastic changes in military architecture. While in the early and middle principate the ramparts of the forts gave only provisional protection against raids, in late antiquity the defensive character of the new military architecture becomes obvious: strong defensive walls of enormous thickness and height (c. 7–8.50 meters up to the rampart walk) and deep and wide ditches protected the garrison – which was reduced in number, but was supposed to endure longer sieges, too. The previous standard shape of camps hardly played a role anymore. Important elements of late antique poliorcetic defense methods are narrowly positioned and protruding towers with a circular or rectangular plan and a probable height of 12–15 meters (Tulln **A**, Traismauer **A**, Portchester **GB**, Richborough **GB**, Qasr Bshir **JOR**); in the Danubian provinces and at some places in Syria regional specialities can be seen, such as fan-shaped towers at the corners of the camps. The number of gates was sometimes reduced and the gates themselves were protected by powerful gate-towers or by horseshoe-shaped to U-shaped terminals and could be closed by a portcullis. The curtain walls stood on especially deep foundations – a measure to avoid undermining.[5]

Already in the third century on the *limes*, especially in North Africa and Raetia (Harlach **D**), small roughly square fortifications (*centenaria*) appeared, which then became common in the frontier zones of North Africa during the fourth century.

The more or less standardized internal camp structure of the principate disappeared in late antiquity. In contrast to the military camps of the principate, architecturally prominent central buildings are almost completely missing in the late antique counterparts; if existent, their measurements are very reduced. The barracks lean against the internal sides of the walls like casemates (Alteium/Alzey **D**, Alta Ripa/Altrip **D**, Oedenburg **F**, Abusina/Eining **D**, Boiotro/Passau **D**). Divitia/Köln-Deutz (**D**) provides the probably complete internal architecture of a late antique fort, including the barracks.

Under the emperor Valentinianus I (AD 364–375) new camps were constructed in the course of a big campaign to fortify the Rhine and Danube *limes*; these new forts profited from the experience of the past and catered for the needs of the time. Forts (e.g. Alteium/Alzey **D** and Alta Ripa/Altrip **D**), small fortified ship landing-places on the hostile river bank (Neuwied-Engers **D**, Biblis-Zullestein **D**, Mannheim-Neckarau **D**, Dunafalva **H**, Nógrádverőce **H**), and stone watch towers (*turres, burgi*) on the Lower Rhine and in the Rhine valley above Lake Constance, on the upper and middle Danube (Goch-Asperden **D**, Asciburgium/Moers-Asberg **D**, Koblenz/Kleiner Laufen **CH**, Etzgen **CH**, Ybbs **A**, Esztergom **H**, Visegrád **H**) date to this period.[6] According to current archaeological research, this was the last time that an extensive building programme took place on the Rhine and Danube frontier.

2 Organization and Structure of Military Camps

Although there is a large number of excavated Roman military camps, not a single one is identical with another. Topographical conditions, the composition of units, strategic and logistic considerations all influenced the appearance of a camp. Vegetius (1.22) provides a list of important criteria for the location of a camp: the existence of firewood, fresh water, and other food in the vicinity. He recommends that a "healthy" place should be chosen if the troops were supposed to stay for a longer period.

Despite variations in plan, size, and internal structure, all are based on a single scheme which provided sufficient protection against hostile attacks, allowing fast construction of barracks and accommodation for the soldiers. The starting point when constructing a camp was the crossing (*locus gromae*) of the two principal roads (*via principalis, via praetoria*, and *via decumana*) which were designed to meet at a right angle. Parallel to these axes lanes divided the interior of the camp. The area between the *via principalis* and the front was called *praetentura*, the rear part *retentura*; in a marching camp the name of the areas next to the *principia* was *latera praetorii* and it is possible that this name was also used for a permanent camp.

The fortifications of Roman military camps mainly consisted of two elements: 1) a simple V-shaped ditch or several V-shaped ditches which were not filled with water, and 2) the rampart (*vallum*). As protection additional obstacles could be installed in front of the ditch–rampart-system, such as pits with pointed posts (*stimuli, cippi, liliae*) and obstacles of thorns, branches, or the like. They are not only known from the written sources, but also from the archaeological record (Rough Castle **GB**, Piercebridge **GB**, Hofheim **D**, Vetera castra I/Xanten **18**). In most cases the *vallum* was constructed from the earth dug out of the ditches. Inside and outside, the wall could be stabilized by layered turfs, and on its top the rampart walk was protected by palisades. If the troops were stationed more permanently the rampart was replaced by a so-called earth-and-timber-rampart – a wooden framework (width of about 3 meters = 10 *pedes*) filled with the dug-out earth of the ditch. On the outer side above the rampart walk there was the wooden parapet (*lorica*) equipped with crenellations (*pinnae*) (Plate 22.2).

Often only after a long period of military presence were the fortifications built of wood and earth replaced by more solid constructions. These were moderately strong stone walls crowned by the rampart walk with crenellations. Sometimes the stone front was enforced by an earth ramp on the inner side. More protection was provided by high towers; the distance separating them seems to have depended on the strength of the enemy; especially short distances are known in the first century for the early Flavian camps I and III at Arae Flaviae/Rottweil (**31**) and for the so-called stone forts at Hofheim im Taunus (**D**) (Plate 22.3). The gates, located on the main road axes, required special protection. Usually a camp could be entered through four gates: the main gate (*porta praetoria*) lay in the center of the camp's front; from here the *via praetoria* led directly to the entrance of the headquarters (*principia*). According to Vegetius (1.23) the *porta praetoria* was supposed to be directed either towards the east, the enemy, or at marching camps in marching direction. The side gates (*porta principalis dextra* and *sinistra*) were connected by the *via principalis* inside the camp, running along the forefront of the *principia*. The *porta praetoria* served as an entrance at the rear side of the camp. The gateways, which were either covered by a gate chamber or a parapet platform, were usually flanked by two towers. Additional protection for the gates was provided by a short ditch (*titulum*) accompanied partly by a rampart. A distinctive feature are the *clavicula*-gates: on both sides

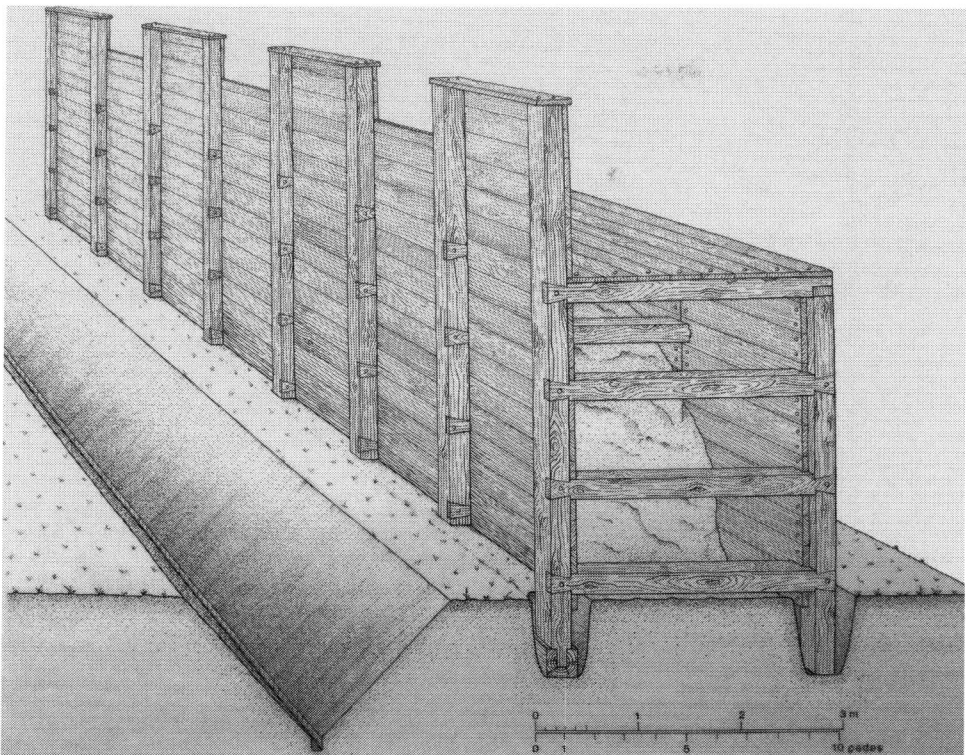

Plate 22.2 Köln-Marienburg (Alteburg). Reconstruction of the earth-and-timber rampart of the principal base of the Classis Germanica (concept N. Hanel; design S. Haase, Römisch-Germanisches Museum, Köln)

the walls receded in a quarter circle towards the inside of the fort and thus produced a kind of bailey.

Between the fortification of the camp and its internal buildings there was a space without buildings (*intervallum*); this served various functions: in case of a siege the defenders could get into position and with the help of an inner ring road (*via sagularis*) move troops to sections of the fortification which were in danger, without being hindered; the *intervallum* was also supposed to prevent missiles coming over the fortification and hitting internal camp buildings. Sometimes in this area the fort latrines, workshops, bread-ovens, sheds etc. were situated.

The centrally-placed headquarters (*principia*) were – comparable to the *forum* in towns – the representative, administrative, and religious center of the camp. The rectangular building had an inner court which was surrounded by a *porticus* and rooms; it could be used as a small place in which to hold the roll-call. At the rear side of the central axis was the shrine of the standards which could be equipped with an

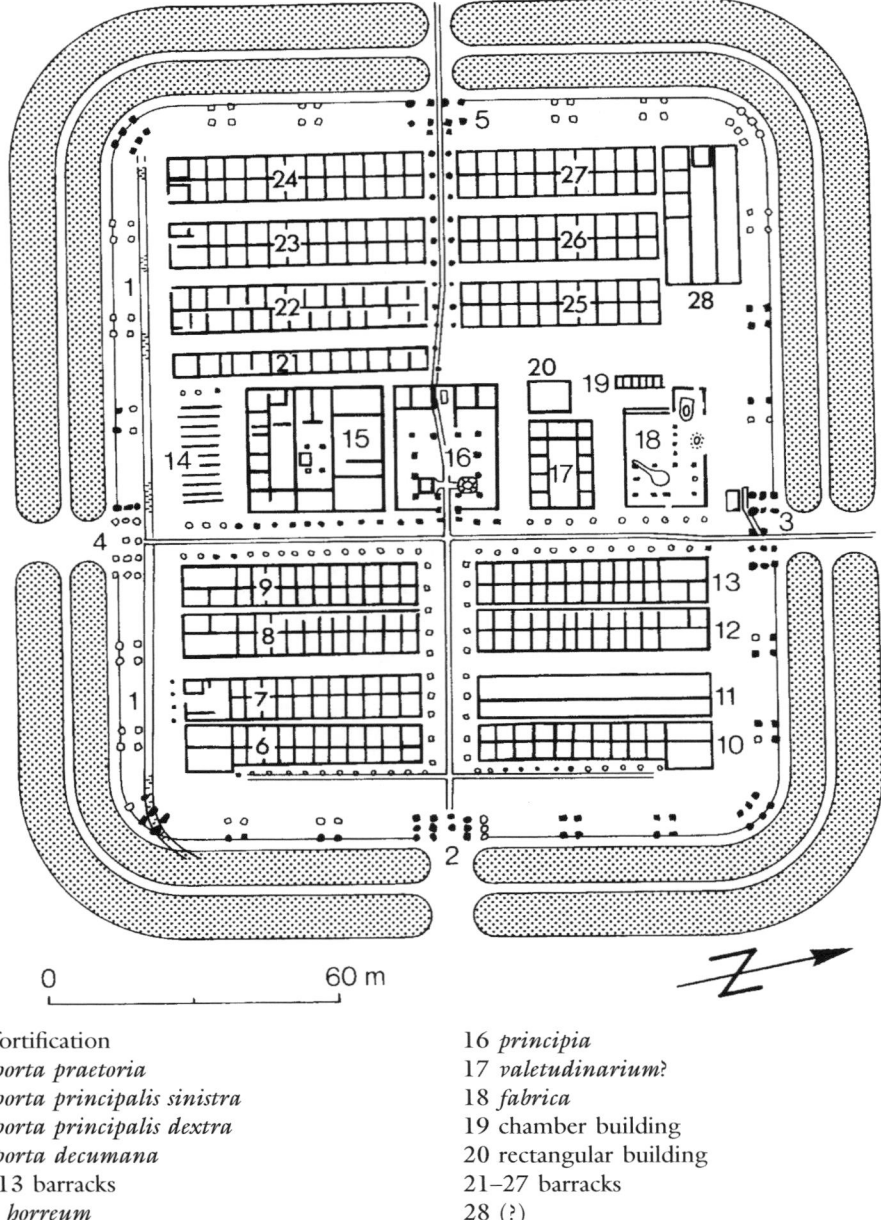

1 fortification
2 _porta praetoria_
3 _porta principalis sinistra_
4 _porta principalis dextra_
5 _porta decumana_
6–13 barracks
14 _horreum_
15 _praetorium_

16 _principia_
17 _valetudinarium?_
18 _fabrica_
19 chamber building
20 rectangular building
21–27 barracks
28 (?)

Plate 22.3 Hofheim (Taunus). Plan of the "Steinkastell" (stone-built fort) (after Nuber, H. U. "Das Steinkastell Hofheim [Main-Taunus-Kreis]," in _Studien zu den Militärgrenzen Roms III_. 13. Internat. Limeskongreß Aalen 1983, Vorträge. Forsch. u. Ber. Vor- u. Frühgesch. Baden-Württemberg 20, Stuttgart 1985, 227 fig. 1)

Plate 22.4   Lambaesis. Entrance hall of the headquarters (*principia*) of the legionary fortress (Forschungsarchiv für Antike Plastik, Cologne)

apsis (*aedes principorum*); here the military colors and the standards of the unit were stored.[7] During the principate this place came to serve the imperial cult. As the shrines of the standards often had a cellar we can assume that in the cellar the strong room of the unit was kept. The rooms on both side of the *aedes* were used as offices (*tabularia*), registrar's offices, and common and ritual rooms (*scholae*) for the officers and corporals. Along the rear side of the *principia* there was a transversally orientated often tripartite basilica with a speaker's platform. Statues of emperors and deities, and altars of the unit were placed in the basilica as well as in the court-yard of the headquarters.[8] The rooms in the wings were used as offices and, presumably, armories (*armamentaria*). These rooms were either continued along the front of the building or replaced by a spacious hall which is interpreted as a drill space. The end of the *via praetoria* was marked by the entrance of the *principia* which could be architectonically emphasized (cf. Lambaesis/Tazoult-Lambèse 77) (Plate 22.4).

    In the legionary fortresses the commander (*legatus legionis*) was often accommodated in a luxurious building of generous dimensions (*praetorium*) which was regarded as suitable for his senatorial rank. The *praetorium*, in which he not only lived but also worked, was located directly next to the *principia* either on its side or rear. These buildings consisted of several groups of rooms around peristyles and atriums. In the Neronian period of the two legionary fortresses Vetera castra at Xanten (**18**) the two commanders' palaces were also equipped with a 80-meter long arrangement similar to a hippodrome. Comparable but smaller buildings (*domus tribunorum et praefectorum*) with peristyles served in legionary fortresses to accommodate senatorial and equestrian tribunes and prefects.

Accommodation for the troops (*centuriae*), which covered the largest part of the interior of the camp, surrounded the central buildings in a ring. They could be arranged parallel (*per scamna*) or orthogonally (*per strigas*) to the *via praetoria*. Usually one barrack consisted of a spacious part on one of the short sides of the building for the centurion and 8–10 men's quarters (*contubernia*) in a row; these were again divided into an anteroom and a bedroom at the rear (*papilio*).[9]

A special type of barrack was found in camps with cavalry (*alae*) or mixed units (*cohortes equitatae*). These are so-called stable-barracks with horsemen and horses sleeping in rooms in a row under the same roof (e.g. in the camps of Heidenheim **D**, Lopodunum/Ladenburg **D**, Durnomagus/Dormagen **D**, Gelduba/Krefeld-Gellep **D**, South Shields **GB**, Wallsend **GB**). To the larger room at the short side of the barrack could be added another room which protruded over the front of the *contubernium*. Its function is unclear; it is assumed that men under the rank of a *centurio* were accommodated here.

Apart from the central buildings, the buildings for the officers and the barracks, there were various so-called utility buildings in the military camps, catering for the needs of the unit: in the legionary fortresses hospitals (*valetudinaria*) can be recognized by a characteristic type of building and finds of medical equipment. They have a standardized longitudinal or square shape and a large yard inside. Three or four wings of the building each consist of two rows of sick-rooms, which can be entered from a circular corridor (e.g. Vetera castra/Xanten **18**, Novae/Steklen **57**). Also some large auxiliary forts seem to have had hospitals (e.g. Künzing **D**, Vercovicium/Housesteads **GB**).

An important part of health provision in Roman military camps were the baths. Recently, buildings inside military camps of the early principate which hitherto were thought to be farm out-houses, have been re-interpreted as small baths (Anreppen **21**, Marktbreit **26**), which shows that already the earliest camps of the principate had sanitary installations.[10] The baths of the legionary fortresses were usually situated inside the fortified area; often they are in the right *praetentura*. In contrast, the baths of the auxiliary forts are outside the camp – either inside the *vicus* or in a separate annex. Such baths had to be supplied with running water through aqueducts. Apart from subterranean pipes (Novaesium/Neuss **22**, Oberstimm **D**) at some garrisons wooden over-ground pipes are probable. Furthermore, wells and cisterns supplied drinking water.

Catering for soldiers and animals required the long-term storage of food in special warehouses (*horrea*). These storage buildings were mainly erected along the *via principalis* next to the *principia* to provide better access for (transport) vehicles. To prevent the cereal and hay from self-ignition these buildings were equipped with suspended floors which guarantied sufficient airing. Buttresses on the outside of the warehouses were supposed to resist the pressure of the cereal inside. For the provision of the troops there were common baking ovens and large mills which were partly situated in the *intervallum*, partly in special camp buildings (Hofheim-Steinkastell **D**).

Fabricae and workshops existed to repair weapons and equipment, as well as for many other craftsman's tasks which belonged to the daily routine in a camp. This is documented, apart from the written sources, by characteristic building types and industrial installations, such as furnaces, numerous finds such as ingots, waste material, semi-finished products, and tools. Whereas – especially in the period of occupation – the military workshops were situated for safety reasons inside the camp, later they were gradually moved outside; apart from the most indispensable ones, they found their places in the *canabae, vici,* or in outposts far away from the garrison (lime-kilns, brickworks etc.).[11]

Great experience and all-round expertise were necessary when planning and organizing the material and work required for the construction of military camps. Most tasks were carried out by the unit itself, with single divisions being allotted certain tasks for construction. The *praefectus castrorum* was in charge of all construction work in the camp. The surveying unit probably was the *pes monetalis* (0.296 meters) or respectively the *actus* (35.52 meters).[12] The quantity of building material was enormous. Calculations demonstrate that for the fortification of the camp Oberaden (**20**) on the river Lippe alone 3,339 square meters or 3,673 tons of wood had to be cut. The weight of the necessary building wood for the Flavian legionary fortress Deva/Chester (**12**) was estimated at about 25,000 tons, whereas the stone re-building of the same garrison in Severan times needed roughly 310,000 tons of stone.[13]

3 Types of Camps (units and functions)

The terminology of ancient sources hardly differentiates between the functions of camps. The main criterion is whether the camp was solely a protected place to stay overnight during a (summer) campaign (*castra aestiva* or *aestivalia,* cf. Tacitus, *Ann.* 1.16.31; Ps.-Hyginus 45; 48) or whether it was constructed as a permanent garrison, e.g. as a winter camp for the troops (*castra stativa* or *hiberna,* cf. Velleius Pat. 2.107, 111, 114–115; Tacitus, *Ann.* 1.27, 37–38, 45; Vegetius 2.11; 3.8). In the case of summer camps the internal buildings probably mainly consisted of leather tents (*papiliones*) and simple wooden buildings. In contrast to this, in winter camps relatively solid barracks in frame-work construction (*hibernacula*) were erected.[14]

With the help of various methods, modern research tries to differentiate between the numerous types of military camps and to understand their characteristics. Important evidence is provided by the literary sources and epigraphy, which directly or indirectly indicate the unit or the size of the unit in a garrison. Roman camps are categorized according to the type of the stationed unit (*legiones, auxilia, numeri, classes*) and according to their function (supply camp, siege camp, training camp etc.).

Combining the written information and the results from excavated garrisons, the following regular camp sizes have been recognized: a legion needed a space of 18–24 hectares. Consequently a two-legionary fortress (Vetera castra I/Xanten **18**, Oberaden **20**) covered an area of more than 50 hectares. For a cavalry unit of 1,000 men (*ala milliaria*) a camp of up to 6.1 hectares was necessary; for an infantry cohort of an auxiliary unit with c. 500 men 1.4–3.2 hectares. The smallest military posts were the so-called *numerus* fortlets with 0.6–1.0 hectares. Thus if the garrison is unknown the camp size can provide information on the type of unit stationed there. However, problems occur in identifying the size of a unit if, for instance, not just one legion but also further auxiliary troops not mentioned in the sources were accommodated in the fortress, or if detachments (*vexillationes*) of various units were housed in the same camp with their size being unknown. Because of their size (8–12 ha), their short period of use, and the lack of associated settlements, the camps at e.g. Carpow (**GB**), Longthorpe (**16**), and Eining-Unterfeld (**D**) have been interpreted as vexillation forts;[15] in the forts at Tisavar/Ksar Rhilane (**TN**) and Gholaia/Bu Njem (**LAR**) on the Tripolitanian *limes* vexillations of the Legio III Augusta were temporarily stationed.

Very little is known about the structure, size, and internal buildings of Roman naval bases and camps; this applies especially to the two principal bases of the praetorian fleet of the Mediterranean at Misenum (**I**) and Ravenna (**I**), and its detachments distributed around the Mediterranean and the Black Sea according to literary and epigraphic sources (Piraeus **GR**, Chersonesos **UA**, Ephesus **TR**, Seleuceia Pieria **TR** etc.). Units of marines of unknown size were sent from both Italian posts to Rome where they were garrisoned in two camps. From the northern provinces of the empire we know of many more naval bases: large parts of the site Dubris/Dover (**GB**) on the English Channel coast could be investigated. The main camp of the Classis Germanica at Köln-Marienburg (Altenburg) (**D**) was excavated and analyzed both some time ago and more recently when considerable areas of the east and west side were uncovered.[16] In late antiquity characteristic fortified landing places were built on the middle and upper Rhine as well as on the middle Danube (Neuwied-Engers **D**, Biblis-Zullestein **D**, Lopodunum/Ladenburg **D**, Contra Florentiam/Dunafalva **H**, Nógrádveröce **H** etc.); these were small places on the hostile side of the river. Connecting walls protected a landing place for small mobile patrolling boats (*lusoriae*) and in their center there could be a *burgus*-like construction.

If large parts of a camp were covered with storage buildings (*horrea*) we can identify its function as a supply camp with certainty: in the first century this is for instance the case for Rödgen in the Wetterau (**D**). The rebuilding of the former auxiliary fort at South Shields (**GB**) (phase 5) to become a supply camp in the Scottish campaigns of the emperor Septimius Severus (AD 208–211) is especially remarkable; at least 17 stone *horrea* could be identified within the fortification, the number of which was even augmented in the following period. A good example from late antiquity is the evidence from Veldidena/Innsbruck-Wilten (**A**) where two large storage buildings with three aisles were enclosed by a strong fortification in a later phase.

In order to protect river crossings one or both sides of the river were equipped with military posts. Numerous fortified bridgeheads are known from the river frontiers along the Rhine and Danube, dating to the whole period of the Roman occupation: whereas on one side of the river a larger garrison or a fortified urban settlement was situated, the crossing or bridge was protected on the hostile side by a smaller fort (colonia Agrippina/Köln–Divitia/Köln-Deutz **D**, Mogontiacum/Mainz–Mainz-

Plate 22.5 Masada. View of siege camp C and the *circumvallatio.* Photograph by the author

Kastel **D**, Tenedo/Zurzach–Rheinheim **CH/D**, Brigetio/Szőny–Celamantia/Iža-Leányvár **H/SK**, Aquincum/Budapest, Contra- and Transaquincum **H** etc.).

Siege camps are integral parts of siege systems (*circumvallationes*) which were erected in order to lay siege to an enemy town or fortification (e.g. Alesia **F**, Jerusalem **72**, Masada **IL**, Burnswark **GB**) (Plate 22.5). Larger camps to accommodate troops and smaller ones to control the siege systems can be differentiated.

Marching camps were usually erected for one night at the end of a day of marching. During the campaigns they provided protection from hostile attacks for the resting army. In his *bellum Judaicum* the historian Flavius Josephus describes the structure of a marching camp in his time; from a later period we have the descriptions of Ps.-Hyginus, *De munitionibus castrorum*. The structure of the marching camps is similar to that of the permanent camps. For archaeologists it is difficult to recognize marching camps as, except for the enclosing ditch, hardly any structural evidence or objects have survived; these camps are usually discovered from the air. Marching camps are especially known from Britannia, in Germania on the right side of the Rhine, and in front of the Noric-Pannonic *limes* (region around Mušov **SK**). At strategically important locations several camps could be constructed.

The exploitation of natural resources needed military protection in some regions of the empire. In mining areas military camps ("mining camps") were therefore built for the garrison which supervised the work and protected the transport of the ore (cf. Pumsaint **GB**, Nanstallon **GB**, Rüthen-Kneblinghausen? **D**, Valmeda? **E** etc.).

Like marching camps, training camps also leave hardly any traces on the ground because of their short period of use. Most of them are discovered through aerial photography. The photographs show their characteristic elements: the gate construction protected by *titula* and *claviculae* (see above). The size of these rectangular or square camps varies between 0.6 and 2.6 hectares; with the exception of pits, internal buildings cannot be identified. Numerous training camps were discovered especially to the south of the legionary fortress Vetera castra (**18**), further examples were situated close to the posts of Bonna/Bonn (**24**), Haltwhistle (**GB**), Llandrindod Common (Wales) (**GB**), Brigetio/Szőny (**38**), and Celemantia/Iža–Leányvár (**SK**).

Whether there were special "building camps" constructed by the Roman army in order to build the actual camp (e.g. Inchtuthil **13**), is a question still under discussion. As long as circumstances and time allowed it, the Roman troops directly started with the construction work, making a building camp unnecessary.

4 Camp Villages (*canabae* and *vici*)

The villages in the vicinity of Roman military camps, which are already reported for the republican period, and which housed the followers (*lixae*) of the units, are the predecessors of the *canabae* and *vici* of the principate; until late antiquity they feature as an important element of Roman garrisons. Although the Roman state took care of the basic provision of the troops, not all the needs of the professional soldiers could be catered for, as service was long and they were often stationed in remote parts of the Imperium. The main task of the sutlers in the camp villages was to provide the soldiers with food and other goods and to offer varied services. The precondition for the close association between soldiers and sutlers was the enormous purchasing power of the soldiers, based on their regular payment.[17]

As far as we know today, the term *canabae* (Greek: κάναβος > *canaba*; English: scaffold, frame; in a broader sense: barracks, stalls) was only used in context with legionary fortresses; the villages around auxiliary forts were called *vici*. The area covered by the settlements associated with military camps often exceeded that of the camps themselves and it is difficult to provide a general overview of their size, structure, and development. Among the *canabae* with the best known infrastructure are Isca

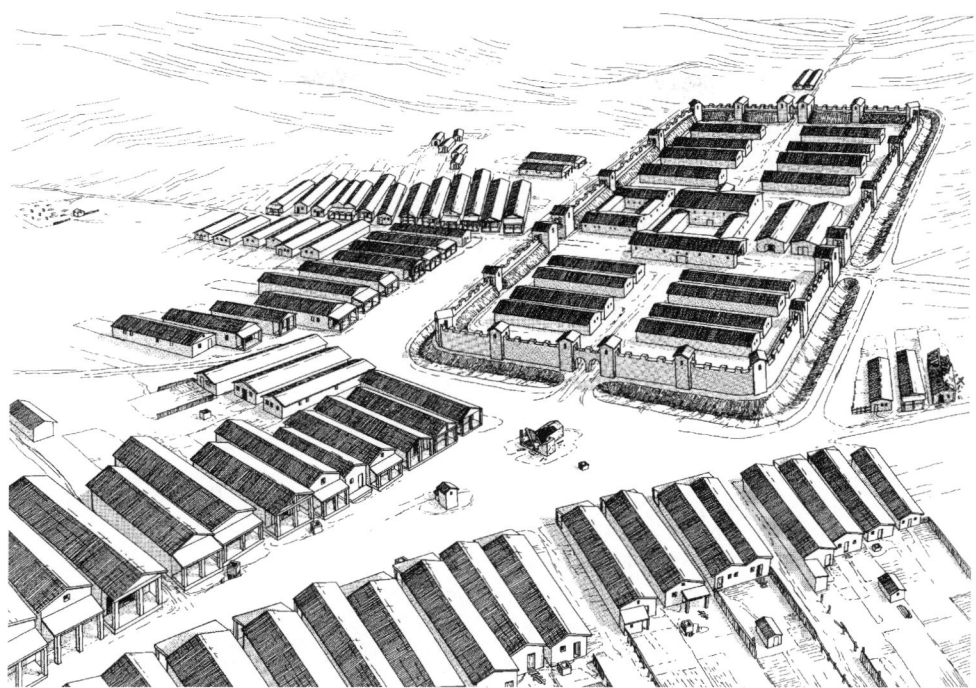

Plate 22.6   Reconstruction of the *limes* fort Zugmantel and the camp *vicus* (after Sommer, C. S. *Kastellvicus und Kastell.* Fundber. Baden-Württemberg 13 [1988] 516 Abb. 12)

Silurum/Caerleon (**8**), Noviomagus/Nijmegen (**17**), Bonna/Bonn (**24**), Carnuntum/ Bad Deutsch-Altenburg (**37**), and Aquincum/Budapest (**39**).[18] The *vici* of the auxiliary forts are better researched and are divided into three types according to their shape: 1) the roadside type with the buildings accompanying the arterial roads; 2) the tangential type with the buildings following a highway passing the camp; and 3) the ring type with the village being orientated along a circular by-pass around the camp.[19] Typical for the camp villages are strip buildings with a narrow front, pointing to the street and mostly equipped with a *porticus*; the house usually occupies a long and narrow plot (Plate 22.6). The front part of the houses contained flats, taverns (*tabernae*), kitchens, shops, and cellars for storage; in the rear part and behind the houses there were outhouses, workshops, stables, wells, toilets (*latrinae*) etc. While agriculture did not seem to play an important role in the camp villages, excavations have demonstrated various industries; finds and features proved the existence of bronze making, pottery kilns, brickworks, the production of glass, bone-working etc. In addition to the strip buildings, occasionally forum-like complexes appear in the camp villages (e.g. in Noviomagus/Nijmegen **17**, Vindonissa/Brugg-Windisch **29**, Mirebeau **28**, and Carnuntum/Bad Deutsch-Altenburg **37**); the question of their function is not yet sufficiently answered. Markets for the produce from the vicinity of the camp might have taken place here. *Mansiones* (hostels), which at some military sites were erected directly in front of the camp gate, served to house travelers with a military-official task. In addition temples and sacral buildings for Roman, native, and oriental cults – the latter especially popular with the army (e.g. temples to Mithras) – were found in the camp villages. Furthermore leisure activities were offered for the soldiers and the inhabitants of the camp villages; especially in the *canabae* of larger legionary fortresses (e.g. Deva/Chester **12**, Vetera castra/Xanten **18**, Carnuntum/Bad Deutsch-Altenburg **37**, Aquincum/Budapest **39**, Lambaesis/Tazoult-Lambèse **77**) there are amphitheaters which compare well with their urban counterparts. However, arenas have also been discovered at auxiliary forts; inscriptions and finds of gladiatorial weapons indicate gladiatorial games during events and celebrations at the garrisons.[20] In contrast to the legionary fortresses, the bath buildings of the auxiliary forts were integrated into the *vici*; in regions with an unstable political situation, and in late antiquity, baths could be situated in fortified annexes or within the camp (e.g. Bewcastle **GB**, Mumrills **GB**, Monheim/Haus Bürgel **D**).

Traces of extra-mural settlements have been detected even at relatively short-lived camps of the Augustan period (Haltern **19**, Dangstetten **30**). However, with the installation of permanent *limites* more or less extensive extra-mural settlements could develop at permanently occupied garrisons. Usually they were preceded by native settlements. The location and partitioning of the house plots, as well as the location of the cemeteries, indicates that the *vicus* was considered during the construction of the camp, often at the price of a higher risk for the actual military settlement. The further development of the camp villages could follow different directions. The close association between the inhabitants of the *vicus/canabae* and the main unit is expressed by the fact that after the withdrawal of the unit not only the camp but also the settlement was often abandoned; in other cases (Viroconium/Wroxeter **11**, Isca Dumnoniorum/Exeter **7**, Nida/Frankfurt-Heddernheim **D**, Lopodunum/ Ladenburg **D** etc.) *civitas* capitals originated from former camp villages. Inscriptions prove that at least some (and possibly all) settlements at military camps had their own magistrates (*magistri*) and a town council (*ordo decurionum*) which probably fulfilled the same administrative tasks as their counterparts in towns of civil origin. The veterans played an important role in taking over offices.[21] So far evidence for public buildings of the magistrates (*forum, curia, basilica*) is lacking from *vici* and *canabae*, and there is hardly any information on the respective responsibilities of the civil magistrates and the military commanders. It is likely that the camp villages were subordinate to the local military command.

According to the epigraphic material, the composition of the inhabitants of *vici* and *canabae* was very heterogeneous: like the soldiers, the sutlers came from various parts of the empire. Some of the troops did not return to their home countries, but for different reasons settled in front of the camp gates. The relationship between the veterans and their comrades from the unit was of great importance, equally their long acquaintance with the region and the excellent financial conditions due to their compensation when leaving the services. Other inhabitants of the camp villages were natives from the neighborhood. *Vici* also housed women of mostly native origin. In the course of long Roman occupations many soldiers were recruited from the off-spring of veterans for the local garrison. The size of the extra-mural settlements of the military camps can only be estimated, as information on the complete extension of the built-up area is lacking. For the *vici* of the auxiliary forts on the Neckar at Lopodunum/Ladenburg (**D**) and Köngen (**D**), for instance, 1,500 people were calculated from 150–170 strip buildings.[22] Comparable calculations would result in several thousand inhabitants for the *canabae legionis.*

Apart from settlements and cemeteries there were other features in the vicinity of the camps: exercise and parade grounds (e.g. Hardknott **GB**, Deva/Chester **12**) and especially military agricultural land (*prata legionis*) known above all from inscriptions, and used for example as grassland, for cutting trees, and as quarries.[23] Outposts further away from the camps, which were occupied by vexillations of the camp unit, served in the first instance to ensure the supply of resources, building materials etc. which were not available in the direct neighborhood of the camp.

As *canabae* and *vici* were probably subject to the military control of the local unit, in some cases (e.g. colonia Ulpia Traiana/Xanten **18**, Carnuntum/Bad Deutsch-Altenburg **37**, Brigetio/Komáron-Szőny **38**, Lambaesis/Tazoult-Lambèse **77**) new settlements of civilian character developed at a certain distance from the camp.[24] Some of them remained without municipal rights during the whole period of the principate (Mogontiacum/Mainz **25**, Bonna/Bonn **24**, Novaesium/Neuss **22**, Argentorate/Strasbourg **27**, Vindobona/Vienna **36**, etc.), while others – in contrast to the majority of the camp villages – were awarded the rank of a *municipium* or even a *colonia* (e.g. Eburacum/York **14**, municipium Batavorum/Nijmegen **17**, colonia Ulpia Traiana/Xanten **18**, Carnuntum/Bad Deutsch-Altenburg **37**, Brigetio/Komáron-Szőny **38**, Aquincum/Budapest **39**, Apulum/Alba Iulia **51**).

5   Future Research

In comparison to the military camps in Britain and the provinces along the Rhine and Danube, the examples in Italy, the Hispanic provinces, but above all in North Africa and the East of the empire are little investigated. In some cases, particularly in the East, the defense walls and internal buildings have been well preserved to the present day because after being abandoned they have not been built on since antiquity. Archaeological research on military camps and their settlements which the written sources associate with concrete historical events and therefore a historical context, is most promising. The complete excavation of a military camp is of course desirable; however, especially for the extensive legionary fortresses and their *canabae*, this is hardly possible in practice and investigation has to be restricted to important areas or parts which are threatened by modern building development. From these selected sites the development of a military camp from its beginning to its end should be followed by analyzing the excavated stratigraphy.

Although many internal buildings in Roman camps can be identified by their characteristic plans, inscriptions, and specific small finds, there are still doubts about the function of some buildings (e.g. special blocks with rows of chambers, so-called *taberna* along the main roads, workshops). Further information is to be expected from careful excavations which combine archaeological evidence and evidence from scientific analysis. As in many cases the fortifications and internal buildings of the camps only left slight traces in the ground, a reconstruction of the excavated features should be aspired to as long as there are enough indications.

NOTES

 1   Steinby 1993, 246–54.
 2   Baatz 1994, 105–54.
 3   Pollard 2000, 39–67.
 4   Jae and Scholz 2002, 415–24.
 5   Pietsch 2000, 9–13. On the *comitatenses* and *limitanei*, see also Strobel (in this volume).
 6   Höckmann 1986, 369–416.
 7   Reddé 2004, 442–62.
 8   Sarnowski 1989, 97–120; Stoll 1992.
 9   Davison 1989.
10   Bidwell 2002, 470f.
11   Von Petrikovits 1976, 612–19; Hanel 2006.
12   Baatz 1984, 315–25.
13   Mason 2001, 47f. (tables 1 and 2).
14   Baatz 1994, 105–54.
15   Frere and St. Joseph 1974, 1–129.
16   Philp 1981; Fischer 2001, 547–64; Fischer and Hanel 2003.
17   Speidel 1992, 87–106.
18   Von Petrikovits 1991, 34.
19   Sommer 1998, 41–52.
20   Wahl 1977, 108–32.
21   Vittinghoff 1974, 111.
22   Reutti and Luik 1988, 26.
23   Mason 1988, 163–89.
24   Piso 1991, 142–51.

BIBLIOGRAPHY

Baatz, D. 1984. "Quellen zur Bauplanung römischer Militärlager," in *Bauplanung und Bautheorie der Antike*. Berlin, 315–25.
—— 1994. *Bauten und Katapulte des römischen Heeres*. Stuttgart.
Bidwell, P. 2002. "Timber baths in Augustan and Tiberian fortresses," in Ph. Freeman et al., 467–81.
Brewer, R. J. (ed.). 2000. *Roman Fortresses and Their Legions*. London.
Davison, D. P. 1989. *The Barracks of the Roman Army from the 1st to 3rd Centuries AD*. Oxford.
Euzennat, M. 1989. *Le limes de Tingitane*. Paris.
Evans, E. 2000. *The Caerleon* Canabae *Excavation in the Civil Settlement 1984–90*. London.

Fischer, Th. 2001. "Neuere Forschungen zum römischen Flottenlager Köln-Alteburg," in Th. Grünewald (ed.), *Germania inferior. Besiedlung, Gesellschaft und Wirtschaft an der Grenze der römisch-germanischen Welt.* Berlin, 547–64.

Fischer, Th., and N. Hanel. 2003. "Neuere Forschungen zum Hauptstützpunkt der classis Germanica in Köln-Marienburg (Alteburg)," *Kölner Jahrbuch* 36: 567–85.

Freeman, Ph., J. Bennett, Z. T. Fiema, and B. Hoffmann (eds.). 2002. Limes *XVIII. Proceedings of the 18th International Congress in Roman Frontier Studies, Amman, Jordan* (September 2000). Oxford.

Frere, S. S., and J. K. St. Joseph. 1974. "The Roman fortress at Longthorpe," *Britannia* 5: 1–129.

Genser, K. 1986. *Der österreichische Donaulimes in der Römerzeit. Ein Forschungsbericht.* Vienna.

Gregory, S. 1995–7. *Roman Military Architecture on the Eastern Frontier. Vol. 1–3.* Amsterdam.

Gudea, N. 1997. "Der dakische Limes – Materialien zu seiner Geschichte," *JRGZ* 44: 497–609.

Hanel, N. 2006. "Fabricae, Werkstätten und handwerkliche Tätigkeiten des Militärs in den Nordprovinzen des römischen Reichs," in Á. Morillo Cerdán (ed.), *Arqueología militar romana en Hispania: Producción y abastecimiento en el ámbito militar.* León, 19–32.

Höckmann, O. 1986. "Römische Schiffsverbände auf dem Ober- und Mittelrhein und die Verteidigung der Rheingrenze in der Spätantike," *JRGZ* 33: 369–416.

Jae, M., and M. Scholz. 2002. "Reduktion von numerus- und Kleinkastellen des obergermanischen Limes im 3. Jahrhundert," in Freeman et al., 415–24.

Johnson, A. 1987. *Römische Kastelle des 1. und 2. Jahrhunderts n. Chr. in Britannien und in den germanischen Provinzen des Römerreiches.* Mainz.

Kennedy, D. 2000. *The Roman Army in Jordan.* London.

Mason, D. J. P. 1988. "*Prata Legionis* in Britain," *Britannia* 19: 163–89.

—— 2001. *Roman Chester. City of the Eagles.* Stroud.

Morillo Cerdán, Á. (ed.). 2002. *Arqueología militar romana en Hispania.* Madrid.

Petrikovits, H. von. 1975. *Die Innenbauten römischer Legionslager während der Prinzipatszeit.* Opladen.

—— 1976. "Militärische Fabricae der Römer," in *Beiträge zur römischen Geschichte und Archäologie 1931 bis 1974.* Bonn, 612–19.

—— 1991. *Beiträge zur römischen Geschichte und Archäologie 1976–1991 II.* Cologne.

Philp, B. 1981. *The Excavation of the Roman Forts of the Classis Britannica at Dover 1970–1977.* Dover.

Pietsch, W. 2000. "Vorbilder für spätantike Turmformen," *Saalburg-Jahrbuch* 50: 9–13.

Piso, I. 1991. "Die Inschriften vom Pfaffenberg und der Bereich der Canabae Legionis," *Tyche* 6: 131–69.

Pollard, N. 2000. *Soldiers, Cities and Civilians in Roman Syria.* Ann Arbor.

Reddé, M. 2004. "Réflexions critiques sur les chapelles militaires (*aedes principiorum*)," *JRA* 17: 442–62.

Reutti, F., and M. Luik. 1988. *Der Römerpark in Köngen.* Stuttgart.

Shirley, E. A. M. 2000. *The Construction of the Roman Legionary Fortress at Inchtuthil.* Oxford.

Sarnowski, T. 1989. "Zur Statuenausstattung römischer Stabsgebäude," *BJ* 189: 97–120.

Sommer, C. S. 1988. "Kastellvicus und Kastell," *Fundberichte Baden-Württemberg* 13: 457–707.

—— 1998. "Kastellvicus und Kastell – Modell für die *Canabae* legionis?" *Jahresberichte Gesellschaft Pro Vindonissa 1997.* Brugg, 41–52.

Speidel, M. A. 1992. "Roman army pay scales," *JRS* 82: 87–106.

Steinby, E. M. 1993. *Lexicon topographicum urbis romanae 1.* Rome, 246–54.

Stoll, O. 1992. *Die Skulpturenausstattung römischer Militäranlagen an Rhein und Donau. Der Obergermanisch-Rätische Limes.* St. Katharinen.

Trousset, P. 1974. *Recherches sur le limes Tripolitanus du Chott el Djerid à la frontière Tuniso-Libyenne*. Paris.

Vittinghoff, F. 1974. "Das Problem des 'Militärterritoriums' in der vorseverischen Kaiserzeit," *Accademia nazionale dei Lincei, Atti* 194: 109–24.

Wahl, J. 1977. "Gladiatorenhelm-Beschläge vom Limes," *Germania* 55: 108–32.

Zahariade, M., and N. Gudea. 1997. *The Fortifications of Lower Moesia (AD 86–275)*. Amsterdam.

FURTHER READING

The huge number, size, and wide distribution of military camps of the principate within and outside the Roman Empire makes a systematic analysis of these fortifications difficult. But a comprehensive handbook sadly is lacking. A review of the progress of excavation and research is provided by the proceedings of the international Limes Congress taking place roughly every three years since 1949 in the former frontier regions of the Imperium. H. von Petrikovits' monograph on the internal buildings of legionary fortresses (1975) is still the best in its field. Questions about the typology and function of camp buildings are discussed and considered against the background of military history.

Research on Roman military camps has developed to different levels in the various regions: the information available about Britain and the Rhine and Danube provinces is very good. The present state of research about the legionary fortresses in the strategically most important frontier zones of the empire has recently been summarized in papers published in honor of G. C. Boon (Brewer 2000). The military camps in the Germanic and Britannic provinces from the period of the first to the second century are described authoritatively by Johnson 1987. The series "Der Obergermanisch-Raetische *Limes* des Römerreiches" (*ORL*) consisting of 14 volumes from between 1894 and 1938, is still an indispensable source for questions concerning the camps of the *limes* section in Upper Germany and Raetia. Important excavation results from the camps along the Lower and Upper German as well as the Raetian *limes* are published in the series "Limesforschungen" by the Römisch-Germanische Kommission, a division of the Deutsches Archäologisches Institut (German Archaeological Institute). An excellent source for the camps along the Danube *limes* in Austria is provided by the monograph by Genser 1986. The publication by Gudea (1997) is a good overview of the camps in the province of Dacia. For the section of the Lower Danube *limes* Zahariade and Gudea 1997 can be consulted.

Gregory 1995–7 provides a summary of the current state of research on the forts from the Turkish coast of the Black Sea up to the Gulf of Aqaba. On the occasion of the eighteenth *limes* congress in Amman Kennedy published a monograph (2000) on the forts along the *limes Arabiae* in Jordan. A similar publication on the Roman military camps in North Africa is lacking. Here the basic works are by Euzennat 1989 and Trousset 1974. Recently archaeological research on the Roman military camps of the Iberian peninsula has been given a new impetus by Morillo Cerdán 2002.

As for the camp villages, the publications especially by H. von Petrikovits and C. S. Sommer deserve special mention.

CHAPTER TWENTY-THREE

Marriage, Families, and Survival: Demographic Aspects

Walter Scheidel

1   Marriage and Families

General context

In the standing army of the principate, the term of service in the legions rose from 16 to 20 and later 25 years, while metropolitan guardsmen served for 12 to 16 or even 20 years. Recruits committed much of their lives to the military: perhaps half of them did not live to see their discharge, and half of those who did would be dead 20 years later. A statistically "average" soldier who enlisted for 25 years at the age of 20 could expect to spend up to three-quarters of his remaining life span on active duty.[1] Under these circumstances, family formation was difficult to reconcile with military service. While republican soldiers had often served in their late teens and twenties and married afterwards in keeping with conventional norms, this sequence became less practicable for imperial soldiers as the length of (continuous) service grew both formally and de facto. In addition, the peripheral deployment of most imperial troops that placed many recruits in alien environments may have further impeded marriage until more localized modes of recruitment became more common from the second century AD onward.

The "marriage ban" for Roman soldiers

Legal provisions only exacerbated this problem.[2] From the early principate, and most likely since the reign of Augustus, Roman soldiers were legally incapable of entering recognized marriages. At the very end of the second century AD, Septimius Severus was said to have granted them the right to "live with" (i.e. marry) their wives. By the fourth century AD, in any case, wives and children had come to be considered typical features of soldiers' lives, although the earliest surviving explicit reference to their formal marital capacity dates from as late as AD 426. We do not know if officers such as *centuriones* were also subject to the ban while it was in effect. Equestrian and senatorial commanders were exempt, yet barred from marrying women from provinces in which they performed their duties.

However, soldiers were not physically prevented from cohabiting with women or raising children: the state merely denied them and their conjugal families the legal entitlements that conventionally accrued from marital unions. Moreover, we do not know of any penalties for soldiers who established such relationships. Thus, "non-recognition" of marriage might be a more precise term than the traditional label "ban." The legal issues involved are elucidated by a number of papyrus documents from Roman Egypt. The most important text lists seven cases that were tried between AD 114 and 142 and show that children born during their fathers' military service were deemed illegitimate, regardless of whether these fathers were Roman citizens and whether they served in legionary or auxiliary units. In consequence, such children had no claims to their father's estate unless they were named heirs in their fathers' wills. Wives likewise lacked the usual legal entitlements, and could not sue for the return of dowries that had been handed over upon (quasi-)marriage, even if they had been concealed as deposits to circumvent the official ban on military unions (and apparently even after soldiers had been discharged). At the same time, gifts between soldiers and their de facto wives, which Roman law prohibited for regular spouses, were permitted in this context, and could not be reclaimed either.

In recognition of real-life practice, sporadic governmental interventions helped ameliorate this situation. In AD 44, Claudius granted soldiers the conventional legal privileges that Augustus had reserved for married citizens. More importantly, and expressly for humane reasons, Hadrian decreed that the children of soldiers who had died intestate be treated as the equivalent of cognate relatives, which meant they were able to inherit if there were no legitimate children or agnate relatives who took precedence. In practice, however, this required illegitimate children to be able to establish descent from soldiers who could not formally count as their fathers. In Roman Egypt, birth declarations (which sometimes noted that registered children were illegitimate because of "military restrictions," i.e., the marriage ban) could presumably be used to support such claims. We cannot tell how such cases were adjudicated in less bureaucratized parts of the empire.

References to dowries show that military unions could in fact be established in much the same way as formal marriages if the parties so desired, and thus point to a wide gap between legal fiat and social practice. This is particularly noteworthy given that soldiers' wives suffered obvious legal handicaps: if their husbands died intestate, they would lose their dowries and consequently find it (even) harder to remarry or support themselves. In this context, wills must have assumed especial importance, and it is tempting to speculate that married soldiers ought to have paid particular attention to this safeguard. Unfortunately, we have no means of determining the relative frequency of intestacy among soldiers.

The state's rationale for its disapproval of military marriage is not discussed in the extant sources and remains the subject of debate. Modern notions that this policy was designed to create a pool of illegitimate sons who grew up in a military environment and had a strong incentive to join the army in order to gain citizenship are implausible: there is no evidence that such individuals would obtain citizen status upon enlistment, and the "internal replacement" model of Roman recruitment is unlikely for demographic reasons as well. In the most elaborate discussion to date, Sara Phang argues that the "marriage ban" was meant to emphasize the masculine qualities of the professional army, restore order after the turmoil of the preceding civil wars, and symbolically dissociate soldier from civilian. While this measure obviously inflicted only disadvantages on soldiers' wives or children, it is unclear to what extent it was considered beneficial to (or by) the soldiers themselves. On the one hand, the lack of formal recognition of their unions shielded active soldiers from legal claims by civilians; yet on the other, the Severan legalization of regular marriage (alongside a pay raise) was supposed to make military service more attractive, which (if true) implies that soldiers may somehow have perceived the "ban" as a handicap as well.

Privileges for veterans

Discharge diplomas, small personal bronze copies of official documents that survive from the reign of Claudius onward, record various privileges that were conferred upon new veterans of the metropolitan guards, the fleets, and provincial auxiliary units. While non-citizens were granted the franchise, all veterans were given the right to marriage (*conubium*) with one (and only one) existing partner or future wife regardless of her civic status: this means that an enfranchised veteran could not enjoy more than a single legitimate union with a non-citizen woman, but was of course free to wed other Roman citizens. Up to around AD 140, existing children of auxiliary soldiers also obtained citizenship, whereas veterans' wives never came to enjoy that status by virtue of their unions. Notwithstanding the inexplicable geographical and chronological limitations of the existing veteran diplomas, these policies seem to have been fairly universal. In addition, imperial edicts on two (known) occasions (in 32/32 BC and AD 88/89) summarily bestowed citizenship on veterans' parents, wives, and children. We cannot tell how exceptional or common these provisions were. Once again, these texts acknowledge the existence of de facto unions with quasi-wives and children.[3]

The demographic character of military unions

Numerous military unions are known from the epitaphs of Roman soldiers. Modern scholarship has focused on patterns of commemoration that are thought to reflect underlying family structure. In their pioneering study of regional samples of tombstone inscriptions from the western half of the empire during the principate, Richard Saller and Brent Shaw observed substantial differences between military and civilian dedications. Wife-to-husband commemorations regularly outnumber husband-to-wife commemorations in military families, while the opposite is true of civilian funerary commemorations (Table 23.1). In addition, we encounter considerable geographical variation. Much like civilian tombstone inscriptions throughout the western provinces, military epitaphs from North Africa, Noricum, Pannonia, and Spain (and to a lesser

Table 23.1 Civilian and military dedications by commemorator (in percent)

Sample	Husband to-wife	Wife-to-husband	Within nuclear family	Heirs and friends
Republican Rome/Latium	41	8	75	10
Italy: Latium	20	11	77	5
Italy: Regio XI	27	7	79	4
Rome: lower orders	20	13	78	2
Rome: Equites singulares	*2*	*5*	*29*	*63*
Rome: other soldiers	*12*	*14*	*61*	*27*
Spain: civilian	13	11	83	8
Spain: military	*9*	*17*	*71*	*15*
Britain: civilian	28	8	80	11
Britain: military	*9*	*17*	*40*	*49*
Germania Inferior: civilian	26	10	86	9
Germania Inferior: military	*6*	*12*	*34*	*75*
Germania Superior: civilian	20	8	89	1
Germania Superior: military	*5*	*4*	*34*	*58*
Noricum: civilian	22	6	91	1
Noricum: military	*6*	*8*	*76*	*12*
Pannonias: military	*13*	*11*	*73*	*17*
Africa: Lambaesis – civilian	23	12	91	3
Africa: Lambaesis – military	*8*	*23*	*82*	*11*
Africa: Caesarea – civilian	15	11	89	6
Africa: Caesarea – military	*4*	*12*	*63*	*33*

Key: military samples in **bold italics**
Source: Saller and Shaw (1984) 147–55

extent for the Praetorian Guards in Rome) are dominated by commemorations within the nuclear family (with rates of 60–80 percent and 70–90 percent for the military and civilian spheres, respectively). By contrast, soldiers' epitaphs from Britain, the Rhine provinces, and the Horse Guards in Rome are dominated by dedications executed by unrelated heirs, while members of their nuclear families commonly account for a mere 30–40 percent of all cases (Table 23.1). To some extent, this discrepancy may be chronological rather than geographical in nature: Sara Phang's more detailed analysis shows that the incidence of commemorations from within the nuclear family consistently increases across different parts of the empire, from generally low rates in the first century AD to higher ones in the second and still higher ones in the third (Table 23.2).

In the first century AD, marital dedications may have been scarce because soldiers commonly manned garrisons far away from home and local same-status women were in short supply. In this environment, soldiers were more readily commemorated by fellow-soldiers, especially by those whom they had designated heirs. Greater troop mobility in the early principate might have been another factor, in as much as it

Table 23.2 Commemorations of soldiers dedicated by their wives (in percent)

Region	Century (AD)		
	1st	2nd	3rd
Africa (legionary)	15	27	37
Danube (legionary)	15	33	45
Danube (auxiliary)	16	39	–
Rome (praetorian)	5	11	28

Source: Phang (2001) 404–9

interfered with the creation of stable de facto unions. Dedications by members of the conjugal (as well as the birth family) increase in the second century AD, a trend that continues into the third. This development may have been spurred by a rise in provincial recruitment that helped preserve links to the birth family and facilitated relationships with local women. Even then, however, the Praetorian Guards in Rome continued to lag behind (Table 23.2), and the ethnically distinct Horse Guards even more so.[4]

Age at marriage can only be indirectly inferred by observed changes in the identity of the principal commemorators. For instance, if teenage women are predominantly commemorated by their parents and women in their twenties more often by their husbands, we may interpret this shift as evidence of widespread female marriage around age 20. The replacement of parents by wives at correspondingly higher ages indicates the same for men. Such readings suggest a typical age of first marriage of around 20 for women and of around 30 for men in Roman Italy, a distribution that is consistent with the later "Mediterranean" type of early female and late male marriage and has been used as the basis of a computer simulation of Roman kinship structure that matches the surge in male marriage around age 30 reflected in the epitaphs from the city of Rome as well as in smaller samples from other parts of imperial Italy. Pertinent information gleaned from the census returns of Roman Egypt points to a more gradual rise in the male marriage rate from the twenties into the forties (Figure 23.1). Conversely, the epitaphs of Roman soldiers generate a markedly different pattern. Dedications by de facto wives appear relatively late and do not exceed one-third of the total until the late forties, that is, for as long as soldiers were in active service. They begin to approach (but nevertheless fall short of) civilian levels only among veterans. The exclusion of samples with a notably low incidence of wife-to-husband commemoration (viz., from the first-century AD frontiers and the first- and second-century AD Praetorian Guards) does not greatly change this picture (Figure 23.1).

Unfortunately, the paucity of civilian funerary commemorations from the main frontier provinces forestalls meaningful comparisons with local marriage customs outside the military sphere. Even so, levels of male marriage as low those as implied by the military epitaphs are inherently unlikely to be representative of any civilian population. It deserves notice that the increase in spousal dedications in the third century

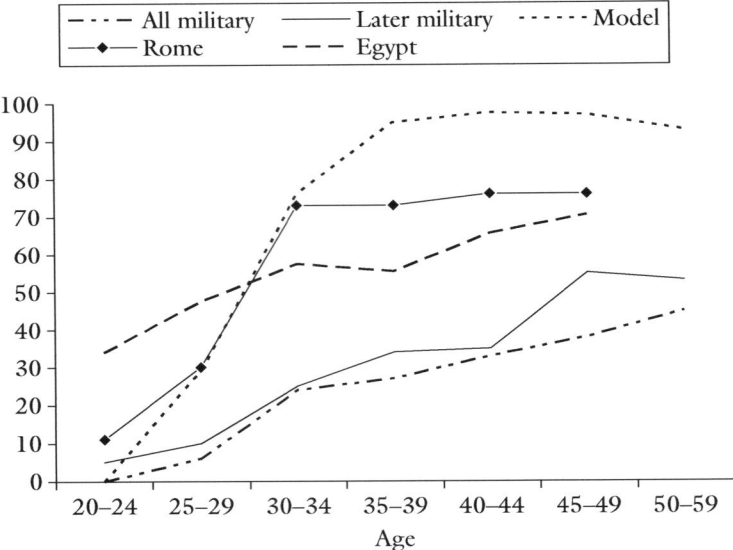

Figure 23.1 Percentage of men currently married ("Model," "Egypt") or commemorated by their wives ("All/later military," "Rome")

Key and sources: "All military" = all military epitaphs from all regions and periods in Phang (2001) 169; "Later military" = all military epitaphs from African and Danube legions and Danube auxilia (2nd/3rd centuries AD) and from Praetorian Guards (3rd century AD) in Phang (2001) 409; "Model" = simulation of Roman kinship structure in Saller (1994) 52; "Rome" = all epitaphs from the city of Rome in Saller (1994) 28; "Egypt" = incidence of male marriage according to the census returns from Roman Egypt (1st–3rd centuries AD) in Bagnall and Frier (1994) 117.

AD is merely the continuation of an earlier trend (Table 23.2), and that marital commemoration remained relatively rare even after discharge: for both reasons, the "marriage ban" cannot have been a crucial determinant of military cohabitation practices. It appears instead that the general circumstances of military life accounted for low rates of spousal commemoration and, by implication, of stable de facto or formal marriage during and after military service.

A narrow focus on those soldiers who were in fact commemorated by their kin reveals striking regional differences: naval crews at Ravenna and Misenum mostly married in their late twenties; legionaries on the Danube in their thirties; and those in North Africa in their forties. This distribution may be causally related to the fact that in the first two groups, soldiers' freedwomen frequently became the wives of their former owners. This practice was rare in North Africa where marriage with free-women appears to have been the norm but was frequently deferred until discharge. These complexities underscore the point that we are dealing with several intersecting variables – space, time, the soldiers' status, and their wives' status – within the confines of small data samples that do not normally permit detailed breakdowns without drowning us in statistical noise.

Under these circumstances, an overly schematic model is the best we can hope for. Compared to the civilian population, active soldiers were less likely to establish relationships with (free) women that were sufficiently stable to ensure funerary dedications in the event of these soldiers' death. Access to women of servile background could mitigate these constraints, and veterans married more frequently than active soldiers but nevertheless lagged behind coeval civilians. We may conclude that military service imposed a "marriage penalty" on the military population both during and after service.[5]

The demographic consequences of this situation are largely a matter of speculation. The one thing that is clear is that in this regime, the "marriage ban" would only rarely interfere with existing unions since men at the typical age of enlistment (mostly in the late teens, see below) would not normally be married (at least outside Egypt). In as much as reproductive success was predicated upon durable unions, soldiers may on average have fathered fewer (surviving) children than male civilians. Delayed marriage and resultant higher paternal age may have produced more orphans who required tutelage, a cost that may have been internalized by the military given that soldiers, whilst exempt from the duty to act as tutors for civilian relatives, could be required to perform this function for the offspring of fellow soldiers.

The soldiers' wives

Who were the (legal or de facto) spouses of Roman soldiers and veterans? In terms of age structure, they conformed to the standard convention that matched brides with significantly older grooms: soldiers' wives recorded in epitaphs are often in their twenties and thirties. The question of their status and background raises more serious problems and has been much discussed in recent scholarship, especially in connection with the broader question of how well the imperial army was integrated into provincial society. Sporadic literary allusions to soldiers' intermarriage with local women (as far apart as Syria and Germany) are vague and do not elucidate the civic status of these wives (Tacitus, *Hist.* 2.80; 4.65). In the epigraphic record, about 90 percent of all recorded wives of soldiers and veterans bear "Roman" names (*duo nomina* with a Latin *nomen gentile* and a Latin or Greek *cognomen*), leaving little room for indigenous single names or "Roman" names with an indigenous *cognomen*, commonly indicating recent enfranchisement. Taken at face value, this would seem to suggest that soldiers overwhelmingly formed unions with women who were either "Roman" (in the narrow sense of citizens who were of Italian origin or descended from other citizen soldiers or enfranchised auxiliary veterans, or women who were "Iunian Latins," that is, informally manumitted ex-slaves who had belonged to Roman citizens), or (both legally and culturally) "Romanized" in the sense that they descended from (long?) enfranchised locals. Given that troops were deployed in areas where Roman citizenship long remained relatively rare outside military and civilian elite circles, either one of these variants suggests a strong dissociation of military society from that of the surrounding communities and consequently only limited interaction between (citizen) soldier and (non-citizen) civilian.[6]

This pattern assumes a particularly extreme form in the frontier zone of North Africa, where 185 of 186 epigraphically attested citizen soldiers or veterans are linked to Roman(ized) wives, alongside 507 (out of 514) civilian citizen husbands who had Roman(ized) wives. Thus, no fewer than 99 percent of all married "Roman" men who appear on tombstones seem to have shunned non-Roman(ized) marriage prospects. This raises two problems. First of all, non-Roman(ized) husbands are almost completely absent from this sample, as 99 percent of all documented married men have Roman names, and only a single non-citizen soldier appears together with his wife. This means that we know absolutely nothing about the marriage customs of non-citizen auxiliary soldiers, who were given the right to marry non-citizen women after their own enfranchisement upon discharge. (Most de facto wives recorded in auxiliary veterans' diplomas do in fact bear non-Roman names.) Second, as far as legionaries and other citizen soldiers are concerned, it strains credulity to accept that only 1 percent of long-term military personnel would consider unions with non-Roman(ized) local women, or that such couples consistently shunned epigraphic conventions. Usurpation of citizen status may be the only plausible explanation, in that women of local origin who established stable relationships with Roman soldiers assumed Roman-style names to "fit in." While we cannot even begin to guess at the scale of this maneuver, it is certainly interesting that a law from Roman Egypt addresses the case of non-citizen wives of veterans who unlawfully "style themselves Romans" (*Gnomon of the Idioslogos* §53). This is an issue where the nature of the evidence prevents even the crudest estimates of actual practice. All we can claim with some confidence is that in this environment, non-assimilation was not an option for citizen soldiers' wives, an observation that continues to support the notion that the citizen army kept its distance from non-citizen locals (and/or vice versa).

Corresponding records from the European frontiers are less extravagantly biased in favor of Roman(ized) wives but nevertheless exhibit the same underlying pattern. The eastern garrisons have left little pertinent evidence. A recent study of the Roman army in Syria found only a single clear case of intermarriage with a local woman, as opposed to a number of unions within the military sphere. However, the evidence is far too thin to sustain quantitative analysis. Papyrus documents from Roman Egypt report unions among Romans and between Romans (including recently enfranchised veterans) and Egyptians in small numbers but fairly equal measure. At the same time, other sources indicate that soldiers were relatively well integrated in Egyptian society, although legal distinctions between citizens and non-citizens may well have maintained some barriers.[7]

Sex and the army

The apparent limitations of the military marriage market may seem hard to reconcile with the fact that soldiers were reasonably well remunerated and ought to have represented acceptable marriage prospects. The imperial tradition also jars with the report that by 171 BC, Roman soldiers on duty in Spain had fathered some 4,000 children with local women (Livy 43.3). More generally, access to nubile women had traditionally been a reward of military service and imperial success in early conquest states. In principle, high concentrations of Roman soldiers in relatively thinly populated frontier regions could have put considerable strain on the local marriage market: in what is perhaps the most extreme case, the Roman garrison of Britain of some 40,000 men resided among a mere 200–300,000 women aged 15 to 35, and habitual marriage with indigenes might have created tensions with the local male population. In this connection, it is worth noting that Rome was one of very few early states that enjoined strict (serial) monogamy on its citizenry. Sexual coercion and exploitation appear to have been channeled into the sphere of chattel slavery that provided a functional equivalent to other forms of resource polygyny pursued in more overtly stratified systems. This hypothesis receives some measure of support from high rates of soldiers' commemoration by their own (certain or possible) freedwomen in some segments of the Roman military: 25–59 percent in the Italian fleets, 42–50 percent in the legions of first-century AD Germany, and between 3 percent and 35 percent in various other samples. *Focariae*, kitchen maids, were regarded as customary sex partners of Roman soldiers. The famous will of the veteran C. Longinus Castor in the late second century AD not only freed two of his slave women and made them heirs but also named as substitute heirs four males who are commonly assumed to be his children by those women. Finally, in addition to stable relationships, we must allow for the contribution of prostitution (of uncertain extent) and homosexual relationships with male slaves and military subordinates, which attracted a fair amount of attention in Roman literature. A deficit in spousal commemorations does not denote a sexually inactive Roman army, all the more so as the reproductive consequences of casual relationships necessarily remain unknown.[8]

2   Survival

The demography of the Roman imperial army: mission impossible?

The odds of surviving Roman military service are empirically unknown. While detailed reports of battle casualties for certain parts of the republican period can be used as a basis for more ambitious – if highly conjectural – estimates of overall attrition rates, the nature of the evidence rules out similar attempts for the principate. Scattered epigraphic records barely begin to fill the void. Information about the average age of enlistment and the length of service allows us to predict probable levels of baseline military mortality. Annual discharge rates for troop formations of known size are required to relate actual attrition rates to idealized projections, and to distinguish conditions in different units. In addition to quantifiable data, we also need to consider qualitative evidence for factors that can be expected to have had an impact on life expectancy, above all the quality of the water supply, sanitation, and hygiene (which helped determine the prevalence of infectious disease), and possibly the range of medical services. At best, this eclectic approach sheds some light on broad trends, while firm conclusions will forever remain beyond our reach.

Enlistment

At what age did Roman soldiers join up? Epitaphs of soldiers who died during active service are our main source of information. In those cases in which both the age of the deceased and the length of his service are recorded on the tombstone, the age of enlistment is usually determined by subtracting the number of years of service from the number of years the soldier had lived. As I have shown elsewhere, this method needs to be refined to take account of the widespread custom of age-rounding: the practice of rounding someone's (often imperfectly known) age at death to the nearest multiple of five. Once we control for this distortion, the epigraphic evidence produces a clear picture. Approximately two-thirds of all legionaries enlisted between ages 17 and 20. Most of the others signed on between ages 21 and 25, whereas recruitment at lower ages was negligible. The mean, median, and modal age of enlistment is 20 years, and this figure can therefore be used for computational purposes. More radical but less dependable adjustments for age-rounding suggest an earlier peak around age 18, and a gradual decline in enlistment rates thereafter. Recruitment for the Praetorian Guards, the Urban Cohorts, and the imperial Horse Guards (*equites singulares Augusti*) in the capital is strongly concentrated in the age group from 18 to 20, with resultant means, medians, and modes of around 19 years. Thus, during the principate, most citizen soldiers enlisted within a few years of attaining legal maturity. This suggests considerable continuity between republican and imperial practice.[9]

Life expectancy

The average life expectancy of Roman soldiers is much more difficult to ascertain. We know that in antiquity many lives were short. Occasional quantifiable data and comparative evidence suggest that mean life at birth expectancy normally fluctuated within a band from 20 to 30 years. In the near-absence of reliable primary data, ancient historians have begun to fall back on model life tables, which are modern extrapolations from known to unknown mortality regimes that project probable age distributions for different levels of life expectancy at birth. These models predict that in high-mortality regimes, a large percentage of all fatalities are concentrated in the first few years of life. Thus, we may assume that between one-third and one-half of all newborns were dead by age five. Adult mortality rates were less extreme but nonetheless very high by modern standards. For instance, a simple model life table for adult males suggests that of 100 soldiers who enlisted at age 20, 78 would have survived to age 35, 69 to age 40, and 60 to age 45.[10] For legionaries, this implies a baseline rate of attrition of roughly one-third for 20 to 25 years of service. In reality, violent death, camp-related disease, and early discharge would have raised overall attrition by a potentially significant margin.

Empirical information that would permit us to improve on this generic assumption is rare. In an earlier study, I made use of epigraphic rosters that list the number of soldiers who were discharged from a particular legion in a given year.[11] In three out of seven surviving documents from the second century AD, anomalies caused by military events forestall further analysis. The other four rosters (from the lower Danube, North Africa, and Egypt) all point to annual rates of between 100+ and c. 125 discharges, and in fact mostly to 120–25 cases per year. The underlying median of 120 annual discharges per legion needs to be related to the typical size of a legion and the length of service in order to calculate the rate of attrition during active service. Reckoning with an effective troop strength of slightly under 5,000, 25 years of service, and an average enlistment age of 20, we may project an annual intake of 250–60 recruits and an annual discharge of 120 veterans per legion. In this scenario, slightly more than one-half of all recruits would not complete a full term of active duty. If correct, this estimate suggests that even in peacetime, the imperial legions lost approximately one-and-a-third times as many soldiers as predicted by mortality models alone (say, 50–55 percent instead of 40 percent over 25 years). Due to the probable margins of error, it is impossible to be more precise. Even so, this apparent discrepancy between predicted and observed attrition rates may readily be explained with reference to early discharge – either dishonorable (*missio ignominiosa*) or, perhaps more often, for medical reasons (*missio causaria*). Desertion and transfers to elite units would have added to the drain. Hence, in the absence of major combat operations, actual mortality in the legions need not have been dramatically (or at all) higher than in the civilian population. This notion is easy to reconcile with what we know about the ancient disease environment in general, and more specifically with the range of amenities provided in permanent legionary camps that I discuss in the penultimate section of this chapter.

Records pertaining to the military units stationed in the capital itself create a very different impression.[12] Discharge rosters for the Praetorian Guards suggest much more rapid attrition than in the legions, of some 58 percent during 17 years of service (in the second century AD) and of 45 percent during 13 years (in the early third century AD). These rates are similar to those among legionaries who served for much longer periods of time, and therefore imply bigger losses overall. Much the same is true for the *equites singulares Augusti*, who appear to have suffered 60 percent attrition within 20 years of service. Various factors may account for this imbalance, including elevated levels of combat mortality in the emperors' campaigns of the Antonine and Severan periods, a greater degree of outward mobility in the form of promotions into the officer corps, and the notoriously severe disease environment of the city of Rome (see below).

Combat mortality

The demographic impact of campaigning is impossible to quantify. For the period from 200 to 168 BC, Nathan Rosenstein calculated an average combat mortality rate of 8.8 percent for Roman troops that were actively involved in – documented – battles (ranging from 4.2 percent for victories to 16 percent for defeats). If troops that did not see battle are included in the tally, the mean annual combat fatality risk for those years drops to 2.6 percent even when we allow for some unreported deaths in minor engagements.[13] These estimates are tenuous and in any case cannot be applied to later periods: for the standing army of the principate, annual combat mortality of the order of 2.6 percent of total troop strength would translate to some 8,000–10,000 battle fatalities per year. Given what we know about the scale and frequency of large-scale military activity in this period, this notion is wildly implausible. We may conclude that relative to total manpower, combat mortality in the principate was much lower than it had been in the mid-republic.

How much lower? In the absence of hard data, this issue is best approached by way of a thought experiment. In the first two centuries AD, war deaths must have been strongly concentrated in particular episodes of intense warfare: the Illyrian and German uprisings under Augustus, the civil wars after Nero and under Septimius Severus, the three Jewish Wars, the Dacian Wars under Domitian and Trajan, the Parthian Wars under Trajan, Verus, and Septimius Severus, and the Marcomannic Wars under Marcus Aurelius. Together, these events covered approximately 50 years. If we generously assume that one-third of the Roman army, or at least 100,000 men, were actively involved in these conflicts (i.e., on average, every fourth year), this translates to a mean annual risk of serious combat of one in twelve in any given year, or a notional total of two years for each soldier surviving to discharge. If soldiers had faced a 10 percent chance of being killed in combat in each year of intense campaigning, the average risk of violent death would have amounted to 0.8 percent per year (or 2,400 fatalities in an army of 300,000), which equals one-half of the regular annual mortality rate predicted by model life tables. Yet again, this figure seems too high, implying as it does the death of 10,000 soldiers in each year of large-scale campaigning. Actual battle deaths need not have raised overall military morality rates by more than 10 or 20 percent. It seems impossible to assign more than a purely notional magnitude to this factor.

All we can say is that on average and in the long term, battle mortality was by no means negligible. At the same time, it was very unevenly distributed: while some units, at certain times, would have suffered disproportionately heavy losses, others would have remained largely untouched for extended periods. For instance, for all we can tell, the 239 veterans (representing two year's worth of releases) who were discharged from Legio VII Claudia around AD 160 had not experienced substantial combat operations during their 25 or 26 years of service (*CIL* 3.8110). By contrast, the ranks of the 230+ veterans who left the same unit in AD 195 (as a single-year cohort) appear to have been swollen by numerous replacements for heavy losses incurred in war and epidemics at the end of the 160s AD (*CIL* 3.14507). Much like today, military mortality risks varied hugely depending on unpredictable changes in strategic conditions.

Health

Infectious disease was the single most important determinant of life expectancy in the ancient world. Direct information about Roman soldiers' exposure to pathogens is scarce. The annalistic record contains sporadic references to epidemic outbreaks during military campaigns of the republican era, and plausibly suggests that sieges were particularly conducive to fatal infections. Unfortunately, the lack of comparably detailed reports for the principate forestalls straightforward comparisons. The fevers that decimated Vitellius' Rhine legions in Rome in AD 69 (Tacitus, *Hist.* 2.93) and the dramatic military fatalities caused by the so-called Antonine Plague (probably smallpox) in the late 160s AD (Galenus 19.17–18; Hieronymus, *Chron.* 204–205 (ed. Helm); *HA, Marc.* 17.2; Orosius 7.15.5–6) are probably the most noteworthy instances. However, it is doubtful whether the overall paucity of references to disease in army camps or during campaigns can be taken as evidence of its relative insignificance. After all, in the more recent past, infections usually carried off more soldiers than did actual combat: in the American Civil War and the Boer War, deaths from disease outnumbered battle fatalities by about two to one, and earlier rates may have been higher still.[14]

Even so, a number of factors may have helped to lessen the impact of disease in the principate. Prolonged sieges, traditionally a major risk factor, were comparatively rare in this period, and even Josephus' detailed account of the sieges of the Jewish War of AD 66–73 contains no reports of epidemics among the Roman forces. More importantly, several of the greatest scourges of early modern armies appear to have been rare or unknown in the ancient Mediterranean, above all louse-borne typhus but also cholera, smallpox, and plague. Conversely, tuberculosis may have been an issue in cramped living quarters that facilitated transmission. Malaria is arguably the most important unknown quantity. It is hard to determine to what extent periodic fevers were common near the major camps outside the capital itself. The coast near Alexandria was said to be relatively safe from that disease, and while we know too little about the suburban camps of the eastern provinces to draw any conclusions, a dry climate may well have curtailed seasonal fevers. Then again, the legionary fortress of Carnuntum on the Danube (at the eastern border of Austria) was situated in close proximity to extensive wetlands that remained malarious well into the nineteenth century, while in nearby Hungary (formerly heavily-garrisoned Roman Pannonia), widespread malaria infections persisted into the 1940s. The Rhineland, which came to house up to one-third of the Roman legionary forces in the early first century AD, experienced high levels of endemic malaria until massive regulations of the river were finally completed in 1879. As a consequence, many Roman army camps may have been exposed to seasonal infection. Although Roman manuals recommended the construction of military (as well as civilian) sites away from infested marshes, the logistical constraints of riverine supply lines appear to have superceded such precautions.

We cannot be sure if the observation that, in AD 208, Septimius Severus' army in Scotland was "badly affected by the waters" (Cassius Dio 77.13.2) refers to malaria (subsequently common in other parts of Britain), or whether a lost inscription from a fort north of Hadrian's Wall had actually been dedicated to Dea Tertiana, the goddess of tertian fever (*CIL* 7.999). We have moreover no reason to assume that frontier troops routinely faced hazards as severe as those that ravaged the city of Rome, with its deadly mix of hyperendemic quotidian and malign tertian fevers (caused by the most potent malaria parasite, *P. falciparum*) and numerous other density-dependent diseases which were capable of inflicting massive fatalities on troops used to less hostile surroundings and may arguably have contributed to the high attrition rates observed among various urban guard units. Nonetheless, the relatively warm climate of the early imperial period and the army's dependence on unregulated waterways raises the very real possibility that malaria took a significant toll on stationary garrisons. It deserves notice, however, that the characteristic variants of the European interior, benign tertian (*P. vivax*) and quartan fever (*P. malariae*), were insufficiently pernicious to kill many adults on their own: rather, they would have boosted mortality by exacerbating unrelated but concurrent illnesses.[15]

In this environment of synergistic superinfection, the prevalence of other diseases acquires especial significance. Given the deployment and routines of the frontier armies, living conditions in the permanent camps of the legions and auxiliary units must have been the principal determinant of military health. The standing army of the principate was concentrated in hundreds of camps with 500 to 1,000 residents each, and in two dozen or more legionary camps with adjacent *canabae* (and sometimes regular cities) whose combined population commonly exceeded 10,000 each. In such high-density clusters, contaminated food and water and resultant gastro-enteric diseases such as dysentery and typhoid fever posed the most serious health risks. In a world without antibiotics, infrastructural provisions for uncontaminated water supply, efficacious waste disposal, and general cleanliness represented the only credible line of defense against such threats.

Excavations in and around imperial army camps have unearthed an impressive range of pertinent amenities. Aqueducts are attested on a number of military sites: a mere auxiliary camp on Hadrian's Wall such as Great Chesters boasted an aqueduct that was six miles long. Other camps relied on draw-wells (no fewer than 99 of which have been located inside the auxiliary fort of Saalburg), used large filtration tanks with multiple chambers, and also drew on rivers. In the southern and eastern provinces, cisterns were used to collect rain water. Bathhouses, where available, offered the standard array of hot, warm, and cold pools, and could be equipped with latrines. Water-flushed latrines have been found in Roman camps as far apart as Britain and North Africa, sometimes with hand basins that improved hygiene. The sophistication of these installations varied considerably, from stone-built latrines that were continually flushed and equipped with elaborate drains to simpler wooden structures with cesspits. The latter were common in auxiliary forts which lacked the dedicated drainage systems that were typical of the much larger legionary encampments. Egyptian papyri mention soldiers who were charged with clearing out such cesspits. According to one estimate, a legionary camp may have been equipped with five or six latrines that could accommodate up to 20 men each. In addition, there is some circumstantial evidence for the existence of separate smaller latrines for private use by officers. The absence of large centralized messes may have helped to curtail food poisoning: rations were prepared by each *contubernium* of eight soldiers on small hearths at the barracks.[16]

A substantial body of epigraphic and archaeological evidence sheds some light on the medical service of the imperial army. *Medici*, the most frequently documented category, were trained soldiers who performed medical functions both in the garrisons and during campaigns. Although it is often assumed that medical personnel could be common soldiers as well as officers, the question of rank continues to be much debated: our readings primarily hinge on the interpretation of the title *medicus ordinarius*, which may denote common soldiers or officers of the rank of *centurio*. *Capsarii* served as dressers, while specialists included the *medicus chirurgus* (surgeon), *m. clinicus* (internist), and *m. ocularius* (oculist), as well as the *marsus* (specialist for snake bites). A reference to trainee dressers (*discentes capsariorum*) points to the existence of on-site instruction.

The strength of military medical personnel is unclear. We only know for certain that each of the *cohortes vigilum* in Rome was endowed with four *medici* (i.e., one per 250 men), while large warships with a crew of 200 to 250 appear to have carried one doctor each. *Medici* are repeatedly attested for auxiliary formations (and even in irregular *numeri*), but there is currently no evidence for the presence of more than one such person in any one unit. Thus, if we conservatively reckon with one *medicus* per 500 men in most units, a legion may have had at least ten (although we may have to allow for the presence of additional specialists in large units), and the armed forces as a whole might have employed up to 1,000 medical staff.[17]

Permanent legionary camps were equipped with sizeable military hospitals (*valetudinaria*) located in quiet areas and run by an *optio valetudinarii*. The best-known examples are those at Vetera (Xanten) and Novaesium (Neuss) on the Rhine. The latter boasted a *valetudinarium* that measured 50 by 90 meters (or more than an acre) and contained a large number of small cubicles that may have accommodated some 260 patients, or 5 percent of the total unit. Substantial collections of medical instruments and assorted remains of medicinal plants have been found at these and comparable sites. Correspondingly smaller establishments are attested in some auxiliary camps in Britain, the Rhineland, and on the upper Danube. It is unclear to what extent this reflects genuine geographical limitations or merely the relative thoroughness of excavations in different parts of the former empire. However, we know that even in these regions, not every camp contained dedicated medical facilities. Papyrological records from Roman Egypt demonstrate that the army kept track of illness: sick soldiers could be listed on a daily basis, and we even hear of arrangements that allowed convalescents to recover away from their camps.[18]

Army surgeons in particular were famed for their skills and practical experience, and we have osteological evidence of demanding surgical procedures. Even so, the demographic benefits of military healthcare remain doubtful. Due to the lack of sterile operating theaters, even seasoned surgeons must have faced serious constraints, and their services would have been useful in the first instance during campaigns.[19] In peacetime, infectious diseases must have been a far greater threat to the soldiers' health. As in all pre-modern societies, the lack of vital medical knowledge gravely limited both prevention and intervention: inoculation, vaccination, and antibiotics – the only effective means of combating serious infections – were as unavailable to Roman army doctors as to any other early medical practitioners. In this context, non-medical prevention necessarily assumed a much greater importance than medical services. Thus, in as much as clean drinking water, proper toilets, and bathhouses were not only set up but routinely used and maintained, Roman garrisons may well have enjoyed basic protection against infection and premature death far beyond the primitive standards of most other pre-modern armies. This notion is consistent with my thesis that peacetime mortality rates in the frontier garrisons need not have been significantly higher than in the general population.

General implications

If we accept an annual baseline rate of 120 discharges per legion, 25 to 30 legions would have produced some 3,000 to 3,600 new veterans each year, as would the various auxiliary formations. The annual creation of 6,000–7,000 45-year-old veterans would have sustained a total veteran population of about 100,000–120,000 men, equivalent to between one-third and one-quarter of the active army. Every year, somewhere around 15,000 fresh recruits were required to staff the legionary, auxiliary, and naval units, or – assuming a total population of 60 to 70 million – about 2½ percent of all 20-year-old men in the Roman empire. Needless to say, this overall mean may conceal potentially massive regional variation in actual recruitment rates.[20]

The question to what extent the imperial army was capable of reproducing itself (via the enlistment of the sons of soldiers) is impossible to answer. Suffice it to note that several factors would have militated against high levels of internal replacement. They include excess mortality caused by combat and other professional risks, attrition due to early discharge or other departures, and the relatively late age of male de facto marriage indicated in many of the soldiers' epitaphs. In purely demographic terms, it is unlikely that the imperial army could ever become a "closed institution."

NOTES

1   Based on section 2 below, with select projections from Coale and Demeny 1983, 42–3.
2   Phang 2001, 16–52, 86–133, 326–83 is now the fundamental study and the basis for this section.
3   Phang 2001, 53–85.
4   Saller and Shaw 1984, 139–45, 152–5; Phang 2001, 142–64.
5   Saller 1994, 25–41; Bagnall and Frier 1994, 116–17; Phang 2001, 164–76, 193–4.
6   Phang 2001, 190–5.
7   Cherry 1998, 101–40; Pollard 2000, 151–9; Alston 1995, 117–42.
8   Phang 2001, 193–4, 240–3 (freedwomen), 204–7 (*focariae*), 231–40 (slave women), 244–51 (prostitution), 262–95 (homosexual relationships). For a general theory of sexual exploitation in early empires and the nexus between Roman chattel slavery and polygyny, see Scheidel forthcoming. For the latter, cf. also Phang 2004.
9   Scheidel 1996, 97–116.
10 Coale and Demeny 1983, 43 (Model West Level 4 Males). Standard model life tables may well underestimate adult mortality rates in archaic mortality regimes: cf. Scheidel 2001b, 1–26.
11 Scheidel 1996, 117–24.
12 Ibid. 124–9.
13 Rosenstein 2004, 107–40.
14 E.g. Prinzing 1916; Rosenstein 2004, 130–1.
15 Relative prevalence of diseases in antiquity: Scheidel 2001a, 67–8, 94–101. For Alexandria, see ibid. 20–1, 78–9; for Britain, see Sallares 2002, 156–7. See Scheidel 2003, 158–76, for a reconstruction of the disease pool of the capital, and Scheidel 1996, 129 n.107 for military mortality there.

16 Water supply: Von Petrikovits 1975, 105–6; Johnson 1983, 202–10; Davies 1989, 211. Latrines, drains, and cesspits: Von Petrikovits 1975, 106; Jackson 1988, 131; Davidson 1989, 233–6; Davies 1989, 211. Cooking: Jackson 1988, 133. See also Hanel (in this volume).
17 Medical staff: Davies 1989, 212–15 (functions); Wilmanns 1995, 68–70 (numbers); 75–86 (rank), 117–24 (functions).
18 Military hospitals: Watermann 1978; Jackson 1988, 134–6; Davies 1989, 218–25; Wilmanns 1995, 103–16.
19 Jackson 1988, 112–29. Cf. also Salazar 2000.
20 Cf. Scheidel 1996, 93–7 for conjectures about regional enlistment rates.

BIBLIOGRAPHY

Alston, R. 1995. *Soldier and Society in Roman Egypt: A Social History*. London.
Bagnall, R. S., and B. W. Frier. 1994. *The Demography of Roman Egypt*. Cambridge.
Cherry, D. 1998. *Frontier and Society in Roman North Africa*. Oxford.
Coale A. J., and P. Demeny. 1983². *Regional Model Life Tables and Stable Populations*. New York.
Davidson, D. P. 1989. *The Barracks of the Roman Army from the 1st to 3rd Centuries* AD, vol. I. Oxford.
Davies, R. W. 1989. *Service in the Roman Army*. Edinburgh.
Jackson, R. 1988. *Doctors and Diseases in the Roman Empire*. Norman.
Johnson, A. 1983. *Roman Forts of the 1st and 2nd Centuries* AD *in Britain and the German Provinces*. London.
Petrikovits, H. von. 1975. *Die Innenbauten römischer Legionslager während der Prinzipatszeit*. Opladen.
Phang, S. E. 2001. *The Marriage of Roman Soldiers (13* BC–AD *235): Law and Family in the Imperial Army*. Leiden.
—— 2004. "Intimate conquests: Roman soldiers' slave women and freedwomen," *The Ancient World* 15: 207–37.
Pollard, N. 2000. *Soldiers, Cities, and Civilians in Roman Syria*. Ann Arbor.
Prinzing, F. 1916. *Epidemics Resulting from Wars*. Oxford.
Rosenstein, N. 2004. *Rome at War: Farms, Families, and Death in the Middle Republic*. Chapel Hill.
Salazar, C. F. 2000. *The Treatment of War Wounds in Graeco-Roman Antiquity*. Leiden.
Sallares, R. 2002. *Malaria and Rome: A History of Malaria in Ancient Italy*. Oxford.
Saller, R. P. 1994. *Patriarchy, Property and Death in the Roman Family*. Cambridge.
——, and B. D. Shaw. 1984. "Tombstones and Roman family relations in the principate: Civilians, soldiers, and slaves," *JRS* 74: 124–55.
Scheidel, W. 1996. *Measuring Sex, Age and Death in the Roman Empire: Explorations in Ancient Demography*. Ann Arbor.
—— 2001a. *Death on the Nile: Disease and the Demography of Roman Egypt*. Leiden.
—— 2001b. "Roman age structure: Evidence and models," *JRS* 91: 1–26.
—— 2003. "Germs for Rome," in C. Edwards and G. Woolf (eds.), *Rome the Cosmopolis*. Cambridge, 158–76.
—— Forthcoming. "Sex and empire: A Darwinian perspective," in I. Morris and W. Scheidel (eds.), *The Dynamics of Ancient Empires*.
Watermann, R. 1978. *Valetudinarium. Das römische Legionskrankenhaus*. Neuss.
Wilmanns, J.C. 1995. *Der Sanitätsdienst im Römischen Reich*. Hildesheim.

FURTHER READING

Phang 2001 offers the most comprehensive discussion of military unions in the principate. Saller and Shaw 1984, 124–55 is a pioneering quantitative analysis of family relations that puts Roman military families in a broader context. For regional studies of military unions, see Alston 1995, 117–42; Cherry 1998, 101–40; and Pollard 2000, 151–9. Scheidel 1996, 93–138 is the most detailed attempt to quantify military participation rates, the typical age of enlistment in the imperial army, and the mean life expectancy of Roman soldiers in the legions and metropolitan guard units. Estimates of overall combat mortality are not feasible for the principate: for an earlier period of Roman history, compare Rosenstein 2004, 107–40. Davies 1989, 209–36 remains the best survey of sanitation and medical services in Roman imperial army camps. Jackson 1988, 112–29 focuses on the role of army surgeons.

CHAPTER TWENTY-FOUR

Recruits and Veterans

Gabriele Wesch-Klein

It should come as no surprise to find recruits and veterans dealt with in a single chapter: entrance into the army meant a young man's separation from civilian life, a life to which he could not return to until after his retirement from military service in middle or old age. Honorable discharge was followed by a "second life" as a civilian. Veterans were respected members of society, and in many cases were financially better off than other civilians. In the course of their military service they had received a glimpse into the administration of the Roman Empire, obtained skills, and made contacts that would prove useful in their civilian lives.

1 Recruits

Personal status

The reforms of Augustus included the creation of a professional army that consisted of legions, auxiliary forces, fleets, and units within the city of Rome itself. While only Roman citizens served in the legions and the Praetorian Guard, the other branches were open to all freeborn men. Thus, men of different ethnic and social origins from the most varied parts of the Roman Empire were to be found in the lower ranks (*militia caligata*) of the Roman armed forces. Freedmen (*liberti*) could also enter the army, although there were always reservations about their admission: the old Roman concept of a citizen army recruited from freeborn men was never entirely forgotten. The admission of slaves into the armed forces was strictly forbidden. Only in moments of extreme necessity was this basic rule violated; and under such extraordinary circumstances slaves became freedmen upon their entrance into the army (Suetonius, *Aug.* 25.2; *Cod. Theod.* 7.13.16; AD 406). Nevertheless, in spite of this ban, slaves were continually found among the ranks of the soldiers. Why they joined the army is open to question: some may have been escaped slaves who sought a hiding place and a new identity; other unfree men may have been illegally enrolled by their owners as substitutes.

Recruiting

At the beginning of the third century AD, Isis wrote to her mother from Alexandria: "And if Aion wants to be a soldier, he only need come, since everyone is becoming a soldier!" (*BGU* 7.1680). The attractiveness of military service in the imperial period reflected in these words was grounded for the most part in the high degree of social security soldiers enjoyed, and especially in soldiers' receiving a regular income over a long period. Anyone who, having passed the suitability test (*probatio*), was entered onto the list (*matrix*) of a unit, had, depending on his branch of service, from at least 16 to around 30 years of service before him. During these years, he would have to accept reductions in his personal freedom, but would enjoy regular pay, lodging, and access to medical treatment. Thanks to the organization of the army, he would always have enough to eat. Moreover, he could count on both financial rewards and legal privileges upon his honorable discharge.

The counterbalancing risk of enlisting as a soldier, that the volunteer might die in war, was evidently considered slim by many. The imperial period was characterized by long periods of peace, and only a small part of the Roman Empire commonly faced armed enemies. Even in the event of a major conflict, only some of the troops would be ordered into the actual theater of war. Moreover, if one had to die, death in the field was honorable.

A young man's decision to become a soldier met mostly with approval from his family, and the more so if they themselves had been soldiers. Those brought up near a military camp were familiar with the soldier's life and its demands from childhood on. Fathers were frequently proud to be soldiers and anticipated the same career for their sons. Evidence for this expectation is to be found in the matching cognomina of M. Aurelius Militio ("Soldier") and his son Aurelius Militaris ("Military") (*CIL* 3.5955). The grave monument which a horn player (*cornicen*) of the Legio II adiutrix erected for his four-year-old son shows the father's expectations for his child: the deceased boy is presented on the stone wearing the *cingulum militare* (army belt) and holding a rolled-up papyrus on which his right index finger is placed, as if taking an oath (*CIL* 3.15159). There were of course other views: in a papyrus (*BGU* 4.1097; AD 41–54), a wife is angry with her husband because he had advised their son to become a soldier.

As a rule, there were enough men in the Roman Empire who freely enrolled in military service; it was seldom necessary to recruit forcibly. However, the general obligation of all citizens to do service in the army was never lifted, which meant that in emergencies eligible men could always be drafted. The consequence of forcible recruiting that some men attempted to remove themselves and their children from eligibility. Suetonius mentions the case of a knight (*eques Romanus*) who amputated the thumbs of his sons to make them ineligible for the draft. The first emperor, Augustus, punished him by confiscating his fortune and sold him into slavery; he then reduced the punishment to confinement in the countryside under the supervision of a freedman (Suetonius, *Aug.* 24.1). The punishment of sale into slavery corresponded to republican custom (*Dig.* 49.16.4.10), but later Trajan decreed that fathers who amputated body parts of their sons in the face of a draft should be punished instead with exile (*deportatio*; *Dig.* 49.16.4.12). Fathers who attempted to save their sons from military service without mutilating them were punished less severely. In a time of war, the father was threatened with banishment and partial confiscation of his property. In peacetime, the father could expect a beating and the forcible recruitment of his son *in deteriorem militiam* (at a lower rank or in a more humble branch of service than his status entitled him. Naturally, this was only relevant to the sons of high-status persons; sons of *equites Romani*, for example, were normally entitled to enter the services as officers) (*Dig.* 49.16.4.11).

Recruiting in the later Roman Empire was achieved through a mixture of volunteering, inheritance of an army career, and the draft. It was mostly the sons of soldiers who inherited military careers, from which they could only be freed through an imperial dispensation. All men who were not assigned to a guild or farming could be drafted, including unsettled and homeless people (*vagantes, vagi et otiosi*). For the most part recruits were presented by localities, as had been true in previous centuries. Guilds and landowners were obliged to present recruits. Around AD 376, there was a major change to the recruiting system, since the Goths, who had crossed the Danube, had to be incorporated into the Roman army. From now on it was allowed, and in many cases preferred, for a levy of men to be commuted into a cash payment (*adaeratio*), because the Goths provided the actual men.

Individuals tried to escape military service in the late Roman Empire as well. Constantine ordained that the sons of veterans who had been mutilated to avoid military service should be compelled to undertake duties in the city senates; thus, they had to serve the state with liturgies rather than with weapons (*Cod. Theod.* 7.22.1; AD 319). This procedure was confirmed in the year 367, and extended to all self-mutilators (*Cod. Theod.* 7.13.4). A little later, however, it was decreed that those who mutilated themselves in order to avoid military service should be burned alive, while their *domini*, who failed to stop them, should also expect to be severely punished (*Cod. Theod.* 7.13.5; AD 368? 370? 373?).[1] Finally, a decree of 381 changed the procedure and compelled the self-mutilated to serve in the army nevertheless (*Cod. Theod.* 7.13.10). Provincials, moreover, were allowed to provide two mutilated recruits instead of one non-mutilated one.

It is uncertain to what extent consideration was given to the personal situation of recruits. The archive of Abinnaeus contains the petition of a man who asked that the only son of a widow either be spared military service or at least not be sent to a *comitatus*, that is, to a combat unit (P. Abinn. 19; AD 342–344). However, we do not know if the petition was successful.

In fact, scooping up fighting men was a tested means of preventing unruly or recently subjugated peoples from rebelling. This was one of the reasons that the Romans often demanded soldiers from ethnic groups they controlled. The names of numerous cohorts and cavalry units (*alae*) reflect the unit's original founding area; examples include the *cohortes* Asturum, Breucorum, Dalmatarum, Thracum, Vindelicorum, or the *alae* Hispanorum, Illyricorum, Ituraeorum, Noricorum, and Pannoniorum. In contrast to their names, the actual ethnic composition of these units soon changed, since men were recruited to fill the ranks from the area of the unit's camp, from the province in which the unit was stationed, from other provinces, and from the place from which the unit originally came. Units that practiced special fighting methods or types of riding were the exception to this rule: they preferred to recruit men who had been brought up with the necessary skills. Thus the Cohors I Aurelia Antoniniana milliaria Hemesenorum sagittaria equitata civium Romanorum, a partly mounted archery unit, while stationed in Lower Pannonia at Intercisa (c. AD 175 to the middle of the third century AD), preferred either to recruit men from the unit's Syrian homeland, or men brought up in the area of their camp.[2]

The conventional view, that local conscription became predominant only under Hadrian, can no longer be accepted. As K. Kraft has established, recruitment from the hinterland of the camp had slowly set in by the first half of the first century AD.[3] Recruits from Egypt were often sent to the fleets. Familiarity with the Nile, the life-giving river of Egypt, and the fact that Egyptians were not Roman citizens and could not seek the more exalted branches of service, may have had something to do with this preference. It seems to have become a tradition for Egyptians to serve in the fleet; there is evidence for Egyptian recruits in the navy up to the fourth century.[4]

Up to the era of Vespasian the Roman military employed, as support, contingents drawn from allied tribes (*sociae cohortes*), which fought for the Romans under their own native leadership. However, following the Batavian rebellion (AD 69/70), the use of ethnic units under their own leaders for the reinforcement of regular troops ceased.

In the Roman army the unfamiliarity of life in the camp, the grueling training, or a first encounter with the enemy saw some recruits drop away from their units. This behavior was regarded with some understanding: for such deserters, the short period of time in which they had been in the army, their status, and their inexperience in *disciplina militaris* would be taken into account (*Dig.* 49.16.3.9). Even in later periods, there was an inclination to pardon recruits who fled from their standards. According to the Theodosian Code (7.18.14.1; AD 403), runaway recruits of the last indiction were not to be punished:

> This condition, however, shall be observed, that the punishment shall not be inflicted in the case of those recruits who are being collected at the present time for the last indiction, because they must be restored by the provincials, within the time prescribed by law, to those standards for which they had been destined. In this way the landholders shall not suffer the loss of replacing those recruits who have fled from military service when they had scarcely been initiated into it.[5]

The age of recruits

The Roman army did not have a prescribed age of entrance. According to the *Historia Augusta*, the Emperor Hadrian, who regularly concerned himself with military affairs, formulated the age criteria in very general terms: "Furthermore, with regard to length of military service, he issued an order that no one should violate ancient usage by being in the service at an earlier age than his strength warranted, or at a more advanced one than common humanity permitted."[6]

To judge by existing epigraphic testimony, young men typically entered the army between the ages of 17 and 20.[7] Around 35 seems to have been the upper limit in periods when there were sufficient volunteers. In the imperial cavalry guard (*equites singulares Augusti*) in the third century AD, a tendency towards a younger entrance age can be observed. This is likely connected to the fact that in this period there was an increased need for mounted troops, and, since the use of a horse in battle required training lasting for years, it generally seemed advisable to begin this training as young as possible.

2   Veterans

Discharge and citizenship (civitas Romana)

The Romans used the term "veteran" (*veteranus*) for all soldiers who were honorably discharged after the end of their service. However, veterans as a social group are a result of changes within the Roman armed forces. The change from the citizen militia of the republican period, summoned as needed, to the standing army of the imperial period with its long periods of service, meant that the soldiers, who left the service at a more advanced age, had to be properly taken care of. As a retirement bonus each man who was honorably discharged received a piece of land (*missio agraria*) or was given a considerable cash payment (*missio nummaria*). On top of this, veterans could look forward to various remissions of the legal burdens of civilian life. In this respect an age-old concept was upheld: the soldier who dedicated his life to the *res publica* was, as compensation for his service to the community, allowed as a veteran to enjoy exemption from all remaining duties. Augustus regularized the land and cash payments to veterans in the year AD 5/6 at the latest, as part of the establishment of the military's own financial office (*aerarium militare*). He had already arranged, in 30 and 14 BC, for extensive land grants. In 13 BC, he introduced a staggered retirement bonus in the form of a payment along with the land assignment (*Res Gestae* 16–17; Cassius Dio 54.25.5).

At retirement, many soldiers had passed their fortieth birthdays, if not their fiftieth. Therefore, it is understandable that we read on the gravestone of one Christian veteran (*ILAlg.* 1, 2766; fourth century AD) that he had sacrificed his youth to military service. For some veterans military service formed only a relatively short period of their lives: the gravestone of L. Pomponius Felix informs us that he entered the army at 20, served 25 years, then lived a further 35 years afterwards. Even if these are rounded figures, Felix was granted a long life, of which he spent approximately one-third in military service.

The regular period of service for those who served in the fleet in the imperial age was 26 years (*stipendia*), or 28 in the last years of the reign of Septimius Severus. In the *auxilia*, men served 25 years; legionaries under Augustus served first 16, then 20, years. The praetorians under Augustus served 12, and afterwards 16, years. There was no formal legal right of discharge after the completion of the specified period of service. The observance of these periods of service was based solely on tradition (*consuetudo*) and humanity (*humanitas*). In addition, since discharges did not regularly take place, longer periods of service were common. Starting in the late first century AD, legionaries were generally expected to serve 25 years.

In the later period honorable discharge (*honesta missio*) was also granted after 20 years, but only soldiers who had completed 24 *stipendia* received the full privileges of veterans.[8]

Although it is customarily assumed that discharges occurred every year, there is a great deal of evidence that they took place only once every two years (e.g. *AE* 1973, 553). The conscious deferral of discharge relieved financial pressure. December, January, and February were militarily quiet, and were the preferred months for both discharge and the enrollment of new recruits (e.g. *CIL* 16 p. 143 no. 1; *CIL* 16 p. 146 no. 13 = PSI 9, 1026; P. Oxy. 1022 = Fink 87; *AE* 1980, 647; *AE* 1998, 1618–1619). Thus, there was time to execute the formalities, complete training, and acclimatize the troops to the soldier's life, before there was any likelihood of actual fighting. For units stationed in Rome, January first became the fixed date for discharge. After Elagabalus, at the latest, the imperial *constitutiones* of discharge for the imperial cavalry guard (*equites singulares Augusti*) were posted on the 7th of January.[9]

The granting of discharge was, ultimately, the prerogative of the emperor. He usually entrusted the discharge of soldiers stationed in the provinces to the governor. The emperor personally discharged soldiers serving in the provincial armies only in special cases, something that is to be seen as a particularly special mark of distinction. The proper discharge of a soldier, his release from the oath of allegiance and his retirement, must be imagined to have taken place in a festive ceremony before the collected troops, comparable to events such as taking the military oath or the granting of decorations to soldiers on active duty. The honorable discharge was mostly granted to those soldiers who had completed their regular service periods, but honorable discharges from military service were also allowed earlier, based on failing health (*missio causaria*). To prevent malingering, this form of retirement was only allowed after a careful examination of the case and with medical advice. On the other hand, a soldier discharged for reasons of health who subsequently recovered could not simply be taken back into military service. A decision of the emperor Gordian (*Cod. Iust.* 12.35.6) shows that even in periods of crisis, a man discharged by *missio causaria* could only be taken back into the service on the recommendation of at least two doctors and a competent magistrate (*iudex competens*). The years of service completed prior to discharge for medical reasons would be reattributed to a soldier upon his return.

A soldier who retired for reasons of health was not usually any worse off – in the long term – than other veterans. He received the rewards pertaining to veterans, as well as the land grant or cash bonus (*praemium militiae*). This changed under Caracalla: men discharged for medical reasons under him had to accept reductions. From this point on only soldiers discharged by *missio causaria* with 20 years of service and a flawless reputation could receive the full privileges of the veteran (*Cod. Iust.* 5.65.1; AD 213). The high number of years in service required was probably the consequence of a desire not to burden the imperial treasury (famously empty under Caracalla), and of a desire to prevent abuse. This stern rule was relaxed by Caracalla's successors. According to the jurist Modestinus, healthy soldiers who had completed at least five years of service before being discharged on the basis of injury were to be accorded privileges in relation to their length of service (*Dig.* 27.1.8.2–3): depending on the length of their military service, they were released from the duties of undertaking wardships or assuming public offices. When a soldier had served for five years, he was given an exemption for one year, after eight years, a two-year exemption, after 12 years a three-year exemption, and after 16 years, a four-year exemption. In contrast, veterans who had served for at least 20 years enjoyed a permanent exemption from wardships (*tutela*) of the children of civilians, but not of the children of soldiers. They could be compelled to undertake such wardships after a limited exemption period (*vacatio*) of one year.

Diocletian and Maximian also implemented laws demanding 20 years of service before all the privileges of retirement could be enjoyed. They decreed that only veterans who had served 20 years would be freed from all obligations, public offices, and personal liturgies (*onera, honores, munera personalia*) (*Cod. Iust.* 7.64.9; 10.55.2–3). Finally, Constantine the Great granted that soldiers who had to be discharged early as the result of a wound taken in battle should be, along with their wives, exempted from the poll tax (*capitatio*) (*AE* 1937, 232 = *FIRA* I^2 no. 94 l. 16ff.).

A graphic example of discharge on grounds of health in late antiquity is provided by the papyrus *ChLA* 43, 1248, according to which numerous soldiers had to be let go early on account of colic, poor health, or continuous illness (*colicus, debilis, aegrotus*). Only about half of the men discharged left the service after 27–35 *stipendia* as old men (*senex*). One soldier was honorably discharged as a *senex* after 20 years. He must have been abnormally old when recruited.[10] Overall, this document confirms the research of W. Scheidel. According to his calculations, given a norm of retirement after 25 *stipendia*, fewer than half of the soldiers in the imperial army will have completed the full term of service.[11]

Up to the time of Hadrian, auxiliary soldiers often served 30 years beneath the standards before they were given veteran status. The length of service of centurions knew no limits. The reason for this is related to the protracted length of time it took to reach the centurionate. One of the most remarkable attested spans of service is that of L. Maximius Gaetulicus: as the first centurion of the Legio I Italica in AD 184, he could already look back at 57 *stipendia* (*AE* 1985, 735). On the other hand, we know of cases in which soldiers were let go *ad diem* (on the exact day on which they were entitled to be discharged). Under Antoninus Pius, in AD 139 and after, the *equites singulares Augusti* obtained regular discharges after the expiration of a standard period of service of 25 years, a period that in earlier times had varied between 27 and 29 years.[12] As already mentioned, longer periods of service of up to 35 years are known in late antiquity (*ChLA* 43, 1248).

With their honorable discharge, Roman soldiers obtained discharge certificates, with which they could prove their honorable discharge and, above all, their claim to legal privileges. Discharges of the imperial period survive in the form of writing tablets and, rarely, in metal versions. These metal examples seem to be copies ordered by the veterans as private duplicates of their own discharge certificates: it seems that the recipients of discharge certificates sometimes wished to have their discharge vouched for in durable material, and in representative form. For the late period, the *Codex*

Theodosianus mentions written certification of the honorable discharge of veterans (*emeritae missionis epistulae*; *Cod. Theod.* 7.20.4; AD 325). We know that a veteran who wanted to settle in Egypt had to undergo the judicial examination called the *epikrisis*. In the course of the examination, he was required to prove that he was honorably retired from the army. In other provinces, veterans were surely also required to prove their status in order to settle in a particular place, not least in order to enjoy their promised privileges there. Corresponding documents were therefore a necessity, and of commensurate importance.

Soldiers who served in the auxiliary units or fleet after Claudius normally received Roman citizenship (*civitas Romana*) on their discharge. What motivated Claudius to take this step is unknown. Claudius probably felt that after decades of service to Rome such veterans were probably "better Romans" than many others, and for this reason it was only logical that they should receive citizenship. According to the scholarly *communis opinio*, citizenship was accorded to all honorably discharged soldiers. Yet, it is not to be assumed that this occurred in every single case. The granting of citizenship always remained in the gift of the emperor: although the emperor usually delegated discharge to the governor, it remained the prerogative of the ruling Augustus or Augusti. It was a gift the emperor could award, refuse, or change. And in special cases auxiliary soldiers in the imperial period received Roman citizenship as a reward before the completion of their service: thus, Trajan honored a unit of soldiers in Dacia with a grant of citizenship while it was still on the battlefield (*CIL* 16.160). This corresponded to old custom, since originally the award of citizenship was not a privilege of veterans, but a distinction for serving soldiers who had proven themselves heroic in battle.

Citizenship certificates made out in the name of the emperor, and which always began with his name, are called "military diplomas" (*diplomata militaria*) by modern scholars. They are official copies made for individual soldiers from imperial constitutions engraved on metal tablets (*tabulae aeneae* or *aereae*) posted in the city of Rome. Thanks to numerous new discoveries in recent years, some hundreds of these military diplomas on metal are known. The practice of issuing metal diplomas was only interrupted in times of emergency, as under Marcus Aurelius, a period of war and financial need, when there are indications that the practice was suspended. Perhaps the metal was needed more urgently for weapons production. The choice of durable materials for military diplomas should be explained not only by the desire to imitate the material of imperial constitutions posted in Rome: given that these citizenship certificates also had great significance for the descendants of veterans, it is understandable that veterans wanted certificates in a durable material.

The issuing of military diplomas to auxiliary soldiers ceased at the beginning of the third century AD. At the time of writing, the latest known diploma for an auxiliary soldier is dated to AD 203 (*RMD* 3.187). Clearly, even before the *constitutio Antoniniana* of AD 212 there were hardly any soldiers discharged from the *auxilia* who were not already Roman citizens. On the other hand, there may still have been interest, as before, in the right to contract a legal marriage (*conubium*) with peregrine women, as is sufficiently demonstrated by the military diplomas that continued to be given to the praetorians, to the imperial cavalry guard (*equites singulares*

Augusti), and to the sailors in the fleet. These are attested up to the middle of the third century, and again under the first and second tetrarchies. It is not clear how to explain the temporary disappearance of diplomas: perhaps for a period they were temporarily produced in non-durable materials and thus do not survive.[13]

Benefits and privileges

Retired soldiers, who were founding a new life at a advanced age, were endowed with substantial money and significant privileges.[14] In contrast to the reward of money or land (*praemium militiae*), the prerogatives and privileges granted to a veteran were called an *emeritum* (Suetonius, *Aug.* 24.2; *Dig.* 49.16.5.7; cf. 49.16.3.8). The bestowal of a whole series of privileges was, next to the reward of the *praemium militiae*, an important contribution to a soldier's construction of a civilian existence after military service. These privileges varied over time. Moreover, they were dependant on the number of years of service, on military rank, and on the soldier's branch of service. The legal exemptions accorded to a *veteranus* were not always permanent; more often they were valid only for a specified period. There were also privileges that were only granted to specific branches or ranks of soldiers. Thus, Vespasian granted retiring praetorians immunity from taxation for the land that they had received from him, and for any property they had owned up to the granting of this privilege (*CIL* 16.25). In the year AD 44, by order of Claudius, all soldiers were made the equals of married men, which improved the position of veterans: now a veteran enjoyed, along with his younger counterpart, the tax benefits of a married man (Cassius Dio 60.24.1). Admittedly, we do not know whether a veteran enjoyed this status in perpetuity, or whether he was obliged to marry within a certain period to keep it.

Veterans were freed from undertaking municipal duties (*munera personalia* and *mixta*) and civic offices (*Dig.* 49.18.2 and 49.18.5; *Cod. Theod.* 7.20.2), but not from local taxes (*vectigalia* and *munera patrimonii*; *Dig.* 49.18.2.4; 50.5.7). In this category another series of privileges made their lives easier. *Veterani* were bequeathed exemptions from tolls by Augustus, as were their nearest relatives; their wives, children, and parents. These rights were confirmed by the emperor Domitian (*CIL* 16 p. 146 no. 12 = *FIRA* I² 76 l. 15ff.) and by later emperors (*Cod. Theod.* 7.20.2 [AD 326]; 7.20.9 [AD 366]). Constantine the Great and his successors once again confirmed for veterans exemptions from taxes on trade (*Cod. Theod.* 7.20.2.4; 13.1.2 [AD 360]; 13.1.7 [AD 369]). In the year AD 385 this tax-exemption was limited to transactions of up to 15 *solidi* (*Cod. Theod.* 13,1,14; AD 385). The privileges vouchsafed to veterans comprised, essentially, freedom from taxes and obligations in the realms of *munera personalia* and *munera mixta*. The number of a veteran's relatives who participated in the privileges granted to a veteran was reduced over time, although the details are not known. At the latest, at some time in the third century AD a veteran's descendants no longer enjoyed immunity, or enjoyed it only conditionally. The *tabula Brigetionensis* differentiates exemptions from the poll tax (*capitatio*) according to the number of *stipendia* the veteran had completed (*AE* 1937, 232 = *FIRA* I² 94): after the fulfillment of the complete service period (*completis stipendiis legitimis*) five people were exempted, while – in contrast – with an honorable discharge after 20 years, or with a discharge on account of wounds, only two exemptions were granted, for the veteran and his wife. At the same time, this means that it was possible, as before and after, to take honorable discharge after 20 years, but that the number of years of service expected from a soldier was over 20. Consequently, it is also to be assumed that the granting of privileges differed from branch to branch. This is attested by a decree of Diocletian and Maximian, who refused an auxiliary soldier exemption from political offices and personal services (*honorum et munerum personalium vacatio*), since this was customarily granted only to men discharged prematurely but honorably from a *vexillatio* or *legio* after 20 years of service (*Cod. Iust.* 10.55.3).

On June 17, AD 325, Constantine made a new determination about veterans' immunities in relation to their status (*Cod. Theod.* 7.20.4). Henceforth a soldier who had served with the *comitatenses* or *ripenses* received freedom from the poll tax for himself and his wife after his full term of service. If he were honorably discharged after just 20 years of service, he received the exemption only for himself. This was a novelty for the *ripenses*. Up to then, they had received these privileges only after the completion of 24 years of service. All other veterans received only a single exemption from one *capitatio*. Soldiers let go for reasons of health from the *comitatenses* received a tax exemption for two persons (*capita*), while the war-invalids of the *ripenses* who had 15 to 23 *stipendia* at the time of their discharge received exemption only for themselves, and for one further person only after 24 years.

The economic situation of veterans

After Augustus, praetorians received a retirement bonus of 5,000 denarii, legionaries 3,000 denarii (Cassius Dio 55.23.1). Caracalla raised this in AD 215 for the praetorians, but by an unknown amount; for legionaries he increased the bonus to 5,000 (Cassius Dio 77.24.1). Higher ranks received correspondingly more. We do not know if, from what age, or in what amount auxiliaries received a retirement bonus. Possibly Claudius and his successors regarded the granting of Roman citizenship as a sufficient reward for auxiliary veterans, and therefore did not consider the granting of a donative. If a veteran were given an allotment of land, the value of the apportioned land must have at least compensated for a money award. The *missio agraria* (discharge on the land) up to the time of Hadrian mostly took the form of closed settlements of large groups of veterans in colonies, rather than man-by-man (*viritim*) grants. However, in the period after Hadrian the individual settlement of soldiers became the norm. It was preferred that veterans be settled in populated areas to strengthen the infrastructure (Tacitus, *Ann.* 14.27.2), or in areas that had belonged to the Roman Empire for only a short while. There were good reasons for settlement in newly won areas: war-hardened veterans could make a real contribution to the defense of their new homes in an emergency. Under some circumstances, settlement in a particular place was not well received by veterans. Sometimes there was loud discontent voiced about the poor quality of the soil (Tacitus, *Ann.* 1.17.3). Repeatedly veterans turned their backs on their new homes, and went back to where they had performed their military service (Tacitus, *Ann.* 14.27.2).

Amongst other such returns, in the Claudian period veterans of the Legio XV Apollinaris who had been settled in Savaria returned home to where their former unit was stationed, Carnuntum.[15]

An edict of Constantine, which set out new regulations for veteran bonuses, gives a glimpse into late-antique circumstances. A veteran wanting to undertake a business received 100 *folles* tax-free. If he preferred agriculture, he received a piece of land, a pair of oxen, 100 bushels (*modii*) of seed, 25 *folles* for purchases, and lifelong tax-exemption for his land (*Cod. Theod.* 7.20.3). In AD 364 Valentinian rescinded the monetary gift. Henceforth a former soldier from the bodyguard (*protector*) received two pairs of oxen, and 200 bushels (*modii*) of seed. All other soldiers, regardless of whether they were honorably discharged at the end of their term or let go for reasons of health, received a pair of oxen and 100 bushels (*modii*) of grain (*Cod. Theod.* 7.20.8).

If a veteran received a payment of more than 3,000 denarii and invested it at 6 percent annual interest, he could receive 300 denarii every year for 14 years, and so receive more than the minimum required for his existence. With yearly payments of 225 denarii, the sum would last 24 years and provide, de facto, for his entire old age.[16] On top of this, there were likely to be savings amassed during service, continuous income from rents and leases, and miscellaneous windfalls. Sometimes veterans or their families increased their fortunes through private loans of smaller amounts of money with interest.[17] Now and again, soldiers and veterans received large inheritances. These bequests came either from their own family or their comrades. C. Iulius Nepotianus enjoyed a respectable lifestyle, which, surely, military savings alone had not provided. He received 1,200 drachmae from the lease of a palm garden (P. Strasb. 3.336; AD 212/213). The legionary veteran L. Bellienus Gemellus should also be considered to have had an income outside the military. He acted as a moneylender in the middle of the second century AD, and as the owner of numerous lands and farming establishments in the region of Arsinoe.[18] Similarly, in the late second century AD, C. Iulius Apolinaris, a former soldier of the Cohors I Apamenorum, lived in his Egyptian hometown, *Karanis*, as a very wealthy landowner (*BGU* 1, 18 = *W.Chr.* 398; AD 69; *BGU* 1, 180 = *W.Chr.* 396; AD 172). He repeatedly appears as a guardian; he served as the tutor of his sister, of a Roman citizen possibly related to him, and of the sons of a veteran (*BGU* 1.168; 4.1032; 15.2461).

Veterans had a good basis for a profession, if they had learned a skill in the army that they could continue to use in civilian life. This includes particularly men who had specialized in crafts or technical and medical skills. The veteran who established himself as a ship-builder in Mainz, and thereby on the Rhine, probably learned his skills with his former unit that was garrisoned there, the Legio XXII Primigenia pia fidelis, and profitably exercised them as a civilian. In general, we have little evidence for the professional occupations of veterans apart from agriculture. We know, among others, of veterans who earned their living by acting as traders of various items, such as clothing- and sword-dealers (*vestiarius, negotiator gladiarius*), as shipbuilders (*naupegus*), and as a proprietor of an oil-press, a dyeing works, and probably of a brickworks.[19] It is unclear to what extent veterans who owned farms (*villae rusticae*), workshops, stores, and small businesses did the work themselves, or let others do the work. To be sure, veterans also had heavy burdens. Not only did they have to provide for their own daily needs and perhaps also for those of a family, but provisions for the new civilian life had to be acquired and, for the first time, a home had to be paid for. In the year AD 136 a former legionary from Karanis rented a house, perhaps with the intention of finding a property to purchase at leisure (*SB* 6.9636). On February 3, AD 154, the 47-year-old C. Iulius Niger, who had served in the Ala veterana Gallica, purchased a house and its yards for 800 drachmae. The date of purchase suggests that Niger had recently been discharged (P. Mich. 6.428).

Choice of place of retirement

The multi-cultural quality stamped on the Roman army is reflected in the places where the veterans retired. In Mainz (Mogontiacum, Germania Superior), we find retired soldiers stemming from Mediolanum, Placentia, Lucus, Vienna, Arelate, and Dertona (*CIL* 5.5747, 13.6882, 6885, 6912; *AE* 1995, 1167–1168). One Helvetian (*civis Helvetius*) spent his twilight years in the capital of Germania Superior (*CIL* 13.6985). The capitals of provinces elsewhere also attracted veterans. L. Baebius and his family, who came from Veleia in northern Italy, as well as the family of the (surely) Campanian veteran L. Poblicius (*CIL* 13.8286; *AE* 1979, 412), settled in Cologne (colonia Ara Agrippinensium), the capital of Lower Germany. L. Baebius had served in the area of the Ubii with the Legio XX, L. Poblicius with the Legio V alauda in Xanten. M. Valerius Celerinus, who was born in Astigi in Spain and served with the Legio X, also chose to stay in Cologne as a veteran, and enjoyed his retirement there with his wife (*CIL* 13.8283). Veterans of the Legio VII gemina, the only legion stationed in the province, established themselves in Tarraco, the *caput provinciae* of Hispania Citerior. In the second century, these included Q. Moneius Verecundus and C. Iulius Proculus, who were born in Narbo (*CIL* 14.1081, 14.1082). We do not know whether both learned to esteem the excellence of this metropolis on the sea during their service there in the office of the governor and had come to feel at home there, or whether they merely preferred a lively city life to the tranquility – monotony – of the country.

   Veterans who did not want to live out their retirement in the province where they had served preferred to return to their old homes, even if these in fact lay thousands of miles away. It used to be thought that discharged soldiers only seldom returned to their places or regions of birth, but recent finds of military diplomas from the Danube and Balkans show that auxiliary soldiers recruited outside the province where they were stationed returned home on a large scale, particularly to Thrace and Moesia.[20] Legionaries also returned to their homelands. In the year AD 170 a soldier from the Legio V Macedonica, who grew up in Troemis, the "Lagerdorf" (*canabae*) of this legion – later transferred to Dacia – returned to where he had grown up after 25 *stipendia* (*CIL* 3.7505). In a few cases, the choice of retirement spot can no longer be explained. We can only speculate as to what induced M. Aurelius Macenius, who was born in Cappadocia and served in Bonna (Lower Germany) with the Legio I Minervia, to retire to Novae (Lower Moesia) (*AE* 1987, 861).

Participation in society

Veterans constituted an important force for Romanization, particularly in the border provinces. Even if veterans did not form a large part of the population in many provinces, they differentiated themselves clearly from the normal population through their privileges, and especially, during the first and second centuries AD, by their Roman citizenship. In addition, they had greater wealth at their disposal than the majority of the local population in many places. Soldiers and veterans normally cultivated close friendships and close contact with each other, so that in at least some provinces we can speak of a distinct military society. Soldiers chiefly married the daughters of comrades, and married their own daughters to other soldiers. Above all, soldiers who were already Roman citizens could often only find Roman-citizen and thus lawful wives among the daughters of soldiers and veterans who had been granted Roman citizenship.

Accustomed to hard physical work, veterans mostly maintained country farms (*villae rusticae*), practiced a trade, or undertook a business. In contrast, they played only a very limited role in political events. This is even more surprising given that veterans from the time of Hadrian (since AD 119?) had been numbered among the *honestiores* of society, along with Roman senators, knights (*equites Romani*), and the elite of the communities (*decuriones*). As *honestiores*, veterans were thus also spared degrading forms of punishment (*Dig.* 49.18.1 and 49.18.3).

Many reasons for veterans' well-known lack of interest in political and administrative affairs can be suggested. Veterans were older, and possibly for this reason had little appetite for undertaking additional duties. No doubt, too many veterans lacked the mindset needed for a political life. Strikingly, significantly more former legionaries took an active part in municipal life than veterans who had served in auxiliary units. Clearly, legionaries, who were either born Roman citizens or who at some point had received citizenship (*civitas Romana*), found municipal institutions and Roman administration less foreign than their peregrine fellow-soldiers. Nonetheless, there must have been further reasons. Of the former legionaries who took part in civic life, many had risen to higher ranks in their earlier military service. This suggests that veterans who had been discharged as simple soldiers shunned the costs associated with the exercise of municipal offices, since the tax exemption (*immunitas*) extended to veterans did not cover the obligations resulting from municipal duties (*Dig.* 49.18.5; *Cod. Iust.* 10.44.1–2).

That means that the veteran who became a city councilor lost his immunity; which must mean that (if he took on this duty) he had negotiated a special arrangement with the community in advance. It was normal for municipal officials to pay an entrance fee (*summa legitima* or *summa honoraria*) for their positions. Apart from this, further expenditures on behalf of a city and its inhabitants were expected. The veterans of the legions could more easily meet these obligations than those of the auxiliaries. Furthermore, he who took on a municipal post could take only a limited interest in his own property. Moreover, typical former soldiers who, in contrast to the higher ranks, had not been entrusted with administrative responsibilities during their military service, may also have had doubts about the performance of administrative responsibilities. It may well also have had something to do with the fact that in cities whose existence bore a clear civilian imprint and in which a municipal upper crust was already extensive and established, the incorporation of veterans into political life was considered to be of little value. City councils (*ordo decurionum*) in cities founded as veteran colonies certainly seem to include few veterans or their descendants. That means that although when the colony was founded the original members of the *ordo* must have been mostly veterans, soon also civilians, perhaps administrators and crafts-men, who settled in the same spot, the descendants of freedmen, new citizens, and even peregrines all obtained access to the decurions' council. The sons of veterans also seem to have had little interest in municipal duties. At any rate, in the com-munities on the Rhine and Danube only around 1 percent of the sons or grandsons of veterans ascended to membership in the local council (*ordo decurionum*). Of those who did take part in municipal life, most were content simply to sit as *decuriones* in the council of the community.

In the first three centuries AD, according to the calculations of L. Mrozewicz, only some 5.8 percent of the known veterans in the Rhine and Danube provinces took an active part in municipal life.[21] The majority of these had served in the legions, about half of them as simple soldiers, the rest in higher ranks. The inscriptions, which evidence the municipal activities of veterans in the area, belong overwhelmingly to the period from Antoninus Pius to Severus Alexander. This observation aligns with the general high rate of inscription production, the general social dynamism, and the increasing urbanization of these regions at this time. Amongst those concerned with the welfare of their fellow citizens was C. Sertorius Tertullus, veteran of the Legio XVI who acted as the *curator civium Romanorum Mogontiaci* (*CIL* 5.5747). T. Florius Saturninus also took up political life in Mainz as a member of the city council (*ordo civium Romanorum Mogontiaci*) after he had finished his military service as a standard bearer (*signifer* Legionis XXII Primigeniae piae fidelis Alexandrianae) (*CIL* 13.6769).

Provinces other than those on the Rhine and Danube offer much the same pic-ture. In Egypt, veterans are only rarely seen amongst the municipal elite. Even in North Africa, one of the oldest provinces of the empire, veterans seem to have taken up honorable civic offices only hesitantly. However, offices of a religious character seem to have held interest for veterans. The respectable position of *flamen* seems to have been particularly esteemed, although admittedly the number of veterans in the entire count of *flamines* is very small. As might be expected, those who served as *flamines* after retirement were usually soldiers from the middle or higher ranks.

Veterans gladly participated in the religious life in their area as members of and donors to cult societies. Numerous monuments dedicated by veterans speak of their close connection to the Roman state gods, to the gods of eastern origin, to local deities, and to those gods fused with Roman gods and goddesses. Thus a certain C. Caesellius Vitalis, veteran of the Legio I Italica, at that time stationed in *Novae*, donated a larger-than-one-meter-high altar there to Iupiter Optimus Maximus and Iuno Regina (*AE* 1998, 1136). Veterans often thanked the gods that they had reached a fortunate retirement, or finally fulfilled vows made on enlistment into the army upon their return to civilian life.

The extent to which veterans integrated themselves into their social environment rested, finally, upon themselves, their health, and their willingness to make and maintain personal contacts, to participate in social and economic life, and to position themselves within that specific ethnic, cultural, and social milieu. This may well have been the chief reason why veterans preferred to return either to their childhood homelands, or the place where they had served. But even this offered scant protection against the hardships of growing old: the veteran C. Iulius Apolinaris (mentioned above), who returned to his homeland in retirement, reports in his own words that he was at the end of his life an old and lonely man, to whom it is unlikely that either family or friends remained (*BGU* 1.180 = *W.Chr.* 396, 22f.).

NOTES

1   The type of capital punishment and fact that the people sentenced to be burned have a master (*dominus*) indicates that they are serfs (*coloni*), since this type of capital punishment penalty was not extended to other people without further justification. – I would like to thank Philip Kiernan for the translation of this article into English, and Professors J. E. Lendon and E. A. Meyer for their kind review of the English version.
2   Kraft 1951, 60 and 176; Lőrincz 2001, 35–6 and 247–66.
3   Kraft 1951, 139.
4   Palme 2004, 113.
5   Translation: Pharr 1952, 178.
6   *HA, Hadr.* 10.8.
7   Scheidel 1992, 281–97.
8   Mann 2000, 153–61. For late antiquity see also *Cod. Iust.* 10.55.3; *AE* 1937, 232; *Cod. Theod.* 7.20.4.
9   Weiß 2004, 119.
10 Rea 1984, 79–88.
11 Scheidel 1996, esp. 121f. and table 3.13.
12 Speidel 1994, 30 table 12, 45–7 no. 11; Weiß 2004, 120.
13 Weiß 2002, 529–32.
14 See also Herz (in this volume).
15 Mann 1983, 32 and 58.
16 Wierschowski 1984, 89 with n. 305.
17 P. Oxy. 12.1471 (AD 81; 38 drachmae) *SB* 1.7 (AD 216; 72 drachmae; renter: a veteran or his son); *SB* 1.4370 (AD 229; 900 drachmae); *BGU* 7.1658 (AD 234; 160 drachmae; the renter is the son of a veteran); *BGU* 7.1657 (240 drachmae, wheat, barley, vegetable seeds; AD 231); P. Yale 1.60 (6/5 BC; 102 drachmae).
18 Hohlwein 1957, 69–91; Mitthof 2000, 393f.
19 *Vestiarius*: CIL 5.774; *negotiator gladiarius*: CIL 13.6677 + 13, 4 p. 107; *naupegus*: CIL 13.11861; owner of an oilpress: P. Fay. 91; a dye works: P. Osl. 3.139; for a brickworks: CIL 13.6458; Paret 1926, 67–70; Kuhnen 1994, 255–64.
20 Eck, MacDonald, and Pangerl 2004, 100.
21 Mrozewicz 1989, 65–80; Ardevan 1989, 81–90; Królczyk 1999, 165–70.

BIBLIOGRAPHY

Alföldy, G., B. Dobson, and W. Eck (eds.). 2000. *Kaiser, Heer und Gesellschaft in der Römischen Kaiserzeit. Gedenkschrift für Eric Birley.* Stuttgart.

Ardevan, R. 1989. "Veteranen und städtische Dekurionen im römischen Dakien," *Eos* 77: 81–90.

Eck, W., D. MacDonald, and A. Pangerl. 2004. "Neue Militärdiplome für Truppen in Britannia, Pannonia superior, Pannonia inferior sowie in Thracia," *REMA* 1: 63–101.

Hohlwein, N. 1957. "Le vétéran Lucius Bellienus Gemellus, gentleman-farmer au Fayoum," *Études de Papyrologie* 8: 69–91.

Kraft, K. 1951. *Zur Rekrutierung von Alen und Kohorten an Rhein und Donau.* Bern.

Królczyk, K. 1999. "Veteranen in den Donauprovinzen des römischen Kaiserreiches (1.–3. Jh. n. Chr.)," *Eos* 86: 165–70.

Kuhnen, H.-P. 1994. "Die Privatziegelei des Gaius Longinius Speratus in Großbottwar, Kreis Ludwigsburg. Handel und Wandel im römischen Südwestdeutschland," *Fundberichte Baden-Württemberg* 19: 255–64.

Lőrincz, B. 2001. *Die römischen Hilfstruppen in Pannonien während der Prinzipatszeit, Teil 1: Die Inschriften.* Vienna.

Mann, J. C. 1983. *Legionary Recruitment and Veteran Settlement during the Principate.* London.

——— 2000. "*Honesta Missio* from the legions," in Alföldy, Dobson, and Eck, 153–61.

Mitthof, F. 2000. "Soldaten und Veteranen in der Gesellschaft des römischen Ägypten (1.–2. Jh. n. Chr.)," in Alföldy, Dobson, and Eck, 377–405.

Mrozewicz, L. 1989. "Die Veteranen in den Munizipalräten an Rhein und Donau zur hohen Kaiserzeit (I.–III. Jh.)," *Eos* 77: 65–80.

Palme, R. 2004. "Die römische Armee von Diokletian bis Valentinian I.: Die papyrologische Evidenz," in Y. Le Bohec and C. Wolff (eds.), *L'armée romaine de Dioclétien à Valentinien Iᵉʳ. Actes du Congrès de Lyon (12–14 septembre 2002).* Lyon.

Paret, O. 1926. "Der Privatziegler G. Longinius von Großbottwar," *Germania* 10: 67–70.

Pharr, C. 1952. *The Theodosian Code and Novels and the Sirmondian Constitutions.* Princeton.

Rea, R. 1984. "A cavalryman's career, AD 384(?)–401," *ZPE* 56: 79–88.

Scheidel, W. 1992. "Inschriftenstatistik und die Frage des Rekrutierungsalters römischer Soldaten," *Chiron* 22: 281–97.

——— 1996. *Measuring Sex, Age and Death in the Roman Empire. Explorations in Ancient Demography.* Ann Arbor.

Speidel, M. P. 1994. *Die Denkmäler der Kaiserreiter. Equites singulares Augusti.* Cologne.

Weiß, P. 2002. "Ausgewählte neue Militärdiplome," *Chiron* 32: 529–32.

——— 2004. "Das erste Diplom für einen *eques singularis Augusti* von Antoninus Pius," *REMA* 1: 117–22.

Wierschowski, L. 1984. *Heer und Wirtschaft. Das römische Heer der Prinzipatszeit als Wirtschaftsfaktor.* Bonn.

CHAPTER TWENTY-FIVE

The Religions of the Armies

Oliver Stoll

1 Introduction

The phenomenon of an official Roman army religion is closely connected to the creation of a standing professional army under the first emperor Augustus. Service life in the militia armies of the republic was admittedly "framed" by cultic actions belonging to the sphere of state religion (like the *sacramentum*, the "service oath" of the soldiers, the commander's *auspicia*, the ritual of the army's *lustratio* with its sacrifices and processions, or the victorious magistrate's triumph in Rome). Yet it lacked the characteristics of the principate in terms of the regularity of cultic dates, prescribed by the calendar, or the synchronization and simultaneous celebration of cultic occasions, which now were bound to a great extent to the emperor cult as the core of state religion throughout the empire. Rituals had the function of creating, consolidating, and demonstrating loyalty to the supreme, imperial commander – the emperor cult being the hub of political integration covering the entire empire – while simultaneously promoting discipline and the emergence of a corporate identity within each regiment and the professional army as a whole. Rituals served to strengthen and to display power.

Notwithstanding the character, at first glance, of the army (*exercitus*) as one unified military body belonging to the emperor (see "*exercitus meus*" in *Res Gestae* 30), the plural "religions of the armies" is well justified: Below the level of the "homogenized" official army religion, the provincial armies (*exercitus Britannicus, e. Germanicus, e. Syriacus*, etc.), because of their close cohabitation with the civilian population in the garrison-provinces, developed a unique and unmistakable religious characteristic of their own, determined to a great extent by the native cults of the provincials. The focal points of these cultural contacts were individual garrisons and places of deployment, where the military and the population entered into complex relationships not restricted to the area of the cults. Here the sources occasionally speak of *exercitus* as well, the *exercitus Aquileiensis* or the *exercitus Alexandrinus* for example, pertaining to the garrison of the respective city (*CIL* 5.899).

2   The Religion of the Army: A Complex "System"

The religion of the Roman army is a complex structure, mainly consisting of two components. Firstly, the regulated official army religion, comprising the emperor cult, identical throughout the empire and obligatory for all regiments, and the cult of the state gods. Secondly, the private cults of the soldiers ("native" gods from the area of recruitment or deities from the former site of deployment, as well as, most prominently, local gods at the current site of the garrison), practiced by groups or individual servicemen out of a fundamental longing for protection. Broadly speaking (!), collective dedications are characteristic of the first level, reflecting collective performances of regiments or groups. Individual dedications are to be regarded primarily as expressions of private religious life. Resting as it does upon epigraphic evidence, i.e. certain formulae and, in some cases, archaeological criteria (locations of finds), this auxiliary system of distinction is frequently blurred. Hence, in analyzing and evaluating cults recorded epigraphically, their significance for soldiers, groups, regiments, or the army as a whole has to be enquired into.[1] Does a certain piece of evidence pertain to a private religious need, or is it testimony of an obligation of service duty and of prescribed rituals of state religion and emperor cult?

Due to the mobility peculiar to their profession, soldiers and regiments are "culture bearers," "transporting" and transplanting not only material cultural items, but also cults themselves. The army is considered the principal agent of processes of acculturation. Beside processes of transfer, those of integration are discernible in the field of private religion. The gods at unfamiliar or new places of deployment are identical with those of the local provincial population. Due to the practice of local recruitment, congruence is frequently a given fact anyway, for, since the end of massive relocations of troops from the beginning of the second century onward, there is an ever-increasing tendency to replenish outfits from within the border provinces, from regional areas, or from the immediate vicinity of the military sites themselves. Nevertheless Roman regiments tend to retain their mixed tribal and national character. An influx of recruits from distant areas was, in certain situations, always a possibility (PSI 9.1063: recruits from Asia Minor for an Egyptian cohort). The "congruence" of soldiers recruited locally and the civilian population explains the high degree of cultural compatibility. Therefore, an analysis of religious conditions at the site of deployment in a local and regional context is helpful. Regarding these fundamental phenomena, no significant differences between service branches (legions, auxiliaries, fleet units) apply.[2]

Possibilities of contact between the military and the civilian population provided by both levels of religion are manifold, not the least because the emperor cult was a concern of the population as a whole. A special case within this system are cultic phenomena peculiar to the military, like the veneration of certain *genii*, tutelary deities, or the so-called flag cult, which has to be considered as closely connected to the emperor cult.

3   The Official Army Religion and Cults Specific to the Military

The essence of the official army religion, identical for every regiment of the empire from Britain and Germany to the Sahara and the Euphrates, was made clear in a papyrus found at the Mesopotamian garrison city of Dura Europos. This so-called "*Feriale Duranum*" (P. Dura 54 = Fink 1971: 422–29, no. 117) contains the January–September section of the festival calendar from the regimental archive of the Cohors XX Palmyrenorum. The papyrus, dating from the period between 225 and 227 AD, in the reign of emperor Severus Alexander, is a copy of an official standard list, universally valid, giving dates and occasions of festival days and stating what cultic actions and sacrifices (wine and incense = *supplicatio*, blood sacrifices = *immolatio*) had to be performed by the unit and its commander, for instance: "9 June: On occasion of the Vestalia for Vesta mater, one *supplicatio*" (Fink 1971: 425 no. 117 col. II l. 15).

Three different kinds of festive occasions can be distinguished, namely festivals of the state gods (e.g. of Mars Pater, Vestalia, or the *dies natalis urbis Romae*, the "birthday" of Rome), festivals specific to the military (like *rosaliae signorum* and *honesta missio*, the ceremony of honorable discharge), and celebrations of the emperor cult, i.e. dates pertaining to the incumbent emperor, such as his birthday (*dies natalis*), the day of his taking power (*dies imperii*) or dynastically relevant dates of the deified predecessors.[3] Due to the date of the document, the Severans and Antonines are especially prominent, but the birthdays of Caesar, Augustus, and that of Germanicus, the adoptive son of Tiberius, are mentioned no less than the day of Trajan's accession. The significance of the emperor cult was paramount. Of the 41 entries, 27 bear reference to it. Shaped and determined by the emperor cult, official army religion provided a solid cultic frame of reference for military life. The sacrificial calendar "politicized" the annual cycle through ritualized symbolic interaction between emperor and army. Its main function was to strengthen the army's loyalty and to create an "imperial consciousness," borne by the army religion, engendering a close relationship between the soldiers and their emperor.

The celebration of festivals, rituals, and ceremonies such as parades had the additional effect of strengthening discipline (Vegetius 3.4.3), which was considered, like religiosity itself, to be the secret behind Roman mastery of the world (Vegetius 1.1.2). Its guarantor was the emperor, regarding himself as *curator* or *conditor disciplinae* (Pliny, *Pan.* 6.2). The existence of a cult of the goddess "Disciplina" in Britain and North Africa (*RIB* 2092; *ILS* 3810), and its direct reference to the imperial dynasty as "Disciplina Augusti," is no coincidence. Notwithstanding the origin of the *Matres Campestres* in Celtic-Germanic religion (*ILS* 2417; *RIB* 2135), the cult of the *Campestres*, the motherly deities being worshipped near the parade ground (*campus*) especially among cavalry units (*CIL* 13.6449), belongs to this "Roman" context of a connection between religion and *disciplina* as well. The *Campestres* became members of that circle of 20 deities of diverse origins, which the *Equites Singulares Augusti*, the horse-guard of

Plate 25.1 Scene from the Bridgeness distance slab (*RIB* 2139, Antonine Wall) depicting a ritual of the official army religion (*suovetaurilia*). The commanding officer is sacrificing on an altar in the presence of the *vexillum* of Legio II Augusta. The Trustees of the National Museums of Scotland

the emperors, worshipped collectively from what is best described as "regimental tradition" (*CIL* 6.31139–46, 6.31148–49). Their reinterpretation and syncretistic "appropriation," even their transfer to the center of power, Rome itself, exemplifies the scope of the role the military played in processes of transfer. The example shows furthermore the proclivity of foreign cults, in some cases, of taking after the "official army religion proper," in terms of significance and circle of dedicators, to a point where both are hardly distinguishable. By the same token, the emperor's horse guard, heirs to a "Germanic tradition," were the agents of the wide diffusion of Celtic Epona and the *Matres Suleviae*, who originated from the Germanic Rhine.[4]

The stock of the official festival calendar dates back to the Julio-Claudian dynasty. Inscriptions from the military provinces giving the exact dates of their dedications, which correlate with those prescribed in the *Feriale Duranum*, indicate that this calendar, updated by every government and managed centrally, is binding for all regiments and in operation throughout the empire: Rome's birthday on April 21 is celebrated in High Rochester (*RIB* 1270) and Novae (*AE* 1975, 755) no less than in Dura Europos. The date of the dedication of a bronze genius "in honour of the imperial house" in Niederbieber in Upper Germany on September 23, 246 AD (*CIL* 13.7754) is not coincidental, since it is the date of the first emperor's, Augustus', birthday as handed down by the *Feriale*. The army calendar does not heed ethno-religious conditions within the regiments or circumstances peculiar to the province where troops are deployed. Being, in a way, the bearer of a tradition of imperial unity as *exercitus populi Romani*, the army contributed to the diffusion of concepts that were Italic or Roman (i.e. from the city of Rome) in origin, by the observation of typically Roman festivals like the Vestalia or Saturnalia. Although the army calendar does not fulfil a decided purpose of "Romanization," it does have an effect toward an emerging "identity." It does not touch, however, upon religious traditions of individual soldiers or "regimental traditions" stemming from the original area of recruitment that might have established themselves in units with a certain degree of ethnic homogeneity at the time of their creation. These belong to a different level of the religion of the army and, in order to strengthen battle morale, were actively encouraged by commanders.[5]

Many details of military life illustrate the close relationship between emperor and army[6] as manifested by the army calendar. First and foremost, mention has to be made of the oath of allegiance to the emperor, taken in front of the regimental colors, that was binding by religious law (Vegetius 2.5; Herodian 8.74), and that had to be formally dissolved in a solemn ceremony upon discharge (*sacramentum solvere* – PSI 1026, *Dig.* 49.18.2). Next is the endowment with the regimental colors through the emperor, the imperial names within the titles of regiments, the ubiquity of the emperor's image on the equipment and flags or crowning a standard of its own, the emperor's *imago* carried by an *imaginifer*. Not least, one has to think of the emperor's image on everyday currency, transmitted to servicemen by regular payment or by way of donative, a gift of the emperor that was made a solemn ritual. Donatives were frequently occasioned by festivals pertaining to the emperor, like his birthday or a "jubilee" (Tertullianus, *Cor.* 1.1–3). As the soldiers saw it, "their money" came from the emperor anyway ("elaba . . . para Kaisaros": *BGU* 423, second century).

Plate 25.2   Bronze Genius from Niederbieber in Upper Germany, dedicated "in honor of the imperial house" on September 23, 246 AD (*CIL* XIII 7754) by some NCOs of the Niederbieber garrison. Universität zu Köln, Archäologisches Institut, Forschungsarchiv für Antike Plastik

The emperor cult provided a link between the provincial population and the military. Joint performances are demonstrable, for example in the *nuncupatio votorum* (on January 3 and the respective emperor's *dies imperii*) or in the emperor's birthday. The younger Pliny, in his letters to the emperor Trajan from Pontus-Bithynia, never fails to report due execution of the oaths of allegiance by the military *and* the provincials under his jurisdiction (Pliny, *Epist.* 10.52f., 100f., 102f.). Similar proceedings are recorded in a papyrus (Mitteis, *Chr.* I 2: 59–66 no. 41) referring to the celebrations of the birthday of Severus Alexander on October 1, 232 in Syene/Aswan. It lists joint *vota*, solemn parades of the garrison cohort, and banquets. In the fourth century, Ammian emphasizes the boisterousness of these joint celebrations (Ammianus Marc. 22.12.6). In this case, the soldiers are so outrageously drunk "that they had to be carried from the public buildings where the feast had been taking place to their quarters by passers-by." Even in the military camps themselves, the celebrations were accompanied by banquets and substantial consumption of alcohol (*Tab. Vindol.* 1 4, ll 27ff. – festival of Fors Fortuna). Joint participation in cultic acts of state religion was painstakingly recorded, as witnessed by the letters of Pliny and the replies made by Trajan. There was no fundamental difference between the calendar of the military and that of the civilians, although the soldiers might have been involved more thoroughly in the succession of rituals due to the obligations of their service. Urban administrative and garrison sites, with military and civilian society living closely together in one place, were especially suitable for joint execution of the essential components of festivals. Classifying the Roman army as a "total institution" is as inappropriate here as it is in other respects.[7] Garrison towns were "nota et familiaria castra" to the soldiers, long-known and well-familiar "home" garrisons, with a close cohabitation between *provinciales* and *milites* (Tacitus, *Hist.* 2.80.3). They were the focal points of a contact the effects of which were manifold in a number of sectors, among them that of religion.

A peculiar characteristic of the Roman army is the immense symbolic importance of the *signa*, the ensigns:[8] Standards and flags played an outstanding role in both the everyday and the cultic lives of the troops. They were omnipresent at all rituals – the service oath was taken before them, sacrifices were made in their presence, and parades were led by them. The *signa* were symbols of the regimental spirit and fulcra of regimental pride. The standards bore on their shafts the name of the regiment and the decorations it had been awarded by the emperor in the course of its service. The *vexilla*, resembling modern standards, examples of which are known to have been the flags of entire units, bore the unit's name on the cloth. The mention, in inscriptions, of *victoria legionis* (the legion's victoriousness), *honos* (honor), and *virtus legionis* (valor or virtue of the legion) in a context pertaining to the "flag cult," is not accidental (*CIL* 13.6749, *CIL* 3.7591). The exploits of the regiment's history were handed down as models for emulation, as can be seen in the Legio XIV Martia Victrix, which was regarded as the "conqueror of Britain" and considered itself invincible (Tacitus, *Hist.* 2.11.1; 5.16.3). The battle honors of the Legio III Gallica, deployed in Syria until the fourth century, even went back as far as the late republic (Tacitus, *Hist.* 3.24.2)!

Nevertheless, it is an exaggeration to say that "religio Romanorum tota castrensis signa veneratur . . ." (Tertullianus, *Apol.* 16.8 and *Ad nat.* 1.12), that the religion of the camps was limited to the worship of the *signa*, which enjoyed pre-eminence over all other gods. That contention was made by Christian and Jewish authors who objected to the idolatry, the icon-worship (Tertullianus, *Idol.* 17f.) taking place in army religion, before the representations of the emperor and the gods that were, as *imagines*, affixed to the *signa* themselves. The so-called "martyr acts" of Christian soldiers are often underrated in their value as sources for this, as well as for the rituals of army religion. The birthday of the flags, the day of conferment by the emperor (Tacitus, *Ann.* 1.42.3) was simultaneously that of the regiment, and was solemnly celebrated. This is hinted at by dedications *ob diem natale aquilae* (*ILS* 2293, *AE* 1967, 229). The "eagle" (*aquila*) was the "most outstanding symbol of the legion" (Vegetius 2.6.2). Further examples are dedications "for the honor of the eagle" of the Legio XXII Primigenia, stationed in Mainz (*CIL* 13.6679, 6690). From Spanish auxiliaries we know of dedications *ob natalem aprunculorum*, "on occasion of the birthday of the boars," or *ob natalem signorum* (*ILS* 9127, 9129), since auxiliaries possessed *signa* of their own, "boar standards" in this case.

In the context of the veneration of the eagle and the standards, the *primipilus*, or top-most centurion of a legion, makes a frequent appearance (*AE* 1935, 98; *CIL* 13.6679, 6694). Vegetius (2.6.2; 2.8.1) lists the "sacral duties" concomitant with this position: supervision of the legion's eagle and keeping of the emperor's images. The eagle was regarded as the symbol of the primipilate (Pliny, *Nat.* 14.9; Artem. 2.20). *Primipili* would (and did) die to spare their legion the disgrace of its loss (Tacitus, *Hist.* 3.22.4), for that meant the end of the regiment. Their cultic activity had more to do with the religious life of their own regiments and regimental traditions than with the discharge of duties conferred upon them by official army religion. Hence inscriptions by soldiers of this rank do not belong unambiguously to either of the two main categories of the religion of the Roman army. On the one hand, the addressees of the dedications do not number among the "state gods." On the other, they are closely related to cults of this nature since they share with these the circle of their dedicators, the purpose of evoking group identity or shared tradition, and the use of formulae referring to the emperor cult. The monuments are often dedicated in a ceremony performed by the legate, the governor, or both, resembling even more the customs of official army religion, of which such official cultic proceedings were a conspicuous characteristic (*CIL* 3.11082). The dedications of the *primipili* are expressions of the *ésprit de corps* manifesting itself in the army religion as well: Roman units had an "unmistakable personality of their own."

Another kind of principal "coat of arms" the regiments bore were the so-called animal-emblems. The exact meaning of symbols such as Capricorn, Pegasus, the boar, or the ram, is not clear. They are displayed on the *signa* or on standards of their own referring to the unit as a whole. Their heraldic significance is illustrated by the fact that pieces of a unit's equipment, primarily helmets, cuirasses, and shields, were adorned with them (e.g. the bull of the Legio VIII Augusta on a bronze shield boss from the River Tyne – *RIB* 2426,1), as were building inscriptions, brick stamps, and donative and funerary inscriptions. Their use on the "legion coins" of third-century imperial coinage, where an animal symbol and the name of the legion appear together on the reverse (*RIC* V2 468 no. 57–59 – Legio II Augusta/Capricorn)

Plate 25.3a   Grave monument of Cn. Musius, *aquilifer* (eagle-bearer) of Legio XIIII
Gemina (*CIL* XIII 6901, Mainz), early 1st century AD: Musius is depicted in parade-uniform,
with his military decorations, presenting the *aquila* of his legion. Landesmuseum, Mainz

Plate 25.3b Monument of Q. Luccius Faustus, soldier of the Legio XIIII Gemina Martia Victrix (*CIL* XIII 6898, Mainz), ca. 70–80 AD: Faustus is depicted as a *signifer*. The shaft of his standard shows among other common decorations the individual animal-emblem of the legion, in this case a capricorn on a globe. Landesmuseum, Mainz

implies a knowledge of their meaning on the part of the public. Equally in the third century, the garrison towns of the Near East applied the "regimental arms" of their garrisons to the reverses of their local coinage (Zeugma: Capricorn of the Legio IIII Scythica; Rhesaena: Centaur of the III Parthica), usually in combination with the city god and the respective principal sanctuaries. The legions and their symbols evolve into "new city patrons" beside the traditional city gods. The union of the symbols expresses *concordia*, a basically sound relationship between garrison and civilian society. The most eloquent manifestation of this is the third-century Bostra coinage, where, on the reverses, the Legio III Cyrenaica's god, Zeus Ammon-Sarapis, shakes hands with the city's Tyche. The legend of the representation is *concordia Bostrenorum*.[9] In inscriptions, cities occasionally define themselves through "their" garrison or, conversely, military units through "their garrison town." The garrison of Dura Europos terms itself "*Europaioi*," while the town councillors call their own city "holy garrison of the *Europaioi*" (*AE* 1933, 223; *AE* 1984, 921).

Like the colors of uniforms, shield covers, and other equipment, these "arms" contributed to the individuality of the units. They furthered regimental consciousness and morale. The logical consequence is the *aemulatio virtutis*, the competition for honor and valor and the regimental pride thence derived (Ammianus Marc. 29.6.13). Obviously, the "corporate rites" of official army religion have to be placed within this framework of constituting regimental "corporate identities" as well. Battle morale, *disciplina*, and cultic structuring of military life belong together, as shown by an analysis of the sources considering the roles of the commanders. Their occupation with army religion expresses consciousness of their social role as well as being an obligation of duty and a demonstration of loyalty. Since military office was not distinguished from the duty of acting as a "priest," the person of the officer was representing his unit as "bearer" of the emperor cult and state religion (*necessitas immolationum* – Tertullianus, *Idol.* 19.1). He was responsible for executing the required actions while it sufficed simply for the troops to be present.

The ceremonies of the official army religion are reflected in collective inscriptions, like dedications to the gods or homage to the emperor in the form of statues, dedicated jointly by a regiment (*AE* 1991, 1573 – Syria; *CIL* 13.6531 – Upper Germania), a group of soldiers holding the same rank (*IGLSyr.* XIII 9051), or veterans having been discharged in the same year (*AE* 1955, 238). The latter monuments were oversized bronze statues of the cuirassed emperor. The occasional mention of the governor or commander ("dedicante": *CIL* 8.18067) hints at a formal consecration ceremony for the monuments otherwise dedicated by the unit itself, an act which is mirrored by the dedication of similar monuments in city fora. Roman literature tends to liken military camps to cities in any case. Both the military and the civilian honorary statues signify collective loyalty to emperor and state, frequently emphasized by formulae of consecration and devotion (e.g. "pro salute (imperatoris)," "devota numini maiestatique eius": *AE* 1986, 529; *CIL* 13.7495).

Further to be named among collective regimental dedications are those to gods which mention the commander and the regiment. For example we know of larger series of altars to the highest state god Iuppiter Optimus Maximus from second- and third-century Maryport (*RIB* 814–835) or Bölcske. These give either the regiment and the commander concerned ("cui praeest" – *RIB* 817, 823, 830), or just the commander (usually with "his" regiment appended in the genitive – *RIB* 824, 829) as dedicators. The celebration of an annual routine ritual is indirectly hinted at by officer's names recurring several times within one series. The probable occasion for the dedications is the *nuncupatio votorum* of the army calendar (a vow for the well-being of the emperor, the stability of the state, and the renewal of the service oath) on January 3 each year. The locations where some of the stones were discovered make it possible that the ceremonies took place near the parade grounds, or in special cultic areas near the military camps.

The cult of certain *genii* particular to the military contributed to the soldiers' morale and their cohesiveness as a group. This extends to administrative or tactical sub-divisions, occupations and ranks below the regimental level.[10] Evidence for this is abundant (e.g. *Genius armamentarii* – *AE* 1978, 707; *G. Signiferorum* – *AE* 1958, 303). An intact social environment, which is equally visible in funerary inscriptions documenting a "comradeship," is shown especially by the popular *Genius centuriae* or *G. Turmae* (*CIL* 3.6576 – Egypt; *CIL* 13.7494a–d – Upper Germany). Although not occupying the level of official army religion, these cults serve essentially the same purpose. This is made clear by their pertinence to the group and by instances of a *Genius signorum* (*RIB* 1262) or the genius of a unit as a whole (*Genius legionis*: *RIB* 327; *Genius cohortis*: *CIL* 3.5935; *Genius alae*: *RIB* 1334) or even that of an *exercitus* (*ILS* 2011, 2216 – Rome) being invoked. It makes sense to distinguish these from the actual private cults, although the scope of dedicators is large and ranges from individual private soldiers and high-ranking officers to groups (*AE* 1926, 69; *ILS* 2292). Conversely, evidence exists for "group dedications" made by regiments or their subdivisions in observing private cults like that of Iuppiter Dolichenus (*AE* 1998, 1156; *CIL* 13.11780). These even imitate official formulae of "regimental dedications" (unit and commander with *cui praeest*: *CIL* 13. 11782). These instances confirm the significance, value, and effectiveness of those collective identities that had been created on the official level. Cultic acts of "private religion" are evidently modeled upon "official cultic acts," even down to formal criteria. Evolving relatively late, especially at the beginning of the third century, the military *collegia* probably had the function of fortifying these group identities, although at first glance their purpose was to provide for basic social necessities (material welfare, ensuring an honorable funeral etc.). Religious proceedings like dedications to a genius (*Genius scholae*: *ILS* 2376) went on as a matter of course, frequently in close association with the emperor cult (*CIL* 3.2554, 2555).

The bond thus tied endured. Veterans tended to remain at their former place of service or in the province where their social and economic contacts had grown. Perpetuating the social forms of military life, the veteran associations of certain regiments (*CIL* 8.3284: Collegium veteranorum legionis III Augustae, Lambaesis) are found in those border provinces where the units had been deployed for a longer spell of duty. Here survive collective inscriptions by veterans, dedicated together with civilians on what was evidently an annual footing (*AE* 1924, 144–146: 175–177 AD), probably on occasion of the joint *nuncupatio votorum* for the well-being of the emperor (*AE* 1980, 779–781; *AE* 1924, 142–146). In an inscription from Durostorum,

Plate 25.4 Second-century altar from Maryport (*RIB* 817): The monument is dedicated to Iupiter Optimus Maximus by a regiment of Spaniards (Cohors I Hispanorum) while a certain C. Caballius Priscus was its commander. The tribune will also have supervised the religious routine ritual and the (later) following setting up of the altar. Senhouse Museum, Maryport

veterans, active soldiers, and Roman citizens appear together as dedicators (*AE* 1974, 570). These inscriptions, which have to date not been investigated systematically, offer insights into the processes of integration and the role of the veterans as "mediators." Some hold the highest sacral offices, like the veteran of a cavalry unit who became *flamen coloniae perpetuus* in Djemila (*AE* 1915, 69). It goes without saying that close ties and contacts existed in the broadest possible sense (see Tacitus, *Hist.* 4.65.2). Veteran families were an integral part of the social structure at garrison sites.

In cultic practice, civilian cults of cities and landscapes adopted components of the state cult and the emperor cult, like formulae, cult names, and pictorial representations. An example of the influence of the military is a third-century cultic relief of Atargatis/Hadad from Dura Europos, which shows between the two deities the "semeion," a cult standard as portrayed by Lucian in his description of the temple of Atargatis in Hierapolis. Lucian calls this *semeion xoanon chryseon* ("gilt wooden image"), that "has no character of its own, but bears the qualities of the other gods" (Lucian, *de dea Syria* 33). But here, on the Dura relief, the *semeion* emulates the appearance of military standards. Similar examples are triangular standard finials of the cult of Iuppiter Dolichenus like those from Iasen and Mauer a.d. Url, depicting cult standards the appearance of which reflect military standards. After his absorption into the Roman cultural sphere, Dolichenus wears the imperial officer's armor and the eagle-hilted sword. A similar change in the representations of local gods can be observed with "armed" gods of the Near East, like Iarhibol and Malakbel in Syria, and the gods of Egypt, like the hawk god Horus, Harpocrates or jackal-headed Anubis, all of whom appear, during the principate, in Roman arms and armor, owing to the influence of their worshippers in the military.

4   The Private Cults in the Religion of the Roman Army

Local cults at the place of deployment

When off duty, soldiers were free to observe any cult conceivable as long as it did not conflict with "public law and order" or keep them from fulfilling the obligations of their service.[11] Sometimes far distant from home or place of birth, through military service they became acquainted with a broad spectrum of religious ideas. The local gods of the province or area of deployment demanded their attention and offered protection: as a possible consequence, their attachment to the new social environment, including the civilian population, became more intense. Every single provincial army and every garrisoned site acquired, through contacts with the provincial population and processes of integration, a specific character. These differences call for a regional and local point of view and make possible the identification of "religious profiles" of soldiers of different regiments.

A good example of this phenomenon, but insufficiently researched as yet, are the soldiers of the Rhine legions. The men of the Legio I Minervia at Bonn were enthusiastic followers of the cult of local motherly deities, the "matrons," in particular of

Plate 25.5 Bronze statuette of the Egyptian falcon-headed god Horus (London, British Museum, *EA* 36062): The god is clad in "roman" uniform, wearing the officer's cuirass and high military boots, reflecting the influence of his worshippers in the military. © Copyright the Trustees of The British Museum

the Matronae Aufaniae. One-third of the dedications this legion's soldiers made refer to this cult, while there is virtually no evidence for worship of the matrons among the legions of Upper Germany. In some individual cases this local cult of the Aufaniae was "transported" along the Rhine *limes* by soldiers of said legion. The cults of the regional civilian population, whence came many of the soldiers, are responsible for the contrasting behavior of the two adjacent army groups, and individual legions: the soldiers turned to local gods, which were those of the civilian population as well.

Even the sacrificial ceremonies of Roman magistrates, save those regular performances of state religion and emperor cult, differed according to province. The prefect of Egypt for instance, acting for the "imperial Pharaoh," had to present the Nile with a sacrifice of bullion receptacles at Philae (Seneca, *Nat.* 4.2.7), regularly, officially, and in accordance with tradition. Naturally, high-ranking Roman magistrates or officers would turn to local cultic traditions in private as well, as the altar of a praetorian prefect to the Germanic war goddess Dea Vagdavercustis in Cologne (*ILS* 9000: 164–167 AD) shows.

A dedication from Gerasa (Speidel 1994: 57f no. 22) shows how urgent the need for protection was among the soldiers in their new, unfamiliar surroundings: The altar, dedicated by a detachment of Emperor Hadrian's mounted escort, is consecrated to Deania Augusta, being the principal goddess of the city, Artemis of Gerasa. The Equites Singulares spent only a brief interval there in the winter of 129/130 AD. The inscription must have been conceived about the time of arrival of the emperor and his escort (". . . qui hibernati sunt . . ."). Tutelage of a local deity was immediately sought after. Two dedications from Hatra testify to similar cases. The tribune of a unit having garrisoned the caravan city only for a short spell under Emperor Gordian III (238–240/41 AD) without delay paid homage to the local sun god Schamasch styled Sol Invictus (*AE* 1958, 239: "religio loci"), the main god of Hatra, and to Hercules Sanctus, who is identical with the local tutelary god Nergal. The latter was even adopted as the regiment's patron deity (*AE* 1958, 240: "Genius cohortis").

This phenomenon can be observed in every military site throughout the empire. The locally established Dea Coventina of the Britannic Carrawburgh, venerated as tutelary goddess by the Cohors I Cugernorum (*RIB* 1524: "dea . . . cohortis") originally recruited among Germanic Cugerni, had a strong influence on other units deployed there as well. In Benwell, on Hadrian's Wall, the Cohors I Vangionum recruited in the Worms area collectively worshipped the local god Antenociticus (*RIB* 1328). A wealth of sources is available for Egypt. Local deities were invoked as tutelary gods in "proskynemata," praying formulae set at the beginning of a letter for the addressee, e.g. in the ostraca from Mons Claudianus (O. Claud. II 225). Similar "proskynemata" have been found on the walls of Egyptian temples with a Roman garrison nearby (e.g. *SB* 1018, 1020, 1332; *IGR* I 1278): the graffiti-like inscriptions assure the writer, relatives, and fellow soldiers of the respective god's protection. Similar invocations survive in the correspondence between soldiers, written on papyrus, either of a local god, like Isis Trischomatos of Koptos (P. Mich. 8.502) or simply unspecified "local gods" or "those among whom I am" (from the writer's point of view). These formulae reflect the necessity for protection the servicemen felt at their respective sites (P. Mich. 8.480, 490, 491). Especially in the temples of

Nubia, we see evidence of the participation by Roman soldiers in local cults, as in Talmis and Pselkis. In the temple of Toth in Pselkis, many *proskynemata* and dedications by military men to this local god who was referred to by them as "Hermes" survive; from Talmis stems evidence for soldiers from at least ten Roman regiments. Occasionally, a more concrete display can be made of the way in which "native" concepts of a god's influence were attributed to a local god. This is clearly hinted at by the oracle-administering sun god Mandulis of Talmis/Kalabsha considered to be "Apollo" by a soldier from western Asia Minor (*SB* 4607), since that man would have been well familiar with the concept of Apollo as an oracle god from the widely-known Apollo sanctuaries of his home region like Didyma or Klaros.

Long-term social integration in garrison cities led soldiers to participate intensively in urban, local, and regional cults, the protection of which they tried to obtain. During the battle of Cremona in 69 AD, the soldiers of the Syrian Legio III Gallica, according to Tacitus (*Hist.* 3.24.3) saluted the rising sun "in the Syrian fashion." Herodian (5.3.8–10) testifies that legionaries from that regiment, deployed in Raphanaea in the third century, were regular visitors to the sanctuary of the sun god at Emesa, located near the permanent camp, where they had no small part in lifting the god's young priest Varius Avitus Bassianus to the throne as Emperor Elagabal (218–222 AD). Participation in local cults can best be seen in the epigraphic evidence. Frequently, the centurions appear as dedicators of temples or furnishings, or in prominent roles in extending local sanctuaries. The Tychaion of Aere, 50 kilometers south of Damascus, was built by a centurion of the III Gallica in 191/192 AD (*IGR* III 1128). The officer terms himself "Euergetes Airesion kai Ktistes," "benefactor and founder," high honorary titles probably conferred by the Koinon of the Airesians, which can be found thus or similarly in urban honorary inscriptions for military men. The gospel of Luke (Lk 7.2–5) records the dedication of a centurion in Capernaum. This officer had contributed a generous amount to the building of the local synagogue and was therefore regarded as a "friend of the Jewish people." Attendance at the same temples by the military and civilian community was a matter of course in the garrison towns of the Near East like Dura Europos, while in Egypt military camps even came to comprise temples already in existence (Pselkis and Tzitzi, temples of Thot and Isis), where the integration of the soldiers into cultic life is consequently easily demonstrable.

Even the sacred areas of the *beneficiarii consularis*, the beneficiaries of the governor, are part of this cultic activity at the place of deployment: Among the beneficiaries, dedicating an altar to Iuppiter Optimus Maximus, the highest state god, occasionally to Juno, and most importantly and frequently to the *Genius huius loci*, the tutelary spirit of the previous place, was customary and possibly obligatory when leaving one place ("expleta statione" – *CBFIR* 752, 753) to take on a new assignment, showing gratitude for a successful and prosperous spell of service there. The according cultic areas were located at the place of the *stationes*, the "offices," as in Osterburken and Sirmium, and are testimony to an explicitly local cult, commending the soldiers and their subordinates to the protection of the respective local god.

Naturally, soldiers would sometimes transport such cults as they had become acquainted with during their service at some place of deployment back to their homes, if they returned there. An example is a third-century veteran whom bishop Epiphanius of Salamis (*Adv. haeres.* 66.1) reports to have been the first to introduce Manichaeism to Eleutheropolis (Syria Palaestina) upon his return from military service in Mesopotamia.

The role of the military in the diffusion of foreign cults

The stimuli of local cults at new garrison sites did not necessarily change the belief in the gods of home or of the previous place of deployment. Rather, they complemented the latter or possibly influenced the soldiers' perspective on the gods surrounding them. By its mobility in particular, the Roman military contributed to the diffusion of cults.[12] This quality of military life, and the concurrent potential, is clearly shown by the example of the former centurion Petronius Fortunatus (*ILS* 2658), who had served in a large number of legions during a career spanning 50 years of the late second and early third century – criss-crossing the empire from Britain and Lower Germania, Italy, Lower Moesia, Pannonia, to Cappadocia, Syria, Arabia, and Africa. Permanent transfer of individuals and entire units led to a proliferation of religious traditions. In this manner, even cults of limited local tradition could reach the most distant parts of the empire. I.O.M. Balmarcodes, the Phoenician Iuppiter, whose main sanctuary was situated in Beirut, had an altar built in Rome (*ILS* 4328) by a centurion of the Legio IIII Scythica from Zeugma, upon his being ordered to the capital. An altar was dedicated in Numidia to the slightly better-known I.O.M. Heliopolitanus from Baalbek by a Syrian centurion (*CIL* 8.2627). Documenting the continuity of Lower Germanic cults and cultic organizations (*pagi*) in Britain, the dedications to the deities Ricagambeda, Viradecthis, and Harimella (*RIB* 2096, 2107, 2108) at Birrens, the garrison of a Tungric cohort, are characteristic as well. The same holds true for Housesteads, garrisoned by a *cuneus Frisiorum*. There the Germanic war god Thincsus, likened to Mars, had accompanied the Frisian warriors, now clad in Roman uniforms, together with an entire pantheon of other deities (*RIB* 1593, 1594). In Rome in 227 AD, 21 soldiers from eight Praetorian cohorts, all natives of Philippopolis in Thrace, jointly worshipped their home god Asclepios Zimidrenus (*ILS* 2094).

An individual example is that of the soldier C. Iulius Apollinaris of the Legio III Cyrenaica. He writes to his father in Egypt, March 26, 107 AD, of Sarapis having provided him a safe passage from Nicopolis near Alexandria to Bostra (present-day Syria), where the legion was redeployed after Trajan's annexation of the kingdom of Nabatea (P. Mich. 8.466, ll 18f.). Later, Sarapis protects him on an official journey to Rome via Syria, Asia, and Achaea (P. Mich. 8.501, ll 17ff.). Religious transfers could by no means take place in an east–west direction only, as has often been contended with a view to the so-called "oriental" religions like the cults of Mithras and Iuppiter Dolichenus. The army was considered the vehicle of these religions. Orientals, or units from the East were implied to have an according part in the diffusion of these cults.

There are, in fact, sections of the *limes*, like in Upper Germania, where temple compounds of the cults of Mithras and Iuppiter Dolichenus form an integral part of the sacral topography of the civilian settlements surrounding the forts. On the other hand, entire sectors of the *limes*, like Lower Germania or Egypt, yield virtually no military evidence of the Mithras cult, and nothing at all can be found of Dolichenus in Egypt, which in the second and third centuries boasted an army group of 14–15,000 men. Examination of the adherents to the so-called "soldier religions" show that less than 20 percent of Mithras worshippers and less than 40 percent of those of Dolichenus are military men. There is no prominent role of soldiers from the Orient in the emergence of these "congregations." We are looking at a cultic community characterized by joint cultic practice of civilians and military personnel. Nevertheless, in the transfer of the two cults, a formative role of high-ranking officers can occasionally be discerned: the earliest instance of the cult of Dolichenus outside of Commagene, namely a building inscription of a temple in Lambaesis of 125/126, has at its roots the activity of the Legio III Augusta's legate (*ILS* 4311a). Military men have exported the cult of Dolichenus to Balaklava in the southwest of the Crimean Peninsula, and thus beyond the borders of the empire, where an outpost was manned by a vexillation comprised of troops from Lower Moesia. A small second- and third-century temple contained mainly dedications to Dolichenus, who granted protection to the soldiers in this temporary place of service (*AE* 1998, 1156–1160).

A small number of examples for transfers of cults in the opposite direction, from West to East, must suffice here. I have selected one individual example, one concentration of inscription finds apt to shed light on a transfer and its effects, and finally, one component of army religion the significance of which has as yet not been fully recognized, the cultic regimental traditions.

A dedication from Dura Europos, the altar of the soldier Aurelius Diphilianus (*AE* 1933, 226), betrays straight away, by its wording, that it was made to a foreign god. The soldier, a member of the Legio IIII Scythica Antoniniana in the first half of the third century, dedicated the item to "the god of home Zeus Baetylos, God of those living on the river Orontes." The dedicator, evidently coming from Northern Syria, alluded to a god at home in Antiochia or the surrounding territory.

The evidence concerning the cultic transfer of Silvanus, a god from the Danube or from Italy, is important in terms of methodology. Although his worship was rather common among military personnel, he decidedly did not belong to the spectrum of cults of official army religion. A concentration of inscriptions for the god was found in the quarry of Aroulis/Ehnesh (*IGLSyr.* I 67–71), run by the soldiers of a vexillation of the IIII Scythica from nearby Zeugma. The significance of these Silvanus inscriptions becomes clear when we examine the diffusion pattern of the cult. The 1,100 inscriptions dedicated to the god come from Italy and the western provinces, mainly from Dacia and Pannonia. From the eastern provinces come only nine inscriptions, of which the five items from Ehnesh stand out very prominently. The fact that these pieces are isolated in the Greek East hints at a transfer of the cult thither, from the West, by military units. The inscriptions from Severan times show that a private cult, imported through the relocation of units from the Danube area or Italy on behalf of Eastern campaigns, or through the mobilization of recruits into the legion and the military province, took root with the soldiers of the Legio IIII Scythica in Syria and was continued there. Searching the third-century papyri from Dura Europos for the theophoric *cognomen* "Silvanus" among the soldiers of the garrison (e.g. Aurelius Ulpius Silvanus – P. Dura 100 col. I l. 14, col. XL l. 1), comprising, since the times of the Severans, a vexillation of the IIII Scythica, clearly indicates that the god was worshipped by a far larger portion of the Syrian civilian population, whence the soldiers of the Cohors XX Palmyrenorum had been recruited, than epigraphic evidence alone can show. This is supported by the survival of the *cognomen* in Syrian units in general, as in Intercisa on the Danube *limes* with its Syrian-dominated military community and the related civilian population.

It was possible for regiments originated in a certain region, or from warriors of a certain tribe or a group of tribes, after their dislocation to the most diverse parts of the Roman Empire, to transfer as one body their native cults ("*dei patrii*") into these areas and maintain them by way of tradition, even if the original "ethnic" context had long been subject to dissolution due to new recruitments. In Porolissum, for instance, a *numerus Palmyrenorum* dedicates a temple to the Deus Patrius Bel (Birley 1978: 1517 ref. 54), another *numerus* of Palmyrenes in Castellum Dimmidi/Numidia worship their native god Malagbel, even styling him *deus numeri*, "god of the regiment" (*ILS* 4340). In Micia/Dacia, the Cohors II Flavia Commagenorum votes an altar to the god Iuppiter Turmazgadus (*ILS* 9273) known from Commagene. The Cohors I Hamiorum, originally recruited in Syria, collectively sacrifices to the Dea Syria, the "Syrian Goddess," in Carvoran (*RIB* 1792). In Intercisa in Hungary, a "Syrian community" turning out a large number of dedications and building inscriptions to the *deus patrius Elagabal* or Sol Invictus, their ancient sun god, constituted itself around the Cohors I milliaria Hemesenorum, which was originally recruited from "Emesans." The documents comprise collective inscriptions of the regiment using official formulae (*ILS* 9155; *AE* 1910, 133, 141); Elagabal is the *deus cohortis* and probably the *Genius cohortis* as well (*RIU* 5, 1112; *CBFIR* 394).

"Regimental traditions" – a special case of cult transfer

Cults peculiar to individual regiments are those of certain tutelary deities, serving, like the "flag cult," to confirm regimental identity, and whose worship is traceable, in some units, over a considerable length of time by way of regimental tradition. Thus they should be seen as existing alongside – or rather in between – the two components of the religion of the Roman armies: official army religion and the soldiers' private cults. One can speak of a "regimental tradition" in cases where the source material allows more than a glimpse of a specific instance. It has to be documented by a certain volume of testimonies from one and the same unit. The observance of these cults from a newly-formed regiment's "native soil" or their original, long-time area of deployment is ideally to be traced over a long period, through several "generations" of soldiers, and to several consecutive locations of the unit's service, even with the ethnic coherence of the unit having dissolved at some point.

This is best exemplified by the role of Zeus-Ammon-Sarapis with the Legio III Cyrenaica in Bostra. Redeployed from Egypt to the former Nabataean kingdom during its annexation (106 AD), the regiment "imported" their god Ammon-Sarapis or Zeus-Ammon, as shown by dedicational and building inscriptions and even private correspondence (the Apollinarius archive already mentioned). The unit maintained a link to its previous area of deployment (P. Oxy. LXIV 4434; *AE* 1909, 98). The god of the Cyrenaica is documented epigraphically in Bostra and many of the legion's quarters in the province of Arabia (*CIL* 3.13587, 13604; *IGLSyr.* 13.9010). According to the inscriptions and local Bostrean coinage, he was a special tutelary god of the regiment, called *Genius sanctus* (*IGLSyr.* 13.9010) or "Theos Patroos," the "god of home" and "*Conservator*" (*IGLSyr.* 13.9014), the preserver. His was a temple with a silver statue near the garrison, documented, among other evidence, by an inscription reporting the reconstruction, in the time of Aurelian, of the sanctuary which had been destroyed by the Palmyrenes in 270 AD (*IGLSyr.* 13.9107). The issues of the urban mint from the middle of the second to the middle of the third century make it possible to grasp the reaction of the urban elites to the presence of legion and god and their everyday interaction: Zeus (= Iuppiter) Ammon, in the designs and legends of the coins, gradually advances from the god of the legion to the tutelary god of the entire metropolis, and the guarantor of the city's security. During one and a half centuries, an intimate relationship between god and regiment is visible, from Trajan to Aurelian (106/107–270 AD), which makes it safe to speak of a "regimental tradition." Furthermore, the prominent role of Zeus-Ammon-Sarapis in the garrison city's coinage exemplifies the changes that cults "imported" by soldiers were able to precipitate in the religious world of the respective civilian society.

5   Demise of the "Old" Army Religion

It is wrong to assume that with the privileged position Christianity attained in the imperial house under Constantine (after 312), and before its proclamation as state religion under Theodosius I (395 AD), the army's pagan tradition from the time of the principate met with a swift end.[13] Admittedly, from the later second century onward, a growing number of Christians, apparently less at odds with idolatry, the army's icon-worship, than the church fathers, entered the army (Tertullianus, *Apol.* 37.4). There was not an ethical problem to start with, and military service was by and large an accepted way of life. For many Christians it sufficed to remain silent during public ceremonies or clandestinely cross themselves (Tertullianus, *Cor.* 12.3; Lactantius, *Mort. Pers.* 10). Nevertheless, at the beginning of the Constantinian epoch, and for some time after, the widespread pagan element within the army, indifferent to religious change at the top, still determined not only the outlook of the army itself, but the behavior of the princeps as well (Eusebius, *Vit. Const.* 2.6 and 4.20; Zosimus 2.29.5). Before the battle of the Milvian Bridge, the place of the imperial court's bishops was – like that of the soldiers' private cults of centuries ago (e.g. the oriental religions) – outside the military camp (Eusebius, *Vit. Const.* 2.12.14 and 4.56). Tradition and novelty abided side by side; changes took place but gradually. Nothing illustrates early conditions better than the silver medallion of the Ticinum mint (315 AD), showing on the obverse Constantine's helmet bearing a christogram, besides a shield with the Roman She-Wolf and her twins. On the reverse, the *imperator* is receiving a wreath from the Goddess Victoria (*RIC* 7.36). The christogram-adorned "labarum,"

Plate 25.6a From the god of the legion to the tutelary god of the entire metropolis, and the guarantor of the city's security: The bust of Zeus-Ammon-Sarapis, god of Legio III Cyrenaica on the reverse of an urban coin-issue from its garrison town Bostra, capital of *provincia Arabia* (second century AD). Kadman Numismatic Pavilion, Eretz Israel Museum, Tel-Aviv

Plate 25.6b Zeus-Ammon-Sarapis, god of Legio III Cyrenaica, on the reverse of an urban coin-issue from Bostra: The god, clad in armor, shaking hands with the city-goddess Tyche, is now the guarantor of the city's peace, unity and security (third century AD). The legend is: *CONCORDIA BOSTRENRUM* (sic). Kadman Numismatic Pavilion, Eretz Israel Museum, Tel-Aviv

the imperial standard introduced by Constantine, bore the image of the emperor and his sons (Eusebius, *Vit. Const.* 1.31.1f.). This example and others, like the overall status ascribed to the standards in "Christian late antiquity" or the general focus of the army on the person of the emperor, as shown for example by the continuance of the service oath – which now included the invocation of the holy trinity as witnesses (Vegetius 2.5.3–5) – illustrate the legacy of pagan antiquity. The doctrine of divine rights demanded absolute devotion to the person of the emperor "as to a god present in person," and determined the soldiers' religiosity, although many servicemen of the fourth century, especially those from Gaul, Illyricum, and from outside the empire, like Germans in Roman services, continued their heathen practices to a very high degree. The reign of Theodosius (379–395 AD), with its executive measures aimed at making Christianity the sole religion and displacing pagans from public office, is generally regarded as a turning point in the breakthrough of Christianity also within the army. Eventually, in 416 AD, pagans were formally excluded from military service (*Cod. Theod.* 16.10.21). Consequently, from the fifth century onward one finds evidence for the office of "military chaplain." Now, even soldiers of barbaric origins increasingly became subjects to Christianization. Without disavowing them completely, the now omnipresent state religion henceforth robed the lingering pagan traditions in Christian garb.

NOTES

1 Ankersdorfer 1973, 24–6, 215; Birley 1978, 1506–41; Helgeland 1978, 1470–555; Clauss 1986, 1073–114 s.v. Heerwesen/Heeresreligion; Herz 2001, 92–100; Stoll 2001a, 133ff., 210ff.

2 Transfer: Speidel 1995, 187–209. Integration: Bauchhenss 1990, 425; Herz 2002, 81.

3 Festivals: Herz 2002, 82–3. Parades: Stoll 2001b, 235ff.

4 Speidel 1994, no. 688, 688c, 688d. Irby-Massie 1996, 293–300.

5 Date and purpose of the *Feriale*: Nock 1972, 736–90, here on 740, 743; Haynes 1993, 141–57 *contra* Fink, Hoey, and Snyder 1940, 202–11; Herz 2002, 85f. Inscriptions: Fishwick 1988, 349–61. Effects: Haynes 1999, 168ff.; James 2001, 79–80, 86.

6 Oath of allegiance: Campbell 1984, 19–32; Rüpke 1990, 76–91; Herz 2001, 101–2. Solving the oath: Stoll 2002, 267ff. Images of the emperor: Stoll 2001b, 222ff. Donatives: Campbell 1984, 186–98.

7 "Total institution": Pollard 1996, 211–27. *Contra*: Speidel 1995, 188–90; Stoll 2001b, 96–101.

8 Symbols of the regiment: Ankersdorfer 1973, 28–44; Stoll 2001b, 257ff., see also James 2001, 79. Problem of "flag religion": Helgeland 1978, 1475; Helgeland 1979, 738–43; Clauss 1986, 1095; Stoll 2001b, 281–93. "Acts of the martyrs": Stoll 1998, 134–8; Stoll 2002, 272–5. Dedications: Ankersdorfer 1973, 38–42; Herz 2002, 87–9. The role of the *primuspilus*: Kolendo 1980, 49–60.

9 Animal Emblems: Stoll 2001b, 271ff., 504–71. "Regimental arms" on the reverses of local coinage: in general see Stoll 2001b, 380–417, 551–64. For the Bostra coinage see Kindler 1983, 123 no. 48 with ill. on plate IV 48 (CONCORDIA BOSTRENORUM). Emblems, morale, and *aemulatio virtutis*: Stoll 2001a, 106–36. Corporate rites and the

role of the officers: Stoll 1998, Stoll 2001b, 230–3. Collective dedications and statues of the emperor: Ankersdorfer 1973, 85ff., 98ff.; Stoll 2001b, 223ff. Altar series at Maryport and Bölcske: Wilson 1997, 67–104; Szabó and Tóth 2003, 131ff. no. 22–26; 136ff. no. 29–32; 140f. no. 34–5.

10 *Genii* and their function: Ankersdorfer 1973, 194ff.; Speidel and Dimitrova-Milceva 1978, 1542–55; Clauss 1986, 1092f.; *Genius centuriae*: Speidel 1978, 1546; Stoll 1992, 142ff, 179ff. Military influences on civilian cult practice: e.g. cult standards/Atargatis (Speidel 1978, plate 16); Gods in roman uniform [Dolichenus]: Speidel 1978, 55ff. with plate 8.11; Irby-Massie 1999, 66f.; Egyptian gods: Stoll 2001b, 187f.

11 Helgeland 1978, 1496f.; Birley 1978, 1525f. Soldiers of the Rhine legions and the *Matronae*: Bauchhenss 1990. Soldiers and local cults in Britannia: Irby-Massie 1999, 11ff., 155ff. Officers as benefactors in local cults: Stoll 2001b, 332ff. Sacred areas of the *beneficiarii consularis*: Ankersdorfer 1973, 157–93; Nelis-Clément 2000, 193–202, 269–88.

12 Oriental religions: Daniels 1975, 249–74, Speidel 1978, 38ff.; transfer of the god Silvanus: Stoll 1998, 99–145; Regimental traditions: Stoll 2001b, 349ff.

13 Helgeland 1979; Clauss 1986, 1105–12.

BIBLIOGRAPHY

Ankersdorfer, H. 1973. *Studien zur Religion des römischen Heeres von Augustus bis Diokletian.* Ph.D. Konstanz.

Bauchhenss, G. 1990. "Inschriftliche Götterweihungen rheinischer Legionssoldaten," in H. Vetters and M. Kandler (eds.), *Akten des 14. Internationalen Limeskongresses 1986 in Carnuntum.* Vienna, 419–30.

Birley, E. 1978. "The religion of the Roman army," in *ANRW* II 16.2. Berlin, 1506–41 = *The Roman Army. Papers 1929–1986.* Amsterdam, 397–432.

Campbell, J. B. 1984. *The Emperor and the Roman Army 31 BC–AD 235.* Oxford.

Clauss, M. 1986. s.v. Heerwesen/Heeresreligion, in *RAC* XIII. Stuttgart, 1073–114.

Daniels, C. M. 1975. "The role of the Roman army in the spread and practice of Mithraism," in J. R. Hinnells (ed.), *Mithraic Studies II.* Manchester, 249–74.

Fink, R. O., A. S. Hoey, and W. F. Snyder. 1940. "The *feriale duranum*," *YCS* 7: 1–222.

Fishwick, D. 1988. "Dated inscriptions and the *feriale duranum*," *Syria* 65: 349–61.

Haynes, I. 1993. "The Romanisation of religion in the *auxilia* of the Roman imperial army from Augustus to Septimius Severus," *Britannia* 24: 141–57.

—— 1997. "Religion in the Roman army: Unifying aspects and regional trends," in H. Cancik and J. Rüpke (eds.), *Römische Reichsreligion und Provinzialreligion.* Tübingen, 113–26.

—— 1999. "Military service and cultural identity in the *auxilia*," in A. Goldsworthy and I. Haynes (eds.), *The Roman Army as a Community.* Portsmouth, RI, 165–74.

Helgeland, J. 1978. "Roman army religion," in *ANRW* II 16.2. Berlin, 1470–555.

—— 1979. "Christians and the Roman army from Marcus Aurelius to Constantine," in *ANRW* II 23, 1. Berlin, 724–834.

Herz, P. 2001. "Das römische Heer und der Kaiserkult in Germanien," in W. Spickermann, H. Cancik, and J. Rüpke (eds.), *Religion in den germanischen Provinzen Roms.* Tübingen, 91–116.

—— 2002. "Sacrifice and sacrificial ceremonies of the Roman army," in A. I. Baumgarten (ed.), *Sacrifice in Religious Experience.* Leiden, 81–100.

Irby-Massie, G. L. 1996. "The Roman army and the cult of the Campestres," *ZPE* 113: 293–300.
—— 1999. *Military religion in Roman Britain*. Leiden.
James, S. 1999. "The community of the soldiers: A major identity and centre of power in the Roman Empire," in P. Baker et al. (ed.), *TRAC 98. Proceedings of the Eighth Annual Theoretical Roman Archaeology Conference, Leicester 1998*. Oxford, 14–25.
—— 2001. "Soldiers and civilians: Identity and interaction in Roman Britain," in S. James and M. Millett (eds.), *Britons and Romans: Advancing an Archaeological Agenda*. London, 77–89.
Kindler, A. 1983. *The Coinage of Bostra*. Warminster.
Kolendo, J. 1980. "Le rôle du Primus Pilus dans le vie religieuse de la Légion," *Archeologia* 31: 49–60.
Nelis-Clément, J. 2000. *Les beneficiarii: militaires et administrateurs au service de l'empire (Ier s.a.C.–VIe s.p.C.)*. Bordeaux.
Nock, A. D. 1972. "The Roman army and the Roman religious year," *Harvard Theological Review* 45: 187–252 = *Essays on Religion and the Ancient World*. Vol. II. Oxford 1972, 736–90.
Pollard, N. 1996. "The Roman army as 'total institution' in the Near East? Dura Europos as a case study," in D. L. Kennedy (ed.), *The Roman Army in the Near East*. Ann Arbor, 211–27.
Rüpke, J. 1990. *Domi Militiae. Die religiöse Konstruktion des Krieges in Rom*. Stuttgart.
Speidel, M. A. 1995. "Das Römische Heer als Kulturträger," in R. Frei-Stolba and H. E. Herzig (eds.), *La politique édilitaire dans les provinces de l'Empire romain IIème–IVème siècles après J.-C. Actes du IIe colloque roumano-suisse, Berne 12–19 septembre 1993*. Bern, 187–209.
Speidel, M. P. 1978. *The Religion of Juppiter Dolichenus in the Roman Army*. Leiden.
—— 1994. *Die Denkmäler der Kaiserzeit. Equites Singulares Augusti*. Cologne 1994.
——, and Dimitrova-Milceva, A. 1978. "The cult of the *genii* in the Roman army and a new military deity," in *ANRW* II 16.2. Berlin, 1542–555 = *Roman Army Studies I*. Amsterdam 1984, 353–68.
Stoll, O. 1992. *Die Skulpturenausstattung römischer Militäranlagen an Rhein und Donau. Der Obergermanisch-rätische Limes I, II*. St. Katharinen.
—— 1998. "Silvanus im Steinbruch. Kulttransfer durch Soldaten der *legio IIII Scythica* in Syrien?" in L. Schumacher (ed.), *Religion – Wirtschaft – Technik. Althistorische Beiträge zur Entstehung neuer kultureller Strukturmuster im historischen Raum Nordafrika/Kleinasien/Syrien*. St. Katharinen, 99–145 = *Römisches Heer und Gesellschaft. Gesammelte Beiträge 1991–1999*. Stuttgart 2001, 222–68.
—— 2001a. "De honore certabant et dignitate. Truppe und Selbstidentifikation in der Armee der römischen Kaiserzeit," in *Römisches Heer und Gesellschaft. Gesammelte Beiträge 1991–1999*. Stuttgart, 106–36.
—— 2001b. *Zwischen Integration und Abgrenzung. Die Religion des Römischen Heeres im Nahen Osten. Studien zum Verhältnis zwischen Armee und Zivilbevölkerung im römischen Syrien und den Nachbarprovinzen*. St. Katharinen.
—— 2002. "'Entlassungsweihungen' aus Bostra und die *honesta missio*," *JRGZ* 49: 235–80.
—— 2003. "Der Gott der arabischen Legion: Zeus Ammon-Sarapis und die *legio III Cyrenaica* in der römischen Provinz Arabia," in L. Schumacher and O. Stoll (eds.), *Sprache und Kultur in der kaiserzeitlichen Provinz Arabia*. St. Katharinen.
Szabó, A., and E. Tóth (ed.). 2003. *Bölcske. Römische Inschriften und Funde*. Budapest.
Wilson, R. J. A. (ed.). 1997. *Roman Maryport and its Setting. Essays in Memory of Michael G. Jarrett*. Nottingham.

FURTHER READING

Comprehensive treatments are: Ankersdorfer 1973; Birley 1978; Helgeland 1978; Clauss 1986. The "religious construction of war" is treated by Rüpke 1990. Rituals connected with the festival calendar and the emperor cult: Herz 2001 and 2002. The festival calendar reflected by inscriptions: see Fishwick 1988; for "collective monuments" compare Herz 2001 and 2002; Stoll 2002; statues of the emperor: Stoll 1992. The role of religion for the identities of soldiers and *esprit de corps*: Haynes 1993; James 1999. The question of a "flag religion": Stoll 2001b. Endurance of religious traditions in spite of a "romanizing" effect of service: Haynes 1993 and 1999. Private religions and the military as "cult bearers": Speidel 1995; Stoll 2001b. Attachment of soldiers to the provincial population by integration into local cults/religious peculiarities of provincial armies and frontier-sections: Bauchhenss 1990; Irby-Massie 1999; Stoll 2001b. The emperor cult as a link between army and society: see Stoll 2001b. For the complex view of a "religion system of the Roman army" see Helgeland 1978. The aspect of Christianity and army religion is treated by Helgeland 1979; Clauss 1986.

PART IV

The Late Roman Empire (up to Justinian)

CHAPTER TWENTY-SIX

Warlords and Landlords

Wolf Liebeschuetz

Conflict between the central ruler and local and regional magnates, whose power was based on the possession of large estates, is a constant theme in the history of the kingdoms of medieval Europe. This theme hardly occurs in the history of the Roman Empire up to the late fourth century. The military power of the emperor was so overwhelming that no local magnate or even combination of magnates could think of challenging it. There were some very wealthy landowners in Italy and the provinces, but they were civilians, and they commanded tenants and clients but not armed followers. Emperors were often challenged, and not rarely overthrown by usurpers, but these were almost invariably the emperor's own officers, most typically generals who had been successful in a major campaign.

Clearly there is a problem with how and when the Roman situation changed into the medieval one. In an extremely stimulating chapter of an extremely stimulating book C. R. Whittaker has discussed this problem and traced the beginnings of the process to the later fourth and fifth centuries.[1] In his view this period saw the fading of a sharp boundary between lands belonging to the empire and lands outside it as a result of the establishment in frontier regions of a variety of practically independent principalities, large and small, governed by locally based rulers, whom he groups together under the collective title of "warlords." This "model" is the starting point of the present chapter.

1 Delegating Defense of the Frontier

There can be no doubt that the later fourth century saw a weakening of the monopoly of the military power of the emperors and their armies. But the process was complex and driven by a number of seemingly independent factors. As might be expected the weakening was most notable in frontier regions. But even there a number of causal factors were involved. The empire's loss of control was certainly not entirely due to pressure from across the frontier. A significant factor was that both in Africa and along the edge of the Arabian Desert the imperial government adopted a policy of delegating frontier defense to tribesmen settled in frontier regions, whose regular transhumant movements also took them into areas beyond the frontier.[2] The empire eventually lost control of this strategy, but it was first adopted voluntarily.

Along the North African desert fringe large stretches of frontier were assigned to local tribesmen. The *Notitia Dignitatum* lists the local divisions that made up this system, and the titles of their commanders, the *praepositi limitis*.[3] But to reconstruct the functioning of the system, and incidentally also how it related to the organization of this region under the early empire, we have to look elsewhere, to inscriptions and the campaign narratives. The *praepositi* were Roman officers, but they were drawn from the local tribes. They were powerful locally, as they possessed their own fortified headquarters (*centenaria*).[4] But some were more powerful than others. Outstandingly powerful was the family of Nubel, "petty king" (*regulus*) among the Moorish people (Ammianus Marc. 29.5.2), whose son Firmus in 373 led a large-scale revolt against the Roman government. Nubel had been a Roman officer. His brother Gildo helped the Romans to defeat Firmus, and was given the command of the Roman forces in Africa. His daughter married a nephew of the empress Flacilla. In 397 he too rebelled, only to be defeated by a Roman army commanded by his brother Mascezel. His property was confiscated and a separate financial department created to administer it (*Not.Dig.Occ.* 12.5). These men were warlords in the full sense of Whittaker's model.

We have little information about the African frontier during the fifth century, apart from the light thrown on military affairs by the career of the general Bonifatius 3, much of which was spent in Africa.[5] Our next detailed account is in Procopius' narrative of the Justinianic reconquest of Africa from the Vandals. At this time the frontier zone was occupied by a series of Moorish kingdoms whose rulers were still formally Roman appointees (Procopius, *Bella* 3.25.5–9), but who were in practice independent, and who were to encroach on the reconstituted Roman provinces as they had previously expanded at the expense of the Vandal kingdom.[6] They presumably were the descendants of the Roman *praefecti gentium* and *praepositi limitum*.

According to the lists of the *Notitia Dignitatum*, which in this case seem to represent the organization of the early fourth century,[7] the desert frontiers of Syria and Palestine were guarded by units of *limitanei*, stationed in forts scattered along the frontier region, but for the most part situated along the military high way, the *strata Diocletiana*, running from the Euphrates to Damascus, and possibly beyond that to the Red Sea. But the empire was already allied to some of the nomad tribes who were settled within the empire but whose transhumant movements took them across the frontier region and into the desert beyond the jurisdiction of Roman officials.[8] We are told that after the eastern field army had been almost destroyed in the battle of Adrianople in 378, soldiers sent by the Saracen queen Mavia helped to defend Constantinople (Socrates, *Hist. Eccl.* 5.1.3; Sozomen *Hist. Eccl.* 7.1.1; Ammianus Marc. 31.16.5–6). In the fifth century groups of Arab tribes under their own leaders (phylarchs) of the Salih tribe seem to have played a growing part in the defense of the eastern frontier, not least against raids of the Lakhmids, the powerful tribe that had established its center at al-Hira on the lower Euphrates and was allied to the Persians. In the sixth century, in the reign of Justinian, the imperial government placed the various allied tribes under the single command of the Ghassanid dynasty. At the same time many, but not all, the frontier forts seem to have been evacuated, so that the tribesmen under Ghassanid leadership now appear to have been given principal responsibility for control of passage in and out of the frontier zone, and defense of the region from raiders, though certainly not from a large scale invasion, which was not anticipated from the desert. The Ghassanids seem to have established several small towns south of Damascus, and some of the monumental residences on the fringe of the desert may have been theirs. The Ghassanid phylarch might well qualify for the title of warlord. But even in the sixth century the frontier region in the east was not entirely denuded of Roman units, and the phylarchs and their followers were formally integrated into the Roman administrative system; Justinian made the Ghassanid phylarch subject to the "moderator" of Arabia, that is to the official responsible for both the civil and military administration of the province (*Nov. Iust.* 102). It is not known how the spheres of authority of the Roman officials, and that of the phylarch were delimited. Later in the century the imperial government dismantled the Ghassanid federation. But it continued to rely on tribesmen to protect the frontier from raids by other nomad tribesmen, particularly when the Romans and the Persians were at war to repel raids by tribesmen allied to the Persians, and to raid the Persians' allies in turn.[9]

Among the factors which induced the government to adopt a defensive strategy of delegation along the desert fringe in the Near East and in North Africa consideration of geography may well have been decisive. Nomads and semi-nomads would be more at home in desert or semi-desert conditions than regular soldiers. In Syria there was the need to protect frontier areas from raids of the Lakhmids. In North Africa too the sedentary population was subject to raiding by nomads, even though not by nomads allied to a rival empire. As the tribesmen assisted the empire while carrying out their own nomadic pursuits, they were probably cheaper than regular troops would have been. At any rate we are told that it was the prospect of financial advantage that induced Valens to admit the Visigoths into the empire, because it would enable the government to spend the recruiting tax on other expenses (Ammianus Marc. 31.4).[10]

2 Over-Mighty Generals: West

Phylarchs and other tribal leaders operating in the frontier regions of North Africa and Syria were one kind of "warlord," and army commanders sufficiently powerful to be able to defy or even dominate the emperor were another, though it would seem that the factors which empowered them were quite different. The over-powerful army commander was in the first place a western phenomenon. With Merobaudes, the commander of the troops in Gaul and on the Rhine 375–385, there begins a line of commanders-in-chief who rivaled and often surpassed the emperor in power. It is a formidable line: beginning with Arbogast, followed by Stilicho, who from

394–408 practically governed the western empire, followed by Constantius (411–421), whose victories enabled the empire to recover from the Alaric crisis, and who married Placidia, the daughter of Theodosius I, and during the last months of his life from April to September 421 held the rank of Augustus. Then came Aetius (435–454) whose victories postponed the collapse of the imperial organization in Gaul, Ricimer (456–472), Orestes (475–476), and finally Odovacer (476–493) who deposed Romulus Augustulus, the last emperor of the west, and reigned as king for the rest of his life.[11] To give an adequate account of these warlords one would have to tell the history of the western empire, but the highlights of the career of Ricimer dramatically illustrate the reversal of the traditional relationship of emperor and commander-in-chief. For Ricimer took a decisive part in the deposition of the emperor Avitus (455–456) and subsequently played a leading part first in the appointment and then in the deposition and killing of the emperors, Maiorian (457–461), Libius Severus (461–465), and Anthemius (467–472).

How is the evolution from powerful commander-in-chief to warlord and finally monarch to be explained?[12] One factor was the range of the command given to Stilicho by Theodosius I after the defeat of the usurper Eugenius in 394. As *magister militum utriusque militiae* Stilicho commanded all field army units in the west, wherever they were stationed, with the *duces* commanding the frontier troops under his disposition as well.[13] Stilicho's successors inherited this plenitude of power, at least in theory. In the long run, as the central government's control over the more distant provinces weakened, the geographical range of commander-in-chief in the West became less and less important. What was ultimately decisive was control of the army that mattered, the army based in Italy.

Accident helped to strengthen the position of the western commander in chief relatively to that of the emperor. Honorius (393–423) the son and successor of Theodosius I was quite incapable of leading an army, and Valentinian III (425–455) became emperor at the age of five and never had any military experience. Institutional changes had made it easier for civilian emperors to remain in power. It had been a central feature of the Diocletianic organization of the empire that civil and military administrations should form two distinct hierarchies, united only by the person of the emperor, who headed both. This division remained. At the same time the activities and interests of the emperors tended to become increasingly civilian. Starting with the successors of Theodosius, both in the east and the west, the emperor as a rule no longer led his army against the enemy, but left this to professional generals, and this was done even if, as in the case of Leo and Zeno,[14] the reigning emperor had been an officer, and even commanded an army earlier in his career.

In the East this worked reasonably well throughout the fifth and sixth centuries. But not in the West, where after the murder of the civilian emperor Valentinian III in 455, the general Ricimer was in a position to make and unmake emperors. The fact that both Maiorian and Anthemius had led armies, and continued to do so as emperor,[15] did not enable them to stand up to Ricimer. One reason was surely that each in turn got discredited as a result of a disastrous expedition against the Vandals in North Africa. But throughout Roman history we can observe that successful generals were likely to become a danger to the central government, whether republican or imperial. Successful campaigning resulted in close bonds between general and troops, which the general could, and often did, try to exploit to his advantage. The proclamation of Julian is only the best documented example of a victorious general being proclaimed Augustus by his troops (Ammianus Marc. 20.4.1–5.10). The numerous military crises of the later fourth century, which continued through most of the fifth, produced many opportunities for bonding of general and other ranks.

Institutional developments of the later fourth century greatly strengthened an inherent tendency. Changes in recruiting strengthened the bond between commander and his troops. The campaigning armies were now very largely composed of miscellaneous units of federates. Many of the federates had probably been recruited for a specific campaign by the commander himself. This is particularly well documented in the cases of Stilicho and Aetius. It was therefore the commander who instilled a sense of unity among his units, and it was to him, as much and often more than the emperor that they looked for reward for their service. Moreover armies now included a category of elite troops who enjoyed a close relationship with the commander, because they acted as his bodyguard.[16] These were the so-called *bucellarii* who had sworn loyalty not only to the emperor but also to their commander, and who were also maintained, at least in part, at his expense.[17] At the same time the settlement of barbarians in western provinces, and above all the loss of the rich provinces of North Africa to the Vandals progressively destroyed the emperor's financial resources, and therefore his ability to reward his soldiers. All these developments increased the dependence of the soldiers on their commander, and consequently their readiness to support him rather than the head of state.

In important respects the power-basis of these powerful *magistri militum* resembled that of the Germanic leaders like Alaric or Geiseric or the Burgundian rulers who established kingdoms within the empire. Of course the generals owed their original appointment to the emperor, while the kings owed theirs to the their people. But even this distinction is not as fundamental as it might seem, for the tribal leaders too sometimes insisted on being given an imperial command, while the generals depended on the loyalty of their army to assert themselves against the emperor.[18] Perhaps the most important difference between the two types of leaders was that the army of an imperial general was multi-ethnic, while the "people" of one of the great tribal leaders, that is the leaders of one of the major barbarian *gentes*, though far from being ethnically monolithic, nevertheless was united by a single, or at least dominant, sense of ethnic solidarity.[19] Eventually the two positions fused. Odovacer, who deposed the last emperor of the west, was a general who had been made king by his Germanic federates, and he was eventually deposed by Theoderic, king of the Ostrogoths, but after the campaign had been authorized by Zeno, the eastern emperor.[20]

3 Over-Mighty Generals: East

The history of the east was quite different. There the generals did not prevail, and the emperor and the civil administration did not lose control over the army. How can we account for the difference? It is clear that the factors which enable the *magister militum praesentalis* (and some regional commanders) to become over-powerful in the West were operative in the East also. On two occasions a *magister militum praesentalis* achieved a position at Constantinople comparable to that of the over-mighty generals in the West: Gainas for less than one year in the reign of Arcadius (399–400), and Aspar from the late 450s to 471 in the reign of Leo. Vitalianus, commander of the federates in Thrace, achieved similar but regionally circumscribed power in the lower Danube region from 513, in the reign of Anastasius, to his assassination perhaps at the instigation of the later emperor Justinian in 520. But Gainas was defeated, and Aspar and Vitalianus were murdered, and the supremacy of the emperor's civilian government restored, so that the phases of military dominance remained episodes. There remains the unique career of the man who was to end up as the emperor Zeno.[21] This was an Isaurian chieftain originally named Tarasicodissa, who took the Greek name of Zeno, and became a Roman officer. His position in Isauria enabled him to recruit troops, so he was a kind of war lord. But he recruited and used the Isaurian soldiers in the service of the emperor Leo, giving him the military backing he required to rid himself of Aspar. So this is a case of a warlord helping to destroy a warlord. Zeno's reward was to became Leo's son-in-law, and eventually legitimate ruler of the empire.

How did civilian government retain control in the East? There is not the space here to go through the whole story of the rise and fall of Gainas, Aspar, and Vitalianus, but it is possible to suggest some reasons why the emperor and his government managed to remain in control of their generals in the East but not in the West. In the West too the government was sometimes able to rid itself of over-mighty generals: Stilicho was executed, Aetius was murdered. But the execution of Stilicho was followed by a flood tide of disasters. The restoration of stability required the rise of another mighty commander in Constantius. The consequences of the murder of Aetius were even worse. It is no exaggeration to say that the western empire never recovered from them. It would seem that it could not function without leadership of a powerful military figure.

A very important difference between East and West was that the former was not under continuous military pressure. The fall of Gainas in 400 was followed by 20 years of peace. A competent civilian administration was able to establish itself. The indecisive Persian war of 420–421 inaugurated another period of large-scale warfare on different fronts, against the usurper John in Italy, against the Vandals in Africa and, very close to the center of power, against the Huns in the Balkans. These wars gave rise to the mighty military dynasty of Ardaburius and his son Aspar, the kind of dynasty Stilicho had hoped to found in the West. Perhaps as early as 420 a powerful group of Goths was settled in Thrace, which was later to be led by Theoderic Strabo (Theophanes, *Chron.* 5931). Somewhat later another group was settled in Pannonia (Jordanes, *Getica* 50.262ff.); a section of this group was to become the people of the famous Theoderic of the Amal dynasty, and to be led by him into Italy. So it seemed for a time in the 450s as if the East would develop in the same way as the West. But Aspar did not have at his disposal a large standing army, for the eastern field army was divided into five independent commands, and even the striking force stationed in or near the capital was probably still split into two regular "praesental" armies.[22] Judging by the emperor's regular need for federates, the two regular armies were probably not very large, and Aspar commanded only one of them. His military power therefore depended to a considerable extent on his ability to call on the support of the Gothic federates settled in Thrace. This of course was very different from the position of *magister militum utriusque militiae* in the West, who was theoretically at least in command of all field army units in the West no matter where they were stationed (*Not.Dig.Occ.* 115–132). The emperor Leo was able to exploit the relative weakness of military resources at Aspar's immediate disposal when, with the help of Zeno, he was able to utilize an abundant source of mercenaries in Isauria whom he recruited in to a new bodyguard, the *excubitors*, and thus established firm military control of Constantinople. So Leo was in a position in which he could kill Aspar and his sons, and subsequently with the aid of geography contain Theoderic Strabo and his Goths in Thrace. Later Zeno was able to ward off the two groups of Goths by getting them to fight each other. Finally he got rid of them for good by encouraging Theoderic the Amal to lead the now united Goths to "liberate" Italy from Odovacer. In these complicated maneuvers the eastern emperors had one very important advantage over those of the West: a very large income from taxation. While Italy had been devastated and the western emperor was losing the revenue from large parts of Gaul, Spain, and, most important of all, North Africa, the heartlands of the eastern empire in Asia Minor, Syria, and Egypt continued to pay taxes. This made the eastern government less dependent on generals and large standing armies. The government had the resources to buy off invaders and dangerous federates, and their relatively strong finances enabled them to pay their soldiers adequately and to raise recruits when they needed them. From the assassination of Vitalianus in 520 to the successful usurpation of Phocas in 602 the emperors of the east were threatened neither by over-mighty generals nor warlords.

4 Self-Help in a Disintegrating Empire

The Roman Empire did not collapse suddenly. It dissolution, or transformation, was a gradual process. The most dramatic development was the establishment of a large Germanic kingdom in what had been the provinces of the Roman Empire by Vandals, Visigoths, Ostrogoths, Franks, and Lombards.[23] But the setting up of barbarian kingdoms within the empire still left very large areas where imperial administration remained, though its functioning was made very much more difficult, or even impossible, by the existence of barbarian kingdoms, which were often in a state of war with the empire and whose very existence greatly reduced the empire's financial resources. The results were untidy. What happened was not abandonment and evacuation of provinces by the central government, but rather a gradual loss of control, leaving provincials to defend and administer themselves, using what was left of the military and civil institutions of the empire, together with what organization they could improvise. The most important of these relics of the Roman system were cities and their territories, the *civitates*, which in Gaul at least seem to have continued to exist as functioning units of administration.[24] The relics also included fragments of the Roman army, for the frontier troops of the late empire tended to remain permanently stationed in their garrison towns, and as service was in practice hereditary, the men became deeply rooted in the local society. In the fifth century in some provinces at least certain frontier lands were reserved for cultivation by *limitanei*, so that at least some frontier troops had become peasant soldiers. But it was probably much more important that soldiers, whether *limitanei* or *comitatenses*, owned private houses and land, and this made them reluctant to be moved from their frontier stations.[25]

Laeti still are rather an obscure institution of the late Roman army. Probably they were descendants of barbarians settled on land with the hereditary duty of serving in the Roman army when called up. Some of them seem to have continued in the same role under the Franks.[26] Units of the field army (*comitatenses*) were mobile by definition, but evidence from Egypt suggests that in practice they too often remained stationed in the same garrison town for very long periods.[27] Consequently they came to see it as their first duty to defend their own locality, and it became difficult, or even impossible to move them (Theophylact 7.3.1–10).

When Justinian ordered the *limitanei* of the African *limes* to be reconstituted, he recommended enrolling men who had been soldiers under the Vandals (*quos antea milites habebant, Cod. Just.* I.27.2.8 (AD 534). He evidently thought that they would watch over the frontier irrespective of whether they did it under Vandal or under Roman command. It is likely that the Vandals, when they took over Roman Africa, had similarly continued to employ such Roman *limitanei* as remained in the frontier zone. We are told that in Gaul Roman frontier troops continued to serve, first Visigoths and then the Franks, and that they even kept their dress uniform and ensigns (Procopius, *Bella* 5.12.13–19). Similarly the settlements of Laeti, which had furnished soldiers for the imperial army, continued to do so for the armies of the Merovingian kings.[28] In Noricum many units garrisoning in frontier towns broke up when they ceased to get their pay, but the garrison of Passau (Batavis) remained and continued to draw pay, long after the others had gone. In Mauten (Favianis) too a small unit appears to have remained after the regular provincial administration had disappeared (*Vita Severini* 20, ibid. 4).

We are best informed about the dissolution of the imperial organization in Gaul, though even there the evidence is far from abundant.[29] The territories north of the Loire experienced an interregnum in the course of which the imperial authorities became less and less effective. In this difficult and dangerous situation the population of frontier areas had to organize its own defense, and there came into existence a number of more or less independent territories – some large, some small – based on *civitates*, and defended in various ways. A unit of the imperial army might have remain in the locality, or the inhabitants might be able to hire a band of roaming federates,[30] or they might take up arms themselves. Some militarization of the *civitates* is suggested by the fact that the Merovingians would be able to use them to organize local levies, a function they do not seem to have had under the empire. No doubt bishops often provided leadership, as they did all over the empire in crisis situations. But leadership was very varied. We are told that St. Genovefa, a nun, kept up morale when Paris was threatened by Attila's Huns, and that later, when the city was threatened or perhaps even occupied by Childeric king of the Franks, she interceded for captives and brought in corn during the siege (*V. Genovefae*, MGH, Script.rer.Merov. III, pp. 26, 35). In Noricum the holy man[31] St. Severinus organized resistance against the Alamanni and Rugi (*V. Severini*, MGH, AA, I.2, pp. 1–30).

However in most cases leadership was provided by officers of the imperial army. Outstanding among these were Aegidius and his son Syagrius in northern Gaul 461–486. Aegidius, a Gaul and almost certainly a Gallic noble, was appointed commander-in-chief (*magister militum*) of the Roman army in Gaul in 456/7. The evidence is scanty, but it is clear that Aegidius was sometimes an ally and sometimes an enemy of the Franks. He evidently won their respect, for, after he had exiled their king Childeric, they made him their king. When the emperor Majorian was murdered 461 Aegidius refused to recognize his successor, and subsequently operated as an independent warlord, controlling a considerable territory centered on Soissons, and defending it against both the Goths in the south and the Franks in the north. It could well be that he had taken over some of the units of the federate army Majorian had disbanded after his unsuccessful campaign against the Vandals. When Childeric returned from exile to reign over his Franks once more he allied himself with Aegidius, and together they won a victory over the Visigoths at Orleans in 363. In 465 Aegidius was killed, but his son Syagrius continued to rule the Roman enclave from Soissons.

Why from Soissons? I would suggest that its position between the *civitates* of central Gaul and the territory of Frankish settlement in what is now Belgium made it a convenient center for Aegidius, particularly when he was king of the Franks as well as the Romans, as it was for Clovis after he had taken over the "kingdom of Soissons." Soissons was the center of a Roman *civitas*, but that was perhaps not what made it important. At least it is not among the *civitates* which are mentioned in our sources as having provided troops for a Frankish army. But it certainly came to be a center of a cluster of estates of the Merovingian family, second in size only to the cluster centered on Paris.

It would seem that Syagrius continued to rule as king (*Lib.Hist.Franc.* 8) until 486, when he was defeated and killed, and his kingdom seized (Gregory of Tours, *HF* 2.27: *regnoque eius accepto*), by Clovis king of the Franks, the son of his father's ally, Childeric. A similar situation existed in Dalmatia where one Marcellinus rebelled against the emperor Valentinian III, and for some years kept Dalmatia independent both of the emperor and of barbarian rulers. He built up for himself a personal power base there, but it is not clear how. He was a highly educated man, with links to Neoplatonist circles. A nephew of his, Julius Nepos, was married to a relative of the empress Verina. So Marcellinus was obviously a man of very good family, in this respect resembling Aegidius and Syagrius in Gaul. But this cannot have been enough to enable him to raise troops and to lead them successfully. We know nothing of his early years, but if he established his position on the basis of nothing more than his private wealth and personal prestige among his fellow Dalmatians he would have been almost unique among the military leaders of the time. The likelihood is that he started as an officer, who rose to be commander of a major military force. We do not know for certain that such a force was stationed in Dalmatia in the 450s, but it is extremely likely that it was. The prosperous coastal strip and the important ports along the Adriatic needed to be protected from Huns and other barbarians in the Danube provinces.[32] Procopius tells us that Marcellinus was one of γνωριμοι of Aetius, and then that he "got all the others to rebel." It is quite unclear who are meant by the γνωριμοι and by "all the others" (Procopius, *Bella* 3.65.7–8). I would suggest that in this context they must be the same people, and that γνωριμοι here stands for officers of the *bucellarii* of Aetius. On that assumption what happened was that after Aetius was murdered his leading *bucellarii* were dispersed,[33] with a number of them, including Marcellinus, being given commands of units in Dalmatia. I suggest that these men and their regiments were the "others" whom Marcellinus persuaded to join him in his revolt. In 461 the emperor Majorian was murdered and it was thought that Marcellinus would invade Italy to depose Ricimer's puppet emperor Libius Severus, but Marcellinus was dissuaded by the eastern government (Priscus fr. 39 Blockley). So by then Marcellinus was in some sense also an officer of the eastern empire. The situation recurred in 374 when Julius Nepos, Marcellinus' nephew and successor, made precisely the intervention in Italy which his uncle had been expected to make, but this time the eastern emperor ordered the intervention (John of Antioch fr. 209). Nepos even became emperor, though not for long. Marcellinus is said to have ruled Dalmatia justly and well (Damascius fr. 155, 158). His success led to his being appointed to important military commands by different emperors, first to defend Sicily against the Vandals with a force of "Scythians," presumably either Goths or Huns (Priscus fr. 38.1 Blockley), and later to lead the western contingents in the great expedition against the Vandals of 468. He drove the Vandals out of Sardinia, but was murdered soon after. His nephew Nepos evidently succeeded to his position and rank, for a law was addressed to him as *magister militum Dalmatiae*. This law, issued by the eastern emperor Leo, is concerned with dowries (*Cod. Just.* 6.61.5). Nepos would therefore seem to have been concerned with civil jurisdiction as well as defense, just like his uncle Marcellinus. Nepos was murdered in 480. His murderer, Ovida, ruled Dalmatia briefly, only to be overthrown by Odovacer in 481/2. So the warlord Odovacer reunited the warlordship of Dalmatia with Italy, but Odovacer would in turn be overthrown and killed by Theoderic king of the Ostrogoths.

5 Landlords Do Not Become Warlords

So far this chapter has dealt with a variety of military leaders, all or most of whom enjoyed some degree of irregular and personal power that allows us to classify them as warlords. It remains to discuss how far this irregular power was based on landownership. It is safe to say that all the individuals discussed were landowners on a considerable scale. The ruling class of the Roman Empire was a class of landowners, and under the late empire the great estates were probably larger than ever before. So the military leaders sprung from this class – that is in all likelihood Aegidius, Syagrius, Marcellinus, Julius Nepos, and probably Aetius – were almost certainly from the start a great landowners. Gildo, the *magister militum* and hereditary tribal leader in Africa, was also a very great landowner. Moreover public office in the Roman Empire, whether it was civil or military, was a route to greater landed wealth. So Libanius' speech on patronage (*Orat.* 47) illustrates some of the ways in which local commanders could amass wealth. The higher the rank, the more numerous the opportunities. So it is likely that by the time a man had risen to the highest post in the army he was very wealthy indeed. Merobaudes, *magister militum* under Gratian, and Arbogastes, *magister militum* under Valentinian II, founded powerful local families. The *magistri militum* might even marry into the imperial family: Eudoxia, daughter of the Frankish general Bauto, married Honorius; Stilicho married Serena, a niece of Theodosius I;[34] Gildo's daughter married Nebridius, a nephew of the empress Flaccilla (Jerome, *ep.* 79); Constantius married Galla Placidia, the daughter of Theodosius I; Ricimer married the daughter of Anthemius (Sidonius Apollinaris, *Carmina* 2.484–86); and Julius Nepos married a relation of the empress Verina (Malchus, *fr.* 10 [14] Blockley).

But it is safe to say that while increased wealth and brilliant marriages were a consequence of these men's rise to power, they were not what had gained them that power in the first place. Under the conditions of the Roman Empire great landed wealth on its own was not convertible into military power. The great landowners may well have been in a position to obstruct tax collectors and to exercise local leadership, but when it came to warfare on a larger scale, whether it involved barbarian invasion or war between contenders for the empire, they were simply swept aside. It was not the great landowners who decided whether Odovacer or Theoderic should reign in Italy. Syagrius could not stand up to Clovis. His 7,000 *bucellarii* could not keep Belisarius in his command when the emperor Justinian wanted to depose him (Procopius, *Anecdota* 4.13–15). When the Arabs invaded Egypt, the great Apion family simply disappeared from the historical record.

Military power that was to count more than locally needed to based on more than just large estates. It required above all one of two starting points: a high command in the army or ethnic leadership, and ideally a combination of the two. Moreover, the two starting positions were not totally distinct. The great army commanders became excessively powerful because they were indispensable for the defense of the empire, but also because they became the patrons of barbarian federates. The power of ethnic leaders was based on an ethnic core; but leaders like Alaric, Geiseric, Theoderic, or Clovis also presided over a process of ethnic expansion in which their original group absorbed and assimilated large numbers from other groups. Power based on an imperial command alone did have a tendency to become hereditary, as is shown by the cases of Bauto, Stilicho, Boniface, Aegidius, and Marcellinus in the West, and Ardabur the elder, father of Aspar, in the East. But only in the case of Ardabur did the power survive to the third generation, and the younger Ardabur was of course put to death in 471, at the same time as his father Aspar.

Historical sources inform us only about the most important leaders. We have seen that the needs of regional self-defense created centers of independent power in frontier regions. There were certainly far more of these than we know about, and far more men who performed the role of an Aegidius or a Sidonius Apollinaris or even a St. Severinus, but on smaller scale, in a more obscure place, or without being lucky enough to obtain a hagiographer. But these local concentrations of power were provisional, and did not last. For a position of power greater than that conferred by high military office to last over generations, it had to have a basis in ethnic leadership, and be in a position to bring about ethnogenesis.

The term ethnogenesis describes the process by which an ad hoc grouping of individuals, for instance a war band, acquires a sense of ethnic identity, which continues to evolve as the group's circumstances change. There were very many processes of ethnogenesis going on at this time. As the administrative structure of the empire dissolved a shared sense of ethnic identity reinforced by religion became by far the most powerful basis of political and military power. Much research of the last 50 years[35] into the character of the peoples (*gentes*) of the Age of Migrations, as well as into that of numerous other "tribes" whether contemporary or historic, has shown that in most cases the sense of tribal kinship is a shared myth, which has little or no biological basis, and which undergoes continuous transformation as the circumstances of the "tribe" change, and as it incorporates new members, or subdivides, or shrinks. But this does not mean that the sense of ethnic solidarity was unimportant. In fact new major political and military groupings within the old empire seem only to have been able to survive for significantly longer than the life of their founder if they had been constructed around an ethnic center.

Great landed wealth on its own could not do it. The senatorial aristocracy of the later Roman Empire was remarkably civilian. Its young men did not become officers and their fathers did not command armies. The great estates seem to have become ever larger, and landowners might even have *bucellarii*, but the estates were not like medieval baronies. They certainly had great regional power and they could obstruct the provincial administration's efforts to collect taxes or to recruit soldiers. In some areas the great landowners might seriously hinder enforcement of the law, but they got their way by using influential connections rather than through military power. They did not as a rule play an independent military role, either in civil war, or in defense of the frontiers. In the gathering crisis of the fifth century things began to change. But the reported cases of aristocrats organizing significant armies, whether to resist invaders, or on one side or the other in civil war, are remarkably few. Spanish landowners mobilized their peasants against the usurper Constantine (Zosimus 6.40). Ecdicius, along with 18 comrades, broke a Gothic siege of Clermont Ferrand (Sidonius Apollinaris, *ep*. 3.3.3–6). Synesius led resistance to invading nomads in Cyrenaica (Synesius, *ep*. 107–108, 122, 125, 130, 132–133, *Catastasis* [*PG* 66, 1572–1573]). It is also the case that to date really very few fortified villas have been found. The western medieval castle does not go back to the fifth and sixth centuries.[36] It may be that many of the very numerous fortified hills-settlements that are found in many of the western provinces owed their existence to dominant local landowners, but, if so, this does not show in their archaeology, which very rarely or never includes a seigniorial residence. It is the case that the aristocracy was becoming remilitarized.[37] Ancestors of men like Syagrius, Marcellinus, Avitus, and Anthemius would in all probability have shunned a military career. We hear that Roman aristocrats fought for the Visigoths against Clovis (Gregory of Tours, *HF* 2.37). A passage in Malalas suggests that Justinian ordered some senators of Constantinople and their followers to garrison cities in Mesopotamia and Phoenicia during a military crisis (Malalas 18[442]). However none of these men were feudal magnates with their own military resources sufficiently great to enable them to play a decisive part in power struggles on more than a local scale. In Justinian's Gothic War (AD 535–54) the extremely wealthy senatorial aristocracy of Italy played no active part. In fact it was one of the war's victims. The class as such was destroyed and a new militarized aristocracy grew up in Byzantine Italy. The Germanic peoples were led by a warrior aristocracy. In the Germanic kingdoms Roman and barbarian aristocracies gradually merged. We hear of descendants of senatorial families who held military commands under the Merovingian rulers of Gaul. Laws from the last decade of Visigothic Spain order landowners who have been called up to fight for the kingdom to present themselves together with their retainers, including armed slaves.[38] This was the way armies were to be assembled for centuries to come.

NOTES

1   Whittaker 1994, 243–78.
2   Shaw 1985.
3   *Notitia Dignitatum*, ed. O. Seeck, 174–5, 184–5, 186–7. While the chapter lists *praepositi limitis* it does not name military units. Other than in Africa the *Notitia* invariably names the units guarding the frontier army. The units listed in the *Distributio numerorum*, ibid. 141–2, as stationed in Africa, belong not to the frontier army, but to the mobile field army.
4   Lepelley 2001, 307–17. See the detailed discussion in Matthews 1976, 157–86. More generally: Whittaker 2000, 518–31.
5   On Bonifatius see s.v. Bonifatius 3, *PLRE* 2, 237–40.
6   See Brett and Fentress 1996; Camps 1984, 183–218.
7   Jones 1964, 57–9, but the lists themselves are later than 395 (ibid. 349).
8   Sometimes only intermittently: Ammianus 25.6.10. The evidence is very scanty, see Conrad 2000, 689–95; Isaac 1990, 239–41.
9   On the Salih tribe, Sartre 1982, 146–9; Kawar 1958, 145–58, Isaac 1990: withdrawal of only some units: 210–13; nomad allies 235–49. Gaube 1984, 61–6. Shahid 1984.
10   Carrié 1995, 27–50.
11   On all the generals O'Flynn 1983; on Ricimer *PLRE* 2, 942–5, s.v. Fl. Ricimer 2 and MacGeorge 2002, 209–68; on Odovacer: MacGeorge 2002, 269–93.
12   Heather 2000, 5–10, 25–7, links the weakening of imperial authority with the shrinking of its financial resources.
13   Jones 1964, 174–5.
14   *PLRE* 2, 663–4 s.v. Leo 6, ibid. 1200–2, s.v. Fl. Zeno 7.
15   *PLRE* 2, 702–3, s.v. Fl. Iulius Valerius Maiorianus, ibid. 96–8, s.v. Anthemius 3.
16   Federates: Liebeschuetz 1990, 37–8; Liebeschuetz 1993, 265–76.
17   Basic on this still quite obscure topic: Gascou 1972, 143–56; discussed from different poins of view also by Carrié 1995, 27–60, esp. 52–9; Whitby 1995, 61–124, esp. 116–19, and recently Schmitt 1994, 147–74. The evidence for their maintenance is mainly sixth century.
18   Note also that it seems that an important group of Franks chose the Roman *magister militum* Aegidius to be their king (Gregory of Tours, *HF* 2.12), and that the Ostrogoths

on one occasioned offered their kingship to the Roman general Belisarius (Procopius 6.29.18). However in 411 a combination of federates supported Jovinus in a bid to become emperor, *PLRE* 2, 621–2 s.v. Jovinus 2, and in 455 the Visigoths and the nobles of Gaul combined to proclaim Avitus 5 (ibid. 196–8 s.v. Eparchius Avitus 5).

19 See the chapters on various peoples in Goetz et al. 2003, which however, to my mind at least, tend to overstress the features showing adaptation and change, in fact continuous "reinvention," at the expense of those representing tradition and continuity in the functioning of the *gentes*.

20 MacGeorge 2002, 269–93; Moorhead 1992, 17–31.

21 Gainas: Liebeschuetz 1990, 104–25; Fl. Ardabur Aspar *PLRE* 2, 164–9; Fl. Vitalianus 2: *PLRE* 2, 1171–7; Zeno: *PLRE* 2, 1200–2, s.v. Zeno 7.

22 The Aspar dynasty: *PLRE* 2, 138, s.v. Fl. Ardabur 3; ibid. 164–9, s.v. Fl. Ardabur Aspar and the family tree of his descendants (*PLRE* 2, 1310). The family survived the fall of Aspar. His descendants still figured among the high aristocracy of Constantinople in the sixth century. On the two groups of Goths: Heather 1991, 242–71; the two praesental armies: Jones 1964, 177–8, a list of commanders *PLRE* 2, 1290.

23 See the chapters on Vandals, Franks, Ostrogoths, and Lombards in Goetz et al. 2003, and Heather 1996 on Visigoths.

24 Frye 1995; Loseby 2006.

25 Jones 1964, 663–4; but some *limitanei* could be promoted to *pseudocomitatenses*: ibid. 99, 126, 609–10; private land of soldiers: ibid. 662–3.

26 Bachrach 1972, 33–34.

27 Jones 1964, 660–1 (soldiers of Alexandria and Arsinoe).

28 Bachrach 1972, 5, 33–4, 124–8.

29 McGeorge 2002, 71–81.

30 For instance the band of Saxons which Odovacer, later king of Italy, led in Gaul in the 360s (Gregory of Tours, *HF* 2.18–19), or perhaps the force Franks and Romans with which the *comes* Paul operated around Angers around 469 (Gregory of Tours, *HF* 2.19).

31 Lotter 1976, identified him with a Severinus of *illustris* rank, who had once held high office in Noricum, but the letter of Eugippius introducing the *Vita Severini* shows that the origins of the holy man were obscure (*Ep. Eugippii* 7–11).

32 On Marcellinus: *PLRE* 2, 708–10 s.v. Marcellinus 6 and MacGeorge 2002, 15–67; his neoplatonism: Damascius fr. 151: Athanassiadi 1999, 181 (69A–E).

33 Dispersal of *bucellarii* of Belisarius: Procopius, *Secret History*, 4.13–14; *Histories* 7.10.1, 12.10.

34 Dynasties and marriages: *PLRE* 2, 756–58, s.v. Fl. Merobaudes 2; ibid. 128–9, s.v. Arbogastes; Philostorgius *HE* 11.6, *PLRE* 2, 410 s.v. Aelia Eudoxia; *PLRE* 1, 159–60, s.v. Flavius Bauto; ibid. 824, s.v. Serena; *PLRE* 2, 888–9, s.v. Aelia Galla Placidia.

35 Though the findings of this research were already assumed by Max Weber (in his *Grundriss der Sozialekonomik* III, Wirtschaft und Gesellschaft, Tübingen 1925): "Dieser Sachverhalt dass das 'Stammesbewusstsein' der regel nach primär durch politisch gemeinsame Schicksale, und nicht primär durch Abstammung bedingt ist" (p. 223). This did not of course stop the extreme exploitation of this already refuted view of ethnicity by the Nazis.

36 The fortified villa of Pontius Leontinus (Bourg-sur-Gironde) described in Sidonius Apollinaris (*ep.* 2.9) is far from typical, cf. Harris 1994, 131–3; see also Chavarria and Lewitt 2004, 28–9; Percival 1976, 174–82.

37 Heather 2000, 441–3.

38 Thompson 1969, 262–7; *Leges Visigothorum* IX.2.8 (673), 9(681); V.7,19.

BIBLIOGRAPHY

Athanassiadi, P. 1999. *Damascius, The Philosophical History, Text with Translation and Notes.* Athens.

Bachrach, B. S. 1972. *Merovingian Military Organisation (481–751).* Minneapolis.

Brett, M., and E. Fentress. 1996. *The Berbers.* Oxford.

Brogiolo, G.-P., and A. Chavarria. 2005. *Aristocracie e campagne nell' Occidente da Constantino a Carlo Magno.* Florence.

Brown, T. S. 1984. *Gentlemen and Officers. Imperial Administration and Aristocratic Power in Byzantine Italy* AD *554–800.* Rome.

Cameron, A. (ed.). 1995. *The Byzantine and Early Islamic Near East. Vol. III: States, Resources and Armies.* Princeton.

Camps, G. 1984. "Rex gentium Maurorum et Romanorum, recherches sur les royaumes de Maurétanie au VIe et VIIe siècles," *Antiquités Africaines* 20: 183–218.

Carrié, J.-M. 1995. "L'état à la recherché de nouveaux modes de financement des armies, Rome et Byzance, IVᵉ–VIIIᵉ siècles," in Cameron, 27–50.

Chavarria, A., and T. Lewitt. 2004. "Archaeological research on the late antique country-side," in W. Bowden, L. Lavan, and C. Machado (eds.), *Recent Research on the Late Antique Countryside.* Leiden, 3–51.

Conrad, L. I. 2000. "The Arabs," in *CAH* 14. Cambridge, 678–700.

Frye, D. 1995. "Transformation and tradition in the Merovingian civitates," *Nottingham Medieval Studies* 39: 1–11.

Gascou, J. 1972. "L'institution des buccellaires," *Bulletin de l'Institut Français de l'Archéologie Orientale* 72: 143–56.

Gaube, H. 1984. "Arabs in sixth-century Syria, some archaeological observations," in M. A. Bakhit (ed.), *Proceedings of the First International Conference on Bilād al-Shām.* Amman 1984, 61–6.

Goetz, H.-W., J. Jarnut, and W. Pohl (eds.). 2003. Regna *and* Gentes, *the Relationship between Late Antique and Early Medieval Peoples and Kingdoms in the Transformation of the Roman World.* Leiden.

Harris, J. 1994. *Sidonius Apollinaris and the Fall of Rome* AD *497–8.* Oxford.

Heather, P. 1991. *Goths and Romans.* Oxford.

—— 1996. *The Goths.* Oxford.

—— 2000. "The western empire 425–76," in *CAH* 14. Cambridge, 1–32.

Isaac, B. 1990. *The Limits of Empire. The Roman Army in the East.* Oxford.

Jones, A. H. M. 1964. *The Later Roman Empire. A Social, Economic and Administrative Survey 284–602.* Oxford.

Kawar, I. 1958. "The last days of the Salih," *Arabica* 5: 148–58.

Lepelley, C. 2001. "La préfecture de tribu dans l'Afrique du Bas Empire," in C. Lepelley, *Aspects de l'Afrique romaine, les cités, la vie rurale, le christianisme.* Bari.

Liebeschuetz, W. 1990. *Barbarians and Bishops.* Oxford.

—— 1993. "The end of the Roman army in the western empire," in J. Rich and G. Shipley (eds.), *War and Society in the Roman World.* London, 265–76.

Loseby, S. 2006. "Decline and change in the cities of late antique Gaul," in J.-U. Krause and C. Witschel (eds.), *Die Stadt in der Spätantike-Niedergang oder Wandel?* Stuttgart.

Lotter, F. 1976. *Severinus von Noricum.* Stuttgart.

MacGeorge, P. 2002. *Late Roman Warlords.* Oxford.

Matthews, J. 1976. "Mauretania in Ammianus and the Notitia," in R. Goodburn and P. Bartholomew (eds.), *Aspects of the Notitia Dignitatum.* Oxford, 157–86.

Moorhead, J. 1992. *Theoderic in Italy*. Oxford.

O'Flynn, J. M. 1983. *Generalissimos of the Western Roman Empire*. Edmonton.

Percival, J. 1976. *The Roman Villa*. London.

Sartre, M. 1982. *Trois etudes sur les Arabes romaines et Byzantines*. Brussels.

Schmitt, O. 1994. "Die Bucellarii, eine studie zum militärischen Gefolgschaftswesen in der Spätantike," *Tyche* 9: 147–74.

Shahid, I. 1984. *Byzantium and the Arabs of the Fourth Century*. Washington, DC.

Shaw, B. D. 1985. *Rulers, Nomads and Christians in Roman North Africa*. Brookfield, VT.

Thompson, E. A. 1969. *The Goths in Spain*. Oxford.

Whittaker, C. R. 1994. "Warlords and landlords in the later empire," in *Frontiers of the Roman Empire, a Social and Economic Study*. Baltimore, 243–78.

—— 2000. "Africa," in *CAH* 11. Cambridge, 518–31.

Whitby, M. 1995. "Recruitment in Roman armies from Justinian to Heraclius (ca. 565–615)," in Cameron, 61–124.

Williams, S., and G. Friell. 1999. *The Rome that did not Fall, the Survival of the East in the Fifth Century*. London.

CHAPTER TWENTY-SEVEN

The *Foederati*

Timo Stickler

1 Some Observations on Terminology

The *foederati* – everyone with more than a passing knowledge of Roman history will probably have a fairly precise idea of what this chapter has to be about: the barbarian peoples of mainly northern origin that during the fourth and fifth century managed to get access to the empire in increasing numbers, at first in small, isolated groups, but soon at least partly in large and more or less homogeneous ethnic formations. In this context, the Goths, who in 382 concluded a *foedus* with the emperor Theodosius the Great which was a sign of things to come, could serve as a good example for the impact of these developments on both the empire in general and the late Roman army in particular. One could indeed come to the conclusion that – together with a number of other internal as well as external factors – these events ultimately brought about the collapse of the civil and military structures of the western empire as well as creating a serious threat to the eastern empire, even though the latter eventually managed to consolidate itself.

This chapter will indeed deal with much of what has just been mentioned. The subject, however, poses a number of problems. Mainly it is the term *foederati* itself that creates difficulties, as it is a traditional term that was already in use under the Roman Republic, when it applied to allies of Rome with whom a *foedus* of either limited or unlimited duration was agreed upon that included certain sacral elements such as invoking curses on oneself if one violated its terms.[1] The Romans saw in these *foederati* separate and independent political entities and counted them among the *gentes externae*. Therefore they did not form a part of the Roman Empire proper, however close their actual relationship with the empire in reality may have been. Roman legal writers stuck to this definition right up to late antiquity (cf. *Dig.* 49.15.5 and 7), a fact that still exerts not inconsiderable influence on today's scholarly discussion – if the *foederati* of the fourth and fifth century were not a part of the Roman Empire, how was their integration into it possible?

It has been suggested that this problem could be avoided by ignoring legal theory and concentrating on the actual integration of allies into the empire instead. This would make it possible to apply the term *foederati* to a diverse range of barbarian groups settling within the empire and serving with the Roman military. Other interpreters have however quite rightly stressed that Roman law even in the fourth and fifth century had not lost its validity in external affairs; this line of thought resulted in repeated attempts to find a suitable definition for the term *foederati* and to explain how this definition had evolved in late antiquity. Thus it has been recently suggested – with some quite remarkable arguments – that the literary evidence for Gothic *foederati* in the fourth century is anachronistic and that it reflected a new and specifically western interpretation of the term *foederati* that had been created as late as during the reign of the emperor Honorius at the beginning of the fifth century.[2] This may be in more than one respect speculative and probably gives rise to at least as many questions as it answers. However, it nevertheless serves to highlight one important point deserving attention in the present chapter: the structural changes undergone by the late Roman army cannot have been effected by the *foederati* alone, as the title of this chapter might suggest. Instead, there evidently existed several different ways of integrating barbarian populations in the empire, and the granting of the status of *foederati* to barbarians who had already settled within the empire was only one of them, and possibly even a late one.[3] As most of the relevant sources from late antiquity lack either legal expertise or interest in legal matters it is rather difficult to get even a vaguely correct idea about these matters. This is all the more deplorable as the transformation of the late Roman army in the fourth and fifth centuries, and in its wake the transformation of the whole empire, is one of the most important aspects of Roman history of late antiquity.

2   Continuity from the Principate

There can be little doubt that the mass recruitment of barbarian mercenaries and the settlement of their families within the empire had a profound effect on the late Roman military and ultimately brought about significant changes. It should, however, be remembered that the practice of taking barbarians into military service was not invented by the late Roman emperors. Quite on the contrary, it was Caesar who during his Gallic war recruited Germanic cavalrymen who proved to be very useful in the final confrontation with Vercingetorix (Caesar, *B. Gal.* 7.65.4). During the following centuries of the principate it is then possible to observe that the relations between the Roman emperor and the barbarians beyond the Rhine and Danube were being steadily intensified. Sometimes, this could result in situations not too dissimilar from those found in late antiquity. Thus Marcus Aurelius, according to a fragment of Cassius Dio, in the course of the Marcomannic wars allowed 3,000 Naristi who had capitulated to settle within the boundaries of the empire (Cassius Dio 71.21). A surviving inscription shows that they later provided valuable military service to the empire in a cavalry unit (*AE* 1956, 124; see also *CIL* 3.4500). The case of the Naristi is in many ways comparable to what happened 200 years later – after the capitulation (*deditio*) the defeated were allowed to settle within the empire and in return had to serve in the emperor's army.

Another example serves well to illustrate the political implications of these relations between the Romans and the barbarians (cf. Tacitus, *Ann.* 2.63; Velleius Pat. 2.129.3 and Suetonius, *Tib.* 37.4): After the disintegration of the kingdom of Maroboduus in 19 AD, Tiberius not only allowed both the deposed king and his opponent Catualda into the empire but also gave each of them an estate, where they could live in retirement, Maroboduus in Italy and Catualda in Gaul. Far from leaving the former kingdom of Maroboduus to itself and thus creating a power vacuum immediately north of the Danube, the Romans instead installed Vannius, a Quadi tribesman, as the new king. His kingdom then lasted for several decades, well into the reign of the emperor Claudius. Taking a closer look at these events reveals elements of an imperial policy that in late antiquity was still regularly employed not only against the barbarians beyond the northern frontier of the empire. One example of this policy is the practice of allowing bankrupt potentates to live in retirement within the empire and keeping them in readily available reserve for any future eventualities. Another example is a certain reluctance on the side of the Romans to extend direct rule; instead, in some areas the establishing of client states under changing kings was preferred. Some scholars went too far in seeing these client states as directly under Roman rule as well; they assumed accordingly that the frontiers of the Roman Empire were effectively "invisible."[4] It is, however, quite clear that by establishing and maintaining intensive contacts into the *barbaricum* the Roman emperors of the principate had a profound influence on the political landscape immediately beyond the provincial frontiers. Indeed, it is possible to say that much of the barbarian world of *gentes* was to a great extent the result of Roman policy: "The Germanic world was perhaps the greatest and most enduring creation of Roman political and military genius."[5] Gaining control over this "Germanic world" was more important to the emperor than the creation of new provinces, as it significantly increased the security of a broad cordon of land separating the empire from the *barbaricum*. Within this cordon the construction of fortified provincial borders (e.g. the *limes* in Germany) was only one, albeit important, measure to mark the course of the frontier and at the same time to control the exchange of people and goods.[6]

3   The So-Called Barbarization of the Late Roman Army

During the principate the Romans in their relations with the *barbaricum* enjoyed a position of political, military, and cultural superiority. This usually had enabled the emperors both to prevail among their northern neighbors, who were in any case subdivided into many smaller political units, and – if necessary – to act from a position of strength. The already mentioned settlement of the Naristi by Marcus Aurelius is a particular case in point. This was to change significantly during late antiquity. Already during the third century the rising number of internal and external conflicts had led emperors and usurpers alike to increasingly recruit barbarian mercenaries.

Even the overall consolidation of the empire following the establishment of the tetrarchy did little to slow this development. Instead, barbarian mercenaries were recruited steadily throughout the fourth century, with Germanic officers soon quite regularly gaining the highest military and eventually even civilian positions. A majority of scholars have described this process as "barbarization," a term that is intended to signify that the army of the principate underwent a significant change through the mass recruitment of barbarian mercenaries. This change is thought to have eventually resulted in the Roman army no longer being able to cope with the new challenges facing it. It is argued that in assimilating its equipment, strategy, and tactics to that of the barbarians the Roman army is supposed to have squandered the superiority it once had enjoyed over its enemies, while the raising of private armies consisting of barbarian mercenaries, the so-called *bucellarii*, by high-ranking military and eventually even civilian officials seriously eroded the state's monopoly of the use of military force.[7] Continuing this line of argument the settlement of barbarian mercenaries and their families west of the Rhine and south of the Danube supposedly resulted in these areas becoming effectively barbarian land as early as the fourth century, a development ultimately culminating in the total collapse of the frontier defense in the fifth century.

In recent years however this concept of a "barbarization" of the late Roman army has met with increasing criticism. It has been stressed that in late antiquity the army particularly in the frontier zones was still able to display considerable military capabilities. Where earlier interpreters had stressed structural changes in the army the emphasis is now laid on the elements of continuity linking the army of the principate with its successor from late antiquity. It is also pointed out that many of the barbarian recruits were in fact loyal to Rome. In all, the fighting quality of the late Roman army is supposed to have been far from being seriously degraded through the influx of barbarian mercenaries; instead, in most cases it was still well able to fulfill its tasks.

As in other areas where no *communis opinio* has been established among the scholars, both the conflicting positions referred to above seem to be too extreme.[8] It is obvious that even the increased recruitment of barbarian soldiers did not degrade the fighting quality of the late Roman army at once. When employed as an emergency expedient to meet short term needs the recruiting of such mercenaries quite on the contrary often yielded the hoped-for results. Yet it nevertheless cannot be denied that in the long run the large numbers of barbarian soldiers in Roman service did indeed have significant effects for both Romans and barbarians. That a Germanic king like the Alaman Crocus could play an important role in the accession of the emperor Constantine in 306 (*Epit. de Caes.* 41.3) would have been unthinkable during the principate, and so would have been the fact that roughly 90 years later the half-Vandal Stilicho, at that time *magister utriusque militiae* in the western empire, could claim the guardianship over the children of the emperor Theodosius and succeed in gaining at least the tutelage over young Honorius (cf. e.g. Claudianus, *III Cons. Hon.* 151–159). It could of course be argued that Crocus and Stilicho were two rare and exceptional examples of barbarians who were particularly well integrated into the Roman world; but that was simply not the case.

Instead, there is even evidence suggesting that some barbarian officers apparently "wandered" between the Roman and the barbarian world – thus, Mallobaudes, who held the important office of *comes domesticorum* under the emperor Gratian is at the same time known as the king of a Frankish tribe (Ammianus Marc. 30.3.7 and 31.10.6). Similarly Hariulfus, who was born into the Burgundian royal family, later served as *protector domesticus* with an unknown Roman emperor or usurper (*CIL* 13.3682 = Dessau, *ILS* 2813). Germanic aristocrats enjoyed a variety of opportunities; even if they returned home after their military service they were able to use the prestige they had gained in the service of the emperor for either winning new followers or increasing an already existing following. And even if they did that, Rome could still reap some benefits. Just as had been the case under the principate men like Mallobaudes and Hariulfus helped Rome to distinguish friends from foes in the area beyond the frontiers of the empire, singling out potential supporters of Rome and providing early warning of possible threats. "Barbarization" of the Roman army was therefore not necessarily bad for the late Roman military, nor should it be seen as a symptom of a decaying empire in late antiquity. Instead it was an attempt, fundamentally similar to policies of the principate yet far more intensively pursued, to cope with potential troublemakers at the frontier of the empire and, if possible, to make them serve Rome's purposes.

4 "Reichsfränkisches Kriegermilieu" – An Example of a Successful Integration Policy

Any success of the "barbarization" outlined above depended entirely on whether the barbarian mercenaries and their families who had been allowed into the empire could be turned into "Romans" in the long term; in other words, successful integration could only be achieved if the Romans managed to replace any ties the barbarian soldiers still had to their old homes with newly formed bonds of loyalty towards the empire. Unlike under the principate the risk of failure was considerable during late antiquity, as the barbarian communities which the Romans targeted for their recruitment were different from those of the time of Marcus Aurelius. Now they were both larger and – because of their increased size – less stable than the communities the Romans had dealt with before. As they had usually evolved around a nucleus of tradition ("Traditionskern") of a particular ethnic group (*gens*), taking their name as well as their sense of identity from it, these formations are also called "gentile Verbände." From the third century onwards they became the partners as well as the adversaries of the Romans beyond the Rhine and Danube. They were led by kings, who were on the one hand ideally suited for negotiations with the Romans on matters of military service, but on the other hand difficult to control, as they were under constant pressure from their followers to secure them a basic livelihood as well as opportunities for winning booty and glory. Thus it is not really surprising to find the relationship of the empire with these "gentile Verbände" and their leadership from the third century onwards to be one of a constant alternation of aggressions, negotiations, broken treaties, and renewed attempts at reconciliation. With a large number of barbarians nonetheless serving in the Roman army, it was therefore crucial for the future of the empire in general and the Roman army in particular whether these "gentile Verbände" beyond Rhine and Danube could be successfully integrated into the military structures of the empire, or not.[9]

The first region of interest in this context is northern Gaul; because of its proximity to the Rhine frontier it allows valuable insight into how the defensive structures worked in late antiquity.[10] From the third century onwards, it is possible to observe how the imperial government and the provincial administrations by a host of different measures reorganized the defense of the provinces; in these schemes settlers and soldiers of barbarian origin assumed an increasingly important role. Thus from 297 onwards the so-called *laeti* (*Pan. Lat.* 8[5].21.1) are attested in the surviving sources; these were farmers of mainly Germanic origin who after their defeat had been allowed to settle in homogeneous settlements (*terrae laeticae*), which were under the control of the military administration. In times of war these *laeti* served under *praefecti laetorum*, officers appointed specifically for that task. Already in 232 the so-called *gentiles* are mentioned (*CIL* 13.6592 = Dessau, *ILS* 9184), who apparently were barbarian settlers as well, and they too, albeit not as often as the *laeti*, are mentioned as serving in the Roman army. It is still not totally clear how these *gentiles* differed from the *laeti* as far as their origin, legal status, and military deployment are concerned.

In any case both *laeti* and *gentiles* were people who had been allowed into the empire after they had been militarily defeated, but who had been settled on the territories assigned to them entirely according to the imperial administration's long-term strategy as well as the current needs of the military authorities. As they were ethnically heterogeneous, they did not develop any "*gens*-identity" around a nucleus of tradition of their own; this is apparently the reason why they were integrated fairly rapidly into the Roman population around them, leaving little original archaeological material in the process. A particular class of burials that until fairly recently were called *laeti*-graves ("Laetengräber") have nothing to do with the *laeti*. These graves are characterized by a distinct mixture of items of Germanic origin (weapons, certain types of brooches) and others clearly of Roman origin (mainly products of late-Roman mass production). They begin to appear around the middle of the fourth century and are closely connected to garrisons of any size in northern Gaul. Apparently they represent a population that had been settled by the emperor or his officials within the empire primarily in return for military service (in contrast to the *laeti* who were settled primarily as farmers and were only called up as the need arose). This has recently led to associating these graves with the term *foederati* ("Föderatengräber"); however, as archaeological finds obviously cannot yield any information on the legal status of those buried in these graves, this association is problematical, too. Rather, taking together the archaeological finds and the literary sources, the following picture emerges: the communities burying their dead in these graves preserved over several generations certain elements of a way of life that is commonly regarded as Germanic; yet at the same time these people evidently were open to Roman influence. Apparently it seemed to be a kind of "Mischzivilisation" that characterized the frontier regions of northern Gaul in the second half of the fourth century.[11] As the literary sources suggest that the people living there were Franks, Horst Wolfgang Böhme coined the term "reichsfränkisches Kriegermilieu."[12]

Looking at the various developments in northern Gaul in the fourth and fifth century makes it fairly obvious that the employment and settlement described above of barbarian mercenaries – of presumably Frankish origin – and their families north of the Loire had far-reaching consequences. From the 350s onwards – when the *Caesar* Julian and later the emperor Valentinian I began to restore the border defenses which had suffered during the preceding civil war – well into the fifth century, generations of these soldiers served the empire loyally, minor incidents notwithstanding. Countless Frankish noblemen served as officers in the Roman army, and during the second half of the fourth century men like Merobaudes, Bauto, and Arbogast not only gained the highest command posts in the Roman army, but also – in the case of Bauto – managed to marry into the imperial family (Philostorgis 11.6). And even if in the fifth century Frankish leaders did not enjoy the same influential positions at the imperial court as in the previous century, the situation in northern Gaul still remained by and large unchanged. Equipped with weapons from imperial *fabricae* the Frankish soldiers continued to serve the emperor even in times of crisis as in 406/7 and 451. Childeric, father of Clovis, the founder of the Merovingian Empire, in the 460s still preferred to cooperate with Roman generals and was buried with the insignia of the officer's rank the emperor had bestowed on him. Basically it was only during the final decline of the western empire that the cooperation between Romans and Franks in northern Gaul did change significantly, but even then the transition from late Roman to Merovingian times was a remarkably smooth one; those belonging to the "reichsfränkische Kriegermilieu" now served with the Merovingian kings instead of the emperor. Thus at many places, for example at the well-known Gelduba (Krefeld-Gellep), this transition is not marked by any archaeological disturbances; late Roman times simply faded away into the early medieval era. The last "Roman" enclaves like the principalities of the *Romanorum rex* Syagrius (Gregory of Tours, *HF* 2.27) and of *comes* Arbogast around Trier could easily be eliminated in the 480s; they had simply lost their function.[13]

In looking at the role these barbarian soldiers in northern Gaul had in the overall transformation of the late Roman defense structures in the area one cannot fail to notice that it proved to be quite a constructive one. It is of secondary importance that the surviving sources do not allow a precise determination of their legal status. Even if, as in the case of the Salic Franks, who were settled in 358 by *Caesar* Julian within the empire (Ammianus Marc. 17.8), literary sources survive, these usually take little interest in purely legal matters. Of much more importance is the simple fact that the system – based on a continuing cooperation and mutual integration as far as military affairs were concerned – did in fact work and survived even in times of dangerous crisis right up to the end of the Roman Empire in the west, when with the collapse of the last structures in Italy and Gaul that were directly focused on the emperor it had finally become obsolete. Defending northern Gaul had been successful over several decades not because the Romans had in every case destroyed the ethnic structures that had characterized the barbarians in Roman

service (even though this was the case with the *laeti* and the *gentiles*), but quite on the contrary because they had learned to make use of them. After the western empire – and with it the one point of reference common to Romans and barbarians alike – ceased to exist, these ethnic formations in whose creation the Romans once had had a part could replace it. In that respect the emerging Merovingian kingdom is the result of the transformation of Roman military structures in northern Gaul.

5   The "Hunnic Alternative" – Incompatible with the Defense Policies of the Empire

On the Rhine and in northern Gaul Roman border defense was, as has been out-lined in the previous paragraphs, quite successful; this is also amply illustrated by comparing this success with the results of Roman efforts elsewhere in the empire. The Roman defensive system on the Danube collapsed in the second half of the fourth century, with consequences for the whole Balkan region. The Romans eventually managed to stabilize the situation again; this however involved shifting barbarian attention away from Thracia and Macedonia towards the West, a process that in the long run was to have far-reaching consequences.

There is an established consensus that the Huns, rooted in central Asian nomadic traditions played a crucial role in the aforementioned events by initiating and con-tinuously enforcing them. The mass exodus of Gothic groups into the empire in 376 that the Romans struggled to solve by means of treaties, the catastrophic defeat inflicted on the eastern mobile army in 378 at Adrianople, and the formation of new barbarian entities like the one of King Alaric in the 390s had all been ultimately caused by the Huns' appearance in Europe. A closer look at their way of ruling and waging war reveals both the limitations and the strengths of a late Roman defense strategy which rested primarily on the integration of barbarian mercenaries.[14]

One of the main characteristics of the Huns was that the bands that went under their name did not constitute an ethnically defined entity. Although their leaders were indeed of Hunnic origin, this apparently did not stimulate a process of ethno-genesis, as a comparable situation often did in the case of Germanic peoples. Thus Charaton, one of the prominent figures north of the Danube in the years after 410 appears in the sources as "first among the kings" of the Huns (Olympiodorus fr. 19 Blockley: ὁ τῶν ῥηγῶν πρῶτος), and likewise Attila 40 years later was by no means the master of all Huns. It is evident that the Huns, far from being the result of an ethnogenesis of enormous dimensions, in fact were a constantly changing coalition of diverse groups of warriors, its size as well as membership depending on short-term military successes. It is therefore not surprising that even in the inner circle around Attila – the group of persons called λογάδες in Priscus' famous account (cf. Priscus fr. 11–14 Blockley) – not only Huns but also men from other barbarian peo-ples could be found, like the Gepid Ardaric or even "Romans" like Orestes, the father of the later Roman emperor Romulus Augustulus. After the death of Attila in 453 this warrior coalition as a result disintegrated into the small groups it was originally formed from. The ethnically homogeneous Hunnic element then turned out to be so small that it could be fairly easily controlled by the Romans.

From a Roman point of view far more important than the suddenness of their appearance around 375 or certain peculiarities of their weaponry and equipment was the fact that the barbarian armies led by the Huns did not constitute a huge single ethnical entity; this made them both incalculable and uncontrollable and hence particularly dangerous. Ethnically defined groups ("gentile Verbände") had a nucleus of ethnic traditions providing the whole group both with cohesion and a tendency to close its ranks even further, however diverse its origins may have been. Here the civil and military authorities of the empire could come into the play: they could actively support this process by allowing small and controllable ethnic groups to settle within the empire. Furthermore the emperor, by taking their chieftains into his military service as officers, or by acknowledging them as kings, offered them the possibility of participation while at the same time binding their longer-term interests to that of the empire. Thus a network of relations was established beyond the river frontiers that, apart from occasional interruptions by elements who saw themselves as the losers from these arrangements, in the long run had a positive effect on security along the borders rather than a negative one.

With the Huns however everything was different. Their leaders did not want to establish any friendly long-term relations with the emperor and were even less interested in the prospect of integration into the military or civil structures of the empire. Quite on the contrary they maintained a sharp separation between themselves and the empire, and any attempts of "Hunnic" barbarians to join the Roman side were prevented by force and met with brutal punishment (Priscus fr. 2 Blockley). In a sequence of acts of aggression and treaties the Hunnic kings year after year managed to extort large amounts of money and other benefits, which in turn increased their prestige in a way that meant they were eventually able to control most of the military potential beyond the Danube. It was only in the 440s under Attila that Hunnic policies underwent a significant change. Apparently realizing that the conventional Hunnic patterns of behavior of alternatively blackmailing and fighting the Romans had finally reached the limits of their usefulness, he tried to seize some territories within the empire (Priscus fr. 11.1 Blockley), get a military office for himself (Priscus fr. 11.2 Blockley: στρατηγοῦ' Ῥωμαίων), and even marry into the emperor's family (e.g. John of Antioch fr. 199.2 = Priscus fr. 17 Blockley). All these are patterns of behavior that were typical for leaders of ethnically defined groups. The untimely death of Attila however brought this to a premature end.

The confrontation with the Hunnic alternative, in comparison to the quite successful integration policy the Romans applied to the Franks in northern Gaul, left the defense structures on the Rhine and Danube frontier in a precarious position as it did not allow the Romans to employ the military strategies they had applied so successfully in northern Gaul. Instead, the dominant position that the Huns – despite temporary setbacks – managed to maintain in the *barbaricum* effectively denied the Romans access to much of what had been one of their key areas of mercenary recruitment. As a result, the imperial government especially in the West was in times of military crisis faced with the problem of hardly getting any troops at all. Also, the

Hunnic pressure on other barbarian communities beyond the Rhine and Danube had made an organic development of the political and military relations between the latter and the Romans impossible. Instead, Rome was repeatedly forced to react swiftly in a way that often overstressed the capabilities of its military structures on the border as well as in the hinterland. The years after 400 are a case in point here, when Germanic and Alanic contingents who did not want to join forces with the Huns moved towards the West, invaded the provinces of Raetia and Noricum and ultimately crossed the Rhine on December 31, 406. In the face of such a sudden and massive threat the existing defense system, well-tried though it was, failed, even if some Frankish contingents operating in northern Gaul and close to the Rhine still continued to serve loyally with the emperor (Orosius 7.40.3; Gregory of Tours, *HF* 2.9). Now, as had already been the case in 376, the "protracted process"[15] which the Huns' actions in Europe resembled had initiated a development that proved to be crucial not only for the defense of the empire but for its very existence.

6   Roman Military Policy South of the Danube after AD 376/8

The appearance of the Huns around 375 had led to dramatic changes in the Balkans which did not spare the Roman defense structures. As the relevant events are well known,[16] it will be sufficient to give only a brief summary. The elimination of the Gothic kingdom of Ermanaric by the Huns had resulted in several smaller barbarian groups, who did not want to submit to the victors, trying to escape. Their options however were severely limited. Apart from acknowledging the Huns as their new masters their only alternative was crossing the Danube and by doing so entering the Roman Empire. Negotiations with the emperor Valens were at first promising, and in 376 a large number of mainly Gothic refugees were accepted into the territories south of the Danube. Only a short time later, however, in a general atmosphere of mistrust and corruption, the situation escalated. Minor friction eventually gave way to open hostilities which in turn culminated in the epoch-making battle of Adrianople on August 9, 378. At the end of that fateful day the emperor Valens lay dead on the battlefield together with two-thirds of the eastern mobile army, while barbarian hordes were sweeping freely through the Balkans, spreading terror and confusion – a result no Roman would ever have thought possible. Even though the existence of the empire as a whole was not immediately threatened by this defeat it was nevertheless clear that a huge effort, as well as a new approach to the problem of securing the borders, was needed to address this situation.

Therefore the solutions actually found by Valens' successor Theodosius during the following years were of great importance both for the fate of the empire as a whole and the late Roman army in particular. There were two aspects in particular that had a profound influence on the actions of the new emperor. On the one hand it was obvious that the victorious Goths and their allies would not leave the empire again voluntarily. On the other hand – as from a military point of view the empire was at that moment seriously weakened – they could be put to good use in replenishing the ranks of the Roman army which had been depleted by the disaster of Adrianople. These two aspects were reflected by the treaty between the Romans and the Goths that was agreed upon in 382.[17] The Goths were settled as a separate community, enjoying a certain degree of autonomy within the empire while owing military service to the emperor in times of war. But although the Gothic contingents were theoretically to serve under a Roman *dux*, they in reality followed their own leaders. Similarly a complete civil integration into the population of the empire was apparently not aimed at, as the right of intermarriage (*conubium*) between Goths and Romans was not part of this treaty. While scholars differ over details, there is nevertheless a consensus that these regulations were new and rather special.[18] Although the term *foederati* (φοιδεράτοι) that was applied by Jordanes (*Get.* 145) and Procopius (*Bella* 4.5.13) to the new allies has to be regarded as an anachronism of the sixth century,[19] it can certainly be said that due to the pressing needs Theodosius found a new way to deal with the critical situation after Adrianople. This in turn paved the way for the consolidation of the Goths in the Balkans in the following years and ultimately made possible the creation of a kingdom based on an ethnically defined group within the boundaries of the empire by Alaric in the 390s, something that would not have happened without the treaty of 382.

This turn of events was furthered at the same time by other developments in the empire. Within a decade Theodosius had to campaign twice against usurpers, in 388 against Magnus Maximus and in 394 against Eugenius; then in 395, just after the civil wars finally had ended, the "friend of the peace and of the Goths" (Jordanes, *Get.* 146: *amator pacis generisque Gothorum*) died, leaving the empire to his underage children. Now any coordinated policy by the two imperial governments aiming at integrating the Goths into the military and civil structures of the empire from a position of strength was out of the question. Quite the contrary, those who had appeared at the frontier of the empire in 376 as refugees succeeded in the 390s in firmly establishing themselves in a central position in the Balkans between the western and the eastern empire. From there they were actively involved in the intrigues that followed the death of Theodosius, supporting now the court at Milan or Ravenna, now that at Constantinople according to their current intentions. In the course of these events Alaric showed how high a king of a *gens* could rise by cleverly exploiting the strengths and weaknesses of his Roman opponents. He soon gained the title of *magister militum per Illyricum* (Claudianus, *In Eutr.* 214–220 and Claudianus, *B. Get.* 535–539) from the eastern emperor Arcadius – an office in which he was confirmed a few years later by Honorius out of short-term motives as well – combining thus the authority of a Roman official with that of a Gothic king. Alaric's position was therefore markedly different from that of barbarian officers like Arbogast or Bauto, as he – although he was still formally integrated into the empire – in reality apparently followed his own objectives which were at odds with the interests of the empire in some crucial aspects. As a result of his successful veering between east and west his wandering army, which had long ceased to consist only of Gothic contingents, steadily increased in size. This was, however, not without problems for Alaric since in order to fulfill the demands of his growing number of followers he in turn had to set his aims higher and higher. Although the eastern government may have felt a certain relief when the Goths turned their attention after the turn of the century mainly to Italy, this proved to be short-sighted. When Alaric's wandering army finally left the Balkans in 408 in search of a new territory capable of sustaining it, more and more damage was caused by it. The Goths now roamed through Italy, Gaul, and Spain, putting the already crippled structures of the Roman Empire under strain to the point of collapse wherever they tried to establish themselves permanently. As a result, the emperor Honorius and his successors had to run even greater risks while trying to retain at least some of the civil and military structures of the empire.

7   The Dilemma of the Western Empire in the Fifth Century

The way the Romans dealt with Alaric and his successors clearly shows that already at the beginning of the fifth century and even before the collapse of the Rhine frontier in 406/7 the western empire was in grave trouble. Neither the *magister militum* Stilicho, who de facto held power in Milan and Ravenna respectively nor his adversaries in Constantinople wanted to do without the military services of the Gothic army roaming through the Balkans. For Stilicho the possibility of regaining the disputed dioceses of Macedonia and Dacia for Honorius was far too tempting. After all, wasn't Alaric a "Roman" officer and those serving in his army therefore "Roman" soldiers?

One of the reasons why the Gothic military potential seemed to be so attractive to Stilicho and his successors lies no doubt in the internal power struggles the empire was engaged in at the time. A reason of a more technical nature, but equally important, was the difficulty in recruiting troops in the traditional manner which the Roman military administration in the West was experiencing towards the end of the fourth century. Not only did wealthy landowners stop providing recruits for the army for fear of weakening their own economic situation (Vegetius 1.28 and Symmachus, *Epist.* 6.64; cf. also *Cod. Theod.* 7.13.8 dating from 380 AD); the military challenges the empire faced around 400 also often presented themselves with little or no forewarning, making it increasingly difficult to meet them with armies that had been regularly recruited and equipped. The conscription of complete barbarian contingents in times of an emergency was both easier and cheaper (Ammianus Marc. 31.4.4),[20] and after the end of the hostilities these troops could be paid and sent back home, freeing the state from the need to support a standing army. In this manner Stilicho had acquired his troops during his inspection tours of the Rhine in 396 and the Danube in 401. A master of improvisation, he managed after the defeat of the barbarian army of Radagaesus, which had invaded Italy in 405/6, to recruit 12,000 elite soldiers from the remnants of the defeated army (Orosius 7.37.14–16; Olympiodorus fr. 9 Blockley).

This approach to the structural problems of the late Roman army – which did not have its origin with Stilicho even though it was consistently employed by him – was however fraught with danger, as was made abundantly clear after Stilicho's assassination. In 408 the empire was nearly paralyzed militarily, as the loyalty of many of the barbarian soldiers recruited by Stilicho ended with the latter's death; many who suddenly found themselves without a leader and were additionally threatened by the newly influential circles at the court then turned to Alaric and his Goths (Zosimus 5.35.5f.). This makes both the uselessness of oaths of loyalty and the fragility of the military command structure at the time abundantly clear. One of Stilicho's successors, the *patricius* and later emperor Constantius III, then managed to consolidate the western empire during the years up to 421; he was however unable to address the fundamental problems that had already been revealed at the beginning of the century. Thus improving the recruitment of citizens of the empire, something that has already been mentioned conflicted with the economic interests of the landowners, continued to be a subject of lawmaking (cf. e.g. *Novellae Valentiniani* 6.1–3 from the 440s). On the other hand the recruiting of barbarian mercenaries became increasingly attractive as a "cheap" stop-gap solution and was accordingly more and more used; it brought, however, great dangers with it, as the fate of Alaric's Goths clearly shows.

The death of Alaric in 410 had not resulted in his wandering army breaking up. Instead his successors Athaulf and Vallia managed to keep it together as well as preserving its military edge at first in Gaul (from 412) and afterwards in Spain (from 415). The emperor repeatedly tried to take the Goths into his service, but without success; as a result they remained a permanent cause of unrest, being involved in several usurpations and revolts. Only the aforementioned Constantius III managed to corner the Goths by employing the logistical capabilities of the empire, which were still superior to those of its adversaries. As a result the Goths accepted a new treaty by the terms of which they had to provide military service to the emperor in return for land in Aquitaine.[21] However, although in 418 such an outcome had to be seen as acceptable, it was nevertheless obvious that the Goths still remained as a homogeneous group with their own military organization. It took rather little to push the new treaty beyond its limitations: after the unexpected death of the emperor Constantius III in 421 and new civil war in 423/5 the Goths in Aquitaine again had the opportunity to evade their treaty obligations. Soon there was no mention of Goths serving under Roman commanders any more, the sources instead indicating that with an increasing frequency Gothic leaders or kings sought a direct confrontation with the empire. Thus the whole history of the Gothic kingdom of Toulouse after 418 shows how the western emperor slowly but steadily lost control over his former treaty partner in a continuous process that was only interrupted by a few retarding moments.[22] One of these was without doubt Attila's invasion into Gaul in 451. On that occasion Goths and Romans fought together against the Huns, but although Aetius had invested a huge amount of time and effort in bringing together his coalition, it rapidly dissolved again after the battle. Already at that time the main dilemma of the western empire was obvious: by making itself militarily dependant on ethnically defined barbarian contingents led by kings the empire had to rely entirely on their goodwill. During the conflict with Attila, the truly "Roman" forces, i.e. troops that were not recruited among the barbarians, played only a minor role.

8   Roman Military Policy on the Rhine after AD 406/7

It is beyond the scope of this chapter to describe in full the effects of the Hunnic incursion into Europe and Alaric's movements to the West. A few selected examples will suffice to show how the emperors dealt with the challenges these two processes represented as well as how the Roman military tried to cope with the new threats it faced – ultimately without success.

The invasion of the Vandals, Alans, and Sueves who crossed the Rhine on December 31, 406, proved to be a turning point not only for those areas immediately affected by it, but for the western empire as a whole. As has already been mentioned above, the defense structures on the Rhine which had been reorganized in the second half of the fourth century had worked properly even in the face of this unexpected threat. In fact, the allies of the Romans, among them undoubtedly also those belonging to the "reichsfränkische Kriegermilieu" loyally fulfilled their treaty obligations, but in the end they succumbed to the invaders' superior military strength. As a result numerous barbarian groups of widely differing sizes gained access into the Gallic interior throughout 407. And when in 409 some of them crossed the Pyrenees the opportunity for containing this danger within the Gallic provinces had already been lost. Hastily proclaimed emperors like Constantine (III), Iovinus, and Maximus managed to achieve some military successes, but these were only of a temporary nature, and the usurpers disappeared from the scene almost as rapidly as they had appeared.[23]

With hindsight the failure of the Roman civil and military structures in Gaul and Spain would seem to have been both predetermined and inevitable. It is, however, often overlooked that throughout the whole time right until the end of the western empire in 476 the imperial government repeatedly and actively attempted to remedy the situation caused by the events of 406/7, or at the very least to lessen the damage it was doing to the empire. This will be illustrated by taking a closer look at two of these attempts – the case of the Vandals and that of the Burgundians – of which the first was a failure while the second was successful.

The Vandals, after they had arrived in Spain in 409, became a major target for aggressive Roman military policy. This amply shows that Ravenna refused to consider the new situation brought about by their invasion as irreversible and at the very least still hoped to be able to roll back the barbarians. In the case of the Vandals, however, all attempts to that end failed. Neither the offensives of Constantius III in 416/18 nor the campaign of his successor Castinus in 422 brought any lasting success; quite the contrary, while they managed to decimate the Vandalic and Alanic groups, they also caused the two groups to join together to form one large entity which then at the end of the decade was led by Geiseric, adopting the title of *rex Vandalorum et Alanorum* (Victor of Vita 2.39 and 3.3). Personally experiencing the aggressive Roman policy aimed at containing the Vandals seems to have had left a lasting impression on him, for during his long reign which spanned almost half a century he carefully avoided offering the Romans an opportunity for such action again. After his invasion of North Africa in 429, and even after he had acquired new territories and secured his position through various treaties he continued to act with great care, launching from time to time raids against the Romans that to them seemed to be of an arbitrary nature yet in reality were part of a well-calculated policy. The example of the Vandals clearly shows how aggressive policies of the Romans could have disastrous results if they were unsuccessful; one wonders what would have happened had Geiseric and his *gens* been offered a place in the army of the emperor and had their integration into the civil and military structures of the empire been successful.

The case of the Burgundians may hint at an answer to that question. The history of their relationship with the Romans was also far from trouble-free; after they had crossed the Rhine in the wake of the events of 406/7 they founded a short-lived kingdom on the left bank of the Rhine, which was eliminated by Aetius as early as 435/7 for reasons that are not completely clear. Remnants of these Burgundians then surfaced a few years later in the lands around Lake Geneva; apparently they served there to protect vital passes over the Alps into Italy. The Burgundians were a far smaller group than either Alaric's Goths or the Vandals led by Geiseric, which is probably the reason why they were not able to offer much resistance to the demands of the Romans. Their successful integration into the defense organization of Gaul after 443 is nevertheless quite remarkable: when Attila invaded Gaul in 451 they readily served in Aetius' army in the defense of Gaul (cf. Jordanes, *Get.* 191). And even afterwards they stayed loyal to the rapidly changing emperors in Ravenna, serving the Roman cause so well that their kings Gundioc and Chilperic were eventually rewarded with the title *magister militum per Gallias* (cf. e.g. Hilarius, *Epist.* 9 Thiel: *viri illustris magistri militum Gunduici*). One of the leaders of this *gens*, named Gundobad, even became the most important general in the empire as well as kingmaker in the last years of the western empire between 472 and 474. The Burgundians, by the 460s at latest, did of course gradually increase their autonomy in the territories they controlled. Nevertheless Aetius' original intentions of integrating them into the civil and military structures of southern Gaul had not failed, and the Burgundians fulfilled their treaty obligations right up to the end of the western empire. It was not their fault that their main point of reference, the emperor, faded away from the 450s onwards; they kept their loyalty far longer than other allies of the Romans.

9 Conclusion

As has already been shown at the beginning of this chapter, finding a suitable terminology for the many different ways the Romans developed to integrate barbarian soldiers into their army structure poses a number of problems. *Foederati* is just one possible term among a number of others, and perhaps not even the most likely one. It has indeed been widely applied in the fifth century to barbarian soldiers serving in the Roman army whether for a longer period of time or only for the duration of one campaign. However, no certainty can be attained as to whether the term *foederati* really describes a coherent concept that was created in the fourth century and that was universally employed for the integration of barbarian soldiers into the military of the late empire. In fact, the military structures in late antiquity seem to have varied as much as the challenges the imperial administrations in the West and in the East had to face. These difficulties notwithstanding this chapter can be concluded with some summarizing remarks that should make developments during that period more transparent and easier to understand.

First of all it is necessary to stress that there was a significant continuity of patterns and practices established under the principate into late antiquity. Neither settling barbarian groups inside the boundaries of the empire, nor employing them as soldiers, nor integrating even comparatively large populations through military service was entirely unheard of before. In northern Gaul the incorporation of successive groups of mainly Frankish immigrants over a period of several generations proved that the Roman military was still quite capable of successful integration even during the fourth and fifth century. Likewise, the settlement of the Burgundians in southern Gaul which – in contrast to the integration of the Franks – took place at comparatively short notice, yielded good results. Burgundians and Franks styled themselves later as descendants of the Romans (Ammianus Marc. 28.5.11; Orosius 7.32.12) or at least of being of Trojan origin (Ps.-Fredegar, *Chron.* 2.4–6 and 3.2); could integration have been any more successful?

Yet incorporating barbarian populations into the empire was for a variety of reasons not always as easy as in these two cases. Among the most important of these certainly was the interdependency between Rome's internal affairs and the policy towards the *gentes* across the Rhine and Danube. Whenever the Romans were preoccupied with internal strife, in the process turning their attention away from potential enemies beyond the frontiers of the empire, they effectively encouraged the barbarians to take advantage of the situation by invading the empire or, if they already settled within its boundaries, by extending their spheres of influence. This phenomenon can already be observed in the fourth century, for instance between 350 and 353 during the civil war between Constantius II and the usurper Magnentius, and later decades right up to the end of the western empire provide ample examples of it. Thus even during its last years Roman rule was significantly weakened by internecine conflict raging mainly in Gaul following the murder of the emperor Majorian in 461; as a result, the last barbarian allies finally joined those trying to divide up the remnants of the empire among them. At that point it was practically impossible to mobilize for military service the barbarian kings still bound by treaties to the emperor, and the garrisons on the Rhine and Danube silently faded away into the early Middle Ages (cf. Eugippius, *Vit. Sev.* 20). When the western emperor as the guarantor of the treaties they once had agreed upon finally ceased to exist, they once and for all lost a crucial point of reference connecting them to Ravenna and the empire.

NOTES

1   Cf. Schwarcz 1995, 290: "Vertragspartner Roms, mit denen ein befristetes oder unbefristetes *foedus* unter Einbeziehung sakraler Elemente wie der Selbstexsekration für den Fall des Vertragsbruchs abgeschlossen worden war."

2 Cf. Scharf 2001, 28ff. Cf. also Schwarcz 1995, 290ff.

3 Cf. in this context also Heather 1997, 57–74.

4 The concept of the "invisible borders of the Roman empire" has somewhat fallen out of favour; cf. Wolters 1990, 11ff. In recent years the discussion has been revived mainly by Anglo-American studies. For references, see Wheeler (in this volume) n.1.

5 Geary 1988, vi.

6 For the concept of a border zone between the empire and the *barbaricum* see Whittaker 1994, *passim*.

7 This traditional interpretation of the *bucellarii*, which Liebeschuetz 1986, 463–74 advocates, has in recent years increasingly met with criticism; cf. Schmitt 1994, 147–74 and Carrié 1995, 27–59.

8 Liebeschuetz 1990, 7ff. may be mentioned here as an example of the position that the "barbarization" of the Roman army in late antiquity brought about grave dangers to the empire. This position was quite vehemently contested by Elton 1996.

9 Modern scholarship on the *gentes* in late antiquity goes back to the study of Wenskus 1961. The following decades have seen a marked increase in research based on the study of Wenskus, for which the series edited by I. Wood under the title *The Transformation of the Roman World* is an example; see recently Goetz et al. 2003. Wenskus' position has however also found critics; the collection of Gillett 2002 serves well to illustrate the debate. See also Liebeschuetz (in this volume) with n.20.

10 See also Liebeschuetz (in this volume).

11 Cf. also Périn 1998, 59–81.

12 Böhme 1974 is still the most important work of reference. Recently Halsall 2000 has repeatedly questioned Böhme's interpretation of the archaeological findings from northern Gaul. Even Halsall has to admit, however, that those buried in the "*foederati*-graves" "looked inwards – to Rome – for the justification of their power" (ibid., 178). They therefore had a connection to the empire and wanted to maintain it; this seems to suggest that they were indeed, as Böhme has suggested, fully integrated into the defense structures of northern Gaul.

13 There is a rich documentation of the finds from Krefeld-Gellep/Gelduba; see Reichmann 1999, 129–44. Bridger and Gilles 1998 covers the whole Rhine and Danube frontier and is mainly based on the most recent archaeological research. On the principality of Syagrius around Soissons cf. MacGeorge 2002, 111ff.

14 The main work of reference on the Hunnic rule is Maenchen-Helfen 1973. In recent years Pohl 1992, 165–207 has made further valuable contributions; cf. also Stickler 2002, 85ff. The term "Hunnic alternative" ("*hunnische Alternative*") goes back to Wolfram 1990b, 183.

15 Heather 1995, 37.

16 Heather 1991, 122ff.; Burns 1994 and Wolfram 1990a, 125ff.

17 For a detailed account of the treaty regulations and the relevant sources cf. Schulz 1993, 178f. See also ibid., 57ff.

18 Cf. Pohl 2002, 51ff. A more skeptical view is held by Scharf 2001, 21ff. and Kulikowski 2002, 77ff.

19 See also Heather 1997, 57ff. and Scharf 2001, 28ff. with valuable arguments.

20 On this particular way of recruiting mercenaries and the dangers that came with it, cf. Liebeschuetz 1993, 265–76 and Cesa 1993, 21–9.

21 For the sources on the treaty of 418 see Schulz 1993, 181.

22 Cf. Stickler 2002, 203ff.; see in this context also Drinkwater and Elton 1992.

23 Cf. Drinkwater and Elton 1992.

BIBLIOGRAPHY

Anke, B. 1998. *Studien zur reiternomadischen Kultur des 4. bis 5 Jahrhunderts.* Weißbach.

Barnwell, P. S. 1992. *Emperor, Prefects and Kings. The Roman West, 395–565.* London.

Bierbrauer, V. 1994. "Archäologie und Geschichte der Goten vom 1.–7. Jahrhundert. Versuch einer Bilanz," *Frühmittelalterliche Studien* 28: 51–171.

Böhme, H. W. 1974. *Germanische Grabfunde des 4. bis 5. Jahrhunderts zwischen unterer Elbe und Loire. Studien zur Chronologie und Bevölkerungsgeschichte,* 2 vols. Munich.

Bridger, C., and K.-J. Gilles (eds.). 1998. *Spätrömische Befestigungsanlagen in den Rhein- und Donauprovinzen.* Oxford.

Burns, Th. S. 1994. *Barbarians within the Gates of Rome. A Study of Roman Military Policy and the Barbarians, ca. 375–425 AD.* Bloomington.

Cameron, A., and P. Garnsey (eds.). 1998. *CAH* 13. *The Late Empire, AD 337–425.* Cambridge.

Cameron, A., B. Ward-Perkins, and M. Whitby (eds.). 2000. *CAH* 14. *Late Antiquity. Empire and Successors, AD 425–600.* Cambridge.

Carrié, J.-M. 1995. "L'Etat à la recherche de nouveaux modes de financement des armées (Rome et Byzance, IVᵉ–VIIIᵉ siècles)," in A. Cameron (ed.), *The Byzantine and Early Islamic Near East. Vol. III: States, Resources and Armies.* Princeton, 27–59.

Cesa, M. 1993. "Römisches Heer und barbarische Föderaten: Bemerkungen zur weströmischen Politik in den Jahren 402–412," in F. Vallet and M. Kazanski (eds.), *L'armée romaine et les Barbares du IIIᵉ au VIIᵉ siècle.* Condé-sur-Noireau, 21–9.

Drinkwater, J., and H. Elton (eds.). 1992. *Fifth-Century Gaul: A Crisis of Identity?* Cambridge.

Elton, H. 1996. *Warfare in Roman Europe, AD 350–425.* Oxford.

Geary, P. J. 1988. *Before France and Germany. The Creation and Transformation of the Merovingian World.* New York.

Geuenich, D. (ed.). 1998. *Die Franken und die Alemannen bis zur "Schlacht bei Zülpich" (496/97).* Berlin.

Gillett, A. (ed.). 2002. *On Barbarian Identity: Critical Approaches to Ethnicity in the Early Middle Ages.* Turnhout.

Goetz, H.-W., J. Jarnut, and W. Pohl. 2003. *Regna and Gentes. The Relation between Late Antique and Early Medieval Peoples and Kingdoms in the Transformation of the Roman World.* Leiden.

Halsall, G. 2000. "Archaeology and the late Roman frontier in northern Gaul: The so-called 'Föderatengräber' reconsidered," in W. Pohl and H. Reimitz (eds.), *Grenze und Differenz im frühen Mittelalter.* Vienna, 167–80.

Heather, P. 1991. *Goths and Romans 332–489.* Oxford.

—— 1995. "The Huns and the end of the Roman Empire in western Europe," *English Historical Review* 110: 37.

—— 1997. "*Foedera* and *foederati* of the fourth century," in W. Pohl, *Kingdoms of the Empire. The Integration of Barbarians in Late Antiquity.* Leiden, 57–74.

James, E. 1988. *The Franks.* Oxford.

Jones, A. H. M. 1964. *The Later Roman Empire, 284–602. A Social, Economical and Administrative Survey,* 4 vols. Oxford.

Kulikowski, M. 2002. "Nation vs. army: A necessary contrast?" in Gillett, 69–84.

Liebeschuetz, J. H. W. G. 1986. "Generals, federates and *bucellarii* in Roman armies around AD 400," in Ph. Freeman and D. Kennedy (eds.), *The Defence of the Roman and Byzantine East. Proceedings of a Colloquium held at the University of Sheffield in April 1986.* Oxford, 463–74.

—— 1990. *Barbarians and Bishops. Army, Church, and State in the Age of Arcadius and Chrysostom.* Oxford.

—— 1993. "The end of the Roman army in the western empire," in J. Rich and G. Shipley (eds.), *War and Society in the Roman World*. London, 265–76.

MacGeorge, P. 2002. *Later Roman Warlords*. Oxford.

Maenchen-Helfen, O. J. 1973. *The World of the Huns. Studies in Their History and Culture*. Berkeley.

Périn, P. 1998. "La progression des Francs en Gaule du Nord au Ve siècle. Histoire et archéologie," in D. Geuenich (ed.), *Die Franken und die Alemannen bis zur "Schlacht bei Zülpich" (496/97)*. Berlin, 59–81.

Pohl, W. 1992. "Konfliktverlauf und Konfliktbewältigung: Römer und Barbaren im frühen Mittelalter," *Frühmittelalterliche Studien* 26: 165–207.

—— 2002. *Die Völkerwanderung. Eroberung und Integration*. Stuttgart.

Reichmann, Ch. 1999. "Germanen im spätantiken Gelduba (Krefeld-Gellep)," in Th. Fischer et al. (eds.), *Germanen beiderseits des spätantiken Limes*. Cologne, 129–44.

Scharf, R. 2001. *Foederati. Von der völkerrechtlichen Kategorie zur byzantinischen Truppengattung*. Vienna.

Schulz, R. 1993. *Die Entwicklung des römischen Völkerrechts im vierten und fünften Jahrhundert n.Chr.* Stuttgart.

Schwarcz, A. 1995. "Foederati," *Reallexikon der germanischen Altertumskunde* 8: 290–99.

Schmitt, O. 1994. "Die Bucellarii. Eine Studie zum militärischen Gefolgschaftswesen in der Spätantike," *Tyche* 9: 147–74.

Stickler, T. 2002. *Aetius. Gestaltungsspielräume eines Heermeisters im ausgehenden Weströmischen Reich*. Munich.

Wenskus, R. 1961. *Stammesbildung und Verfassung. Das Werden der frühmittelalterlichen Gentes*. Cologne.

Whittaker, C. R. 1994. *Frontiers of the Roman Empire. A Social and Economic Study*. London.

—— 1997. *Frontiers of the Roman Empire. A Social and Economic Study*. Baltimore.

Wieczorek, A., P. Périn, K. von Welck, and W. Menghin (eds.). 1996. *Die Franken – Wegbereiter Europas. Vor 1500 Jahren: König Chlodwig und seine Erben*. Mainz.

Wolfram, H. 1990^{3}a. *Die Goten. Von den Anfängen bis zur Mitte des sechsten Jahrhunderts. Entwurf einer historischen Ethnographie*. Munich.

—— 1990b. *Das Reich und die Germanen. Zwischen Antike und Mittelalter*. Berlin.

Wolters, R. 1990. *Römische Eroberung und Herrschaftsorganisation in Gallien und Germanien. Zur Entstehung und Bedeutung der sogenannten Klientel-Randstaaten*. Bochum.

FURTHER READING

The relevant volumes of the *Cambridge Ancient History*, Cameron and Garnsey 1998 and Cameron 2000, represent an excellent general overview of all important aspects of the history of late antiquity, including those addressed in the present chapter. Additionally, Jones 1964 has still to be regarded as a standard work of reference. Barnwell 1992 addresses the fundamental structural developments in the western empire during late antiquity, while Whittaker 1997 focuses on the border regions in the West.

Indispensable for dealing with the fourth- and fifth-century movements of Germanic peoples is still Wenskus 1961; the discussion his study sparked is well documented in Gillett 2002, citing both arguments in favor of and opposing Wenskus. A sound general overview on the Migration Period is presented by Pohl 2002, incorporating recent research on the subject. Listing the relevant literature on all the different peoples would be beyond the scope of this short bibliographical overview; therefore, only some notes on the Franks, Goths, and Huns follow, as they feature most prominently in the present chapter. Valuable information on all aspects of the Migration Period can additionally be found in the relevant articles of the *Reallexikon der germanischen Altertumskunde.*

James 1988 is a good introduction on the Franks; relevant research of a more recent date can be found with Geuenich 1998 and Wieczorek et al. 1996. Any study of the archaeological evidence still has to start with Böhme 1974. On the Goths see Wolfram 1990a, Heather 1991, and Burns 1994. For a good introduction into the most important archaeological aspects see Bierbrauer 1994. On the Huns Maenchen-Helfen 1973 still has to be regarded as a standard work of reference. The Romano-Hunnic relationship has most recently been covered by Stickler 2002; the archaeological evidence has been documented by Anke 1998.

CHAPTER TWENTY-EIGHT

Army and Society in the Late Roman World: A Context for Decline?

Michael Whitby

1 Introduction

The *Life* of Daniel the Stylite records stories (chs. 60–63) about a man called Titus who became one of the saint's devotees in the late 460s. In his previous existence Titus had been a soldier, an inhabitant of Gaul who was of sufficient substance to have a band of trained companions. He traveled to Constantinople in response to a summons from Emperor Leo, who had heard of his prowess and gave him the rank of *comes* to be available for whatever military need might arise. Leo sent Titus to Daniel's column at Anaplus to be blessed, with the unfortunate consequence that Titus was seduced by the Stylite's strange example and renounced his military profession; two of his followers chose to remain and minister to his ascetic regime, being suspended by ropes under the armpits so that his feet could not touch the floor with three dates or dried figs and a measure of wine as daily sustenance, while the remainder took their money and departed. Although Leo was angered by the loss of a useful military leader, his remonstrations were futile. Titus stayed until his death, when he was replaced by one of his former military attendants, a barbarian whom Daniel had chosen to name Anatolius. Whether Titus was really as famous as the story implies is immaterial: he might well have traveled east to seek employment as Roman imperial authority in Gaul collapsed after the death of Majorian (461), rather than being individually summoned by Leo. His story, though, introduces a number of key aspects of late Roman military service which have been seen as relevant to the empire's decline: recruitment; the role of outsiders; the relationship between emperors and their soldiers; the relationship between East and West and an understanding of their different fates; and the impact of Christianity on military activity.

Titus belonged to a western generation which experienced substantial change: a rapidly growing economic imbalance between East and West; the Vandal sack of Rome in 455, a far more serious blow to the prosperity of the Eternal City than the capture by Alaric in 410; and repeated interruptions to the imperial succession as occupation of the western throne became an irrelevance, with real power resting with the commander of the army of Italy and the rulers of the new tribal states in Gaul and Africa. It is a generation which might appear to justify the traditional "Decline and Fall" approach to the later Roman Empire and its armed forces, since it was ultimately the inability of western rulers to sustain a powerful army of their own which surrendered their fate to non-Roman commanders such as the Sueve-Visigoth Ricimer or notional allies such as the Visigoth ruler Theoderic. Key elements of the "Decline and Fall" approach are that citizen-soldiers were outnumbered by foreigners as Romans became progressively demilitarized, the infantry backbone of the traditional Roman army was eclipsed by cavalry units in which non-Romans predominated, and frontier units (*limitanei*) were reduced to an inferior economic and legal status; overall the increasingly un-Roman armies declined in discipline, morale, effectiveness, and loyalty, while a gap opened between the interests of the army and the civilian society it was meant to serve.[1]

When analyzing these issues, however convenient it is to attempt to impose an overarching framework on military developments, one must think of armies rather than army. In part this is obvious, since during three-and-a-half centuries there will have been significant military changes, just as there had been in any comparable period of earlier Roman history. In part, however, the distinctions are regional. In the early empire differences could perhaps be detected between legions stationed in distant provinces, between "softer" eastern legions and northern troops toughened by constant exposure to German tribes, but when it came to civil war there was little to separate their combat effectiveness. In the late empire the pressures of logistics and recruitment, not to mention repeated campaigning against increased frontier threats, meant that there was less mobility and flexibility: the regular splitting of units into detachments for service on separate frontiers, which had contributed to the uniformity of the second-century imperial army, could no longer be managed. The age of Ammianus, the mid- to late fourth century, is the last time at which it is realistic to discuss a single Roman army;[2] thereafter there is separation between East and West, and then further subdivisions, rapidly in the West into Gallic and Italian elements, and more gradually in the East into Balkan and eastern frontiers. When Titus traveled east from Gaul to serve Leo he was moving within what was still notionally a single Roman world, but which was in reality already fragmenting into discrete and sometimes competing elements. With respect to soldiering, he was moving from a world where most significant military activity had been outsourced to one where the state had managed to retain control of a more balanced organization.

Because of the diversity of late Roman armies some of the "Decline and Fall" criticisms will be applicable to certain times and places, but I would propose that such failings are reflections of other, more significant, problems rather than prime causes of those problems. In contrast to the negative image of the military capacity of the late empire, I see the Roman military as an organization with sufficient flexibility to cope with quite significant changes while still remaining an effective and Roman institution. Sustainability is a current buzz-word in economic and political analysis, and it offers a measure for late Roman armies, both in terms of their ability to sustain the empire which they existed to serve and protect, and of the empire's ability to allocate sufficient human and material resources to the military sector to sustain its effective operation. It was a concept familiar to the Romans, being encapsulated in Emperor Tiberius' response to an over-zealous provincial governor that he wanted his sheep shorn not fleeced, and underpinning the various suggestions for economic and military reform contained in the anonymous memorandum on military improvements from the late fourth century known as *de Rebus Bellicis* (e.g. ch. 5, on the reduction of military expenditure). Sustainability requires the capacity to adapt to changing circumstances and without flexibility the Roman Empire could not have prospered for as long as it did; important military developments in the late empire need to be reviewed with regard to their impact and consequences rather than on the principle that all departures from early imperial practice must be signs of decline.

2   Manpower

A first issue is the overall size of the late Roman military establishment, since this had always been the largest item of imperial expenditure, and the strains of supporting it were already evident in the Severan period.[3] The military problems of the third century occasioned a significant expansion of numbers as imperial frontiers were stabilized during the tetrarchy. Writing in the sixth century, John Lydus recorded the Diocletianic establishment as 389,704 in the armies and 45,562 in the fleets (435,266 in total), and alleged that Constantine doubled Diocletian's army (*de Mensibus* 1.27). Slightly later than John Lydus, Agathias offered 645,000 as the total military establishment at an unspecified date, in the context of a rhetorical attack on the depleted Justinianic military forces (5.13.7–8). These figures have to be calibrated against the evidence of the *Notitia Dignitatum*, a list of the disposition of military units in the eastern and western parts of the empire which was produced in at least two stages in the late fourth and early fifth centuries. This information has occasioned much debate, but the general picture is not implausible, especially once it is realized that a large overall military establishment was required to generate the mobile armies of 20–30,000 attested in the sources. Such an overall increase in size from the Severan period intensified the problems of stable support, straining relations between soldiers and tax-payers, especially when the empire's overall prosperity was being affected by persistent invasions. Thus the taxation and other economic reforms effected by Diocletian and Constantine were essential elements of the stabilization of the empire's military position, the foundation for a prolonged period of relative security, almost a century in the West and three centuries in the East.

Roman superiority in manpower had long been recognized as the basis of republican military success (e.g. Polybius 2.24 on the war against Hannibal); in the empire Rome was collectively outnumbered by its enemies, though local superiority could be preserved by restricting the frontiers engaged in active warfare and relying on the empire's overall demographic prosperity. Until recently the later empire was seen as a period of demographic decline, to be traced back to the plague of the late second century; problems increased as invasions ravaged frontier provinces, harsh taxation drove farmers from their lands, and the increasingly powerful church annexed economic and human resources. The combination of these factors supposedly led to pressure on internal sources of recruits and greater reliance on external barbarian recruitment. Archaeological work over the last generation, especially in the countryside, has changed this picture so that the fourth century is now recognized as a time of demographic strength throughout much of the empire, especially the East; by about 400 the balance had swung in many northern and western provinces, but in Anatolia and the Levant settlement remained dense until the later sixth century when repeated waves of bubonic plague reinforced the effects of protracted warfare.[4] Demographic decline, though relevant, no longer offers the easy answer to all late Roman military change, though if weakness in certain areas could not be offset by transfers from elsewhere the sustainability of some armies would be compromised.

A healthy level of population is not sufficient by itself to sustain armies, since men need to be transferred regularly from the civilian to the military sector and might be dissuaded if conditions were wrong. Thus in the second century BC the republic appeared to face a recruitment crisis because it proved difficult to persuade soldiers to present themselves for dangerous and unprofitable service in Spain. In the early empire soldiering was probably seen as a relatively attractive and safe career, and this permitted the empire to replenish its forces through voluntary recruitment rather than conscription. By contrast in the late empire it is believed that conscription was often needed to coerce manpower into the ranks, since the greater dangers of regular fighting on frontiers as well as civil wars increased risks and reduced rewards; legislation attempted to tighten the conscription process, but its repetition merely demonstrates the unpopularity of military service among Romans who came to rely increasingly on non-Roman recruits.[5]

Book 7 of the *Theodosian Code* is devoted to military legislation, including one substantial chapter of 22 extracts from laws relating to recruitment. Taken out of context these laws appear to demonstrate that Romans strongly disliked military service: people mutilated themselves or offered slaves to escape conscription, while exemption from the levy was a privilege. However, most of this recruitment legislation is directly linked to specific military crises, periods when heavy losses increased demand but when the clear dangers or loss of enthusiasm or prestige among local recruiters made military service less attractive: the aftermath of Julian's failed invasion of Persia in 363, the defeat at Adrianople in 378, and the bloody suppression of western usurpations in the late 380s and 390s. Laws on desertion (*Cod. Theod.* 7.18), another indicator of hostility to military service, show the same distribution. The most urgent legislation was issued by Honorius in the early fifth century as the western court attempted unsuccessfully to squeeze recruits from senatorial estates and drum up volunteers with special incentives. In 406 ten *solidi* were offered to freeborn recruits, and freedom and a grant of two *solidi* to slaves (*Cod. Theod.* 7.13.16–17), with the state resorting to Rome's extreme manpower solution, employed during the Hannibalic War or after the Varian disaster. This legislation applied across the whole empire, but does not prove that recruitment problems were similarly widespread.

In the late empire membership of a military unit continued to be a considerable asset in terms of dealings with civilians, giving soldiers better status and opportunities to exploit and so attracting citizen recruits: in a settled unit in a reasonably peaceful province, such as that based at Syene in Upper Egypt in the sixth century, there was an entry fee for enrolling in a group which constituted a local elite; hereditary service could be a privilege as well as an obligation. Remuneration could also be significant: in addition to payments in kind and money, there were privileges for veterans including tax relief for their families and immunity from compulsory municipal duties which were the envy of others (*Cod. Theod.* 7.20.12).[6] When weighed against the struggle to eke out a living in a harsh and overcrowded landscape, military service still appeared attractive to the rural populations who constituted the preferred recruits throughout the ancient world: thus two future emperors, Marcian (Evagrius 2.1) and Justin I (Procopius, *Anecdota* 6.2), left the rugged central Balkans to seek fortune in Constantinople. The commitment of local elites to channel manpower in the required direction – the secret of the recruitment strength of republican Italy – was also required; an impoverished state with a weak ruler could not command the necessary support.

A system tuned to delivering 30,000 recruits each year from across the whole empire was likely to be put under strain if the requirement suddenly doubled, particularly if much of the extra manpower was to be extracted from a limited number of provinces. Such a crisis might be surmounted, especially if the state's finances were strong: thus through the fifth century and into the late sixth the East's wealth stimulated recruitment from recognized areas such as the Balkan highlands, mountainous Isauria in southern Asia Minor, and Armenia. In the West Honorius' problems are revealed as much by his capitulation to the Senate over the application of conscription to senatorial properties and the admission that the enrolment bonus for free men would not be paid in full until "affairs had been settled" (*Cod. Theod.* 7.13.12–14; 17) as by the appeal for slaves. In these straitened circumstances different solutions might be necessary, with profound effects on the balance between Roman and non-Roman in the armies.

3 Outsiders

Roman military success had always depended upon non-citizen recruits. In the republic of the third and second centuries over half "Roman" manpower was furnished by Latin and Italian allies; on the rare occasions when casualty figures are broken down, it appears that the allies often endured the heaviest fighting. In the imperial armies of the first two centuries AD non-citizen *auxilia* were crucial, being responsible for Agricola's victory at Mons Graupius and dominating the active fighting on Trajan's Column. What counted was not so much the place of origin as the degree of attachment to the empire, with the offer of citizenship being a powerful incentive. These outsiders wanted to share the benefits of membership of the dominant community, which the republican allies achieved after the bitter Social War and the imperial *auxilia* secured individually on retirement. After Caracalla's extension of citizenship, the military pressures of the third century ensured that there was a continuing need for extra manpower, which it was hard to meet from internal resources when many provinces were being ravaged. Urgent demands for troops, as in civil wars and after military defeat, or for special expeditions, were more easily met by turning to non-Romans than squeezing extra manpower from internal processes. In the fourth century Constantine's campaigns between 310 and 325 to re-unify the empire were one crucial stimulus for external recruitment, while another was the aftermath of Adrianople in 378.[7]

To a pagan historian such as Zosimus these particular instances demonstrated the treachery of the two most important Christian rulers of the fourth century, with the abandonment of the proper gods paralleled by the demise of a traditional army (2.15, 4.26–33; also 2.33–4 for other criticisms): unreliable mercenary barbarians were now entrusted with the empire's defense, and their indiscipline and treachery contributed to Roman defeats. Zosimus' preferred terminology of "barbarians" is a distortion which underlies some of the negative scholarly assessments of the late imperial army: it is a convenient descriptor for tribesmen from beyond the Rhine and Danube who made up many of the foreigners in Roman service, but the pejorative implications of decline which attracted this jaundiced author need to be resisted. The military "outsiders" were in fact often excellent soldiers, men for whom fighting was the regular way of life; they provided reliable bodyguards for emperors and generals, whose personal retinues of *bucellarii* (biscuit-men) might represent the elite part of an army. Roman pay and the prospect of rewards within the imperial frontier, coupled with the uncertainties and competition of life outside, ensured that there was a regular supply of volunteers for military service, often by individuals of some status who would enlist along with a military retinue. Such people may already have been familiar with many aspects of "civilized" Roman life, or have easily become detached from their native origin during their military service.[8] The relationship is revealed in Ammianus' account of the dilemma of the general Romanus, a Frank by descent: when machinations at the court of Constantius II rendered his position untenable, he contemplated flight to his fellow Franks but recognized that they would immediately kill him as a servant of Rome (15.5.16).

Non-Roman units played an important part in late Roman armies and are often prominent in contemporary accounts of major military events. They may often have been selected for the important actions which attracted the attention of our sources, but the explanation might be expendability as much as quality: at the Frigidus River in 394 the Goths in Theodosius' army found themselves being used in traditional Roman fashion as shock troops and suffered heavy casualties. It is, however, difficult to determine the varying proportions of non-Romans in the armies, since we have very little evidence about individuals below the senior ranks and our most common type of information, personal names, is a poor indication of ethnic affiliation.[9] Specific ethnic labels are rarely provided, and are usually attached to people who had made it to the top, men such as Silvanus the Frank or Victor the Sarmatian, whose attitudes and habits may have been as Roman as their names. General comments about the barbarity of the army cannot be pressed: to the educated urban elite who created most of our written evidence, late Roman armies may have looked barbaric and undisciplined, but the same was also said about early imperial armies. What matters more than the presence of a significant but unquantifiable non-Roman element in the army is how effectively the hybrid army fought for the state and who exercised real authority over it.

In modern states units of outsiders such as the French Foreign Legion or the Ghurkhas in the British army are elements of unquestionable loyalty and quality, with the Nepalese Ghurkhas demonstrating how a particular external group can forge a close community of interest with the employing state. An alternative use of outsiders is represented by the contracting out of military responsibilities, perhaps to corporations specializing in the provision of security, perhaps to groups of mercenaries to conduct the actual fighting. In the latter case the state is prepared to renounce its monopoly of force, since it no longer has outright control of all military operations, although it can attempt to limit the consequences by creating long-term financial incentives for the contractors. In a given set of circumstances, perhaps a political or economic crisis, the benefits to the state of such military devolution are perceived to outweigh the risks, at least in the short term.

In the Roman context the majority of outsiders recruited into the army can be characterized as "Ghurkhas," certainly until the late fourth century, and much later in the East; in some cases the tribal groups may have come to enjoy similarly close long-term relations with their employers. Such a relationship undoubtedly benefits the state, which secures higher-quality recruits than can be obtained internally but has only limited financial obligations outside the period of service. Limited outsourcing could also permit a particular military problem to be surmounted at acceptable cost, provided imperial authority was maintained: in the East the Gothic leader Alaric failed to extract concessions from Arcadius (395–408), in spite of a decade of threats and ravaging in the Balkans, the attempt by Gaïnas to dominate Constantinople in 399/400 was thwarted, and in the 470s the Gothic bands led by the two Theoderics were played off against each other by Zeno, even though they saw through the emperor's duplicity (Malchus 18.2), since the lure of official position and land proved stronger. Fuller-scale devolution is a different matter, as is revealed by the evaporation of western emperors' ability to determine the direction of affairs when the complex economic and social organization which underpinned the Roman army collapsed.[10]

4 Composition

The balance between Romans and outsiders in the army is relevant to the questions of the composition of the army and the competence of Roman frontier troops, *limitanei*, since it has been assumed that unenthusiastic Roman recruits were primarily suitable for the less military *limitanei* whereas more bellicose "barbarians," with better cavalry skills, dominated central units. During the third century the balance of Roman armies did shift. Heavy-armed infantry had always been the particular strength of the Romans, with the necessary diversity of light-armed elements and cavalry being provided primarily by allies or non-citizens. Cavalry units became more numerous in late Roman armies and performed more important roles than during the republic or early empire, a shift which affected the economic sustainability of the armies since horsemen were significantly more expensive to equip and support than infantry. Cavalry, however, did not supplant infantry: the Romans were well aware that they faced enemies with differing capabilities, against whom different military combinations were likely to be most effective. This point is made in the late-sixth-century *Strategicon* of Maurice, a training manual of obvious practical intent. Book 11 contains advice on how to defeat the empire's principal enemies: the Persians are seen as vulnerable to a rapid cavalry charge that would minimize the impact of their superior archery and permit the more heavily equipped Romans to fight at close quarters; by contrast the mighty Avars, who overwhelmed opponents through repeated charges of cavalry groups, had to be faced by a balanced army in which infantry provided a steady platform.[11]

From at least the third century, the Romans had a few units of mailed lancers, *clibanarii* or boiler-boys, in imitation of Parthian and Persian units, but such specialist heavily-armored units were always an expensive minority. From the fifth century onwards mounted archers on the Hunnic model, or horsemen capable of using both bow and lance, were more common. Some of this expertise was provided by mercenary outsiders or from tribal groups permitted to settle within the frontiers, but Maurice's *Strategicon* reveals that internal recruits were also being enrolled: the handbook is largely devoted to the improvement of equestrian skills and the coordination of cavalry units, the military aspect in greatest need of training for Romans recruits. The *Strategicon*'s lack of attention to infantry can be seen as recognition that this element of the army was in better shape, or at least that its traditional training techniques and methods of deployment continued to be effective. Late Roman infantry was probably less heavily-equipped than in the early empire, but the evidence for this development in Vegetius (1.20) must be detached from his moral criticism, that recruits found the old style of armament too heavy: infantry were now expected to perform a wider variety of roles, so that a reduction in the weight of equipment reflected their greater flexibility, the late Roman equivalent of the emergence of the peltast in the fourth century BC. Late Roman cavalry also had to be sufficiently versatile to fight on foot when the situation required.

Another development in the late Roman army which bears on the infantry–cavalry balance is that distinctions were drawn, in terms of status as well as rewards, between *limitanei* and *comitatenses*, in other words between more static provincial units and those which accompanied the emperor or senior generals. The distinctions may go back to Constantine, and were certainly entrenched by the mid-fourth century since there are passages in Ammianus which suggest that some units of *comitatenses* were already linked to specific regions and reluctant to be transferred. Thereafter the key distinction developed between palatine or praesental troops, which were genuinely attached to the court and so fully mobile, and the rest which usually operated in a particular region or sector of the frontier. The unsurprising preference for many recruits for service close to home indicates that one explanation for the legal evidence for superior pay and conditions of service for *comitatenses* is that recruits to these units had to be encouraged to serve away from home by better terms; by itself it does not prove the inferiority of the *limitanei*. The *limitanei* are also often disparaged as soldier-farmers, amateurs who had lost their military quality along with their professional training. There was, however, a persistent belief in the ancient world that to secure good service soldiers needed to have a personal stake in what they were expected to defend; the anonymous *de Rebus Bellicis* (5) advocated allocating land grants along frontiers to veterans to improve local security. There is no reason to suppose that all (or even many) soldiers who owned property actually cultivated the land themselves; the evidence for the property dealings of the military unit stationed at Nessana in Palestine in the early seventh century suggests that they were traditional rentiers who relied on the labors of others and whose extended families and households were available to assist in administering their possessions.[12]

Adherents of the negative thesis about the *limitanei* have to contend with the fact that they were reinstated in Africa after its recovery from the Vandals and were also used in conjunction with mobile troops on major eastern campaigns during the sixth century. Such evidence might be dismissed as desperation in the face of recruitment difficulties, but that is to ignore the contribution which *limitanei* could genuinely make to a campaign. Analysis of the lists of units and dispositions in the *Notitia Dignitatum* reveals that the *limitanei* included substantially more cavalry units than the *comitatenses*. Although this contradicts the old notion of emperors from the late third century relying on a central cavalry force as a mobile reserve to support frontier zones under threat, the balance does reflect the military reality that infantry retained their fighting strength when required to move long distances quickly, whereas cavalry would be rendered ineffective as their horses succumbed after four or five days of repeated pressure. Most of the armies assembled for particular provincial campaigns combined different categories of troops, some local and some more central; this would have increased the incentives for all units to maintain quality and helped to ensure that they preserved an attachment to the center. Even if there is probably some basis to the jaundiced assertion in Procopius' *Anecdota* that Justinian deprived *limitanei* of their salaries (24.12–14), Procopius has undoubtedly exaggerated whatever was done: for example, Justinian may have introduced a modest reform of payments, possibly along the lines that provincial troops whose basic needs were already provided by public grants of land would only receive imperial salaries when on active service or on duty outside their own province. Although payment was a powerful aid to loyalty, the absence of monetary reward in the ancient world did not necessarily entail that soldiers were second rate. Exploitation of land, a resource of which there was a reasonable supply in frontier regions, as a supplement or alternative to payment of salaries will have contributed significantly to the affordability of armies.

Changes in the composition of late Roman armies, and especially the increased recruitment of barbarians have been associated with a decline in military effectiveness and the breakdown of discipline, but as with other aspects of military change the position in the early empire should not be regarded as perfect. Evidence can be cited, though it is of dubious value: before the battle of the Catalaunian plains Attila encouraged his troops to disregard their Roman opponents as completely ineffective and concentrate instead on the Goths and Alans (Jordanes, *Getica* 204–205). If poor discipline is used to explain the rapid succession of mutinies in the third century, the experience of the Year of the Four Emperors and the various civil wars of the Severan period show that the problem was not entirely new. In fact a distinction needs to be drawn between a decline in the capacity of emperors to control their armies and a decline in the disciplined fighting capability of those armies, between disloyalty and indiscipline. Armies that were prepared to oppose a current emperor by supporting their own commander were also capable of fighting each other ferociously, as the expensive victories of Constantius at Mursa and Theodosius at the Frigidus River demonstrate. Discipline itself may have suffered during civil wars as commanders had to maintain the loyalty of their troops, but success would probably be followed by a reassertion of normal standards. Evidence for lapses of discipline in late Roman armies can be collected (e.g. Ammianus Marc. 16.12.33; 25.6.11–13; 27.2.9), but republican and early imperial armies were far from perfect (e.g. Livy 22.6.11; 25.21; Caesar, *B. Gall.* 1.40; 7.47–52; Tacitus, *Hist.* 1.64–9; 2.56; Cassius Dio 80.4.1–5.1). With regard to discipline, things may not have changed all that much.[13]

5 Organization

Apart from manpower, another traditional Roman advantage was logistical organization, with the Romans possessing the capacity to sustain a large establishment overall and sufficient troops in the field to cope with all challenges. During the early imperial centuries armies had been supported by an empire-wide circulation of goods and money which redirected tax surpluses from provinces in credit, primarily those away from frontiers where few soldiers were stationed, towards the main centers of consumption, the legionary camps sited near the frontiers and the imperial city of Rome itself. During the third century this system came under pressure, and troops had relied increasingly on payments in kind which ensured that they received the necessary supplies and protected them to a certain extent from the ravages of monetary inflation. Units came to be linked with specific areas, with troops often being quartered in or near major cities, probably to ease the logistical problems of transporting and storing large quantities of bulky supplies. The supply system was administratively complex, as legislation on collection, storage, and disbursement in the Theodosian Code reveals (*Cod. Theod.* 7.4; 36 extracts, the longest chapter in Book 7), but any failure in the fiscal underpinning of the army, the stomach which fed the arms to adopt the imagery of Corippus (*Laud. Iust.* 2.249–53), was disastrous: in 444 Valentinian III desperately introduced a new sales tax since "neither for new recruits nor for the old army can sufficient supplies be raised from the exhausted taxpayers to provide food and clothing" (*Novellae Val.* 15.1). The movement of troops across Roman territory was even more complex, with the questions of billets and exactions en route compounding the problems (*Cod. Theod.* 7.8–10).[14] Extensive invasions, such as occurred in the West in the early fifth century, quite apart from undermining the state's financial resources, reduced the Roman capacity to move forces without resort to the pillaging which they were supposed to prevent. The difficulties of organizing expeditions across devastated countryside are revealed in accounts of campaigns in the Balkans in the late fifth and early sixth centuries, when advances inland, away from Constantinople and naval support, were slow and vulnerable (Marcellinus Comes *ss.aa.* 499, 505).

6 Loyalties

An almost boundless enthusiasm for warfare is another traditional Roman advantage, but alleged recruitment problems and reliance on outsiders have been taken as signs of a profound demilitarization in the late empire. This thesis proposes that active loyalty to the Roman state waned: traditional civic patriotism declined as imperial officials increasingly took over local affairs such as taxation and justice; citizenship was no longer a privilege, and there was little to demonstrate that distant emperors had any concern for the provinces other than as a source of heavier tax payments. As a result manpower could not be channeled into the army unless there were direct threats to the recruits' home region.[15]

These issues are complex and range beyond the scope of this chapter, but with regard to the military it is worth focusing on the question of loyalties. There were occasions when a divide did open up between local and imperial agendas, particularly when the failure of an emperor to protect a region or to assert his authority over it led local groups to elevate their own imperial figure, for example during the "Gallic" empire of the third century or the fragmentation of the West in response to the tribal incursions of the early fifth century. On such occasions, however, the danger was not so much of a demilitarization of the Roman population but of the direction in which their military energies were being directed; the solution was not some vague cultivation of outmoded civic patriotism but the specific attachment of local elites and provincial armies to the imperial center. This was achieved through the reforms of Diocletian and Constantine which created powerful imperial courts that served as magnets for the careers of ambitious local elites; this may have affected the vitality of provincial cities who lost some of their leading citizens and suffered from the redirection of their spending power, but overall the empire benefited.[16]

The strength of imperial authority was the crucial factor in sustaining this system, and here the geography and dynamics of the eastern empire gave it considerable advantages over the West. Although Antioch was frequently used as an imperial capital between the 340s and 370s, Constantinople thereafter had no competitor as the focus of an efficient and centralized administration, the magnet for senatorial, bureaucratic, military, and much ecclesiastical ambition. Here emperors manipulated credit for victories through ceremonies in the Hippodrome and used the allegiance of the circus factions to extend vociferous loyalty to all major provincial cities; here the different branches of the bureaucracy competed for prominence, but within a framework overseen by the emperor, while religious ceremonies bolstered the emperor's status. By contrast in the West there was fragmentation as Rome, increasingly "Old" Rome, remained the home of the Senate and developed as the ecclesiastical center, whereas secular administration and military matters were directed from elsewhere: initially this was wherever the itinerant emperor happened to be – Trier, Carnuntum, Milan – but in the early fifth century Ravenna, a remote and insalubrious minor city, emerged as the most common administrative center, while the armies were directed from wherever their commander was located. In the East Constantinople ensured cohesion and generals had to maintain their influence there; in the West there were clashes between senators and emperors, or emperors and generals, and men of power could ignore Ravenna. The direction of loyalties rather than demilitarization is the issue.

One element of imperial authority was military command: this had always been part of an emperor's duties, encapsulated in the very name of the office, and most rulers showed some interest in the activity which was the basis for their power. During the troubles of the third century, the military element of emperors' duties increased in importance and personal success became crucial for survival in imperial office; direct involvement in campaigns was advertised on coins whose slogans were predominantly military or in statues such as the "Venice Tetrarchs." Aurelius Victor's comment on the tetrarchs encapsulates the new requirements: "although they were deficient in culture, they had nevertheless been sufficiently schooled by the hardships of the countryside and of military service to be the best men in the state" (*de Caes.* 39). The multiplication of imperial figures under the tetrarchy, which continued through most of the dynastic arrangements of the fourth century, brought rulers into closer contact with the people who mattered for imperial strength and security, the provincial armies and the local aristocracies.[17]

The nature of the bonds between soldier and ruler, between province and emperor, changed in 395 when Theodosius I, the last campaigning emperor of the late Roman period, was succeeded by his two young sons, Arcadius and Honorius, who in their turn were followed by their own underage offspring, Theodosius II and Valentinian III. Current practice was reversed and emperors now rarely left their capital city, a change which provoked criticisms. Arcadius was urged by Synesius that "he should regularly associate with soldiers and not stay in his chamber, for it showed that goodwill, the one solid safeguard of kingship, was strengthened by this daily contact" (*Regn.* 21); Synesius contrasted the foreign luxury of the imperial palace with the traditional austerity which had gained Rome its empire (*Regn.* 14–17). The story, doubtless apocryphal, that Honorius reacted to news of Rome's capture by grieving for his pet cockerel which was also called Roma (Procopius, *Bella* 3.2.25–6) suggests that he was the object of similar comments.

It was, however, possible for emperors to control armies and apportion military authority without being personally involved: of the Julio-Claudian rulers only the unmilitary Claudius participated in a campaign, but the armies remained loyal to the dynasty. What was required were checks and balances to pure military authority and mechanisms to control credit for victory. If these could be achieved there might even be advantages for emperors in distancing themselves from the repeated competition for military glory, the pressure which led Valens to engage at Adrianople before Gratian's arrival to avoid sharing credit for the expected victory (Ammianus Marc. 31.12.7); defeat became the responsibility of the individual commander rather than an immediate threat to the emperor's position. Diplomatic business could also be conducted more effectively and safely away from the frontier where Valens had been forced to meet Athanaric on equal terms in the middle of the Danube and Valentinian died during a reception for Quadi envoys (Ammianus Marc. 27.5.9; 30.6).

The transition was achieved in the East, though not without some scares: the advantages of Constantinople as capital were reinforced by the fortunate fact that a century of almost unbroken peace with Persia, with no external disruption to the empire's main sources of wealth in Egypt, Syria, and Anatolia spared the eastern administration the complexity and intensity of military crises which shook the West in the early fifth century. In the West the change in imperial behavior had profound military consequences which ultimately destroyed the political authority of emperors. Authority over what survived of imperial armies rested with commanders such as the half-Vandal Stilicho or the Sueve-Visigoth Ricimer,[18] while much military power in the provinces was devolved to outsiders such as the Visigoth or Burgundian ruler or seized by the Vandal king. Money was the final lever available to western emperors to influence the operation of delegated or outsourced military power, but the legislation of Honorius and Valentinian III reveals that this was in short supply (*Cod. Theod.* 7.13.17; *Novellae Val. III* 15.1): their only recourse was further military devolution, alienating revenue-generating territories, and finally, in 440, encouraging civilians to arm themselves against Vandal raids (*Novellae Val. III* 9). The state which had for centuries sustained a professional army to protect its citizens was now forced to the ultimate renunciation of power.

7   Soldiers and Civilians

In the Roman Empire military and civilian worlds had always been connected by logistical and manpower factors, but it is arguable that the interpenetration of these worlds became much more visible in the late empire. In earlier centuries most troops had been stationed on distant frontiers, and most military action occurred beyond, or at least close to, these frontiers. In the late empire a higher proportion of troops was located in internal provinces, and the location of conflict had changed with more fighting occurring inside the empire, often deep inside it. As a consequence most cities acquired sets of defenses, a reassurance in which the civilian population might take pride as well as a reminder of the heightened threat to their prosperous existence. The closer proximity of soldier and civilian inevitably led to problems. Billeting was an obvious source of dispute, with owners being required to surrender one-third of their house to their military "guest" who might then proceed to claim additional resources and even sexual services. The legislation against such abuses (*Cod. Theod.* 7.8) is more telling than a disingenuous comment by Libanius about the enthusiasm of the Antiochenes for the arrival and billeting of Constantius' troops who were allegedly received like relatives (*Orat.* 11.178); in 398 Arcadius legislated to prevent soldiers from pasturing their animals on the public lands of Apamea and Antioch (*Cod. Theod.* 7.7.3). When Edessa had to serve as the base for the main eastern army during the Persian War of 502–505, a contemporary local source records the impositions on the population: ten pounds of iron per household, compulsory baking of bread, and a catalogue of abuses including rape and murder (Ps.-Joshua the Stylite 86.93–96). These sacrifices might be regarded as worthwhile if the city survived, but the imperial treasurer Ursulus bemoaned the cost of the army when he saw the ruins of Amida which the Persians had captured in 359 (Ammianus Marc. 20.11.5).

This evidence for intimidation and exploitation has been factored into analyses of the decline of the empire and its army, but these negative assessments need to be challenged. The archive of Abinnaeus, commander of troops at Dionysias in Egypt in the mid-fourth century, contains several documents about the alleged misdemeanors of his troops who, for example, had stolen animals or engaged over-enthusiastically in tax-collection, but there is also a complaint that a soldier had been beaten up by villagers (P. Abinn. 48; 27; 12). In all these cases, however, we are only provided with one side of the dispute, and we do not know how Abinnaeus responded. A very different picture of the interaction between a military unit and its civilian environment is provided by the papyri from Syene in Egypt and Nessana in Palestine, which appear to show soldiers pursuing a normal range of commercial dealings with their non-military neighbors; much depends upon the nature and provenance of the evidence preserved for us. Libanius devotes a speech to the protection provided to villagers by military patrons, including soldiers billeted on them, against attempts by landowners such as Libanius himself to extract due taxes (*Orat.* 47). The proximity of troops might bring other benefits, with the arrival of a large, almost captive market, as Diocletian noted in the preamble to his Edict on Maximum Prices, and opportunities for employment on military contracts such as the construction of Dara (Ps.-Zachariah 6.6).[19] It must also be remembered that, whatever the disadvantages of the close proximity of troops, in any site under threat from enemy attack a garrison was a precious asset whose departure might lead to disaster (Theophylact 7.3, Asemus; Eugippius, *Vit. Sev.* 20, 22.4–5, 27.3 Batavis).

8   Christianity

Christianity is the final issue relating to late Roman warfare that I wish to review. The conversion of Constantine has been regarded as a major factor in the Roman military decline,[20] partly through the adoption of a moral code which had traditions of opposition to military activity and hostility to the empire, and partly through the competition for scarce resources which it introduced, the "idle mouths" of modern critics. These are relevant considerations, and the story of Titus' switch from military to religious service provides one specific example of a transfer of resources. But one of Christianity's strengths was the diversity of models afforded in the Bible, and the Old Testament could be cited in defense of military service (e.g. Augustine, *contra Faustum* 22.74–5; *Epist.* 189.4). Armies seem not to have been affected by the religious changes of the fourth century, with Christianity taking over the role of traditional religion as the foundation of the military oath of allegiance (Vegetius 2.5), providing a new military standard and chants, and being acknowledged on coinage. Even the wealth and size of the church are unlikely to have grown sufficiently to have caused the weakness of the West in the early fifth century, and in the eastern crisis of the early seventh century ecclesiastical wealth constituted a resource which Emperor Heraclius annexed to finance his military plans. Christianity in fact supported the state through aligning civilian energies with imperial interests, as the experience of frontier cities such as Nisibis in the fourth century, Clermont in the fifth, Edessa in the sixth, and Thessalonica in the seventh reveal. The Christian emperor in Constantinople sat at the center of the state's secular and religious hierarchies, a dominant position which no western ruler managed to secure.

9 Conclusion

In considering the history of the late Roman Empire it is essential to give due weight to military issues, since the inability of imperial armies to continue to defeat external enemies and provide provinces with reasonable security led to imperial collapse. But these military failures should not be taken as proof that late Roman armies had abandoned the standards of the earlier empire. These armies faced new challenges, which they had to adapt to overcome. Provided that emperors could generate the money to finance military activity and devise means of retaining authority over far-flung operations, their armed forces generally served the state effectively and loyally whether or not the ruler was present in person. The scale of the enterprise was massive, especially in a world of increasing threats; the size of the empire offered a certain degree of resilience, but the sheer complexity of the system was also a weakness since disruption to some elements could trigger a spiral of decline. When it came that spiral was a violent and destructive process, not a relatively peaceful integration.

NOTES

1 E.g. Liebeschuetz 1990; MacMullen 1963; Southern and Dixon 1996; Ferrill 1986.
2 On Ammianus, see Crump 1975; Matthews 1989.
3 There is substantial discussion: Jones 1964, 679–86 is clear; Treadgold 1995, chapter 2 is detailed, but his precision may be self-defeating; Nicasie 1998, 67–76; MacMullen 1980, 451–60 is skeptical but his arguments are countered by Nicasie 1998, 202–6. See also Elton (in this volume) for specifically sixth-century evidence.
4 Traditional picture in Jones 1964, chapters 20–1. There is a useful survey of more recent work in Banaji 2002, chapter 1. See also Ward-Perkins 2000, 315–45, esp. 320–7, and Duncan-Jones 2004, 20–52.
5 For detailed discussion of recruitment and conscription, see Whitby 1995, 61–121, at 75–87 with references to earlier views; Elton 1996, chapter 5; Nicasie 1998, chapter 3; Zuckerman 1998, 79–139; Whitby 2004, 156–86, at 169–70.
6 Terms and conditions are discussed by Jones 1964, 668–79; Treadgold 1995, 149–57.
7 Jones 1964, 611–13, 663–8; Speidel 1975, 202–31; Liebeschuetz 1990, chapters 1–2.
8 Whitby 1995, 103–10; Elton 1996, 136–52; Nicasie 1998, chapter 4; Stickler (in this volume).
9 Nicasie 1998, 97–9; Elton 1996, 145–52, though note the sensible caution of Janniard 2001, 351–61. 357–8.
10 Heather 1991, chapters 5–6; Cameron and Long 1993, 199–223, 250–2, 323–33. The Theoderics: Heather 1991, chapters 8–9. The early fifth-century West: Blockley 1998, 111–37, at 129–33. See also Stickler (in this volume).
11 Southern and Dixon 1996, 11–14; Elton 1996, 103–7; Nicasie 1998, 35–41, 60–5; Whitby 2004, 160–3; Syvänne 2004, esp. chapter 2; Rance 2006. For the sixth-century army, see also Elton (in this volume).
12 Jones 1964, 649–54, 661–3; Isaac 1990, 208–13; Whitby 1995, 68–75, 110–16; Elton 1996, 89–101; Southern and Dixon 1996, 35–7; Nicasie 1998, 14–22.

13   Negative views on discipline in MacMullen 1963; Ferrill 1986; counter-arguments in Whitby 2004, 173–5.
14   Early empire: Hopkins 1980, 101–25. Jones 1964, chapter 13; Elton 1996, chapter 4; Treadgold 1995, chapter 6.
15   Liebeschuetz 1990, chapter 2; Liebeschuetz 2001, chapter 13.
16   More detailed discussion in Whitby 2004, 179–86; Whitby 2005, 372–80.
17   Fuller discussion with references in Whitby 2004, esp. 179–86; Whitby 2005, 373–8.
18   For further discussion, see Liebeschuetz (in this volume).
19   Negative discussion in MacMullen 1963. Abinnaeus archive: Bell et al. 1962. Syene: Keenan 1990, 139–50. Nessana: Kraemer 1958.
20   Negative assessments in MacMullen 1963; Jones 1964, 1045–8; positive in Tomlin 1998, 21–51; Whitby 1998, 191–208; 2004, 175–9.

BIBLIOGRAPHY

Banaji, J. 2002. *Agrarian Change in Late Antiquity. Gold, Labour, and Aristocratic Dominance*. Oxford.
Bell, H. I., V. Martin, E. G. Turner, and D. Van Berchem (eds.). 1962. *The Abinnaeus Archive: Papers of a Roman Officer in the Reign of Constantius II*. Oxford.
Blockley, R. C. 1998. "The dynasty of Theodosius," in Cameron and Garnsey, 111–37.
Cameron, A. (ed.). 1995. *The Byzantine and Early Islamic Near East. Vol. III. States, Resources and Armies*. Princeton.
——, and P. Garnsey. 1998. *CAH* 13. *The Late Empire, AD 337–425*. Cambridge.
——, and J. Long. 1993. *Barbarians and Politics at the Court of Arcadius*. Berkeley.
——, B. Ward-Perkins, and M. Whitby (eds.). 2000. *CAH* 14. *Late Antiquity, Empire and Successors, AD 425–600*. Cambridge.
Crump, G. A. 1975. *Ammianus Marcellinus as a Military Historian*. Wiesbaden.
Duncan-Jones, R. 2004. "Economic change and the transition to late antiquity," in Swain and Edwards, 20–52.
Elton, H. 1996. *Warfare in Roman Europe AD 350–425*. Oxford.
Ferrill, A. 1986. *The Fall of the Roman Empire: The Military Explanation*. London.
Heather, P. J. 1991. *Goths and Romans 332–489*. Oxford.
Hopkins, K. 1980. "Taxes and trade in the Roman Empire (200 BC–AD 400)," *JRS* 70: 101–25.
Isaac, B. 1990. *The Limits of Empire: The Roman Army in the East*. Oxford.
Janniard, S. 2001. "L'armée romaine tardive dans quelques travaux récents. 2eme partie. Stratégies et techniques militaires," *Antiquité Tardive* 9: 351–61.
Jones, A. H. M. 1964. *The Later Roman Empire, 284–602, A Social, Economic and Administrative Survey*. Oxford.
Keenan, J. G. 1990. "Evidence for the Byzantine army in the Syene Papyri" *BASP* 27: 139–50.
Kraemer, C. J. 1958. *Excavations at Nessana conducted by H. D. Colt, Jr., III. Non-Literary Papyri*. Princeton.
Lee, A. D. 1998. "The army," in *CAH* 13. Cambridge, 211–37.
Liebeschuetz, J. H. W. G. 1990. *Barbarians and Bishops. Army, Church, and State in the Age of Arcadius and Chrysostom*. Oxford.
—— 2001. *The Decline and Fall of the Roman City*. Oxford.
MacMullen, R. 1963. *Soldier and Civilian in the Later Roman Empire*. Cambridge, MA.
—— 1980. "How big was the Roman imperial army?" *Klio* 62: 451–60.

Matthews, J. F. 1989. *The Roman Empire of Ammianus*. London.

Nicasie, M. J. 1998. *Twilight of Empire. The Roman Army from the Reign of Diocletian until the Battle of Adrianople*. Amsterdam.

Rance, R. 2006. "Combat," in Van Wees, Sabin, and Whitby.

Southern, P., and K. Dixon. 1996. *The Late Roman Army*. London.

Speidel, M. P. 1975. "The rise of ethnic units in the Roman imperial army," *ANRW* II.3, 202–31.

Swain, S., and M. Edwards (eds.). 2004. *Approaching Late Antiquity: The Transformation from Early to Late Empire*. Oxford.

Syvänne, I. 2004. *The Age of the Hippotoxotai*. Tampere.

Tomlin, R. 1998. "Christianity and the late Roman army," in S. N. C. Lieu and D. Montserrat (eds.), *Constantine: History, Historiography, and Legend*. London, 21–51.

Treadgold, W. 1995. *Byzantium and its Army 284–1081*. Stanford.

Van Wees, H., P. Sabin, and M. Whitby (eds.). 2006. *The Cambridge History of Greek and Roman Warfare*. Cambridge.

Ward-Perkins, B. 2000. "Land, labour and settlement," in Cameron, Ward-Perkins, and Whitby, 315–45.

Whitby, M. 1995. "Recruitment in Roman armies from Justinian to Heraclius (ca. 565–615)," in Cameron, 61–124.

—— 1998. "*Deus nobiscum*: Christianity, warfare and morale in late antiquity," in M. Austin, J. Harries, and C. Smith (eds.), *Modus Operandi, Essays in Honour of Geoffrey Rickman*. London, 191–208.

—— 2000a. "The army," in *CAH* 14. Cambridge, 288–314.

—— 2000b. "Armies and society in the later Roman world," in *CAH* 14. Cambridge, 469–96.

—— 2004. "Emperors and armies, AD 235–395," in Swain and Edwards, 156–86.

—— 2005. "War and state in late antiquity: Some economic and political connections," in B. Meissner, O. Schmitt, and M. Sommer (eds.) *Krieg, Gesellschaft, Institutionen. Beiträge zu einer Uergleichenden Kriegsgeschichte*. Berlin, 355–85.

Zuckerman, C. 1998. "Two reforms of the 370s: Recruiting soldiers and senators in the divided empire," *REB* 56: 79–139.

FURTHER READING

Jones 1964 is essential, especially chapter 17, although also consult the index s.v. "army." More recent surveys are provided by Lee 1998 and Whitby 2000a and 2000b. The new *Cambridge History of Greek and Roman Warfare* (Van Wees, Sabin, and Whitby 2006) contains six chapters devoted to the later Roman world, covering external relations, organization, combat, war, political aspects, and social issues. Another important forthcoming study is a monograph on the late Roman army by A. D. Lee, due to be published in 2007.

A traditionally negative view of the later army is available in the short volume of MacMullen 1963; much more authoritative, but also from a negative perspective is Liebeschuetz 1990. Elton 1996 and Nicasie 1998 provide more positive assessments of the fourth-century army. Southern and Dixon 1996 is useful for discussion of equipment, but is derivative in other respects. Treadgold 1995 discusses numbers and economics with a precision that must be treated cautiously. My own views on various issues are presented in Whitby 1995, 2004, and forthcoming.

CHAPTER TWENTY-NINE

Army and Battle in the Age of Justinian (527–65)

Hugh Elton

Three actions, in Lazica, Italy, and Africa, illustrate the difficulties of summarizing army and battle in the age of Justinian. In 556, Rome and Sassanid Persia were at war. In the kingdom of Lazica in the Caucasus, the Persians had made a surprise crossing of the River Phasis by pontoon bridge and were hastening to capture the city of Phasis (modern Poti). The Romans, under the *magister militum per Armeniam* Martinus, sent troops overland to garrison the city, but also sent a smaller force, a fleet of "triremes" and 30-oared ships, by water. The Persians anticipated the naval move and their commander had "laid a barrier of timber and small boats right across the river, massing his elephants behind it in lines which extended as far as they could wade." The Roman fleet withdrew, but the garrison was reinforced in time (Agathias 3.20.1–8).

In the second action, in Campanian Italy, a Roman force of 18,000 men under the command of the general Narses faced a mixed Frankish and Alamannic force of 30,000 led by Butilinus at Casilinum in 554.

> When Narses reached the place where he intended to fight, he immediately drew the army into battle formation and deployed. The cavalry were placed on the wings at either side . . . the infantry occupied all the ground in the centre . . . a place had been reserved for the Heruli in the middle of the line of battle and it was still empty since they had not yet arrived.

According to Agathias, the Heruli were late because they were sulking, the cause of their bad temper being Narses' summary execution of one of their officers for murder. The Franks, seeing the gap, formed a wedge and charged at it. Unable to penetrate the line, they were surrounded by the Romans and "being virtually caught in a net, were slaughtered on all sides." Only five escaped, while only 80 Romans were lost. "Laden with booty, crowned with laurels of victory, and singing songs of triumph, they led their general back in state to Rome" (Agathias 2.8–10).

In a third action in North Africa in 535, the *magister militum* Solomon faced a Moorish army at Mammes. Solomon's army made a traditional marching camp with ditch and palisade. While Solomon deployed for battle in a traditional line, the Moors had made a 12-deep circle of camels, with their troops standing between the animals. The horses of the Roman cavalry were unsettled by the camels, so Solomon dismounted them and then led an infantry assault into the laager. Once the circle of camels was broken, the Moors collapsed (Procopius, *Bella* 4.11.47–55).

1   Sources

These three examples show some of the battlefield challenges that faced the Roman army in the age of Justinian. Battle was a complicated combined arms affair, but beyond tactical considerations lay a host of logistical and political problems, themselves conditioned by the strategies chosen by the generals to carry out the orders of the emperor with the resources he provided. These examples also show the importance of understanding the limits of our sources, since we have only one description of each action. The two major historians for the period are Procopius and Agathias. Procopius served on Belisarius' staff between 527 and c. 540, and accompanied his general to Persia, Africa, and Italy. He subsequently wrote a *History* covering the wars of Justinian's reign down to 553. Despite its title, it focuses more on Belisarius than on all of Justinian's Wars.[1] Procopius' work was continued to 559 by Agathias, a lawyer with no field experience.[2] Agathias' work in turn was continued by Menander who was a professional historian (his rank of *protector* appears honorary).[3] The works of Procopius and Agathias survive complete, but that of Menander survives only in fragments. Several church historians also provide useful information, including Evagrius and John of Ephesus. Although focusing on ecclesiastical history, contemporaries felt that secular matters reflected God's judgment, so these works often included details of military affairs. There are many useful inscriptions, including an interesting collection of cross-shaped stones from a sixth- to eighth-century cemetery next to the Theodosian Walls in Constantinople.[4]

All of these histories, however, are academic and literary works and we have no memoirs or works written by serving soldiers or commanders, even if Procopius occasionally gives us a snapshot of the discussions or some revealing cameos. They are thus very different from Mauricius' *Strategikon* which was written in the late-sixth century. Most of Mauricius' work is clear, practical advice about organization, equipment, tactics, and operations, focusing on cavalry. It includes a chapter on infantry that was incorporated from a similar and (possibly earlier) treatise. This army appears little different in organization and equipment from that of Justinian's reign.[5]

2   Attitudes

Procopius and Agathias make it very clear that modern concepts of how and why wars should be fought differ greatly from those of the ancients. For many of these writers, battle was a distant concept, a world of heroism and glory rather than of death through septicaemia, and the places described were exotic. What was known of the horrors of the battlefield often came from writers like Corippus (author of a Latin epic about a general in Africa) or Agathias, writing for aristocrats. But others, including Procopius and Mauricius, did have a very good idea of how big the Roman world was, how far away Africa and Lazica were from Constantinople, and what it felt like to hear men dying. What Roman farmers and shepherds thought is unknown to us, probably a combination of fear, ignorance, and complacency. But both popular and aristocratic concepts of war acknowledged its necessity without question. This included acceptance of the way in which defeated cities were treated, with men killed, women and children sold into slavery. At Antioch in 540, "the Persians did not spare persons of any age and were slaying all whom they met, old and young alike" (Procopius, *Bella* 2.8.34). But attitudes varied, and Procopius seems less concerned about this than Agathias, who was horrified both by the destruction wrought by the Kutrigurs in 559 (Agathias 5.2) and by the Roman slaughter of women and children at Tzachar in 557 (Agathias 4.19.3–6).

Nor is it easy to know how Justinian himself felt. Unlike many earlier Roman emperors, Justinian did not lead troops on the battlefield, but directed operations from the imperial palace at Constantinople. But he had many close brushes with military matters, with an uncle who under Anastasius rose to the rank of *comes excubitorum*, a cousin Germanus who had won a major victory over the Antae, and his own career as a *scholarius* and *candidatus*. He would have seen the destruction of Vitalian's fleet off the imperial city in 515, even if he did not take part (as his uncle did), and early in his reign, he was forced to commit troops in the Nika riot. Although he inherited one Persian war and was forced to respond to a second Persian war and events in the Balkans, other wars were launched on his initiative. The reconquest of Africa was begun in 533 almost as soon as the Persian war was brought to an end in 532. For Justinian, war was an instrument of policy, as well as a chance to earn glory comparable with his predecessors. But personal factors were also important, and the deposition and imprisonment of two friendly rulers, Hilderic in Africa and Amalasuntha in Italy, may have provoked genuine outrage from Justinian, even if combined with opportunism. Some of Justinian's concern for the West was also driven by his upbringing in Thrace as a Latin speaker.

When it came to discussions about warfare, he did not have to rely on his experiences or those of his family. Most decisions were discussed in some sort of imperial council, whose members included the *magister officiorum*, two *magistri militum praesentales*, the Urban Prefect of Constantinople, and the Praetorian Prefect of Illyricum. These men, even if they listened to Agathias for pleasure, understood the realities of war. They could also oppose the emperor; the eastern Praetorian Prefect John argued fiercely against the invasion of Africa in 533 (Procopius, *Bella* 3.10.7–17). Even in these debates, although there were clear differences between soldiers and civilians, there was no conception of the army as a body separate from the government. The only political question that might be raised was that of the loyalty of individual officers to the emperor. The recent revolt of Vitalian, *magister militum per Thracias* was an event confined to the Balkans. But such a revolt was rare, and both generals and soldiers were usually loyal to the emperor if he faced a challenge. At the Nika riot of 532, although the emperor had lost popular and political support in Constantinople, Belisarius and Mundo still led their troops against the city population, killing large numbers before they restored order.[6]

This loyalty was felt because soldiers were always the emperor's men, as suggested by a pre-battle speech given for a general by Procopius:

> As you came from the fields with your knapsacks and smocks, [Justinian] brought you together in Constantinople and has caused you to be so powerful that the Roman state now depends on you. (*Bella* 4.16.13)

Possibly a cliché, but it was also true. However, this loyalty was not unconditional. Vitalian could exploit religious tensions and pay was always a problem. Procopius mentioned Isaurian troops betraying Rome in 549, "men nursing a grievance because for many years nothing had been paid them by the emperor" (*Bella* 7.36.7). The regions most favored for recruiting were Isauria, Illyricum, Thrace, and Armenia. However, troops were occasionally recruited from other areas of Anatolia and from other parts of the empire, e.g. Italy, Africa, and Egypt.[7] Although regiments were named after their recruiting regions, these labels were not always exact. Procopius mentioned a regiment of Isaurians at the battle of Callinicum in 531, but added a note that these men were in fact, not Isaurians but Lycaonians (*Bella* 1.18.38).

Most soldiers were volunteers, though some conscription did continue. However, there was a general problem in obtaining troops, particularly in Italy. This reflected a shortage of money to pay the signing bonus, not a shortage of manpower. The regular system was supplemented by generals recruiting before their own campaigns, as with Belisarius in 544 or Narses in 551 before they went to Italy. Although large armies could be assembled in this fashion, it suggests difficulty in focusing resources for new tasks. Defeated enemies were sometimes formed into their own regiments and sent elsewhere in the empire. Thus after the reconquest of Africa, five regiments of Iustinianivandali were created and sent to the eastern front (Procopius, *Bella* 4.14–17 –18). Defeated Goths from Italy also served in the east (Procopius, *Bella* 2.14.10) and Persians in Italy (2.19.25). Individual prisoners or deserters were treated in the same way. Thus Aratius, who deserted to Rome from the Persians in 530, led troops in Italy in 538–540 and in the Balkans in 549–552 (*PLRE* 3: Aratius). Such men were often given positions of great responsibility. The Armenian Artabanes, who as a Persian ally was responsible for the death of the *magister militum praesentalis* Sittas in 538/9, was by 546 *magister militum per Africam*. Though in 549 accused of plotting against Justinian, he was sent to Italy in 550 and later fought at the battle of Casilinum (*PLRE* 3: Artabanes 2).

The emperor was the critical figure in starting Roman offensives. However, our lack of detailed information about Roman resources, especially of money and manpower, makes understanding how he thought about strategy difficult. Justinian's actions are presented by Procopius as both niggardly and often driven by suspicions, but it is impossible to judge these comments objectively without more information. For example, attempting to assess whether Rome was short of troops is made difficult by our lack of knowledge of how big the army was. The only information we have comes from Agathias, who says that in Justinian's reign there were 150,000 men to defend the empire (Agathias 5.13.7). Although Agathias' figure is plausible, it cannot be supported in any detail.[8] However many troops there were, it was not enough to keep all enemies beyond imperial frontiers all the time. Such a goal was probably impossible to achieve. Justinian's success was remarkable, given that the strategic commitments of Rome were little different than they had been in the fourth or fifth centuries, but with less territory, both financial and manpower resources were smaller. Procopius is explicit that when Belisarius was sent to Italy for the second time in 544, he had few troops because of existing commitments in Persia (*Bella* 7.10.1). The events of 559 could suggest an empire that was overstretched. At this point, although there were no major hostilities in Persia or Italy, when the Kutrigur Huns raided the Balkans and approached Constantinople, there were few troops available and Justinian had to recall the retired Belisarius to manage the defenses. But though annoying, these raids caused little long-term damage, and the Danube remained the frontier for the rest of the sixth century. The empire may have been stretched in 559, but it was not wasting resources in the years before or after.

The relative importance of these theaters can be glimpsed through the size of field armies. The central army at Constantinople rarely served in its own right and by 559 had been severely run down, with many units detached to expeditionary armies. The eastern army fielded 25,000 men at Dara in 530 (Procopius, *Bella* 1.13.23) and 20,000 men at Callinicum in 531 (1.18.5). After peace was made here, Belisarius took 16,000 men from these forces to Africa (3.11.2.11). The army that was sent from Constantinople to Italy in 535 was c. 8,000 men (5.5.2–4), at the same time as Mundo was fighting in Dalmatia with the Illyrian army; this was 15,000 strong in 548 (5.29.3). The Italian expedition was reinforced by c. 1,600 men in 536 (5.27.1), c. 5,000 in 537 (6.5.1), and 7,000 in 538 (6.13.16–18). However, we can say very little about losses, so estimating its total size at any point after 535 is difficult; Narses' 550 expedition drew on troops from Constantinople, Thrace, and Illyricum. At Busta Gallorum, this force, together with some troops from Italy, included 8,500 barbarian allies and over 9,500 Romans (8.26.7–13 and 31.5–6).[9] Another Balkan force included over 11,500 Romans under Constantianus in 549 (7.34.40–42). Although sketchy, the largest commitment was clearly to the eastern frontier, followed by the Balkans.

3   Operations

With the topic of operations, we can return to our opening anecdotes, posing the question of how battle worked in the age of Justinian. With forces raised and committed to a region for a campaign, how did a Roman general of the sixth century maneuver his resources to achieve his objectives? Wars were won by forcing the enemy to make peace. This was accomplished by depriving their commander of the will and ability to win. Enemy armies could be worn down, destroyed in battle, or their fixed assets (usually towns or fortresses) could be occupied. It was preferred to avoid pitched battle if possible, since it was unpredictable and dangerous, and to use other methods. This, however, depended on having a Roman army in the field.

The core of the Roman army was the standing regiments of *katalogoi*. The older divisions into field army and border troops appear to have become operationally meaningless. Infantry regiments were about 1,000 men, but were often brigaded together into larger units. The main line of battle infantry were usually armed with spears, though most had a sword as a secondary weapon. They were protected by body armor (usually mail), helmets, and large oval shields; troops in the front rank usually had more armor, and could on occasion wear greaves. Some men further back had javelins. They were supported by light troops, armed with a variety of distance weapons (bows, javelins, crossbows, slings), but either lightly protected or unarmored.[10] Cavalry regiments were usually 300–500 strong, with body armor, helmets, and small shields. As with infantry, the troops in the front ranks of cavalry units had more and better armor; sometimes horses were armored (Mauricius, *Strat.* 1.2). Most were contact cavalry, with lances and swords, and although many units were armed with both bows and lances, not every trooper was able to shoot (Mauricius, *Strat.* 2.8; cf. Procopius, *Bella* 1.1.12–15). These units were supplemented by light cavalry with bows or javelins, best suited for skirmishing. There were also standing regiments of *foederati*, paid and recruited differently from the *katalogoi*, but operationally used in the same way. Many of these were cavalry units with a barbarian identity, like Huns or Heruls; a particular effort was made to recruit horse archers.[11]

The *katalogoi* and *foederati* were often supported by allied forces, either mercenaries or acquired through treaties. In 552, Narses had over 5,500 Lombards in Italy, paying them off immediately after the battle of Busta Gallorum because of their poor discipline (Procopius, *Bella* 8.33.2). In 556, a force of 2,000 Hunnic Sabiri fought as heavy infantry with the Roman army in Lazica. At the end of the campaign they were paid off by the Romans, and are then found fighting for the Persians in 557 (Agathias 3.17.5, 4.13.7–9).

The land forces were supplemented by naval forces. Roman warships, generally known as dromons, were oared galleys, with crews varying from 100 to 200 depending on their size. The oars were used for combat and when becalmed, but for long-distance movement sails were used. Dromons could be equipped with rams, and sometimes bolt-shooting artillery. The eastern waters were a Roman lake, but in the West the Ostrogoths had a few ships and the Vandals had a large fleet (120 ships went to Sardinia in 533). Belisarius' fleet in 533 contained 92 warships, though presumably others were left at Constantinople. Naval battles were rare, and the only major clash was when 50 Roman ships defeated 47 Gothic ships at Sena Gallica in 552 (Procopius, *Bella* 8.23.1–42).

4 Regions

Some of the army was deployed along the frontiers, to deal with small raids and to provide intelligence, but the core of the army was a series of field armies. The largest of these was at Constantinople, technically commanded by two equally ranked *magistri militum praesentales*, though it served mainly as a source of troops for expeditionary armies. There were also three regional field armies, in Illyricum at Thessalonica, in Thrace at Marcianopolis (modern Reka Devniya in Bulgaria), and in the East at

Antioch. In 528, the eastern army was divided. The forces in the north (supplemented by some troops from Constantinople), now came under the command of the *magister militum per Armeniam* (based at Theodosiopolis, modern Erzurum); the southern command was still under the *magister militum per Orientem* at Antioch and watched the middle Euphrates and Tigris regions.

These regional armies were explicitly configured to fight local enemies. The *Strategikon* contains four short essays giving strategic and operational recommendations for fighting the Persians, Slavs and Antes, Huns and other Scythians, and Western barbarians. The introduction to these essays says that

> The purpose of this chapter is to enable those who intend to wage war against these peoples to prepare themselves properly, for all nations do not fight in a single formation or in the same manner and one cannot deal with them all in the same way. (Mauricius, *Strat.* 11 preface)

These essays could be dismissed as stereotypes, but they fit closely with attitudes and practices described in the historians. While the enemy could be clearly identified, the local population were a different matter. It is often difficult to escape the idea of Roman armies grappling with their enemies like strangers in a strange land. Although Italy, Africa, Spain, Lazica, and Armenia had all been ruled directly by Rome at some point, Roman armies campaigning in all these regions spoke a different language from the locals, had to work with or against local monarchs, and were frequently treated as enemies. In many ways they had more in common with their enemies than they did with the local populace. It is thus not too surprising that when a regiment of Heruli withdrawing from Italy in 539 met a Gothic army "they sold all the slaves and animals they were taking with them to the enemy and thus having gained a great amount of money, they took an oath that they would never array themselves against Goths or do battle with them" (Procopius, *Bella* 6.22.6).

Persia and the eastern front

Justinian fought two wars against the Sassanids. These wars took place in several different theaters; the Caucasus (mostly involving the Lazi), central Anatolia (also known as Armenia), and Mesopotamia (mainly direct conflict between Rome and Persia). In Mesopotamia and Syria, the Romans had semi-permanent alliances with a number of Arab dynasties, perhaps most useful in ensuring that these peoples did not instead ally with the Persians. First, there were the final stages of the 502–532 war, closed by the Endless Peace. Hostilities restarted in 540, though after 545 they were confined to Lazica where they lasted until 557. Finally, the Fifty Years Peace was negotiated in 561. The campaigns in Mesopotamia involved large armies that moved on predictable routes. Sieges and field battles attempting to relieve besieged cities thus dominated campaigns. In Lazica and Syria, there were also widespread skirmishes.

Balkans

In the Balkans, the Romans faced a complex array of problems. The whole region can be divided into three major zones, the western Balkans, the lower Danube, and the

Crimea, united by the lands to the north of the Danube. This is well demonstrated by the arrival of the Avars. In 558 they sent ambassadors to Justinian's court and fought against the Utigurs in the Ukraine, but by 582 they were living on the Great Hungarian plain and had occupied Sirmium. Roman defense of the area south of the lower Danube was carried out by the *magister militum per Illyricum* based at Thessalonica and the *magister militum per Thracias* at Marcianopolis. The field armies were supported by border troops, local militias, and numerous fortified cities and strongpoints. However, Roman control of areas beyond the cities and the major communication routes was often weak. Most of the threats were from Slav, Antae, and Hun raiders who made little attempt to conquer this territory, even though there were occasional settlements. These raids were frequent and widespread, stretching even as far south as the Greek Peloponnese and as far east as Constantinople. However, as events since the mid-fifth century had shown, control of the area south of the Danube was not critical to imperial survival and provided a field army remained in being, Roman control could always be restored. This meant that Roman strategy was usually based on an avoidance of battle. Instead, it was considered better to dog the flanks of the raiders and to wear them down until they withdrew. Thus in 551 at Adrianople, a Roman army was defeated by the Slavs and plundered as far as the Long Walls near Constantinople. When the Roman force recovered, it counterattacked the retreating Slavs and recovered much of the booty and prisoners (Procopius, *Bella* 7.40.33–45). Though effective at a strategic level, the cost to the inhabitants was often severe. But such a policy allowed the empire to fight simultaneous wars in Italy and Persia, while concentrating on building walls rather than armies in the Balkans.

North Africa

After the Vandal occupation of North Africa in the fifth century, the Romans had attempted to reoccupy it in 431, 441, and 468, in part because of the wealth it produced. Justinian had had good relations with Hilderic (523–530) who had stopped persecuting Catholics. But when Hilderic was deposed by Gelimer, as soon as peace had been made with the Persians on the eastern front, Justinian sent an expedition against Africa. Belisarius landed in 533 and defeated the Vandals in a minor action at Ad Decimum, then occupied Carthage before winning a major victory at Tricamarum. The duties of the army now included keeping the peace against a number of Moorish and Numidian tribes, a task that involved frontier skirmishes and occasional battles for the rest of Justinian's reign. There were also serious mutinies in 536 and 545–546, with the mutineers joined by Moors.

Italy

Italy, the home of the Roman Empire, had been controlled by Theoderic's Goths since 493. After the death of Theoderic's grandson Athalaric in 534, the imprisonment and murder of Amalasuntha, Theoderic's daughter, gave Justinian a justification to invade. In 535, Mundo was sent against Salona and the still-young Belisarius was sent with an army to Sicily, landing in Italy in 536. The subsequent war, until the final Gothic collapse in 552 and defeat of the Franks in 554, was dominated by sieges

and skirmishes. Roman resources were especially limited after the waves of reinforcements stopped being sent following the outbreak of the Persian War in 540.
Then after the Roman defeat at Faventia in 542, the Romans lost the strategic initiative because they could not assemble a new field army. When Belisarius was sent back
to Italy in 544, he was never able to assemble enough troops to regain the initiative,
so was restricted to sieges and skirmishes. He was withdrawn in 548 and eventually
replaced by Narses in 551. Narses raised a large army, including allied Lombards,
Heruli, and Gepids, arriving at Ravenna in 552. With this new force, he was able to
challenge Totila directly. The two armies met in the Gothic War's only major field
battle, at Busta Gallorum, near Sentinum. Totila died in the battle, and the occupation of Rome and a second action at Mons Lactarius finished the major fighting.
During these years, the Franks made several efforts to occupy north Italy, most
seriously when an army under Butilinus and Leutharis invaded the Po Valley in 553,
but were destroyed by Narses in the second major battle, at Casilinum in 554. The
surrender of the garrison at Campsa marked the effective end of the war, though a
few diehards fought on until 562.

Each regional army thus had its own characteristics, a product of local terrain, resources,
and objectives. Cavalry were important numerically and doctrinally within the army,
and increasingly so as the sixth century went on, but the core of most armies was
always infantry. Procopius' emphasis on the bow- and lance-armed cavalry of Belisarius'
army is not always borne out by his narrative, and Mauricius' *Strategikon* shows that
Procopius was describing an ideal. Such troops were especially useful in the low-
intensity warfare in Italy, Lazica, and the Balkans, but could never replace infantry
which remained important for field battles and for operations in woods or mountains. Thus, the African expeditionary force of 533 contained 10,000 foot and 6,000
horse, selected from the field army of Constantinople. The army at Busta Gallorum
(552) contained at least 8,000 foot and 1,500 horse, though there were other troops
in this force (Procopius, *Bella* 8.31.5–6). On rare occasions, forces could be composed mostly or entirely of cavalry, and Constantianus helped lead 10,000 horse to
help the Lombards in 549 (7.34.40–42).

Operations were also shaped by the enemies of Rome. Both Vandal and Gothic
armies had many aristocratic cavalry, but few horse archers. Huns, on the other hand,
had many horse archers, but few effective infantry. Unlike the other enemies, the Persian
Empire had large resources of money and manpower. Thus in 530, they had 50,000
men in Mesopotamia and 30,000 in Armenia (Procopius, *Bella* 1.13.23, 1.14.1,
1.15.11). The core of Persian armies was heavy cavalry, provided in a feudal manner
by aristocrats, but there was also a royal elite regiment known as the Immortals.
However, the bulk of the numbers were poor quality infantry and mercenary or allied
contingents of infantry (Daylami) and light cavalry (Turks and Huns).

Managing Roman armies to break the will of the opposition required more than
simply providing troops. An efficient system of supplying campaigning armies was
critical, if commanders were to have full freedom of maneuver. A wide range of supplies had first to be obtained, then transferred to the armies, and finally distributed
to the troops themselves. These materials included food, firewood, water, clothing,

equipment, arms, and ammunition. Without any of these, the ability of commanders to operate was limited. Ammunition was required in large quantities, even though individuals carried only 30–40 arrows each (Mauricius, *Strat.* 1.2, 12.B.5). A tenth-century treatise regarding a naval expedition in 911 mentions a proposed requisition of 800,000 arrows and 10,000 javelins for an army of about 34,000 men. Such figures are large, but this is only a partial figure, since each of the 102 dromons on this expedition should also have been equipped with 50 bows and 10,000 arrows (*De Caer.* 657.10–15, 669.13–670.5).[12]

The impact of the supply system on local populations would have varied. In constantly fought over areas, like Italy or Mesopotamia, it would have been heavy, though in more distant regions like Egypt or Pamphylia, there would have been little or no impact. Usually it was an efficient system, making use of the sea wherever possible, especially in the Italian wars (Procopius, *Bella* 3.13.15–20, 8.22.32). Although the performance of the army in the field suggests that the system worked well, it is the failures that are noted by historians. Thus Procopius mentions the failure to double bake the biscuit for the Vandal campaign, though this was clearly an exception to standard practice (*Bella* 3.13.15–20).

Good logistics gave commanders freedom of action, but they had to be combined with intelligence for effective operations. Scouts were continuously sent out to monitor the enemy's location and intentions, while masking those of the Romans. Interpreting the information gained was often difficult and involved generals making critical decisions. Deserters were common, which meant that information could be planted by men pretending to be deserters. When some Isaurians promised to betray Rome to Totila in 547, his first reaction was to believe that this was a trap (Procopius, *Bella* 7.20.4–16). Such doubts could be well founded. In the same year, Martinianus pretended to desert to the Goths, then persuaded 15 other Roman deserters to return to Roman service and with these men opened the gates of Spolitium to Roman troops (Procopius, *Bella* 7.23.1–7). Martin, when besieged inside Phasis in 556, spread rumors of the impending arrival of a relieving force to encourage his own men. When the news reached the Persians (a good example of the way in which information moved), it led the Persian commander to despatch a force to ambush the putative relievers and to launch a hasty attack on Phasis that failed badly (Agathias 3.23.5–24.4). Good intelligence allowed freedom of movement, as when Stephanus with 200 men in 553 marched from Lucca to Faventia by night, avoiding Frankish foragers as they went. As the troops marched, "the anguished cries of the peasantry could be heard and the lowing of cattle being driven away and the crash of trees being felled" (Agathias 1.17.4–5).

Such night marches were rare, not least because of the ease of getting lost. But close to the enemy, day or night, infantry would have carried their kit on their backs, though cavalrymen could use their horses. In addition to arms and armor, personal items included boots, woollen tunic, trousers and cloak, a water bottle, and a blanket. Men wearing mail would have worn an extra padded undergarment. Sometimes the men also carried some rations, pickaxe, tent quarter, and palisade stake, though these were usually carried on a mule or in a cart (Mauricius, *Strat.* 5.4). All of these would be carried for a day in which perhaps 8–10 hours would be spent marching, probably starting around dawn (Mauricius, *Strat.* 12.B.22). Outside the combat zone, most kit would have been carried in carts or by animals. In many areas, the most characteristic feature of the day would have been the dust raised by the thousands of feet, human and animal. Dust was often accompanied by intense heat. In Mesopotamia, for example, in July and August noonday heat often exceeds 45° C (≈ 115° F), but summer temperatures in most regions would often have been in the mid-30s° C (≈ 100° F).[13] At the end of the day, a marching camp was set up, a tiring task involving digging a ditch and erecting a palisade.

Many long-distance movements, e.g. from Constantinople to the eastern frontier, were carried out on foot, but sometimes troops were moved by sea. The lift capacity of the Roman fleet was quite large, with Belisarius' transports in 533 carrying 10,000 infantry and 6,000 cavalry, most of the latter in specially designed ships (Procopius, *Bella* 3.11.13–16). Subsequent expeditions to Italy and Spain were smaller. Most of these transports were converted merchant vessels, powered by sails. Cavalry, however, were moved in dedicated horse transports.[14] Though this might be easier than marching, there was little shelter on the ships, and there was always the fear of encountering poor weather. This happened in 550 when Artabanes' fleet, sailing from Dalmatia to Sicily was hit by a storm near Calabria; ships were scattered along the Adriatic coast from Melita to the Peloponnese (Procopius, *Bella* 7.40.14–17).

As armies moved, losses would inevitably occur. Violence and criminal activity, going absent without leave, and desertion are factors that affect all armies, not simply those of late antiquity; without official records, we can say little about how serious these problems were.[15] Although on campaign minor pilfering, drunkenness, and indiscipline were mostly overlooked, more serious crimes were dealt with fiercely and swiftly. Belisarius' public impaling of two soldiers at Abydus in 533 for murder was not exceptional (Procopius, *Bella* 3.12.8–9). Minor medical issues would have continuously taken men from the ranks, but on occasion there were more serious problems that did not just sap armies' strengths, but actually affected operations. As the siege wore on at Mesopotamian Theodosiopolis (Resaina) in 541, illness blamed on the heat weakened the Roman army (Procopius, *Bella* 2.19.31–32) and in 527 some Roman troops died of thirst on the march near Dara (Zacharias of Mytilene, *Hist. Eccl.* 9.1). However, care for hygiene means that we rarely hear of the Romans suffering like the Frankish army in the Po Valley in 539 which was forced to abandon the campaign, in part because diarrhoea and dysentery had ravaged their ranks (Procopius, *Bella* 6.25.16–18). The Frankish expedition to Italy in 554 was also weakened by disease (Agathias 2.3.4–8).

5 Combat

The processes involved when men fight are difficult to understand. Even in better documented modern eras there remain great uncertainties as to what actually happened at various battles. We cannot expect a single picture of any action, since a soldier's battle would have been different from that of a regimental commander or the commanding general, while the battles of two regimental commanders would differ according to their place on the battlefield. Recording what did happen was difficult for many reasons. Sometimes participants were dead before they had an opportunity to write. The ability to observe events was often limited, with line of sight being blocked by bodies of men, trees, or hills, the clouds of dust caused by movements of men and animals in the summer, and the limitations of human vision before the introduction of optical glass. Assembling reports from those involved into a coherent narrative was thus difficult, particularly as there was no accurate time-keeping. Comparing battles is also difficult. Synthetic approaches, like that used here, thus tend to stress common elements of what were not generic events. Although there were similarities, every battle was unique.

Even if writers like Procopius understood what happened, other writers like Agathias knew of battle only in a theoretical sense. Although a bowshot was often used as a unit of measurement of c. 300 meters, this does not mean that missile shot actually took place at such a range.[16] The effective range of archery was about 100 meters, though at this distance a human being on foot appears to be 1.8 centimeters tall. In other words, effective aimed shot at individuals at such range was impossible. Such facts, as well as a knowledge of heat, dust, and horses, would be second nature to Procopius, if not to Agathias, but need careful explication for a modern audience.

Combat was intensely personal. As death or injury from missile weapons at long range was unlikely, most participants in battles stood up and could see and be seen. Battles took place in phases, so that there were gaps between actions, opportunities for deeds to be discussed and noted. It was also a world of leaders and followers, in which men were expected to perform in public, to be seen to do so, and then to be rewarded. At the siege of the walls of Chersonese in 559, the commander of the garrison Germanus, son of Dorotheus, personally led a sortie against the Kutrigur Huns. He was wounded in the thigh by an arrow, but continued to fight (Agathias 5.23.2–3). And in Italy, after carelessly leading his men into an ambush, the Herul Fulcaris died fighting and refused his attendants' pleas to save himself, saying: "how could I endure the sting of Narses' tongue when he reproaches me for my folly?" (Agathias 1.15.1–3). Courage and care were important in ensuring victory, but there were other factors. Procopius listened to Belisarius speaking to his men before departing to Africa in 533. His version of Belisarius' speech claimed that

> you are not ignorant, I think, that while it is men who always do the fighting in either army, it is God who judges the contest as seems best to him and bestows the victory in battle. (*Bella* 3.12.13)

It was thus important that God be respected, and so the army at Callinicum fasted for Easter, even though they were expecting to fight a battle, and in fact suffered for it (Procopius, *Bella* 1.18.15). Events in battle could often be interpreted in religious terms, particularly if they appeared inexplicable. According to Evagrius, at the siege of Edessa in 543, the Romans were only able to fire their mine below a Persian siege mound after they had brought a divine image up to the timbers. Procopius also records problems in igniting the timbers, but says nothing about an icon (Evagrius,

Hist. Eccl. 4.27; Procopius, *Bella* 2.27.1–17). Evagrius' report, whether true or not, shows how some men could rationalize events in battle.

The problems involved with moving men to the battlefield also recurred in battle. Here, though, there was often little chance to avoid the hot parts of the day. The battle of Dara in 530 was fought in July, one of the hottest months of the year, when regional maximum temperatures now average 34° C/94° F; the main clash started only at noon, when temperatures were probably closer to 45° C/115° F. When to eat was a concern, and Narses at Busta Gallorum fed his men in the ranks (Procopius, *Bella* 8.32.4). Waiting was also tiring, and the *Strategikon* encouraged commanders to have men sit down in formation to rest, rather than standing all day (Mauricius, *Strat.* 12.B.23). Weather had effects too. Rain could make bowstrings damp, reducing the effectiveness of archery or even prohibiting it, and wind could make archery more or less effective, depending on its direction. Sometimes these factors could combine, and then it could all go horribly wrong, as at Callinicum in 531 when the Romans were exhausted by the march to battle and had not eaten because of the Easter fast. When the Persians broke through the Roman cavalry and hit the main line from both sides, it is hardly surprising that the Roman force collapsed.

6 Skirmishing and Attrition Warfare

As Callinicum showed, full-scale field battles were risky and the Romans tried to avoid them, even when they outnumbered the enemy. Skirmishes were thus common as the Romans tried to restrict the ability of the enemy to gather forage and intelligence. This would also wear down the enemy and sap their morale and initiative. Roman cavalry, many of whom had bows, were well-suited for this. In late 553, 300 mounted bodyguard troops led by Narses attacked a foraging force of 2,000 Frankish cavalry and infantry at Ariminum. When attacked, the Franks formed a dense formation that was resistant to the Roman arrows. The Romans then carried out a feigned retreat, which broke up the Frankish formation, and then proceeded to cause heavy casualties on the scattered Franks (Agathias 1.21–22). These actions required aggression and confidence, but allowed small numbers of Romans to dominate large forces. Thus Dabregezas and Usigardus with 600 cavalry met 3,000 Persian cavalry in Lazica in 555. Their immediate response was to attack, despite being outnumbered by six to one (Agathias 3.7.1–5). Similar aggressive maneuvers with horse archers were employed by Belisarius at the siege of Rome in 537 (Procopius, *Bella* 5.27.4–14) and at Constantinople in 559 against the Kutrigurs. Such aggressiveness appears normal. At Tzachar in the Caucasus in 556, a group of 40 Roman cavalry was attacked by a mixed force of 600 Misimians. Instead of evading, they occupied high ground and engaged the enemy until the main force arrived (Agathias 4.16.5–7). However, such operations were limited to open country, and in wooded or mountainous areas, in particular at passes and water crossings, infantry were used (Mauricius, *Strat.* 9.4). Surprise in these actions could be critical, and the *Strategikon* was concerned to keep polished armor and weapons covered before a clash (Mauricius, *Strat.* 7.B.15).

7 Battle

At most battles, Roman armies formed up into an infantry center and two wings of cavalry, as at Dara and in a modified fashion at Callinicum, where the left flank was protected by a river. This general purpose formation was good against the Persians, but was also used in Italy at Busta Gallorum and Casilinum. The Roman battlefield commander usually fought in the center, surrounded by his mounted bodyguard with his personal standard flying. Sometimes reserves or outflanking forces were employed, as at Dara and Busta Gallorum. Behind the army was the baggage, with its own guard. This was of great importance for the soldiers and in Mauricius' words, if this is not kept safe, "the soldiers become distracted, hesitant and dispirited in battle" (*Strat.* 5.1).

Troops could deploy in deep formations. In the case of infantry, there seems to have been a preference for eight ranks deep, possibly with light troops interspersed. Shallower formations were possible, though four ranks deep was a minimum. Cavalry deployments seem to have varied between five and ten ranks, though in a far more loose formation than the infantry. Even at this stage, it might be hard for many men to see the enemy. Men further back might have an obstructed view, while clouds of dust caused by deployment would already be raised over the battlefield. Before the battle of Satala in 530, the Persians were confused by the size of a cloud of dust raised by Sittas' troops, "since owing to the summer season a great cloud of dust hung over them" (Procopius, *Bella* 1.15.12). At the battle of Chettus in 559, the Huns were unable to see because of the cloud of dust raised, so could not tell how few Roman troops there were (Agathias 5.19.9). In these conditions, the importance of unit flags is clear (though units also had other means of identification, including painted shields and colored plumes and pennons).[17]

As a preliminary to the battle, there were negotiations, demonstrations, speeches, and champions. At Busta Gallorum, the Gothic leader delayed the start of the battle to give time for Gothic reinforcements to arrive.

> Totila went alone into the space between the armies, not in order to engage in single combat, but in order to prevent his opponents from using the present opportunity. . . . And he himself, sitting upon a very large horse, began to perform the dance under arms skilfully between the armies. For he wheeled his horse round in a circle and then turned him again to the other side and so made him run round and round. And as he rode he hurled his spear into the air and caught it again as it quivered above him, then passed it rapidly from hand to hand, shifting it with consummate skill, and he gloried in his practice in such matters, falling back on his shoulders, spreading his legs and leaning from side to side, like one who has been instructed with precision in the art of dancing from childhood. (Procopius, *Bella* 8.31.17–20)

The habit of champions issuing forth from the ranks of Gothic and Persian armies often prompted Roman responses. Success or failure could impact morale. Outside Dara in 530, when Andreas defeated a Persian champion, "a mighty shout was raised from both the city wall and from the Roman army. But the Persians were deeply distressed at the outcome" (Procopius, *Bella* 1.13.32–33). For these events to have been seen the armies would have been close together, within a few hundred meters of each other.

The armies then closed. Whether infantry or cavalry led the attack depended on many factors, including the personality of the commander (Belisarius was more innovative in this respect than Narses), the troops available, and the enemy faced. This was the moment for a final psychological boost. According to the *Strategikon*, there was a tight sequence. One bowshot from the enemy, the command "Ready" (*parati* – commands were still given in Latin) was given. This was immediately followed by a single officer shouting "Help Us" (*adiuta*), to which the entire army replied "O God" (*Deus*) (Mauricius, *Strat.* 12.B.16). The process began with exchanges of missiles between light troops. More dust would be raised, and shouted commands heard. The Persians were notorious for their speed of archery and so rapid closing was important when engaging them. But as soon as enemy missiles began to strike home, it was time for the main bodies to charge. Since effective archery range was around 100 meters, it would take infantry in formation less than two minutes to contact a stationery foe. The first clashes were usually between the cavalry on the wings, followed by a collision of the main bodies. If there was an infantry main body, then they would be supported by light troops firing missiles overhead. If the infantry formed a maneuver base for the cavalry, then they would provide a hedge of spears, supported from behind by archery. This tight formation was known as the *foulkon* and was usually successful. This could also be formed by cavalry in difficulties if they dismounted.[18]

This was perhaps the noisiest moment of the battle, with horses rearing, the clash of weapons on weapons and armor, and the shouting and screaming of men. The leadership provided by commanders was critical, but armies could be demoralized if they fell. Gothic attempts to kill Belisarius in the skirmishes outside Rome in 537 provided the focus for some of these actions (Procopius, *Bella* 5.18.4–15). Capture or loss of a standard often occurred at this point. Then as one side was pushed back, there was an opportunity for the lines to settle and reserves to be committed. It was probably here that luck played the greatest role. At Phasis in 556, the Persians were retreating in good order until an elephant was hit in the face with a spear. It then stampeded through the Persian army, turning an orderly retreat into a rout (Agathias 3.26.8–27.7).

The battle could be brought to an end by nightfall, or by the withdrawal on one side. As the enemy fell back, the men faced the temptation of plundering the enemy corpses. The frequent prohibition of this practice suggests that it was a common problem (Mauricius, *Strat.* 7.A.14). Procopius described the events as the enemy camp was captured at Scalae Veteres in North Africa in 537. "There the soldiers, finding it easy to plunder the goods of the camp, neither took any account of the enemy nor paid any heed to the exhortations of their general since booty was at hand" (Procopius, *Bella* 4.17.28–29).

The withdrawal might be an orderly retreat to a town or fort, but was sometimes a total collapse, pursued by the enemy. For the Romans as they pursued, keeping good order was important, since losing formation in the pursuit meant being vulnerable to a counterattack. Thus pursuits were often limited in extent, as after the battle of Dara in 530. Even in these situations, casualties could occur. In the confusion of the pursuit at Scalae Veteres, the general Germanus had his horse killed underneath him, but after the battle of Edessa, the Romans captured four Persian standards (Procopius, *Bella* 4.17.23, 8.14.43).

After the battle, many of the wounded would go on to die slow and painful deaths. But septicaemia did not afflict all. After a skirmish outside Rome in early 537, a certain Visandus was left for dead on the battlefield, with 13 wounds. He was found on the battlefield a few days later, desperately hungry and thirsty, but still alive (Procopius, *Bella* 5.18.29–33).

8   Sieges

Capturing cities and fortresses was a key process. We have no siege manuals, though manuals existed, giving Roman commanders an advantage over many barbarians. Most cities were walled (though defenses could often deteriorate if not maintained; immediately after entering Carthage in 533 and Rome in 536, Belisarius began repairing the defenses). Certain key sites were besieged repeatedly. Rome was besieged by the Goths three times, in 537–538 (a year and nine days), 546, and 549, falling to treachery on the latter two occasions, and Dara was attacked in 530 and 540. Large armies, however, could not defend cities from the inside, but had to stand outside and fight, thus generating frequent field battles. Garrisons were always small compared to besieging armies, so that once enemy troops entered the city, it usually surrendered.

The defenses could be breached in several ways. There were several types of indirect approaches. Gates could be opened by treachery, as at Rome in 546, and keeping morale up and guards alert was important (Procopius, *Bella* 7.20.14–16). The attackers could also infiltrate to open gates, as at Naples in 536 when some Isaurians were sent into the city through an aqueduct (Procopius, *Bella* 5.9.11–21), or at Tzachar in Lazica in 557 when troops climbed a rocky crag overlooking the fortress (Agathias 4.17.4–19.1).

Failing these, direct methods were used. Missile fire was especially important here. If the attackers could win missile superiority, or at least dominate the approaches, then they could approach the wall and assaults and/or siege engineering could take place. Walls could be assaulted by scaling ladders, as at Petra in 551 (Procopius, *Bella* 8.11.39–47). And siege operations could attempt to cross the wall by a mound, as at Edessa in 543 (Procopius, *Bella* 2.26.23–24), or create a breach by undermining the wall as at Cumae in 554 (Agathias 1.10.3–8). At the siege of Dara in 540, the Persians were intercepted while tunneling under the walls (Procopius, *Bella* 2.13.20–27).[19] There were several types of siege artillery, though often described generically as "engines" or "machines." Tension-powered bolt shooters were useful for sniping. Torsion driven catapults were useful for bombarding towers, gates, personnel targets, and other engines but, like the traction trebuchets introduced at the end of the sixth century, were unable to breach most walls.[20]

The various enemies of Rome had different skills when it came to sieges. Procopius was contemptuous of Arab abilities: "the Saracens are by natural disposition incapable of storming a wall. The worst kind of fortification, even if put together with mud, becomes an impediment to their attack" (*Aedificia* 2.9.4). The Persians were very good at sieges, but Gothic abilities varied. At Rome in 537, Vitigis was able to organize siege equipment, including ladders, rams, fascines to fill ditches, and siege towers, but he did not have the required expertise in their use. When the towers were drawn by oxen within bowshot of the walls, all the draught animals were rapidly shot down (Procopius, *Bella* 5.22.1–9). But this sort of Roman supremacy could not be counted on, and the Goths learned quickly; a siege tower at Rimini in 538 was solely man propelled, even though it was unsuccessful for other reasons (Procopius, *Bella* 6.12.2).

During long sieges, sorties could take place. These happened particularly often during the Gothic siege of Rome, where the exceptional length of the walls (c. 19 km) meant control of the area by both sides was very loose. These sorties were usually similar to the skirmishes described above, though were sometimes focused on destroying siege works or siege engines.

The ability to attack or defend fortified sites was, however, in the end dependent on logistics. Prolonged sieges could cause difficulties on both sides. As the Romans besieged the Goths at Auximum in 538, the countryside was devastated by a famine, but Belisarius was able to rely on supplies brought in by sea to Ancona (Procopius, *Bella* 6.24.14). Ports had to be blockaded on the sea side as well. At Salona in 537, the Romans were able to defeat the Gothic fleet, so were able to bring in supplies from the sea. During the siege of Rome in 537–538, the Romans were able to bring in supplies up the Tiber, but in the two sieges in the 540s, although the Romans controlled both Portus and Rome, the Goths were able to interdict the river (Procopius, *Bella* 6.7.1–13, 7.19.1–34). Eventually, however, starvation would force all fortresses to surrender, as with Gelimer at Papua (after three months), the Romans at Milan in 539, or the Goths at Auximum in the same year.

9   Conclusion

Understanding the nature of battle in this period is difficult. Battle itself was a complex combined arms process, and commanders needed to be able to combine cavalry and infantry in various fashions to achieve their objectives, while at the same time assessing the terrain and intentions of the enemy. Many campaigns were decided on the battlefield, but activity beyond the battlefield could also be decisive, and mastery of these elements was also important for success. Although the institutional framework was strong, it was conditioned by the often over-stretched resources, while all actions had to be carried out by men.

NOTES

1   Cameron 1985; Greatrex 2003; Kaegi 1990.
2   Cameron 1970.

3   Blockley 1985.
4   Kalkan and Şahin 1995; Zuckerman 1995.
5   Text and German translation, Dennis and Gamillscheg 1981; English translation, Dennis 1984; Rance 2005: a sixth-century date has been suggested for Syrianus, Zuckerman 1990, but see Cosentino 2000.
6   Greatrex 1997, 60–86.
7   Whitby 1995; Haldon 1989.
8   Treadgold 1995.
9   Hannestad 1960.
10 Coulston 1990; Haldon 1975; Kolias 1988.
11 Haldon 1984.
12 Haldon 2000.
13 Kaegi 1991.
14 Elton 1996, 98–9, 100; MacGeorge 2002, 306–11.
15 For comparison, in northwestern Europe 1944–5, US infantry divisions in the combat zone lost on average 8 percent of their strength per month from non-battle losses, as compared to 10 percent from battle losses, for a total monthly loss of 18 percent.
16 McLeod 1965.
17 Dennis 1982.
18 Rance 2004.
19 Crow and Croke 1983.
20 Haldon 1999, 134–8.

BIBLIOGRAPHY

Blockley, R. C. 1985. *The History of Menander the Guardsman*. Liverpool.
Cameron, A. 1970. *Agathias*. Oxford.
—— 1985. *Procopius*. London.
Carrié, J. M., and S. Janniard. 2000/2001/2002. "L'armée romaine dans quelques travaux récents," *Antiquité Tardive* 8: 321–41; 9: 351–61, and 10: 427–42.
Cosentino, S. 2000. "Syrianos' *Strategikon* – A ninth-century source?" *Bizantinistica* 2: 243–80.
Coulston, J. C. 1990. "Later Roman armour, 3rd–6th centuries AD," *JRMES* 1: 139–60.
Crow, J., and B. Croke. 1983. "Procopius and Dara," *JRS* 73: 143–59.
Dennis, G. T. 1982. "Byzantine battle flags," *Byzantinische Forschungen* 8: 51–9.
—— 1984. *Maurice's Strategikon*. Philadelphia.
——, and E. Gamillscheg. 1981. *Das Strategikon des Maurikios*. Vienna.
Elton, H. W. 1996. *Warfare in Roman Europe, AD 350–425*. Oxford.
Evans, J. A. S. 1996. *The Age of Justinian*. London.
Greatrex, G. 1997. "The Nika riot: A reappraisal," *JHS* 117: 60–86.
—— 1998. *Rome and Persia at War, 502–532*. Leeds.
—— 2003. "Recent work on Procopius and the composition of Wars VIII," *Byzantine and Modern Greek Studies* 27: 45–67.
Haldon, J. F. 1975. "Some aspects of Byzantine military technology from the sixth to the tenth centuries," *Byzantine and Modern Greek Studies* 1: 11–47.
—— 1984. *Byzantine Praetorians*. Bonn.
—— 1989. *Recruitment and Conscription in the Byzantine Army c. 550–950*. Vienna.
—— 1999. *Warfare, State and Society in the Byzantine World, 565–1204*. London.

—— 2000. "Theory and practice in tenth-century military administration," *Travaux et Mémoires* 13: 201–352.

Hannestad, K. 1960. "Les force militaires d'après la guerre gothique de Procope," *Classica et Mediaevalia* 21: 136–83.

Jones, A. H. M. 1964. *The Later Roman Empire*. Oxford.

Kaegi, W. E. 1990. "Procopius the military historian," *Byzantinische Forschungen* 15: 53–85.

—— 1991. "Challenges to late Roman and Byzantine military operations in Iraq (fourth–ninth centuries)," *Klio* 73: 586–94.

Kalkan, H., and S. Şahin. 1995. "Epigraphische Mitteilungen aus Istanbul II," *EA* 24: 137–46.

Keegan, J. 1976. *The Face of Battle*. London.

Kolias, T. 1988. *Byzantinische Waffen*. Vienna.

MacGeorge, P. 2002. *Late Roman Warlords*. Oxford.

McLeod, W. 1965. "The range of the ancient bow," *Phoenix* 19: 1–14.

Moorhead, J. 1994. *Justinian*. London.

Rance, P. 2004. "The *Fulcum*, the late Roman and Byzantine *testudo*: The Germanization of late Roman tactics?" *GRBS* 44: 265–326.

—— 2006. *The Roman Art of War in Late Antiquity: The Strategikon of the Emperor Maurice. A Translation with Commentary and Textual Studies*. Aldershot.

Teall, J. 1965. "The barbarians in Justinian's armies," *Speculum* 40: 294–322.

Treadgold, W. 1995. *Byzantium and Its Army, 284–1081*. Stanford.

Whitby, M. 1995. "Recruitment in Roman armies from Justinian to Heraclius (ca. 565–615)," in A. Cameron (ed.), *The Byzantine and Early Islamic Near East. Vol. 3: States, Resources and Armies*. Princeton, 61–124.

—— 2000. "The army c. 420–602," in *CAH* 14. Cambridge, 286–314.

Zuckerman, C. 1990. "The military compendium of Syrianus Magister," *JÖB* 40: 209–24.

—— 1995. "Le δεύτερον βάνδον Κωνσταντινιακῶν dans une épitaphe de Pylai," *Tyche* 10: 233–5.

FURTHER READING

There are two recent narratives on Justinian's reign, Moorhead 1994; Evans 1996. These, and similar works, avoid detailed consideration of military matters, even if they contain a sizeable military narrative. Justinian's army was little studied before the 1980s. The fundamental works are Jones 1964 and Teall 1965. More recently, a number of works have been partly or entirely devoted to sixth-century warfare: Greatrex 1998; Haldon 1999; Treadgold 1995; Whitby 2000. These form part of a renewed focus of interest in warfare in general, covered in the forthcoming *The Cambridge History of Greek and Roman Warfare*, Cambridge 2006, which includes the sixth century. Many of these recent works are discussed in a series of review articles by Carrié and Janniard 2000, 2001, 2002. Since the publication of Keegan 1976, more complex evaluations of ancient warfare have begun to appear in other periods, though they have not yet been applied to the age of Justinian.

Index locorum

LITERARY SOURCES

Agathias
  5.13.7–8 517, 536
Appian
B.Civ.
  1.7 148
  1.9 118
  1.11 118
  1.27 118
  1.55–57 170
  1.96 159
  2.94 161
  3.68 72
  4.3 161
Apuleius
Met.
  9.39 301
Arrian
Ekt.
  22–23 274
Aurelius Victor
Caes.
  33–4 271–2
  39 526
Caesar
B.Gal.
  7.3.1 108
Cassius Dio
  43.18.1–2 379
  54.25.5–6 369

  69.9.1–4 353
Cicero
Agr.
  2.73 153
Att.
  5.21.8 110
  6.3.2 107
Rep.
  2.40 32, 81, 125–6
Marcus Diaconus
Vita Porphyrii
  41 375
Diodorus
  11.53.6 16
  23.2.1 53–4
Dionysius of Halicarnassus
  4.16–21 18
  6.95.2 117
  20.11.2 70
Florus
Epit.
  1.13.26–7 48
A. Gellius
NA
  6.13 17, 32
  10.15.4 32
  16.10.5 32
  16.10.10 125
  16.13.9 151

JURIDICAL SOURCES

EPIGRAPHIC SOURCES

OSTRACA, TABLETS, AND PAPYRI

Index

Ghadames 400
Ghassanid dynasty 481
Gheriat al Garbia 400
Gheriat-es Shergia 400
Gholaia *see* Bu Njem
Ghurkhas 521
Gildo 480, 488–9
Gladiators 212, 278
Gloucester 230
Gnaeus Marcius Coriolanus, *Cn.* 16
Goch-Asperden 401
Gordianus I 389
Gordianus II 389
Gordianus III 250, 270, 279, 374–6,
 389, 466
Goths 253–4, 269, 437, 484–91, 495–6,
 502, 504–7, 509, 520–1, 523, 535,
 538–41, 545–8; *see also* Ostrogoths;
 Visigoths
Granaries 290, 328, 332–3, 406–8
Gratianus 391, 489, 499, 526
Grave-goods 17, 25
Grave-stele 17
Graves 29
Great Chesters 430
Greece 55, 82–3, 109–10, 171–2, 207,
 325, 539
Gundioc 509
Gundobad 509
Gunpowder 97

Hadrian 243, 246, 249, 261–3, 275, 277,
 339, 348, 352–4, 386, 399, 418, 438,
 441, 444, 466
Hadrian's Wall 215, 229–32, 286, 326,
 399, 430, 466
Halmyris 214
Haltern 208, 332, 398, 412
Haltwhistle 329, 410
Handbooks, military 115, 139, 141,
 323–4, 522, 533
Hannibal 67, 71–2, 74–5, 140, 142
Harbors 204–5, 207, 215, 290
Hardknotte 413
Hariulfus 499
Harlach 401
Hasdrubal 75
Hastati see triplex acies
Hatra 251, 466
Hebdomon 255
Heeresgefolgschaft 164–76

Heidenheim 406
Helmets 17, 27, 31, 54, 89, 91, 192,
 260, 274, 277, 280, 458, 537
Helvetii 93, 224–5, 446
Heraclea 46, 51
Heraclius 528
Hercules 466
Hermes 467
Hernici 11–14, 45–6, 53, 99
Herod the Great 242, 331
Heruli 532, 537–8, 540, 543
Hierapolis 464
Hieronymus of Cardia 70
High Rochester 455
Hilderic 534, 539
Hippodrome 525
Hipponium 50
Hirpini 152
Hirtius 175
Hispaniae 63–4, 66, 68, 70–1, 75, 81,
 85, 96, 103, 106, 109–10, 123–4, 145,
 160, 166–7, 173–4, 205, 314, 325, 386,
 419, 424, 446, 485, 491, 506–7, 518,
 542
Hod Hill 221
Hofheim 402, 406
Holzhausen 399
Homeric Greece 15
Honorius 482, 489, 496, 498, 505–6,
 518–19, 526–7
Hoplite equipment 17–18, 27–8, 31–2, 54
Horace 350
Hordeonius Flaccus 385
Horn blowers 29, 192, 436
Horse Guard *see equites singulares Augusti*
Horsemanship 87
Horses 88, 102–3, 203, 223, 259–61,
 274, 315–17, 325–6, 406, 439, 542
Horus 464–5
Hospitals *see* medical care
Housesteads 399, 406, 468
Hungarian Plain 539
Huns 256–7, 484, 486, 488, 502–4,
 507–8, 522, 536–40, 543, 545
Hyrcania 259
Hyssi Portus 246

Iasen 464
Iberia, Iberians (Caucasus) 195, 241–3,
 251–2, 256, 258, 260
Iberians (Spain) 54, 72–5, 85

Printed in Great Britain
by Amazon